THE democraTic eXPeRiENCE

THE
DEMOCRATIC
EXPERIENCE

A SHORT AMERICAN HISTORY

VOLUME II

THIRD EDITION

Carl N. Degler   Stanford University
Thomas C. Cochran   University of Pennsylvania
Vincent P. De Santis   University of Notre Dame
Holman Hamilton   University of Kentucky
William H. Harbaugh   University of Virginia
Arthur S. Link   Princeton University
Russel B. Nye   Michigan State University
David M. Potter
Clarence L. Ver Steeg   Northwestern University

Scott, Foresman and Company
Glenview, Illinois   Brighton, England

Library of Congress Catalog Card Number: 72-189444
ISBN 0–673–07916–3

Regional offices of Scott, Foresman and Company are located in Dallas, Texas;
Glenview, Illinois; Oakland, New Jersey; Palo Alto, California; Tucker, Georgia;
and Brighton, England.

The reception accorded the original and second editions of THE DEMOCRATIC EXPERIENCE has justified the continued belief that there is an increasing need in colleges and universities for a concise yet scholarly textbook of American history. The number of short introductory courses continues to multiply, while many instructors of more extensive courses have come to prefer a brief text that leaves room for the instructor to introduce source materials, add to the variety of the reading, and develop emphases of his own choice. The third edition is now available in two volumes, furthermore, to provide greater flexibility in course scheduling and to accommodate the needs of those students who elect only one semester of the traditional two-semester American history course. For those instructors who prefer to begin the second semester with the Civil War period, the chapter on the Civil War and Reconstruction is here reprinted as the Prologue to Volume II.

pREFACE

In this newly revised edition of THE DEMOCRATIC EXPERIENCE, the text has been reworked, and new material has been added, to reflect a growing interest in the histories of American minority groups and women. While the Part Introductions continue to indicate the thrust of central issues of their respective periods, they include a new emphasis on changing historical interpretations which seeks to show how, to successive generations of historians, the historical significance of a period changes over time. In addition, the Part Introductions each conclude with a series of questions designed to stimulate judgment and interpretation rather than mere factual recall; the reader is invited to draw out for himself the significance of earlier periods to his own experience and to exercise his intelligence on the historical materials presented in each of the Parts. Numerous changes have been made elsewhere, including a new book design, a new illustration program which presents eight photo-essay variations on themes from the Preamble to the Constitution, and the updating of bibliographies, charts, and tables.

The Publishers wish to express their appreciation to the following: to Louis B. Wright of the National Geographic Society for his contribution to a previous edition; to James M. McPherson of Princeton University for assistance in the revision of Part 4 of Volume I; and to David Hall of Boston University for special help in the preparation of this edition.

THE PUBLISHERS

CONTENTS

PHOTO ESSAYS   The photo essays which appear in these volumes are
                intended as pictorial variations on eight themes em-
                bodied in the Preamble to the United States Constitution.
                In contemporary visual terms, the picture essays suggest
                our conflicting feelings of fulfillment vs. frustration of the
                ideals set forth by the Constitution.

MAPS AND CHARTS

PHOTO CREDITS

THE
DEMOCRATIC
EXPERIENCE

CIVIL WAR AND RECONSTRUCTION 1861–77

"CAUSES" OF THE CIVIL WAR

Ever since 1861, writers have disputed what caused the Civil War and whether it was an "irrepressible conflict" in the sense of being inevitable. Southerners have argued that the war was fought not over slavery but over the question of states' rights; several of the Confederate states, they point out, seceded only when the others had been attacked. Economic determinists have contended that the Northern public never would support the abolitionists on any direct question (which is certainly true), that Lincoln did not even venture to issue the Emancipation Proclamation until the war had been in progress for a year and five months (which is also true), and that the conflict was really between an industrial interest which wanted one kind of future for America and an agrarian interest which wanted another. Other historians, going a step beyond this, have pictured the North and the South as two "diverse civilizations," so dissimilar in their culture and their values that union between them was artificial and unnatural. In the 1940s another group of writers, known as revisionists, emphasized the idea that Northerners and Southerners had formed distorted and false concepts of each other and that they went to war against these images rather than against the people they were really fighting. The war, they argued, grew out of emotions, not out of realities.

Every one of these points of view has something to be said for it. The causes of the Civil War were certainly not simple. But though each of the explanations points to something other than slavery, it is significant that the factor of slavery was involved in all of them. It is true that the South believed in the right of the states to secede whereas the North did not, but this belief would have remained an abstraction and never been acted upon if the Republican crusade against slavery had not impelled the South to use the secession weapon. It is also true that the economies of the North and of the South were very different, but the United States has always had certain great regional diversities in economy—for instance between the urban, industrial Northeast and the rural, grain-producing Middle West—and these diversities have not led to war.

It is hard to believe that without slavery the general dissimilarities of North and South—their economic divergence, their specific disagreements on issues like the tariff, or even their social and cultural separateness—would have been brought into such sharp focus as to precipitate a war. That North and South could live together in harmony despite great dissimilarities was proved by experience before 1846 and again after 1877. Furthermore, when one speaks of a "distinctive Southern civilization," one is speaking to a very great extent of slavery, for slavery lay at the foundation of the plantation system, which was the very heart and center of Southern society. Finally, it is true that in the 1850s extremist leaders came to the fore and each section formed an emotional stereotype rather than a realistic picture of the other. But this is a process which always occurs as antagonism deepens.

The point is that slavery furnished the emotional voltage that led to deep distrust and dislike in each section for the people of the other. In his second inaugural, Abraham Lincoln said, "All know that slavery was somehow the cause of the war." The operative word in his statement was "somehow," for the war was not in any simple sense a fight between crusaders for freedom all on one side and believers in slavery all on the other. Robert E. Lee, to name but one Southerner, did not believe in slavery at all, and many a Northern soldier who was willing to die, if need be, for the Union was deeply opposed to making slavery an issue of the war. But both antislavery Southerners and proslavery Northerners were caught in a web which could never have been woven without the issue of slavery.

Could this issue have been settled without war? Was the crisis artificial? Was the territorial question a contest over "an imaginary Negro in an impossible place"? Was war really necessary in a situation where it seems doubtful that a majority of Southerners wanted to secede (only seven out of fifteen slave states seceded before the firing on Fort Sumter) or that a majority of Northerners wanted to make an issue of slavery? (Lincoln had only 39 percent of the popular vote, and he promised security for slavery where it was already established.) Were the American people, both North and South, so much alike in their religion (overwhelmingly evangelical Protestant), their speech (an American variant of English), their ethnic descent (mostly from British, Irish, and German stock), their democratic beliefs, their pioneer ways, their emphasis upon the values of self-reliance and hard work, their veneration for the Constitution, and even their bumptious Americanism—were they so much alike that a war between them could and should have been avoided? This question raises the more general question whether disagreements are any less bitter when the parties disagreeing share much in common.

What was happening in America was that the center of gravity was gradually shifting from a loosely organized agricultural society to a modern industrial society with much greater concentration of power. As this happened, the government was being transformed from a loose association of separately powerful states to a consolidated nation in which the states would be little more than political subdivisions. In America's startling growth the North had outstripped the South and the equilibrium that previously existed between them had been destroyed. The proposal of the victorious Republicans to confine slavery—and in this sense to exclude the South from further participation in the nation's growth—dramatized this shift in equilibrium. It seems most unlikely that the South would ever have accepted the political conse-quences of this basic change without a crisis, especially since Southern whites greatly feared the possibility that a preponderant North in control of the federal government might ultimately use its power to abolish slavery. The brooding presence of race permeated this issue. Slavery was more than an institution to exploit cheap labor; it was a means of controlling a large and potentially threatening black population and of maintaining white supremacy. Any hint of a threat to the "Southern way of life," which was based on the subordination of a race both scorned and feared, was bound to arouse deep and irrational phobias and to create a crisis. Whether this crisis had to take the form of armed conflict and whether this phase of armed force had to occur precisely when it did, or might have come a month, or a year, or a decade sooner or later, would seem to be a matter for endless speculation.

THE BLUE AND THE GRAY

The "American" War.   The American Civil War lasted four years, from April 1861 to April 1865. It was fought over more than half of the United States, for battles took place in every slave state except Delaware, and Confederate forces made incursions into Pennsylvania, Ohio, West Virginia, Kansas, and (raiding from Canada) Vermont.

From a total of 14 million free males, 2.8 million were in uniform—two million for the Union and 800,000 for the Confederacy—a higher proportion than that in any other American war. The Union total included 180,000 black soldiers—almost one in ten of the manpower in the Union Army—and more than 20,000 black sailors. Either as battle casualties or as victims of camp maladies, 618,000 men died in service (360,000 Union troops and 258,000 Confederates); more than one soldier in five lost his life—a far heavier ratio of losses than in any other war in our history.

Partly because the cost was proportionately so heavy, and partly because the Civil War was distinctly an American war, this conflict has occupied a place in the American memory and the American imagination which other wars—more recent, greater, and more crucial in terms of survival—have never held. On both sides, men were fighting for what they deeply believed to be American values. Southerners were convinced that their right to form a Confederacy was based on a principle of the Declaration of Independence—that governments derive their just powers from the consent of the governed. Northerners were equally zealous to prove that a democracy is not too weak to hold together, and that, as Lincoln said, the principle of self-government is not an absurdity.

The Resources of North and South.   In later years, after the Confederacy had gone down to defeat, men said that the Lost Cause, as Southerners called it, had been lost from the beginning and that the South had been fighting against the census returns. In many respects this seems true, for the South was completely outnumbered in almost all the factors of manpower and economic strength which make up the sinews of modern war. The eleven Confederate states (not counting Kentucky and Missouri, which were divided) had a white population of 5,450,000, while the nineteen free states had 18,950,000. These figures leave out both the population of the four border slave states of Missouri, Kentucky, Maryland, and Delaware and the slave population of the Confederate states. Slaves strengthened the Confederate war effort indirectly, since by serving as workers they could release some of the whites to serve as soldiers.

The Union was far ahead of the Confederacy in financial and economic strength, too. It had a bank capital two and a half times as great as that of the South. It led the South in the number of manufacturing enterprises by three and a half to one; in the number of industrial workers by six to one; and in the value of its manufactures by five and a half to one. In railroad mileage, it led by approximately two to one.

But against these ratios of strength must be placed the fact that the Union was undertaking a vastly more difficult military objective. It was seeking to occupy and subdue an area larger than all of western Europe. This meant that armies had to be sent hundreds of miles into hostile territory and be maintained in these distant operations. This necessity involved the gigantic task of transporting the immense volume of supplies required by an army in the field and defending long lines of communication, which would be worthless if they were cut even at a single point. In wars prior to the Civil War, armies had depended upon the use of great wagon trains to bring supplies. As the supply lines lengthened, the horses ate up in fodder a steadily increasing proportion of the amount they could haul, until there was scarcely any margin left between what the supply lines carried and what they consumed in carrying it. During the Civil War, for the first time in the history of warfare, railroads played a major part in the supply services. If these more efficient carriers of goods had not changed the whole nature of war, it is questionable whether invading armies could ever have marched from the Ohio to the Gulf of Mexico. Ten years earlier the United States had not possessed the railroad network which supplied the Union armies between 1861 and 1865. At an earlier time the defensive position of the South would have been far stronger.

But even with railroads, superior munitions, and superior industrial facilities, the military tasks of the Union were most formidable. America was a profoundly civilian country. The peacetime army numbered only sixteen thousand, and few people on either side had any conception of the vast problems involved in recruiting, mobilizing, equipping, training, and maintaining large armies. It was an amateur's war on both sides, and many of its features seem inconceivable today. Most of the troops were recruited as volunteers rather than by conscription. There were no conscription laws in operation until the war was more than half over, and when these laws were adopted, their real purpose was not to put recruitment on a conscription basis but rather to stimulate volunteering. Even when conscripted under the Union's law, a man could still gain exemption by paying a fee of $300 or by hiring a substitute. Conscription was applied only in localities which failed to meet their quotas, and thus communities were impelled to pay "bounties" to encourage men to volunteer. This resulted in the practice of "bounty-jumping"—a man would enlist, collect his bounty, desert, enlist again in some other locality, collect another bounty, and desert again.

Volunteers often enlisted for limited periods, and when their terms of enlistment expired, there was nothing to prevent them from quitting the service and going home, even if the army in which they were enrolled was on the eve of battle. Volunteer units in most cases elected their own officers, up to the rank of colonel, and they frequently preferred officers who were not strict in matters of discipline.

Preparation for military service was negligible. Physical examinations for recruits were a farce. Men were placed in positions of command without prior training as officers, and recruits were often thrown into combat without any basic training as soldiers. This was, to a great extent, a do-it-yourself war.

THE WAR IN THE FIELD

The Virginia Front. From the very outset of the war, attention was focused on the Virginia front. After fighting had begun at Fort Sumter and the states of the upper South had joined the Confederacy, the Confederate government moved its capital to Richmond, Virginia, about one hundred miles south of Washington. With the two seats of government so close together, the war in the East became a struggle on the part of the Union to capture Richmond and on the part of the South to defend it.

Between Washington and Richmond a number of broad rivers—the Potomac, the Rappahannock, the York, the Chickahominy, and their tributaries—flow more or less parallel with one another from the Allegheny Mountains in the west to Chesapeake Bay in the east. This grid of rivers afforded a natural system of defense to the South and presented an obstacle course to the North. Southern armies on the defensive could lie in wait for their attackers on the south banks of these streams, as they did at Fredericksburg or at Chancellorsville. If the Southern army was driven back after going on the offensive, it could recross to safety, reorganize, and recoup, as it did after Antietam (Sharpsburg) and Gettysburg.

For four years the principal army of the North, the Army of the Potomac, struggled against the principal army of the South, the Army of Northern Virginia, over this terrain. Here each side placed its foremost commander: Robert E. Lee headed the Army of Northern Virginia after Joseph E. Johnston was wounded in 1862, while Ulysses S. Grant was brought east to take overall command of Union armies in 1864 after his great successes in the West. Public attention centered primarily upon these campaigns, and they have continued to receive more than their share of attention in history.

During the first half of the war, the Union met with a long succession of disappointments and defeats on the Virginia front. In July 1861, when both armies were still raw and unseasoned, the Union sent General Irvin McDowell south with the slogan "Onward to Richmond" and with expectations of an easy victory. But when he encountered the Confederate armies of Generals Pierre Beauregard and Joseph E. Johnston at Manassas Junction (the first battle of Bull Run), he was defeated, and his army, which was too green to absorb a defeat, lost all organization and retreated in panic to Washington. McDowell was replaced by George Brinton McClellan, who had campaigned successfully in West Virginia—a little man of supremely self-confident manner who was inevitably compared with Napoleon. McClellan possessed real ability as an organizer, and he had the good sense to realize that he must make his troops into

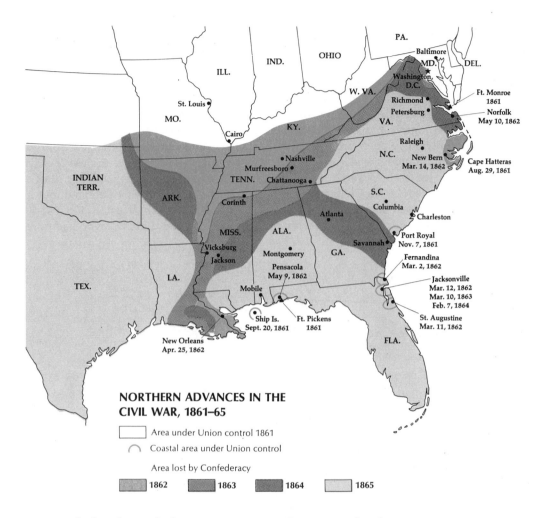

NORTHERN ADVANCES IN THE CIVIL WAR, 1861–65

☐ Area under Union control 1861

⌒ Coastal area under Union control

Area lost by Confederacy

| 1862 | 1863 | 1864 | 1865 |

Labels on map:
PA.
IND.
OHIO
ILL.
Baltimore
MD.
DEL.
Washington, D.C.
W. VA.
Richmond
Petersburg
Ft. Monroe 1861
Norfolk May 10, 1862
VA.
St. Louis
MO.
Cairo
KY.
Raleigh
N.C.
New Bern Mar. 14, 1862
Cape Hatteras Aug. 29, 1861
Nashville
Murfreesboro
TENN. Chattanooga
INDIAN TERR.
ARK.
Corinth
S.C.
Columbia
Charleston
Atlanta
Port Royal Nov. 7, 1861
MISS. ALA.
Savannah
Vicksburg
Jackson
Montgomery
GA.
Fernandina Mar. 2, 1862
Pensacola May 9, 1862
Jacksonville Mar. 12, 1862 Mar. 10, 1863 Feb. 7, 1864
LA.
Mobile
TEX.
Ship Is. Sept. 20, 1861
Ft. Pickens 1861
St. Augustine Mar. 11, 1862
New Orleans Apr. 25, 1862
FLA.

an army before he took them campaigning. Consequently, there was no more major fighting on the Virginia front for almost a year. When McClellan did at last move in April 1862, he persuaded President Lincoln to let him transport his troops by ship to a point (Fort Monroe) on the Virginia coast within striking distance of Richmond. From this point he proposed to move up the peninsula between the York and the James rivers (hence called the Peninsula Campaign) and to capture the Confederate capital.

McClellan's plan was a brilliant solution to the difficult problem of supply, for he could now bring provisions to his army by ship without fear of Confederate raiders getting to his rear and cutting his lines. But the plan had one important drawback: it left, or appeared to leave, Washington exposed to the Confederates. President Lincoln therefore insisted on withholding, for the defense of the capital, part of the troops that McClellan wanted, and McClellan, who was never willing to fight unless he had a sure thing, refused to push the offensive without these troops.

While these developments were in progress, the Confederate commander, Joseph E. Johnston, was badly wounded and was replaced by Robert E. Lee. Lee, a Virginia aristocrat, mild of speech and gentle of manner but gifted with a daring that was terrible to his adversaries, quickly perceived that he could play upon the Union's fear that Washington was too exposed. Accordingly, he sent his brilliant subordinate, Thomas J. ("Stonewall") Jackson, on a raid up the Shenandoah Valley, appearing to threaten Washington and causing the administration to hold there defensive troops which had previously been promised to McClellan. When Jackson returned from his raid with phenomenal speed, Lee's reunited forces took the offensive against McClellan's original forces in a series of engagements known as the Seven Days' Battles (June 26-July 1, 1862). McClellan fought hard and was not decisively defeated, but he lost his nerve, moved back to a base on the James River, and sent Washington a series of hysterical messages that the government had deserted him. Lincoln, who had never

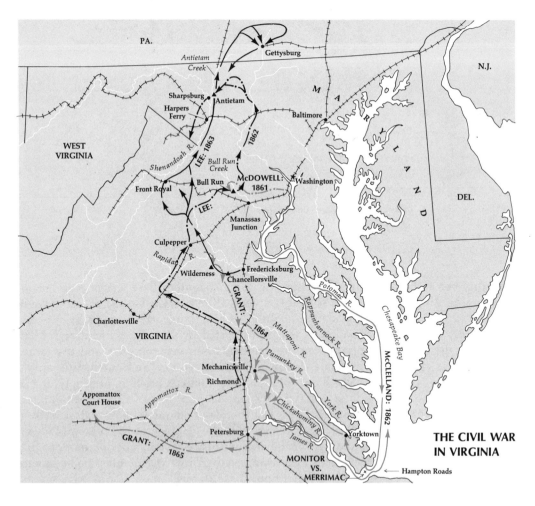

THE CIVIL WAR
IN VIRGINIA

fully accepted the basic idea of operating by sea, removed him from command and placed most of the troops under John Pope, who had gained a reputation in the West.

Pope promptly ran afoul of the Lee-Jackson combination at the Second Battle of Manassas (the second battle of Bull Run) in August 1862, and McClellan was restored to command and given a second chance. When Lee marched north, crossed the Potomac, and advanced into Maryland, McClellan shadowed him. Again Lee divided his forces, sending part of his army to capture Harper's Ferry. But even when a copy of Lee's secret orders fell into McClellan's hands and he knew exactly what to expect, he still did not move quickly or decisively. After a supremely hard-fought engagement at Antietam (Sharpsburg), Lee withdrew, undefeated and unpursued, to the south bank of the Potomac. Lincoln again replaced McClellan, this time with Ambrose E. Burnside.

In December 1862 Burnside made an unimaginative frontal attack across the Rappahannock at Fredericksburg, Virginia, against prepared Confederate defenses. Fighting the Confederates on ground of their own choosing, he sustained terrible losses and was replaced by Joseph Hooker. Hooker seemed a man of boldness and decision, but in May 1863, when he was trying to cross the Rappahannock at Chancellorsville, Lee and Jackson caught him with his army straddled across the river. The Confederates won another victory, but Hooker saved his army and the South paid a fearful price: Jackson was accidentally shot by a Confederate and died of his wound a few days later.

Hooker remained in command until Lee launched a second offensive against the North, this time into Pennsylvania. When Lee escaped from Hooker on the northward march, Lincoln again changed commanders, turning this time to George Gordon Meade. Meade's army and Lee's army met at Gettysburg, though neither side had planned it that way, and on July 2 and 3, 1863, the South made its supreme effort. The little town in Pennsylvania became the scene of the greatest battle ever fought in North America. Lee, facing Meade across a valley, threw his troops against the Union positions in a series of bold attacks, the most famous of which was Pickett's Charge. But Meade was too strong to be dislodged. Lee's forces, which had been fearfully punished, waited for more than a day to receive a counterattack that never came and then marched south. Meade did not pursue until too late, and ten days after the battle Lee recrossed the Potomac unmolested. The Army of Northern Virginia had still never been driven from a battlefield, but its great offensive power was forever broken.

The War in the West. On July 4, 1863, the day on which Lee began his uncontested withdrawal, another Confederate general, John C. Pemberton, at Vicksburg, Mississippi, surrendered an army of about thirty thousand men—the largest that has ever been captured in North America. The man to whom he surrendered was Ulysses S. Grant, and the event marked the culmination of a series of campaigns in the West which had been much more decisive in their results than the eastern campaigns.

The whole region beyond the Alleghenies was far vaster and more broken up geographically than the Virginia theater, and the campaigns in the West never had a single focus as they did in Virginia. Operations along the Mississippi were scarcely coordinated with operations in the central and eastern parts of Tennessee and

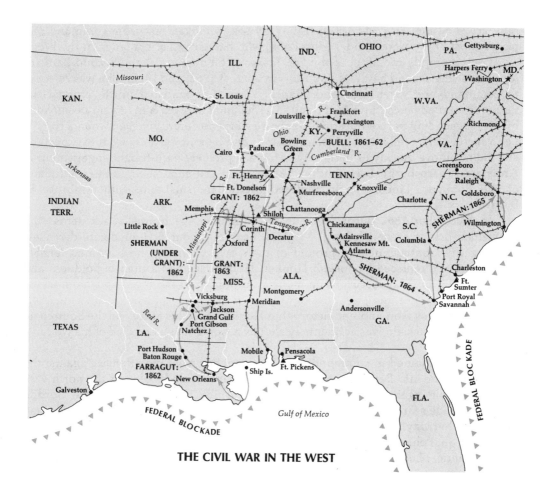

THE CIVIL WAR IN THE WEST

Kentucky, and neither of these was synchronized with activities "west of the River" in Missouri, Arkansas, most of Louisiana, and Texas. Essentially, however, it was the objective of the Union to gain control of the Mississippi and thus to cut off the western wing of the Confederacy. In this way Confederate armies would be deprived of reinforcements and supplies—especially of Texas cattle—which they vitally needed. A further division of the Confederacy would be undertaken by driving southeast through Kentucky and Tennessee, cutting vital Confederate rail connections at Chattanooga in eastern Tennessee, and continuing thence into the heart of the Confederacy, across Georgia to the sea. Such an operation would cut off the Gulf Coast region from the Atlantic seaboard and leave only Virginia, the Carolinas, and part of Georgia to support a hopeless cause.

It took three years and eight months for the Union to carry out these plans, but they began sooner than the great campaigns in Virginia. In February 1862, Grant, a man who had left the army in 1854 as a failure because of excessive drinking, successfully captured two forts, Henry and Donelson, in western Kentucky, which controlled the Tennessee and the Cumberland Rivers. Unlike the streams of Virginia, which cut across the paths of advancing armies, each of these rivers flowed in a "U" shaped course from the southern Appalachians southward into northern Alabama (in the case of the Tennessee) or central Tennessee (in the case of the Cumberland) and then, reversing their course, almost due north to the Ohio River. Control of these river highways gave Grant easy entry deep into the South. On the Cumberland, Nashville, the capital of Tennessee, fell to the Union as soon as Fort Donelson was captured, and by April Grant had advanced up the Tennessee almost to the border of Mississippi. In that same month, when all was still very "quiet along the Potomac," the Union army and navy, by skillful combined operations, captured New Orleans, the largest city of the Confederacy.

After these early successes, the Union forces found themselves blocked for some time. A Confederate army under Albert Sidney Johnston struck Grant unexpectedly at Shiloh, Tennessee, on April 6, 1862, drove his army to the edge of the Tennessee River, and might have destroyed it if Johnston had not been killed in action. When Grant was later able to resume the initiative, he turned his attention to the Confederate stronghold at Vicksburg, where towering bluffs command the Mississippi. Deep in enemy country, Vicksburg was rendered almost impregnable by vast swamps, a succession of steep hills, and by the river itself. After making a series of unsuccessful moves against this natural fortress, Grant at last hit on the bold and unorthodox plan of moving down the west side of the river, crossing below Vicksburg, abandoning his lines of communication, and living off the country during a final drive against the Confederate defenses. It was by this plan that he finally captured Pemberton's entire army at Vicksburg on July 4, 1863, and gained complete control of the Mississippi artery.

Grant Takes Command. After Vicksburg, in March 1864, Lincoln brought Grant east to serve as general-in-chief and to take personal charge of the Army of the Potomac (Meade was not removed but was under Grant's command).

By this time the Confederacy, outnumbered from the beginning, was fearfully handicapped by losses of men which could not be replaced as Union losses could. Grant, recognizing this handicap, settled upon a plan of operations that was far less brilliant than his operations in the West, but no less decisive. By steadily extending his flanks, he forced the Confederacy to extend also and to make its lines very thin; by continuing pressure, he gave his adversaries no rest. Lee resisted with immense skill, and Grant sacrificed men so freely in the Campaign of the Wilderness (May 5–6, 1864) that his losses exceeded the total number of men in Lee's army. In June 1864, after being terribly punished at the Battle of Cold Harbor, Grant decided to move his base to the James River (as McClellan had done two years earlier), to attack from the south. He succeeded in this maneuver and thus pinned Lee's forces at Petersburg, which is actually south of Richmond. With Petersburg under siege and Lee no longer mobile, it was only a question of time, but Lee held on for nine long months while Richmond remained the Confederate capital.

Sherman's March. While Grant and Lee faced each other across the trenches at Petersburg, the Confederacy was being cut to pieces from the rear. Grant had first cut it at Vicksburg on the Mississippi, and the next cut was to take place from central Kentucky and Tennessee. By the end of 1863 the Union armies had won control of eastern Tennessee through a series of battles, principally at Chickamauga and at Missionary Ridge outside Chattanooga. When Grant left for Virginia, William T. Sherman, a trusted subordinate, was left to face the Confederate forces under Joseph E. Johnston in the mountains of north Georgia.

Johnston, "retreating general" but a resourceful obstructionist, blocked and delayed Sherman at every step, all the way to Atlanta. There he was removed because of his unwillingness to take the offensive, and John B. Hood was put in his place. Hood made the mistake of challenging Sherman in a general engagement and was so badly defeated that Sherman, after taking Atlanta on September 2, 1864, was able to march unopposed across Georgia to the sea. Sherman reached the port of Savannah on Christmas 1864, while Grant was still outside Petersburg.

Appomattox. From this time, the South was completely fragmented and the Confederacy's cause was hopeless. But Johnston, having returned to his command in the Southeast, held together a force which retreated across the Carolinas, with Sherman pursuing and burning Columbia, South Carolina, as he pursued. Lee, meanwhile, held against steadily increasing odds at Petersburg. By April 1865, however, the inevitable defeat could be put off no longer. Petersburg fell and Richmond was evacuated. Lee met Grant on April 9 at a farmhouse near Appomattox Court House, and in a moving scene surrendered the Army of Northern Virginia to Grant, who accorded generous terms and told his troops not to cheer because, he said, "the rebels are our countrymen again." Johnston also surrendered at Greensboro, North Carolina, before the end of the month, and the Confederate government, which had fled south after the fall of Petersburg, simply evaporated.

THE WAR BEHIND THE LINES

The Problems of the Confederacy. Writers on the Civil War have piled up a vast literature—one of the largest bodies of literature on any historical subject—detailing the military aspects of the war: the battles and leaders, the campaigns and maneuvers, the strategy and tactics. This military record, however, does not fully explain the outcome of the war. For, in terms of strategy and tactics, the Confederate performance equaled that of the Union and, on the Virginia front, surpassed it until the last year of the war. The final result was registered on the battlefield, but the basic factors which caused Confederate defeat lay behind the lines. Essentially, the Confederacy failed to solve the problems of organizing its society and its economy for war. It faced these problems in a particularly difficult form, and when it proved unable to solve them, it went down to defeat.

One basic handicap of the Confederacy lay in the fact that while the North had an industrial economy that was invigorated by war, the Southern economy was based on cotton production, which was dislocated and almost paralyzed by the war. In the North, war stimulated employment, and while wages failed to keep pace with inflation, civilian morale was generally high except among the underpaid urban poor. In the South, economic conditions deteriorated so badly that what may be called economic morale declined even while fighting morale remained good. During the spring of 1863 "bread riots" occurred in Richmond and several other Southern cities.

Essentially, the Confederacy, with its rural and agricultural society, needed two things. First, it needed access to the products of European—especially British—industry. Second, it needed to stimulate production of food, of horses, and of strategic supplies within the South. Ultimately, it was unable to meet any of these needs.

In order to be able to draw on British industry, the Confederacy needed to have buying power in the European market and to be able to ship goods freely to and fro across the Atlantic. Once war broke out, Lincoln proclaimed a blockade, which meant that federal naval vessels would try to seize the merchant vessels of any neutral country bringing goods to Confederate ports. But Southerners thought that the blockade would not work, partly because there were not enough Union ships to enforce it and even more because they believed in what has been called the "King Cotton delusion." They were firmly convinced that cotton was an absolute economic necessity to Britain, because textiles were the heart of British industry, and without cotton this industry would be prostrated; Britain's factories would stand idle; its workers would be unemployed and would literally starve. When this started happening, the British government would decide to intervene to get cotton, and the British navy, which still dominated the seas, would break the blockade.

Southerners were so confident of this idea that they were quite willing to see the British supply of cotton cut off for awhile. In the first months of the blockade, while it was still largely ineffective, they deliberately kept their cotton at home instead of sending a part of it abroad to be held in British warehouses so that it could later be sold to give them funds for the purchase of supplies. Thus, their only important economic asset, a store of cotton which was worth ten times as much as the gold supply of the Confederacy, was never put to constructive use.

The Importance of Sea Power. This faith in cotton ultimately proved to be a fallacy for several reasons. Britain succeeded in getting a certain amount of cotton elsewhere; British antislavery sentiment generated a strong resistance to taking steps that would help the Confederacy; and Britain was pleased to see America adopting a doctrine of international law concerning the right of blockade which she had always advocated and which was bound to be favorable to a nation with large naval power. But most of all, British industry was not paralyzed because Northern wartime purchases stimulated it. Britain, as a neutral, enjoyed an economic boom from supplying war materials to the Union—a boom very similar to the booms which the United States later enjoyed in 1914–17 and 1939–41 as a neutral supplying war materials to Britain.

Consequently, Britain and France, which was following Britain's lead, never did give diplomatic recognition to the Confederate government, although they did recognize the existence of a state of war in which they would be neutral. This meant that they would treat Confederate naval vessels as warships and not as pirates. The

British recognition of belligerency was much resented in the United States, but in fact the real danger for the Union cause lay in the possibility of diplomatic recognition of the Confederacy, which would probably have resulted in British efforts to break the blockade. Such efforts would, in turn, have led to war with Britain. But this recognition, for which the Confederacy waited so anxiously, never came.

In November 1861 Confederate hopes were high when an eager Union naval officer, Charles Wilkes, stopped a British ship on the high seas and took off two Confederate envoys to Britain, James Mason and John Slidell. Britain, at this point, actually prepared to fight, but President Lincoln wisely admitted the error and set the commissioners free. Meanwhile, the blockade steadily grew tighter. One Confederate port after another was sealed off. Small Confederate vessels, built for speed and based in the Bahama Islands, continued to delight the South by running the blockade freely and bringing in cargoes of goods with high value in proportion to their bulk. But their volume was small, and they did not in any sense provide the flow of goods which the Confederacy so vitally needed.

In addition to depending on British naval might, the Confederacy made two important efforts to establish sea power of its own. To begin with, it fitted out the first large ironclad vessel ever to put to sea. A powerful steam frigate, the U.S.S. *Merrimac,* which the federals had scuttled in the Norfolk Navy Yard, was raised, renamed the *Virginia,* covered with armor plate, and sent out in March 1862—an iron giant against the wooden vessels of the Union navy. In its first day at sea it destroyed two large Union vessels with ease. The entire Union navy appeared to be in acute danger, and there was panic in Northern coastal cities. But the Union had been preparing a metal-clad vessel of its own—a small craft that lay low in the water, with a revolving gun turret. This *Monitor,* as it was called, challenged the *Virginia* on March 9, 1862. The battle ended in a draw, but with Monitor-type vessels the Union navy was again safe.

The Confederacy's second major endeavor at sea was to buy in England vessels and equipment which, under the technicalities of British law, could be combined on the high seas to produce fighting ships without violating Britain's neutrality. These vessels could then raid merchant vessels flying the Union flag. There were five such raiders, most famous of which was the *Alabama.* This great marauder, commanded by Admiral Raphael Semmes, roamed the seas for two years, from Newfoundland to Singapore, captured sixty-two merchant ships (most of which were burned, after careful attention to the safety of their crews and passengers), and sank the U.S.S. *Hatteras* in a major naval battle. It was at last cornered and sunk off Cherbourg, France, by the U.S.S. *Kearsarge,* but its career had made the American flag so unsafe on the high seas that prohibitive insurance costs caused more than seven hundred American vessels to transfer to British registry. The American merchant marine never again attained the place in the world's carrying trade it had held before the *Alabama* put to sea.

The Confederacy sought to have additional raiders built in British shipyards, and two immensely formidable vessels—the Laird rams—were actually constructed. But strenuous American diplomatic protests, coupled with British awareness that in spite of technicalities this was really a violation of neutrality, led the British government to stop their delivery in October 1863. After this the Confederate cause was lost at sea as well as on land, and the federal blockade tightened like a noose to strangle the Confederacy economically.

Economic Failures of the South. Meanwhile, on the home front, the Confederacy failed economically because it was caught between the need to stimulate production and the need to keep down prices and to control inflation. The Southern government began with almost no financial assets other than land and slaves, neither of which could be readily transformed into negotiable currency. It faced a dilemma: it could either encourage production by buying goods in the open market at an uncontrolled price, in which case inflation would mushroom; or it could control inflation by a system of requisitioning goods for its armies at arbitrarily fixed prices, in which case production would be discouraged rather than stimulated. Only a program of heavy taxation, by which the government would take back the inflationary dollars that had been spent, could have helped at all in reducing this problem, but the Confederacy was afraid to use its taxing power. It raised less than 1 percent of its revenue from taxes—a smaller proportion than any other nation in a modern war—and it procured funds by borrowing, which is the most inflationary method of all. Ultimately it failed either to stimulate production or to control inflation. Goods grew scarcer while money grew more plentiful: it was grimly said that at the beginning of the war people took their money to market in a purse and brought their goods home in a basket, but that by the end they took the money in a basket and brought their purchases home in a purse.

In short, the Confederacy died of economic starvation—an insufficiency of goods. Its government was too weak to cope with the nearly insoluble economic problems the war had caused. President Jefferson Davis was a bureaucrat who thought in legalistic rather than in dynamic terms; he was not an innovator but a conservative miscast as a revolutionist. The state governments competed against the Confederate government for the control of manpower and supplies; they insisted upon their sovereign status so strenuously that it has been said that the Confederacy was born of states' rights and died of states' rights. The only chance the Confederacy ever had, and it was perhaps a fairly good one, was to win a short war before the results of economic malnutrition set in. Once that failed, the cause was hopeless. A few Confederates, like Josiah Gorgas in the Ordnance Department, improvised brilliantly, and others did so desperately; but in a country where a vitally necessary rail line could be laid only be tearing up the rails somewhere else and re-laying them, a long war against a dynamic adversary could have but one ending.

Northern Industrialism and Republican Ascendancy. The problems and limitations of the Confederacy—problems of localism and decentralization, of an agricultural economy and of small-scale economic activities—were characteristic features of the kind of folk society the Confederacy was defending. But while the South was making a last stand against the forces of the modern mechanized world, the war was rushing the North along the path toward industrial domination. Before the Southern states withdrew from the Union, they had blocked some of the governmental measures most conducive to the new industrial economy. Southern secession, however, left the new Republican party in control; and though this party seemed what we call liberal in its opposition to slavery, it was from the outset Whiggish, or conservative, in its economic policies. It believed in using federal power to promote economic growth through the encouragement of various forms of private enterprise; and while this was believed to work to the advantage of everyone, it meant in direct terms the encouragement and sponsorship of measures favorable to industry and to private capital. Thus, in February 1861, while the empty seats of the departing Southern congressmen were still warm, and even before President Lincoln took office, Congress adopted the Morrill Tariff, which, though not very high, was higher than the existing tariff of 1857. This was the first of many tariff increases; there was not another perceptible reduction until 1913. Meanwhile Congress repeatedly strengthened the measures by which it gave American industrial producers more exclusive control in the American market, even if this forced American consumers to pay higher prices than they would have had to pay on the world market.

The Transcontinental Railroad.   In 1862 Congress broke the long deadlock the sectional conflict had created over the building of a railroad to the Pacific. For a decade, advocates of a southern route and supporters of a northern route had blocked each other; but now, with the Southerners absent, Congress created the Union Pacific Railroad Company, incorporated with a federal charter, to build westward from Omaha and to meet another road, the Central Pacific, a California corporation, building eastward from Sacramento. To encourage this enterprise, Congress placed very large resources at the disposal of the railroads. It gave to the roads ten square miles of land, running back in alternate blocks from the tracks, for each mile of track built, and it granted loans (not gifts) of between $16,000 and $48,000 a mile—according to the difficulty of the terrain where construction took place. The value of the lands at that time was not great, and the munificence of this largesse has often been exaggerated. But the point is that the government was paying most of the costs of construction, and it might well have controlled or even owned the railroad. Instead, it placed these resources in the hands of private operators, who, if they succeeded, would become owners of the world's greatest railroad and, if they lost, would be losing the government's money rather than their own. It was "venture capitalism," as it is now called, but the government was doing most of the venturing and the private interests which constructed the road were getting most of the capital.

In 1869, four years after the war ended, the Union Pacific and the Central Pacific met at Promontory Point in Utah, and a golden spike was driven to mark the event. Travelers to California no longer were obliged to sail around Cape Horn, and the United States was a long step closer to being a transcontinental, two-ocean republic in an operative sense as well as in a purely geographical one.

The National Banking System.   One other major economic measure resulting from Republican ascendancy was the creation of a new and far more centralized system of banking and money. Ever since Andrew Jackson's overthrow of the Bank of the United States in 1832, the country had had a decentralized, loose-jointed financial system—one which today it is difficult even to imagine. The United States, of course, issued coins and also bills; for each bill in circulation, a corresponding value of precious metal was held in the Treasury and could be claimed by the holder of the bill. The government handled all its own transactions in such currency and was thus on a "hard money" basis. Actually, this kind of money was not nearly sufficient to meet the economic needs of the country for a circulating medium. The principal circulating medium, therefore, had been provided by notes issued by banks operating under charters from the various states. State laws governing the incorporation of banks naturally varied, which meant that the financial soundness of the various banks also varied; this in turn meant that some of the notes circulated at face value, and others circulated at various degrees of discount from face value. Although the government was on a hard money basis, the economy of the country was not, and the federal government exercised no control whatever over the principal component in the monetary system of the country.

The National Bank Act of 1863, which changed all this, grew out of the government's need to raise the immense sums required for fighting a war. At times the government's need of funds was so acute that it resorted to the issue of "green-backs"—bills which could not be redeemed in bullion. But primarily the Treasury relied upon borrowing—that is, upon selling bonds—and to borrow it had to make the bonds attractive as holdings for the banks. Accordingly, the National Banking Act provided that a bank which purchased government bonds to the amount of one third of its paid-in capital (not less than $30,000) might receive federally guaranteed notes, known as national bank notes, in an amount equal to 90 percent of its bond holdings. The bank would, of course, lend out the notes at interest, and thus would receive interest both on the bonds and on the notes it received for holding the bonds. At the same time, a tax was laid on the notes issued under state authority by state-chartered banks; the tax had the effect of making these notes unprofitable and thus driving them out of circulation. As a result of government borrowing policy, therefore, the United States acquired a new, uniform, federally sanctioned circulating medium of national bank notes.

These notes became the principal form of money for the next fifty years, but they had a great defect—they made the amount of money dependent upon the volume of federal debt rather than upon the economic needs of the country. They were inflexible, and in 1913 they were largely replaced by Federal Reserve notes as a result of the establishment of the Federal Reserve System. But the principles that the United States should have a uniform currency in use throughout the nation, and that the federal government should be responsible for this currency, had come to stay.

Women and the War. Although the Civil War brought suffering and loss to hundreds of thousands of American women, for women as a group the war meant progress toward independence and equality. It meant new opportunities for employment, broadened social and political interests, demonstrations of competence in activities previously reserved for men. Some women went to war, as nurses, spies, even as soldiers. But the vast majority who served at home—including those who stayed in the home—did most damage to the myth of the helpless female.

As in earlier wars, but in much greater numbers, women had to take their husbands' places as heads of households, running shops, managing farms and plantations, finding jobs to earn food for their families. In the South, many had to do housework—and field work—for the first time; some had to face armed, hostile blacks as well as enemy soldiers. In Minnesota and elsewhere on the frontier, women had to survive Indian uprisings.

Job opportunities for women multiplied as men went off to fight or quit old occupations for better paying ones. Schoolteaching paid so poorly that many men left it, and women—who were paid even less than the men they replaced—began their advance toward dominance of the profession. In both the Union and the Confederacy, women also went to work for the government. By the end of the war hundreds held government office jobs. Here, too, the change was permanent: Washington, D.C., would never again be without its corps of women workers. Many were employed, and some were killed, in government arsenals.

When the war began, women dominated the work force in the mills and factories of New England, while in the South women industrial workers were a small minority—another situation that favored the Union war effort. As men joined the service, women took their places in industry and helped produce military equipment and supplies. The demand for what was considered women's work also expanded: sewing women were hired by the thousands, and brutally exploited. In self-protection, the women organized, protested, and went out on strikes.

In addition to work for pay, there was a tremendous amount of unpaid activity by women in both South and North. Women volunteered to nurse and to teach; they joined aid societies; they organized activities to raise funds. They wrote and spoke for the causes they believed in. They were often brave, noble, self-sacrificing. They were also passionately partisan, pushing men and boys into enlisting and preaching hatred of the enemy to their children. In the South some turned food riots into excuses for looting; in the North some helped turn draft riots into murderous assaults on blacks.

The Civil War went a long way toward destroying the myth of the helpless female. It gave American women a chance to prove themselves quite as capable as men in many areas. They proved their smartness and their toughness. When the war ended, many lost their jobs to returning veterans. Some returned gratefully to domesticity. But there was no turning back the clock.

EMANCIPATION AND RECONSTRUCTION

The Road to Reunion. Wars always bring results which are not intended by the men who fight them. The Civil War accelerated the growth of mass production and economic centralization in the North while it destroyed much of the economic plant in the South and convinced the rising generation of Southern leaders that future regional prosperity would depend upon industrialization. The war also caused an increase in federal power at the expense of the states, for no government could spend the funds, organize the forces, and wield the strength the federal government did, without increasing its power. But the main purpose of the war was to reunite a broken union of states, and there was a question whether the abolition of slavery was necessary to the objective of reunion. Some Republicans wanted to make emancipation one of the objects of the war, simply because they deplored slavery and did not believe that a Union which had slavery in it was worth saving. Others, who were relatively indifferent to the welfare of the blacks, believed that the slaveholding class, which they called the "slave power," was guilty of causing disunion, that to make the Union safe this power must be destroyed, and that the way to destroy it was to abolish slavery. Still others, including many of the "War Democrats" and the Unionists in the border states, regarded the war as one against secession, having nothing to do with slavery.

Emancipation. For his part, Abraham Lincoln had stated his belief, long before he became President, that the Union could not endure permanently half-slave and half-free. He knew, however, that he could not free any slaves unless he won the war and that he could not win the war if he antagonized all the Unionists in the slave states of Delaware, Maryland, Kentucky (his own birthplace), and Missouri. As a result, he moved very slowly on the slavery question, and when two of his generals tried to move more quickly by emancipating slaves in the areas they had occupied, he countermanded their orders. Few people realize it today, but the war had raged for seventeen months and was more than a third over before Lincoln moved to free the slaves in the Confederacy. In July 1862 he made up his mind to proclaim the freedom of slaves in the insurrectionary states, but he decided to wait for a victory before doing so. The Battle of Antietam (Sharpsburg) in September was not a great victory, but it sufficed; in that month Lincoln issued a proclamation that after January 1, 1863, all slaves in areas which were at that time in rebellion should be "forever free." This still did nothing about slaves in places like New Orleans, which was occupied by federal forces, nor in the border slave states, and it gave all the states of the Confederacy more than ninety days during which they could save slavery by coming back into the union. Strongly believing in persuasion rather than force, Lincoln in December 1862 proposed a constitutional amendment for the gradual emancipation of slaves in the border states by the year 1900, with compensation to the owners. But this was defeated in Congress by a combination of proslavery men who thought it went too far and antislavery men who thought it did not go far enough.

The caution with which Lincoln had proceeded with emancipation reflects his own scruples about the Constitution and the prudence of his own temperament, but it also reflects the fierceness of the divisions within the North and the dangers which these divisions held for the administration. On one flank, Lincoln was assailed by the Democrats. A minority of War Democrats gave him vigorous support, but a majority of "Copperheads" constantly called for peace, and especially assailed any move against slavery. Democratic propagandists helped convince white workingmen that they were being used in a war to free blacks who would take their jobs away; this conviction turned the "draft riots" in New York in July 1863 into mob assaults on blacks, in which hundreds were killed (most of them white rioters shot down by police).

On the other flank, the more militant antislavery men in the Republican party denounced Lincoln because he did not instantly take drastic action. These "radical

Republicans" hoped to dominate the administration by forcing all moderates on the slavery question out of the cabinet, and in 1864 some of them sought to prevent Lincoln's nomination for a second term. But by unrivaled political dexterity and skill Lincoln frustrated these attacks from both directions and maintained a broad base of support for the war.

As late as 1864 the House of Representatives defeated a constitutional amendment for the abolition of slavery. The Thirteenth Amendment was not finally voted by Congress for submission to the states until January 31, 1865. Maryland, Tennessee, and Missouri abolished slavery by state action at about this same time, but slavery was still legal in Kentucky and Delaware when the Civil War ended, and the amendment for the abolition of slavery was not ratified until eight months after Lincoln's death.

Lincoln as a War Leader.　Long after these events, people who had grown up with an oversimplified image of Lincoln as a Great Emancipator became disillusioned by this record, and in the twentieth century some critics have sought to tear down his reputation. But in fact, he remains a figure of immense stature.

Born in 1809 in a log cabin in Kentucky, Lincoln grew up on the frontier in Indiana and Illinois, doing rough work as a rail splitter and a plowboy and receiving only a meager education. Later he became a self-taught lawyer with a successful practice in Springfield, served in the state legislature as a Whig, and rode the circuit on horseback to follow the sessions of the court. Except for one term in Congress, 1845–47, he virtually never went East and was unknown until the debates with Douglas gained him a reputation in 1858. In 1861, at a moment of crisis, this tall, gangling, plain-looking man, whose qualities of greatness were still unsuspected, became President.

Lincoln's relaxed and unpretentious manner masked remarkable powers of decision and qualities of leadership. Completely lacking in self-importance, he seemed humble to some observers. But in fact he acted with the patience and forbearance of a man who was very sure of what he was doing. Refusing to let the abolitionists push him into an antislavery war which would antagonize Union men who did not care about slavery, and refusing to let the Union men separate him from the antislavery contingent by restricting war aims too narrowly, he saw that the causes of Union and emancipation must support each other instead of opposing each other, or both would be defeated. Patiently he worked to fuse the idea of union with that of freedom and equality ("a new nation conceived in liberty and dedicated to the proposition that all men are created equal"). Thus he reaffirmed for American nationalism the idealism of freedom and gave to the ideal of freedom the strength of an undivided union. Knowing that in a democracy a man must win political success in order to gain a chance for statesmanship, he moved patiently and indirectly to his goals, and his opportunism greatly offended many abolitionists. But in the end he struck slavery a more deadly blow than any of them could ever strike.

Black Americans and the War.　For black Americans, the Civil War years were a time of elation and rejoicing, frustration and despair. Many Northern blacks felt that, as a preliminary to emancipation and reconstruction, the separation of the slave states from the free states was long overdue. Men and women alike worked hard for the Union cause. Black intellectuals wrote and lectured, at home and abroad. Blacks organized their own aid and relief societies for the great numbers of freed slaves and went to them as teachers. Black women volunteered their services as nurses and hospital aids; black men by the hundreds of thousands went to war for the Union as sailors in the navy and as servants, cooks, and laborers with the army. When they were finally allowed to, they also went as soldiers.

But for a long time blacks were not allowed to serve in the army. Not until the summer of 1862 were blacks officially permitted to enlist, and it was another year before the bravery of black regiments in battle began to change the scornful attitude of whites, in and out of the service. Overall, black servicemen established an admirable record: twenty-one received the Congressional Medal of Honor. But they were denied commissions, and not until June 1864 were they given as much pay as their white counterparts.

Throughout the war, then, blacks continued to face injustice and discrimination, despite their major contribution to the Union cause. From the beginning, their most influential spokesman, Frederick Douglass, looked on Lincoln as much too conservative, and when the President took no decisive steps toward freeing the slaves, Douglass was outspoken in his criticism. Although Lincoln had his black supporters, including the beloved Harriet Tubman, he also gave offense by his continuing interest in some programs to move blacks out of the country to a colony in the tropics. There were some already so embittered that they welcomed the possibility of such separation. Martin R. Delany, who later joined with Douglass in working for black recruitment, favored the migration of American blacks to Haiti, a project that was tried unsuccessfully early in the war. After the rejection of black volunteers by the army, the subsequent mistreatment of black soldiers, and attacks on both black soldiers and black civilians in several Northern cities, there were blacks who agreed with white racists that the Civil War was indeed a white man's war—in a white man's country to which blacks owed no allegiance.

Nevertheless, there was progress. The Emancipation Proclamation was finally issued; the Thirteenth Amendment was adopted. The great slave population (which, as Douglass had repeatedly pointed out, enabled the Confederacy to put so large a proportion of its whites into uniform) was finally freed. Many blacks, Union soldiers as well as former slaves, were also freed from the bonds of illiteracy by dedicated teachers—both black and white—and through their own efforts. Blacks were recognized as full citizens by the federal government, and campaigns against discrimination in the law courts, the polling places, the schools, and public conveyances won victories in several states. In 1864 black representatives from eighteen states formed the National Equal Rights League. The long, agonizingly slow march toward equality was begun.

The Question of the Former Slave. If the Union was slow to face the question of slavery, it was even slower to face the question of racism in America. From the perspective of the twentieth century we can now see the great misfortune of the Civil War: while it solved the problem of slavery, it did nothing whatever to solve the problem of racism, which was so closely linked with slavery. People recognized that slavery must end, but this was a negative decision, for it did not clarify what should be put in slavery's place. Was the former slave to occupy a subordinate status in American society, or was he to be put on the path toward equality? The answer was by no means clear, for although there were twenty-one free states, only a part of these permitted blacks to vote, and though Abraham Lincoln opposed slavery ("If slavery is not wrong, then nothing is wrong"), he did not accept the idea of racial equality ("I am not, nor ever have been, in favor of bringing about in any way the social and political equality of the white and black races"). In fact, to the end of his life he wanted to colonize the former slaves in Haiti or Central America, because he believed that whites and blacks could not live harmoniously together. (This belief, it should be noted, did not necessarily mean that he was discriminatory in his personal attitude; it might mean simply that he was pessimistic about biracial adjustments.)

Lincoln's Policy of Reconstruction. Along with this lack of conviction concerning racial equality, Lincoln and the Northern moderates were deeply impressed by a feeling that victory in war could not really restore the Union; it could only prevent secession. After that, if the Union were really restored, it would be because the Southern people again accepted the Union and gave their loyalty to it. To bring them back, Lincoln wanted a moderate and conciliatory policy. When in 1864 Congress adopted a measure known as the Wade-Davis Bill, imposing drastic terms for the restoration of the former Confederates, Lincoln vetoed it, and when people raised technical questions about the legal status of the Confederate states (Were they still states, or conquered territories? Had they committed "state suicide"?), he was impatient about such "pernicious abstractions." All that mattered was whether the states could be brought back into their proper relationship with the Union.

By 1864 the Union had regained enough control in Louisiana and Arkansas to start a process of restoring these states to the Union, and Lincoln laid down generous terms on which this could be done. He would grant amnesty to former Confederates who took an oath of allegiance, and when as many as one tenth of the number who had been citizens in 1860 did so, he would permit them to form a new state government. When this government accepted the abolition of slavery and repudiated the principle of secession, Lincoln would receive it back into the Union. It did not have to recognize the rights of blacks nor give a single one the vote. Louisiana was the first state reorganized on this basis, and despite its denial of black suffrage, Lincoln accepted it, though he did ask the governor "whether some of the colored people may not be let in, as for instance the very intelligent, and especially those who have fought gallantly in our ranks." In Virginia, Tennessee, and Arkansas, also, Lincoln recognized state governments which did not enfranchise the black American. But it was clear that Republicans in Congress were suspicious of these states—more because of their leniency toward the former Confederates than because of their treatment of the black—and that Congress might deny them recognition by refusing to seat their newly elected senators and representatives.

In 1864, when the time came for a new presidential election, the Democrats nominated General McClellan to run against Lincoln. Some of the so-called Radical Republicans, who were dissatisfied with Lincoln's leniency, tried to block his renomination and put up the Secretary of the Treasury, Salmon P. Chase, in his stead.

But this effort failed, and Lincoln was, of course, renominated. In an effort to put the ticket on a broad, bipartisan basis, the party dropped the name Republican, called itself the Union party and nominated for the vice-presidency a Southern Democrat and former slaveholder who had stood firmly for the Union, Andrew Johnson of Tennessee.

In November 1864 Lincoln and Johnson were elected, carrying all but three states (New Jersey, Delaware, and Kentucky). In the following March, the new term began, and Lincoln delivered his Second Inaugural Address, calling for "malice toward none and charity for all," in order "to bind up the nation's wounds." On April 9, Lee surrendered the Army of Northern Virginia; it was clear that the work of Reconstruction must now begin in earnest. On April 14, Lincoln attended a performance at Ford's Theater, where he was shot by an assassin, John Wilkes Booth. He died the next morning, without ever recovering consciousness, and Andrew Johnson became President of the United States.

Johnson's Policy of Reconstruction. Although a Southerner, Johnson was expected to be more severe in his Reconstruction policy than Lincoln. Johnson, a former tailor who had been illiterate until his wife taught him to write, and a man of strong emotions, hated both aristocrats and secessionists. But when his policy developed, Johnson proved even more lenient toward the Southern states than Lincoln had been.

On May 29, 1865, he issued a broad amnesty to all who would take an oath of allegiance, though men with property valued at more than $20,000 (in other words, planters) were required to ask special pardon, which was freely given. In the six weeks after May 29 he appointed provisional governors in each of the remaining Southern states to reorganize governments for these states. Only men who had been voters in 1860 and who had taken the oath of allegiance could participate in these reorganizations. This meant, of course, that blacks were excluded. When the new governments disavowed secession, accepted the abolition of slavery, and repudiated the Confederate debt, Johnson would accept them. As to what they were going to do about the blacks, no questions would be asked.

The Southern states moved swiftly under this easy formula. Before the end of the year, every state except Texas, which followed soon after, had set up a new government which met the President's terms. But two conspicuous features of these governments were deeply disturbing to many Republicans. First, these Southern states had adopted a series of laws known as "Black Codes," which denied to blacks many of the rights of citizenship—including the right to vote and to serve on juries—and which also excluded them from certain types of property ownership and certain occupations. Unemployed Negroes might be arrested as vagrants and bound out to labor in a new form of involuntary servitude. Second, the former Confederates were in complete control: the newly organized states, between them, elected to Congress the vice-president of the Confederacy, four Confederate generals, five Confederate colonels, six Confederate cabinet officers, and fifty-eight Confederate congressmen.

Congressional Radicals. When Congress met at the end of 1865, it was confronted by the fact that Reconstruction (on the President's terms) had been virtually completed without Congress having any voice in the matter. At this point, the Republicans were far from ready for the kind of all-out fight against Johnson which later developed, but they were not willing to accept the reorganized states, especially since they felt that these states would now claim a larger representation in Congress because of the free black population (only three fifths of the blacks had been counted when they were slaves), without actually allowing the blacks any voice in the government. It would be ironical indeed if the overthrow of slavery should increase the representation of the South in Congress and if the Rebels should come back into the Union stronger than when they went out.

For some months, the Republicans in Congress moved slowly, unwilling to face a break with a President of their own party, and far from ready to make a vigorous stand for the rights of blacks. But they would not seat the Southern congressmen-elect, and they set up a Joint Committee of the Senate and the House to assert their claim to a voice in the formulation of Reconstruction policy. They also passed a bill to extend the life and increase the activities of the Freedmen's Bureau—an agency created to aid blacks in their transition from slavery to freedom. When Johnson vetoed this measure and also vetoed a Civil Rights bill, tensions increased, and in June 1866, Congress voted a proposed Fourteenth Amendment. This amendment clearly asserted the citizenship of blacks; it also asserted that they were entitled to the "privileges and immunities of citizens," to the "equal protection of the laws," and to protection against being deprived of "life, liberty, and property without due process of law." The determination of exactly what these terms meant has kept lawyers busy for almost a century now, but one thing was clear:the amendment did not include a right of black suffrage. It did, however, provide that states which disfranchised a part of their adult male population would have their representation proportionately reduced. It almost seemed that Congress was offering the Southerners a choice: they might disfranchise the blacks if they were willing to pay the price of reduced representation, or they might have increased representation if they were willing to pay the price of black suffrage. This might not help the blacks, but it was certain to help the Republicans: it would either reduce the strength of Southern white Democrats or give the Republicans black political allies in the South.

The Fourteenth Amendment also excluded from federal office any person who had held any important public office before the Civil War and had then gone over to the Confederacy. This sweeping move to disqualify almost the entire leadership of the South led the Southern states to make the serious mistake of following President Johnson's advice to reject the amendment. During the latter half of 1866 and the first months of 1867, ten Southern states voted not to ratify.

Radical Reconstruction. Southern rejection of the Fourteenth Amendment precipitated the bitter fight which had been brewing for almost two years. Congress now moved to destroy the Johnson governments and to set up new governments of its own. Between March and July 1867, it adopted a series of Reconstruction Acts which divided ten Southern states into five military districts under five military governors. These governors were to hold elections for conventions to frame new state constitutions. In these elections adult males, including blacks, were to vote, but many whites, disqualified by their support of the Confederacy, were not to vote. The constitutions these conventions adopted must establish black suffrage, and the governments which they established must ratify the Fourteenth Amendment. Then and only then might they be readmitted to the Union. Thus, two years after the war was over, when the South supposed that the postwar adjustment had been completed, the process of Reconstruction actually began.

The period that followed has been the subject of more bitter feeling and more controversy than perhaps any other period in American history, and the intensity of the bitterness has made it hard to get at the realities. During 1867 the military governors conducted elections; in late 1867 and early 1868 the new constitutional conventions met in the Southern states. They complied with the terms Congress had laid down, including enfranchisement of the black, and within a year after the third Reconstruction Act (of July 1867), seven states had adopted new constitutions, organized new governments, ratified the Fourteenth Amendment, and been readmitted to the Union. In Virginia, Mississippi, and Texas the process was for one reason or another not completed until 1870.

All of these new governments, except the one in Virginia, began under Republican control, with more or less black representation in the legislatures. In one state after another, however, the Democrats, supporting a policy of white supremacy, gained the ascendancy. Military and "Radical" rule lasted for three years in North Carolina; four years in Tennessee (never under military government) and Georgia; six years in Texas; seven years in Alabama and Arkansas; eight years in Mississippi; and ten years in Florida, Louisiana, and South Carolina.

The experience of this so-called "carpetbag" rule has been interpreted in completely different terms by historians of the past and those of the present. The earlier interpretation reflected the feelings of the Southern whites who resented this regime bitterly as one of "military despotism" and "Negro rule." According to this version, later elaborated by a pro-Southern school of historians, the South was at the outset the victim of military occupation in which a brutal soldiery maintained bayonet rule. Then came the "carpetbaggers"—unscrupulous Northern adventurers whose only purpose was to enrich themselves by plundering the prostrate South. To maintain their ascendancy, the carpetbaggers incited the blacks, who were essentially well disposed, to assert themselves in swaggering insolence. Thereupon, majorities made up of illiterate blacks swarmed into the legislatures, where they were manipulated by the carpetbaggers. A carnival of riotous corruption and looting followed, until at last the outraged whites, excluded from all voice in public affairs, could endure these conditions no longer and arose to drive the vandals away and to redeem their dishonored states.

This picture of Reconstruction has a very real importance, for it has undoubtedly influenced Southern attitudes in the twentieth century, but it is an extreme distortion of the realities. Historical treatments since 1950 have presented quite a different version, stressing the brief nature of the military rule and constructive measures of the "carpetbag" governments. As for bayonet rule, the number of troops in the "Army of

Occupation" was absurdly small. In November 1869 there were 1000 federal soldiers scattered over the state of Virginia and 716 over Mississippi, with hardly more than a corporal's guard in any one place. As for the carpetbaggers, there were indeed looters among the newcomers who moved into the South, but there were also idealists: many Northern women came to teach the freed slaves; many men came to develop needed industry; many others worked with integrity and self-sacrifice to find a constructive solution for the problems of a society devastated by war and left with a huge population of former slaves to absorb and provide for. Many native Southerners, who joined with the "carpetbaggers" in their programs and who were therefore denounced as "scalawags," were equally public-spirited and high-minded.

As for "Negro rule," the fact is that the blacks were in a majority only in the convention and the first three legislatures of South Carolina. Elsewhere they were a minority, even in Mississippi and Louisiana, where they constituted a majority of the population. In view of their illiteracy and their political inexperience, the blacks handled their new responsibilities well. They tended to choose educated men for public office; many of the black legislators, congressmen, and state officials were well qualified. They were, on the whole, moderate and self-restrained in their demands, and they gave major support to certain policies of long-range value, including notably the establishment of public school systems, which the South had not had in any broad sense before the Civil War.

As for the "carnival of corruption," the post-Civil War era was marked by corruption throughout the country, and it is true that corruption presented especial hardships for the Southern states, already stripped of their resources by the war. Carpetbag governments in several states issued bonds pledging the state to pay one hundred cents on the dollar and then sold the bonds at immense discounts for whatever they would bring, pocketing the money as it came in. In South Carolina, corruptionists even stole a fund which was created to buy homesteads for blacks. But corruption was not confined to the South, and within the South it was not confined to the Republicans. Democrats also were among the guilty.

Finally, it should be noted that the Southern whites were never reduced to abject helplessness, as is sometimes imagined. From the outset they were present in all of the Reconstruction conventions and legislatures—always vocal, frequently aggressive, and sometimes dominating the proceedings.

The Fall of Radical Reconstruction. For an average of six years the regimes of Radical Republican Reconstruction continued; then they gave way to the Democratic Redeemers—delaying further action on the question of the rights of blacks until the twentieth century. When one considers the fact that the South had just been badly defeated in war, that Radical Reconstruction was the policy of the dominant party in Washington, and that blacks constituted an actual majority of the potential electorate in several Southern states (with a certain proportion of the former Confederates disfranchised), it is difficult to understand why the Radical regimes were so promptly—almost easily—overthrown. Several contributing factors must be recognized.

First of all, of course, the former slaves were poorly fitted to assume political responsibility. Largely illiterate and conditioned for many decades to defer to the white man, they grasped their opportunity with uncertain hands. Very often they seemed to wish, quite realistically, for security of land tenure and for education more than for political rights. At the same time, however, a number of articulate and able black men, some of them former slaves, came to the fore and might have provided effective leadership for their race if Reconstruction had not been abandoned so soon. Second, and more important, one must recognize the importance of the grim resistance offered by the Southern whites. With their deep belief in the superiority of their own race, these Southerners were convinced that civilization itself was at stake, and they fought with proportionate desperation, not hesitating to resort to violence and terror. In 1867 a half-whimsical secret society formed in Tennessee and known as the Ku Klux Klan began to take on a more purposeful character and to spread across the South. Soon every Southern state had its organization of masked and robed riders, either as part of the Klan or under some other name, who, by use of threat, horsewhip, and even rope and gun, spread fear not only among blacks but perhaps even more among the Republican leaders. The states and even Congress passed laws to break up this activity, but the laws proved almost impossible to enforce, and the Klan ceased to operate only when its purposes had been accomplished.

The dramatic quality of the Klan has given it a prominent place in the public's mental picture of Reconstruction. But though the Klan played a prominent role, the white South had other, less spectacular weapons which were no less powerful. Southern whites owned virtually all of the land; they controlled virtually all employment; they dominated the small supply of money and credit that was to be found in the South; and they could, in unspectacular ways, make life very hard for individuals who did not comply with the system. This, perhaps more than the acts of night riders and violent men, made the pressure against Radical rule almost irresistible.

But still more important, perhaps, than either the limitations of the Southern blacks or the fierce determination of the Southern whites was the fact that, when all was said and done, neither the Republican party nor the Northern public was really committed to racial equality. Patterns of discrimination against the black, which still prevail today, had become well established in the Northern states long before the Civil War. Even antislavery men like the Free Soilers had taken the position they did because they wanted to keep blacks—whether slave or free—out of their bailiwicks. More than one free state had laws to prevent blacks from entering. Significantly, after emancipation all efforts to provide the former slaves with land ("forty acres and a mule") or to set up a federal program of education for blacks failed even in Congresses with large Radical majorities.

There were just not enough people who really cared about the freedmen. The decision to give the vote to the black was reached very reluctantly, as has been shown above, and it was really adopted not because of any belief that it was right in principle but because black participation in politics appeared to be the only alternative to Confederate rule—an unwelcome choice, but the only one. Later, Republicans found that the Northern voters did not support them in this choice; that the white South would not consent to a real reunion on this basis; and that the former Confederates had political objectives quite similar to the Republicans' objectives. As a result, the

Republicans let the existing forces in the South find their own resolution—which was one of white supremacy.

Yet Reconstruction was not a total failure. It established public schools in the South. It brought abolitionists and missionaries from the North to found such colleges as Howard, Fisk, Morehouse, and Talladega, which trained future generations of black leaders who in turn led the black protest movements of the twentieth century. Reconstruction also left as a permanent legacy the Fourteenth and Fifteenth Amendments, which formed the constitutional basis for the civil rights movements of the post-World War II generation.

Johnson versus the Radicals. The Radicals did not abandon their program all at once. Indeed, it faded out very gradually. While Johnson remained President, the Radicals remained militant, and in 1868 they tried to remove him by impeachment. Though he had denounced the Radicals in intemperate terms, he had done nothing to justify impeachment proceedings except to remove the Secretary of War, Edwin M. Stanton, from his post in the cabinet. In March 1867 Congress had passed a law, the Tenure of Office Act, which forbade such removals without senatorial consent and which has since been held by the courts to be unconstitutional. But when Johnson removed Stanton, who was reporting to the Radicals what went on in administration councils, there had been no judicial ruling, and the House of Representatives voted to impeach Johnson, which meant that he must be tried by the Senate on the articles of impeachment. The trial was conducted in a tense atmosphere and scarcely in a judicial way. Immense pressure was put on all Republican senators to vote for conviction. When a vote was finally taken on May 16, 1868, conviction failed by one vote of the two thirds required. Seven Republicans had stood out against the party; Johnson was permitted to serve out his term; and the balance between executive and legislative power in the American political system, which had almost been destroyed, was preserved.

The determination of the Republican leaders in Congress to beat down the opposition regardless of cost showed up in a parallel attack on the judiciary. When a Mississippi editor named McCardle appealed to the Supreme Court to rule on the constitutionality of one of the Reconstruction Acts, under which he had been arrested by the military, Congress in March 1868 passed an act changing the appellate jurisdiction of the Court so that it could not pass judgment on McCardle's case.

The Grant Administration. In 1868 the country faced another election, and the Republicans turned to General Grant as their nominee. He was elected over the Democratic candidate, Governor Horatio Seymour of New York, by a popular majority of only 300,000—a surprisingly close vote. Grant was not supported by a majority of the white voters: some 700,000 black votes helped to elect him. (The importance of the black vote in this election inspired Congress to propose the Fifteenth Amendment, forbidding any state from denying any citizen his right to vote "on account of race, color, or previous condition of servitude.")

President Grant supported the measures of the Radicals and in some ways gave his backing to their policies. Like the good military man he was, he believed that where violence broke out, it should be put down uncompromisingly. Accordingly, he favored the adoption of Enforcement Acts for the use of federal troops to break up the activities of the Ku Klux Klan. When these laws were adopted, he did not hesitate to invoke them, and troops were sent in on a number of occasions.

Fundamentally, however, Grant did not care much about politics or the rights of the black. He wanted to see tranquillity restored, and this meant reuniting North and South on any basis both would be willing to accept. Accordingly, he urged a broader extension of amnesty to all former Confederates, and he grew to resent the frequent appeals of Republican governments in the South for troops to uphold their authority. Though he realized that the tactics of the Redeemers were very bad—"bloodthirsty butchery," "scarcely a credit to savages"—he became convinced that constant federal military intervention was worse in the long run.

During the eight years of Grant's presidency, while the Radicals controlled the Congress and presumably the executive department, Radical governments were overthrown in eight of the Southern states. As Grant's second term neared its end, only three states—Louisiana, Florida, and South Carolina—remained under Radical rule.

The program of Radical Reconstruction still remained official policy in the Republican party, but it had lost its steam. The country was concerned about other things. In foreign affairs, Secretary of State Hamilton Fish was busy putting through an important settlement by which Great Britain and the United States adopted the principle of international arbitration as a means of settling American claims that had grown out of the raiding activities of the *Alabama,* which British shipyards had built for the Confederacy.

In financial circles there was a bitter contest over what to do about the greenback dollars issued during the war. Since greenbacks were not backed by gold, people had saved the more valuable gold dollars and spent the less valuable greenback dollars, thus driving gold out of circulation. The government was willing to give gold for greenbacks even though such a policy would tend to increase the value of the dollar. Debtor interests (such as farmers), who wanted a cheap dollar, fought hard against the policy of redemption, but the policy was adopted in 1875.

In politics, public confidence in the government was very much shaken by a series of disclosures concerning government corruption. In 1872 it was revealed that several congressmen had accepted gifts of stock in a construction company, the Crédit Mobilier, which was found to be diverting the funds of the Union Pacific Railroad—including the funds the government had granted to it—with the knowledge of the officers of the road. In 1875 Grant's private secretary was implicated in the operations of the "Whiskey Ring," which, by evading taxes, had systematically defrauded the government of millions of dollars. The following year, the Secretary of War was caught selling appointments to Indian posts. Meanwhile, in the New York City government, the Tweed Ring, headed by Tammany boss William Marcy Tweed, was exposed as guilty of graft and thefts which have seldom been equaled in size and never been surpassed in effrontery.

The epidemic of corruption inspired a revolt by reform Republicans, who bolted the party in 1872, organized the Liberal Republican party, and nominated Horace

Greeley, editor of the New York *Tribune,* for President. Although the Democrats also nominated Greeley and formed a coalition with the Liberal Republicans, Grant easily won reelection because most Northern voters were not yet prepared to trust the Democrats.

In the economic orbit, the country was trying to weather the financial depression that began with the panic of 1873. All in all, the problems posed by the South and the black seemed more and more distant, less and less important, to the people of the North.

The Hayes-Tilden Election of 1876. The election of 1876 brought to an end the program of Reconstruction, which probably would have ended soon in any case. In this election the Republicans, who were badly divided, turned to a Civil War veteran and governor of Ohio, Rutherford B. Hayes, as their nominee. Hayes was a conspicuously honest man, and so was his Democratic opponent, Samuel J. Tilden of New York, who owed his reputation to his part in breaking up the Tweed Ring.

When the votes were counted, Tilden clearly had a popular majority (obtained only by the suppression of black votes in several Southern states) and was within one vote of an electoral majority. But there were three states—Florida, Louisiana, and South Carolina—in which the result was contested, and two sets of returns were filed by rival officials. Congress had to count the votes, and the House of Representatives, with a Democratic majority, was in a position to prevent an election by refusing to go into joint session with the Senate, which the Constitution requires for the count. Congress agreed to appoint an Electoral Commission to provide an impartial judgment, but the commission divided along party lines, voting eight to seven for Hayes. As late as two days before the inauguration it was doubtful whether the Democrats in the House would allow the electoral count to proceed.

Many Northern Democrats were prepared to fight to a finish against what they regarded as a stolen election, but the Southern Democrats had found that one civil war

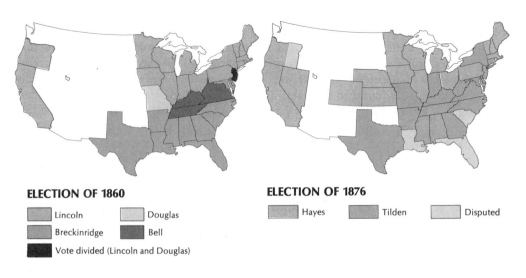

ELECTION OF 1860

Lincoln	Douglas
Breckinridge	Bell
Vote divided (Lincoln and Douglas)	

ELECTION OF 1876

| Hayes | Tilden | Disputed |

was enough. Moreover, various negotiations had been in progress behind the scenes. Important groups of Southern Democrats who had been left out when the government largesse of the Union Pacific-Central Pacific was distributed now hoped for a Texas and Pacific Railroad which would provide bountiful federal grants for Southern interests. They received assurances from friends of Governor Hayes that he would look with favor upon such programs of internal improvement. Moreover, they were assured that he would withdraw the last remaining federal troops from Louisiana and South Carolina, which meant that their Republican governments would collapse and the score of states would be: redeemed, eleven; reconstructed, none.

With these understandings in mind, Southern congressmen voted to let the count proceed so that Hayes would be elected. Later, when they were explaining their conduct to their constituents, they thought it best to say quite a great deal about how they had ransomed South Carolina and Louisiana and very little about their hopes for the Texas and Pacific Railroad and other such enterprises. Thus a legend grew up that there had been a "compromise" by which Reconstruction was ended. What had really happened, however, was that Southern Democrats and Northern Republicans had discovered that there were many features of economic policy on which they were in close harmony. The slaves were emancipated; the Union was restored; bygones were bygones; and the harmony of their views made reconciliation natural and Reconstruction unnecessary. There was still the question of the blacks; but only a few whites had ever supported black suffrage or racial equality for its own sake. It had been an expedient, and now that the expedient was no longer needed, it could be laid aside. Such was the spirit of reconciliation.

Thus, the country ended a period of intense friction and entered upon a long era of sectional harmony and rapid economic growth. But this was done at the expense of leaving the question of racial relations still unattended to, even though slavery itself had, at immense cost, been removed.

1

THE
AGE OF
INDUSTRIALISM

AMERICANS IN THE GILDED AGE LIVED IN A NATION QUITE DIFFERENT from that of their fathers—a nation where traditional ideas of democracy were modified by the values of a new industrial and urban society. The most important change was the burgeoning of industrial and financial corporations controlling nationwide industries. In addition, American life was fundamentally altered by other far-reaching developments: settlement of the last American West, revolutionary changes in agriculture, construction of the transcontinental railroads, the growth of cities with all their attendant urban problems, the rise of the labor movement, the great influx of immigrants, and the emergence of the United States as a world power. These developments gave the period its dramatic character and its importance in our history. They also provided the foundations for modern America.

The triumph of industrialism in the post–Civil War generation launched the United States on the road to becoming the richest and most powerful nation in the world. But at the same time it transformed the country from one of economic democracy and opportunity for all to one of economic plutocracy and opportunity for only a few. Industrial growth led to extreme economic inequities and sharpened class differences. At the end of the nineteenth century few Americans could regard themselves as economically secure and independent; most of them were dependent for their livelihood on the workings of a vast, complex economic system.

Although the old agrarian ideals of freedom, personal dignity, and worth steadily gave ground under the impact of industrial expansion, they still remained the core of the American view of life in the industrial age. Most Americans wanted a society based on these ideals, and many continued to believe—despite evidence to the contrary—that big business was compatible with such a society. But they were either misled or confused about what was going on, because industrial growth could not help but create inequities. A small class of businessmen, whose economic stakes were protected by the government, organized American industry and employed in its factories a large class of workers who had practically no economic rights. In the process a fundamental change occurred in American life. The ordinary American became the hired employee of a large corporation and, as a consequence, lost much of his freedom along with his sense of responsibility and initiative. Economic equality had largely given way to economic progress.

The term "Gilded Age," created by Mark Twain and Charles Dudley Warner in their novel of that name, was used by contemporaries, and has been used by historians ever since, to describe the era that followed the Civil War. It seemed a fitting epithet for the "all-pervading speculativeness" of the times and the "shameful corruption" which, Twain observed, had "lately crept into our politics." In portraying Colonel Beriah Sellers with his gilt cane, overblown rhetoric, easygoing ethical standards, inflated dreams, and fanciful optimism, Twain and Warner set forth a view of the whole generation that has largely persisted to our own day. Other contemporaries presented portrayals of the age that were substantially similar. "The

American thought of himself as a restless, pushing, energetic, ingenious person, always awake and trying to get ahead of his neighbors," noted Henry Adams. And the American in those years was so interested in making money that he "had been deflected by its pursuit till [he] could turn in no other direction."

History is often not what actually happened but rather what historians say happened, and, in light of what historians have said, the Gilded Age has fared badly. When twentieth-century historians began to study the era closely, most adopted the interpretation of Mark Twain and Henry Adams. Vernon Louis Parrington in the widely read and profoundly influential third volume of his *Main Currents in American Thought* (1930) set the modern tone when he wrote of these years: "Exploitation was the business of the times." The politicians of the period made government "a huge barbecue . . . to which all presumably were invited" except "inconspicuous persons" such as industrial workers and farmers. And society had become "only too plainly mired . . . in a bog of bad taste," producing a "triumphant and unabashed vulgarity without its like in our history."

Two other very influential figures who dealt with the period, Charles A. Beard and Matthew Josephson, writing in the thirties, strengthened and expanded this view. Like Parrington, Beard deplored the accumulation of power by the business leaders, and he condemned "the cash nexus pure and simple" that produced the era's vulgarities and inequities. Josephson saw the period in terms of economic, political, and social exploitation of the many by the few, for whom he popularized the damning phrase "Robber Barons."

The impulse to spring to the aid of the underdog has brought forth champions of the cultural, literary, and technological achievements of the Gilded Age, but the stereotype of its business leadership, industrial development, and political activity has not changed substantially despite the study given to the period since the 1940s. This is because few students have seriously attempted to investigate the Gilded Age in its own context, in accordance with the standards and ideas that prevailed then, and for the things that it produced in itself. In addition, historians have largely accepted the harsh indictments that contemporary reformers and intellectuals made of the era, preferring men like E. L. Godkin, Henry and Brooks Adams, and Thomas Nast to figures such as James G. Blaine, Roscoe Conkling, and Daniel Drew. And possible liberal historians, usually Democrats, have not been much impressed by a supposedly predominantly conservative and Republican era.

Without glossing over the flaws and shortcomings of the Robber Barons, these later historians have nevertheless sought to present a fuller, more balanced picture by emphasizing the important contributions the businessman of the Gilded Age made to the economic development of the nation, the technology he introduced in industry, and the social good he sometimes did with his money. While showing the mogul to be destructive, they also depict him as a creative, pioneering entrepreneur. Allan Nevins, Thomas C. Cochran, Edward C. Kirkland, and others in the 1940s and 1950s launched this reevaluation of American business leadership in the Gilded Age, and the trend has continued without interruption and with only occasional dissent. Recent historians have also stressed the impersonal forces and standardization of life under industrialism, the growing dependence of people upon one another, the increasing feeling of insecurity, and the decline of interest in nonmaterial things, all of which still characterize and affect our life today.

Likewise, modern historians, in an effort to counterbalance the traditional censure of the political life of the Gilded Age for its barrenness, dreariness, and monotony, have tried to show the importance of politics to Americans of that period and the vitality of the democratic spirit. They point out that public interest in government was very much alive and that the political issues were deeply significant, attesting to the emergence of the United States as a great industrial nation and an international power. They dismiss the charge that no basic issues divided the major parties and argue that politics, in the words of H. Wayne Morgan, was "an ever-present, vivid, and meaningful reality to that whole generation." In the last few years Morgan and others, making extensive use of primary sources and without blinking away the corruption and blandness in many areas of politics, have led the way in reassessing the politics and politicians of the Gilded Age.

Finally, whatever its shortcomings and flaws, the Gilded Age believed in itself, something we in our time cannot always claim. It was also a time of peace, of relative prosperity, and of growth and change, when, unlike today, the United States was almost entirely free of international affairs and could devote itself to its own self-interest.

FOR THOUGHT AND DISCUSSION

1. What evidences are there that the attitude of the federal government and the courts toward big business has changed since the Gilded Age?

2. Is the primary responsibility of a corporation to its owners—the stockholders—or to society? Is it to make money, or is it to protect the environment, provide job opportunities for the underprivileged, and, in other ways, contribute to the general welfare?

3. Do you believe that the morality of politics today has improved over what it was in the late nineteenth century? What is the current attitude of the American public toward its political parties and their spokesmen?

4. Was American democracy working during the Gilded Age? Is it working successfully today?

5. The belief that the acquisition of wealth is evidence of hard work and virtue and that poverty is evidence of idleness and worthlessness was particularly widespread in the late nineteenth century, but it can be traced all the way back to colonial times. Do many Americans still believe it? What facts support your opinion?

proVide
for The
commoN
deFense

CHAPTER 1

INDUSTRIALIZATION AND URBANIZATION
1865–1900

THE AMERICAN INDUSTRIAL REVOLUTION

The Growth of Industrial Capitalism. In the years following the Civil War there occurred in the United States a series of notable economic changes that resulted in what is frequently known as the American Industrial Revolution. The most important feature of this phenomenon was a rapid and vast economic expansion. Between 1860 and 1900 the total railroad mileage increased from 30 thousand to 193 thousand, while the capital invested in manufacturing jumped from $1 billion to almost $10 billion, the number of workers from 1.3 million to 5.3 million, and the value of the annual product from under $2 million to over $13 million. Industry had come of age, and the United States had become the greatest industrial nation in the world.

This enormous economic growth not only made the United States potentially the most powerful country in the world but transformed it from a rural and agrarian nation into an urban and industrial one. By 1890 the value of this country's manufactured goods exceeded that of its agricultural products; ten years later manufactured products were worth twice as much.

Big business came to dominate economic life. Antebellum factories and plants—where the relationship between the owner and his help was close, where the workshop was small and the market was local, where the ownership comprised an individual or a partnership—gave way to large, impersonal corporations. The hitherto scattered banking institutions now became concentrated in four or five financial centers. And east of the Mississippi River factory and foundry workers and their families helped build towns into cities and create sprawling industrial centers. Into these centers swarmed millions of immigrants, who were to alter the racial composition of the nation.

Although the Civil War is generally regarded as marking the beginning of the triumph of industrial capitalism, it did not produce the Industrial Revolution. The forces responsible for the rapid postwar expansion of American industry had been developing for more than half a century. In the 1850s railroads revolutionized transportation, and at about the same time inventions transformed both industry and agriculture. The sewing machine paved the way for the ready-made clothing industry, and a similar machine, adapted to leather, provided the possibility of factory-made boots and shoes. The Hoe rotary printing press brought large-scale mechanization to the newspaper business.

In agriculture, the introduction of such machinery as the reaper brought new methods of farming to this country. The new machines enabled the North to meet the food needs of its military forces and yet have a surplus of wheat for shipment to Europe. At the time of the Civil War, Colt revolvers were considered the best in the world; vulcanized rubber—made through a process discovered in 1839 by the American, Charles Goodyear—was commonplace; American iron manufacturers had experimented with the Bessemer process; and Boston was the leading boot and shoe center in the world.

The Effect of the Civil War.   It has been customary to credit the Civil War with a major role in bringing about the Industrial Revolution through the great impetus that it supposedly gave to the growth of manufacturing in the North. In fact, however, the Civil War may have retarded American industrial development, for growth rates slowed during the conflict. Between 1839 and 1899 total output of commodities, including agricultural products, increased elevenfold, or at an average rate per decade of slightly less than 50 percent. But growth rates varied widely from decade to decade. The 1840s and 1880s were periods of considerably more rapid advance than the 1850s, 1860s, and 1870s, and the lowest level of industrial growth occurred during the decade of the Civil War.

Nevertheless, the government gave strong encouragement to entrepreneurs during the Civil War. The Republican party, seeking the votes of businessmen in the 1860 campaign, promised them favorable legislation. In power, the Republicans carried out their pledges and through tariff, railway, banking, and immigration legislation created conditions suitable for industrial capitalism.

The Post–Civil War Boom.   A number of factors were responsible for the post–Civil War industrial boom. The United States possessed bountiful raw materials, and the government was willing to turn them over to industry for little or no money. Coupled with the abundance of natural resources was a home market steadily expanding through immigration and a high birth rate. Both capital and labor were plentiful. The increase in trade and manufacturing in the Northeast in the years before the war produced an accumulation of savings, while additional millions of dollars came from European investors. Unbroken waves of European immigration provided American industry with workers as well as with customers. From 1860 to 1900 about 14 million immigrants came to the United States, most of whom settled in cities and became industrial workers.

The Role of Government in Business.   An essential factor in the growth of industrialism was the continuation of the government's friendly attitude toward business. The protective tariff—beginning with the Morrill Tariff of 1861 and expanded by the McKinley bill of 1890, the Wilson-Gorman law of 1894, and the Dingley Tariff of 1897—allowed American manufacturers to charge high prices without fear of foreign competition. The national banking system and the financial policies pursued by the Treasury Department resulted in a currency deflation that benefited creditors at the expense of debtors. Additional favors to businessmen came in the form of grants of land and of natural resources.

Equally helpful to the development of business was government inertia. There were no sweeping investigations of business practices, no legislation to protect labor and consumers, and no effective regulatory commissions or laws. Businessmen knew they could with impunity do very nearly what they wished. This fitted in well with the prevalent idea in post–Civil War America that the government, beyond protecting property rights and maintaining law and order, should not meddle with the economic and social life of the country. American businessmen professed to believe in the laissez-faire economic theory set forth by the English economist Adam Smith in his *Wealth of Nations* (1776). But the protective tariff violated the laissez-faire economic doctrine, for it was a form of government intervention in the economy on behalf of American manufacturers.

The Role of the Courts.   Just as beneficial to business as protective tariffs and a hands-off attitude was the protection given by the Supreme Court in its interpretation of the Fourteenth Amendment. This amendment, added to the Constitution in 1868, was presumably designed to safeguard the newly emancipated black. But the original intent of the amendment disappeared, and it became instead a refuge for private enterprise.

In its first section the Fourteenth Amendment declares: "No state shall make or enforce any law which shall abridge the privileges or immunities of citizens of the United States; nor shall any state deprive any person of life, liberty, or property, without due process of law." It is true that in the first postwar cases involving the question of governmental regulation of business, the Court interpreted this "due process" clause in favor of the state governments. In the Slaughterhouse Cases of 1873, involving a Louisiana law that granted a monopoly of the slaughterhouse business in New Orleans to one corporation, the Court declared the law to be a legitimate exercise of the police powers of a state to protect its citizens. In *Munn* v. *Illinois* (1877) the Court approved an Illinois law that fixed maximum storage rates for grain elevators on the grounds that a state could regulate "a business that is public in nature though privately owned and managed."

These decisions so alarmed American businessmen, however, that some predicted the end of private property. Others believed that the only remedy lay in a constitutional amendment to protect business against state regulation. Then a change occurred in the make-up of the Court with the appointment of more conservative justices. The end of the depression years of the mid-eighties quieted radical demands, and a series of decisions beginning in the Santa Clara case of 1886 and culminating in *Smyth* v. *Ames* in 1898 made the Fourteenth Amendment into something quite new. In these cases the Court greatly broadened the scope of the amendment by holding that the word *person* in its first section included corporations as well as individuals. It widened the application of the "due process" clause (which had originally been intended only to prohibit confiscation of property or other arbitrary violations of individual rights) to invalidate any regulation that would prohibit a corporation from making a "reasonable" profit on its investment. And, finally, the Court held that the courts and not the states should decide how much profit was reasonable. With these last cases the Fourteenth Amendment had practically been rewritten. Businessmen who denounced the rule laid down in *Munn* v. *Illinois* found protection in the later decisions. Lower courts handed down injunctions that tied the hands of regulatory commissions, and the Supreme Court became the stronghold of laissez-faire.

THE RAILROAD AGE

The new industrialism could never have been possible without the tremendous expansion of the railroad systems in America. In fact, they played such a dominant role that the period could well be called the railroad age. Between 1831 and 1861, 30,000 miles of railroad created a network connecting the Atlantic seaboard and the Mississippi valley. The war slowed down construction, but between 1867 and 1873 about 30,000 miles of railroad were added, and during the 1880s a record-breaking 73,000 miles were constructed. In 1900 the American railroad system, extending into every section of the country, measured 193,000 miles. This represented 40 percent of the world's railroad mileage and was more than the mileage of all European countries combined. Railroad building increased more rapidly than the population. In 1865 there was one mile of track in operation for every 1150 Americans; twenty years later there was one mile for every 450. Capital invested in railroads jumped in this period from $2 billion to nearly $10 billion.

After the war most of the short lines were consolidated into a few large systems. Cornelius Vanderbilt, who had already made a fortune in steamboats, led the way. Before his death in 1877 he had extended the New York Central System to Chicago, offering improved service at reduced rates.

The New York Central's chief competitor for the traffic between the East and the Middle West was the Pennsylvania Railroad, which became the most important railroad and one of the foremost business enterprises in the country. At the end of the nineteenth century the Pennsylvania had lines tapping the most important Middle Atlantic and North Central industrial centers.

The Erie Railroad was a competitor for much of this traffic, but in the 1860s and 1870s it suffered from being in the hands of three of the most disreputable railroad manipulators of the era: Daniel Drew, Jay Gould, and Jim Fisk. Through bribery, chicanery, and fraud they made the Erie synonymous with all the vices of the Industrial Revolution. Consolidation enabled the Baltimore and Ohio to push into the Middle West, and the New York, New Haven, and Hartford to fan out into New England. By 1900 railroad consolidation had reached such vast proportions that more than two thirds of the railroad mileage of the country was controlled by groups led by Cornelius Vanderbilt, James J. Hill, E. H. Harriman, Jay Gould, John D. Rockefeller, and John Pierpont Morgan.

The Transcontinentals. More spectacular and more important than railroad building in the older sections of the country was the construction of the transcon-

SELECTED TRAVEL TIMES AND COSTS 1870

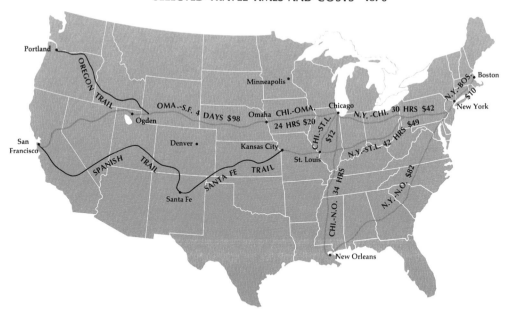

Portland

OREGON TRAIL

Minneapolis

OMA.-S.F. 4 DAYS $98

Chicago

N.Y.-BOS. $10

Boston

Omaha CHI.-OMA. 24 HRS $20

CHI.-ST.L. $12

N.Y.-CHI. 30 HRS $42

New York

Ogden

San Francisco

SPANISH TRAIL

Denver

Kansas City

St. Louis

N.Y.-ST.L. 42 HRS $49

SANTA FE TRAIL

CHI.-N.O. 34 HRS

N.Y.-N.O. $82

Santa Fe

New Orleans

SELECTED TRAVEL TIMES AND COSTS 1900

Portland

MINN.-PORT. 4 DAYS

DEN.-PORT. 48 HRS

Minneapolis

N.Y.-BOS. 6 HRS

Boston

Chicago

N.Y.-CHI. 20 HRS $23

New York

$6

Ogden

Omaha

CHI.-ST.L. $7

San Francisco

DEN.-S.F. 26 HRS

Denver

K.C.-DEN. $20

Kansas City

St. Louis

N.Y.-ST.L. 29 HRS $27

Los Angeles

Santa Fe

CHI.-N.O. 25 HRS

N.Y.-N.O. 37 HRS $40

El Paso

Houston

New Orleans

—— Railroad

—— Wagon Trails

tinentals. In 1862 Congress chartered the Union Pacific and the Central Pacific railroads (see p. 16). Upon their completion in 1869, the two railroads had received 54 million acres of government land and government loans amounting to about $60 million. In addition the Union Pacific issued one million shares of stock at $100 a share.

Much of the profiteering that accompanied the building of both roads can be ascribed to the separation of ownership and control in modern corporate enterprise. Managers systematically bled their companies for their own profit. The public first became aware of the large scale of this practice in the Crédit Mobilier scandal of 1872. Officers of the Union Pacific Railroad had used a dummy construction company (the Crédit Mobilier), which they owned, to build the road and had turned over most of the assets of the road, including loans from the government and investments by shareholders, to themselves as constructors, paying, by a conservative estimate, $73 million for a $50 million job. Their bribery of congressmen in connection with this deal was only incidental. More fundamental to an understanding of this form of corruption is the fact that executives were placed in a position which gave them constant opportunity to enrich themselves at the expense of the investors and of the enterprise itself.

The Crocker Company, which built the Central Pacific, amassed a profit of about $63 million on an investment of $121 million. Most of this went to the four leading officials of the Central Pacific—Leland Stanford, Collis P. Huntington, Charles Crocker, and Mark Hopkins—each of whom left a fortune of $40 million or more at his death.

Government Aid to Railroads. While individual initiative and enterprise played a large part in the building of America's great railroad empire, it is doubtful if American railroads would have become so highly developed had it not been for the generosity of the federal, state, and local governments. Between 1850 and 1871 the railroads received from the federal government alone more than 130 million acres of land—an area as large as the New England states, Pennsylvania, and New York combined—and from the states about 49 million acres of land. It is nearly impossible to assess the value of this land, but a conservative estimate (based on $2.00 an acre) would place the value at $360 million. Some estimates have been as high as $2.5 billion.

Because they failed to meet all the conditions under which this land was granted, the railroads were able to retain only about 116 million acres. Even so, at the end of the land-grant era it was discovered that railroads had been granted one fourth of the entire area of Minnesota and Washington; one fifth of Wisconsin, Iowa, Kansas, North Dakota, and Montana; one seventh of Nebraska; one eighth of California; and one ninth of Louisiana. And at one point (1882) Texas discovered that its donations of land to railroads exceeded by 8 million acres the amount remaining in the public domain.

To such grants of land were added loans and subsidies. Towns, cities, and counties gave the railroads about $300 million, and the states, at a conservative estimate, furnished an additional $228 million. The federal government made loans of approximately $65 million, most of which went to the Union and Central Pacific. A town was at the mercy of a railroad, which could bypass it and thereby cause it to dry up. By this threat the railroads were able to secure cash grants, loans, exemption from taxation, and subscription to their stocks. Yet many loans were made voluntarily and enthusiastically to get local railroad advantages. For, as the governor of Maine asked in 1867, "Why should private individuals be called upon to make a useless sacrifice of their means when railroads can be constructed by the unity of public with private interests, and made profitable to all?" By 1870, according to one estimate, public subsidies plus land grants contributed 60 percent of the costs of all railroad construction.

The national railroad system no doubt brought great benefits to the economy. In addition to facilitating the movement of goods, the railroads used enormous amounts of iron and steel, coal, lumber, and other products and provided employment for hundreds of thousands of workers. In the decade of the 1880s the railroad companies bought nearly 15 million tons of rails, purchasing in some years over 90 percent of the rolled steel manufactured in the United States.

The railroads were also one of the most active colonizers of the last West. They possessed vast tracts of land grants to sell, and they stood to gain in increased passenger and freight business as settlement expanded. They offered prospective settlers and buyers of land rail tickets at reduced prices and sometimes even provided free transportation for a settler's furniture. The railroads kept agents at eastern seaports to welcome immigrants and to arrange for their transportation to the West. And they had immigration agencies in Europe to persuade Europeans to come to America.

THE INDUSTRIALISTS

"Robber Barons" or "Captains of Industry"?   It is important to recognize that the foregoing factors were not wholly responsible for the American Industrial Revolution. It required the superb talent found among those Americans who mobilized the nation's productive energies to build the railroads and factories. The new industrialists were ambitious, resourceful, and extremely able. At times they were ruthless and dishonest but probably no more so than many other Americans of their day. They displayed the vigor, cleverness, and strength of will that have characterized the great entrepreneurs of all epochs of capitalistic expansion. They lived at a time when the highest goal was to acquire wealth and when one's position in society was determined by the amount amassed. In their day they were known as Captains of Industry and praised for the economic growth of modern America; but in time they came to be described in many quarters as Robber Barons who exploited the working class and exacted tribute from the public.

Few of the industrialists were guided by the morality and ethics that had prevailed in business before the Civil War. To eliminate competitors and get around legal and political obstacles, they did not hesitate to use trickery, bribery, and corruption. Their attitude toward complaints about their methods was summed up in William Vanderbilt's famous "The public be damned," uttered in reply to a reporter's question about the motives for his management of the railroads. H. O. Havemeyer boasted that he did not know enough about ethics to apply them to business; Cornelius Vanderbilt exclaimed, "Law, what do I care about law? Haint I got the power?"; and J. P. Morgan told a reporter that he "owe[d] the public nothing."

The industrialists came mostly from lower- or middle-class families. The majority of them were native white and of Anglo-Saxon and New England descent. They had little or no formal education. Usually they were Protestants, strict denominationalists and pious men; scarcely any were high livers like Jim Fisk, who had a flair for publicity, splendid gestures, and the gilded life. Many of them had bookkeeping training and experience.

While these men accumulated large fortunes, they insisted they were not materialistic. "I know of nothing more despicable and pathetic than a man who devotes all the waking hours of the day to making money for money's sake," wrote John D. Rockefeller in his *Reminiscences.* He maintained it was "the association with interesting and quick-minded men," not money alone, that prompted him to follow his course to success. Andrew Carnegie expressed a similar view when he said that many of his "clever partners" in the steel business had been his friends from boyhood and when he emphasized the joy he found in "manufacturing something and giving employment to many men."

A number of the new industrialists were of military age during the Civil War, but most of these took advantage of a law that allowed them to hire a substitute or to pay a certain amount of money in lieu of military service. Writing from Pittsburgh in 1863, Thomas Mellon, the founder of an aluminum fortune, declared that "such opportunities for making money had never existed before in all my former experience." When his son James asked permission to enlist, the elder Mellon wrote, "Don't do it. It is only greenhorns who enlist. Those who are able to pay for substitutes do so, and no discredit attaches." Then he added, "It is not so much the danger as disease and idleness and vicious habits. . . . I had hoped my boy was going to make a smart, intelligent businessman and was not such a goose as to be seduced from his duty by the declamations of buncombed speeches."

Simon Cameron, as Secretary of War, handed out war contracts left and right and asked only for production in return. Gigantic frauds and great fortunes resulted from shoddy contracts and shady deals. Vanderbilt supplied the government leaky ships. J. P. Morgan, who was twenty-four years old in 1861, purchased five thousand discarded carbines and sold them back to the army for $112,000. Both Morgan's and Vanderbilt's deals were exposed, but neither man was punished. Jim Fisk went south to smuggle out cotton and sell it in the North for large profits. Jay Gould's inside information enabled him to cash in on railroad deals and speculation in gold. And so it went during the war years.

Social Darwinism. Invaluable to the new industrial order was social Darwinism. Herbert Spencer, a leading English disciple of Charles Darwin, applied Darwin's law of biological evolution to social and economic life. Spencer held that evolution was leading inevitably to a society in which men would enjoy "the greatest perfection and the most complete happiness" and that competitive struggle was the means by which this would come to pass. In this unremitting strife the weak fell by the wayside, and the strong pushed forward. Any governmental attempt to alter this situation impeded progress.

The Darwinian theory seemed to prove that those who survived were the fittest. Translated into economic and social terms, this assumption brought science to the support of predatory capitalism. Spencer enjoyed a great vogue in the United States from 1870 to 1890, and his theories considerably helped the new industrialism. In fact, they provided American businessmen with a rationale for their conduct. John D. Rockefeller told his Sunday-school class, "The growth of a large business is merely the survival of the fittest. . . . The American Beauty rose can be produced in the splendor and fragrance which bring cheer to its beholder only by sacrificing the early buds which grow up around it. This is not an evil tendency in business. It is merely the working-out of a law of nature and a law of God." Andrew Carnegie exclaimed when he first read Spencer, "I remember that light came as in a flood and all was clear. Not only had I got rid of theology and the supernatural, but I had found the truth of evolution."

According to Spencerianism the American economy was governed by a natural aristocracy that had risen to the top through the struggle for profits that rewarded the strong and eliminated the weak. The country could be served best by the economic independence of this natural aristocracy. The new doctrine crippled reform movements by justifying poverty and slums. These conditions were natural for the unfit who, by lack of thrift and industrious habits, had not survived the economic struggle, and any governmental effort to relieve poverty was a perversion of the natural law; for as Spencer declared, "there shall not be a forcible burdening of the superior for the support of the inferior."

Somewhat paradoxically, philanthropy also was expected to play a part in the behavior of a businessman. On the one hand, he was expected to be humanitarian and to relieve distress in whatever form it appeared; on the other, he was forbidden by the dictates of social Darwinism to offer any aid that might undermine self-reliance, initiative, and ambition. The solution to this dilemma was offered by Andrew Carnegie in *The Gospel of Wealth* (1889). While asserting that wealth must necessarily be concentrated in the hands of the few, Carnegie also set forth the maxim that the man who dies rich dies disgraced. The duty of the man of wealth, he maintained, was to administer his surplus funds as a trust to yield the greatest value to the *community*. Funds should be given, for example, to help found public libraries, improve education, and promote world peace. To support a needy *individual*, on the other hand, was wrong. Carnegie argued that every man maintained by charity was a source of moral infection to his neighborhood and asserted that of every thousand dollars spent for poor relief nine hundred fifty would better be thrown into the sea.

And the large gifts of businessmen to religious and charitable organizations and to colleges, libraries, and other educational institutions suggest that they were not entirely selfish and that they were philanthropic. While Carnegie and Rockefeller were the greatest benefactors, they were not unique in this respect. Other wealthy men like Ezra Cornell, Johns Hopkins, Leland Stanford, Cornelius (Commodore) Vanderbilt, and James B. Duke gave generously to educational institutions.

The Trust. Before the Civil War, American business was highly competitive and consisted of small units, mostly individual enterprises or partnerships. After the war, businessmen sought ways to check increasing competition, which they had come to regard as inefficient, wasteful, and threatening to their profits. They established trade agreements, associations, and pools to limit competition; but because these devices depended upon voluntary cooperation and were not enforceable in the courts, none proved sufficiently reliable. The answer seemed to lie in the formation of industrial trusts, which provided businessmen with more efficient control over the policies of all members within a single industry.

Under the trust system the stock of several competing companies was placed under the control of a group of trustees in exchange for trustee certificates. Ownership remained with the original companies, but management was consolidated in a single board of directors. John D. Rockefeller was by far the most important figure in the trust movement, and the formation of his Standard Oil Company in 1879 established the trust pattern in the United States.

Rockefeller and the Standard Oil Trusts. Rockefeller was a young merchant in Cleveland, Ohio, when he decided to enter the oil industry during the Civil War. Here he found violence, lawlessness, and waste, and, being no exponent of such free enterprise, he took steps to end this competitive strife. Rockefeller adopted the most efficient methods of production, regularly saved a part of his profits, and surrounded himself with some of the ablest men in the industry. By 1867 he was the largest refiner of oil in Cleveland, and in 1870 he organized the Standard Oil Company of Ohio with a capitalization of $1 million and eliminated his Ohio competitors. He now proceeded to take on the refiners in New York, Pittsburgh, and Philadelphia. Those who accepted Rockefeller's terms shared in the large profits, but those who continued to resist him were attacked with every weapon in cutthroat competitive warfare. He usually crushed his competitors with ruthless price cutting, but he also had an immense competitive advantage in the rebates and drawbacks (see footnotes, p. 50) which he received from the railroads. By 1879 Rockefeller controlled about 90 percent of America's refining industry.

Within a comparatively short time after entering the highly competitive oil industry, the Standard Oil Company was able to dominate it. In accomplishing this domination, Rockefeller created the original *trust*—a word that came to be applied to any large combination with monopolistic powers. Of all the trusts that appeared in the eighties and nineties, none aroused more alarms or pointed up more moral issues than the Standard Oil Trust. Even the means Rockefeller used to gain a monopoly in the oil industry produced conflicting opinions. "I ascribe the success of the Standard Oil Company to its consistent policy of making the volume of its business large through the merit and cheapness of its products," declared Rockefeller. But Senator James K. Jones of Arkansas offered another explanation on the floor of the United States Senate in 1889: "The iniquities of the Standard Oil Company have been enumerated and recounted until some of them are familiar to everyone," said Jones, "and the colossal fortunes which have grown from it, which in all their vastness do not represent one dollar of honest toil or one trace of benefit to mankind, nor any addition to the product of human labor, are known everywhere."

And the controversy has continued. Some writers see in the rise of Standard Oil a dark record of unfair trade practices, railroad favors, bribery and blackmail, and an alliance between the corporation and politics by which legislators, officials, and judges closed their eyes to practices that violated the law. Others have argued that Standard Oil straightened out a disorderly industry and, by introducing efficiency and competency, lowered prices and created a great industry. Both sides, however, agree that Standard's methods frequently were ruthless and that they would not be tolerated today.

Rockefeller had a way of being ahead of the law most of the time. William Vanderbilt, testifying about the leaders of Standard Oil before a congressional committee in 1879, expressed an opinion prevalent in those years: "Yes, they are very shrewd men. I don't believe that by any legislative enactment or anything else, through any of the States or all of the States, you can keep such men down. You can't do it! They will be on top all the time. You see if they are not." Be that as it may, in 1892 the Supreme Court of Ohio ordered the dissolution of the Standard Trust on the grounds that it was designed to "establish a virtual monopoly" and was "contrary to the policy of our state." But this decision did not produce the desired results, for the Standard trustees, although they returned the stock to the stockholders, continued to manage the member concerns as "liquidating trustees" until 1897, when the court forced them to abandon this stratagem.

Prior to this, in 1889, New Jersey had changed its corporation laws in such a way as to make legal the formation of a holding company—a company which owned a majority of the stock in a number of subsidiary corporations and was established to unify their control. In 1899 the various subsidiaries of Standard were legally combined through the creation of a giant holding company, the Standard Oil Company of New Jersey, capitalized at $110 million (as compared to the first Standard Oil Company of Ohio, capitalization of $1 million). Standard's control over the refining business continued as complete as ever. In 1911 the United States Supreme Court held that Standard had violated the Sherman Antitrust Act, but this decision, like earlier ones in the state courts, had little effect upon the management of Standard's affairs.

Carnegie and Steel. Just as Rockefeller captured the refining market from his competitors, so Andrew Carnegie captured much of the steel market, although he never achieved a monopoly. He had made money in various ways in the fifties and sixties and was already a millionaire when he turned to steel production in the early seventies. Like Rockefeller, Carnegie secured rebates from the railroads. He also was materially aided by the depression of the seventies, for as he said about it afterward, "so many of my friends needed money, that they begged me to repay them [for their investments in early Carnegie enterprises]. I did so and bought out five or six of them. That was what gave me my leading interest in this steel business."

From this time on, Carnegie led the field in the steel industry. He bought out and took into his business Henry Clay Frick, who in the seventies had gained control of most of the coke ovens around Pittsburgh. Together they created a great vertical combine of coal fields, coke ovens, limestone deposits, iron mines, ore ships, and railroads. In 1892 the Carnegie Steel Company was formed at a capitalization of $25 million; it controlled all its sources of supply and was soon making one fourth of all unfinished steel in the United States. At the turn of the century it became a New Jersey corporation with a capitalization of $160 million.

Carnegie was essentially an industrial capitalist in that his money came from industry and not from bankers. He put a large part of his profits back into his business, and he did not allow his corporation's stock to be sold to persons outside his organization. He was successful because of his efficient business methods and driving energy and because he skillfully chose partners of almost equal ability, such as Frick and Charles Schwab. His labor policy, like that of most of the corporation leaders of this era, was one of long hours, low wages, and hostility to trade unions. Carnegie was willing to make innovations in methods and machinery, ready to discard equipment whenever better came along. He made improvements in times of depression, and when prosperity returned, he was ready to produce. Carnegie was a skeptic and also something of an intellectual. He had many friends in the political and literary worlds and contributed pieces to serious magazines.

The Growth of Trusts. Soon after Standard Oil Company had set the trust pattern, other business enterprises of this type appeared. The McCormick Harvester Company of Chicago secured almost a monopoly of mechanical farm equipment. James B. Duke's American Tobacco Company, established in 1890, and Henry O. Havemeyer's American Sugar Refining Company, founded in 1891, gained almost complete monopolies, while Philip D. Armour and Gustavus Swift won domination of the meat packing business. Other consumer goods controlled by trusts were salt, whisky, matches, crackers, wire, and nails.

Eventually, prosecution by states or state legislation declaring trusts illegal ended these organizations. But though the original form of trust disappeared, the term *trust* continued in use and was applied to any type of monopoly. Many of the former trusts reorganized themselves into holding companies under the friendly corporate laws of New Jersey. Others became corporate combines created by mergers of separate firms. Fewer combinations occurred during the depression of 1893–97, but after this they increased at an extraordinary rate.

Opposition to the Trusts. As the American people watched the proliferation of trusts and millionaires, they became convinced that something must be done to restore competition. There arose a popular outcry against monopolies, and by the eighties public speakers and writers began to condemn them. In 1881 Henry D. Lloyd attacked the Standard Oil Trust in "The Story of a Great Monopoly" in the *Atlantic Monthly;* similar articles against other examples of big business followed. Edward Bellamy in his *Looking Backward* (1887) assailed economic conditions of the time and pictured a future socialist utopian state where life's necessities and luxuries would be produced by a cooperative society for the benefit of all. Henry George in his *Progress and Poverty* (1879) maintained that the problems of the times were largely the result of a monopoly of land. "All who do not possess land," he argued, "are toiling for those who do, and this is the reason why progress and poverty go hand in hand." Land took on value not because of anything that the owner did, but because people came to live on it. George proposed, therefore, that the unearned increments in land values be confiscated by the government in the form of a single tax on land. This would benefit the whole of society and adjust those economic disparities from which American society in the industrial age suffered.

During the eighties a number of states passed laws prohibiting trusts, but these failed to check the increasing concentration of industry. Some trusts appeared more powerful than the states that attempted to regulate them, and when one device for creating monopoly ran afoul of the law, another was substituted. State legislation also proved ineffective so long as such states as New Jersey, Delaware, and West Virginia placed few restrictions on the chartering corporations and permitted the creation of holding companies.

The Interstate Commerce Act. These frustrations aroused the opponents of monopoly to demand federal action. Between 1873 and 1885 more than thirty measures were introduced in the House of Representatives providing for the regulation of interstate railroads. Some of them were passed, only to fail in the Senate. But under the pressure of Easterners as well as Westerners, the Senate yielded at last and appointed the Cullom Committee to investigate. In 1886 the committee made its report, concluding: "It is the deliberate judgment of the Committee that upon no public question are the people so nearly unanimous as upon the proposition that Congress should undertake in some way the regulation of interstate commerce." This recommendation together with the Wabash decision in 1886, forbidding the states to continue their regulation of *interstate* railroad traffic, led to the Interstate Commerce Act of 1887.

This law provided that all railway rates "shall be reasonable and just." It prohibited such discriminatory practices as rebates[1] and drawbacks[2] and made illegal some of the long and short haul abuses.[3] It forbade pooling agreements[4] and required

---

[1] Powerful industrial shippers, in a strong bargaining position with railroads, often demanded—and received—secret "rebates," or discounts from publicly posted shipping rates. Rebates sometimes were given in return for a specified volume of business or in return for the shipper's distributing his traffic in accordance with a pooling agreement made among competing lines.

[2] In exchange for the privilege of transporting the freight of a large shipper (e.g., Standard Oil), railroads agreed to pay the shipper "drawbacks," or subsidies drawn from a percentage of all receipts of its competitors.

[3] The "long and short haul" abuse pointed up the fact that railroads charged rates based not on operating costs but on what the public could be forced to pay. Over "long hauls"—e.g., from Chicago to New York—competition between railroads was keen and freight charges were low (sometimes lower than operating costs); but over "short hauls"—i.e., between local points serviced by only one line—a railroad, in a noncompetitive situation, could charge rates as high as the public could bear, thereby recouping whatever losses the railroad may have suffered on long hauls.

[4] By means of "pooling agreements" competing railroads sometimes agreed to maintain uniformly high rates in a particular locality by apportioning traffic among themselves or dividing accumulated earnings. Pooling was intended to avoid competitive rate wars.

that all rates and fares be printed and publicly posted. The act established a five-man Interstate Commerce Commission, with power to investigate the railroads and to require reports from them. The Commission could hear complaints of violations of the law, but it had to depend upon the courts to enforce its rulings; thus the Commission did not receive the powers necessary to regulate the transportation system. Also, the commissioners were virtually required by the act to be inexperienced in railroad practices, so they had difficulties fully understanding and acting on the complaints of the shippers. The chief weakness of the law, however, was its vagueness: what were "reasonable and just" rates? Such grave defects in the act were recognized even by such a staunch opponent of federal regulation as Senator Nelson Aldrich of Rhode Island, who described the new law as a "delusion and a sham, an empty menace to great interests, made to answer the clamor of the ignorant and unreasoning."

The Commission soon discovered that it could not compel witnesses to testify and that appeals to the courts produced endless delays. Even in those cases that reached the Supreme Court, the decisions generally favored the railroads over the Commission. Between 1887 and 1905 the Court heard sixteen cases appealed by the I.C.C., and in fifteen it upheld the railroads.

The Sherman Antitrust Act. When the states proved unable to curb the industrial trusts, it was clear that the federal government would have to step in. Senator John Sherman of Ohio outlined the issue when he said in 1890:

> Congress alone can deal with the trusts, and if we are unwilling or unable there will soon be a trust for every production and a master to fix the price for every necessity of life.

In 1890 Congress passed the Sherman Antitrust Act by an almost unanimous vote. Although Sherman introduced it, it was written mainly by Senators George F. Edmunds of Vermont and George F. Hoar of Massachusetts. The act declared that "every contract, combination in the form of trust or otherwise, or conspiracy in restraint of trade or commerce" was illegal. But Congress left it to the courts to determine the meaning of the terms and phrases in the law, and it could not be enforced without the cooperation of the Attorney General. Senator Orville Platt of Connecticut in commenting on the act stated, "The conduct of the Senate . . . has not been in the line of honest preparation of a bill to prohibit and punish trusts. It has been in the line of getting some bill with that title that we might go to the country with." Senator Shelby Cullom of Illinois thought that if the act "were strictly and literally enforced the business of the country would come to a standstill."

But it was not enforced. From 1890 to 1901 the Justice Department instituted only eighteen antitrust suits. And the Supreme Court—in *U.S.* v. *E. C. Knight Co.* (1895)—vitiated the law by holding that manufacturing, being wholly intrastate in character even though ultimately affecting interstate commerce, was not subject to federal regulation. This limited definition of the "commerce clause" in the Constitution put trusts beyond federal control.

The Growth of Finance Capitalism. During the 1890s industrial capitalism began to give way to finance capitalism as investment bankers became more influential in the development of American industry. The industrial capitalists like Rockefeller and Carnegie were producers who had grown up with their own industries. Finance capitalists like J. P. Morgan and August Belmont came to power not because they were skilled industrial organizers but because they had enormous sums of money with which they could purchase control of an industry. The influence of the bankers derived from their control of funds available for investment. A corporation in need of capital could ask a banking house to sell the corporation's securities. In return the investment banker demanded a share in the management of concerns in which his customers had invested. Hard-pressed industrialists could not refuse, and gradually the bankers assumed supervision of corporate policies. By the turn of the century control of a number of corporations had passed from industrialists to bankers.

The leading American finance capitalist was J. P. Morgan, who was also a dominant figure in the entire national economy, but the New York banking houses of August Belmont and Company and Kuhn, Loeb and Company and the Boston banking houses of Lee, Higginson and Company and Kidder Peabody and Company were also important. Morgan worked to bring about order and stability in one industry after another, for he wanted to make sure that dividends would be paid regularly to stockholders. He disliked competition because he felt it would lead to cutthroat price cutting, which would be bad for business. Instead, he wanted corporations to make prices and markets. Morgan's policies meant more protection to stockholders but higher prices to consumers.

Probably the biggest of Morgan's ventures was his launching of the United States Steel Corporation in 1901. He bought out the Carnegie Steel Corporation and combined it with ten other steel companies into one vast corporation capitalized at the unprecedented figure of slightly over $1 billion plus a bonded debt of over $303 million. The Bureau of Corporations later estimated that the total value of the combined assets of all the merged companies was $676 million. Thus, only two thirds of the $1 billion capitalization represented real assets; the remaining one third was in the form of "watered" stock, representing fictitious values. The bonded indebtedness and the $75 million which Morgan personally drew from the corporation to pay for his services made the corporation worth even less than $676 million.

With Carnegie's sale to Morgan the era of industrial capitalism came to a close. Finance capitalism brought even greater economic consolidation. In 1893 there were twelve great companies with an aggregate capital of about $1 billion. By 1904 there were 318 industrial combinations—one of them being Morgan's United States Steel Corporation—with an aggregate capital in excess of $7.25 billion. Together these 318 companies controlled more than 5000 separate plants.

LABOR

Labor had a difficult time in the industrial age. While businessmen solicited government assistance in the form of tariff protection and did not regard this as government intervention, they bitterly opposed any attempt to improve the conditions of labor by legislation on the ground that this would be unwarranted interference with the economic system. Most businessmen regarded as absurd the notion that employees had the same right to government protection and aid as had already been afforded business. Businessmen believed that they alone had the right to determine terms and conditions of employment, and they dismissed the idea of collective bargaining.

But as business formed combinations, so did labor. The National Labor Union, organized in 1866, was mainly a reform organization that summed up various grievances labor had had since the 1840s. It demanded an eight-hour day, the abolition of slums, and the establishment of cooperatives. It favored arbitration over strikes in labor disputes, and it frowned, at first, upon independent political action. Its most important leader was William Sylvis, who died in 1869 after heading the organization for only a year. Had he lived longer, the union might have played a greater role in the history of labor; but after his death it turned more and more to political activity, and in 1873 its trade-union aspect disappeared when it became the National Labor Reform party. Even so, the National Labor Union prepared the way for more effective labor organizations.

One of these was the Knights of Labor, organized in Philadelphia in 1869 under the leadership of Uriah Stephens. The main objective of the Knights was to secure the solidarity of labor through secrecy, the organization of cooperatives, and education and propaganda. Secrecy was of prime importance to the members, for their jobs were at stake: industries locked out workers belonging to unions. Even the name of the organization was not made public until 1881. Their secrecy caused the Knights trouble with the churches: only the intercession of Cardinal Gibbons of Baltimore kept the pope from excommunicating the Catholics in the federation.

The Knights were of national importance from 1879 to 1893, while Terence V. Powderly was their Grand Master Workman. Although Powderly himself was opposed to use of the strike as a weapon and was willing to come to terms with capital at almost any price, the hard times of the mid-eighties led to boycotts and strikes, notably on the Union Pacific in 1884 and Jay Gould's Wabash in 1885. Spontaneous strikes by shopmen and trainmen caught the companies off guard and compelled Powderly's support of his followers. These were labor's first major victories, and they forced Gould to negotiate with the Knights. An illusion of easy success arose, and suddenly the Knights were flooded with members. In 1886, their peak year, membership shot up to 700,000.

But fast on the heels of success came the Great Southwestern Strike of 1886 and failure. Powderly had agreed in the Wabash settlement to have no more strikes without notifying the railroads in advance. It was an agreement he could not enforce; the strikes that had occurred were not of his making but were strikes of local origin that had drawn him in only after they had begun. In the Southwestern strike Gould refused to negotiate, because the Knights had given no advance notice to the railroad, and the workers were unable to hold out.

Of all the labor upheavals of the period, none was more frightening to men of property and order or did more damage to the prestige of labor than the bombing at Haymarket Square in Chicago in 1886. On May 1 a number of independent trade unions struck for recognition of the eight-hour day, and two days later the police shot and clubbed some of the strikers who were beating up strikebreakers. The violence of the police prompted growls of resentment and threats of retaliation in the labor press. The next day, May 4, a group of anarchists called a protest meeting in Haymarket Square. As the speeches were coming to a close, almost two hundred policemen arrived on the scene and ordered the crowd to go home. Before anyone could move, however, a bomb exploded, killing one policeman outright and fatally wounding several others. Almost immediately the police opened fire on the workers, and soon a riot was in full swing. A number of civilians were killed, dozens wounded, and in the confusion and excitement several of the policemen shot each other. The reaction in Chicago and throughout the nation was one of horror. In the resulting hysteria, eight men were arrested, tried, and convicted on what later has come to be seen as flimsy, inconclusive evidence. Four were executed and the others imprisoned.

Although the Knights of Labor had nothing to do with the Haymarket Riot, they were identified in the public mind with the anarchists, and skilled workers began to desert the Knights in large numbers. From this time on, the Knights declined in influence, and by 1890 the membership had fallen to 100,000. Other reasons, such as the failure of their cooperatives and their identification with some of the other labor violence of the eighties, also contributed to the downfall of the Knights.

With the onset of depression in the summer of 1893, however, unrest and dissatisfaction among the working class deepened. Among the most violent of the labor upheavals, which aroused national apprehension, was the Pullman strike called by the American Railway Union in sympathy for the distress of Pullman workers. By the end of June 1894 some twenty thousand railroad men were on strike in and around Chicago, tying up every Midwestern railroad. In retaliation the railroad companies appealed to a federal court for an injunction against the strikers on the basis of the Sherman Antitrust Act, arguing that the strike was a restraint on trade such as the act forbade. The court issued the injunction.

At the same time, violence broke out in Chicago, and President Cleveland (over the protest of Governor Altgeld of Illinois) sent in two thousand federal soldiers to "protect the mails." Before order was restored, some twenty people were reported killed and two thousand railway cars destroyed. Eugene V. Debs, president of the American Railway Union, and other labor leaders were arrested, convicted of contempt of court—for violating the injunction—and sentenced to six months to a year in jail. The conviction of the A.R.U. leaders was upheld later by the Supreme Court of the United States, which declared the injunction issued against the union to be a legitimate device for the protection of interstate commerce and the mails.

For thirty years after the Debs case, a federal court injunction was a potent weapon in the hands of employers threatened with a strike. Although the Clayton Act of 1914 appeared to limit the court's authority to interfere in labor disputes, many antilabor injunctions continued to be granted by the federal courts, and it was not until the Norris–La Guardia Anti-Injunction Act was passed in 1932 that labor gained the protection against injunctions it had long sought.

Outside of the railroad brotherhoods, the only national union of sizable membership to weather the antilabor pressures of these years was the American Federation of Labor, founded in 1886. However, the AFL at this time was a somewhat reactionary movement. Under the presidency of Samuel Gompers, it devoted itself solely to trade unionism, organizing skilled workers but doing little for the unskilled. By 1904 the AFL claimed 1,676,200 of the nation's 2,072,700 unionists.

Most American workingmen in these years accepted existing working conditions as inevitable and made the best of them. Though they might be discontented, they did not always protest. Industrial workers were a minority group and were much influenced by rural values. They were also awed by the enormous achievements of the new industry and were proud of being a part of it. As a class, American workers were noticeably silent. Many were unskilled, poorly educated, and socially underprivileged. According to John Garraty, "Negroes and immigrants particularly had little influence, and lacked the self-confidence necessary to seek influence aggressively." Workers of the upwardly mobile type generally identified with their employers and accepted the values of American capitalism. They did not consider themselves exploited or underprivileged, and their attitude helped to reduce the discontent of workers generally.

The national labor organizations of the post–Civil War decades were confronted with the race issue. Should they organize black workers; and if they did, should they allow them to join the same union with white workers, or should they put them in segregated unions? This was a difficult problem for labor leaders, because they recognized that the black was a potential competitor for the white worker. The National Labor Union, owing to the wide diversity of opinion among its members, never took any specific action on this matter. But the Knights of Labor, whose goal was to organize all workers, skilled and unskilled, sought to bring blacks into the labor movement. And thus it organized black as well as mixed locals, not only in the North, but in the South, where Knights organizers were attacked by vigilantes and lynch mobs. It is not possible to tell from the available records how many blacks became members of the Knights. At the 1886 convention of the union the general secretary reported that "the colored people of the South are flocking to us, being eager for organization and education . . . ," and in that same year, the peak year for the Knights, it has been estimated that there were no fewer than sixty thousand blacks in the Knights of Labor.

Since the American Federation of Labor was comprised of national craft unions, it had little place for blacks, for few of them had ever been admitted to craft unions. Gompers' position on the black worker was made clear in his annual report of 1890 when he emphasized the "necessity of avoiding as far as possible all controversial questions." It was not until the First World War, according to Spero and Harris in their history, *The Black Worker*, that blacks became "a regular element in the labor force of every basic industry."

THE LAST FRONTIER

The West. While industrial expansion was transforming post–Civil War America, there took place another movement of momentous consequence, the settlement of the western half of the country. It was a migration probably unparalleled in the history of the world. In one generation Americans established more than a million farms in this last West and occupied more new land than earlier Americans had settled in two and a half centuries. From 1607 to 1870 Americans had occupied 407 million acres and had placed 189 million of them under cultivation. In the last three decades of the nineteenth century they took up 430 million acres and brought 225 million of them under cultivation.

The Mining Frontier.   Miners were the first to reveal to the nation the resources and potentialities of the territory between the Missouri River and the Pacific. The discovery of gold in 1848 had lured many miners to California, and later, throughout the 1860s, miners hurried to "strikes" in Colorado, Arizona, Idaho, Montana, and Wyoming. In each case gold attracted the first settlers, the miners. When the pay dirt was exhausted, ranchers and farmers, aided by the government and railroads, laid the foundations of the territory.

The discovery of gold in the foothills of the Rocky Mountains close to Pike's Peak, near Lake Tahoe on the eastern slopes of the Sierra Nevada, on the reservation of the Nez Percé Indians in the eastern part of Washington territory, in Last Chance Gulch in Montana, and in the Black Hills region of South Dakota on the reservation of the Sioux Indians brought thousands upon thousands of persons to these areas. Into them crowded all the elements of a rough and active civilization. A large number of the miners, such as those in Idaho, "were like quicksilver," said H. H. Bancroft, the historian: "A mass of them dropped in any locality, broke up into individual globules, and ran off after any atom of gold in their vicinity. They stayed nowhere longer than the gold attracted them." Others, as in Colorado, stayed on, once the mining boom had spent itself, to farm and to help their area become a territory.

The story of the mining towns is a familiar one in fiction and motion pictures. Their lawlessness has attracted much attention. To be sure, it existed. But it would be a mistake to represent the mining communities as mere nests of lawlessness, or to argue, as most Easterners did, that mining camps had abandoned the institutions of civilized society. Mining camps did have few churches, schools, newspapers, theaters, and so forth, but they quickly established them. For example, in the town of Deadwood, South Dakota, known as the most lawless place in the country and consisting mainly of two long rows of saloons, a stage company played Gilbert and Sullivan's *Mikado* for a record run of 130 nights. Each mining camp was a separate administrative and judicial district having its own governing officials who passed and enforced its own laws. The legal codes and practices of these mining camps were eventually recognized in American courts, and a number of them were incorporated into constitutions and laws of the Western states.

The miners' frontier came to an end in the 1880s. No more important discoveries were made, and the individual prospector was gradually replaced by big corporations usually run by Eastern financiers. Between 1860 and 1890, $1,242,000,000 in gold and $901,000,000 in silver were taken out of the mines in the West. These amounts enabled the federal government to resume specie payment and helped precipitate the money question, a major political issue during the last quarter of the nineteenth century (see Chapter 2).

The Settlers. The opportunities for obtaining cheap or free land induced many a settler to go West. He could buy a farm outright from the national government under the terms of the Preemption Act of 1841, which allowed him to obtain a quarter section (160 acres) at the nominal price of $1.25 an acre. Or he could purchase his quarter section from one of the land-grant railroads or from one of the states whose holdings of public domain were greatly increased by the passage of the Morrill Act of 1862. (The Act had given every state establishing a public agricultural college thirty thousand acres for each senator and representative then in Congress.) Finally, the western settler could secure his quarter section free of charge under the Homestead Act of 1862. This law made it possible for any American citizen, or any alien who had declared his intention of becoming a citizen, to acquire 160 acres of unoccupied government land by living on it or by cultivating it for five years. If the homesteader wished to gain ownership sooner, he could, after six months of residence, buy his quarter section at the prevailing minimum price, usually $1.25 an acre. The residence requirement went up to fourteen months in 1891.

The Homestead Act has been called "the greatest democratic measure of all history," but it had a number of faults. The best farming lands east of the 100th meridian (the line approximately bisecting the Dakotas and Nebraska east and west) were largely preempted by 1862, and in the region from the Great Plains to the Pacific, to which the law chiefly applied, small homesteads were inadequate. Moreover, the Homestead Act did not end land speculation. Larger purchases than ever were made by individuals. For example, William S. Chapman bought a million acres in California and Nevada, and Francis Palms and Frederick E. Driggs together procured 486,000 acres of timberland in Michigan and Wisconsin. There was also fraudulent administration of the law. False claims were made; claims were turned over to speculators and to land, mining, and timber companies, and perjury and bribery of land officials were common. In practice the act was a perversion of the land reformer's ideas.

During this period a generous Congress passed other measures to dispose of the public domain. The Timber Culture Act of 1873 provided free grants of 160 acres in certain regions on condition that the settler plant 40 acres (later reduced to 10 acres) in trees and keep them growing for ten years. Under the terms of the Desert Act of 1877 the government offered semiarid lands in 640-acre tracts to those who would irrigate them. But since irrigation projects usually required more capital than most settlers had, the law primarily benefited large-scale grazing companies. The Timber and Stone Act of 1878 permitted the sale of quarter sections of land not suited for agriculture but valuable for timber, and large corporations and speculators managed to get possession of more than thirteen million acres of such government lands.

The Ranching Frontier. Flourishing on the Great Plains for about two decades after the Civil War was an open-range cattle industry, originating with the Long Drive of cattle from Texas northward to railroads on the Great Plains for shipment eastward to the large cities. One of the most accessible meeting places for ranchers and packers was at Abilene, Kansas, on the Kansas Pacific railroad line. Here Joseph G. McCoy, an enterprising meat dealer from Illinois, built a hotel and erected barns, stables, pens, and loading chutes. In 1868 Abilene received 75,000 head of cattle and in 1871, a record year, 700,000 head. Over the next dozen years a total of four million cattle were driven over the Chisholm Trail to Abilene and other Kansas cow towns. The cattle were moved slowly in herds of two or three thousand head. This procedure required the services of sixteen or eighteen cowboys, a cook with a chuck wagon, and a wrangler with extra cow ponies.

It was on the Long Drive that the cowboy came into his own as a unique character of the frontier. He was a picturesque figure, usually clothed in a flannel shirt, with a brightly colored handkerchief loosely knotted around his neck, high-heeled boots into which his trousers were tucked, a pair of leather chaps—or heavy riding overalls—and a broad-brimmed felt hat; heavy spurs and a revolver completed his costume. The cowboy's work was hazardous. With only a cow pony, a lasso, and a six-shooter, he and his companions tried to keep under safe control several thousand head of steers during two months of continuous travel. There were many risks along the trail—the danger of stampedes, which could be set off by a sudden noise or lightning flash, of thefts by rustlers, and of raids by Indians. One of the veterans of the Long Drive wrote, "It was tiresome grimy business for the attendant punchers who travelled ever in a cloud of dust and heard little but the constant chorus from the crackling of hoofs and of ankle joints, from the bellows, lows, and bleats of the trudging animals."[5] The cowboy's life was also a lonely one. He sang sentimental words to soothe the restless cattle and to cheer himself as he whiled away the lonely hours on the Chisholm Trail. Although fans of Western stories and movies might never suspect the fact, blacks were numerous among the cowboys who drove the herds to market.

The cattle business reached its peak in the early 1880s, when profits of 40 to 50 percent were common. But such returns quickly attracted so many prospective ranchers that they overstocked the range. The unfenced plains of the public domain were bountiful and free, and the ranchers made use of this public land. Between 1882 and 1884 they sent as many young steers north to the ranges as they shipped east to the markets. But the two disastrous winters of 1885–86 and 1886–87 and the blistering summer of 1886 destroyed most of the feed and the cattle. What steers eventually reached market were so inferior in quality that the bottom fell out of beef prices despite the great shortage. Also at this time large numbers of sheepherders began to cross the plains. The sheep stripped the range of grass, so when the sheepmen came to stay, the cattlemen had to fight or leave. Farmers were also homesteading the plains and fencing the open range, and many of them turned to cattle raising. Soon they were able to produce beef of higher quality than that found on the open range. With the increase of railroad facilities, the Long Drive became unnecessary. Gradually this stage of the colorful cattle industry was ending, and with it came an end to the last frontier.

The Indian.   An essential step in the conquest of the last West was the solution of the Indian problem. The Indians of the Great Plains and the Rocky Mountains, about 250,000 in number, actively opposed white settlement in their areas. The land had been theirs for centuries, and they were determined to fight, if necessary, to keep it. The strongest and most warlike were the Sioux, Blackfoot, Crow, Cheyenne,

[5]Philip Ashton Rollins, *The Cowboy* (New York: Charles Scribner's Sons, 1922), p. 253.

Comanche, and Apache tribes. They clung tenaciously to their land and fought valiantly for it. Mounted on swift horses and armed with bows and arrows, the Indians of the Great Plains were more than a match for the white man until he perfected the repeater rifle.

Until the time of the Civil War, the Plains Indians had been relatively peaceful. Then the miners invaded the mountains, cattlemen moved into the grasslands, and white settlers followed the railroads across the prairies. Wanton destruction of the buffalo by the intruding whites threatened the Indians' very existence, because they depended on the animal for food, fuel, clothing, robes, bowstrings, tools, and other essentials. Faced with all these pressures, the tribes became dissatisfied with their treaties with the federal government. During the war, whites clashed with the Apache and Navaho in the Southwest and with the Arapaho and Cheyenne on the Great Plains, and for the next twenty-five years Indian warfare constantly recurred. In the mountain areas most of the tribes were eventually persuaded to give up their lands and move to reservations, but the tribes on the plains were not willing to abandon their hunting grounds to the encroaching whites.

In 1867, Congress enacted legislation providing for the removal of all Indians to reservations and thereby breaking the promises given to the Plains Indians in the 1820s and 1830s that they could keep their lands forever. The federal government decided to create two reservations for the Plains Indians—one in the Black Hills of Dakota, the other in present-day Oklahoma. But then there were difficulties. While the tribal chieftains signed the treaties, individual Indians often refused to be bound by them. General W. T. Sherman expressed a prevalent white attitude when he wrote, "We have . . . provided reservations for all, off the great roads. All who cling to their old hunting grounds are hostile and will remain so till killed off. We will have a sort of a predatory war for years—every now and then be shocked by the indiscriminate murder of travelers and settlers, but the country is so large, and the advantage of the Indians so great, that we cannot make a single war to end it."

Sherman's prediction was accurate. Between 1869 and 1875 more than two hundred battles between the United States army and the Indians took place. What went on in these conflicts can be derived from a statement of General Francis A. Walker, Commissioner of Indian Affairs, in 1871: "When dealing with savage men, as with savage beasts, no question of national honor can arise. Whether to fight, to run away, or to employ a ruse, is solely a question of expediency." A few years earlier General S. R. Curtis, United States Army commander in the West, had told his subordinate officers: "I want no peace till the Indians suffer more."

And the Indians did suffer. A white trader reported that Cheyenne "were scalped, their brains knocked out; the men used their knives, ripped open women, clubbed little children, knocked them in the head with their guns, beat their brains out, mutilated their bodies in every sense of the word." This barbarity surely raises the question: Who were the savages, the Indians or the whites?

The Indian wars after 1865 cost the federal government millions of dollars and hundreds of lives, yet a solution to the problem seemed to be nowhere in sight. Much of the failure rested with the national government, whose officials regarded each tribe as a sovereign but dependent nation. Indians frequently misunderstood the terms of the tribal treaties, and many individual Indians did not feel obligated by them. Moreover, authority over Indian affairs was divided between the Department of the Interior and the War Department, and each pursued different policies and objectives. Then, too, frontiersmen in general believed that the only good Indian was a dead one, and most soldiers agreed. Easterners, far removed from the scene of strife, had a different attitude. Here churchmen and reformers united to urge a policy of humanitarianism toward the Indians.

As the War Department followed its policy of fighting the Indians, new ideas about the problem began to have some influence at Washington. A new civilian Board of Indian Commissioners, created in 1869, attempted to convert the nomadic Plains Indians to agriculture on the reservations and sought to persuade the government to break down tribal autonomy. In 1871 Congress abolished the policy of dealing with tribes as though they were independent nations. In the seventies, too, the government began to establish Indian boarding schools removed from the reservations. To give Indians greater incentive, the Indian Commissioners recommended individual land holdings and the gradual elimination of the system of reservations. Books on behalf of the Indian began to appear, among them Helen Hunt Jackson's *Century of Dishonor* (1881), which had the greatest influence in stirring up public opinion behind efforts to improve the Indians' lot.

Finally, in 1887, the Dawes Act initiated a new Indian policy that reversed the old military policy of extermination. The Act provided for the dissolution of tribal autonomy and the division of tribal lands, with each family head receiving 160 acres. To protect the Indian in his property, the right of disposal was withheld for twenty-five years. At the end of this probationary period the Indian received full rights of ownership and full United States citizenship.

The new policy did not work well. In dividing up the reservations, the best tracts were usually sold to white settlers and the worst given to the Indians. Often the Indian owners were disheartened and failed to cultivate adequately the land they kept. And when individual Indians, without experience as property owners, acquired good land, they were too easily persuaded to sell it. (The Burke Act of 1906 gave the Secretary of the Interior discretionary authority to reduce the probationary period preceding legal sale.) The policy was not universally applied: some tribes, especially in Arizona and New Mexico, retained their tribal organizations and continued to hold their land in tribal fashion.

Gradually the feeling developed that it had been a mistake to have the Indians abandon their traditional way of life. And an effort was made to reverse the policy laid down by the Dawes Act and to allow the tribes to hold their land as communal property. This was realized in the Indian Reorganization Act of 1934. For a continuation of the record of the government's Indian policies, see pp. 219–20.

CHAPTER 2

THE POLITICS OF
CONSERVATISM AND DISSENT
1877–1900

POLITICAL DOLDRUMS

Critics of the Gilded Age. In contrast to its dramatic industrial and economic progress, the political activity of the United States in the post-Reconstruction years seemed to lack the vitality and productivity of earlier periods. The Presidents had executive ability and high principles, but they, like most of the important men in Congress, proved to be mediocre and uninspiring leaders. "No period so thoroughly ordinary has been known in American politics since Christopher Columbus first disturbed the balance of power in American society," wrote Henry Adams, that mordant commentator of the Gilded Age. "One might search the whole list of Congress, Judiciary, and Executive during the twenty-five years 1870 to 1895 and find little but damaged reputation. The period was poor in purpose and barren in results."

This era in American politics has been kicked and scuffed by historians until little remains of its reputation. Most critics believe that at no other time in American history was the moral and intellectual tone of political life so uniformly low, nor were political contests so preoccupied with patronage. "Even among the most powerful men of that generation," said Henry Adams, speaking of the politicians, there were "none who had a good word for it." It has become a historical convention to censure the politicians of these years for degenerating into a group of spoilsmen who served the business community as they were themselves served by business.

The most serious charge leveled against the major parties was that they failed to meet the problems generated by the Industrial Revolution. Far-reaching economic changes necessitated extensive social readjustments, and problems arising from recurrent industrial crises and depressions demanded vigorous governmental action. But both parties chose to ignore these new issues; problems of the new economic order were seldom aired in the political arena except when the third parties joined battle.

The Parties. The common explanation for this failure is that there were no important differences on major issues between Democrats and Republicans. "Neither party has any principles, any distinctive tenets," wrote James Bryce, a contemporary English observer of the American party system. "The two major parties in this period," concluded Bryce, "were like two bottles. Each bore a label denoting the kind of liquor it contained, but each was empty." Historians have called the period the "age of negation" and its politics "the politics of dead center."

To account for the seeming impotence of political parties during the era, it must be remembered that the consensus of opinion in America was that government should "let well enough alone"; consequently, government rarely concerned itself with economic and social problems. However, there were other deterrents to governmental action. Probably most important was the sharp contest between the parties and the failure of either to control the national government for any appreciable length of time. Contrary to popular belief, these were not years of Republican supremacy; rather, they were a period of party stalemate and equilibrium.

In the six presidential elections from 1876 to 1896, the Republicans, while winning four, gained a majority of the popular vote in only one (1896) and a plurality in only one (1880)—and even that plurality was less than one tenth of 1 percent. In three of these elections the difference between the popular vote for the two major party candidates was less than 1 percent, although electoral vote majorities ranged from 1 in 1876 to 132 in 1892. The Democrats, while electing a President twice (1884, 1892), won a majority of the popular vote in 1876 and a plurality in 1884, 1888, and 1892. Each party managed to control the presidency and Congress at the same time for only four years—the Republicans from 1889 to 1891 and the Democrats from 1893 to 1895.

Victory in national elections depended heavily on the "doubtful" states, which had enough shifting voters to swing the results either way. These were Connecticut, New York, and New Jersey in the East and Ohio, Indiana, and Illinois in the Midwest. These states, especially New York and the three Midwestern ones, enjoyed strong bargaining power with which they secured favorable posts for their politicians and obtained most of the funds from the campaign treasuries at election time. The doubtful states were wedded to neither party but courted by both. The parties chose presidential and vice-presidential candidates from these areas and awarded their congressmen important committee assignments.

Congressional Supremacy. National political power was then vested chiefly in Congress and not in the presidency. Congressional leaders had almost overthrown Andrew Johnson, had gained nearly complete control of Grant, and tried to put subsequent Presidents in the Gilded Age at their mercy. The office of President was at low ebb in power and prestige. Senator John Sherman, Republican leader of Ohio and a perpetual aspirant to the office, wrote: "The executive department of a republic like ours should be subordinate to the legislative department. The President should [merely] obey and enforce the laws." Congressional leaders acted accordingly. "The most eminent Senators," observed George F. Hoar, Republican of Massachusetts, about his colleagues in the Senate, "would have received as a personal affront a private message from the White House expressing a desire that they should adopt any course in the discharge of their legislative duties that they did not approve. If they visited the White House, it was to give, not to receive advice."

Big Business in Politics. The considerable power that business wielded also contravened governmental action. Businessmen were usually able to obtain what they wanted from either party, because rival political machines either could be purchased or were so tractable that they did not need to be bought. It should be remembered that a majority of Americans were sympathetic to business. They believed that laissez-faire and free competition reduced prices and assured a higher rate of employment; therefore, they considered government regulation unnecessary, unjust, and immoral. Even the reformers crusaded for only the most urgent reforms, and then only after a careful study had confirmed the need. "Government supervision among Anglo-Saxons is apt to degenerate into jobbery," wrote Charles Francis Adams, Jr. "In America, particularly, the whole instinct of the people leads them to circumscribe rather than to enlarge the province of government. This policy is founded in wisdom."

But despite its favored position, business did not control American politics. Businessmen had to pay heavily for political favors, and often they were blackmailed by threats of regulation or withdrawal of government assistance. Businessmen complained that politicians treated them simply as customers, compelling them to pay for protection, selling political benefits to the highest bidders, and refusing to do the proper thing without pay. These facts alone furnish proof of the independence of the politician, which was so complete that it was necessary for the businessman to bribe him. Politicians were eager to deal with businessmen because they were well organized and had money to spend. Farmers and workers also were able to win political favors once they became organized and began to put pressure on politicians.

The Republicans. The Republican party was a loose combination of Northeastern business groups and upper Midwestern farming groups—an alliance that had been formed in 1860 and had fought and won the Civil War. In much of the North and West, Republicans were the party of wealth and respectability.

Two other large groups attached to the party were blacks and Union army veterans. The blacks, loyal to the party of emancipation, were able to elect a few congressmen from the South. But after the Republicans abandoned them in 1877, they became more openly critical of the party and rapidly lost what little political power they had previously enjoyed. War veterans, on the other hand, increased their political importance by organizing the Grand Army of the Republic in 1866 and pressuring Congress into voting for generous pension laws.

Sharply divergent views between Northeastern businessmen and Western farmers occasionally threatened party unity, but Republican orators tried to sidestep their differences by "waving the bloody shirt"—equating party loyalty with national patriotism and charging the Democrats with having fought under the Confederate flag.

The Democrats. The Democratic party was a more regional coalition than the Republican. Its support came chiefly from the "solid South" and the city machines of the Northeast, but it also had some support from the industrial workers of the big cities and from those Northeastern bankers and merchants—"sound money" men—who opposed protective tariffs and government subsidies to special interests and who favored contraction of the currency.

In the South the Democrats were the party of white supremacy. Southern party leaders, often of Whig background, called themselves "Conservatives" and frequently were labeled "Bourbons" by their opponents. They had much in common with Democratic leaders in the Midwest, who shared their conservative economic views and were also known as "Bourbons." In large Northern cities the Democratic party had the allegiance of most immigrants, who were attracted by the name of the party and whose leaders had sometimes risen to places of influence in it. The rank-and-file Democrats—farmers, industrial workers, and small businessmen—were often restive under their conservative leaders, but those leaders prevailed in the party until the mid-1890s.

Today the big cities of the country will usually vote Democratic, but in the Gilded Age most of the large urban centers outside the South were more likely to be Republican than Democratic. New York and Boston ordinarily went Democratic, but in the three presidential elections of the 1880s, for example, a majority of the cities of over fifty thousand outside the South went Republican. The Republican party in these years was able to appeal successfully to urban voters and immigrants as the party of prosperity and economic growth. In contrast the Democrats appeared as the more conservative and economy-minded party and did not have the same appeal.

The Party Bosses. The political rulers of the day were not the titular leaders but the party bosses, many of them United States senators, who headed powerful state machines and rewarded their followers with public offices. Among the important bosses were Senators James G. Blaine of Maine, Roscoe Conkling of New York, Zachariah Chandler of Michigan, and John A. Logan of Illinois, all Republicans; and Arthur P. Gorman of Maryland, a Democrat. Before 1883 these party bosses had at their disposal an enormous amount of spoils in the form of federal, state, and local offices. They controlled a hierarchy of workers down to the ward heelers, to whom they gave offices in return for faithful service. The assessment of office holders and the sale of nominations and offices tightened the bosses' grip on local machines.

When the Civil Service Reform Act of 1883 (see pp. 69–70) began to remove these resources by eliminating the spoils that produced them, politicians turned increasingly to businessmen for money and support. A new type of political boss appeared—a business type who resembled and worked closely with the corporation executive, made few speeches, and conducted his activities in anterooms, caucuses, and committees. Matthew S. Quay of Pennsylvania, Leland Stanford of California, Philetus Sawyer of Wisconsin, Thomas Platt of New York, and Nelson W. Aldrich of Rhode Island were bosses of the new type. Some had been prosperous bankers and businessmen and had entered the Senate to protect their interests. In 1889 William Allen White could say: "a United States Senator . . . represented something more than a state, more even than a region. He represented principalities and powers in business." According to White, one senator "represented the Union Pacific Railway System, another the New York Central. . . . Coal and iron owned a coterie from the Middle and Eastern seaport states. Cotton had half a dozen senators. And so it went." Many labeled this imposing body the "Millionaires' Club." Senator George Hearst of California, one of the group, expressed what these men thought of themselves: "I do not know much about books; . . . but I have traveled a good deal and have observed men and things and I have made up my mind after my experiences that the members of the Senate are the survivors of the fittest."

Besides these prominent Establishment bosses, there were the backroom bosses, who often ruled without ever holding elective office. The principal effect of the spoils system was to transfer party control from publicly elected leaders to "inside" rulers. The most flagrant examples of "invisible government" occurred in the cities, many of which were run by corrupt political machines. Whether Democratic, like Tammany Hall in New York, or Republican, like the Gas Ring in Philadelphia, their methods were the same. Bryce expressed the opinion that municipal government was "the one conspicuous failure of the United States," and Andrew D. White in an article in *Forum* in 1890 stated that "with very few exceptions, the city governments of the United States are the worst in Christendom—the most expensive, the most inefficient, and the most corrupt."

New York City furnished the country its most notorious example of a municipal machine. There Tammany Hall, an organization dating back to the eighteenth century, controlled the Democratic party and the local government. William Marcy Tweed and his followers A. Oakey Hall, the mayor, Peter B. Sweeney, county and city treasurer, and Richard B. Connally, the city controller, ran Tammany Hall and plundered the city. By every type of peculation this repulsive crew robbed the city treasury year after year until, at the height of their power, they were splitting among themselves 85 percent of the total expenditures made by the city and county. Their technique was simple. Everyone who had a bill against the city was instructed to pad it—at first by 10 percent, later 66 percent, finally 85 percent. Tweed's gang received the padding. For example, the courthouse, originally estimated at $3,000,000, cost the taxpayers $11,000,000. The plastering bill alone amounted to $2,870,000 and the carpeting to $350,000, "enough to cover the whole City Park three times." The loot taken by the Tweed Ring has been variously estimated at from $45,000,000 to $100,000,000.

Although respectable citizens protested, they were powerless for several years to move against Tweed because he controlled every arm of the government. Finally, courageous editorials in the New York *Times* and the cartoons of Thomas Nast in *Harper's Weekly* exposed the corruption of the Tweed Ring and aroused the general public. His own followers, Tweed said, could not read, but they could "look at the damn pictures." Tweed offered George Jones, owner of the *Times,* a million dollars to quiet his paper and Nast a half million to study art in Europe, but they refused. A citizens' committee headed by Samuel J. Tilden and Charles O'Conor launched an investigation that was able by the end of 1872 to drive every member of the Tweed Ring out of office. Tweed himself died in jail.

Yet the traditional view of the boss as nothing but a corrupting force in American politics needs to be modified. Some recent studies of Boss Tweed and of the Cox and Pendergast machines in Cincinnati and Kansas City show that these political organizations furnished some element of order and stability in a rapidly expanding and disordered society. They point out that the boss provided a valuable service in giving expression to the needs of many people who had no other institutional or social order to respond to.

Moreover not all bosses used politics to advance their material interest. Common as the various forms of graft and corruption were in the Gilded Age, not all bosses sought material profit. Boies Penrose, Republican boss of Pennsylvania, apparently never made a dollar out of politics. And according to Theodore Roosevelt, "Senator Platt [Republican boss of New York state] did not use his political position to advance his private fortunes—therein differing from many other political bosses. He lived in hotels and had few extravagant tastes."

The Reformers. In this age of cynicism and corruption, voices such as those of the "single-tax" advocate Henry George and the socialist Edward Bellamy called for reform. Probably the most respectable of all the reformers were the "Mugwumps," as they were called by their opponents. (The term was first used politically in 1884 to describe the independent Republicans who refused to support presidential candidate James G. Blaine.) Mugwumps generally were newspapermen, scholars, and intellectuals, earnest men of high ideals and prominent social position, of conservative economic views, and usually of Republican background. Foremost among them were George William Curtis, editor of *Harper's Weekly;* E. L. Godkin, editor of the *Nation;* Carl Schurz; William Cullen Bryant; Whitelaw Reid; and Samuel Bowles. They lashed out against the spoils system and worked to purify politics through civil service reform. Since they believed in laissez-faire, they restricted their economic program to tariff reform and sound money.

The Mugwumps spoke in moralistic terms rather than in economic ones. They appealed primarily to the educated upper classes and seldom identified themselves with the interests of the masses, whom they viewed with an aristocratic disdain. They regarded the reform movements of labor and farmers as radical and dangerous and had little use for other reform movements of the period. But this was a characteristic of most contemporary reform movements. They had little in common and had great difficulty in understanding one another. Thus reformers were divided and mutually suspicious and exerted little influence.

FROM HAYES TO HARRISON

Hayes and the Presidency. Historians have portrayed Rutherford B. Hayes as a respectable mediocrity with an average capacity and an impeccable public and private life. True, there was no dramatic flair in his personality, and he lacked brilliance, but he was a man of integrity and honest intentions, and his determination and steadfastness of purpose eventually frustrated even his bitterest foes. Hayes' presidency is an excellent illustration of how party stalemate and equilibrium can hamper effective executive leadership. Hayes worked under severe handicaps that have not been fully appreciated. His right to the office was disputed (see pp. 30–31), and Republicans and Democrats alike referred to him as "the *de facto* President" and "His Fraudulency." His programs for the South and for civil service reform, plus his show of independence, caused such a deep split within his own Republican party that he was nearly read out of it. At one time Hayes had but three supporters in the Senate, one of them a lifelong friend and relative. Moreover, the Democrats controlled the House of Representatives throughout his administration and the Senate the last two years of his term. Under these circumstances it is amazing that he could accomplish anything.

Hayes endeavored to reestablish presidential power and prestige and to redress the balance between the executive and legislative branches. He first challenged congressional dominance in the make-up of his cabinet when he picked men who were most unwelcome to the bosses, particularly the liberal Republican Carl Schurz for Secretary of the Interior and the Southern Democrat and former Confederate David M. Key for the important patronage-dispensing position of Postmaster General. At first the Senate balked and refused to confirm the entire cabinet list, but under much public pressure it finally gave in to the President.

Hayes gained another victory over congressional encroachment by refusing to yield the right given him by the Force Acts of 1870–71 to intervene in federal elections in the states. Democratic majorities in Congress sought to nullify these Reconstruction laws by attaching to army appropriation bills riders aimed at removing federal supervision of elections. Hayes fought these attempts because they would have placed him under the "coercive dictation" of a "bare" majority in Congress and because he wanted to make the executive "an equal and independent branch of the government." He vetoed eight such bills, and Congress lacked enough votes to override him.

Hayes struck a daring and spectacular blow for reform against the spoils system and its greatest champion, Senator Conkling. Hayes had already vexed the bosses with his inaugural statement: "He serves his party best who serves his country best," and he really angered them with his comment, "Party leaders should have no more influence in appointments than other equally respectable citizens." He appointed a commission headed by John Jay of New York, grandson of the first Chief Justice, to investigate the largest patronage office in the federal service, the New York Custom House—long an example of the spoils system at its worst. The commission found that most of the employees had been appointed in the interest of the Conkling machine, that 20 percent of them were superfluous, and that the place was ridden with "ignorance, inefficiency, and corruption." When Conkling's lieutenants, Collector of the Port Chester A. Arthur and Naval Officer Alonzo B. Cornell, refused to clean up the corruption or to resign, Hayes boldly removed them and named two others to the posts. On Conkling's insistence the Senate refused to confirm the nominations, but Hayes persisted and within a year his choices were approved. He had won a battle, but he had not routed the spoilsmen.

The End of Reconstruction. Hayes removed the last of the federal troops from the South and ended military Reconstruction. He acted to restore harmony between North and South and between whites and blacks. He responded to a general demand for a change in policy in the South. He considered that Reconstruction governments had lost so much support they had become completely unable to sustain themselves even with the use of force. And he dreamed of building in the South a strong Republican party that would no longer depend upon the black for its main strength and that could command the esteem and support of Southern whites. He became the first Republican President to experiment with the plan of appointing regular Democrats to important posts in the South in the hope of gaining Republican success there. He seldom was credited with any honest motives, for the public in 1877—and many years later—believed this was part of the bargain that had made him President. His experiment was a sharp departure from the strategy of the Radicals during Reconstruction; had it worked, the "solid South" as a Democratic stronghold might not have come into being.

Depression and the Silver Question. When Hayes entered the presidency, the country was experiencing the worst years of a depression that had begun in 1873. Almost immediately he was confronted with the first great industrial conflict in our history—a railroad strike that began on the Baltimore and Ohio and spread through fourteen states, affecting two thirds of the railroad mileage in the country outside New England and the South. At the request of four state governors, Hayes sent federal troops to intervene in the strike and restore order.

Hayes ran further afoul of labor, especially on the West Coast, when he vetoed a bill passed in 1879 to restrict Chinese immigration. He felt the bill violated the Burlingame Treaty of 1868, which had given the Chinese the right of unlimited immigration to the United States. (However, Hayes sent a mission to China to negotiate a new treaty, and the resultant Treaty of 1880 gave the United States the right to regulate or suspend Chinese immigration. The Exclusion Act, passed by Congress in 1882, suspended such immigration for ten years.)

The President also took an unpopular stand on the currency question. Discontented agrarians wanted "cheap money" and the repeal or modification of the Resumption Act of 1875, which obligated the Treasury to redeem greenbacks in specie at full face value on January 1, 1879. Many predicted that such redemption would wreck the monetary system, for everyone would want gold rather than paper notes. But Hayes resisted the pressure and aided Secretary of the Treasury John Sherman in accumulating a gold reserve to redeem the currency. Greenback dollars, which were worth only sixty-seven cents in 1865, rose to one hundred cents before the deadline of resumption, and people realizing this preferred the notes, which were easier to handle; thus no run on the gold reserve developed.

Inflationists now pushed demands for free coinage of silver, and once again Hayes took the unpopular side. The old ratio between gold and silver had been 16 to 1: there was sixteen times as much silver in a silver dollar as there was gold in a gold dollar. But when the Gold Rush of 1849 lowered the price of gold, an ounce of silver became worth more than one sixteenth of an ounce of gold, and Americans sold their silver on the open market rather than have it coined at a loss. Silver dollars nearly disappeared from circulation, and in 1873 Congress abolished their coinage. Then silver mines in Nevada, Arizona, and Colorado produced such large quantities of silver that the price of silver fell, and miners and agrarians called for a return to the coinage of silver at the old ratio.

Congress responded by passing over Hayes' veto in 1878 the Bland-Allison Act, authorizing the Treasury to purchase not less than $2 million and not more than $4 million worth of silver each month and coin it into dollars at the former ratio of 16 to 1. The act, however, did not fully meet the demands of the silverites, who wanted the "free and unlimited coinage of silver"; moreover, the Treasury consistently purchased only the minimum amount of silver required by the act.

The Election of 1880. Hayes did not seek reelection, and the Republican convention of 1880 was divided in its support: the "Stalwart" faction, led by party boss Roscoe Conkling, sought a third term for Ulysses S. Grant; but James G. Blaine of

Maine and John Sherman of Ohio also had Republican supporters. When it became clear that none of the three could secure a majority, the delegates nominated Congressman James A. Garfield of Ohio on the thirty-sixth ballot. To appease the Stalwarts, second place on the ticket went to one of Conkling's closest associates, Chester A. Arthur, whom Hayes in 1878 had dismissed as head of the New York Custom House. When Samuel J. Tilden declined to run, the Democrats picked General Winfield Scott Hancock, a Pennsylvanian and a Union hero in the Battle of Gettysburg. His running mate was William H. English of Indiana.

The platforms of the two parties revealed few basic differences on policy and no real understanding of the country's problems. The campaign, which turned largely on personalities and irrelevant issues, produced a great deal of sound and fury but nothing of importance. Five sixths of the voters turned out, and Garfield won by fewer than 40,000 popular votes, although his electoral vote was 214 as compared to 155 for Hancock. Despite the failure of the major parties to discuss the vital issues of the day, less than 4 percent of the electorate voted for a protest party candidate—General James B. Weaver of Iowa of the Greenback Labor party, which advocated inflationary policies and stricter federal regulation of interstate commerce.

Garfield and Arthur.   Garfield had been an effective speaker and an able party leader in the House, but many of his contemporaries found him timid and vacillating. Overwhelmed with the demands of office seekers, he exclaimed, "My God! What is there in this place that a man should ever want to get into it?" After accepting the aid of the Stalwarts during the campaign and apparently reaching some understanding with them on patronage matters, Garfield antagonized Conkling by making Conkling's great rival, Blaine, Secretary of State and by appointing a Conkling opponent in New York Collector of the Port. In the ensuing fight between the President and the Stalwarts, Conkling and his colleague from New York, Thomas "Me Too" Platt, resigned their seats in the Senate and were not reelected by the New York legislature. At the height of the conflict, on July 2, 1881, Charles J. Guiteau, a disappointed office seeker who was mentally unbalanced, shot Garfield and shouted, "I am a Stalwart and Arthur is President now." Garfield died of the wound on September 19, and Arthur became President.

To many Americans the succession of Arthur was a calamity, for he had the reputation of a New York machine politician. Reformers shuddered at the thought of a spoilsman in the presidency, and there was a widespread feeling that the Stalwarts would take over. But in spite of his unsavory past, Arthur was personally honest and did have ability. The responsibilities and dignity of the high office caused him to rise to the occasion and to give the country a good administration. He did not turn over the patronage to Conkling, as many thought he would. He supported civil service reform, prosecuted frauds in the Post Office, cleared the way for the construction of a modern navy, and had the Chinese immigration question settled. He also tried to check federal spending on unnecessary public works by vetoing an $18 million rivers and harbors bill and to bring about a reduction in the tariff, but both efforts were defeated by Congress.

The Civil Service Act.   The most important legislation during Arthur's presidency was the Pendleton Civil Service Act of 1883. Since the end of the Civil War, reformers had been denouncing the spoils system and advocating the establishment of a permanent civil service based on merit. Garfield's murder dramatically advanced their cause. The Pendleton Act authorized the President to appoint a Civil Service Commission of three members to provide "open competitive examinations for testing the fitness of applicants for the public service now classified or to be classified." In addition, the act forbade the levying of political campaign assessments on federal office holders and protected them against ouster for failure to make such contributions. At first the act affected only the lowest offices—about fourteen thousand, or 12 percent of the total number of federal employees, leaving the remainder under the spoils system—but the President was given authority to extend the classified list at his discretion. Arthur demonstrated good faith by making excellent appointments to the Commission. Every subsequent President extended the classified list, and at the end of the century it included 40 percent of all federal positions.

The Election of 1884.   In 1884 the Republicans turned their backs on Arthur and nominated James G. Blaine of Maine for President. The Democrats named Grover Cleveland of New York. Viewing Blaine as an old guard politician inimical to good government, William Curtis, Carl Schurz, and other reformist Mugwumps bolted the Republican party and supported Cleveland. As in 1880 there were few real issues, and the campaign degenerated into one of personal abuse and vilification. "The public is angry and abusive," observed Henry Adams. "Everyone takes part. We are all doing our best, and swearing like demons. But the amusing thing is that no one talks about real issues." The Democrats publicized the "Mulligan letters" to prove that Blaine, as Speaker of the House, had been guilty of unethical conduct in connection with land-grant railroads, and the Republicans retaliated with the charge that Cleveland was the father of an illegitimate child, the responsibility for whom he had accepted. Since Blaine seemed to have led an impeccable private life but a culpable public one and Cleveland just the reverse, one Mugwump suggested that "we should elect Mr. Cleveland to the public office he is so admirably qualified to fill and remand Mr. Blaine to the private life which he is so eminently fitted to adorn." Overall, the decision in 1884 was even closer than in 1880. Cleveland's plurality in popular votes was only 29,000 and his electoral vote was 219 to Blaine's 182. So narrow was the margin of victory for Cleveland that he carried the pivotal state of New York by a mere 1149 votes.

Cleveland and the Presidency.   Cleveland, a strapping figure of well over two hundred pounds, came to the White House in 1885 with a reputation as a reformer and a man of courage, integrity, and prodigious work habits. Actually he was unimaginative, stolid, obdurate, and brutally candid, and he lacked a sense of timing. He was also a thoroughgoing conservative, a believer in sound money, and a defender of property rights. In his inaugural he promised to adhere to "business principles," and his cabinet included conservatives and business-minded Democrats of the East and South. His administration signified no break with his Republican predecessors on fundamental issues.

Cleveland faced the task of pleasing both the Mugwumps and the hungry spoilsmen of his own party, who had been cut off from federal patronage for twenty-four years. At first he refused to yield to the bosses on appointments and thereby won the acclaim of reformers. But faced with a revolt within his own party,

Cleveland gave in to the spoilsmen and replaced Republicans with "honest Democrats." Carl Schurz wrote, "Your attempt to please both reformers and spoilsmen has failed," and Cleveland broke with the Mugwumps. At the end of his presidency he had removed about two thirds of the 120,000 federal officeholders. On the credit side he increased the civil service classified list to 27,380, almost double the number when he took office.

Cleveland had more success as a watchdog of the Treasury. He halted the scandalous pension racket by vetoing hundreds of private pension bills that congressmen pushed through for constituents whose claims had been rejected by the Pension Office. Cleveland signed more of these bills than had all his predecessors since Johnson put together, but he was the first President to veto any. The Grand Army of the Republic screamed at the vetoes, and in January 1887 Congress responded by passing a Dependent Pension Bill, which provided a pension for all honorably discharged disabled veterans who had served as little as three months in the Union army, irrespective of how they had become disabled. Cleveland vetoed it and angered the G.A.R.

Aside from the Interstate Commerce Act (see pp. 50–51), for which Cleveland deserves no credit and which he signed with reluctance and "with reservations," little significant legislation was enacted during his term. He did compel railroad, lumber, and cattle companies to give up 81 million acres of public land that they had fraudulently occupied. In 1886 Congress passed a Presidential Succession Law, which provided that after the Vice-President, the succession should pass to the members of the cabinet, beginning with the Secretary of State, in the order of the creation of their departments. In 1887 the Dawes Act inaugurated a new Indian policy (see p. 60).

The Tariff Issue.   For the first time in this era both major parties were forced to take a position on the tariff issue. Cleveland devoted his entire annual message of December 1887 to the tariff question, advocating a drastic reduction in duties. The Democratic-controlled House responded with a low tariff measure, but the Republican-dominated Senate turned it down and passed a highly protective bill that the House would not accept. This led to a deadlock and the injection of the tariff question into the 1888 election.

The Election of 1888.   The Democrats renominated Cleveland and chose the elderly ex-Senator Allen G. Thurman of Ohio as his running mate. The Republicans nominated Senator Benjamin Harrison of Indiana for President, and Levi P. Morton, a wealthy New York banker, for Vice-President. Two labor parties, voicing the industrial unrest of the period, entered the campaign. Union Labor and United Labor condemned the major parties for being under the control of monopolies and for being indifferent to the welfare of workers.

The campaign was waged largely on the tariff issue, with Republicans defending protection and Democrats advocating a reduction of duties. The Republicans appealed to the manufacturing interests, who would profit from a high tariff, and to veterans, who were promised generous pension legislation. Both parties used money freely; throughout the country voters were bribed in probably the most corrupt presidential election in our history. Although Cleveland had a plurality of more than 90,000 popular votes, Harrison carried the crucial doubtful states of Indiana, New York, and Ohio and gained 233 electoral votes to Cleveland's 168. Despite all the campaign talk about the tariff, the vote did not indicate a national decision against Cleveland on that issue. Cleveland carried the manufacturing states of New Jersey and Connecticut and increased his strength of 1884 in such pro-tariff states as Ohio, Michigan, and California. The decisive factors were probably the efficiency of the Republican organization and the purchase of the floating vote in the doubtful states.

Harrison and the Republicans. Harrison possessed intellectual and oratorical gifts, but he was very cold in his personal relationships. "Harrison sweats ice water" became a popular phrase, and one of his close associates remarked, "Harrison can make a speech to ten thousand men and every man of them will go away his friend. Let him meet the same ten thousand in private, and every one will go away his enemy." Although Harrison had ability, he lacked forcefulness, and the leadership passed largely to the Republican leaders in Congress, especially to Senator Nelson W. Aldrich of Rhode Island and Speaker of the House Thomas B. Reed of Maine. Reed pushed through the House a revision of the rules that gave him almost dictatorial powers over proceedings and earned him the title of "czar."

For the first time since 1875 the Republicans had the presidency and a majority in both houses of Congress, and they began to pay off their political debts. The McKinley Tariff of 1890 raised rates to a higher level and protected more products than any previous tariff in American history. In the same year the Dependent Pension Act, substantially the same measure vetoed by Cleveland, granted pensions to all G.A.R. veterans suffering from any disability, acquired in war service or not, and to their widows and children. In the same year, to meet the demands of the silverites, the Sherman Silver Purchase Act increased the amount of silver to be purchased by the Treasury to 4.5 million ounces a month. To appease the popular clamor against monopolies, the Sherman Antitrust Act was also passed in 1890 (see p. 51).

This same Congress earned itself the label "the Billion Dollar Congress." By distributing subsidies to steamship lines, passing extravagant rivers-and-harbors bills, offering large premiums to government bondholders, and returning federal taxes paid by Northern states during the Civil War, it handed out so much money that by 1894 the Treasury surplus was gone. The United States has never had a surplus since.

Instead of the widespread support that such policies were expected to bring, the public reaction was one of hostility, and in the congressional elections of 1890 the Republicans were severely rebuked. They retained only 88 of the 332 seats in the House and had their majority in the Senate reduced from 14 to 6. The appearance of nine new congressmen representing farm interests and not associated with either of the major parties indicated that a third-party revolt was shaping up and that a new phase in American politics was under way.

THE AGRARIAN REVOLT

The Plight of the Farmer. The third-party revolt took the form of agrarian insurgency in the West and South, which had been coming on since the Civil War and which reached its culmination in the 1890s. There were a number of causes for agrarian discontent. The conversion of American agriculture to a commercial basis made the farmer a specialist whose role was to produce a surplus by which the United States could adjust an unfavorable balance of trade. But unlike the manufacturer, the farmer had no control over his market or his prices. He worked alone and competed with other farmers, American and foreign. Rather than benefiting from the new order of things, he was one of its victims.

Prices for agricultural products had declined. Between 1870 and 1897 wheat prices dropped from $1.06 to 63.3 cents a bushel, corn from 43.1 to 29.7 cents a bushel, and cotton from 15.1 to 5.8 cents a pound. These were market prices, after warehouse and transportation charges were added; the net prices paid to the farmer were even lower. Farmers of the Old Northwest received only 42 cents a bushel for wheat which government economists estimated cost 45.1 cents a bushel to produce. In Kansas in 1889 corn sold for ten cents a bushel and was commonly used for fuel, and in 1890 a farmer in Nebraska shot his hogs because he could neither sell them nor give them away.

Farmers increasingly were shackled with debts and loss of proprietorship over their land. In 1900 nearly one third of the country's farms were mortgaged. In the Middle West the percentages were highest—45 percent in Wisconsin, 48 percent in Michigan, and 53 percent in Iowa. Mortgages were few in the South because of the crop-lien system, by which local merchants advanced seed, equipment, and personal necessities to planters in return for a first lien on the planter's future cotton crop. Throughout the country the number of tenant farmers increased from 25.9 percent of all the farms in 1880 to 29.4 percent in 1890 and to 35.3 percent in 1900.

Naturally the farmer blamed others for his plight, in particular the railroads, the middlemen, and the banks. He resented railroad rate differentials and discriminations against him. On through routes and long hauls rates were low, because the railroads competed with one another, but on local or short hauls, where there was little or no competition, rates were high. Sometimes the Western local rate was four times that charged for the same distance and commodity in the East, where rail lines were more numerous. Farmers paid more to ship their grain from Minnesota towns to St. Paul or Minneapolis than a shipper in Minneapolis had to pay for a haul to New York. Farmers also disliked the way railroads favored big shippers and dominated state politics.

The farmer also believed himself to be at the mercy of the middlemen—local merchants, grain dealers, brokers, and speculators. He attacked the national banks because their rules precluded loans on real estate and farm property and because they did not respond to his seasonal needs for money.

The farmer complained that he bore the brunt of the tax burden. The merchant could underestimate the value of his stock, the householder might exclude some of his property, the owner of securities could conceal them, but the farmer could not hide his land. Finally, the protective tariff hurt the farmer because he purchased his manufactured goods in a highly protected market and sold his crops in an unprotected one. He shared none of the benefits of protection; instead, he contributed heavily to the subsidization of business. This injustice was all the more difficult to bear in view of his belief that the tariff was "the mother of trusts."

The Granger Movement. Feeling they were being left behind and suspecting politicians of indifference and even hostility to their interests, farmers decided to organize and protest against their condition. In 1867 Oliver Hudson Kelley, a government clerk, founded the Patrons of Husbandry, which became better known as the Grange. The farmers saw in the Grange a weapon with which to fight their foes. By 1874, its peak year, it had an estimated membership of 1.5 million. The Grangers established a number of cooperatives in an effort to eliminate the profits of the middleman, but mismanagement and business opposition doomed most of them. Although the Grange officially declared itself "nonpolitical," individual members joined various agrarian third parties organized in the Midwest; in coalition with either the Democrats or the Republicans, these third parties gained control of several state legislatures and enacted Granger laws to regulate the rates charged by grain elevators and railroads. They were challenged in the courts, but in *Munn* v. *Illinois* in 1877, the most important of these cases, the Supreme Court upheld the "police power" of state regulation. After 1875 Grange membership decreased rapidly; out of the twenty thousand local granges extant in 1874 only four thousand remained in 1880. Many farmers had been attracted by the novelty and vogue of the Grange, and others believed it would provide a panacea for all their ills; they left when they found there was not immediate and universal success.

The Greenback Movement. Farmers next were attracted to the Greenback movement. From 1867 to 1872, in the social-reform or wage-earners' period, Eastern labor dominated the movement, and its primary objectives then were to lower the interest rate on money and to reduce taxation. After 1873, in the inflationists' or farmers' period, farmers favored an expansion of the currency in the hope it would bring higher prices for their products. When the panic of 1873 intensified the agricultural depression and the Granger movement failed to relieve the situation, farmers took over the Greenback movement. Its high-water mark was the election of fifteen congressmen in 1878. But with the resumption of specie payment in 1879 and with the rise of the price of corn in 1880, farmers lost interest in Greenbackism and its support rapidly declined. In the presidential election of 1880 the Greenback candidate, James B. Weaver of Iowa, received only 300,000 votes, about 3 percent of the total, and by 1888 the party was dead.

The Farmers' Alliance. With the decline of the Grange and the disappearance of Greenbackism, a new set of farm groups appeared. Most important were the Farmers' Alliances, two distinct organizations of different origins. The Northwestern Alliance was organized by Milton George in Chicago in 1880. The Southern Alliance was formed in 1875 in a frontier county of Texas for protection against horse thieves and land sharks. It remained small until 1886, when it expanded throughout the South under the vigorous leadership of C. W. Macune and absorbed rival farmers' organizations. For blacks there was a Farmers' National Alliance and Cooperative Union.

The Alliances experimented with cooperatives more than the Grange had but with no greater success. A merger of the Northwestern and the Southern Alliance was unsuccessfully attempted in a meeting at St. Louis in 1889. The Southern Alliance insisted upon the retention of its secret rituals and the exclusion of blacks, at least from the national body. The Northwestern Alliance wanted a federation in which each organization would keep its identity. Then the Southern Alliance changed its name to the National Farmers' Alliance and Industrial Union and induced the three strongest state alliances of the Northwestern Alliance, those of Kansas and North and South Dakota, to join it. In the same year it gained the endorsement of the Knights of Labor.

The Emergence of Populism. Though the Alliances proclaimed themselves nonpolitical organizations, each year they issued demands which could be realized only by political means. For example, the Ocala, Florida, platform of 1890 called for the abolition of national banks, establishment of subtreasuries, a graduated income tax, direct election of United States senators, and government control of communication and transportation facilities. By 1890 the Northwestern Alliance concluded that nonpartisan activities were a failure and decided to enter politics. Kansas led the way by organizing a People's (Populist) party in June 1890, and Alliancemen in other Western states set up independent parties under other names. The West was in the throes of a mighty upheaval; a later commentator called it "a pentecost of politics in which a tongue of flame sat upon every man and each spoke as the spirit gave him utterance."

"Sockless" Jerry Simpson, Ignatius Donnelly, Mary Elizabeth Lease, Anna L. Diggs, and General James B. Weaver were among the leaders of Western Populism. The party, though hastily constructed, was successful in Kansas, where it elected five congressmen and one senator in the 1890 elections; in Nebraska, where it gained control of both houses of the legislature and elected two congressmen; and in South Dakota, where it elected a senator.

In the South the Alliance, fearing that the establishment of a third party might bring the black into power, first tried to gain control of the Democratic party machinery. It attacked the industrial and urban leadership of the Democrats and endorsed candidates who pledged themselves to the Ocala platform. The Alliance appeared to have captured the Democratic party in the elections of 1890 when four governors, eight state legislatures, forty-four congressmen, and three senators promised to support Alliance demands, but nearly all these elected officials reverted to Democratic orthodoxy once in office. This disillusioning experience, plus the prospects of Cleveland's renomination by the Democratic party, stimulated southern Alliancemen to become Populists. In July 1892 the national People's party was formally organized in Omaha.

The Election of 1892. The Populist platform of 1892 restated earlier Alliance demands, including the free and unlimited coinage of silver at the ratio of 16 to 1; government ownership and operation of railroads and the telephone, telegraph, and postal systems; prohibition of alien ownership of land; restriction of immigration; and a graduated income tax. The death of L. L. Polk of North Carolina just before the convention met in Omaha on July 4 probably deprived the Populists of their strongest candidate. They nominated General James B. Weaver of Iowa for President and General James G. Field of Virginia for Vice-President. Both Cleveland and Harrison were renominated by the major parties; their running mates were Adlai E. Stevenson of Illinois and Whitelaw Reid, editor of the New York *Tribune.* The free silver plank was the only exciting issue in the campaign, and Weaver polled 1,040,000 popular votes and 22 electoral votes. Populists became the first third party since the Civil War to break into the Electoral College. They also elected 10 representatives, 5 senators, 3 governors, and 1500 members of state legislatures. Cleveland defeated Harrison with 277 to 145 electoral votes and 5,555,426 to 5,182,690 popular votes.

Cleveland and the Depression of 1893. Shortly after Cleveland assumed the presidency in 1893, the country began to experience the worst financial panic in years. Following the failure of a number of prominent firms, the stock market suddenly collapsed. Banks called in their loans, and credit just about dried up. Businesses failed daily. Before the year was out, 500 banks and nearly 16,000 businesses had gone into bankruptcy. According to the *Commercial and Financial Chronicle,* never before had there been such a sudden and striking cessation of industrial activity. And no part of the nation escaped it. Everywhere mills, factories, furnaces, and mines closed down in large numbers, and hundreds of thousands of men were thrown out of work. By the fall of 1893, the *Banker's Magazine* of London reported the American people to be "in the throes of a fiasco unprecedented even in their broad experience" and declared that "Ruin and disaster run riot over the land."

The panic developed into a major depression. There was no agreement as to its causes. Conservative business leaders attributed it to the Sherman Silver Purchase Act and to radical attacks on property. Labor leaders and agrarians blamed it on the capitalists. The Democrats blamed the Republicans, and the Republicans accused the Democrats. In fact, nearly every American had his own explanation of what had caused the panic and the depression.

There had been periodic panics followed by depressions ever since the end of the Civil War. In each instance reckless speculation overinflated values. Then confidence collapsed with attendant business failures and unemployment. The primary cause for the debacle of 1893 was the overexpansion of transportation facilities and industrial production, accompanied by stock manipulation and reckless speculation. And as usual it had been preceded by a similar depression abroad.

Like his predecessors in office, Cleveland believed it was not the duty of the federal government to alleviate suffering in a depression; as he complacently stated in his second inaugural, ". . . while the people should patriotically and cheerfully support their Government, its functions do not include the support of the people." In his view the Sherman Silver Purchase Act had caused the depression, and his proposed remedy was to repeal the act and maintain the gold standard. The silverites disagreed. They contended that the cure lay in the free and unlimited coinage of silver at a ratio of 16 to 1 of gold and that the Sherman Act had provided inadequate relief. Many debtor agrarians agreed.

But Cleveland was convinced that the silver certificates issued under the Sherman Act and redeemed in gold were responsible for the drain on the gold reserve that was being lowered to the established minimum of $100 million. This was an oversimplification, for there were several causes for the drain on gold. Cleveland summoned Congress into special session in 1893 and, through a combination of Gold Democrats and Republicans, had the Sherman Act repealed. Most Western and Southern Democrats voted against the Democratic administration, widening the split within the party on the currency issue.

Repeal failed to restore prosperity. The Treasury's gold reserve continued to fall, and to keep the country on the gold standard, Cleveland had the Treasury sell government bonds for gold. A group of bankers headed by J. P. Morgan absorbed three bond issues in 1894 and 1895, but it was not until 1897, when the depression had finally run its course, that the Treasury crisis ended. Although the gold purchases enabled the Treasury to meet its obligations, the bond sales intensified the silverites' hatred of the President. Many Americans became alarmed over the government's dependence upon a syndicate of New York bankers.

Cleveland failed to bring about any substantial reduction of the tariff. The Democrats, fulfilling their campaign promises, had passed a tariff bill in the House, drawn up by William L. Wilson of West Virginia, which provided for a modest reduction in rates. In the Senate, though, a group of protectionists from both parties, led by Senator Arthur Gorman, influential Democrat from Maryland, attacked the bill with more than six hundred amendments, restoring some old rates and raising others. The resultant Wilson-Gorman Tariff of 1894, which Cleveland denounced as "party perfidy and party dishonor" and which became law without his signature, was a far cry from reform. It did provide for a small income tax of 2 percent on incomes over $4000, but the Supreme Court, as unpopular as Cleveland, held the tax to be unconstitutional, even though an income tax had been collected during the Civil War.

For the remainder of his presidency, Cleveland confined his role to that of protector of the status quo. He vetoed the Seigniorage bill, which would have increased the supply of the currency. Through subordinates he rudely rejected the petitions of "armies" of unemployed workers who, under the nominal leadership of men like Populist Jacob S. Coxey, marched on Washington in 1894 to plead for public works relief programs. In the same year, Cleveland sent federal troops to crush the Pullman strike.

The Election of 1896. The Republicans met in St. Louis in June and nominated William McKinley of Ohio for President and Garret A. Hobart, a corporation lawyer of New Jersey, for Vice-President. Marcus Alonzo Hanna, a wealthy Ohio industrialist, was largely responsible for McKinley's nomination. Hanna is a good example of the new kind of political boss then emerging—the businessman holding office and actually running the party instead of remaining in the background and paying out political favors. As a leader of the Republican party in Ohio, soon to become Republican national chairman, Hanna gathered the necessary delegate votes for McKinley's nomination and financed and managed his preconvention campaign.

On the monetary question McKinley's record was not consistent. He had voted for both the Bland-Allison Act and the Sherman Silver Purchase Act. Yet in 1891, in running for governor, he condemned the free coinage of silver and advocated international bimetallism. Hanna had already decided upon a gold standard plank, but at the convention he gave the impression he had to be "persuaded" by the Eastern delegates that "the existing gold standard must be maintained." After a gold plank was adopted, a small group of silver advocates led by Senator Henry M. Teller of Colorado dramatically left the hall and organized the Silver Republican party.

The Democrats were torn by bitter strife when they met in Chicago in July. The agrarians looked upon Cleveland as an enemy; he personified the Northeastern conservatism against which they were in revolt. Within the Democratic party insurgency was rampant. In the elections of 1894 the Democrats had barely retained control of the Senate and had lost the House. The take-over by the farm elements of the convention of 1896 was not a sudden coup; it had been well planned. Insurgent Democrats prepared to outdo the silverites in denouncing Cleveland and advocating free silver. They hoped to win back the Populists and take over the Democratic party. Their work was so effective that by the summer of 1896 they had gained control of every state Democratic organization south of the Potomac and west of the Alleghenies except South Dakota, Minnesota, and Wisconsin.

The silverites dominated the convention, and Cleveland was denounced in resolutions and speeches. The platform repudiated the Cleveland program and attacked the protective tariff, national banks, trusts, and the Supreme Court; it called for an income tax and the free coinage of silver at the ratio of 16 to 1. The leading contender for the nomination was Congressman Richard P. ("Silver Dick") Bland of Missouri, who had fought for free silver since the seventies. But the convention passed him by and on the fifth ballot nominated William Jennings Bryan of Nebraska, who had captivated the silver delegates with a speech that rose to a stirring peroration: "You shall not press down upon the brow of labor this crown of thorns, you shall not crucify mankind upon a cross of gold."

Bryan, only thirty-six at the time, seemed to have been nominated by the accident of a spontaneous speech. But he had been rounding up support for several years and had presented his ideas many times to other audiences. His convention speech was simply the last step, and that step became certain when the silverites gained control of the convention. Bryan's running mate was Arthur Sewall of Maine, a wealthy shipbuilder, banker, and protectionist but an advocate of free silver.

The Populists faced a dilemma when their convention met in St. Louis in July. If they nominated their own candidate, they feared they would split the reform vote and permit McKinley to win. If they endorsed Bryan, they would surrender their identity to the Democrats and sacrifice their broad program of reform for one that placed a disproportionate emphasis on the silver question. Western Populists were eager to nominate Bryan, but Southern Populists, who regarded fusion with the Democrats as anathema, wanted a separate ticket. The Populists finally were induced to nominate Bryan through trickery. Senator William V. Allen of Nebraska, chairman of the convention, told the Southerners that the Democrats had promised to withdraw Sewall and accept Thomas E. Watson, Populist leader of Georgia, as their vice-presidential candidate if the Populists would nominate Bryan. Watson's decision to accept this compromise persuaded Southern opponents of fusion to vote for Bryan's nomination. This would have created a true Democratic-Populist partnership, but the Democrats refused to withdraw Sewall. Henry Demarest Lloyd watched the convention with great disgust and finally concluded, "The People's party has been betrayed, . . . but after all it is its own fault."

The campaign was a highly emotional and dramatic one. Bryan spoke in twenty-one states, traveled eighteen thousand miles, and addressed some five million people in more than six hundred speeches. McKinley remained at his home in Canton and read well-prepared speeches from his front porch to carefully coached delegations that visited him. But Hanna did the real work. The powerful response to Bryan's appeal frightened Eastern conservatives, and Hanna took advantage of their panic to collect campaign funds. From trusts, banks, railroads, and tycoons he raised a sum estimated at between $3.5 million and $15 million as against a bare $300,000 for Bryan.

Hanna used the money lavishly but wisely, and he received great assistance from the press, which heaped all kinds of abuse upon Bryan. The *Louisville Courier Journal* called him "a dishonest dodger . . . a daring adventurer . . . a political faker," and the New York *Tribune* referred to him as a "wretched, rattle-pated boy." The Philadelphia *Press* described the "Jacobins" of the Democratic Convention as "hideous and repulsive vipers," and Theodore Roosevelt was reported as saying that the silver men might well "be stood up against the wall and shot." John Hay, writing to Henry Adams in London, said of Bryan, "The Boy Orator makes only one speech—but he makes it twice a day. There is no fun in it. He simply reiterates the unquestionable truths that every man who has a clean shirt is a thief and should be hanged, and there is no goodness or wisdom except among the illiterates and criminal classes." In addition there were dire warnings that Bryan's victory would bring disaster. Farmers were told that mortgages would not be renewed. Workmen were informed that factories would be closed or wages cut.

Out of almost 14 million popular votes cast, McKinley won with a margin of over a half million and with 271 electoral votes to 176 for Bryan. Bryan failed to carry a single industrial and urban state and did not win a single state north of the Potomac and east of the Mississippi. Despite the widespread unrest among labor, he failed to elicit its support, and this failure was one of the principal reasons for his defeat. But also he had nowhere near the material resources backing McKinley, and he represented the party charged with the depression. The Republicans gained a majority in both houses of Congress.

McKinley lost all the mining states and the wheat-growing states of South Dakota, Nebraska, and Kansas, where Republicans had always been strong. But he held onto the corn-producing states of the Middle West, where the farmers were better off than those on the Plains. And he gained an ascendancy in the Northeast such as no previous Republican President had had. From Maine south to Virginia and from the

ELECTION OF 1896: ELECTORAL VOTE

McKinley: 271   Bryan: 176

Great Lakes to Tennessee he carried every state. While the margin by which he carried some was narrow, McKinley had a majority of the popular vote in the nation—the first Republican presidential candidate to achieve a majority since Grant in 1872. The Republicans continued to hold the bulk of the Northern farmers and had gained new strength among the commercial and industrial interests of the North and the Upper South. For the first time since 1872, New England and the Middle Atlantic, Central, and North Central states were solidly Republican, and these sections were strong enough, if united, to control the electoral college and thereby the presidency itself.

Historians are generally agreed that the election of 1896 was the most important one since 1860, and they have regarded it as a turning point in American history. For one thing it gave the Republicans a clear majority of the popular vote in the country as a whole for the first time since Reconstruction. For another it ushered in a series of Republican triumphs and a period of Republican supremacy in the national government that was to last, except for Wilson's two terms, until 1932. McKinley's victory also marked a triumph for conservatism and industrialism. The backbone of agrarian resurgence was broken in 1896.

In the mourning for Bryan the fate of Populism was largely forgotten. Its passing seemed to be the concern of few, yet it was one of the most significant results of the election of 1896. Fusion with the Democrats and the abandonment of a broad program of reform for the sake of silver had all but destroyed the Populist party on the national level. It was Populism, not Bryanism, that furnished the backbone of agrarian resurgence, and when that backbone was broken in 1896, it meant that agrarian radicalism had made its last aggressive stand against capitalist industrialism.

McKinley and the End of an Era.   The McKinley administration was ushered in under highly favorable circumstances. Businessmen knew that their interests would be safeguarded for four years. There was a return to prosperity which was to continue for several years. Farmers largely dropped politics and were busy raising crops. Politicians were happy and looked forward to a long period of abundance. McKinley, well aware of the economic distress that had affected Americans, promised in his first inaugural that this would be his chief concern. To maintain recovery he advocated two principal measures—a higher tariff and a gold standard act. Congress responded with the Dingley Tariff of 1897, which raised duties to an average of 52 percent, the highest in our history, and the Gold Standard Act of 1900, which declared the gold dollar from that time on would be the sole standard of currency.

With these two laws the McKinley administration made good its campaign promises. Beyond this neither the President nor Congress intended to interfere with the country. They planned to let it alone and to allow business to create prosperity. McKinley's inauguration marked the beginning of the greatest consolidation movement in American industry (1897–1904). This, coupled with the Spanish-American War, produced the golden years of prosperity under McKinley and Hanna.

McKinley's presidency marked the beginning of a new era not only in national politics but in the running of the national government; as Professor Wilfred Binkley, a leading authority on the President and Congress, writes: "Not since the presidency of Thomas Jefferson, had there been achieved such an integration of the political branches of the federal government and such consequent coherence and sense of direction in its functioning." The equilibrium and stalemate of the preceding two decades had given way to Republican supremacy.

THE DISFRANCHISEMENT OF BLACK AMERICA

America's greatest and most tragic problem in the post–Civil War years was the plight of the blacks who comprised one tenth of the population. Though the Civil War had settled the question of human slavery, it did not settle the problem of securing for all Americans the inalienable rights set forth in the Declaration of Independence. Nor did it alter the fact that white supremacy was generally taken for granted. During Reconstruction significant constitutional and legislative steps were taken to insure the freedman's political and civil rights, but developments during the last quarter of the nineteenth century virtually destroyed these efforts. When President Hayes removed the last of the federal troops from the South, he left Southern blacks in the custody of Southern whites; and when they failed to respect the rights of blacks, as they had promised to do, there was little protest from the blacks' former champions in the North. In effect, Congress turned the problem back to the South. And regardless of the party in power in Washington, the blacks did not benefit. While both major parties made pious statements about equality and constitutional rights for blacks, neither one did anything about them.

As for looking after the rights of blacks, in the two decades after 1890 the Southern states disfranchised practically all black voters by means of poll taxes, white primaries, and literacy or property qualifications that were enforced against blacks but not against whites. In the same years the Southern states also passed numerous "Jim Crow" laws, segregating blacks in virtually every aspect of public life. The old conservative leaders of the South, the "Redeemers" like Wade Hampton of South Carolina, who governed their states from the 1870s and who retained some of the paternalistic attitudes of slavery days toward blacks, were supplanted in the 1890s by a new class of Southern politicians, men like Ben Tillman and James K. Vardaman, whose chief appeal was frequently an invidious racism. At the same time the growth of scientific racism and the cult of Anglo-Saxon supremacy, together with the northward migration of blacks, produced a widening of antiblack sentiment in the North as well.

Not only was the black American forsaken by the federal government in the post-Reconstruction years, but he was also abandoned by the courts. After 1877 practically every Supreme Court decision affecting blacks nullified their rights or curtailed them somehow. The Court drastically limited the powers of the federal government to intervene in the states to protect the rights of blacks, and to all intents and purposes it invalidated the Fourteenth and Fifteenth Amendments as effective safeguards for the black. When in 1883 the Court set aside the Civil Rights Act of 1875 on the ground that the Fourteenth Amendment was binding on states but not individuals, it ended federal attempts to protect blacks against discrimination by private persons. There would be no federal civil rights legislation thereafter until 1957.

And in the 1870s when the Court held that the Fifteenth Amendment did not confer the right to vote upon anyone and that Congress did not have the authority to protect the right to vote generally, sections of the Enforcement Act of 1870 were declared unconstitutional because they provided penalties for hindering a person in voting. In 1894 Congress repealed the entire law. Again, there was no further legislation on the subject until 1957.

Finally, in two decisions in the 1890s, the Court paved the way for additional curtailment of the rights of blacks. In *Plessy* v. *Ferguson* (1896) the Court laid down the "separate but equal" rule in defense of segregation; this became the law of the land until 1954. Then in *Williams* v. *Mississippi* (1898) the Court opened the road to legal disfranchisement by approving the Southern plans, already noted, for depriving the black of his vote.

Most Northerners shared the Court's attitude toward blacks. They desired reconciliation between North and South, and since the black was the symbol of sectional antagonism, most Northerners deplored agitation on his behalf and accepted the South's racial policies. Even educated, intelligent Northerners believed that the black was racially inferior.

The dominant position of black leader Booker T. Washington among his race from 1885 to his death in 1915 also helped encourage the white assault upon blacks. Washington, founder and principal of Tuskegee Institute in Alabama, proposed that, for the time being, blacks forego agitation for the vote and social equality and devote their efforts to achieving economic security and independence. "In all things that are purely social," he said in a speech at the Atlanta Cotton Exposition of 1895, "we can be as separate as the fingers, yet one as a hand in all things for mutual progress." This submissive principle won the enthusiastic support of the white community and fixed the pattern of race relations for most of the remainder of Washington's lifetime. While most blacks then probably accepted Washington's view, a later generation would repudiate it as an "Uncle Tom" attitude.

In view of these developments, it is no wonder that Rayford W. Logan, a leading black historian, could write, "At the beginning of the twentieth century, what is now called second-class citizenship for Negroes was accepted by Presidents, the Supreme Court, Congress, organized labor, the General Federation of Women's Clubs—indeed, by the vast majority of Americans, North and South, and by the 'leader' of the Negro race." It was indeed the saddest aspect of American life. Congress had repudiated or abandoned the federal government's pledges. Civil rights for blacks were a dead letter; disfranchisement enjoyed federal approval and support; "separate but equal" was the law of the land; racism was not merely a regional but a national creed. In short, by 1900 there was a merging of the Southern outlook and the national outlook and a general acceptance of the theory of white supremacy. This situation would persist without serious disturbance for almost forty years into the twentieth century.

CHAPTER 3

INDUSTRIALISM AND AMERICAN CULTURE

POLITICAL AND ECONOMIC IDEAS OF INDUSTRIALISM

The Gilded Age. The term most commonly used by historians to describe the decades that followed the Civil War is "The Gilded Age," the title of a novel by Mark Twain and Charles Dudley Warren published in 1873. It seemed a fitting epithet for the tawdriness that characterized many features of American life in this period. It captured the cynical spirit and crudeness of the new age and the graft, corruption, and worship of material values that accompanied it. The United States, wrote E. L. Godkin in *The Nation* in 1866, is a "gaudy stream of bespangled, belaced, and beruffled barbarians. . . . Who knows how to be rich in America? Plenty of people know how to get money; but . . . to be rich properly is, indeed, a fine art. It requires culture, imagination, and character." Godkin spoke for a number of perceptive Americans who were appalled by the materialism, crassness, and immorality that had accompanied the new industrialism. They were alarmed especially that the men of new wealth—the new plutocracy—lacked the "restraints of culture, experience, the pride, or even the inherited caution of class or rank." The ideals, character, and moral values of a rural and agrarian America seemed outmoded in industrial America.

But though perceptive social critics of the Gilded Age assailed the captains of industry as robber barons who undermined our moral fiber and imposed their coarse tastes upon the nation, the typical American saw them only in their role as respected members of society, pillars of the churches, and philanthropists who occupied positions of prestige and power both here and abroad. As a consequence, millions of Americans admired and emulated the successful businessmen. Their favorable view of industrialists was given further support by the prevailing economic and social theories of the period—laissez-faire and social Darwinism—both of which extolled the rugged individualism practiced by the industrialists.

Industrialism and Laissez-Faire. The dominant economic philosophy of the times was laissez-faire: beyond what was necessary to maintain law and order and to protect life and property, the government was not to interfere in the conduct of business or in personal matters. According to this view, men pursuing their business interests free of government meddling would achieve the best possible use of resources, would promote steady economic progress, and would be rewarded, each according to his deserts. Acquisition of wealth was considered evidence of merit, for did not wealth come as a result of frugality, industriousness, and sagacity? And poverty carried with it the stigma of worthlessness, for did it not result from idleness and wastefulness? During most of the late nineteenth century these attitudes prevailed in America and were upheld by prominent educators, editors, clergymen, and economists.

Social Darwinism. Free competition and government nonintervention were sanctioned not only by the laissez-faire economic theories of Adam Smith and the English classical school; rugged individualism also found "scientific" support in social Darwinism (see pp. 45–46). Spencer's ideas were especially attractive to American businessmen because they justified free competition and made successful businessmen feel that they themselves were the finest flower of evolution. Many industrialists cited Spencer's views to defend their business activities and to oppose government regulation. The new doctrine opposed poor relief, housing regulations, and public education and justified poverty and slums; Spencer believed that these conditions were the proper lot of the unfit who had been bested in the economic struggle and that any governmental effort to relieve poverty was an interference with the operation of the natural law.

Spencer's ideas had an enormous vogue in the United States in the last quarter of the nineteenth century. By the time of his death in 1903 Americans had bought nearly 400,000 copies of his books, an incredibly high figure for a sociological or philosophical work. Numbered among his many devoted followers in America were Edward Livingston Youmans and John Fiske, who spread the gospel of social Darwinism all over the country through magazine articles, popular books, and lectures. Such leading universities as Harvard, Johns Hopkins, and Yale included the Spencerian philosophy in courses on religion, biology, and social science.

Spencer's most influential American disciple was William Graham Sumner, who taught sociology and political economy at Yale from 1872 until his death in 1910. Sumner vigorously supported economic individualism and hailed the millionaires as products of natural selection. He scornfully derided reformers and their programs to protect the weak; he ridiculed democracy as the "pet superstition of the age"; and he repudiated the idea of equality among mankind. Sumner was interested in the welfare of the "forgotten man," who to him was the middle-class citizen who worked hard, minded his own business, paid his taxes, and never asked the government for help. Sumner remained true to his individualism and incurred the hostility of social Darwinists who were businessmen when he attacked the protective tariff for violating genuine individualism.

Reform Darwinism. The social Darwinists took the position that since society was the outcome of natural processes, man could not hope to control it. Hence they considered the efforts of reformers both mischievous and futile. In the 1880s, however, a number of sociologists and economists revolted against the individualism and fatalism of social Darwinism. These "reform Darwinists" maintained that societies could command their own destinies and that human intelligence could improve the existing system.

A leader among the dissenters was Lester Ward, a largely self-educated sociologist. He came from a poor family in Illinois, endured privations in his early life, worked in factories, fought in the Civil War, and for many years was a government official. When he was sixty-five, Ward became Professor of Sociology at Brown University, where he taught "A Survey of All Knowledge." His ideas were first presented in his *Dynamic Sociology* (1883) but were more readable in *The Psychic Factors of Civilization* (1893). Ward opposed the prevailing theory that "neither physical nor social phenomena are capable of human control," asserting "that all the practical benefits of science are the result of man's control of natural forces." Ward argued that man must use his intelligence to plan and direct his future. He distinguished between "telic" forces—those governed by human purpose—and "genetic" forces—those resulting from blind natural processes—and maintained that there was "no natural harmony between natural law and human advantage." Thus he believed that a laissez-faire economic system did not necessarily advance human progress, and he advocated state management and social planning. "Those who dismiss state interference," Ward said, "are the ones who most frequently and successfully invoke it."

Younger professors of sociology, such as Albion Small of Illinois, Charles Horton Cooley of Michigan, and Edward Allsworth Ross of Wisconsin, seconded Ward's assault on social Darwinism. Contrary to Spencer's notion that society was composed of separate individuals operating independently of one another, they asserted that each individual personality was shaped by social institutions which were themselves amenable to social control. In *Sin and Society* (1907) Ross argued that in the new industrial society morality required the impersonal corporation to accept full responsibility for its antisocial acts. Followers of Spencer and Sumner declined in numbers and influence in the universities. In 1906 the American Sociological Society was founded and Ward was its first president. His ideas on government social planning eventually dominated American social thinking in the twentieth century, but for many years the ideas of social Darwinism had prevailed.

The New Economists. Similarly the viewpoint of economists changed. Leading university economists in the Gilded Age—men like Francis Amasa Walker of the Massachusetts Institute of Technology and J. Lawrence Laughlin of Harvard and Chicago—believed in the orthodox laissez-faire economics of the classical school and taught that natural economic laws could function properly only in an unregulated society.

In the mid-1880s, however, a new group of scholars, many of whom had been trained in German universities, began to challenge these sentiments. In 1885 they founded the American Economic Association, which boldly declared that the state was "an agency whose positive assistance is one of the indispensable conditions of human progress" and that "the doctrine of laissez-faire is unsafe in politics and unsound in morals." Among the leaders of this revolt were Richard T. Ely of Johns Hopkins and Wisconsin, Simon Nelsen Patten of Pennsylvania, John R. Commons of Wisconsin and Wesley C. Mitchell of Columbia. Although they differed in their economic and political programs, they all dissented from the classical belief in absolute economic laws valid for all societies. They insisted that society, constantly changing, had to be examined in terms of process and growth. Using the historical approach to study economic realities, they discovered that there were great differences between what actually happened and what, according to classical economics, was supposed to have happened.

Thorstein Veblen.   The leading academic rebel was Thorstein Veblen. Born in Wisconsin of Norwegian immigrants and educated at Yale and Johns Hopkins, he taught at Chicago, Stanford, and Missouri. Veblen bitterly assailed what he called the "kept classes" and their "pecuniary" society. He derided the idea that the wealthy leisure class was the most biologically fit and that millionaires were a product of natural selection. Veblen argued that the millionaire was not responsible for the creation of the industrial technology but rather had taken possession of the wealth produced by the skill and labor of other people.

In his most widely read book, *The Theory of the Leisure Class* (1899), and a number of other volumes Veblen analyzed the role of the upper class in American society. Although he had little popular appeal, he wielded a great deal of influence among intellectuals of the twentieth century, particularly after the Great Depression of 1929.

Reformers.   Outside academic circles, increasing numbers of radical reformers began to attack the existing social and economic system and to propose new plans of economic organization. They, too, rejected Spencer's fatalism and the idea that progress resulted from the struggle for existence and the consequent removal of the unfit.

The most important of these reformers was Henry George. Born in Philadelphia, he moved to San Francisco as a young man and for twenty years watched a frontier society become transformed into a wealthy and class-stratified society. What was the cause of the imbalance that deepened the poverty of the masses and increased the wealth of a few? George believed the explanation lay in the inequities of private land ownership that allowed landowners to enrich themselves solely through the rise of real-estate values. Land took on value not because of anything the owner did but because people lived on it. George maintained that the unearned increment, instead of going to private individuals, ought to be taken by the government in the form of a "single tax" on land values; this would make other taxes and other forms of government intervention unnecessary, leave individual enterprise otherwise free, and promote "the Golden Age of which poets have sung and high-raised seers have told us in metaphor!"

George set forth his theories in *Progress and Poverty* (1879) and found a wide audience both in the United States and abroad. He spent the rest of his life working for the single tax program and continued to develop his theme in subsequent books. In addition, he edited a newspaper, gave many speeches, and came close to being elected mayor of New York City in 1886.

Somewhat more radical than George's program was that of his contemporary Edward Bellamy. Rejecting both classical economics and the fatalism of the social Darwinists, Bellamy concentrated his attack on the free-enterprise system itself. He attacked excessive individualism, private monopoly, and competition, characterizing the latter as "sheer madness, a scene from bedlam" and the price system as "an education in self-seeking at the expense of others." He assailed "the imbecility of the system of private enterprise" and the callousness of industrialists, who "maim and slaughter [their] workers by thousands."

In his utopian novel *Looking Backward* (1888), Bellamy portrayed an ideal community in the year 2000 whose beauty and tranquility contrasted sharply with the ugly industrial towns of his day. In this utopia the government owned all the means of production, and material rewards were shared equally by everyone. At least 500,000 copies of the book were sold. Bellamy called his system "Nationalism," and "Nationalist" clubs sprang up to spread the new faith. "Nationalist" magazines advocated public ownership of railroads and utilities, civil service reform, and government aid to education. This served to renew interest in socialism and caused Americans to consider socialist ideas and programs. But both George and Bellamy rejected Marxian socialism. George regarded Karl Marx as "the prince of muddleheads," and Bellamy maintained that American Marxists were really in the pay of the "great monopolists," employed by them "to wave the red flag and talk about burning, sacking, and blowing people up, in order, by alarming the timid, to head off any real reforms." The word *socialist* "is one I could never well stomach," Bellamy once told the novelist William Dean Howells. "In the first place it is a foreign word itself and equally foreign in all its suggestions. It smells to the average American of petroleum, suggests the red flag with all manner of sexual novelties, and an abusive tone toward God and religion, which in this country we can at least treat with decent respect."

Socialism.   Bellamy and other reformers avoided the word *socialism* not only because they found it distasteful but also because they realized that in the United States it was often identified with *anarchism* and *communism,* labels that frightened most Americans. The first socialist parties in this country appeared in New York, Philadelphia, Chicago, St. Louis, Milwaukee, and other large cities in the years immediately following the Civil War. In the beginning most American socialists, like their European counterparts, were followers of Karl Marx, the founder of modern revolutionary socialism. However, Marxian socialism had little appeal for native Americans. The class warfare Marx wrote of and the foreign sources of his ideas repelled most of them, including the workers who were supposed to gain power according to his theory. Most of the few adherents of Marxian socialism in the United States were immigrants who had been forced to flee to America because of their radicalism.

These socialists sought to develop a revolutionary spirit among American workers. They urged all workers to "offer an armed resistance to the invasions by the capitalist class and capitalist legislatures" and exhorted wage earners to overthrow American capitalism by "energetic, relentless, revolutionary and international action." A National Labor Reform party was organized in 1868 with a platform declaring that "our government is wholly perverted from its true design. . . . In this beneficent country of unlimited resources . . . the mass of the people have no supply beyond their daily wants and are compelled . . . to become paupers and vagrants." These appeals, directed to the workers in an effort to organize them politically, were too radical for the masses of wage earners and found only a small receptive audience among them. The National Labor Reform party's presidential candidate in 1868 polled fewer than thirty thousand votes.

In 1877 a Socialist Labor party was formed. Marxian doctrines were the basis of its program, and recent European immigrants provided most of its members. Its purpose was not to reform but to revolutionize the industrial order. It blamed the plight of the masses on the concentration of economic power in private hands, and it advocated having all the basic means of production run by the government in democratic association with the workers. For some years the Socialist Labor party avoided regular political activities and instead attempted to bore its way into control of the Knights of Labor and the AFL. But while some of the prominent labor leaders of these years were at one time either socialists or under socialist influence, they had become disgusted with socialist rivalry and dissension and had also turned against radicalism. The leaders of post–Civil War unionism successfully opposed the efforts of socialists to control labor and rejected their radical solutions to economic and social problems.

Eventually, in the 1890s, the splintered factions of the Socialist Labor party united under the leadership of Daniel De Leon, who became known as "the socialist pope." Born on the island of Curaçao and educated in Germany, De Leon had come to the United States, where he studied law and taught for a short time at Columbia College. A brilliant orator and pamphleteer, he became a champion of Marxism and took a militant stand against traditional trade unionism. He derided the AFL as "a cross between a windbag and a rope of sand" and called Gompers "a labor faker" and "a greasy tool of Wall Street."

De Leon urged all workers to join an independent political movement that would win control of the government and establish "a socialist or co-operative commonwealth, whereby the instruments of production shall be made the property of the whole people." But again these radical appeals found only a small receptive audience among the workers. In 1892 the Socialist Labor presidential ticket polled only 22,000 votes and in the next election only 34,000. The party was too foreign in its makeup and too radical in its program to attract wide support. To offset some of this deficiency, a rival organization, the Social Democratic party, was organized in 1896 by Eugene V. Debs, president of the American Railway Union. In 1901 the anti-De Leon group in the Socialist Labor party joined Debs to form the Socialist Party of America.

PHILOSOPHY IN THE AGE OF INDUSTRIALISM

"Common Sense" and Idealism. Just as laissez-faire and social Darwinism were increasingly criticized as the nineteenth century came to a close, so formalism in social thought and orthodoxy in philosophy were being subjected to reexamination. The traditional philosophy prevalent in the United States was Scottish or "common-sense" realism. Its main purpose was to explain traditional Protestant theology, but it also justified the status quo and conservative thought. First introduced in the late eighteenth century, it still dominated academic circles. Its leading exponents were the Reverend James McCosh of Princeton and the Reverend Noah Porter of Yale.

From the 1870s on, the most important new influence was German idealism, particularly as expressed by Georg Wilhelm Friedrich Hegel (1770–1831). Hegel viewed the whole course of history as the working out of divine purpose by certain general laws of nature, culminating in the achievement of perfect freedom. But Hegelianism, like the Scottish philosophy, rationalized existing conditions, and what Hegel meant by "freedom" was very different from the traditional American conception. Hegel's philosophy glorified the state and taught that the individual could be free only by subordinating himself to his national government and to his social institutions. These ideas coincided well with the policies of the Republican party during the Civil War and Reconstruction.

Thus, in philosophy as in economics the initial stimulus toward a new outlook came from Germany. Most of the young men who founded new schools of philosophy in America had studied at German universities and had been influenced by Hegel, although they did not accept German idealism uncritically. The earliest centers of new philosophic thought were outside the colleges and universities. Very influential was the Philosophical Society of St. Louis, whose leading figure was William T. Harris, commissioner of schools first for St. Louis and then later in the federal government. Other well-known institutions were the Fellowship of the New Life, founded in 1884 by Thomas Davidson; the Concord Summer School of Philosophy and Literature (1879–88); and the Society for Ethical Culture, founded in 1876 by Felix Adler.

An idealist movement displaced the common-sense school in academic circles in the 1880s. It was strongest in New England, where its leaders were Josiah Royce of Harvard and C. E. Garman of Amherst, but it was not confined to any one part of the country. The idealist awakening was evident also at such universities as California, Columbia, Cornell, Johns Hopkins, Michigan, and Princeton. The idealists believed in the priority of mind over matter and in the fundamental unity of the universe, but they modified these concepts to support American individualism.

Probably the most influential American idealist was the California-born Josiah Royce, who taught at Harvard from 1882 until his death in 1916. Royce accepted the German belief that individuals were parts of a single absolute mind, but unlike the orthodox Hegelians, he asserted that each separate individual was an essential part of this whole and made his own singular contribution to it. Thus he gave to the individual a more significant, active role in the universe.

American Pragmatism.   Meanwhile a school of philosophy more distinctively American and opposed to idealism was growing in popularity. Pragmatism, unlike most earlier philosophies, did not offer theories about God and the universe. It presented instead a way of evaluating acts and ideas in terms of their consequences in concrete experience. Pragmatism says that we cannot reject any hypothesis if consequences useful to life flow from it. The pragmatist's decision regarding the truth or falsity of an idea, then, is based on experimental test; "workability" is the correct method for finding truth. This concept was closely associated with two ideas that had gained wide currency in American thought—the idea of progress through evolution, and the idea of truth obtained through scientific investigation. The forerunners of pragmatism were Chauncey Wright and Charles S. Peirce, but two other men, William James and John Dewey, developed it.

William James, philosopher and psychologist at Harvard, rejected Spencerian determinism, which afforded no place for chance or human will. He upheld the independence of the mind and "the right to believe at our own risk any hypothesis that is live enough to tempt our will." At times he was inclined to suggest that if someone felt happier or behaved better as a result of believing some idea, that idea should be regarded as true. While James repudiated absolutes, he also spoke out against a skepticism that would inhibit impulsively generous commitment. He distrusted all general laws and abstractions that denied man's capacity for free action. James contended that man's decisions would influence the course of events and that, in spite of the existence of God, good or evil would result from human device and intelligence.

In his *Principles of Psychology* (1890), James made the first important American contribution to the scientific study of the mind. In later books he expounded his views on pragmatism. Theories to him were "instruments, not answers to enigmas." Pragmatism "has no dogmas, and no doctrines save its method," which was a method for reaching the truth. "The true is the name of whatever proves to be good in the way of belief," James said, "and good, too, for definite, assignable reasons." Such views were a sharp departure from nearly all the philosophies and religions of the past, and they captivated many Americans. Yet they also laid James open to the charge that pragmatism was simply another name for expedience: anything is good that works.

James' chief disciple was John Dewey, who considered himself an instrumentalist rather than a pragmatist. Born in Vermont in 1859, Dewey taught at Michigan, Chicago, and Columbia and remained an active force in American thought until his death in 1952. Originally an idealist, Dewey was converted to pragmatism in the 1890s after reading James. Though he lacked James' lucidity, he developed his ideas in greater detail.

Dewey believed philosophy should become a tool for society to use in meeting its problems. To him no thinking was valid that did not spring from experience, for while ideas led to action, it was only through action that men could acquire sound ideas. As he himself put it, his philosophy stemmed from the "growth of democracy—the development of the experimental methods in the sciences, evolutionary ideas in the biological sciences, and the industrial reorganization." Dewey put much faith in intelligence as a tool for social reform; he considered the mind "at least an organ of service for the control of environment." Like other social dissenters of this period, Dewey criticized laissez-faire and social Darwinism and argued that life need not be accepted passively but could be shaped by man. Since his instrumentalism meant using philosophy to advance democracy, he urged philosophers to leave their ivory towers, stop speculating about what he felt were meaningless trifles, and occupy themselves with politics, education, and ethics.

The New Legal Theory. There was also a revolt against formalism in law. The preceding generation regarded the law as fixed and unchanging and as a standard measure which the judge applied to the question at hand. But Oliver Wendell Holmes, son of the poet of the same name and friend of William James, declared in his book *The Common Law* (1881):

> The life of the law . . . has not been logic; it has been experience. . . . The felt necessities of the time, the prevalent moral and political theories, intuitions of public policy, avowed or unconscious, even the prejudices which judges share with their fellowmen, have a good deal more to do than the syllogism in determining the rules by which men should be governed.

Law, Holmes felt, should be based upon changing social needs or political policies rather than upon logic or precedent. "It is revolting," he said, "to have no better reason for a rule of law than that it was laid down in the time of Henry iv. It is still more revolting if the grounds upon which it was laid down have vanished long since, and the rule simply persists from blind imitation of the past." A new school of legal theorists arose who not only accepted Holmes' reasoning but went on to contend that the meaning of any general legal principle must always be judged by its practical effects.

RELIGION IN THE AGE OF INDUSTRIALISM

Protestantism and Darwinism. The churches also had to adapt themselves to industrialism and to some of the main currents of thought. This proved to be difficult for the Protestant churches. Most Protestants considered the Bible to be the supreme authority and closely identified their ethics with the economic individualism of the middle class; but the Darwinian theory of evolution undermined confidence in the authority of the Bible, and the rise of large corporations weakened belief in the virtues of economic individualism.

In the eighties and nineties an increasing number of Protestant clergymen accepted the theory of evolution and reconciled it with religious beliefs. Henry Ward Beecher, one of the most celebrated preachers of the time, declared in his *Evolution and Religion* (1885) that evolution was merely "the deciphering of God's thought as revealed in the structure of the world." A few clergymen went beyond this to deny some of the supernatural events in Christianity; this alarmed the "fundamentalists," who reasserted their literal belief in the supreme authority of the Bible as the only solid foundation for religious faith. A struggle ensued between the fundamentalists and the liberals.

Throughout the Gilded Age most Protestant clergymen believed the existing economic order was just. For instance, Beecher condemned the eight-hour day, insisted that poverty was a sign of sin, and advocated the use of force, if necessary, to put down strikes. Commenting in 1877 on the sharp wage cuts suffered by railway workers, Beecher concluded:

> It is said that a dollar a day is not enough for a wife and five or six children. NO, not if the man smokes or drinks beer. . . . But is not a dollar a day enough to buy bread with? Water costs nothing; and a man who cannot live on bread is not fit to live.

Perhaps Beecher and other clergymen like him were conservative because wealthy businessmen in their congregations made heavy contributions to church funds. In any case, the conservative sentiments of many of the clergy and their lack of sympathy for the workingman's demands caused a drop in working-class attendance in the churches.

The Social Gospel.   In the 1880s a few socially conscious Protestant clergymen took issue with Beecher's teachings on current economic questions and began to preach the Social Gospel. They insisted that the problems created by industrialism could be solved only by a universal application of the teachings of Christ. Among the chief exponents of the Social Gospel were ministers Josiah Strong, Washington Gladden, and Walter Rauschenbusch. In his writings and sermons Gladden upheld the right of labor to organize and recommended that industrial disputes be eliminated by an "industrial partnership" that would allow workers to receive "a fixed share" of industry's profits. Gladden espoused the idea of government ownership of public utilities, although he rejected socialism as a system. Rauschenbusch severely censured industrial capitalism as a "mammonistic organization with which Christianity can never be content."

The Catholic View.   The attitude of the Roman Catholic Church toward social reform was more negative than positive, more tolerating than approving. Only in part was the hierarchy moved by consideration of justice and charity. James Cardinal Gibbons, Archbishop of Baltimore, insisted that Catholics cultivate a patriotic citizenship in keeping with the nation's civil institutions and customs. Gibbons asserted, "The accusation of being un-American—that is to say, alien to our national spirit—is the most powerful weapon which the enemies of the Church can employ against her." Only in this sense—as an aspect of Americanization—did the Catholic Church display any marked interest in social reform before the second decade of the twentieth century.

Archbishop John Ireland of St. Paul minimized the economic problems of the time and advocated only temperance and conservative trade unionism. In 1903 he said publicly, "I have no fear of great fortunes in the hands of individuals, nor of vast aggregations of capital in the hands of corporations." Ireland's friendship with James J. Hill, the railroad builder, and President McKinley brought him under the criticism of reformers. Yet he often expressed strong sympathy for organized labor, saying on one occasion, "Until their material condition is improved it is futile to speak to them of spiritual life and duties."

Through this indifference to social reform, the Church jeopardized its hold on the loyalty of its communicants. Catholics in large numbers lost interest in a Church which seemed indifferent, if not hostile, to movements for the promotion of their economic welfare. Many Catholics turned to socialism. As the Church began to lose its members to Protestantism and socialism, it developed a greater interest in social problems. Also helping to change the Church's attitude was Pope Leo xiii's famous encyclical *De Rerum Novarum* (1891), which condemned the exploitation of labor and asserted that it was the duty of the state to bring social justice.

CULTURE IN THE GILDED AGE

Tastes and Manners.   The Gilded Age has often been characterized as one of the most sterile periods in the cultural history of the United States. Everywhere in this generation, according to some critics, materialism so abounded that it perverted tastes and debauched the intellectual life of the country. There is ample evidence to suggest this point of view. But the age has too often been measured by its political record, which frequently misfired, and this criterion alone is not sufficient. Although the times were roundly condemned by such contemporary critics as Walt Whitman, Mark Twain, and Henry George, their reasons were mostly superficial.

It was an age of crassness and vulgarity, and its unhappy aspects must be recognized. But historian and socioliterary critic Vernon L. Parrington, though sharply critical of the period, was fascinated by it. He interpreted the Gilded Age as one in which the energies dammed up by frontier life and inhibitions of backwoods religion were suddenly released.

One of the better known aspects of the Gilded Age was society's freedom to revise its morals and manners. The new rich of the industrial age were unsure of themselves and employed gaudy display to impress outsiders. The conspicuous waste of money was the measure of social status; it prompted the American craze for antiques and European art collections, and launched perhaps the greatest plunder of the Continent since the sack of Rome.

Nothing exhibits better the excesses of the Gilded Age than its architecture and interior decoration, which declined to a new low. It was the age of the jig-saw, the cupola, the mansard roof with its dormer windows, and an orgy of decoration. "A stuffy and fussy riot of fancy," Parrington says of it, "restrained by no feeling for structural lines, supplied the lack of creative imagination, and architecture sank to the level of the jerry-builder. Bad taste could go no further." The same excess can be found in dress, with its bustles, paddings, and corsets, in furniture, and even in machinery. In morals low and broad standards commingled with Victorian prudishness.

Achievements.   Yet despite these obvious cultural excesses, intellectual and artistic developments of the Gilded Age were among the most fruitful this country has ever seen. We have already observed how the original and creative thinkers of the eighties and nineties made these two decades perhaps one of the most intellectually fertile periods in the whole of American history. Unfortunately, too many observers of the period have been preoccupied with the second-rate thinkers and artists and have neglected those who made contributions of the first order.

In scholarship, the age saw the birth of two new social sciences: Lewis Henry Morgan founded anthropology and Lester Ward fathered American sociology. The period also witnessed a revolution in higher education. Until this time colleges and universities concentrated on training ministers and lawyers, but now learning began to shake off its fetters and to range freely in the physical, natural, and social sciences, the arts, and the humanities. The most famous of the daring new university presidents were Charles W. Eliot of Harvard and Daniel Coit Gilman of Johns Hopkins. At

Harvard, Eliot greatly expanded the curriculum and sponsored the elective system, which had originated at the University of Virginia at the time of its founding. He also drastically reformed Harvard's medical and law schools and gave them true professional status. At Johns Hopkins, Gilman built the first great graduate school in America. The graduate school and the seminar method were introduced from Germany in the 1870s, and some graduate work was done at Harvard and Yale in that decade. But Johns Hopkins, designed primarily as a center for graduate work at its founding in 1876, took the lead in this field and held it for the next quarter of a century. At that time also, professional schools got under way—the Columbia School of Mines (1864), the Massachusetts Institute of Technology (1865), Stevens Institute (1871), and the Johns Hopkins Medical School (1893).

Arts and Letters. During the two or three decades following the Civil War, there developed a new realism in American literature, stimulated by Darwinism, the influence of European writers, and a reaction against the sentimental gush that had come to dominate fiction. An early manifestation of the trend was the regional short story. Bret Harte and Hamlin Garland in the West, George Washington Cable and Joel Chandler Harris in the South, and Sarah Orne Jewett in New England gave readers a fresh and exciting view of regional America and contributed to the reunification of the country.

Mark Twain (Samuel L. Clemens), whose works were written in this period, was in his own day considered a regional author, but his novels, essays, and sketches have made a lasting reputation for him as a humorist, moralist, and social critic. The materials for Twain's best narratives—*The Adventures of Tom Sawyer* (1876), *Life on the Mississippi* (1883), and *The Adventures of Huckleberry Finn* (1884)—were his boyhood home, Hannibal, Missouri, and the great Mississippi River which rolled before it. Along with many other writers of the period, he deplored the evils of crass materialism and ridiculed the get-rich-quick schemes of his money-mad countrymen. In *The Gilded Age*, for example, Twain and Charles Dudley Warren pointed out that sober industry and contentment with a modest income honestly earned are infinitely preferable to frantic money-making schemes—yet Twain himself tirelessly sought ways to increase his wealth.

Growing social ills of the Gilded Age called forth specific indictments which became increasingly prominent in the realistic literature of the late nineteenth and early twentieth centuries. William Dean Howells, who by 1900 was considered by many young writers to be the dean of American letters, exhibited the grime and squalor of New York City in *A Hazard of New Fortunes* (1890); Stephen Crane's *Maggie: A Girl of the Streets* (1893) exposed the ugly life of New York's Bowery; and Hamlin Garland in *Main-Travelled Roads* (1891) described the hardships and injustices suffered by farmers in Iowa and Wisconsin. While they emphasized the injustices and abuses of the new industrial order, however, writers were comparatively gentle in their treatment of the captains of industry. In Howells' *The Rise of Silas Lapham* (1884), for example, the author implied that the great majority of American financiers were honest—that robber barons were the exception, not the rule.

Even the much more subtle and sensitive novelist and literary critic Henry James (brother of William James), who lived abroad most of his life, presented American financiers as men of integrity and charm in several of his books. James' particular interest was the interaction of men and women—American and European—in sophisticated international society. *The American* (1877), *The Portrait of a Lady* (1881), and *The Ambassadors* (1903) present Americans who are morally superior to their more cultured European counterparts.

The literature of social criticism contained proposals for specific utopias, the most influential being Edward Bellamy's *Looking Backward* (see p. 87). Bellamy, believing that economic inequality was the cause of all social ills, described a utopia in which wealth was distributed equally among its members. Other writers of the period who proposed a socialist solution were Howells in *A Traveller from Altruria* (1893) and Upton Sinclair in *The Jungle* (1906). Most of the literature dealing with social problems, however, proposed reforms rather than a radical alteration of the American system of free enterprise.

Because many poets—Bryant, Longfellow, Holmes, Lowell, Emerson, and Whittier—whose careers had begun in an earlier period continued to satisfy tastes after the war, much of American poetry showed remarkably few effects of the changing intellectual climate. By the end of the century, however, American poets and prose writers were feeling the impact of the scientific movement. For example, much of Stephen Crane's poetry inferred from the biological struggle for survival and the astronomical immensity of the universe that man is unimportant:

> A man said to the universe
> "Sir, I exist!"
> "However," replied the universe,
> "The fact has not created in me
> A sense of obligation."

The Gilded Age knew nothing of Emily Dickinson, because only seven of her poems were published during her lifetime (1830–86), but she is today considered one of the leading poets of the post–Civil War period. She began to write poetry in the mid-fifties and continued until her death, but she spent the last half of her life as a recluse in Amherst, Massachusetts.

In striking contrast was Walt Whitman, whose revolutionary volume of poetry, *Leaves of Grass,* had been published in three editions before the Civil War and who continued to be an important figure in American poetry of the postwar period. Although many critics objected to his departures from the conventions of versification and to his frankness about sex, he became for many others the very voice of America, enthusiastic, optimistic, energetic, and free. His Quaker inheritance contributed to the independence, love of peace, and sense of brotherhood celebrated in so many of his works—among them *Drum Taps* (1866), a volume of poems recounting the experiences and suffering shared by both North and South, and the richest account of the Civil War to be found in our poetry.

Increasing wealth and leisure after the Civil War contributed to a new awareness of art among Americans, and the work of the artists George Inness, Thomas Eakins,

Winslow Homer, and Albert Pinkham Ryder was of such high caliber that the Gilded Age could be called the most important in American painting. Inness pioneered a new landscape school. Homer and Eakins were the leading American representatives of the naturalistic movement in painting; Homer grounded his art in direct observation of nature, while Eakins depicted ordinary middle-class city life of the United States in the late nineteenth century. Ryder, haunted throughout his life by the sea, was the most original Romantic of his time. Two American expatriates, James McNeill Whistler and John Singer Sargent, both of whom lived for most of their lives in London, enjoyed international reputations—Whistler for his muted, poetic compositions, Sargent as the most sought-after portraitist of the Anglo-Saxon world.

Although in architecture, as has been noted, the Gilded Age marked the nadir of taste, fine and outstanding architects did exist. Henry Hobsen Richardson and Louis H. Sullivan were the first major architects to meet the demands of industrialism upon their art; to these men, buildings had a sociological function as well as an artistic one. In his *Autobiography of an Idea,* Sullivan wrote that "masonry construction was a thing of the past . . . [and] the old ideas of superimposition must give way before a sense of vertical continuity."

While it is true that many of the first-rate writers and artists of the period were overshadowed in reputation and popularity by their second-rate contemporaries, it is obviously a mistake to dismiss these years as a cultural desert. Indeed, from the perspective of history the Gilded Age may be viewed as one of America's richest and most fruitful eras.

The Chautauqua Movement. As in the pre–Civil War generation, an effort was made, through privately sponsored agencies, to keep Americans of limited schooling informed and to make culture popular in the country. There was a mass desire for knowledge, and various efforts were made to meet the demand. Most successful of these ventures was the Chautauqua movement, founded in 1874 by Lewis Miller, an Ohio businessman, and John H. Vincent, a Methodist minister. The two-week summer course they organized for a few Sunday-school teachers at Lake Chautauqua in New York proved to be such an enjoyable experience for those who attended that the word spread and within a few years thousands from all parts of the country were coming to Lake Chautauqua. And the Chautauqua movement, like the earlier lyceum movement, expanded its activities. The founders broadened their range of instruction to include such subjects as economics, government, science, and literature. During the years of Chautauqua's greatest popularity, eminent authorities, including some of the Presidents of the period, gave talks to open-air audiences on every subject conceivable. In addition, the Chautauqua Literary and Scientific Reading Circle was organized and became a national society. This organization provided correspondence courses leading to a diploma. Textbooks were written for the program, and a monthly magazine, the *Chautauquan,* was published to keep the various members informed. According to the Reverend Vincent, the program was formulated to give "the college outlook" to those who did not have a higher education.

Because the Chautauqua movement was so successful, various imitators appeared, until by 1900 there were about two hundred Chautauqua-type organizations in the country. Most of these were of a more commercial character but were designed to satisfy the same craving for self-culture. They furnished a varied fare of music, humor, and inspirational lectures and probably provided more entertainment than enlightenment.

The Chautauqua movement and its imitators helped popularize information that earlier had been the property of experts only. Too, thousands of Americans who sought cultural and intellectual improvement probably felt rewarded by many of the programs and perhaps their interests were broadened by them. Certainly the craving for culture and for facts has remained strong in American society, as has been reflected in the popularity of radio and television quiz shows and in that modern version of Chautauqua, the television "talk" show, with its endless parade of high-, low-, and middlebrow celebrities.

BIBLIOGRAPHY

An excellent survey of industrial growth can be found in Edward C. Kirkland, *Industry Comes of Age: Business, Labor and Public Policy, 1860–1897* (Chicago: Quadrangle Press, 1967). Thomas C. Cochran and William Miller, *The Age of Enterprise* (New York: Harper & Row, 1968) covers industrial and business expansion since 1800. Roger Burlingame, *Engines of Democracy* (New York: Charles Scribner's Sons, 1940) emphasizes inventions and technology. Stewart H. Holbrook, *The Age of the Moguls* (New York: Doubleday, 1953) contains entertaining anecdotes and dramatic incidents of the lives of business leaders. William Miller (ed.), *Men in Business: Essays in the History of Entrepreneurship* (Cambridge, Mass.: Harvard University Press, 1952) has scholarly studies of the business community. Joseph Dorfman, *The Economic Mind in American Civilization, 1865–1918*, vol. 3 (New York: Viking, 1949) and E. C. Kirkland, *Dream and Thought in the Business Community, 1860–1900* (Ithaca: Cornell University Press, 1956) analyze the dominant ideas in the business world. The trust problem is analyzed in H. R. Seager and C. A. Gulick, *Trust and Corporation Problems* (New York: Harper & Row, 1929).

Rendigs Fels, *American Business Cycles, 1865–1897* (Chapel Hill: University of North Carolina, 1959) is an excellent study of cyclical course of American economic development in post-Civil War America. Samuel P. Hays, *The Response to Industrialism, 1895–1914* (Chicago: University of Chicago Press, 1957) studies the impact of industrialism upon American life. Sigmund Diamond, ed., *The Nation Transformed: The Creation of Industrial Society* (New York: George Braziller, 1963) is an excellent anthology.

Thomas C. Cochran, *Railroad Leaders, 1845–1890* (New York: Russell & Russel, 1965) studies the attitudes of leading railroad executives on a number of business matters. R. E. Riegel, *The Story of the Western Railroads* (Lincoln: University of Nebraska Press, 1964) is the most useful general account of the transcontinentals. R. A. Billington and J. B. Hedges, *Westward Expansion*, 2nd ed. (New York: Macmillan, 1960) is an excellent survey of the westward movement. See also Thomas D. Clark, *Frontier America: The Story of the Westward Movement*, 2nd ed. (New York: Charles Scribner's Sons, 1969) and Walter Prescott Webb, *The Great Plains* (New York: Grosset and Dunlap, 1957). T. A. Rickard, *A History of American Mining* (New York: Johnson Reprint, 1932) is the standard account of the miners' frontier. Roy M. Robbins, *Our Landed Heritage: The Public Domain, 1776–1936* (Lincoln: University of Nebraska Press, 1962) is excellent on the disposition of public lands.

On cattle ranching on the plains see Lewis Atherton, *The Cattle Kings* (Bloomington: University of Indiana Press, 1961) and E. S. Osgood, *The Day of the Cattleman* (Chicago: University of Chicago Press, 1957).

W. T. Hagan, *American Indians* (Chicago: University of Chicago Press, 1961) is a good short survey, and Ralph K. Andrist, *The Long Death: The Last Days of the Plains Indians** (New York: Collier-Macmillan, 1969) is a vivid account of the Indian wars on the Plains.

Matthew Josephson, *The Politicos** (New York: Harcourt Brace Jovanovich, 1963) is the liveliest and the most comprehensive, but not the most detached, account of the political history of this period. H. Wayne Morgan, *From Hayes to McKinley, National Party Politics, 1877–1896* (Syracuse: Syracuse University Press, 1969) is a first-rate modern appraisal. A short worthy account can be found in John A. Garraty, *The New Commonwealth, 1877–1890* (New York: Harper & Row, 1969) and H. U. Faulkner, *Politics, Reform, and Expansion, 1890–1900** (New York: Harper & Row, 1959) is a recent synthesis of the nineties. Two excellent sectional studies of politics are C. Vann Woodward, *Origins of the New South, 1877–1913** (Baton Rouge: Louisiana State University Press, 1951) and H. S. Merrill, *Bourbon Democracy of the Middle West, 1865–1898** (Baton Rouge: Louisiana State University Press, 1953). A brilliant but mordant commentary on the period may be found in the appropriate chapters in Henry Adams, *The Education of Henry Adams** (Boston: Mass. Hist. Soc., 1918). James Bryce, *The American Commonwealth,** 2 vols. (New York: MacMillan and Co., 1895) is a classic contemporary account of American government and American politics by a brilliant Englishman. Leonard D. White, *The Republican Era, 1869–1901** (New York: Free Press, 1965) traces the federal administrative history of these years.

Vincent P. De Santis, *Republicans Face the Southern Question* (Baltimore: Johns Hopkins Press, 1959) traces Republican efforts in these years to break up the Democratic South, and Stanley P. Hirshon, *Farewell to the Bloody Shirt: northern Republicans and the Southern Negro, 1877–1893** (Bloomington, Ind.: Indiana University Press, 1962) analyzes Republican strategy in the South. Robert D. Marcus, *Grand Old Party, Political Structure in the Gilded Age, 1880–1896* (New York: Oxford University Press, 1971) is an excellent study of the Republican party and its organizational structure.

E. F. Goldman, *Rendezvous with Destiny** (New York: Random House, 1956) and Richard Hofstadter, *The Age of Reform: From Bryan to F.D.R.** (New York: Random House, 1955) deal with the mentality of reform. Ari Hoogenboom, *Outlawing the Spoils** (Urbana: University of

Illinois Press, 1968) surveys the course of the civil service reform movement in this period.

Ray Ginger, *Age of Excess, American Life from the End of Reconstruction to World War I** (New York: Macmillan, 1965) and H. W. Morgan, ed., *The Gilded Age** (Syracuse: Syracuse University Press, 1963) are two able recent appraisals of the Gilded Age.

F. A. Shannon, *The Farmer's Last Frontier: Agriculture, 1860–1897** (New York: Harper & Row, 1968) examines agricultural conditions and movements. The political repercussions of the depression of the nineties are handled in excellent fashion by G. H. Knoles, *The Presidential Campaign and Election of 1892* (Stanford: Stanford University Press, 1942). John D. Hicks, *The Populist Revolt** (Minneapolis: University of Minnesota Press, 1931) is the standard work on Populism.

General studies of the intellectual history of the post-Civil War generation include Merle Curti, *The Growth of American Thought,* 3rd ed. (New York: Harper & Row, 1964); R. H. Gabriel, *The Course of American Democratic Thought,* rev. ed. (New York: Ronald Press, 1956); H. S. Commager, *The American Mind** (New Haven: Yale University Press, 1959); and V. L. Parrington, *Main Currents in American Thought,** vol. 3 (New York: Harcourt Brace Jovanovich, 1930). Giving a more specialized treatment of ideas in this generation are Richard Hofstadter, *Social Darwinism in American Thought,** rev. ed. (New York: George Braziller, 1959); M. G. White, *Social Thought in America** (Boston: Beacon Press, 1957); and Charles Page, *Class and American Sociology: From Ward to Ross** (New York: Schocken, 1969). Perry Miller, *American Thought: Civil War to World War I** (New York: Holt, Rinehart & Winston, 1954) is a first class anthology.

Biographies and special studies of some of the leading thinkers of the period include A. G. Keller, *Reminiscences (Mainly Personal) of William Graham Sumner* (1933); Samuel Chugerman, *Lester F. Ward: The American Aristotle* (New York: Octagon Books, 1965); C. A. Barker, *Henry George* (New York: Oxford University Press, 1955); Lewis Mumford, *The Story of Utopias** (New York: Viking Press, 1962); Joseph Dorfman, *Thorstein Veblen and His America* (1934); R. B. Perry, *The Thought and Character of William James,* 2 vols. (Cambridge: Harvard University Press, 1948); Sidney Hook, *John Dewey*

(New York: Greenwood Press, 1939); Max Lerner, ed., *The Mind and Faith of Justice Holmes* (New York: Modern Library, 1943). Van Wyck Brooks, *The Confident Years, 1885–1915* (New York: E. P. Dutton and Co., 1952) is a stimulating study of the literary history of the period. Alfred Kazin, *On Native Grounds** (New York: Doubleday and Co., 1942) treats American writing since 1890; so also does M. D. Geismar, *Rebels and Ancestors** (New York: Hill & Wang, 1963).

*Denotes a paperback.

2
THE
EMERGENCE of
A MODERN NATION

Few OF THE GRAVE PROBLEMS CREATED BY THE TRANSFORMATION OF THE United States from an agricultural to an industrial nation had been solved by the turn of the century. On the domestic side, these problems fell into two broad and often overlapping categories, economic and social. Could monopoly and the resultant concentration of economic and political power be modified? Could agriculture be brought under the government's protective umbrella as the tariff and subsidies had already brought much of business under it? Could the virtual serfdom of workers in the steel, mining, and textile industries be eliminated? Could real wages be raised substantially without drying up investment capital? Could the despoilation of natural resources—a process begun by the earliest settlers but intensified by the new industrialists—be halted? Could a tax system be instituted which would fund society's increasingly complex needs without depressing the economy?

Many of the social problems had economic overtones. The employment of hundreds of thousands of children was necessitated by low family incomes. Excessive immigration and the overcrowding of cities were induced in part by the thirst for profit of steamship and railroad companies and by the desire of industrialists for cheap labor. Other problems, such as the need for an unemployment, health, and old age insurance system, grew directly out of urbanization. The packaging of unsanitary food and the mislabeling of drugs were stimulated by the rise of a national marketing system. Still others had historical and cultural roots. The appalling state of medical education was fundamentally a result of the nation's newness, and the uneven quality of legal education reflected in considerable part the society's commitment to easy upward mobility. The inadequate support of education was attributable to the common man's anti-intellectualism and to the aversion of all classes to taxation. Similarly, the exploitation and suppression of blacks long antedated the coming of industrialism.

By 1900 signs were multiplying that influential Americans were prepared to face some of these problems realistically. Nevertheless, the proponents of reform faced formidable obstacles. Politically, they comprised an insignificant minority of the power structure of each party; intellectually they made up an extraordinarily small percentage of the citizenry at large. On many issues, moreover, their potential support was severely circumscribed. In the South the black man was being disenfranchised at that very moment. In the North cultural tensions brought over from Europe worked against formation of a common front on social and economic issues. The Irish-dominated urban Democratic machines had little interest in industrial issues and none whatever in either blacks or the agrarian-oriented program of William Jennings Bryan. More recent immigrants were joining the Republican party in droves, partly because they resented the Irish monopoly of Democratic party offices, partly because they were alienated by Bryan's evangelical Protestantism, and partly because they feared a low Democratic tariff would deprive them of their jobs.

Yet to achieve their ends the reformers would have to induce changes in American attitudes and institutions as far-reaching in some respects as those wrought by the Civil War. For in spite of the growth of cities and the infusion of new ethnic and religious strains, the dominant American values remained rural, individualistic, and Protestant. Regulation of corporations, organization of labor, abolition of child labor, control of natural resources, creation of a central banking system, and, most critically, extension of suffrage to women and of civil rights to blacks depended largely on Washington. This meant the enactment of numerous laws and the staffing of federal agencies by experts. It meant the modification of the old commitment to individualism and states' rights in the interest of the commonweal. And it meant the supplanting of the old survival-of-the-fittest doctrine by the environmentalism of the Reform Darwinists.

The simultaneous emergence of the United States as a world power compounded matters. Here, too, the currents of change had begun to flow long before they became a raging torrent during the Spanish-American War and its aftermath. Here, too, the wellsprings were fed by industrialization. Yet there were barriers to acceptance and performance of the new role. Geographical and intellectual isolation made it difficult for many Americans in small towns and rural areas to realize that there was no escaping the position of international power that the nation's newfound industrial might had forged. A belief in economic determinism made many progressives and labor leaders reluctant at first to support the conservative-nationalist movement to prepare the United States to enter World War I. Ultranationalism caused many conservatives to reject the moral responsibilities of the world power they themselves had fostered.

Historians' interpretations of both the domestic and international aspects of the Progressive Era have broadly reflected the values of their own times. The early 1920s were marked by a spate of favorable assessments. The Great Depression sparked a revival of economic determinism; and this, combined with the relative failure of progressivism in the twenties and with disillusionment over World War I, produced a negative historical judgment on both the domestic and foreign policies of the Progressive Era. After the New Deal gave historians a new basis of comparison, the results were mixed. Some historians writing in the 1940s perceived a causal link between the progressive movement and the New Deal; others saw a fundamental distinction in the failure of progressivism to develop the kind of broad-based political support from labor and agriculture which characterized the New Deal. Meanwhile the rise of Hitler and the participation of the United States in World War II stimulated a favorable reappraisal of American involvement in World War I.

The vogue of behaviorism began to infect the historical profession in the 1950s, and for several years the progressive movement was interpreted as an effort by the upper class and the upper-middle class to preserve their status against the inroads of the nouveaux riches and the lower classes. At the same time, however, some historians continued to characterize the Roosevelt and Wilson administrations in more complex and favorable terms. They regarded the Fair Deal, New Frontier, and Great Society of Presidents Truman, Kennedy, and Johnson as graphic proof of the viability of progressive assumptions and policies. They also viewed the United States' decision to support the United Nations as a vindication of the ideals of

Woodrow Wilson. More recently society's failure to solve the urban, racial, and environmental crises has induced a more cynical reappraisal. By attacking only surface inequities, so New Left historians argue, progressives created an illusion of reform which ultimately strengthened rather than changed the basic economic and social system.

Disillusionment over the Cold War, the prolonged conflict in Vietnam, and the rise of what President Eisenhower defined as the "military-industrial complex"—a loose alliance of military, industrial, and labor leaders committed to an all-powerful defense establishment—has also revived a quasi-Marxist interpretation of American foreign policy. New Left historians regard the United States' Caribbean and Far Eastern policies during the Progressive Era as *prima facie* evidence of the aggressive nature of capitalism. They further contend, as did their progenitors in the 1930s, that economic interest was the root cause of American entry into World War I.

Conversely, probably a majority of historians continue to regard progressivism as the critically important first stage in the evolution of the welfare state. And though many of these same historians question the resultant bureaucratic rigidity and impersonality of big government, they tend on balance to endorse the main outlines. Many also continue to evaluate the basic thrust of American policy toward Europe favorably. Yet even the defenders of our European involvement during the Progressive Era incline toward the conclusion that the United States had no vital interests in the Far East and that acquisition of the Philippines and, especially, the continued effort to maintain the Open Door in China had tragic consequences.

FOR THOUGHT AND DISCUSSION

1. Do you see parallels between the progressive movement and current pressures for change, particularly from your own generation? What major differences are there?

2. To what do you attribute the percentage decline in voter turnout during the Progressive Era? Is a very large turnout desirable? Why or why not?

3. Did progressivism strengthen or weaken the capitalist system?

4. To what extent do you think American foreign policy during the Progressive Era was actuated by idealism? by materialism? by more or less enlightened self-interest? For example, what was our stake in World War I?

5. What workable alternatives can you suggest to American policy in Latin America, then and now?

6. What were the long-term implications of the Roosevelt Corollary to the Monroe Doctrine? of Wilson's doctrine of nonrecognition?

PROMOTE THE GENERAL WELFARE

CHAPTER 4

THE FORGING OF MODERN GOVERNMENT 1900–1917

PROLOGUE TO CHANGE

Enter Theodore Roosevelt.   On a September afternoon in 1901, at the Pan-American Exposition in Buffalo, New York, a young anarchist shot President William McKinley at close range. Eight days later the President died, and the old order began to give way to what became known as the Progressive Era. It was symbolized at first by Theodore Roosevelt, at forty-one the youngest man to occupy the White House, then by Senator Robert M. La Follette of Wisconsin and President Woodrow Wilson.

Two and a half months after being sworn in, President Roosevelt sounded the dominant note of twentieth-century American politics. The old system, he said in his first annual message to Congress, must be changed to meet new social and economic problems: "When the Constitution was adopted, at the end of the eighteenth century, no human wisdom could foretell the sweeping changes . . . which were to take place by the beginning of the twentieth century. At that time it was accepted as a matter of course that the several States were the proper authorities to regulate, so far as was then necessary, the comparatively insignificant and strictly localized corporate bodies of the day. The conditions are now wholly different and wholly different action is called for."

Presidential Initiative.   Action soon followed words. On February 14, 1902, Roosevelt invoked the Sherman Antitrust Act against the Northern Securities Company, a mammoth railroad holding corporation controlled by the bankers J. P. Morgan and Company and Kuhn, Loeb and Company and the railroad operators James J. Hill and Edward H. Harriman.

Morgan was stunned. He exclaimed that Roosevelt had not acted like a "gentleman" and later tried to treat the President like a rival operator. Hill was even more embittered. "It really seems hard," he complained, "that we should be compelled to fight for our lives against the political adventurers who have never done anything but pose and draw a salary." But the proceedings went forward. Two years later the Supreme Court, in a five to four decision, ordered the Northern Securities Company to dissolve.

By the time the Northern Securities case was settled, Roosevelt had added a further dimension to presidential leadership. In May 1902, John Mitchell, the moderate leader of the United Mine Workers, had called anthracite miners of northeastern Pennsylvania out on strike. The strikers demanded an eight-hour day, wage increases, and recognition of their union. The eight railroad companies which dominated the industry would neither recognize the United Mine Workers nor mitigate the workers' near subhuman conditions of life. "[The miners] don't suffer," the operators' chief spokesman expostulated at one point; "why, they can't even speak English." And so the strike continued through the summer and into the fall.

Fearful of a coal shortage and infuriated by the operators' arrogance, Roosevelt considered filing an antitrust suit against the coal combine. But when the Attorney General advised that it would fail for lack of evidence, he decided to invite the contesting parties to the White House. The operators deeply resented this implied recognition of the U.M.W. and vehemently refused to make any concessions at the ensuing conference in October. Roosevelt was so determined to end the strike that he issued secret orders to the army to prepare to seize the mines. He then warned prominent business leaders on Wall Street of his intent. These measures sufficed. The operators agreed to accept the recommendations of an independent arbitration committee appointed by the President. Their plan to crush the U.M.W. had failed. "This is the great distinguishing fact," the Springfield *Republican* proclaimed at the time, "for while the operators still nominally refuse to recognize the mine workers' union, that union nevertheless is a party to the President's plan of arbitration and is so recognized by him."

The political importance of both the Northern Securities suit and the President's intervention in the coal strike far transcended their immediate economic significance. By striking out boldly on his own, Roosevelt had asserted his independence of big business, revitalized the executive office, and helped prepare the way for the progressive movement to reach the national level. He had also given meaning to the Sherman Antitrust Act and had created the impression that the Republican party could become a viable instrument of reform.

THE REVOLT OF THE MIDDLE CLASSES

The New Consensus.   The program that Theodore Roosevelt and Woodrow Wilson were to press on Congress and the nation from 1905 to 1916 was neither revolutionary nor even original. Many reforms of the Progressive Era had been spelled out in the Populist party platform of 1892; almost every major measure that Roosevelt and his successors would sign into law had been suggested earlier by William Jennings Bryan. Even the attack on the Northern Securities Company was based on a law enacted twelve years before. Why, then, did progressivism succeed where Populism and Bryanism had failed?

The critical reason was the character of progressivism's constituency and leadership. Populism, despite its attempt to win labor support, had been essentially a movement of rural protest. Bryanism had been more broadly based; but Bryan's identification with prohibition and evangelical Protestantism had alienated many normally Democratic Catholic and Jewish workingmen, and in 1896 Bryan had failed to win essential middle-class support, even among more substantial farmers. Middle-class voters were frightened mainly by Bryan's alleged financial heresies. "How intellectually snobbish I was about 'sound economics,' " the Kansas editor William Allen White remembered. "I was blinded by my birthright. . . . It seemed to me that rude hands were trying to tear down the tabernacle of our national life."

Progressivism triumphed because White and tens of thousands of other civic-minded Americans who shared both his prejudices and his virtues were drawn into it. They took with them a white-collar middle class almost six million strong. Predominantly old stock, Protestant, and urban this group had numbered less than a million when the Mugwumps had vainly defied the old Republican bosses in the 1870s and 1880s. By 1900, however, its members constituted the new balance of power. Even as they were reelecting William McKinley to the presidency, they were supporting candidates for municipal and state offices on platforms embodying much that post-Civil War reformers had always demanded. "Populism shaved its whiskers, washed its shirt, put on a derby and moved up into the middle of the class—the upper middle class," White also remembered. The result was an urban and rural consensus that cut across the old party lines, changed the character of both major parties, and profoundly altered the course of American history.

Wellsprings of Reform. For the vast majority of its silent, white-collar supporters, progressivism was an economic movement fired by moral indignation. Progressives fed on resentment against poor schools, street car and water monopolies, rising prices, and soaring tax rates induced partly by collusion between politicians and businessmen. They wanted only to "turn the rascals out" and reestablish honest government. They were as yet not much concerned with labor's problems. They were more interested in policing the slums than in eradicating them. They suspected that the influx of southern and eastern European immigrants was the cause of urban blight. Furthermore, the numerous small businessmen among them feared that they would be destroyed by the all-powerful monopolies.

For all their limitations, progressives had both the ability and the desire to gain political control. They were generally well educated by the standards of the times and were accustomed to active participation in local affairs. They were not shackled by the tribal loyalties that made political machines irresponsible agencies of municipal government. They shared with farmers a puritanical heritage that made them fundamentally intolerant of corruption. Most important, they were capable of pursuing goals that transcended their immediate economic interests. They responded enthusiastically when their leaders and spokesmen—editors and clergymen, college presidents and school principals, and, above all, civic-minded businessmen and lawyers—went on to conceive an ever growing reform program.

Their leaders were also partly moved by self-interest. They resented the waste of tax dollars, blamed high prices on the "trusts," and deplored the discriminatory practices of the railroads. They also feared aggrandizement of power by organized labor, the growth of a non-Protestant population, and the morally corrosive effect of slums. Indeed, they evinced the same attitude toward the new immigrants that the new immigrants and their descendants would later take toward blacks. Many of them also thought that they were being squeezed between the upper and nether elements of society. And some may even have been moved by a desire to regain a status supposedly stolen by the new financial and business leaders, those *nouveaux riches* whom one critic described as being "without restraints of culture, experience, the pride, or even the inherited caution of class or rank." Yet on balance their program was based more on hope than on fear, more on moral indignation than on personal resentment, more on concern for the commonweal than on ordinary self-interest.

The Social Problem. Everywhere that progressives looked they saw poverty, injustice, and political corruption in the midst of growing abundance and seemingly limitless opportunity. One percent of the nation's families owned seven eighths of its wealth, and ten million Americans lived in abject circumstances. The average worker toiled sixty hours a week. Almost two million children worked in the fields or in factories, where they were frequently on night shifts. Thousands of workers were killed annually on the railroads alone—by one estimate over seven thousand. As late as 1913 industrial accidents caused twenty-five thousand deaths a year.

Nor did there seem to be much hope that employers would or could cope with these problems. Wages were fixed by supply and demand. In the absence of a strong labor movement or minimum wage laws, even those manufacturers who wished to be humane were forced to keep wages at the subsistence level in order to survive competition. Thus Massachusetts, which had pioneered in strong child labor laws, steadily lost textile mills to the South, where the use of child labor helped keep production costs low.

Labor's attempts to organize and strike for higher wages and shorter hours had been systematically weakened by injunctions and, more important, by management's use of immigrants as strikebreakers. There was no pension system, no automatic compensation for injuries or death sustained on the job. The widow who received $250 from her late husband's employer could consider herself blessed. Relief, when it was available, came largely from private sources.

The Business Problem. The consolidation of several firms into large industrial combines, a movement described in Chapter 1, threatened to make conditions worse rather than better. By 1904 combinations of one form or another controlled two fifths of all manufacturing in the United States. Six great financial groups dominated about 95 percent of the railroads. Some 1320 utilities companies were organized under a handful of giant holding companies. As early as 1902 the United States Industrial Commission reported, "In most cases the combination has exerted an appreciable power over prices, and in practically all cases it has increased the margin between raw materials and finished products." The Commission added that the cost of production had probably decreased and that profits had doubtless increased. A subsequent report revealed that the cost of living actually increased 35 percent between 1897 and 1913.

As we have seen, efficiency was the economic justification for these developments. But the consolidation movement, like the protective tariff movement, was based primarily on fear of competition and its attendant instability. No one, not even J. Pierpont Morgan, whose very gaze "forced the complex of inferiority . . . upon all around him," was immune. Fear of competition had driven him and his associates to buy out Andrew Carnegie and organize the United States Steel Corporation in 1901. The desire for stability and assured profits had also prompted him and James J. Hill to organize the Northern Securities Company in 1901.

The consolidation movement not only tended to destroy competition; more important, it made it difficult for the nation to solve its festering social and political problems. Great corporations had the power to prevent labor from organizing basic industries and used this power ruthlessly. They also transformed economic power into political influence in various ways. If railroad, sugar, oil, and steel interests could not "buy" state legislatures as openly as they had twenty-five years earlier and if they could no longer send as many hand-picked men to Congress as they once had done, they nevertheless exerted great influence over both elections and legislative decisions. They made huge contributions to the Republican party, controlled countless newspaper editors and publishers, and maintained powerful lobbies in Washington and in state capitals. They also assured themselves a disproportionately powerful voice in Congress by arranging the gerrymandering of voting districts to control the election of state legislators; until the adoption of the Seventeenth Amendment in 1913, these legislators elected United States senators.

Among the chief and most active opponents of social and economic change were the small industrialists, organized in the National Association of Manufacturers, which was founded in 1895. These and other comparatively small businessmen and real estate promoters shared responsibility with big business for the already widespread desecration and pollution of America's cities and countryside. Small industry fought minimum wage, child labor, and factory safety bills. Small businessmen lobbied most vigorously for low local and state taxes and thus for inadequate schools and social services.

The obstructionist role of small business should not obscure the major issue that Roosevelt and progressives faced on the national level. The inescapable fact was that big business in 1901 constituted the most potent threat to American democracy. The post-Civil War transfer of power from Washington to Wall Street had been accelerated under President McKinley. By the time of Roosevelt's ascension, the presidency had become a kind of branch brokerage office, with the President himself little more than the Washington director of a nationwide financial operation. There was nothing particularly sinister or even secret about the system. Republican politicians such as McKinley and his friend Mark Hanna believed that national welfare depended upon cooperation between business and government. National policies should promote the prosperity of big business.

But there could be no national progressive movement until the reign of big business was effectively challenged. This was why Roosevelt's action against the Northern Securities Company had such great symbolic importance. It was also one of the principal reasons for the progressives' emphasis on direct democracy—the primary, initiative, referendum, recall of judicial decisions, and, above all, the direct election of senators. These devices, so they believed, would enable them to introduce bills in boss-dominated legislatures, undo the work of conservative legislatures and judges, and replace business-oriented senators with more representative men.

Social Idealism. The men who would march to battle with Theodore Roosevelt when he disrupted the Republican party in 1912 were ten years younger than the stalwarts who manned the bastions for conservatism and the G.O.P. Progressives were college students or impressionable young men of affairs in the 1880s and 1890s when the intellectual revolution described in Chapter 15 challenged the economic and social values of their fathers. They may not have heard of Lester Ward and his *Dynamic Sociology* (1883), but they were thoroughly familiar with Henry George's indictment of poverty and Edward Bellamy's utopian vision of the potentialities of the new technology. They accepted the postulates of reform Darwinism as distinguished from Spencerian social Darwinism, and they believed with varying intensity that man could and should shape his environment to bring out the best in mankind and its institutions.

Assuredly, vestiges of older theories of race, especially of Anglo-Saxon superiority, continued to modify their environmentalism. Even John R. Commons, economist, Christian layman, and zealous friend of labor, favored restriction of immigration on genetic grounds. Fundamentally, however, progressives advocated restriction for reasons that were both practical and idealistic. They believed, correctly, that excessive immigration enabled employers to hold wages down; they feared that immigrants from nondemocratic countries could not be readily assimilated. Unlike conservatives, moreover, many progressives worked hard to create a better environment for the millions of southern and eastern Europeans who had already come. One of the noblest chapters in the history of the United States was written by Jane Addams at Chicago's Hull House, a settlement house devoted to the improvement of community life in the Chicago slums. She worked to restore the immigrants' sense of personal dignity and encouraged them to preserve the best of their own cultures. Roosevelt's appointments of blacks and members of other minority groups were based on more than political expediency. "I grow extremely indignant at the attitude of coarse hostility to the immigrant," the President wrote the Protestant clergyman and editor Lyman Abbott in 1906:

> I have one Catholic in my Cabinet . . . and I now have a Jew . . . and part of my object in each appointment was to implant in the minds of our fellow Americans of Catholic or of Jewish faith, or of foreign ancestry or birth, the knowledge that they have in this country just the same rights and opportunities as every one else.

Scientism. Another powerful influence on the progressives' outlook was the new technology. By 1910, when the progressive movement began to reach full flower, there were a half million automobiles on American roads. By 1917, after the assembly line had enabled Ford to cut the price of his Model T from $950 to $290, there were close to five million. By 1915 over six million telephones were in use and more than fifty corporations were supporting industrial research. When the United States entered World War I in 1917, the country was well on the way to being thoroughly serviced by electricity; by the end of the war more than half of American industry was run by electric power. Meanwhile, scientific management techniques devised by Frederick Winslow Taylor were increasingly applied. Production increased 76 percent between 1899 and 1909, although the labor force increased by only 40 percent. Progress in medicine and development of public health programs reduced the death rate from 17 to 12.2 per thousand and increased life expectancy from 49 to 56 years between 1897 and 1917.

Not all progressives reacted to these developments in the same way. Some were more impressed by large-scale production and scientific management than were others. But virtually all agreed that increased production would decrease poverty and the personal indignities and social effects that accompany it. They further agreed that the art of government had not kept pace with the science of industry. They proposed, accordingly, to apply the new techniques to management of public affairs. And they turned with remarkable unanimity to experts—scientists, economists, social workers, and public health specialists—for counsel, political support, and the staffing of commissions formed to deal with the bewildering complexities of modern society. Had they not thus created a bureaucratic state, chaos would have ensued. But one of the ironic results was a lessening of direct democracy: out of the new bureaucracy came a body of administrative law which fed on empirical, as distinct from purely political and theoretically democratic, findings. The distance between the people and their government actually increased.

Moral Idealism. To their conviction that man could shape his environment creatively by the application of science, progressives added a full measure of Christian idealism. Jews, of course, had brought to America a long tradition of concern for the commonweal. Now, though active proponents of the Social Gospel never constituted more than a small minority of the Protestant clergy concentrated in urban churches, even atheists and agnostics among the progressives became profoundly influenced by the movement (see p. 92). Its most important figure, Walter Rauschenbusch, had become convinced that capitalism was inherently sinful and that the righteous alternative was Christian Socialism. Although his ideology was decisively rejected by churchmen, his graphic analysis of the brutalizing impact of industrial life was widely accepted. In 1908, one year after publication of Rauschenbusch's most important work, *Christianity and the Social Crisis,* the Methodist Episcopal Church came out for abolition of child labor and for a host of other reforms. In that same year the Federal Council of Churches of Christ in America was organized on a platform that placed official Protestantism squarely behind the movement to end exploitative capitalism by means of social welfare legislation.

Nevertheless, American Protestantism actually spent more energy campaigning for prohibition and against parochial schools than fighting man's exploitation of his fellow man. Nor was the influence of Pope Leo XIII's memorable encyclical, *De Rerum Novarum* (1891), substantial among Roman Catholics. The Pope's charge that "a small number of very rich men have been able to lay upon the masses of the poor a yoke little better than slavery itself" spurred numerous parish priests to compassionate works; but partly because of the hierarchy's conservative, Irish character and mainly because of the need of the American Catholic Church to win acceptance by the conservative Protestant power structure, *De Rerum Novarum* continued to be ignored.

In the summing up, the Social Gospel movement quickened many lay consciences and raised profound questions about business ethics and the morality of the laws of the marketplace. Most important, it broadened and strengthened the moral foundations of the progressive movement.

Muckraking. Of all influences affecting progressives, the most sensational was the literature of exposure. In 1902 a group of journalists, later dubbed "muckrakers" by Theodore Roosevelt, began to publish articles about social, economic, and political problems in such middle-class magazines as *McClure's, Collier's, Everybody's,* and *Cosmopolitan.* Their subject matter ranged from the traffic in prostitutes to the perversion of democracy in city halls, statehouses, and the United States Senate. Their output varied greatly in quality. Some, like Ida M. Tarbell, who carefully documented the impersonal ruthlessness of John D. Rockefeller and his associates in the *History of the Standard Oil Company* (1904), established standards of research and reporting that few journalists have ever surpassed. Others resembled David Graham Phillips, author of *The Treason of the Senate* (1906), whose innuendo and misrepresentation obscured much of the real truth that underlay his work.

One muckraker, Lincoln Steffens, brought to his work extraordinary insight into contemporary practices of American politicians, businessmen, and ordinary citizens. His two chief contributions were *The Shame of the Cities* (1904) and *The Struggle for Self-Government* (1906). Steffens was neither unaware of the defects of character that made public officials accept bribes nor indifferent to the moral lassitude that made average citizens indulgent of bad government. But he was much more interested in the bribe givers than in the bribe takers. Refusing to cater to the anti-immigrant biases of his middle-class readers, he showed that the old-stock Republican machine in Philadelphia was more corrupt than Irish-dominated Tammany Hall. He revealed that in Rhode Island it was rural Yankee legislators, not urban Italians, who had sold out to the streetcar and other interests. And he described how the Pennsylvania Railroad in New Jersey and the Public Service Corporation of that state had contrived to have the New Jersey legislature perpetuate low taxes and other special privileges for railroads and public service corporations.

The muckrakers' impact was enormous. Their analysis of political corruption confirmed the progressive leaders' belief that the American republic must be reformed or become a businessman's oligarchy. And the widespread circulation of their articles aroused voters and helped to create the political support necessary for successful action. But it is important to remember that muckraking was not a prime generator of reform. It reached its height in 1906, long after reform Darwinism, scientism, moral idealism, and the Social Gospel had made their impact.

THUNDER IN THE CITIES AND STATES

Early Reform. The foundations of progressivism were laid during the six years between Bryan's defeat in 1896 and Roosevelt's intervention in the coal strike of 1902. During the next decade the movement spread through the entire country, including the South, in one of the most creative political upheavals that the nation has ever experienced.

Starting most often as reformers intent upon restoring honesty to city government, progressive leaders soon found that the trail of privilege and corruption led from the city hall to the statehouse and thence to powerful business interests. They also learned, as their Mugwump predecessors rarely had, that honesty was not enough. Government, they gradually concluded, had to be transformed from a negative to a positive force. Only then could utilities corporations be brought under control, exploitation of men, women, and children stopped, and other urban evils eradicated.

The movement began with the eruption of municipal reform movements across the country between 1894 and 1897. Two years later Governor Theodore Roosevelt of New York pushed through a corporation tax, strengthened factory and tenement inspection laws, and flouted business interests on so many other counts that in 1900 the G.O.P. machine eased him out of the state and into the vice-presidential nomination. In the same year, Robert M. La Follette abandoned the Republican orthodoxy of his years in Congress and won the governorship of Wisconsin. Much of the reform program that he introduced had developed piecemeal in the East, especially in Massachusetts and New York; but La Follette, drawing on a general shift of progressive support from the countryside to urban centers, implemented it so imaginatively that it became a model and gained renown as the "Wisconsin Idea."

The Reform Program. Concluding that they must sever the business-political nexus before economic reforms could be enacted, progressives sought both to transfer power to the people and to apply scientific procedures to government. In city after city progressive candidates—both Republican and Democratic—campaigned successfully for the commission or city-manager plans, for home rule, and for honest elections. And in state after state they won the direct primary, the short ballot, the initiative and the referendum, and the recall of elected officials.

In addition, progressives in state government strengthened child labor laws, created commissions staffed by experts to regulate utilities and railroad rates, and began to impose inheritance, corporation, and graduated income taxes. They also made increasingly large appropriations for schools, state universities, mental and penal institutions, and welfare programs in general. Maryland enacted the first workmen's compensation law in 1902. Oregon limited women workers to a ten-hour day in the next year. Illinois established a public assistance program for mothers with dependent children in 1911. And Massachusetts in 1912 created a commission to fix wages for women and children. By the end of the Progressive Era the number of students in high schools had almost doubled, most of the great industrial states had workmen's compensation laws, and the number of industrial accidents had been dramatically reduced by the adoption—either forced or voluntary—of safety procedures.

To be sure, the strictly procedural reforms never proved as effective as their proponents had anticipated. The initiative, referendum, and recall were little used; the commission plan could be and often was subverted. Bosses eventually returned to most cities. The new "participatory democracy" forced them to make concessions, however, and the movement for social justice steadily advanced and expanded down through the 1920s. The epilogue that Senator La Follette wrote in his *Autobiography* in 1913 was in reality a prologue:

It has been a fight supremely worth making, and I want it to be judged . . . by results actually attained. If it can be shown that Wisconsin is a happier and better state to live in, that its institutions are more democratic, that the opportunities of all its people are more equal, that social justice more nearly prevails, that human life is safer and sweeter—then I shall rest content in the feeling that the Progressive movement has been successful.

PROGRESSIVISM MOVES TO WASHINGTON

In 1904 President Roosevelt was girding for a mighty struggle with conservatives in his own party. He had come into office well aware that his party was a hostage to business and its spokesmen in Congress and that this situation placed limits on his ability to act. As he explained to intimates, he could do something about either the tariff or the trusts, but nothing about both. He had opted for trust reform as the more popular issue, the issue less offensive to Congress, and the issue more vulnerable to executive leverage. On the legislative side, the record of his first administration had been modest. A Democratic-sponsored reclamation measure, the Newlands Act, had been passed in 1902 with the President's support. The Elkins Act to prohibit railroad rebates had gone through in 1903 because the railroads favored it. And a Department of Commerce and Labor, including a Bureau of Corporations with investigatory powers, had been created the same year. But a handful of conservatives, called Old Guardsmen—Nelson W. Aldrich of Rhode Island, William B. Allison of Iowa, Marcus A. Hanna of Ohio, Orville H. Platt of Connecticut, and John C. Spooner of New York—had otherwise kept the legislative hatches closed.

Wealthy, able, and intelligent, these senators were also arrogant and dogmatic. Except for Mark Hanna, who had sought rapprochement with labor in 1900 by joining with Samuel Gompers in forming the National Civic Federation to promote mediation of labor disputes, they were insensitive to social and economic injustice. They supported governmental subsidies and other favors to business even while they invoked the survival-of-the-fittest concept against the mildest reforms. They did not want Roosevelt to run for a full term in 1904. But after he captured the party machinery, they and the financial and business interests helped him win a rousing victory over the Democratic candidate, Judge Alton B. Parker of New York, who was so conservative that he believed the trust problem should be left to the states. As the New York *Sun* put it, it was better to have "the impulsive candidate of the party of conservatism than the conservative candidate of the party which the business interests regard as permanently and dangerously impulsive."

Significantly, not even Roosevelt's extraordinary popularity reversed the downward trend in voter turnout which had started in 1900 and would continue until 1928. This decline was strong in the North as well as in the South, and it was especially pronounced among workers and marginal farmers. The most plausible explanation is that it reflected an alienation induced by the growing impersonality of society and politics, the ethnic and cultural conflicts within both major parties, and the supplanting of political campaigns by other forms of popular entertainment.

Roosevelt would find little support for his legislative program by turning to the Democrats. Bryanism was stronger outside Congress than in it. And although

Democrats were willing to abandon states' rights on some issues, they had scant sympathy for Roosevelt's desire for a more centralized government. Furthermore, their strength in the Senate was too slight for Roosevelt to have forged a viable coalition with them and the small minority of progressive Republicans. He had no choice, therefore, but to work through the men who controlled the party—the conservative Republican leaders.

Still, there were offsetting factors. The President controlled the patronage. He could enforce acts of Congress vigorously or indifferently. He could appoint fact-finding commissions. And he could use the vast moral force of his office to influence public opinion and thus, indirectly, the Congress. Reinforced by his understanding of these powers and emboldened by his popular mandate and the angry excitement whipped up by the muckrakers, Roosevelt prepared in December 1904 to present Congress with a full program of reform.

Railroad Regulation. His first major achievement was the Hepburn Act for railroad regulation. Following publication in *McClure's* of a devastating account of railroad malpractices, a concerted demand for action arose in the Middle West and the South. It came not only from farmers but also from merchants, manufacturers, and civic leaders, whose national organizations protested less against high rates than against the long-and-short-haul evil (see footnote, p. 50), the curtailment of services induced by the consolidation of lines, and similar abuses.

These powerful pressures drove a number of conservative Republican senators part way to the President's side. Spurred by brilliant presidential maneuvering, a coalition then passed a compromise measure in 1906. Although La Follette cried "betrayal" because the bill failed to authorize evaluation of a railroad's worth in determining rates, the Hepburn Act had many salutary features, including extension of the Interstate Commerce Commission's jurisdiction to oil pipeline, sleeping-car, and express companies.

Public Health Controls. Shortly after adoption of the Hepburn Act, the President signed two other significant measures—the Pure Food and Drug Act and the Meat Inspection Amendment to the Agricultural Appropriations Act. Each was necessitated by the callous disregard for the public's health by the industries concerned; each reflected a sharpened awareness by responsible men that federal regulation was the only means of safeguarding the people's health against avaricious businessmen.

The Pure Food and Drug Act was a testament both to the new scientism and to the single-minded dedication of the Department of Agriculture's chief chemist, Dr. Harvey W. Wiley, "a very mountain among men, a lion among fighters." Wiley had long been pressing for a law to prevent the manufacture and sale of adulterated, misbranded, or poisonous foods and drugs. With powerful help from President Roosevelt, the American Medical Association, and the muckraker Samuel Hopkins Adams, his bill finally came to the floor of the Senate in the spring of 1906. Sneering openly at chemists in the Department of Agriculture, Senator Nelson W. Aldrich said that "the liberty of all the people" was at stake. But Senator Porter J. McCumber of North Dakota rejoined that the real issue was the public's right to receive what it asked for and "not some poisonous substance in lieu thereof." An imperfect but pioneering pure-food-and-drug measure became law on June 30, 1906.

The fight for the Meat Inspection Amendment offered an even more penetrating insight into the business mind. Upton Sinclair's muckraking novel, *The Jungle* (1906), graphically exposed conditions in the meat-packing industry:

> There was never the least attention paid to what was cut up for sausage, there would come all the way back from Europe old sausage that had been rejected, and that was mouldy and white—it would be doused with borax and glycerine, and dumped into the hoppers, and made over again for home consumption. There would be meat that had tumbled out on the floor, in the dirt and sawdust, where the workers had tramped and spit uncounted millions of germs. . . .[A] man could run his hand over these piles of meat and sweep off handfuls of the dried dung of rats.

According to Finley Peter Dunne's humorous character "Mr. Dooley," Roosevelt rose from his breakfast table crying "I'm pizened" and threw his sausages out the window. The President ordered an immediate investigation. Meanwhile, lobbyists for the meat-packing industry charged that an inspection measure drawn by Senator Albert J. Beveridge of Indiana was "unconstitutional" and "socialistic." When European sales dropped precipitously, however, the meat packers abruptly reversed themselves and demanded, in the words of Mark Sullivan, "an inspection law . . . strong enough to still public clamor, while not so drastic as to inconvenience them too greatly." The result was compromise in the Rooseveltian pattern.

For Generations Yet Unborn. By then the President was also deep in a bitter struggle for rational control and development of the nation's natural resources. On his side were a great host of governmental scientists and experts headed by Gifford Pinchot, uncounted public-spirited citizens from all over the nation (but especially from the East), numerous homesteaders, and the great lumber corporations. Arrayed against him were small lumber companies, grazing, mining, and power interests of all types, most Western state governments, and, in the end, a decisive majority in Congress.

The issues were simple in some instances and complex in others. Should homesteaders be sacrificed to big cattle and sheep men for reasons of efficiency? Should giant lumber corporations, which had the means to pursue scientific forestry, be favored over small companies, which did not? Should the moralistic and scientific assumptions of Roosevelt and his supporters prevail? These assumptions were that the country's natural resources belong to the people as a whole; that "the fundamental idea of forestry is the perpetuation of forests by use"; that the federal government should reclaim arid lands; that "every stream is a unit from its source to its mouth, and all its uses are interdependent"; and that the electric monopoly is "the most threatening which has ever appeared."

Early in his administration Roosevelt saved what became the heart of the Tennessee Valley Authority in the 1930s by vetoing a bill that would have opened Muscle Shoals on the Tennessee River to haphazard development by private interests. He then set aside governmental reserves in Nebraska for a tree-planting experiment that served as a model for a more comprehensive program under the New Deal. In 1905 he rehabilitated the Bureau of Forestry, renamed it the Forest Service, and appointed Gifford Pinchot as its chief.

A small revolution followed. The new agency was staffed with trained and dedicated foresters. The development of water-power sites by utilities corporations was subjected to enlightened controls. Numerous bills for development under conditions injurious to the public interest were vetoed. More than 2500 potential dam sites were temporarily withdrawn from entry in order to assure orderly and constructive development. In addition, 150 million acres were added to the national forests; half as many acres with coal and mineral deposits were transferred to the public domain; and most large lumber corporations (though not the small ones) were persuaded to adopt selective-cutting techniques which alone assured both the perpetuation and the proper use of timber resources.

Western congressmen beholden to private interests responded with near-hysterical charges of "executive usurpation" and destruction of states' rights. But Roosevelt was undaunted. He skirmished for the preservation of the country's natural monuments even as Congress passed laws depriving him of authority to create new national forests. Before he left office in March 1909 the number of national parks had been doubled, sixteen National Monuments like California's Muir Woods and Washington's Mount Olympus had been created, and fifty-one wildlife refuges had been established. "Is there any law that will prevent me from declaring Pelican Island a Federal Bird Reservation?" Roosevelt had asked. "Very well, then I so declare it."

Meanwhile the President appointed a commission to investigate and make recommendations for multipurpose river valley developments such as the Tennessee Valley Authority later became. Then in May 1908 he urged the first conference of governors to implement the conservation movement in their states. No governor espoused the movement with Roosevelt's zeal and understanding, but spadework for moderate state programs had nevertheless begun. "When the historian . . . shall speak of Theodore Roosevelt," the President's bitter enemy Senator La Follette later wrote, "he is likely to say . . . that his greatest work was inspiring and actually beginning a world movement for . . . saving for the human race the things on which alone a peaceful, progressive, and happy life can be founded."

Variations in Antitrust Policy.   Neither La Follette nor most other progressives were altogether enthusiastic about Roosevelt's later attitude toward big business. The President had followed up action against the Northern Securities Company with a spate of suits; by the end of his second term twenty-five indictments had been obtained and eighteen proceedings in equity had been instituted. His successor, William Howard Taft, intensified the pace, bringing forty-three indictments in four years. In 1911 the Supreme Court implicitly reversed the Knight decision of 1895 in two verdicts decreeing dissolution of the Standard Oil Company and the American Tobacco Company. These decisions made it clear that manufacturing combinations were not exempt from the Sherman Antitrust Act, even though the Court qualified this somewhat with the so-called rule of reason, which said that bigness *per se* was no crime.

"The example of these basic decisions served as a powerful negative factor in business affairs," concludes one recent scholar. "Certain lines of development were denied to ambitious men." Yet they wrought few basic changes in the American economy. Price leadership continued, as the producers in an industry followed the lead of a few dominant corporations. Moreover, control over credit remained highly concentrated in Wall Street.

As his administration progressed, Roosevelt himself experienced a metamorphosis in his attitude toward the "trusts." Because he appreciated the advantages of large-scale production and distribution, he sought to distinguish between "good" and "bad" trusts. Putting his faith primarily in regulation, he repeatedly called on Congress to strengthen and expand the regulatory Bureau of Corporations. Then, after he left office, he came out openly for government price-fixing in basic industries.

Otherwise, Roosevelt maintained cordial relations with the Morgan–U.S. Steel axis. In order to prevent the spread of a severe financial panic that struck New York in 1907, he went to the aid of the banks and acquiesced in U.S. Steel's absorption of a Southern competitor, the Tennessee Coal and Iron Company. In the next year he accepted without protest the inadequate Aldrich-Vreeland banking bill, which progressives and agrarians bitterly opposed.

Trouble on the Labor Front. Labor continued to make modest advances during the Roosevelt and Taft administrations, mainly because of the progressives' work in the states. The American Federation of Labor grew by fits and starts, and the standard of living of its highly skilled members rose appreciably. In the manufacturing industries, real wages seem to have increased all through the period—for a total of 37 percent from 1897 to 1914—while the average work week declined from sixty to fifty hours.

The AFL failed to organize basic industry, however, mainly because of the massive counteroffensive by employers, spearheaded by the National Association of Manufacturers. To prevent labor from organizing, the NAM resorted to weapons ranging from propaganda to violence. The most effective tactic was maintenance of the open shop (a shop in which union membership is not a precondition of employment), their most important ally the middle class. The employers understood that in practice an open shop meant a nonunion shop, but middle-class progressives often did not. Even when they saw the point, a lingering devotion to natural law and inalienable rights made it difficult for them to accept the idea of the closed shop. Roosevelt was unsure on the issue. And men like Woodrow Wilson, president of Princeton, and Charles W. Eliot, president of Harvard, were adamant in their opposition to the closed shop; Eliot actually acclaimed the strikebreaker as "a very good type of modern hero." In consequence, labor received virtually no support during the Progressive Era for the one measure that would have assured it success—active governmental support of the organizing process.

To compound labor's difficulties, the basic right to strike was often grossly impaired by management's private police forces, the actions of corporation-dominated state governments, and the indiscriminate issuance of injunctions by judges who cared more for property than for human rights. In speech after speech from 1905 to 1912,

Roosevelt inveighed mightily against the abuse of the injunction (six special messages to Congress between 1905 and 1908). But the NAM was so influential in Republican councils that he failed even to get an anti-injunction plank in the party platform in 1908.

Campaigns to organize the steel industry meanwhile suffered a series of setbacks and finally collapsed altogether. The United Mine Workers were successful in the East, but they failed in two bloody efforts in Colorado. The first, in 1903–1904, ended in a rout climaxed by the deportation of strikers to the desert. The second, in 1913–14, ended in tragedy when National Guardsmen burned a striker's tent colony at Ludlow on April 20, 1914, accidentally killing eleven women and two children.

Against this background the formation in 1905 of the freewheeling and often violent Industrial Workers of the World ("Wobblies") was almost inevitable. The I.W.W. was concentrated in the West and fought the battles of frontier miners, lumbermen, and migratory workers. Equally predictable was the growth in influence of the Socialist party, especially after the AFL decided to concentrate on winning procedural reforms through the Republican and Democratic parties.

Forecasts of the Welfare State. By 1907 the Republican majority in Congress had had their fill of Theodore Roosevelt. They approved no major domestic legislation during his last two years in office and repudiated him openly on several occasions. Nevertheless, the executive power continued to expand. The President appointed numerous investigatory commissions. He made further advances in conservation. He repeatedly lectured Congress and the people on the need to mitigate the harsh inequities of capitalism by welfare measures. He was outraged by the Supreme Court's ruling in *Lochner* v. *New York* (1905), which held a maximum-hours law for bakers to be unconstitutional on the grounds that it was an unreasonable interference with the right of free contract and an unreasonable use of the state's police power. And after a New York tenement law was invalidated and a workmen's compensation law declared unconstitutional, Roosevelt wrote Justice William R. Day that, unless the judiciary's spirit changed, "we should not only have a revolution, but it would be absolutely necessary to have a revolution, because the condition of the worker would become intolerable."

On January 31, 1908, Roosevelt sent Congress the most radical presidential message to that time. He charged that businessmen had revived the doctrine of states' rights in order to avoid all meaningful regulation. He observed that there was "no moral difference between gambling at cards . . . and gambling in the stock market." He called for stringent regulation of securities, imprisonment of businessmen who flouted the law, and a comprehensive program of business regulation. He upbraided "decent citizens" for permitting "those rich men whose lives are evil and corrupt" to control the nation's destiny. He lashed the judiciary for "abusing" the writ of injunction in labor disputes. He contemptuously dismissed editors, lawyers, and politicians who had been "purchased by the corporations" as "puppets who move as the strings are pulled." Moreover, he came out for workmen's compensation, compulsory arbitration of labor disputes, and acceptance of big unionism as a countervailing power to big business.

THE DISRUPTION OF THE G.O.P.

Taft's Background. Roosevelt's chosen successor, William Howard Taft, lacked the energy, conviction, and political skill to carry on Roosevelt's policies. He had been an enlightened governor in the Philippines, and he seemed to be sympathetic to Roosevelt's progressive views. But he had marked limitations. He believed implicitly in natural law. He was a good but painfully conventional lawyer. And he had no zest for the give-and-take of politics. Although he possessed a strain of courage, he completely lacked political boldness and energy.

Big and small business heartily concurred in Taft's nomination, and he handily defeated William Jennings Bryan by 321 to 162 electoral votes. No sooner were the election returns in, however, than Taft's troubles began. He conceived his mission to be to consolidate the Roosevelt reforms (giving them the "sanction of law," as he privately phrased it), not to embark on new ventures. Actually, he was too steeped in legal traditionalism to accept Roosevelt's dynamic conception of the Constitution, and he therefore failed to seize the executive reins. Taft believed that the counsel of lawyers was superior to that of scientists and other experts, and he deplored Roosevelt's reliance on investigatory commissions.

The Tariff Fiasco. Many persons blamed the tariff for the rise in the cost of living, and by 1908 agitation was so strong in the Republican Middle West that the Republican platform promised tariff revision. But when Taft called a special session of Congress in the spring of 1909 to honor this promise, Nelson W. Aldrich and the Old Guard in the Senate rejected his recommendations. The President accepted a compromise (the Payne-Aldrich Tariff of 1909) and then, to the disgust of agrarian progressives, defended the measure as "the best bill that the Republican party ever passed." Two years later he negotiated a reciprocity agreement with Canada, only to have Canada reject it because of loose talk that it presaged annexation by the United States.

The Rise of Insurgency. Meanwhile, Taft was besieged with troubles on other fronts. In 1910 a group of progressive Republicans in the House, led by George W. Norris of Nebraska, stripped Speaker Joseph G. Cannon of his arbitrary and partisan control over legislation and committee appointments. Taft was secretly pleased, but both insurgents and the public continued to link the President with the uncouth and reactionary Speaker.

Taft's rather curious stand on conservation led to even worse difficulties. He believed in conservation, but he abhorred the freewheeling methods that Roosevelt had used to achieve his objective. Accordingly, he replaced Secretary of the Interior James R. Garfield with Richard A. Ballinger, an honest conservative who had earlier resigned from the Land Office because he disagreed with Roosevelt's view that the public's interest in natural resources had priority over that of entrepreneurs. Construing the law rigidly when government interests were at stake and loosely when private interests were at issue, Ballinger soon provoked Gifford Pinchot, Chief of the U.S. Forest Service, to charge a "giveaway" of Alaskan mineral lands to the Guggenheims, the great mining industrialists. Ballinger was eventually exonerated, but the President was fatally stamped as anticonservationist. The characterization was not wholly unfair. Although he withdrew more lands from public entry (closing them to exploitation by private individuals and corporations) than Roosevelt and put millions of acres of forest lands into new reserves, he never did grasp the Roosevelt-Pinchot conception of controlled development or of multi-purpose river valley projects.

Taft and Insurgency.   Roosevelt returned from abroad in 1910 in high indignation over Taft's ineptitude and the implied repudiation of his conservation policies. At Osawatomie, Kansas, on September 1, the former President amplified the social welfare program he had set forth in his memorable messages of 1908, calling it the "New Nationalism" because it put the national need "before sectional or personal advantage." Roosevelt quoted Lincoln's assertion that "Labor is prior to, and independent of, capital." He asserted that the judiciary's primary obligation was to protect "human welfare rather than . . . property." And he called for graduated income and inheritance taxes, workmen's compensation legislation, a federal child labor law, tariff revision, and more stringent regulation of corporations.

The general elections that fall produced the most sweeping changes since the great realignment of the mid-nineties. From East to West stand-pat Republicans were turned out of office as the G.O.P. lost fifty-eight seats in the House, ten in the Senate, and a net of seven governorships. Most contemporary observers blamed the tariff, but it is more likely that the results reflected, first, Taft's failure to project a dynamic, reform image and, second, the new immigrants' resentment of the Republicans' increasingly fervent commitment to prohibition on the state and local levels.

On balance, the Taft administration's legislative achievements were considerable. Safety measures were adopted for mines, an Employers' Liability Act for government contracts was passed, and a Children's Bureau was created. The I.C.C. was strengthened and its authority extended to telephone, telegraph, cable, and wireless companies. A postal savings bank system was established to serve rural residents. And the Sixteenth (income tax) Amendment was adopted. Some of these measures were warmly supported by the President; others received his half-support; and some got none at all.

Armageddon.   By 1911 Republican progressives were demanding the nomination of La Follette or Roosevelt in 1912. The Wisconsin senator made an early and

ELECTION OF 1912: ELECTORAL VOTE

Wilson: 435   Roosevelt: 88   Taft: 8

earnest bid, then refused to bow out gracefully after his most devoted followers admitted that he could not win. Roosevelt's entry into the race in February 1912 precipitated one of the most bitter pre-convention campaigns in Republican history. Roosevelt outpolled Taft two to one in the thirteen states that held primaries, but the Old Guard refused to let him have the nomination. "We can't elect Taft," a Kansas regular confessed, "but we are going to hold on to this organization and when we get back four years from now, we will have it and not those d----- insurgents."

As a result, more than three hundred Roosevelt delegates stormed out of the convention hall in Chicago. Six weeks later they returned to form the Progressive or "Bull Moose" party, nominate their hero, and synthesize their aspirations for democracy, equality of opportunity, and elimination of injustice.

Roosevelt's following included Social Gospel clergymen and laymen, college presidents and professors, liberal businessmen and editors, Gifford Pinchot and his fellow conservationists, and social workers by the hundreds. But when the Democrats nominated a moderate progressive, Governor Woodrow Wilson of New Jersey, Roosevelt and his party were doomed to defeat. In the election that autumn Wilson won forty states and 42 percent of the popular vote. Roosevelt ran second and Taft a poor third. The Socialist candidate, Debs, drew almost a million votes. Several hundred thousand of these represented a desire for more fundamental economic reform than either Roosevelt or Wilson proposed; many others, probably a majority, were simply a general protest against prevailing conditions, including the unofficial commitment of all three major parties to prohibition. In spite of the campaign's extraordinary personal and ideological drama, moreover, the percentage of eligible voters who voted declined sharply as the alienation of the lower economic classes continued.

THE TRIUMPH OF PROGRESSIVISM

Wilson's Background. Woodrow Wilson was born in a Presbyterian manse in Virginia in 1856 and reared in a South convulsed by Civil War and Reconstruction. As a Ph.D. candidate at Johns Hopkins University, he argued in a brilliant dissertation, *Congressional Government* (1885), that the basic weakness in the American political system was its separation of executive from legislative leadership. Following a distinguished tenure as president of Princeton University, he became governor of New Jersey in 1910 and changed from a rather academic conservative into a practical progressive. He boldly seized control of the Democratic state machine, pushed a comprehensive reform program through a divided legislature, and gave eloquent voice to high ideals and moderately progressive aspirations.

The New Freedom. The program Wilson called the New Freedom differed from Roosevelt's New Nationalism in two essentials: first, it advocated regulated competition rather than regulated monopoly; second, it turned most of the social programs of progressivism back to the states and municipalities. The first and positive goal was to be achieved by downward revision of the tariff, relentless enforcement as well as strengthening of the antitrust laws, and freeing of banks from dependence on Wall Street.

Tariff and Banking Reform. Wilson began auspiciously by calling a special session of Congress the day of his inauguration and then addressing a joint meeting of the Senate and House in person. He aimed to destroy the Republican system of special privilege to industry and the producers of raw materials by reducing tariff protection and thereby increasing competition. He used patronage to hold wavering Democrats in line, and he marshalled opinion against the G.O.P. Old Guard by charging publicly that Washington had seldom seen "so numerous, so industrious or so insidious a lobby" as had invaded the Capitol. This masterful exertion of leadership resulted in the first substantial reduction of the tariff since before the Civil War.

By the time he signed the Underwood tariff bill (which included the graduated income tax) in October 1913, Wilson was embroiled in conflict over banking legislation. Conservative Republicans wanted a single central bank controlled by private bankers. Conservative Democrats insisted on a decentralized reserve system under private control. Bryan Democrats and progressive Republicans called for a reserve system and currency supply owned and controlled by the government. (The latter were roused especially by sensational revelations of Wall Street's influence over the nation's financial and investment system.) Finally, after consultations with Louis D. Brandeis, his most influential adviser on domestic matters, Wilson worked out a series of constructive compromises that were adopted as the Federal Reserve Act in December 1913.

The measure created twelve Federal Reserve Banks owned and controlled by private bankers but responsible to a seven-member central Federal Reserve Board appointed by the President. The reserve banks were authorized to issue currency and to perform numerous other central banking functions. Provision was also made to meet the seasonal needs of agriculture. The Federal Reserve System was not intended to destroy private ownership and initiative in banking. But it did create new centers of financial power to offset the overweening influence of New York bankers.

Wilson planned to round out his program by revising the antitrust laws. There were to be no special benefits to labor, no aid to agriculture, no such conservation program as Roosevelt had envisaged. Child labor, woman suffrage, workmen's compensation, and all the rest would have to come, if they came at all, by haphazard state action. Indeed, when a bill sponsored by the National Child Labor Committee passed the House in 1914 over the protests of states' rights Southerners, Wilson refused to push it in the Senate.

Politics and the Black Man. Throughout the era the political situation of black Americans had become steadily worse. Roosevelt's original objective had been a biracial Southern Republican party led by patrician whites and educated blacks, his immediate end the securing of his own nomination in 1904 through control of the Southern delegations. He had maintained close relations with Booker T. Washington, head of the Tuskeegee Institute, and, unlike McKinley, he had appointed eminently qualified blacks to federal offices in the South. He had also denounced lynching and ordered legal action against peonage—the use of debt to force a worker to remain in a job.

By 1904 these policies had produced a vicious reaction in the South. With the tacit acquiescence of Bryan and Parker, Southern editors and politicians inflamed the region over "Roosevelt Republicanism," and enlightened white Southerners were forced on the defensive. Nor was the situation much better in the North. "Scientific" racial theories were infecting the Northern mind, and even the Socialist leader Eugene V. Debs was deferring to the militantly racist views of one wing of his party.

Against this background, Roosevelt equivocated. He appointed a few more blacks to medium-level offices and continued to denounce lynching. But during a race riot in Atlanta in 1906, he gave no moral leadership, and in the aftermath of an affray at Brownsville, Texas, he arbitrarily discharged three companies of black soldiers. By the end of his presidency he had concluded that the hope of a viable biracial Republican party in the South was an idle dream. As he sadly reflected, "the North and the South act in just the same way toward the Negro."

His successor had no interest whatever in the race problem. "I will not be swerved one iota from my policy to the South . . .," Taft snapped. "I shall not appoint Negroes to office in the South. . . . I shall not relinquish my hope to build up a decent white man's party there."

In 1912 many Northern blacks went over to Woodrow Wilson and the Democratic party. They were soon disillusioned. Blacks were segregated in some federal departments, and virtually no blacks were appointed to any but the lowest-level offices in either the South or the North. During World War I, moreover, discrimination became so rank in the military service that the Federal Council of Churches of Christ in America established a commission to investigate.

Yet there was some advance on the legal front. In separate decisions during the Taft and Wilson administrations, the Supreme Court struck down peonage (the system actually continued with modifications into the late 1920s). It also overturned an amendment to the Oklahoma Constitution—the so-called Grandfather Clause—which was designed to prevent blacks from voting. On balance, only the Indians fared worse. (See pp. 81–82.)

Moving Toward the New Nationalism. By 1914 the progressive movement had gathered too much momentum to be long halted by presidential indifference. While the child labor forces were regrouping for a second assault, new pressures were bearing so heavily on the White House that Wilson had either to accommodate them or risk loss of his office in 1916. They were first felt when the administration introduced its antitrust program in 1914.

Wilson's original measures included legislation to outlaw specific unfair trade practices and to create a federal trade commission with only fact-finding powers. Progressives in both parties thought little of the former and refused to support the latter because it did not grant the commission power to act on its findings. Brandeis and others ultimately persuaded the President that it was impossible to outlaw every conceivable unfair trade practice and that something like Roosevelt's proposal for continuous regulation was the only possible alternative. Wilson signed the Clayton antitrust bill, which was full of ambiguities and qualifications; but he put his energy and influence into Brandeis' measure to create a Federal Trade Commission empowered, in effect, to define unfair trade practices on its own terms and to suppress them on its own findings, subject to broad court review.

Meanwhile the President engaged in a bitter quarrel with organized labor over the Clayton antitrust bill. Samuel Gompers and the AFL hierarchy demanded provisions to exempt labor unions from prosecution for the secondary boycott, the blacklist, and other weapons the Supreme Court had declared in violation of the Sherman Act. In effect, labor wanted special privileges to offset management's power. At this point Wilson adhered rigidly to the New Freedom line. But he did accept an affirmation of rights that labor already possessed in law, if not always in fact, and a few other moderate provisions. His adherence to the New Freedom on this one point did not signify that he was ordinarily unsympathetic to labor; on the contrary, the AFL lobby spoke more decisively in Washington during Wilson's administration than did the National Association of Manufacturers.

"We Are Also Progressives."   As Wilson's tenure lengthened, it became evident that the New Freedom ideology was too confining to permit achievement of the President's own expanding social and economic goals. It also became clear that the Democrats would have to attract a substantial portion of Roosevelt's disintegrating Bull Moose party to retain the presidency in 1916. Accordingly, Wilson became more progressive. He began by signing the La Follette Seamen's Act of 1915, which freed sailors from bondage to labor contracts. He then nominated Brandeis to the Supreme Court over vehement opposition by Old Guard Republicans and leaders of the legal profession. (Brandeis, known as the "people's lawyer," had broken legal tradition in 1908 by presenting a mass of sociological data to the Court in his defense of an Oregon law establishing maximum working hours for women.) Next, the President came out for a languishing rural-credits bill that he had condemned as class legislation two years before. He successfully urged creation of a tariff commission because he feared that Europe would dump its surplus goods in America at the end of the war. And he threw strong support behind the child labor bill and won its adoption. (Enacted in the summer of 1916, it was declared unconstitutional two years later in *Hammer* v. *Dagenhart*.) He also won approval of a model federal workmen's compensation bill.

The flow of legislation continued until the very eve of the election. A measure was adopted to extend federal assistance to the states for the construction of highways. The Revenue Act adopted in the late summer of 1916 increased income taxes sharply and imposed a new estate tax. In September the President personally drove through Congress the Adamson bill to establish the eight-hour day for railroad workers.

Altogether, Wilson's administration embodied the most imposing and important program of reform legislation in American history up to that time. Wilson could claim truthfully, as he did during the presidential campaign that followed, that he and his party had in fact put much of the Progressive platform of 1912 on the federal statute books.

Impressive as Wilson's achievement was, it fell far short of the real needs of American society. It wrought few, if any, fundamental structural changes. It contained no provision for the organization by labor of basic industries, such as steel. It offered no long-term solution to the farm problem. It failed even to urge the states to adopt old-age pension, unemployment insurance, and medical care programs. (The incipient movement for the latter was destroyed by the American Medical Association.) Yet progressivism under Roosevelt, Taft, and Wilson did ameliorate the conditions of life of millions of Americans. Most important of all, it established a tax base for future expansion of the welfare state.

CHAPTER 5

THE RISE OF AMERICA
AS A WORLD POWER
1898–1919

THE NEW FRONTIER

Several decades before the historian Frederick Jackson Turner proclaimed in 1893 that the Western frontier was closed, an influential minority of Americans were straining to extend the nation's power and influence to the remote reaches of the globe. Their motives and emphases varied. Some feared that Europe's penetration of South America threatened the United States' security. Some felt that it was the manifest destiny of a "superior" people to control more than the areas their country then held. Others believed that expansion would divert the people's attention first from slavery and later from pressing industrial problems. But in almost all cases their views were underlaid by the conviction that assured access to the markets of the world was essential to long-term prosperity and that the possession of outlying territories was one of the hallmarks of greatness. Thus, the desire to annex Canada persisted into the twentieth century. A few Americans lusted for northern Mexico until the coming of World War I. And many more never ceased to look at Cuba with annexation in mind.

"Rome expanded and passed away," wrote Theodore Roosevelt, "but all western Europe, both Americas, Australia and large parts of Asia and Africa to this day continue the history of Rome. . . . Spain expanded and fell, but a whole continent to this day speaks Spanish and is covered with commonwealths of the Spanish tongue and culture. . . . England expanded and England will fall. But think of what she will leave behind her. . . ."

The foremost early expansionist was William H. Seward, Secretary of State under Lincoln and Johnson. "Give me . . . fifty, forty, thirty more years of life," he declared in Boston in 1867, "and I will give you possession of the American continent and control of the world." Two months later the United States took over the unoccupied Midway Islands far out in the Pacific. Then, in April 1867, the Senate ratified a treaty with Russia, negotiated by Seward, for the purchase of Alaska for $7,200,000. Most Americans were still too anti-imperialistic to give Seward his rein, however, and he went out of office in 1869 with his major objectives unfulfilled—annexation by one means or another of Hawaii, Cuba, Puerto Rico, the Danish West Indies (now the

Virgin Islands), St. Bartholomew's Island (now St. Barthélemy), Greenland, Iceland, and Canada.

Nevertheless, the expansionist impulse continued to grow. Under President Grant an annexation treaty with Santo Domingo was signed but rejected by the Senate, 24 to 24. And only the consummate diplomacy of Seward's successor, Hamilton Fish, prevented the United States from becoming embroiled in Cuba, where a rebellion against Spain broke out in 1868. Meanwhile the expansionist minority was formulating the intellectual underpinning of its case. As early as 1847 the business-oriented *New York Sun* began to argue that annexation of Cuba would be commercially advantageous. Many Americans who subscribed to the sentiments expressed in the Ostend Manifesto were also prompted by commercial considerations.

More significant in the long run was the growing rapport between naval officers, congressmen, intellectuals, and businessmen. During the 1870s the United States' exports exceeded its imports for the first time, and in the 1880s the aforementioned groups combined forces to promote the revitalization of the navy. Again and again, congressmen justified requests for naval construction in commercial or expansionist terms. "The time has come . . . ," Senator John F. Miller of California declared in 1884, "when manufactures are springing up all over the land, when new markets are necessary to be found in order to keep our factories running." Congressmen also deferred to the professional officers' expertise. "We assembled at the Navy Department," the chairman of the House Naval Affairs Committee explained, "and listened to the advice of naval officers, and our bill was changed in obedience to their views." Finally, in 1890, Captain Alfred T. Mahan published *The Influence of Sea Power upon History.* A brilliant synthesis of ideas current in naval circles for ten years or more, it argued that only a large navy could protect the trade that would be the lifeblood of the new American empire.

Many businessmen agreed. The protectionists among them stopped Secretary of State James G. Blaine from instituting an effective reciprocal trade program with Latin America in 1890, though he did lay the groundwork for later programs. Moreover, the National Association of Manufacturers devoted much of its initial program to promoting expansion of the merchant marine, the navy, and foreign trade.

Expansionist intellectuals and politicians continued, meanwhile, to trumpet for territorial acquisitions. In 1885 the Reverend Josiah Strong equated Christianity in *Our Country* with those "peculiarly aggressive traits" that would impose Anglo-Saxon civilization "upon Mexico, down upon Central and South America, out upon the islands of the seas, over upon Africa and beyond." That same year John Fiske, the most persuasive of the social Darwinists, predicted that "every land on the earth's surface that is not already the seat of an old civilization shall become English in its language, in its religion, in its political habits." And a decade later Henry Cabot Lodge, a disciple of Mahan, put forth the commercial rationale for naval expansion in categorical terms:

> Commerce follows the flag. The great nations are rapidly absorbing for their future expansion and their present defense all the waste places of the earth. . . . The United States must not fall out of the line of march.

Samoa. Hard on the completion of the first transcontinental railroad in 1869, American business and naval groups arranged a treaty for a naval station and commercial coaling rights in Samoa in expectation of a quickening of the Asian trade. A decade of jockeying for power by Germany, Great Britain, and the United States followed. Open conflict was narrowly avoided in 1889, and the German government proposed that the islands be divided. But at the United States' insistence it was agreed instead to establish a tripartite protectorate. Rivalry continued, and in 1899, after the Spanish-American War had committed the United States openly to imperialism, the fiction of Samoan independence was abolished. Germany and the United States divided the Samoan Islands, and Great Britain was compensated with the Gilbert and Solomon Islands.

Hawaii. Another group of naval officers conspired with Hawaiian-American businessmen to formalize American control of Hawaii, the crossroads of the central Pacific. Invoking native misgovernment as their rationale, the white men who dominated the Hawaiian economy virtually disfranchised the natives in 1887. Native resentment was soon compounded by the depressing impact of the McKinley Tariff Act (1890) on the Hawaiian sugar industry, and Queen Liliuokalani in 1892 abrogated the whites' special political privileges. With the support of the American minister and American marines, the whites overthrew the Queen in 1893 and sent a mission to Washington to negotiate a treaty of annexation. They hoped to avoid the sugar tariff and assure orderly government in their own interest.

President Cleveland's refusal to approve the treaty set off a four-year debate. American strategists contended that possession of Hawaii would give naval protection to the Pacific Coast, prevent annexation by Japan, and enable the United States to penetrate the Far East commercially and militarily. Annexation, in their view, was part of a "Large Policy" embracing construction of a Nicaraguan canal and acquisition of Canada. Meanwhile a puppet government ruled Hawaii for white businessmen.

Many influential newspapers and periodicals also supported Hawaiian annexation; the Republican platform of 1896 endorsed it; and William Jennings Bryan came out tentatively for it the next year. President McKinley announced on taking office that he opposed all acquisition of territory, but he soon changed his mind; three months after his inauguration he submitted a new treaty of annexation to the Senate. Although the treaty was rejected, the islands were annexed by joint resolution of Congress in July 1898, after naval operations in the Pacific had dramatized Hawaii's usefulness as a base. "As I look back upon the first steps in this miserable business and as I contemplate the outrage," ex-President Cleveland wrote to his former Secretary of State Richard Olney, "I am ashamed of the whole affair."

Venezuela and the Monroe Doctrine. Yet Cleveland himself had contributed to the jingoism that made the imperialists' triumph possible. Angered by Great Britain's refusal in 1895 to accept American arbitration of a boundary dispute between British Guiana and Venezuela, Secretary of State Olney had bluntly informed the British Foreign Secretary that ". . . . the United States is practically sovereign on this continent, and its fiat is law." The British testily replied that the Monroe Doctrine was not recognized in international law and did not apply to boundary disputes in any event. Cleveland then sent a message to Congress requesting money for an independent investigation. He also warned that British failure to accept the American findings would constitute "a willful aggression." The British thereupon began slowly to back down, and the boundary was fixed by an international commission in 1899 (although largely in accord with Britain's original claims).

Cleveland's rude threat of force had ironic implications. Until then, enforcement of the Monroe Doctrine had actually been dependent on the might of the Royal Navy; now the Doctrine became a viable instrument of American policy. Furthermore, the President's action prompted Great Britain to reappraise its relations with the United States in the context of Germany's rise to world power. This led to a decision of momentous future importance—the formation during the administration of Theodore Roosevelt of a kind of unofficial naval alliance between the United States and Great Britain.

THE SPANISH-AMERICAN WAR
AND THE GREAT DEPARTURE

Trouble in Cuba. In spite of the increasingly strong thrust of the imperialists, American foreign policy until 1898 had been generally grounded on a realistic appraisal of the national interest—one which reflected a sharp awareness of both the possibilities and the limitations of American power. The festering crisis in Cuba during the 1890s precipitated the first fateful departure from this policy.

Cubans had always resented Spain's misrule of their island. When their sugar economy collapsed under the weight of European competition, the international depression of 1893, and the restrictive duties of the Wilson-Gorman Tariff of 1894, their smoldering hostilities flamed into a full-scale revolt. Determined to suppress it, Spain sent over its ablest general, Valeriano "Butcher" Weyler, who soon drove much of the civilian population into concentration camps at an estimated cost of 200,000 lives.

The American people's instinctive sympathies for the Cuban people were intensified by an outpouring of propaganda from a revolutionary junta in New York and by the yellow journalism of the New York *World* and New York *Journal.* "You furnish the pictures," *Journal* publisher William Randolph Hearst wired one of his artists who reported that there was no war in Cuba to portray, "and I'll furnish the war." But it was the press as a whole, feeding voraciously on the junta's releases and reprinting indiscriminately the *World's* and the *Journal's* atrocity stories, that incited the nationwide hysteria.

Genuine sympathy for the Cubans combined with less altruistic attitudes to create a growing demand for a war to liberate the Cubans. Conservative Republicans and Democrats hoped that a war would divert attention from liberal or populist issues such as free silver. Others saw commercial benefits: "Free Cuba would mean a great market to the United States" and "an opportunity for American capital," Senator Lodge asserted. Protestant clergymen felt that American intervention would alleviate suffering and, incidentally, open Cuba to Protestantism. Ultranationalists saw war as a means of testing the nation's military might, uniting the North and South, and even resolving the unemployment problem. As an Atlantan wrote the President, "The South dearly loves a fighter; if you will show yourself strong and courageous in defense of Cuba, you will have a solid South at your call. . . . Strengthen the Army and Navy of this country and in this way give employment to the thousands of idle men who need it."

But Grover Cleveland had a different conception of his duty. He was convinced that the Cuban insurrectionists were as barbarous as the Spaniards, and he was reluctant, in any event, to involve the United States deeply in Cuba's internal affairs. He went out of office in March 1897 without having yielded to the emotion-wrought calls for a positive policy.

Submission. Cleveland's successor, William McKinley, lacked his stubborn courage and iron principle. Neither McKinley nor the industrialists and bankers upon whom he leaned wanted war. The President set out, accordingly, to overcome the raging fever by forcing Spain to make a settlement satisfactory to the insurrectionists. Under American pressure Spain recalled General Weyler in the summer of 1897 and promised abolition of the concentration camps and autonomy for Cuba similar to that of Canada. But though McKinley responded graciously to these concessions, he gradually locked himself into a policy of independence for Cuba.

The war fever mounted in February 1898, when Hearst published a stolen letter, written by the Spanish Minister Dupuy de Lôme, which called McKinley a "peanut politician," a "bidder for the admiration of the crowd." Western Republicans introduced three separate resolutions giving the Cuban insurrectionists the status of a warring power. And the President was bombarded with demands for action. Meanwhile, in a gesture designed to demonstrate the American government's determination to force a settlement, the battleship *Maine* was dispatched to Havana.

Soon after the De Lôme letter was published, the *Maine* was destroyed in Havana Harbor (February 15). The Hearst press, the New York *Tribune,* and a few other newspapers blamed the disaster on Spain and called for war. Lodge, Senator Albert J. Beveridge of Indiana, and other militant politicians joined them. The *Maine* "was sunk by an act of dirty treachery on the part of the Spaniards," Roosevelt charged. But McKinley and most of the financial establishment still hoped for peace. The President appointed a commission of inquiry and resumed negotiations with Spain.

As passions mounted, administration circles began to fear that McKinley could not be reelected if he refused to submit. Important men in the business and financial community—men who had little active interest in the "Large Policy" and none whatsoever in liberating the Cubans or avenging the destruction of the *Maine*—now reluctantly joined the war hawks. Thus presidential adviser Elihu Root warned: "Fruitless attempts to hold back or retard the enormous momentum of the people bent upon war would result in the destruction of the President's power and influence, in depriving the country of its natural leader, in the elevation of the Silver Democracy to power." Under the weight of such counsels McKinley lost the will to resist. "I think . . . possibly the President could have worked out the business without war," one of his intimates later wrote, "but the current was too strong, the demagogues too numerous, the fall elections too near."

On March 27, 1898, the United States sent an ultimatum to Spain demanding an immediate armistice, closing of the concentration camps, and Cuban independence if the United States decided it was advisable. Before Spain could respond, the President began to compose his war message. Then on April 11, two days after Spain had capitulated to his first two demands, he sent the unrevised message to Congress, adding only that Spain had agreed to an armistice. Within two weeks Congress enthusiastically passed, and the President signed, a joint resolution authorizing use of force to compel the Spaniards to evacuate. The Teller Amendment to the resolution pledged the United States to withdraw from Cuba as soon as its independence had been established.

Military Operations. Only the American navy was prepared for hostilities. Modernization and expansion of the fleet had roughly paralleled the rise of interest in the Far East, and by 1898 the United States navy was the fifth largest in the world. The Asiatic squadron was especially strong. Ten days before the destruction of the *Maine,* in accordance with standing plans, Assistant Secretary of the Navy Theodore Roosevelt ordered Commodore George Dewey to attack the Philippines in the event of war with Spain.

Dewey confronted an antiquated Spanish fleet in Manila Bay less than two weeks after the war resolution was signed. Five hours later it had been destroyed and the course of history changed. Troops were hastily dispatched from the United States, and the Spanish garrison in Manila surrendered on August 13.

Land operations in Cuba proceeded less smoothly. The 28,000 men in the regular army were dispersed throughout the United States and lacked any training in large-scale maneuvering. The War Department was inefficient and unimaginative. It proved incapable of properly equipping the new regular and volunteer forces that Congress soon authorized, and the army that landed in Cuba was short of every basic supply from arms to medicine.

The original strategy of commanding general Nelson A. Miles was to occupy Puerto Rico in the autumn and then to proceed to Havana, where Cuban insurrectionists would augment his forces. When the Spanish Atlantic fleet slipped into Santiago harbor in Cuba, however, he decided to send his army to Cuba immediately.

A force of 17,000, including Theodore Roosevelt's volunteer Rough Riders, landed amidst incredible confusion outside Santiago in June. They drove toward the city, winning a fierce engagement at El Caney and a major battle at San Juan Hill. The campaigns produced the usual complement of heroes, but none so dramatic as Roosevelt. "The instant I received the order I sprang on my horse," he later wrote of his exploits, "and then my 'crowded hour' began."

The end of the war swiftly followed. On July 3 the Spanish fleet sailed to its destruction by the American squadron that lay in wait outside Santiago harbor. On July 17 the Spanish army commander in Santiago surrendered on generous terms. Meanwhile, United States troops occupied Puerto Rico almost without opposition, and on August 12 an armistice was signed. United States forces had suffered 450 dead in battle or of wounds and had lost 5200 from disease. Wrote John Hay to Theodore Roosevelt: "It has been a splendid little war."

The Triumph of Imperialism. The self-denying Teller Amendment had reflected the American people's humanitarian strain as distinct from their romantic imperialist impulses. Expansionist sentiment had grown to gale-like proportions during the war. The Hawaiian annexation resolution rolled through Congress three months after hostilities began. Soon afterward the President decided that Puerto Rico and Guam should be ceded to the United States. Meanwhile, he made plans to retain Manila and finally decided to annex the entire Philippine archipelago.

McKinley later explained his decision to a delegation of Methodist clergymen:

> I went down on my knees and prayed God Almighty for light and guidance more than one night. And one night late it came to me this way—I don't know how it was, but it came: (1) That we could not give them back to Spain—that would be cowardly and dishonorable; (2) that we could not turn them over to France or Germany—our commercial rivals in the Orient—that would be bad business and discreditable; (3) that we could not leave them to themselves—they were unfit for self-government—and they would soon have anarchy and misrule over there worse than Spain's was; and (4) that there was nothing left for us to do but to take them all, and to educate the Filipinos, and uplift and civilize and Christianize them, and by God's grace do the very best we could by them, as our fellow men for whom Christ also died. And then I went to bed and went to sleep and slept soundly.

The President's explanation was good as far as it went. The evidence indicated that Spanish rule had actually been worse in the Philippines than in Cuba, that the Filipinos were unprepared for self-government, and that they could not long remain independent on their own. More fundamental, however, was McKinley's desire to satisfy the people's will.

The victory at Manila had broadened horizons dramatically. All through the summer and autumn of 1898, newspapers, religious publications, and civic leaders called for retention of the Philippines for substantially the same reasons that the President gave the Methodist clergymen. The prospect of an expanding trade with China also drew a large and influential phalanx of businessmen and their spokesmen into the imperialist camp. "If it is commercialism to want the possession of a strategic point giving the American people an opportunity to maintain a foothold in the markets of . . . China," Mark Hanna declared, "for God's sake let us have commercialism."

McKinley sensed the force of opinion. As he wrote the American peace commission in August, "It is my judgment that the well-considered opinion of the majority would be that duty requires we should take the archipelago." But he wanted to be certain. So he toured the Middle West in October with a stenographer at his side to time the applause accorded his various soundings. Only after he had convinced himself of the preponderant sentiment for annexation did he cable his peace commissioners in Paris to demand cession of the entire Philippine archipelago.

The Treaty of Paris. By the terms of the treaty signed on December 10, 1898, Spain ceded the Philippines to the United States for $20 million. Spain also acknowledged Cuban independence and ceded Puerto Rico and Guam outright to the United

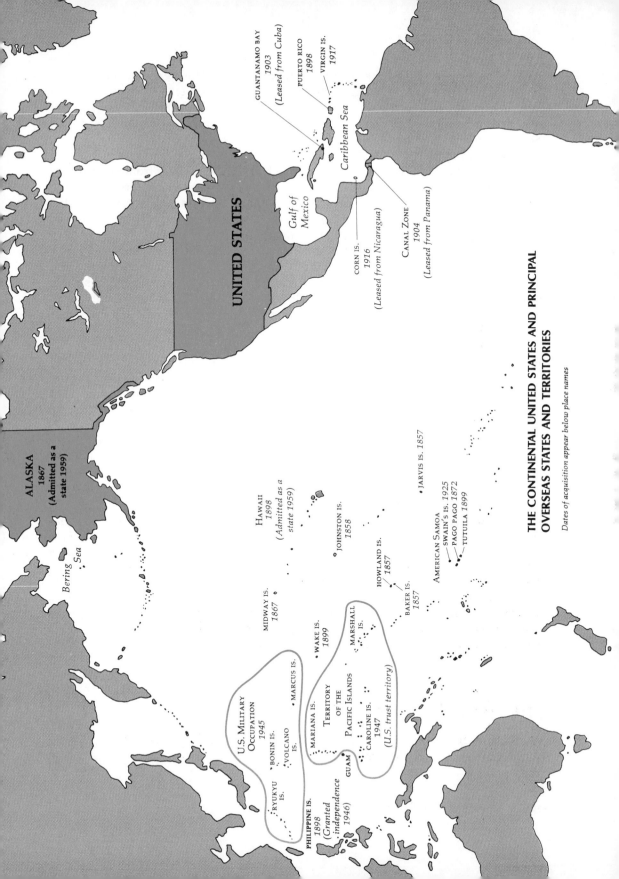

ALASKA
1867
(Admitted as a
state 1959)

*Bering
Sea*

UNITED STATES

*Gulf of
Mexico*

Caribbean Sea

GUANTANAMO BAY
1903
(Leased from Cuba)

PUERTO RICO
1898

VIRGIN IS.
1917

CORN IS.
1916
(Leased from Nicaragua)

CANAL ZONE
1904
(Leased from Panama)

HAWAII
1898
(Admitted as a
state 1959)

MIDWAY IS.
1867

JOHNSTON IS.
1858

• JARVIS IS. 1857

AMERICAN SAMOA
SWAIN'S IS. 1925
PAGO PAGO 1872
TUTUILA 1899

HOWLAND IS.
1857

BAKER IS.
1857

WAKE IS.
1899

MARSHALL
IS.

MARIANA IS.

TERRITORY
OF THE
PACIFIC ISLANDS
1947
(U.S. trust territory)

CAROLINE IS.

GUAM

U.S. MILITARY
OCCUPATION
1945

BONIN IS.
• VOLCANO
IS.

• MARCUS IS.

RYUKYU
IS.

PHILIPPINE IS.
1898
(Granted
independence
1946)

THE CONTINENTAL UNITED STATES AND PRINCIPAL
OVERSEAS STATES AND TERRITORIES

Dates of acquisition appear below place names

States. The Senate ratified the treaty two months later. The treaty would probably have been defeated had not a substantial number of anti-imperialist Republicans put party loyalty above conscience. It would also have been defeated if Bryan had not influenced a handful of Democrats to support it in the hope that imperialism would then become the dominant issue in the presidential campaign of 1900.

The Aftermath. By 1900 the United States was tasting the first bitter fruits of imperialism. Filipino partisans had begun to fight for independence from Spain before the Americans arrived. They turned against their new American masters in 1899 and inflicted losses on the American occupation troops as heavy as those suffered in the war with Spain. Not until the Americans resorted to methods as ruthless as those used by the Spanish in Cuba were the Filipinos finally suppressed in 1902.

Partial restitution followed. McKinley, and especially Theodore Roosevelt, took literally the poet's charge to "Take up the White Man's burden—/Send forth the best ye breed." McKinley instituted and Roosevelt greatly strengthened a political system designed to prepare the Filipinos for self-government. Schools were built; small farmers were installed on lands purchased from the Catholic Church; and numerous other reforms were instituted.

Meanwhile, the United States observed the form of the Teller Amendment by granting nominal independence to Cuba. There, too, the people benefited enormously from the American occupation, especially in public health. After assuring itself control of Cuba's foreign affairs by insisting that Cuba accept the American-written Platt Amendment to the Cuban Constitution (which also authorized U.S. intervention to protect national independence and just government), the United States withdrew.

In the long run such minor economic advantages as accrued to the United States in Cuba and the new island possessions were offset by vast expenditures for civic and social improvement. From the outset, moreover, the Philippines were a military liability—"our heel of Achilles," as Roosevelt soon called them. Despite the eventual institution of democratic forms of government on those islands owned outright, it is also an open question whether the native peoples were better or worse off under American rule. Hawaii prospered materially, but it remained the virtual fief of a half-dozen giant American corporations. Puerto Rico suffered from overpopulation (the result of American public health measures), inadequate natural resources, and absentee ownership. And the Philippines concentrated too much on the production of raw materials for the American market. Assuredly, the material standard of living improved enormously. Yet in the Philippines and elsewhere the old social structure and existent extremes of wealth and poverty remained largely undisturbed, while much of the islanders' cultural integrity was destroyed.

THE FAR EASTERN ABERRATION

The Open Door. The quest for trade, missionary zeal, and illusions of grandeur soon drove the United States into the vortex of Far Eastern affairs. Beveridge summed it all up in January 1900:

The Philippines are ours forever. . . . And just beyond . . . are China's illimitable markets. We will not retreat from either . . . will not renounce our part in the mission of our race, trustees under God, of the civilization of the world. . . . The power that rules the Pacific is the power that rules the world.

During the Spanish-American War the great powers had continued to carve out spheres of influence in China, and the British in 1899 began to evade payment of the tariff, the Chinese government's main source of revenue. If taken generally, such action could only cause the collapse of the Peking government. China would then be dismembered, and American trade, which was privileged by a most-favored-nation agreement, would be foreclosed. McKinley's new Secretary of State, John Hay, accordingly proposed in September 1899 that the powers agree to respect the rights of all nationals within all spheres of influence. Specifically, Chinese officials were to continue to collect the tariffs, and the powers were to refrain from discriminating in levying port duties and railroad charges within their spheres. Reluctant to offend the United States, the powers responded equivocally to Hay's proposal. When the Secretary boldly announced their "final and definitive" acceptance in March 1900, Japan alone protested.

The policy thus inaugurated was the ultimate triumph of the proponents of the "Large Policy." Based on the assumption that trade with the Orient was essential to American prosperity, the policy, in the words of one historian, "commanded a measure of interest and support over the years second only to that accorded the Monroe Doctrine." It led to deep and continuing involvement of the United States in the affairs of the Far East and, ultimately, to conflict with Japan.

The first complications came in the spring of 1900 when a group of fanatical Chinese nationalists, the Boxers, killed foreigners, occupied Peking, and besieged the foreign legations. The United States joined in suppressing the revolt and imposing a huge indemnity on the impotent and impoverished Chinese government. Meanwhile Hay issued a second round of Open Door notes, extending the demand for equal trade rights to the entire Chinese empire and underlining American concern for the preservation of Chinese territorial and administrative integrity.

The Roosevelt Far Eastern Policies. In 1901 Theodore Roosevelt came into office determined to realize the fruits of America's venture into the Far East. "Before I came to the Pacific slope I was an expansionist," he told an export-conscious audience in San Francisco in May 1903, "and after having been here I fail to understand how any man . . . can be anything but an expansionist." Yet even as Roosevelt spoke those words, he realized that the United States could maintain its foothold in the Far East only by accommodating itself to the Japanese in Manchuria. Alone among twentieth-century American Presidents, Roosevelt perceived that Japan's need for raw materials and markets impelled it to look outward. He believed, moreover, that Japan's abandonment of designs on Hawaii and the Philippines, coupled with its alliance with Great Britain in 1902, made it the natural counterpoise to Russia, whose failure to withdraw from China in 1902 he considered an act of "well-nigh incredible mendacity." Roosevelt's first major move was the secret recognition in 1905 of Japanese suzerainty in Korea in return for an explicit disavowal of Japanese designs on the Philippines.

By this time Roosevelt was already mediating the Russo-Japanese War of 1904-1905 at the request of the victorious but nearly insolvent Japanese. His basic objectives were to preserve the balance of power and to protect the Open Door. But he also felt that it was his moral duty to end the carnage as soon as possible. He further hoped to cement Japanese-American relations. His mediation fulfilled the first three of these goals but failed in the fourth: the Japanese blamed him for Russia's refusal to pay a war indemnity or to cede to them all of Sakhalin Island.

A decision by the San Francisco board of education to segregate the ninety-three Japanese students in the city's public schools dealt Japanese-American relations a more serious blow in October 1906. Roosevelt labeled the segregation order "a crime against a friendly nation" and threatened to use "all the forces, civil and military," at his command to rectify it. He then called the board members to the White House. They agreed to reverse the order if Japan would curb the emigration of peasants and laborers. A "Gentlemen's Agreement" to that effect was arranged in 1907.

Having thus deferred to Japanese sensibilities, Roosevelt characteristically decided to flaunt American strength by sending the battle fleet on a world cruise in 1907. Before the fleet returned, however, the President made another realistic concession to Japan. By the Root-Takahira Agreement of November 1908 the United States implicitly recognized Japan's economic ascendancy in Manchuria in return for a reaffirmation of the status quo in the Pacific and the Open Door in China.

New Far Eastern Policies. Neither Taft nor Wilson shared Roosevelt's view that the United States should accept Japanese preeminence in East Asia. Roosevelt warned Taft as early as 1910 that China was "weak and unreliable" and that the United States should abandon its commercial aspirations in Manchuria. But Taft believed too strongly in the fiction of Chinese independence and was too enamored of trade possibilities to pursue so realistic a course. He followed instead what he called a policy of "active intervention to secure for our merchandise and our capitalists opportunity for profitable investment." He permitted his Secretary of State, Philander C. Knox, to demand American participation in an international bankers' consortium to build a network of railways in China. Taft also allowed Knox, who was alarmed by the consolidation of Japanese and Russian influence in Manchuria, to propose the internationalization of that province's railways.

President Wilson was no less determined than Taft to maintain the Open Door. "Our industries have expanded to such a point that they will burst their jackets if they cannot find a free outlet to the markets of the world," he declared in 1912. "Our domestic markets no longer suffice. We need foreign markets." Essentially, however, he conceived of China, which had been penetrated by Christian missionaries, in moralistic terms. He opposed the bankers' consortium because he feared that it would result in European domination, not because he intended to withdraw from the Far East. The United States intends "to participate, and participate very generously, in the opening to the Chinese and to the use of the world the almost untouched and perhaps unlimited resources of China," he declared at the time. He then urged American bankers to act independently.

Wilson perceived that the outbreak of World War I in 1914 created a power vacuum in China. When Japan tried to make China into a satellite by imposing twenty-one far-reaching demands in 1915, the President vigorously defended Chinese integrity and independence. To forestall Japanese economic domination of China, Wilson and Secretary of State Robert Lansing proposed formation of a new four-power consortium to supply China with private capital. With Wilson's approval, Lansing also rejected Tokyo's demand that the United States recognize Japan's paramount interest in China just as Japan had recognized America's in Mexico. Finally, they arranged a *modus vivendi*—the Lansing-Ishii Agreement of November 1917. By this document the United States recognized Japan's special interests in China while Japan reaffirmed its support of the Open Door and agreed not to use the war situation to seek new privileges in China.

THE CARIBBEAN

Panama. President Roosevelt's Caribbean diplomacy was designed to establish stability, security, and U.S. supremacy in the area. Soon after taking office he arranged negotiation of the second Hay-Pauncefote Treaty (1901), by which Great Britain granted the United States the right to build and defend a canal across Central America. Early American planning envisioned a Nicaraguan route. But in 1902 Roosevelt seized an opportunity to buy for $40 million a French company's rights to a more desirable route through Panama. The President also had Secretary of State Hay draw up a treaty to grant Colombia, which owned Panama, $10 million and $250,000 annual rental for the proposed canal zone.

The Colombian senate's understandably indignant rejection of this arrangement infuriated Roosevelt. Privately castigating the Colombians as "Dagos" and "inefficient bandits," he tacitly encouraged agents of the French company to stimulate a Panamanian revolution against Colombia. When the revolution broke out on November 3, 1903, he sent an American warship to the scene under conditions that assured the revolutionaries' success. Three days later he recognized the new Republic of Panama and approved a treaty, negotiated by Panama's new minister (an agent of the French company), authorizing the United States to build the canal.

Roosevelt later claimed that "our course was straightforward and in absolute accord with the highest standards of international morality." But in 1911 he blurted, "I took the canal zone and let Congress debate, and while the debate goes on the canal also does." Ten years after that confession, the United States agreed to pay Colombia $25 million. By then Roosevelt was dead, but the memory of his obtuseness lived on in all Latin America.

Meanwhile, the first great government corporation in American history overcame extraordinary health and engineering problems to complete construction of the Panama Canal. It was opened to the commerce of the world on August 15, 1914, on equal terms to all nations—but only because President Wilson had persuaded Congress to repeal an act of 1912 that exempted American coastwise traffic from payment of tolls.

The Roosevelt Corollary and "Dollar Diplomacy." The need to defend the Panama Canal soon drew the United States deeply into the affairs of the Caribbean. Neither Roosevelt nor his successors wanted this. As the President said of the Dominican Republic, he had "about the same desire to annex it as a gorged boa constrictor might have to swallow a porcupine wrong-end-to." But the poverty, instability, and corruption of the Caribbean republics invited European penetration, and even such an apostle of peace as William Jennings Bryan saw no recourse but to make the Caribbean Sea an American lake.

The first serious incident occurred in December 1902, when the Germans, cooperating with the British in a blockade of Venezuela, bombarded a port town and threatened to take control of Venezuelan customs. Roosevelt and the American people reacted militantly. Kaiser Wilhelm ii, reluctant to add the United States to the growing list of nations hostile to Germany, accepted Roosevelt's suggestion for mediation, as did Britain. The dispute was settled by the Hague Tribunal in 1904.

By then the Dominican Republic had been forced by the German, Italian, and Spanish governments to sign protocols for the payment of debts. The Dominicans thereupon requested Roosevelt "to establish some kind of protectorate over the islands," as the President phrased it. In 1905 the United States assumed control of Dominican customs so that funds could be allotted to the European creditors. Against this background of intervention and threats of intervention by European powers, the President announced in December 1904 what became known as the Roosevelt Corollary to the Monroe Doctrine:

> Chronic wrongdoing, or an impotence which results in a general loosening of the ties of civilized society, may in America, as elsewhere, ultimately require intervention by some civilized nation, and in the Western Hemisphere the adherence of the United States to the Monroe Doctrine may force the United States, however reluctantly, in flagrant cases of such wrongdoing or impotence, to the exercise of an international police power.

By thus expanding the Doctrine to include the right of United States intervention in the internal affairs of Latin America, Roosevelt offended Latin Americans anew. Even more important, he also gave his successors a rationale for deep and continuous involvement.

President Taft devised some new approaches to the Caribbean. One was the dispatch of troops to Nicaragua in 1912 to install and maintain a pro-United States government. Another was what he christened "dollar diplomacy"—use of private American capital to displace European bondholders and concessionaires. These actions, like Roosevelt's, were designed fundamentally to protect the Panama Canal. Over the years, however, the need of the American military and American investors for assured stability resulted in a pattern of United States support of ultra-conservative and often dictatorial governments in Central America and the Caribbean.

The Wilson-Bryan Policies. President Wilson was not averse to using dollar diplomacy when circumstances seemed to require it. But he and Secretary of State Bryan also conceived that they had a mission to democratize the corrupt and revolution-ridden Caribbean republics. "We can have no sympathy with those who seek to seize the power of government to advance their own personal interests or ambition," Wilson warned in a public statement on March 11, 1913. "As friends, therefore, we shall prefer those who act in the interest of peace and honor, who protect private rights and respect the restraints of constitutional provision." The consequence of Wilson's and Bryan's activism was unparalleled diplomatic and military intervention in the Caribbean, to say nothing of Mexico. The Wilson administration regularized the occupation of Nicaragua (which remained occupied by U.S. marines until 1933). It sent marines to Haiti and, by imposing a puppet but nominally democratic regime in 1915, made that state a virtual protectorate of the United States. It dispatched marines to the Dominican Republic in 1916 and governed it directly through military officers. It also fostered road building, school construction, and public health projects.

Triumph and Tragedy in Mexico. Meanwhile, Wilson embarked on a bold new policy toward Mexico, where the classic Latin American alliance of dictator, Church, and foreign investors had provoked a convulsive political upheaval. By 1911 more than half of Mexico's oil, two thirds of its railroads, and three fourths of its mines and smelters were owned by Americans. Much of the remaining oil was British. The Catholic Church was the largest landowner, though William Randolph Hearst and other Americans also had huge holdings. The average Mexican, whether peon or industrial worker, lived in abject poverty. Against this background, a revolution erupted in 1910, and the dictator Porfirio Díaz was finally driven out in May 1911 by a group of middle-class intellectuals headed by a constitutionalist named Francisco Madero. Less than a year later Madero himself was overthrown and murdered by counterrevolutionary forces under the army's chief general, Victoriano Huerta, who became president of Mexico amid revolutionary upheaval.

Wilson's first break with tradition came when he withheld recognition from the dictator Huerta on the grounds that the United States should henceforth cooperate only with governments based on the unquestioned consent of the governed. Next he persuaded the British to withdraw their support from Huerta. Then he brought his new policy to fruition by offering to aid Huerta's chief antagonist, the constitutional reformer Venustiano Carranza. Carranza wanted only arms; and on February 3, 1914, Wilson lifted an arms embargo instituted by Taft.

Huerta's strength nevertheless continued to increase, partly as a result of resentment over United States interference, and Wilson's sense of frustration became more acute. Seizing finally on a trivial incident at Tampico, he asked Congress for authority to move against the Mexican dictator. Congress had not responded when he ordered the fleet on April 21, 1914, to occupy Vera Cruz to prevent a German ship from unloading ammunition. In the resultant action, 126 Mexicans were killed.

The President's militant action horrified peace-loving Americans and provoked even Carranza to threaten full-scale resistance should American troops march on Mexico City. Thus abandoned by the liberals of both Mexico and the United States, Wilson resolved his dilemma by agreeing to mediation by the "ABC powers"— Argentina, Brazil, and Chile—with the eventual result that Huerta resigned in favor of Carranza, who became *de facto* president of Mexico. Yet Wilson continued to press Carranza to accept his guidance. He warned him against mass executions and made it clear that he would oppose expropriation of the vast holdings of Americans and other foreigners. Then, wrongly concluding that Pancho Villa, an unscrupulous military adventurer tinged with Robin Hoodism, was an honest social reformer, Wilson shifted his support to him. Carranza thereupon broadened his own reform program while his leading general crushed Villa's armies in the field.

Back in Washington, American conservatives put the President under tremendous pressure to mount a full-scale invasion of Mexico. The Catholic hierarchy, the Hearst press, oil and other corporate interests, and ultranationalists like Theodore Roosevelt all urged him to act. But Wilson held firm and in October 1915 extended *de facto* recognition to the Carranza regime.

Reduced to banditry, Villa now strove to regain his power by inciting the United States to war. Early in 1916 he murdered eighteen American engineers in northern Mexico, and Wilson once again braved a nearly overpowering call for war. Then, in a bold sortie into New Mexico, Villa killed seventeen more Americans. The President thereupon ordered Brigadier General John J. Pershing to pursue Villa into Mexico. More incidents followed, and for the third time conservatives and ultranationalists called angrily for an all-out invasion. Wilson responded by mobilizing the National Guard along the Mexican border, but he refused to change the expedition's limited objective. Finally, in late January 1917, he ordered its withdrawal because of the impending conflict with Germany.

WORLD WAR I

Outbreak of Hostilities. On June 28, 1914, an obscure Serbian nationalist shot the heir to the Austro-Hungarian throne, Archduke Francis Ferdinand. The resultant crisis between Austria-Hungary and Serbia might have been localized if Europe had not been organized into a network of alliances which reflected deep divisions of militant nationalism, and if the Russian and Austrian governments had not been spurred to reckless action by dangers of national revolt. After Serbia rejected impossible demands by Austria, the Austrians opened hostilities against the Serbs. Russia then went to the aid of Serbia, and Germany declared war on Russia, prompting France to enter the war on the side of Russia. When German troops pushed through neutral Belgium in a vain effort to knock out France immediately, Great Britain went to war against Germany. Four years and three months later a generation of Europeans—almost 8.5 million—lay dead.

President Wilson believed at first that geography would save the United States from the holocaust; he issued a proclamation of neutrality and then adjured the American people to be "impartial in thought as well as in action." But despite an initial resolve to avoid military involvement, the American public was never disposed to be neutral in thought. The dominant British and French bias was compounded of ethnic, business, and cultural ties and was intensified by a vaguely formed feeling that a German victory would adversely affect American interests by putting an aggressive military regime in control of Europe and possibly of the high seas. Indeed, a small minority of American statesmen and intellectuals, including Roosevelt, Mahan, and the brothers Brooks and Henry Adams, had long insisted, as Roosevelt phrased it in 1900, that "if England should fail to preserve the European balance of power, the United States would be forced to step in."

In these circumstances, Germany's violation of Belgian neutrality and subsequent resort to indiscriminate submarine warfare were the real catalysts acting on American opinion. British propaganda served merely to sharpen perceptions and inflame passions that were already present. "The principle of Anglo-Saxon liberty seems to have met the irreconcilable conception of the German State," wrote Elihu Root at the time, "and the two ideas are battling for control of the world."

These sentiments were far from unanimous. The great majority of the country's 8 million Germans and German-Americans were strongly attached to the fatherland. The spokesmen of the nation's 4.5 million Irish-Americans were almost universally anti-British. And several million Poles and Jews were almost fanatically anti-Russian. From the outset these groups fed on German propaganda in their foreign-language newspapers, and neither the pro-Allied cast of the regular press nor German actions changed their sympathies during the period 1914–16. Because these groups were overwhelmingly lower or lower-middle class, however, they never exercised an influence proportionate to their numbers.

The divisions among the American people were accentuated by the impossibility of genuine neutrality. German might was based on dominance of the land mass of central Europe, Great Britain's on control of the seas. To impose an embargo, as the pro-Germans and many pacifists demanded, would be to deal Britain a paralyzing blow; to supply the Allies, as the United States soon did, was to strengthen them in relation to Germany. Hence the impossibility of substantive, as distinct from formalistic, neutrality.

President Wilson's decision to accept Britain's control of the seas seems to have been based on two factors: his desire to adhere to traditional rules of neutrality and his fear of a German victory. As he said to his cabinet in 1915, "the Allies are standing with their backs to the wall fighting wild beasts. I will permit nothing to be done by our country to hinder or embarrass them . . . unless admitted rights are grossly violated." Assuredly, he protested Britain's expansion of the contraband list (goods which they could intercept under international law) to include even food. But at no time did Wilson consider military action against Britain to uphold his shifting and, in some cases, historically untenable construction of neutral rights.

As the war progressed, the President permitted positive action to assure the flow of supplies to the Allies. Anticipating a strain on American gold reserves in the summer of 1914, he had permitted Secretary of State Bryan to declare that the administration disapproved of loans to the Allies because they violated the spirit of neutrality. He modified this policy in March 1915 by permitting the Morgan banking house to extend a $50 million credit to the French government. He rejected a German-American proposal to prohibit the export of all war materials. Then, in the summer of 1915, he completely lifted Bryan's ban on loans.

The President was undoubtedly influenced by the realization that American prosperity had become dependent upon war production. By 1916 exports to the Allies exceeded $3 billion in value, four times their 1914 level. "To maintain our prosperity, we must finance it," Secretary of the Treasury McAdoo warned Wilson in August 1915. "Otherwise it may stop and that would be disastrous." But it does not follow that the United States entered the war to maintain this prosperity or to assure repayment of these loans.

The German Response. On February 4, 1915, the German Admiralty marked out a broad war zone around the British Isles in which neutral vessels would run the risk of being sunk without warning by German submarines. Six days later Wilson replied that Germany would be held to "strict accountability" for illegal destruction of American ships and American lives.

The issue was first joined in March when an American was lost on a British liner torpedoed without warning. Arguing passionately that the United States should not indulge the technical right of its citizens to sail through war zones on belligerent ships, Bryan proposed that the government warn them against it. But before a decision was reached, an event of tragic proportions virtually destroyed all hopes of such a solution. On May 7 off the coast of Ireland the British liner *Lusitania* was sunk without warning, with a loss of 1198 lives, 124 of them American.

The nation was appalled by the immensity of the disaster, but few voices were raised for war. From all over the country, in fact, came fervent appeals for peace, and from Democratic leaders in Congress came a warning that Wilson probably could not obtain passage of a war resolution. As a Kansas progressive leader informed Roosevelt, the Midwest's sense of outrage "died down as suddenly as it had risen." When the President soon afterward declared that "There is such a thing as a man being too proud to fight," Roosevelt was almost alone in denouncing him.

Determined to find a peaceful solution, Wilson called on the German government to renew its allegiance to "the rights of humanity" by conforming to the traditional rules of war. The second of his three notes was so stern that Bryan, who feared that it would provoke Germany into hostilities, resigned in protest. But the President was prepared at the most to sever relations. The Germans proved unwilling to gamble on his intent, and on June 6 the Admiralty ordered U-boats to spare large liners. When a submarine provoked a more severe crisis by sinking the British liner *Arabic* on August 19, 1915, the German government was able to avoid a break with America only by pledging that liners would not be sunk "without warning and without safety of the lives of noncombatants," providing they did not offer resistance or try to escape. Following the torpedoing of the French steamer *Sussex* in March 1916, Wilson sent the Imperial Government an even stronger ultimatum. The Germans again pledged restraint, contingent on British observance of international law. Wilson accepted the pledge but not the qualification, and the crisis was temporarily resolved.

Preparedness. Meanwhile Wilson had begun to prepare the nation for the hazards of an uncertain future. He was reluctant to do so; but under the hammering of Roosevelt and a substantial element of the Republican party, he finally faced the implications of his "strict accountability" policy. He took the first tentative steps in the summer of 1915, came out for major increases in the navy and army in December, and then toured the Middle West in January and February 1916 to whip up support for his new preparedness program.

No other issue of the period proved to be so revealing of the configuration of isolationist sentiment. Progressives of all three parties, including the secondary leadership of the disintegrating Bull Moose organization, opposed preparedness as a movement of munitions makers in particular and capitalists in general. Farmers in upstate New York, in California, in the Carolina Piedmont, and in the valley of Virginia, no less than in Kansas and Nebraska, charged that preparedness would lead to war. Organized labor all over the country—in New York and San Francisco as well as in Chicago, Milwaukee, and St. Louis—agreed.

Conversely, conservatives from every section of the nation supported preparedness enthusiastically. The Chamber of Commerce in almost every state endorsed it overwhelmingly. Bankers' and manufacturers' associations in the Midwest and South came out militantly for it.

The main opposition in Congress came from Bryan Democrats and a few Republican progressives. Attributing the movement to conservative Republicans, they resolved to make them bear its cost. "I am persuaded to think that when the income tax will have to pay for the increase in the army and navy," wrote Claude Kitchin of North Carolina to Bryan, "they will not be one-half so frightened over the future invasion by Germany." Not until Wilson agreed to accept their inheritance, munitions-profits, and progressive income tax program did they relax their opposition; and then it was to approve a severely compromised program. The defense legislation of 1916 provided for only moderate increases in the army.

The Election of 1916. Prewar progressivism had reached full flower by the spring and summer of 1916 (pp. 153–69). In convention at St. Louis in mid-June, the progressive-agrarian Democrats ignored the President's orders to make "Americanism" their keynote and indulged instead in one long and tremendous demand for peace. "He kept us out of war" became their campaign theme, and Wilson had little recourse but to accept it. Compared to the extreme measures advocated by the Roosevelt and Old Guard wings of the reunited Republican party, Wilson's was in fact the policy of moderation. This was widely recognized at the time, and along with the Democrats' remarkable legislative record, it exerted a powerful pull on independents and ex-Bull Moosers.

Divisions within the Republican party also redounded to Wilson's advantage. Although the G.O.P. platform criticized the Democratic preparedness program as inadequate and virtually called for war against Mexico, it deferred to the sensibilities of the more than one hundred German-American delegates at the Republican convention by equivocating on neutral rights. As a result, the Republican campaign lacked consistency. The Republican presidential candidate, former Justice Charles Evans Hughes, was forced, on the one hand, to call for a hard policy toward Germany and to contend, on the other hand, that such a policy would assure peace. The St. Louis *Post-Dispatch* graphically described his dilemma:

To satisfy the pro-Germans he must quarrel with the pro-British, who demand war with Germany. To satisfy Wall Street, he must quarrel with the western radicals. To satisfy the jingoes and the Munitions Trust, he must quarrel with most of the country. To satisfy privilege and plutocracy, he must quarrel with the people. Even as a candidate Mr. Hughes dare not have a policy, because to have a policy is to antagonize one element or another of his followers.

Wilson squeezed through by a narrow, half-million plurality. The resentment of Irish-, German-, Jewish-, and Polish-American voters probably cost him much of the East and such Midwestern states as Illinois and Wisconsin. But he swept most states where isolationism reflected agrarianism rather than ethnocentrism and where the progressive impulse was strong.

The Failure of Mediation.   Hardly were the returns in than the President sought to end the war. For almost two years he had been striving to persuade the belligerents to accept a negotiated peace. His efforts had failed because both the Allies and the Central Powers still aspired to victory in the field. Taking new hope in a German peace overture of December 12, 1916, Wilson six days later called on the belligerents to define their war aims. The British replied privately that they would negotiate on liberal terms (even though the Allies had returned a belligerent public answer), but the Germans answered evasively.

The President thereupon appealed to world opinion in a speech before the Senate on January 22, 1917. He asserted the right of the United States to share in laying the foundations for a lasting peace, set forth his plan for a League of Nations, and added the noblest of all his perorations: "It must be a peace without victory. Victory would mean peace forced upon the loser, a victor's terms imposed upon the vanquished . . . . Only a peace between equals can last."

Men of good will the world over were intoxicated by Wilson's great vision. But realists knew that it was hopeless to expect the German military party to will its own destruction. On January 31 the German government submitted terms that would have assured its hegemony in Europe. It also announced resumption of unrestricted submarine warfare. At that point President Wilson severed diplomatic relations with Germany.

Although Wilson still hoped to avert war, the onrush of events soon overtook him. From British intelligence on February 25 he received a transcript of the "Zimmermann note," a diplomatic message by German Foreign Secretary Zimmermann proposing to Mexico that in the event of war between the United States and Germany, Mexico should join Germany against the United States. As a reward, Mexico should recover "the lost territory in Texas, New Mexico, and Arizona." On the next day the President asked Congress for authority to arm American ships for defense and to employ other measures to protect American commerce on the high seas. Bolstered by the public's militant reaction to the Zimmermann note, he castigated progressive senators who prevented adoption of the armed-ship bill as "a little group of willful men representing no opinion but their own." He then ordered ships armed under the authority of earlier statutes.

A succession of events followed. Three American ships were sunk with heavy losses on March 19. Also in March a liberal revolution in Russia overthrew the czar, thereby giving the Allied cause more the aspect of a popular crusade. Great throngs of Americans called for war in mass meetings in New York and other cities. Reports that the Allies were in such desperate straits that only American intervention could save them came to the White House from London.

Weighed down by these enormous pressures, the President sorrowfully decided for war. He briefly considered a limited naval war but quickly dismissed the idea, perhaps because he thought that the end of the conflict was near and wanted a large role at the peace conference. At eight-thirty in the evening of April 2, 1917, Wilson asked a joint session of Congress to recognize that Germany was at war against the United States and mankind. "The world must be made safe for democracy," he said, ". . . for the right of those who submit to authority to have a voice in their own Governments, for the rights and liberties of small nations, for a universal domination of right by such a concert of free peoples as shall bring peace and safety to all nations and make the world itself at last free."

Four days later, on April 6, 1917, the Senate voted for a war resolution 82 to 6, the House 373 to 50. How much this vote reflected Congress' acceptance of Wilson's concept of a world democratic mission, how much a purely nationalistic reaction against the loss of American shipping, and how much a conviction that British naval supremacy in the Atlantic was in the United States' continuing interest is impossible to say. All that is clear is that many Republican interventionists conceived the war as a power struggle involving American interests and disparaged the proposed League of Nations from the outset. "I am an American," expostulated Congressman Augustus P. Gardner of Massachusetts. "I want no internationalism. I want no conglomerate flag of all nations, with a streak of yellow down the middle."

A PEOPLE AT WAR

The President and his advisers soon learned that disaster loomed on almost every side. On the western front a French offensive had been stopped, and ten French divisions had already mutinied. In the Balkans the Allies were being pushed back. In Italy the Austrians, reinforced by the Germans, were soon to win a great victory at Caporetto. In the east the Russian armies were demoralized. On all fronts the Allies were running out of reserves. More ominous still, the Germans were destroying three times as much shipping each month as the Allies were building. Britain faced starvation unless something could be done.

The Washington administration responded boldly. The navy at once began to patrol the Western Hemisphere and to give assistance to the antisubmarine campaign around the British Isles. By July thirty-five American destroyers were based at Queenstown, Ireland; by the end of the war almost four hundred American ships were overseas. Meanwhile, the American navy virtually coerced the British into adopting the convoy system. The results of this critical decision were spectacular. Shipping losses fell from 881,027 tons in April to half that figure in December. By May 1918 they had dropped to 200,000 tons per month, thus destroying the calculations on which the Germans had based their decision to risk hostilities with the United States.

The War on Land. Six weeks after adoption of the war resolution a selective service law that applied to rich and poor alike was enacted, and by the summer of 1917 a great army was in process of formation. During the winter of 1917–18 a small American expeditionary force held a quiet sector of the front and served generally to bolster sagging Allied morale.

Meanwhile the American commander, General John J. Pershing, systematically prepared a major offensive. Appalled by the defense-mindedness of Allied generals, Pershing was determined "to draw the best German divisions to our front and consume them." But before he could do so, he had to throw two divisions into Chateau-Thierry to support the French in May 1918. Two months later 85,000 Americans helped the Allies turn back the last great German drive to break through the Marne pocket and take Paris. Finally, in mid-September Pershing's army, now greatly reinforced, took the offensive at Saint-Mihiel in its first independent action. It attained its objective after a two-day battle that cost six thousand in dead and wounded. Now more than half a million strong, the Americans turned west and won a fiercely fought battle in the Meuse-Argonne area. This victory, coupled with British and French successes in the central and northern sectors, brought Germany to its knees. An armistice was signed on November 11, 1918. The American contribution had been critical, though slight by comparison to that of the Allies.

Mobilization for Victory. Three months after American intervention the War Industries Board was created to coordinate purchases, allocate raw materials, control production, and supervise labor relations. The WIB made rapid progress in some areas but failed to control military purchases. "The Military Establishment . . . has fallen down," a Democratic senator exclaimed in January 1918. "It has almost stopped functioning . . . because of inefficiency in every bureau and in every department of the Government." Rejecting a Republican demand for a coalition cabinet, Wilson boldly conferred such sweeping authority on the WIB's new head, Bernard Baruch, that the industrial machine was soon hammered into shape.

Meanwhile Herbert Hoover, director of the Food Administration, stimulated dramatic agricultural increases by pegging prices. Food exports to the Allies doubled in 1917–18 and tripled in 1918–19. The Fuel Administration was not so spectacularly successful, but it too performed effectively. Conversely, the ship-building program proved a failure, less than a half-million new tons being afloat by the end of the war. Only by commandeering three million tons already under construction in private yards and by seizing a million tons of German and Dutch shipping did the United States acquire the fleet that saved the Allies. For a while the railroad situation was even worse. The eastern freight system nearly collapsed in December 1917. But conditions rapidly improved after the President put all railroad transportation under the control of William G. McAdoo, and the demands of the great military effort of 1918 were fully met.

Progressivism in War Time. The administration's tax and labor policies continued the powerful progressive surge of 1916. Over the bitter protests of conservatives, almost a third of the $38.5 billion total war bill was raised by war profits, income, and luxury taxes.

Moreover, the government threw its power decisively to labor's side. The National War Labor Board promoted harmony between labor and management. The AFL increased its membership from 2,072,702 to 3,260,168. Hours of labor declined from 53.5 per week in 1914 to 50.4 in 1920. And real wages rose sharply—14 percent above the prewar level in 1917 and 20 percent in 1918. Yet many of the gains proved temporary. The administration failed to devise and implement a viable reconversion plan. Upon the end of hostilities management resumed its old practices. And after a series of long and bitter strikes, labor failed to organize steel and other industries. Conversely, the progressives won their long struggle for prohibition and woman suffrage with the ratification of the Eighteenth and Nineteenth Amendments in 1919 and 1920. (See pp. 191–94.)

Propaganda and Civil Liberties. The record on civil liberties proved far less exemplary, partly because of the need to create a solid front. Millions of Americans believed on April 6 that the United States should not have entered the war. In 1917 mayoral candidates of the antiwar Socialist party polled close to half the vote in Dayton, Ohio, more than a third in Chicago, and nearly a quarter in New York and Buffalo—impressive evidence of both the magnitude and geographic spread of antiwar sentiments.

The administration struck back with a vast propaganda program and legislation to bridle criticism of the war. The Committee on Public Information under George Creel induced the press to accept voluntary censorship and organized some fifteen thousand writers, scholars, and businessmen into a public-speaking and pamphlet-writing bureau. The result was the creation of a necessary national will to fight. The American people accepted the draft, subscribed liberally to numerous bond drives, and adjusted reasonably well to the dislocations and inconveniences wrought by mobilization. They came also to believe the President's reiterated assertions, echoed again and again by Creel and his speakers and writers, that Americans were fighting to make the world safe for democracy. At the same time, however, they indulged in an orgy of intolerance and bigotry. State committees of public safety repressed and persecuted almost capriciously. One German-American was lynched. Conservatives read "Bolshevist" and "German socialist" into almost any sign of labor strife. Meanwhile black servicemen and workers were proscribed from full participation in the "crusade for democracy."

From the outset the administration was determined to suppress opposition that might cripple the war effort. The Espionage Act of June 1917 forbade interference with the draft or any action calculated to help the enemy. This restrictive program was broadened as the war progressed, partly because the activities of the "Wobblies" (the Industrial Workers of the World) caused production of copper to decline precipitously. The Trading-with-the-Enemy Act of October 1917 and the Sedition Act of 1918 imposed virtual closure on free speech in the United States. By war's end some 1500 people had been convicted for violating their provisions or those of the Espionage Act.

The Lost Peace. As early as the spring of 1916 President Wilson had committed himself both to a liberal peace and to American participation in a postwar league of nations. He had amplified this program in his "Peace without Victory" speech of January 22, 1917, and had spelled out its details in the memorable "Fourteen Points" address a year later.[1] Determined to impose this program on the Allies in spite of their secret treaties for the division of the German, Austro-Hungarian, and Turkish empires, he set out for the peace conference in Paris in the first week of December 1918.

The President faced imposing obstacles. A narrow Republican victory in the congressional elections in November 1918 had weakened his moral authority. Many Republicans had already expressed opposition to his program. And Roosevelt and Lodge would soon write Prime Minister David Lloyd George of Great Britain and Premier Georges Clemenceau of France that Wilson did not speak for the American people. Nor did Wilson help matters by failing to select a single prominent Republican as a member of his five-man peace commission.

The President reached France convinced nevertheless that he might well deliver all Europe from the tyranny of history. Triumphal tours of Paris, London, and Rome confirmed his sense of mission. "Wilson heard from his carriage, something different, inhuman or super human," wrote a correspondent who had seen the great men of the age on parade. Hardly conscious of the fear, lust, and vindictiveness that would shatter his hopes, he sat down with Lloyd George, Clemenceau, and Vittorio Orlando of Italy to forge a lasting peace.

The President first rejected a proposal by the French, who were obsessed with the need for security against Germany, to convert the west bank of the Rhine into buffer states under French control. But he did agree that the west bank should be permanently demilitarized and occupied by the Allies for fifteen years. He also

---

[1]Wilson's "Fourteen Points," pronounced on January 8, 1918, may be paraphrased as follows:

(1) "Open covenants openly arrived at."

(2) Freedom of the seas in peace and in war alike.

(3) The removal of all economic barriers and the establishment of an equality of trade conditions among all nations.

(4) Reduction of national armaments.

(5) A readjustment of all colonial claims, giving the interests of the population concerned equal weight with the claims of the government whose title was to be determined.

(6) The evacuation of Russian territory and the independent determination by Russia of its own political development and national policy.

(7) The evacuation and restoration of Belgium.

(8) The evacuation and restoration of France and the return of Alsace-Lorraine.

(9) A readjustment of the frontiers of Italy along national lines.

(10) Self-determination for the peoples of Austria-Hungary.

(11) Evacuation of Rumania, Serbia, and Montenegro and access to the sea for Serbia.

(12) Self-determination for the peoples under Turkish rule and freedom of the Dardanelles under international guarantee.

(13) The independence of Poland, with free access to the sea guaranteed by international covenant.

(14) The formation of a general association of nations (*i.e.*, the League of Nations) under specific covenants for the purpose of affording mutual guarantees of political independence and territorial integrity to great and small states alike.

acquiesced in the return of Alsace-Lorraine to France, the reduction of the German army and navy to cadre strength, and the mandating of Germany's colonies to victor nations under the League of Nations. Finally, he won Clemenceau's acceptance of the league idea by agreeing to join Britain and France in a treaty of mutual defense against Germany.

Wilson also opposed at Paris expansion of Allied intervention in Siberia. Point VI of the Fourteen Points had called for the evacuation of foreign troops from Russia in order to give that country "an unhampered and unembarrassed opportunity for the independent determination of her own political development and national policy." And though Wilson reluctantly supported the anti-Bolshevik campaign in Siberia with American troops, he feared that the intervention would backfire by strengthening the Russian people's support of the Bolsheviks. He hoped that the Bolsheviks would be supplanted by a liberal-democratic-capitalist regime such as he envisioned for the entire world, including Japan and China; and to that end he instituted a policy of nonrecognition of Soviet Russia that persisted until 1933.

More victories and more concessions followed. A new Poland was created without violating unduly the principle of self-determination. Italy was granted control of the Brenner Pass for security reasons, but its plea for a long strip of the Dalmatian coast to include Fiume was rebuffed. And the Covenant of the League of Nations was firmly embedded in the peace treaty. On the other hand, Germany was subjected to a potentially astronomical reparations bill and was compelled to admit war guilt. More important still, nothing was done to remove economic barriers within Europe or throughout the world. Thus Wilson had won considerably more than his critics later conceded and a great deal less than he had hoped.

Returning to the United States on July 8, 1919, the President threw down the gauntlet two days later. "Our isolation was ended twenty years ago," he warned the Senate. "There can be no question of our ceasing to be a world power. The only question is whether we can refuse the moral leadership that is offered, whether we shall accept or reject the confidence of the world."

Wilson's words fell on a divided country. The German-Americans and their powerful journalistic ally, the Hearst press, opposed the treaty's harshness toward Germany. Italian-Americans sulked over Wilson's refusal to allow Italy to take Fiume. Irish-Americans mounted a virulent opposition because of President Wilson's failure to support the movement for Ireland's independence. Furthermore, a small group of sincere and irreconcilable isolationists in the Senate pledged themselves to complete defeat of the treaty because of the provision for the League of Nations. Many intellectuals and idealists were revolted by the treaty. "The European politicians who with American complicity have hatched this inhuman monster," said the *New Republic,* "have acted either cynically, hypocritically or vindictively."

Nevertheless, Wilson might still have won the fight for ratification had he not been so uncompromising, and had not Senator Henry Cabot Lodge and a small group of Republican nationalists, most of whom had been militant interventionists, been so opposed to the concept of collective security and any compromise of American freedom of action. More than two thirds of the Senate approved the League Covenant in broad principle. When the President was greeted by a tremendous response on a trip through the West in September 1919, it looked as though he must win. "My clients are the children; my clients are the next generation," he exclaimed with tears in his eyes to a cheering throng in Pueblo, Colorado. "I intend to redeem my pledges to the children; they shall not be sent [to France]." Seven days after this memorable peroration the President suffered a stroke that paralyzed his left side.

The battle now ground slowly to its tragic end. Lodge, as chairman of the foreign relations committee, presented the treaty to the Senate on November 6 for approval subject to a number of reservations. The most important had been suggested earlier by Elihu Root. It asserted that the United States assumed no obligations under Article X of the League Covenant to preserve the territorial integrity or political independence of any country, to interfere in controversies between nations, or to use its armed forces to uphold any article of the Treaty for any purpose, *unless Congress by joint resolution so provided.*

The ailing President refused to accept the Lodge reservations on the grounds that they crippled the Covenant, and Democrats on November 19 dutifully followed his command and voted against the treaty with reservations. Their vote was sufficient to prevent approval.

So strong was pro-League sentiment throughout the country, however, that the Treaty was brought to a second vote on March 19, 1920. By this time Wilson had recovered sufficiently to take an active part in the controversy. "Either we should enter the League fearlessly," he wrote in a public letter, "accepting the responsibility and not fearing the role of leadership which we now enjoy . . . or we should retire as gracefully as possible from the great concert of powers by which the world was saved." If the Senate failed to ratify without crippling reservations, he concluded, the election of 1920 should then be a "great and solemn referendum" on the issue. In spite of—perhaps because of—Wilson's last stand, the Senate again refused to approve ratification of the Versailles Treaty. A change of seven Democratic votes would have been enough for Senate approval.

CHAPTER 6

CULTURE AND THOUGHT
IN THE PROGRESSIVE ERA

THE PROGRESSIVE MIND AND RACISM

Old and New. The momentous political and social reforms of the Roosevelt, Taft, and Wilson administrations testified eloquently to the richness of progressive thought. Although most of the ideas which nurtured it had come earlier, the progressive mind was an extraordinarily constructive mind—a mind unafraid to apply the imperfect new insights of psychology, philosophy, and science to individuals and society. Almost every aspect of American life felt its impact: theology became infused with social theory; education was transformed; new art forms emerged; the study of history deepened and narrowed; and the law became more creative.

The "New" Immigration and Racism. The most significant exception to these trends was in race relations, which deteriorated during the Progressive Era, as some 3 million Italians, 1.5 million Jews, and 4 million Slavs poured into the United States between 1901 and 1914. No society could have absorbed such a vast number of people without social tension. Moreover, the problem was compounded by the preponderantly peasant origins of the new immigrants, their different values and customs (as compared to the old-stock majority), their tendency to settle in already crowded urban centers, and the persistence of Old World rivalries among them. One result was that employers often prevented unionization by playing one ethnic group against another. Another, as we saw in the configuration of attitudes toward World War I and the election of 1916, was the large-scale injection of ethnic considerations into politics and public policy.

The rise of racist theory, most of which emanated in Europe, enabled old-stock whites to rationalize their often contemptuous view of the new immigrants, to say nothing of the black man. Superficially the racist views of the period seemed convincing. The neo-Darwinian belief that individual characteristics were passed on through the germ plasm regardless of environment was widely accepted by eugenicists. Furthermore, the stability of Anglo-American political institutions suggested, at least to those who wanted so to believe, that Anglo-Americans were a superior race of men. For a while the findings of psychologists buttressed this plausible body of racist theory. They disclosed, for example, that Americans of northern European derivation scored markedly higher than southeastern Europeans on intelligence tests.

During World War I, however, new research suggested that such cultural or

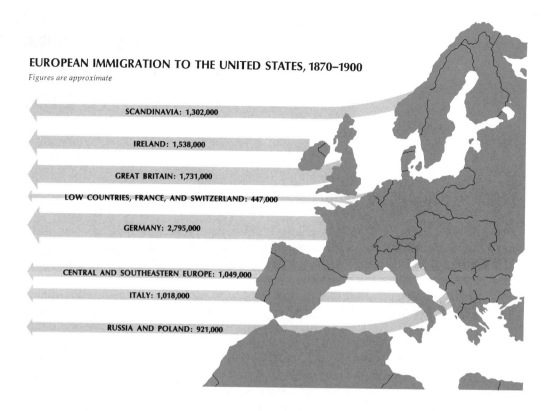

EUROPEAN IMMIGRATION TO THE UNITED STATES, 1870–1900

Figures are approximate

SCANDINAVIA: 1,302,000

IRELAND: 1,538,000

GREAT BRITAIN: 1,731,000

LOW COUNTRIES, FRANCE, AND SWITZERLAND: 447,000

GERMANY: 2,795,000

CENTRAL AND SOUTHEASTERN EUROPE: 1,049,000

ITALY: 1,018,000

RUSSIA AND POLAND: 921,000

environmental factors as rural-urban origin and educational advantages were more important than biological differences. Thus Southern whites scored lower than Northern whites in army intelligence tests, and blacks from some Northern states scored higher than whites from some Southern states.

It bears emphasizing that long before the startling findings of the army intelligence tests, the environmentalist emphasis of reform Darwinism had modified the racism of the progressives, if not of the conservatives. Yet while most progressives neither accepted completely nor rejected totally the neo-Darwinian belief in heredity, they did equate race with cultural nationalism and did believe in "superior" cultures, into which immigrants had to be assimilated. They concluded that the "new" immigrants should eventually be "Americanized." But they also believed that the "new" immigrants were coming in too rapidly to be absorbed successfully, and therefore proposed a literacy test to curtail drastically, though not to cut off entirely, the "new" immigration.

Blacks and Racism.　Whatever the moderation of their racial views, progressives were almost as slow as conservatives to resist the wave of intolerance toward blacks that swept the country during the era. Between 1895 and 1907 all the Southern states except Maryland, Tennessee, and Kentucky disfranchised black voters. Violence or the threat of violence continued to be the ultimate means of race control. And though

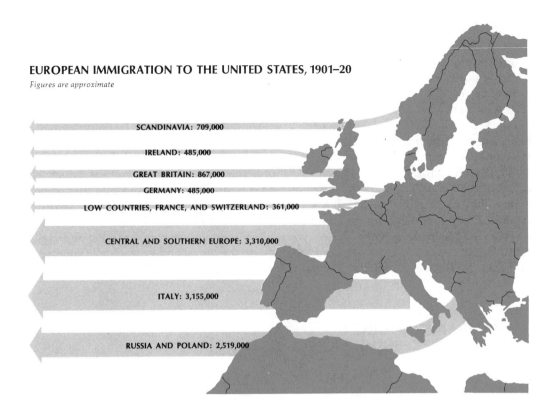

EUROPEAN IMMIGRATION TO THE UNITED STATES, 1901–20

Figures are approximate

SCANDINAVIA: 709,000

IRELAND: 485,000

GREAT BRITAIN: 867,000

GERMANY: 485,000

LOW COUNTRIES, FRANCE, AND SWITZERLAND: 361,000

CENTRAL AND SOUTHERN EUROPE: 3,310,000

ITALY: 3,155,000

RUSSIA AND POLAND: 2,519,000

the total number of lynchings decreased as the result of a sharp decline in the North, the number in the South actually increased. A race riot in Atlanta in 1906 degenerated into a mass slaughter. Two years later an anti-black riot occurred a half mile from Lincoln's home in Springfield, Illinois. Meanwhile, Southern orators like South Carolina's "Pitchfork Ben" Tillman carried the message of white supremacy to receptive Northern audiences. The production in 1915 of Thomas Dixon's violently racist book, *The Clansman,* as a motion picture titled *The Birth of a Nation* stimulated more incidents.

The bright spots were few. Blacks decreased their illiteracy rate from 44.5 percent to 30.1 percent in the first decade of the century. They also benefited slightly from the general upswing in prosperity. A handful of Northern philanthropists expanded their support of colleges for blacks. A minority of Southern whites welcomed blacks into the Progressive party in 1912. And the prestige of the black leader Booker T. Washington continued to grow among whites, though not among militant blacks. But as late as 1910 only 8251 black youths attended high school. Nor did any Southern state make a serious effort to provide adequate or equal educational opportunities for blacks. In South Carolina in 1915, for example, the annual expenditure for each white child was $13.98, for each black child $1.13. The state appropriation for higher education for whites was almost a half million dollars, for blacks less than $24,000.

The first real ray of hope came when the National Association for the Advancement of Colored People was founded on Lincoln's Birthday, 1909, by a group of black intellectuals and a number of white educators, clergymen, editors, and social workers. They dedicated the NAACP to the abolition of all forced segregation and to the promotion of equal justice and enlarged educational opportunities for blacks. For tactical reasons, most NAACP leaders were whites; only one black, W. E. Burghardt Du Bois, served as an official during the organization's first years. A Harvard-trained historian and political activist, Du Bois became one of the nation's early social scientists with his *Philadelphia Negro* (1899). His *The Souls of Black Folk* (1903), a distinguished contribution to American culture, was also a seminal work. Considerably more militant than Booker T. Washington, Du Bois had little faith that the white man would voluntarily give the black man justice; he eventually broke with Washington over the latter's emphasis on vocational education and insistence on political quiescence. Meanwhile other blacks, with Washington's support, founded the National Urban League in 1911. Designed to upgrade the social and economic conditions of blacks in the cities, it fought a largely losing battle.

SCHOOL AND CHURCH IN THE PROGRESSIVE ERA

Public Education. A less dramatic development than the exploitation of immigrants or the rise of racism was the revolution in education. The public school system was in deplorable condition at the start of the Progressive Era. Politics, corruption, and incompetence were rife; rote instruction, oversized classes, and an out-of-date curriculum were the rule. Teachers were poorly prepared and even more poorly paid. They averaged $42.14 per month in 1900, less than a day laborer. The proportion of male teachers had dropped from 43 percent in 1880 to 30 percent in 1900; by 1920 it would fall to 15 percent. Children averaged three years of schooling in the South, seven years in the North. Southern states spent an average of $9.72 per pupil each year, Northern states, $20.85.

The most dramatic changes occurred in the South, which was swept by an educational revival comparable to the one that had transformed Northern and Midwestern schools before the Civil War. By 1910 school budgets had doubled, the enrollment of white children had risen almost a third, and the average school term had been lengthened from five to six months. Meanwhile the illiteracy rate of whites declined from 11.8 to 7.7 percent.

At the same time, a revolution in educational theory and practice was changing the character of the nation's school system. It was spurred by imaginative teachers and experimental psychologists and was already under way when the philosopher John Dewey (see p. 90) assumed leadership around the turn of the century. Dewey's desire to reconstruct society gradually by applying intelligence to social problems made it almost inevitable that he should turn first to educational reform. "The pragmatic theory of intelligence," he said, "means that the function of the mind is to project new and more complex ends—to free experience from routine and caprice."

Dewey called for an educational curriculum that prepared children to live in an urban, democratic society. Subject matter, he felt, should be adapted to the needs and capabilities of children; the learning process should be centered on the child's own experiences; and "learning by doing" should supplant the memorization of data. "To do this," he wrote in *School and Society* (1899), "means to make each one of our schools an embryonic community life, active with types of occupations that reflect the life of the larger society, and permeated throughout with the spirit of art, history, and science."

Against the sustained and often irrational opposition of traditionalists, Dewey and his followers accomplished one of the major cultural revolutions of the century. By the outbreak of World War I, Teachers College of Columbia University was well on the way to inculcating a whole generation of teachers with a potentially creative approach to teaching. Dewey's most influential work, *Democracy and Education,* appeared in 1916. Three years later the Progressive Education Association was organized to advance further the dynamic new program.

As in most creative acts, however, the costs proved high. Traditionalists within the universities failed at first to grasp the intellectual foundation of the reconstruction of education. Moreover, in one of the most critical decisions in American educational history, they irresponsibly refused either to encourage or to cooperate with the proponents of teacher-training. Forced thus to organize outside the liberal arts faculties, departments and colleges of education within universities tended to become autonomous. As a result, they lost contact with the psychologists, philosophers, and historians who might have had a leavening influence upon their curricula. The situation in state teachers colleges was even more paradoxical: they were a distinct improvement over the two-year normal schools from which they had sprung, yet they failed tragically to fulfill their promise. Directed by men and women trained as vocationalists, they offered such a proliferation of overlapping education courses as to make a mockery of the word *education.* (As late as 1970 it was common for prospective elementary school teachers to take more than half their course work in education, or education-related, courses.) On no level—B.S., M.S., or Ph.D.—did the quality of an education degree compare favorably to that of a degree in one of the traditional disciplines.

Professional educationists also began to gain control of the certification of new teachers in this period. The results were mixed. The quality of teachers and teaching in rural areas and small towns improved dramatically, and many well-educated older teachers in the cities and suburbs began to use the new methods imaginatively and constructively. But at the same time, the new certification requirements discouraged countless men and women of superior intellect and liberal education from entering public school systems. More ironical still, thousands of poorly prepared English, history, and science teachers began to spend summers taking graduate education courses, rather than content courses, in order to qualify for salary increases or administrative positions. Most ominous of all, an increasing number of physical education teachers with minimal background in the liberal arts began to qualify for principalships and superintendencies by taking summer courses in education.

Higher Education. Colleges and universities were favorably influenced by the deepening of knowledge, the specialization induced by the new technology, and their own growing commitment to excellence. The quality of graduate and professional study rose notably. States greatly expanded their aid to higher education. Municipal colleges and universities multiplied. Major strides were made in adult education. And between 1900, when the Association of American Universities was founded, and 1914, the total enrollment in colleges and universities increased from 109,929 to 216,493. Concurrently, the status and salaries of college professors rose; the percentage of Ph.D.'s increased; the concept of tenure broadened; and although often violated by college presidents and boards of trustees, the principle of academic freedom received wider and wider acceptance. These developments reflected in part the influence of the American Association of University Professors, organized in 1915. But in the main they marked the coming to age of American higher education.

Increased specialization, expanded research opportunities, and freedom to create led to epochal contributions to almost all areas of knowledge. By the end of the Progressive Era American scholarship had surpassed European scholarship in some fields and equaled it in many others. But once again the cost proved high: the social sciences developed their own vocabularies, often unnecessarily; historians wrote more and more for each other even as the quality of their research improved remarkably; and scientists, physicians, and engineers lost contact with the humanities and social sciences because of their need to specialize early in their undergraduate careers.

Legal education was beset by the same paradoxes. Pre-law training was steadily upgraded; by World War I two years of undergraduate work was a common requirement for admission to reputable lawschools. But except in a handful attached to the great universities, the nature and theory of law were largely neglected. Even though a law degree became a virtual prerequisite for election to public office, most law schools turned out little more than competently trained technicians.

Meanwhile medical education, which had become a national scandal, was dramatically upgraded following publication in 1910 of Abraham Flexner's searching report for the Carnegie Foundation. Enormous strides were also made in public health during the Progressive Era, and for a few years elements of the medical profession seemed genuinely interested in institutionalizing medical care for the poor. By 1919, however, the conservative, entrepreneurial mentality had become dominant in the American Medical Association. Proposals for mild forms of socialized medicine (medicare) were fiercely repelled, and the United States' record of treatment of the poor, both black and white, became one of the worst in the Western world. Conversely, its care of the middle and upper classes was among the world's best, partly as a result of superb advances in medical technology.

Some of the same paradoxes marked agricultural education and development. Science, technology, and the spread of knowledge through the expansion of agricultural colleges, and institution of the county extension system induced striking increases in the quality and quantity of farm production. By and large, however, the burgeoning agricultural educational establishment oriented itself toward large-scale commercial producers to the gross neglect of tenant farmers and sharecroppers.

Meanwhile, undergraduate education in general became increasingly watered with nonacademic subject matter. The burgeoning land-grant colleges sustained an extraordinary amount of theoretical research, especially in the physical and natural sciences, but, hardly less than the teachers colleges, they fell short of fulfilling their promise. Partly because of the influence of Dewey's followers and largely because of the demands of the taxpayers, they too opened their doors to vocationalism and educational trivia. Many coeds spent their energies on home economics courses at the very time that the great Eastern women's colleges were decisively proving the ability of women to excel in academic disciplines. And colleges or departments of business administration committed to the narrow or technical aspects of business education began to be formed in almost all but the finest private colleges and universities. All the while, much of the worst teaching in America was done by college professors who remained impervious to, or contemptuous of, the revolution in teaching wrought by Dewey and his disciples.

Theology.   Another striking phenomenon of the prewar period was the survival of Protestantism after the violent intellectual storms of the last quarter of the nineteenth century. To be sure, the Progressive Era was marked by radical, and often paradoxical, change. Organizations like the Young Men's Christian Association, the International Sunday School Association, and the American Bible Society blurred denominational lines. Modernism, fundamentalism, and the Social Gospel movement cut across them. And the formation of the Federal Council of Churches of Christ in America by thirty-three evangelical bodies with a membership of 17 million created a loose unity after 1908.

At the same time, however, a large number of disgruntled Methodist and Baptist fundamentalists formed new Protestant sects, and the northern Presbyterian church preserved the purity of its doctrines only by expelling several of its most distinguished ministers and losing control of its leading seminary, the Union Theological Seminary in New York. Modernist clergymen largely captured the northern Methodists, the northern Baptists, and the urban Congregationalists. And perhaps a majority of intellectuals left the church in spirit.

Even the Social Gospel ministers failed to agree on a common body of assumptions. Thus one leader of the movement, the Congregationalist Washington Gladden, blamed the world's ills on Protestantism's theological rock bed—the belief that salvation is a private matter between man and God. The result, he charged, was a failure to apply the law of love to the resolution of social problems. Christians must realize that although God did not reveal Himself fully in nature, His partial immanence could be seen in the ever-increasing force of sympathy, love, and self-sacrifice. They should further understand, Gladden held, "that human nature is modifiable, and is constantly being modified, under the influence of the divine Spirit, so that social standards and ruling ideas are gradually changing from generation to generation."

Another eminent Congregationalist, George Herron, argued with great fervor that Christ would be revealed fully with the Second Coming. He would come, however, only after such a self-sacrificing imitation by Christians as would transform the world. The dualism of contemporary life was intolerable:

> A corporation, greedy, godless, vicious in many of its operations, consists of men famous for their piety and benevolence. A nation governed by men of eminent Christian character goes mad with the spoils of unrighteousness. . . . A church containing many sincere, teachable, self-sacrificing Christians is as powerless a moral institution in the community as the town pump.

The two most prominent modernists of the times, Edward Scribner Ames, a Disciple of Christ, and Shailer Mathews, a Baptist, broke still more sharply with traditional theology. Rejecting the supernatural, Ames emphasized both the scientific method and democratic idealism. Man was to revere life, love his fellow man, and have faith in his ability to improve the world. For Ames, as for most of the intellectuals who left the church, social justice rather than individual salvation became the ultimate ideal.

Mathews was more representative of those who stayed in the church. Like Ames, he was enamored of both science and democracy; but unlike Ames, he continued to have faith in the supernatural. Mathews believed that man must be regenerated, and he and a majority of modernists fastened on incarnation as the means to that end. "God's spirit," writes historian Stow Persons, "was believed to be incarnate in the world, working through the social historical process, expressing itself in the highest values of the community, such as love, brotherhood, justice, and good will."

Yet it would be wrong to assume that these views characterized Protestantism as a whole. For every Christian Socialist or near-socialist clergyman, there were probably hundreds of theological and social conservatives; for every layman whose social conscience was aroused by a Washington Gladden, probably a thousand were moved to acceptance of the existing theological and social order by the Reverend Russell Conwell's exhortation to get rich—"to make money honestly is to preach the gospel"—or by the Reverend Billy Sunday's thundering fundamentalism.

ARCHITECTURE, PAINTING, AND LITERATURE

Architecture. The paradoxes of progressivism were even more graphically set off by the popular taste in architecture. Two striking originators, Louis Sullivan and Frank Lloyd Wright, conceived organic styles and profoundly influenced European architecture; a number of talented designer-engineers also built functional and often aesthetically inspiring bridges and factories of steel and reinforced concrete. But most architects and their businessmen-clients emphasized form rather than function. The overwhelming majority of the buildings of the era were more banal than creative, more pretentious than graceful. The same held for private houses. Sullivan, Wright, and a few others did imaginative work, but the preponderance of new construction was eclectic. When historical styles such as Cape Cod, Georgian, or Greek Revival were used, the end product almost invariably violated the lines and proportions that had given the originals their distinction.

Sullivan attributed this failure of taste to the appeal of the Roman façades, false monumentalism, and harmonious lagoons of the Great White City fashioned for Chicago's Columbian Exposition of 1893. "The damage . . . has penetrated deep into the . . . American mind," he wrote, "effecting there lesions of dementia." More likely, however, the Exposition's imperial style touched the same impulses for grandeur that ordained the acquisition of an empire after the war with Spain in 1898.

Sullivan's pupil, Frank Lloyd Wright, also failed to exercise much immediate influence on the American skyline. "Early in life," Wright once wrote, "I had to choose between honest arrogance and hypocritical humility. I chose honest arrogance." Wright's great distinction was his development of Sullivan's concept of "organic" architecture. Professing a regional style (he was in fact influenced by the Japanese), he designed from the inside out, emphasizing always the unique texture of his materials. His use of native woods, horizontal planes, and deep overhangs often succeeded brilliantly in harmonizing man and nature. As early as 1900 the *Architectural Review* recognized Wright's genius, and by 1905 his work had deeply affected the modern movement in Germany, Holland, and France. But only as his ideas were brought back to the United States by Europeans like Walter Gropius did Wright make a vigorous imprint on American architecture. Meanwhile, the skilled traditionalists Stanford White, Ralph Adams Cram, and their disciples continued both to form and to reflect the widespread preference for Roman and Gothic.

The maligned Columbian Exposition did serve at least one creditable purpose: its classic spaciousness sparked a nationwide movement to beautify American cities. Uncounted urban open spaces were converted into parks, and sums commensurate with the nation's wealth were poured into public buildings. Unfortunately, little attention was given to the flow of traffic, and even less to the needs, interests, and habits of pedestrians. Almost always, moreover, the buildings erected were more derivative than original in design.

Painting. "There is a state of unrest all over the world in art as in all other things," the director of the Metropolitan Museum complained in 1908. "It is the same in literature, as in music, in painting and in sculpture." This was the year that eight young painters, spearheaded by the realists Robert Henri, George B. Luks, and John Sloan, protested against the National Academy's near blackout of their work and staged a private show in New York. They rebelled not against the old painting techniques—they never mastered the new ones—but against the class bias that failed to see reality in all human activity, including the seamy. Theirs was a work of social protest closer to the political ferment of the era than to the revolution in art forms that had already swept Europe. Inevitably, Victorian-minded critics dismissed them as "apostles of ugliness," "the revolutionary gang," "the black gang," and, most often, "the ash-can school."

Meanwhile, more creative European currents were beginning to affect American artists. By 1912 the work of the Postimpressionists was familiar to sophisticated habitués of the New York gallery of the revolutionary camera artist Alfred Stieglitz. The next year sixteen hundred paintings, drawings, prints, and pieces of sculpture representing almost every mode in modern art were exhibited in a spectacular show at the New York Armory. Picasso, Matisse, Brancusi, Duchamp, Kandinsky, Cezanne, Van Gogh, Gauguin, and virtually all other prominent artists had their work displayed, to the extreme discomfort of conservative critics. The *New York Times* labeled the show "pathological." *Art and Progress* compared many of its artists to "anarchists, bomb-throwers, lunatics, depravers." And an official of the Chicago Law and Order League demanded that the exhibition be banned from his city because the "idea that people can gaze at this sort of thing without it hurting them is all bosh."

The vehemence of the conservatives' criticism and the desperation of the counterattack they soon mounted served only to underscore their artistic bankruptcy. As the art historian Sam Hunter writes, "They were soon unable to pose with real conviction or enthusiasm a possible alternative, since even the art they defended was becoming a retarded and diluted academic derivative of some form of modernism." Nevertheless, the public proved as slow to accept the highly individualized abstraction-ism of the new painters (including the Americans Max Weber and John Marin) as it did the architecture of Sullivan and Wright.

The Novel. The trend toward realism in literature reached its highest form in the works of Nebraska-born Willa Cather, author of *O Pioneers!* (1913) and *My Ántonia* (1918). More popular were Booth Tarkington, Winston Churchill, and several literary journalists like William Allen White, who blended realism with optimism much as the progressive political leaders were doing.

Meanwhile, Jack London and Frank Norris were writing a raw version of the survival-of-the-fittest doctrine into a host of brutal novels ranging in subject from man's struggle against the elements to his battle with the trusts. But it was in the writings of Theodore Dreiser, the era's only literary giant, that naturalism, as literary determinism was called, proved most profound. The son of German Catholic im-migrants who settled in Indiana, Dreiser early disavowed belief in religion and conventional morality. "Man was a mechanism," he wrote, "undevised and uncreat-ed, and a badly and carelessly driven one at that." Yet Dreiser, no less than his predecessors, was a moralist at heart. All his work was charged by a tension between determinism and its antithesis; in the very act of denying free will and the importance of man, he affirmed them. "To have accepted America as he has accepted it, to immerse oneself in something one can neither escape nor relinquish, to yield to what has been true and to yearn over what has seemed inexorable," this, concludes Alfred Kazin, "has been Dreiser's fate and the secret of his victory."

Dreiser's first novel, *Sister Carrie* (1900), was withdrawn by his publisher because of its harsh reception; critics, many of whom objected to the novel's sympathetic treatment of a "fallen woman," failed to see that its account of the purposelessness of life was counterbalanced by its emphasis on life's sheer vitality. His second book, *Jennie Gerhardt* (1911), like *Sister Carrie* the story of a "kept woman" who was otherwise virtuous, struck at the failure of the conventional moral code to correspond to reality. Similar themes pervaded *The Financier* (1912) and *The Titan* (1914), though they were widely regarded as progressive-type indictments of the "robber barons."

Poetry. The years before World War 1 also witnessed a remarkable renaissance in poetry. Perhaps the most powerful voice was Edwin Arlington Robinson, a traditionalist who dealt with the abiding theme of the individual's search for God and truth amidst darkness and suffering. Robinson failed in his quest; life and human destiny remained mysterious. Yet in the "black and awful chaos of the night" he felt "the coming glory of the Light." Rescued from obscurity by Theodore Roosevelt, who gave him a government sinecure after reading his *Children of the Night* (1897), Robinson failed nevertheless to receive full recognition until after the war.

By 1912, the year Harriet Monroe established the magazine *Poetry* in Chicago, the renaissance was at hand. Vachel Lindsay, now remembered more for his jazz-like odes than his sensitive lyrics, published his "General William Booth Enters into Heaven" in the first issue of *Poetry,* then went on to exalt the common people in numerous other works. Edgar Lee Masters, Clarence Darrow's law partner, startled traditionalists with his masterpiece, *Spoon River Anthology,* in 1915. There he laid bare the sham and moral shabbiness of small-town America in a brilliant compound of irony, sadness, and humor which closed, paradoxically, on an affirmative note. A year later Carl Sandburg's first important volume appeared. A Whitmanesque romantic who employed free verse, Sandburg glorified Chicago as the roaring, brawling butcher and steel-maker to the world. During these same years Robert Frost was writing deceptively simple verse against a rural New England backdrop that masked his passionate, almost terrifying, life-force.

At the same time another revolt against the genteel tradition was brewing among a group of American and English poets in London, the so-called imagists. Led by Ezra Pound and Amy Lowell, they asserted that the poet should re-create impressions caught in the fleeting image. They held that meter and rhyme made the creation of a pure image difficult, if not impossible, and they accordingly rejected them. They also rejected Romanticism as being the literary expression of a decadent humanistic culture. They were soon joined by T. S. Eliot, whose now classic "The Love Song of J. Alfred Prufrock" met a hostile reception when first published in *Poetry* in 1915.

THE SOCIAL SCIENCES

Psychology and Economics.   Man's understanding of himself was further deepened by rapid advances in psychology. Freed from its old metaphysical and theological commitment by the Darwinian revolution, psychology began now to explore the whole range of human activity. By World War I two definite schools—the instinct and the behaviorist—had emerged. Both were European in origin; both found a receptive audience in the United States and exerted considerable impact on American thought.

The founder of the instinct school, William McDougall, felt strongly that psychology should concern itself with social behavior. He contended that man was ruled by deep-seated instincts rather than by rational or moral considerations. And his charge that classical economic theory was "a tissue of false conclusions drawn from false psychological assumptions" reinforced the insights Thorstein Veblen had already written into his *Theory of the Leisure Class* (1899). In *The Instinct of Workmanship and the State of the Industrial Arts* (1914) Veblen echoed McDougall's strictures against the inadequate psychological base of classical economics. He especially charged that modern industrial institutions had failed to play upon man's constructive instincts. F. W. Taussig argued in *Inventors and Money-Makers* (1915) that the instinct of contrivance, or workmanship, did not depend necessarily on prospective gain, as the defenders of the profit-making system contended. However, although instinct psychology undermined classical economic thought, it produced no systematic theory of its own.

The behaviorist psychology of the Russian Ivan Pavlov and the Americans E. L. Thorndike and John B. Watson proved more receptive to the dominant environmentalism of the times. Passing over everything that could not be verified by direct observation, the behaviorists sought to measure all human behavior in terms of stimuli and response. "It is the business of behavioristic psychology," wrote Watson, who later became an executive in an advertising agency, "to be able to predict and control human activity." Since consciousness was not observable, it should not be studied; thought was to be treated as latent speech.

Behaviorism offered too restricted and shocking a view of human nature to be universally acceptable; humanists rejected it decisively. Nevertheless, it sired a powerful school of psychology and markedly influenced all subsequent social science. At its best, behaviorism contributed enormously to social engineering of a constructive sort; at its worst, it lent itself to social manipulation. Its rise was paralleled by the equally spectacular rise of one of capitalism's unique institutions, advertising. On the one hand, that institution served powerfully to spur economic growth. On the other, it inculcated attitudes far removed from the values of the school and the church as it stimulated, even urged, materialistic values.

The New History. The writing of history proved no more immune to the new intellectual currents than did other disciplines; nor did it escape their paradoxes. The influence of German methodology, first felt at Johns Hopkins, continued as historians now severed their ties with literature almost completely. Seeking scientific truth by the use of rigorously exact techniques, they destroyed hallowed beliefs, stripped history of its individual drama and romance, and lost some of their popular audience. Yet they added immeasurably to the general body of knowledge, contributed important new insights about the forces that molded America, and provoked much constructive controversy inside and outside the profession.

The foremost characteristic of much of the new history was present-mindedness. As James Harvey Robinson and Charles A. Beard confessed in their pathfinding *The Development of Modern Europe* (1907), they had "consistently subordinated the past to the present" in the "ever-conscious aim to enable the reader to catch up with his own times." Implicit in this approach was a belief in laws of behavior as formulated by social scientists; the insights of philosophers, poets, and observers no longer sufficed. Implicit, also, was a desire to use history to create a better future. This last was not new. From Thucydides' time historians had concerned themselves with the usable past; some had been great moralists, finding in the past examples of virtue to be imitated in the present. By Robinson and Beard's time, however, probably a majority of America's professional historians conceived their task as being merely descriptive.

It was against them and their failure to search for casual explanations that might indirectly bear on the present—to be, in the new view, truly scientific—that Robinson and Beard revolted.

The seeds of revolt had been sown by Frederick Jackson Turner in his essay "The Significance of the Frontier in American History" (1893). Notwithstanding his effort to cut off Americans from their European past, Turner's environmentalism had opened new vistas to many historians. As Eric Goldman puts it, "The vogue of Turner's idea pulled men away from thinking in terms of political abstractions and shifted their minds to a concept that was close to economic." One of Turner's students, Algie M. Simons, wrote the first semischolarly Marxist history of the United States. Numerous others proved sensitive in some degree to the influence of economic forces on history.

Meanwhile a storm was brewing over the Constitution. In 1907 J. Allen Smith published *The Spirit of American Government,* in which he argued that the Constitution was written by property-holders who aimed to prevent the masses from controlling the government. "The powerful corporate interests . . . ," said Smith in a passage that summed up the progressives' criticism of the judiciary, "are securely intrenched behind a series of constitutional and legal checks on the majority which makes it extremely difficult for public opinion to exercise any effective control over them."

Six years later Charles A. Beard buttressed Smith's hypothesis with mountains of seemingly conclusive evidence. "The Constitution," he wrote in *An Economic Interpretation of the Constitution* (1913), "was essentially an economic document based upon the concept that the fundamental private rights of property are anterior to government and morally beyond the reach of popular majorities." He then set forth data to prove that through their interest in public securities, money, manufacturing, trade, and shipping, the framers of the Constitution had stood to gain directly from the establishment of the new government.

Beard always protested that his work was American-inspired. James Madison, he repeatedly pointed out, had offered "one of the earliest, and certainly one of the clearest" statements of economic determinism. As Morton G. White has observed, however, *An Economic Interpretation of the Constitution* actually reflected the worst, or at least the simplest, aspects of both Marx's and Madison's thought. Thus Marx neither denied man's capacity for high-minded action nor accepted the idea that every political action derived directly from an economic interest. Conversely, Madison believed with Aristotle that factions and interests were rooted in human nature—not, as Marx contended, in economic systems. But in Beard's analysis the framers had been moved by a narrow Marxian view of the deterministic force of economic systems and a similarly narrow Madisonian view of a direct relationship between self-interest and action. Recent scholarship has demolished, or at least seriously challenged, the evidence on which Beard based his economic thesis.

Beard always denied that he had written a tract for the times. "I simply sought to bring back into the mental picture of the Constitution," he said, "those realistic features of economic conflict, stress and strain, which my masters had, for some reason, left out of it, or thrust far into the background as incidental rather than fundamental." Whatever his intentions, the work drove deeper the wedge between progressives and conservatives. In the span of a decade many men's attitudes toward the Constitution and the judiciary that upheld it had moved from reverence to begrudged respect to unbridled contempt.

The impact of *An Economic Interpretation of the Constitution* on the historical profession proved even greater than its impact on progressive politicians. Two generations of historians were nourished on it; and though many were skeptical from the beginning, few failed thereafter to give due attention to economic factors in their teaching and writing. Perhaps the fairest judgment of Smith and Beard's work is the one that Roosevelt passed on the Armory Exhibition of Modern Art: "The necessary penalty of creativity is a liability to extravagance."

LEGAL AND POLITICAL MAIN CURRENTS

Sociological Jurisprudence.   The vast changes in American thought and institutions wrought by progressivism were mirrored in the law. Admittedly, the old absolutes died hard. Not until the new industrial problems became acute did the liberating force of Oliver Wendell Holmes' *The Common Law* begin to be felt; not until judges came abreast of the new psychological and sociological currents did a progressive synthesis begin to be formed. In crudest form the new accommodation reflected the judiciary's realization that since it lacked the power of the purse or sword, it could not indefinitely hold back a nation bent on reform. As "Mr. Dooley" phrased it, "Th' Supreme Court follows th' ilection returns." But in its broadest and highest form it reflected the same impulses that had inspired the progressive movement in general—the quest for social justice, the belief in progress, the urge to create, and the faith in scientism. Thus Harvard's Dean Roscoe Pound, who synthesized the historical insights of Holmes, the methodology of the social scientists, and the pragmatism of James and Dewey, conceived the law as an agency for social reconstruction:

> The sociological movement in jurisprudence is a movement for pragmatism as a philosophy of law; for the adjustment of principles and doctrines to the human conditions they are to govern rather than to assume first principles; for putting the human factor in the central place and relegating logic to its true position as an instrument.

In spite of lingering opposition, the force of these and similar ideas was immediate and widespread, if hardly pervasive. Judges began to probe beyond the crime into its social or psychological origins. Juvenile delinquency came to be viewed as environmental rather than hereditary in origin. And children's courts modeled on the one that Judge Ben Lindsey established in Denver spread throughout the nation and even to Japan.

The law also began to adjust creatively, though again slowly and inadequately, to labor problems. The common law concepts of "fellow-servant rule" and "contributory negligence," which had exempted employers from liability for most industrial accidents, withered away as the courts upheld liability and workmen's compensation laws grounded on sociological realities. No one put the case more graphically than Roosevelt in his remarkable message of January 31, 1908:

> It is hypocritical baseness to speak of a girl who works in a factory where the dangerous machinery is unprotected as having the "right" freely to contract to expose herself to dangers to life and limb. She has no alternative but to suffer want or else to expose herself to such dangers. . . . It is a moral wrong that the whole burden of the risk incidental to the business would be placed with crushing weight upon her weak shoulders.

The most celebrated manifestation of sociological jurisprudence was Louis D. Brandeis' successful defense in 1908 of an Oregon statute regulating the working hours of women. Disposing of the legal precedents in the first two pages of his brief, he spent 102 pages on sociological data designed to prove that excessive hours of labor were injurious to the health of women and to the general well-being of the community. Actually, lawyers had long invoked extralegal evidence to support their arguments; from John Marshall's time, moreover, Supreme Court justices had read their own social and economic biases into their opinions. But the "Brandeis Brief" served to make more scientific and dramatic an established practice. He would have the justices form their extralegal views on the best available evidence rather than on personal prejudice.

Hardly less important than the inroads made by sociological jurisprudence was a renewed emphasis on judicial restraint. This was the belief, best exemplified by Holmes, that the legislature should be reasonably free to pass experimental legislation:

> I think that the word liberty in the Fourteenth Amendment is perverted when it is held to prevent the natural outcome of a dominant opinion unless it can be said that a rational and fair man necessarily would admit that the statute proposed would infringe principles as they have been understood by the traditions of our people and law.

The majority of the Court did not adhere consistently to this doctrine. It struck down the Child Labor Act of 1916, and it ruled numerous state statutes unconstitutional. Yet, as a recent student of the Supreme Court concludes, the vision of judicial tyranny was an exaggeration. The Court did uphold most of the basic progressive legislation of the period even though much of this legislation struck at the core of the free enterprise system—for example, at an employer's right to fix prices and wages.

Political Thought.   While Dewey, Pound, and Beard were reconstructing education, law, and history, three young humanists—Herbert Croly, Walter Lippmann, and Walter Weyl—were calling for a reconstitution of politics. They charged that the existing system was geared to minority interests, and they deplored especially the failure of spiritual and esthetic progress to keep pace with material progress. The remedy, they concluded, was to infuse the political order with the new social and psychological concepts.

In 1909 Croly published the first of the new blueprints, *The Promise of American Life.* Croly accepted the charges of Veblen and the instinct psychologists that industrialism had repressed man's finer instincts. He directed his fire, accordingly, at laissez-faire capitalism's basic precept—the belief that freedom to pursue individual gain led inevitably to social progress. In words that came close to paraphrasing Theodore Roosevelt's presidential messages of 1907 and 1908, Croly called for the replacement of anarchic individualism by social cohesion. By the rigorous exercise of self-discipline, man must create a community loyal to an elevating ideal—a nation-state that would fulfill man's great promise.

Believing in big business' potential for good and despairing of the Democrats' devotion to states' rights, Croly at first fastened on the Republican party as the vehicle to achieve his purposes. He considered Roosevelt almost the ideal statesman: "The whole tendency of his programme is to give a democratic meaning and purpose to Hamiltonian tradition and method. He proposes to use the power and resources of the Federal government for purpose of making his countrymen a more complete democracy in organization and practice." Like Roosevelt, however, Croly finally concluded that Republican nationalism served special interests almost exclusively. In 1912 *The Promise of American Life* became the Bull Moose party's bible and Croly its prophet.

The following year Walter Lippmann wrote a Freudian analysis into his synthesis of the current social wisdom, *Preface to Politics* (1913). Lippmann professed little faith in direct democracy, and he seemed to call for a superman to lead the nation to an unspecified destiny. "He who has the courage of existence," he proclaimed, "will put it triumphantly, crying 'yes' as Nietsche did." Yet Lippmann had too sharp an appreciation of the representative character of American institutions to believe in dictatorship. He really sought leadership that would give voice to the "dynamic currents" and "actual needs" of the people and destroy the corruption, political indifference, and cultural apathy that prevailed almost everywhere. Constitutional fetishism, the conscious belief in the sanctity of private property, vested rights, and competition—all this, said Lippmann, should be reexamined. "The same energies," he wrote, "produce crime and civilization, art, vice, insanity, love, lust, religion. . . . Only by supplying our passions with civilized interests can we escape their destructive force."

Walter Weyl, a young economist well trained in statistics, added solid knowledge in his *The New Democracy,* published in 1912. A democracy, he said, had to soften the harsh condition of its poor in order to survive. Croly, Lippmann, and Weyl all found a public forum in *The New Republic,* a weekly magazine of comment that began publication in 1914 and remained until the 1920s the chief clearing house of progressive political opinion and thought.

Historians have tended in recent years to pass off the progressive intellectuals as superficial and to term their times an age of innocence. These generalizations are not without truth if we measure the progressives by their failures rather than by their triumphs. They are even more persuasive if we tear the progressives from their historical context and fail to compare their program with that of the conservatives or traditionalists. For it was the conservatives, not the progressives, who failed to see that workers had to be treated as more than subhumans; that crime and vice were largely environmental in origin; and that the study of personality by psychologists, and of man and society by sociologists and anthropologists, opened rich possibilities for further human development. More important still, it was the conservatives, not the progressives, who failed to see that big government was all that prevented the American Republic from becoming the feudal domain of the new industrial barons; that the advance of technology and the rise of pure science and the social sciences stripped traditional educational curricula of a large part of their reason for being; and that the law was neither created in a social vacuum nor could long remain static. Most important of all, it was the conservatives who clung to the fiction that nation-states could indefinitely survive under the law of the jungle.

Assuredly, the progressive mind had its faults. It expected and demanded more than most men could give. It was slow to understand that to solve one problem is to create another; and when it did grasp that truth after World War I, it became disillusioned. It flirted dangerously with political authoritarianism because of its uncritical acceptance of the new scientism. It distorted history even as it made history meaningful to its own generation. It placed its faith in an environmental interpretation of society that emphasized physical conditions too heavily and thus proved too simple. It submitted to a philosophical relativism of epochal proportions. It was also enamored of means—with the initiative, the referendum, and the recall as well as with government by commission—at the cost of a clear definition of its ends. In consequence, it failed to realize that the need to change the power structure of American society was more critical than the need to change the forms of democracy. Finally, it fell far short of achieving the synthesis its theoreticians—Croly, Lippmann, and Weyl—envisioned.

But to point up the progressive mind's flaws is not to deny its worth. No cynical appraisal of its motives, no reasoned critique of its paradoxes, no sophisticated rejection of the idea of progress—the virtual hallmark of progressivism—can deprive it of its rightful dignity and historical eminence. If it built imperfectly, it for the most part built humanely. And if it cast down the ancient absolutes, its act of negation was one of affirmation. For above all else, the progressive mind sought to create a society in which individual dignity could withstand the fearful onslaught of raw industrialism.

In the end, of course, both the progressive mind and the political movement it encompassed failed to devise a viable alternative to the corporate state; in fact, the progressives' emphasis on welfarism, scientism, and bureaucratization served ultimately to strengthen the corporate state. But this phenomenon was in no sense unique to American progressivism. On the contrary, it embodied the essential paradox of all advanced technological societies of the modern age, including the Asian nation Japan and the Marxist states that arose after World War I and World War II.

BIBLIOGRAPHY

George E. Mowry, *The Era of Theodore Roosevelt: 1900–1912** (New York: Harper & Row, 1958) is an admirable synthesis of progressivism's early phases. The same author's *Theodore Roosevelt and the Progressive Movement** (New York: Hill & Wang, 1960) is illuminating but dated in its treatment of the trust issue. Arthur S. Link, *Woodrow Wilson and the Progressive Era: 1910–1917** (New York: Harper & Row, 1954) is the best account of Democratic progressivism. A comprehensive regional survey is Russel B. Nye, *Midwestern Progressive Politics, 1870–1958,** rev. ed. (East Lansing: Michigan State University Press, 1959). Richard Hofstadter, *The Age of Reform: From Bryan to F.D.R.** (New York: Alfred A. Knopf, 1955) is suggestive although its central theses have been subjected to sharp and effective attack. Robert H. Wiebe, *The Search for Order: 1877–1920** (New York: Hill & Wang, 1968) offers new insights into the middle-class progressive mind. Ray Ginger, *The Age of Excess** (New York: Macmillan, 1965), Gabriel Kolko, *The Triumph of Conservatism** (Chicago: Quadrangle Books, 1967), and James Weinstein, *The Corporate Ideal in the Liberal State* (Boston: Beacon Press, 1968) are provocative works in the anticapitalist tradition of Matthew Josephson. Three other works of general value and considerable importance are: Sidney Fine, *Laissez Faire and the General Welfare State** (Ann Arbor, Mich.: University of Michigan Press, 1964); Robert F. Bremner, *From the Depths: The Discovery of Poverty in the United States** (New Haven: Yale University Press, 1956); and Horace S. and Marion G. Merrill, *The Republican Command, 1897–1913* (Lexington, Ky.: University of Kentucky Press, 1971).

A number of works treat progressivism in the cities and states. Among the best are: Richard M. Abrams, *Conservatism in a Progressive Era* (Cambridge: Harvard University Press, 1964), Robert S. Maxwell, *La Follette and the Rise of the Progressives in Wisconsin* (Madison: State Historical Society of Wisconsin, 1956), George Wallace Chessman, *Governor Theodore Roosevelt* (Cambridge: Harvard University Press, 1965), William D. Miller, *Memphis During the Progressive Era* (Providence: Brown University Press, 1957), Hoyt L. Warner, *Progressivism in Ohio, 1897–1917* (Columbus: Ohio State University Press, 1964), Zane L. Miller, *Boss Cox's Cincinnati: Urban Politics in the Progressive Era** (New York: Oxford University Press, 1968), and Robert B. Wesser, *Charles Evans Hughes: Politics and Reform in New York* (Ithaca, N.Y.: Cornell University Press, 1967). David P. Thelen, *The New Citizenship: The Origins of Progressivism in Wisconsin* (Columbia, Mo.: University of Missouri Press, 1972) is of special importance. Lincoln Steffens' highly readable and still informative contemporary articles are reprinted as *The Struggle for Self-Government* (New York: McClure, Phillips, 1906)

and *The Shame of the Cities** (New York: Hill & Wang, 1957). Many other works could be added to this sample.

There is no good comprehensive economic study of the era. There are, however, several specialized works. Alfred D. Chandler, Jr., *Strategy and Structure: Chapters in the History of the Industrial Enterprise** (Cambridge: M.I.T. Press, 1969) is a pioneering exploration of the corporation. Among the many other works that make substantial contributions are: Allan Nevins and Frank E. Hill, *Ford: The Times, the Man, the Company*, vol. 1 (New York: Scribner, 1954); Albert Rees, *Real Wages in Manufacturing, 1890–1914* (Princeton: Princeton University Press, 1961); Samuel Haber, *Efficiency and Uplift: Scientific Management in the Progressive Era, 1820–1920* (Chicago: University of Chicago Press, 1964); Morton Keller, *The Life Insurance Enterprise, 1885–1910* (Cambridge: Harvard University Press, 1963); and Harold Williamson and Associates, *The American Petroleum Industry*, 2 vols. (Evanston: Northwestern University Press, 1963).

There is also a growing literature on special aspects of the progressive era. Samuel P. Hays, *Conservation and the Gospel of Efficiency** (Cambridge: Harvard University Press, 1959) analyzes the conservation movement's scientific base. M. Nelson McGeary, *Gifford Pinchot* (Princeton: Princeton University Press, 1960) humanizes it. J. Leonard Bates, *The Origins of Teapot Dome* (Urbana: University of Illinois Press, 1963) carries the story into the Wilson administration. Alan P. Grimes, *The Puritan Ethic and Woman Suffrage* (New York: Oxford University Press, 1967) links the woman suffrage movement to prohibition, and James H. Timberlake, *Prohibition and the Progressive Movement, 1900–1920** (New York: Atheneum, 1970) offers an understanding account of why many progressives supported prohibition. Roy Lubove, *The Struggle for Social Security, 1900–1935* (Cambridge, Mass.: Harvard University Press, 1968) is an important contribution, as is Allen F. Davis, *Spearheads for Reform: The Social Settlements and the Progressive Movement, 1890–1914** (New York: Oxford University Press, 1970). Other recent works of interest include Aileen S. Kraditor, *The Ideas of the Woman Suffrage Movement, 1890–1920** (New York: Doubleday, 1971), Jeremy P. Felt, *Hostages of Fortune: Child Labor Reform* in New York State (Syracuse, N.Y.: Syracuse University Press, 1965), and Daniel M. Fox, *The Discovery of Abundance* (Ithaca, N.Y.: Cornell University Press, 1967).

The literature on labor and the left is voluminous. Ira Kipnis, *The American Socialist Movement: 1897–1912* (New York: Greenwood Press, 1952) should be supplemented by Ray Ginger's brilliant biography of Eugene V. Debs, *Eugene V. Debs** (New York: Collier, 1962), and David Shannon, *The Socialist Party of America** (Chicago: Quadrangle Books, 1967). Bernard Mandel, *Samuel Gompers* (Kent, Ohio: Kent State University Press, 1963) is the standard work on the A.F. of L. leader. Richard Drinnon, *Rebel in Paradise: A Biography of Emma Goldman* (Boston: Beacon Press, 1970) illumines the mind of an anarchist, and David Brody, *Labor in Crisis: The Steel Strike of 1919** (Philadelphia: Lippincott, 1965) puts the abortive effort to organize that industry in historical perspective.

Contrasting interpretations of Theodore Roosevelt are offered in Henry F. Pringle, *Theodore Roosevelt,** rev. ed. (New York: Harcourt Brace Jovanovich, Inc. 1956); John M. Blum, *The Republican Roosevelt** (Cambridge: Harvard University Press, 1954); and William H. Harbaugh, *The Life and Times of Theodore Roosevelt,** rev. ed. (New York: Collier, 1963). Louis W. Koenig, *Bryan: A Political Biography* (New York: G. P. Putnam's Sons, 1971) is the best one-volume work on Bryan. Henry F. Pringle, *The Life and Times of William Howard Taft,* 2 vols. (Hamden, Conn.: Shoe String Press, Inc., 1964) is a standard biography as is Merlo J. Pusey, *Charles Evans Hughes,* 2 vols. (New York: Columbia University Press, 1963). Belle Case and Fola La Follette, *Robert M. La Follette: 1855–1925,* 2 vols. (New York: Macmillan, 1953) is a loving but substantial account of the life of Roosevelt's great rival. Richard Lowitt, *George W. Norris,* vol. 1 (Syracuse: Syracuse University Press, 1963), vol. 2 (Urbana, Ill.: University of Illinois Press, 1971), carries Norris to 1932. Dewey W. Grantham, Jr., *Hoke Smith and the Politics of the New South** (Baton Rouge: Louisiana State University Press, 1958) is an informative account of one of the southern progressives.

Among the many biographies of lesser figures, the following are just a few of those worth examining: John A. Garraty, *Right-Hand Man: The Life of George W. Perkins* (New York: Har-

per & Row, 1960); Warren F. Kuehl, *Hamilton Holt* (Gainesville: University of Florida Press, 1960); Maurice M. Vance, *Charles Richard Van Hise, Scientist Progressive* (Madison: Wisconsin State Historical Society, 1960); Ira V. Brown, *Lyman Abbot* (New York: Greenwood Press, 1953); and Michael Wreszin, *Oswald Garrison Villard* (Bloomington: Indiana University Press, 1965).

The most informed and judicious survey of foreign affairs for this period is in Richard W. Leopold, *The Growth of American Foreign Policy* (New York: Alfred A. Knopf, 1962). Margaret Leech, *In the Days of McKinley* (New York: Harper & Row, 1959) redeems McKinley and adds a little luster he never had. H. Wayne Morgan, *William McKinley and His America* (Syracuse: Syracuse University Press, 1963) is more balanced though also favorable. Ernest R. May, *Imperial Democracy* (New York: Harcourt Brace Jovanovich, Inc. 1961) dissects the diplomacy of the decision to go to war in 1898. It is complemented by Julius W. Pratt, *Expansionists of 1898** (Chicago: Quadrangle Press, 1964) and Walter LaFeber, *The New Empire: An Interpretation of American Expansion** (Ithaca: Cornell University Press, 1963). The Filipinos' view of American expansion is sensitively examined in Leon Wolff, *Little Brown Brother* (Garden City: Doubleday, 1961). Both George F. Kennan, *American Diplomacy, 1900–1950** (New York: Mentor Books, 1952) and William A. Williams,* *The Tragedy of American Diplomacy,* rev. ed. (New York: Dell, 1962) conclude that American intervention in the Far East was deeply unfortunate. Among the more important of the spate of recent books on the United States and the Far East are Robert L. Beisner, *Twelve Against Empire* (New York: McGraw-Hill, 1968), Thomas J. McCormick, *China Market: America's Quest for Informal Empire, 1893–1901** (Chicago: Quadrangle Books, 1970), William A. Williams, *Roots of the Modern American Empire* (New York: Random House, 1969), Paul A. Varg, *The Making of a Myth* (East Lansing, Mich.: Michigan State University Press, 1968), Eugene P. Traini, *The Treaty of Portsmouth* (Lexington, Ky.: University of Kentucky Press, 1969), and Charles Neu, *An Uncertain Friendship: Theodore Roosevelt and Japan: 1906–1909* (Cambridge, Mass.: Harvard University Press, 1967).

Howard K. Beale, *Theodore Roosevelt and*

the *Rise of America to World Power**(New York: Collier, 1966) is a seminal, and in its exposition if not its conclusion, a favorable assessment of Roosevelt's conduct of foreign policy. The first five volumes of Arthur S. Link's *Wilson** (Princeton: Princeton University Press, 1947–65) carry its subject into World War I. TR's post-presidential career, Taft's handling of foreign policy, and the coming of the First World War are treated in the previously cited works by Harbaugh, Pringle, and Link. These works should be supplemented by Tyler Dennett, *John Hay: From Poetry to Politics* (Port Washington, N.Y.: Kennikat Press, 1933); Richard W. Leopold, *Elihu Root and the Conservative Tradition** (Boston: Little, Brown, 1954); Daniel M. Smith, *Robert Lansing and American Neutrality* (Berkeley: University of California Press, 1958); Howard F. Cline, *The United States and Mexico,** rev. ed. (New York: Atheneum, 1963); Dana G. Munro, *Intervention and Dollar Diplomacy in the Caribbean, 1900–1921* (Princeton: Princeton University Press, 1964); Robert E. Quirk, *An Affair of Honor** (New York: W. W. Norton, 1967); and others too numerous to mention.

Frederic L. Paxson, *American Democracy and the World War,* 3 vols. (New York: Cooper Square, 1948) is still a useful survey of the nation at war. H. C. Peterson and Gilbert C. Fite, *Opponents of War, 1917–1918** (Seattle: University of Washington Press, 1968) is a biting account of the suppression of civil liberties in wartime as is William Preston, Jr., *Aliens and Dissenters**(New York: Harper & Row, 1963). Robert K. Murray, *Red Scare** (New York: McGraw-Hill, 1954) is a standard work. Stanley Coben, *A. Mitchell Palmer* (New York: Columbia University Press, 1963) offers a rounded evaluation of the man partly responsible for the excesses of the Red Scare. A highly sympathetic account of Wilson and the peacemaking is Arthur Walworth, *Woodrow Wilson,** 2nd ed. (Baltimore: Penguin, 1969). It should be read against John A. Garraty, *Henry Cabot Lodge* (New York: Alfred A. Knopf, 1953). Thomas A. Bailey, *Wilson and the Peacemakers* (New York: Macmillan, 1947) retains much of its original value. Also see Arthur S. Link, *Wilson the Diplomatist** (Baltimore: Johns Hopkins University Press, 1957) and N. Gordon Levin, Jr., *Woodrow Wilson and World Politics: America's Response to War and Revolution** (New York: Oxford University Press, 1970). The story of the

election of 1920 is ably told in Wesley M. Bagby, *The Road to Normalcy** (Baltimore: Johns Hopkins Press, 1962).

Among the intellectual histories, the following more or less survey the period: Henry F. May, *The End of American Innocence**(Chicago: Quadrangle Books, 1964); Stow Persons, *American Minds* (New York: Holt, Rinehart and Winston, Inc., 1958); and Henry Steele Commager, *The American Mind** (New Haven: Yale University Press, 1950). Charles Forcey, *The Crossroads of Liberalism** (New York: Oxford University Press, 1961) analyzes the thought of Croly, Lippmann, and Weyl, while David W. Noble, *The Paradox of Progressive Thought* (Minneapolis: University of Minnesota Press, 1958) treats them and several others. Morton G. White, *Social Thought in America** (Boston: Beacon Press, 1957) is especially good on the breakdown of formalism.

Many works treat immigrants and ethnic groups including the Negro. Among those which stand out are: Oscar Handlin, *The Uprooted** (Boston: Little, Brown and Co., 1951); John Higham, *Strangers in the Land** (New York: Atheneum, 1963); Donald B. Cole, *Immigrant City: Lawrence, Massachusetts, 1845–1921* (Chapel Hill: University of North Carolina Press, 1963); Gilbert Osofsky, *Harlem**(New York: Harper & Row, 1966); August Meier, *Negro Thought in America, 1880–1915** (Ann Arbor: University of Michigan Press, 1963), one of the few works to take a balanced view of Booker T. Washington; and Elliot M. Rudwick, *W. E. B. DuBois: Propagandist of the Negro Protest* (New York: Atheneum, 1968). Other important works include Louis R. Harlan, *Separate and Unequal: Public School Campaigns and Racism in the Southern Seaboard States 1900–1915** (New York: Atheneum, 1968), Rayford W. Logan, *The Betrayal of the Negro** (New York: Collier Books, 1965), Allen H. Spear, *Black Chicago* (Chicago: University of Chicago Press, 1967), and Charles Flint Kellogg, *A History of the National Association for the Advancement of Colored People, 1909–1920* (Baltimore: Johns Hopkins University Press, 1967).

Lawrence A. Cremin, *The Transformation of the School** (New York: Vintage, 1961) is a work of considerable insight. Henry F. May, *Protestant Churches and Industrial America** (New York: Harper & Row, 1963) and Charles H. Hopkins, *The Rise of the Social Gospel in American Protestantism, 1860–1915* (New Haven: Yale University

Press, 1940) are highly informative. David M. Chalmers, *The Social and Political Ideas of the Muckrakers** (New York: Citadel, 1964) is suggestive. John E. Burchard and Albert Bush-Brown, *The Architecture of America** (Boston: Little, Brown and Co., 1961) interweaves history and esthetics. Alfred Kazin's classic *On Native Grounds** (New York: Doubleday, 1942) should be supplemented by Charles C. Walcutt, *American Literary Naturalism, a Divided Stream* (Minneapolis: University of Minnesota Press, 1956).

The student should also consult the bibliography at the end of Chapter 15 for many titles which are also pertinent to this section.

*Denotes a paperback.

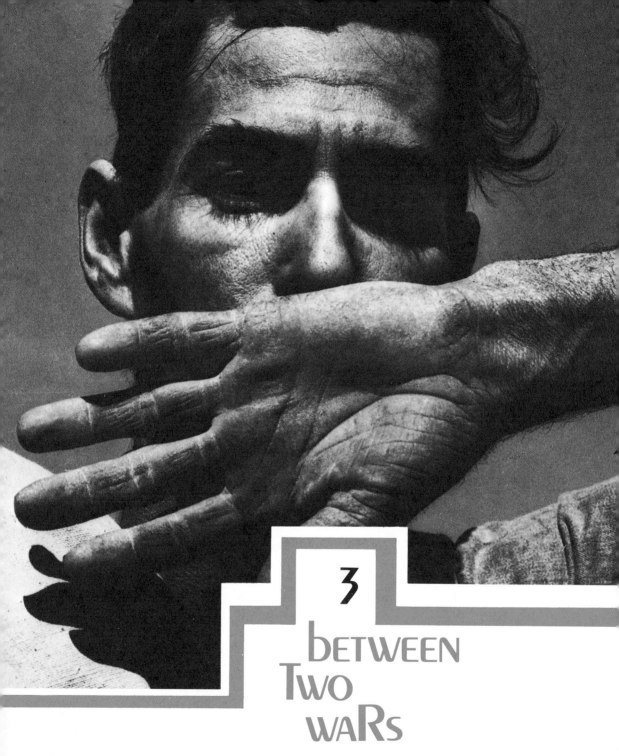

3

bETWEEN TwO waRs

SINCE THE BEGINNING OF INDUSTRIALISM, CHANGES IN THE PHYSICAL basis of society have been continuous. When the changes produce results in harmony with social traditions and values, they have been easily adjusted to. When they threaten such social norms, their effects have been resisted.

In the years between World War I and World War II, progress in technology continued steadily to alter living and working conditions. The true motorization of the United States came in the 1920s. The motion picture displaced live entertainment in all but a few score theaters in the larger cities. Radio, unknown to the general public in 1920, had already reached a high level of social importance by 1932, when Franklin Delano Roosevelt's soon-to-be-familiar salutation, "My friends," began to be heard.

An abrupt political change reversed three centuries of American practice: immigration had been halted by the war, and in 1921 Congress took action to curtail the great influx from abroad. Thereafter, America looked largely to its own underemployed to meet its labor demands. One immediate effect was to open up job opportunities for the rural poor, and since the most depressed farmers were blacks, these men and their families came to the cities by the hundreds of thousands throughout the war and the prosperous twenties. The creation of ghettos of erstwhile rural blacks alongside those of the more recent European immigrants laid the basis for both immediate and future urban problems.

There were important changes in ideas and attitudes as well. The rearing of children came to be scientifically guided. Education for social adjustment reached a peak and produced a generation less bound than its predecessors by traditional values and beliefs. Women assumed a new leadership in the war on Victorian manners and morals. From 1920 Freud's theories of the unconscious and its force in motivating conduct gained wide acceptance; and late in the twenties the popularization of mathematical physics forced intellectuals, at least, to recognize still greater inadequacies in human perception and in the simple verbal logic by which men had always reasoned.

All these changes were important at the time; all have had effects in the decades since. But the changes that struck hardest at the values of the society as a whole were the changes that forced individuals to recognize that they had lost much of their self-sufficiency and forced government to assume new functions. The changes represented a continuation of the march of industrialism: ever-growing corporations, employing more and more thousands of workers; increasingly crowded and less livable cities; and all the countless effects of this trend toward impersonal giantism. But the adjustments went contrary to deeply held beliefs in the self-regulating economy and the virtue of individual initiative and self-help.

Even such an inherently unstable situation may endure with relatively little change until some disruptive event produces a crisis. In the United States, World War I was not disruptive. With the return of peace, businessmen and most other Americans quickly resumed their prewar practices; in fact, much of the dominant middle class tried to reach backward to resurrect earlier political and social attitudes.

The temporary change in production from consumer goods to military supplies, and the creation of a large national debt in private hands, generated a strong postwar consumer demand that made the 1920s, in general, a period of prosperity during which the well-to-do could safely close their eyes to mounting social problems. Meanwhile, the automobile recast the spacial relations of society, slums grew worse, wages were held down, and economic stability came to depend, not on rising mass consumption, but on loans to foreign governments and businesses, through the purchase of their bonds, and on manipulation of domestic securities. Between late 1929 and 1931 the unstable system collapsed, sending upsetting reverberations throughout the world and, particularly in Germany and the United States, ushering in a depression too deep to be long endured.

The major issues of the period center around the partially successful efforts of Franklin D. Roosevelt's administration to cure the lingering, recurrent depression. In general these took the form of providing greater security for all groups—farmers, workers, investors, householders, the aged, and the unemployed—through the regulatory and financial power of the federal government. Although the measures now seem mildly palliative, they nevertheless contradicted the value America traditionally placed on freedom of action and individual responsibility. They were the subject of bitter contemporary debate, and they have undergone varying interpretations by historians.

To the majority of the people, and to an even larger proportion of the historians who personally experienced these "years of hardship," Herbert Hoover seemed an obscurantist conservative, while Franklin D. Roosevelt stood forth as a strong, liberal humanitarian, personally responsible for fundamental reforms that combatted the depression as effectively as could be done by federal action. Henry Steele Commager and Allan Nevins serve as outstanding exemplars of this contemporary view. Among the few anti-Roosevelt historians were unfaltering believers in the self-regulating economy like Edgar E. Robinson, some moderate socialists like Broadus Mitchell who thought the President's actions inadequate, and isolationists in foreign policy led by Charles A. Beard. In the ranks of important professional historians writing on the period, there were no Communists.

Over the next generation the liberal interpretation was eroded by streams of ideas stemming from quite different sources. As economists were gradually won over to the views of the great English theorist, John Maynard Keynes, they learned that there were sound theoretical reasons why the economy was not self-regulating and that had Roosevelt comprehended the importance of government spending, he might have ended the depression by means other than preparation for World War II. The President's most successful biographer, James McGregor Burns, writing in the mid-1950s, saw Roosevelt as a man of limited intellectual ability but with a keen grasp of politics—essentially, the charming politician. As a corollary, the reforms of the period have come to be seen as of the type that any President responsive to congressional and public opinion would have to have made, and Roosevelt as a leader who did no more than was necessary while always trying to conciliate the conservatives. This view gives more credit to the leadership of congressional liberals such as Senator Robert F. Wagner of New York. By the 1960s, members of a New Left movement among historians saw the period much as had the socialist intellectuals of an earlier time. According to both groups, Roosevelt had saved capitalism without substantially improving it and, as Beard had charged earlier, had cured domestic troubles by deliberately leading the country into World War II.

Whatever the interpretations of the era, much of the historic America survived the interwar years, including the years of the Great Depression. For many of its people, the economic breakdown seemed like a final blow after the attacks of science on some of their most cherished beliefs—from how to raise children to how to reason logically. But for all the uncertainty about the nature of man and the universe (not to mention the banking system), many of the traditional values governing American society persisted, and some even thrived on adversity. In many walks of life, the New Deal strengthened the old ideals of equality and democracy. At the end of the era, as they prepared for another war, Americans seemed to be striving to retain as much of their heritage as new circumstances would permit.

FOR THOUGHT AND DISCUSSION

1. Can any conclusions about the American character fairly be drawn from the Great Red Scare and the popularity of the Klan in the 1920s? Is there both hatred and fear of anything "alien" (see the immigration restrictions of 1921, 1924)? Is there a strong, continuing tendency to chauvinsim? to violence?

2. Why has Marxism, a strong tradition in the European labor movement, had so little success among American workers?

3. How much did the depression of the 1930s contribute to today's generation gap?

4. Do you think FDR started America down the road to socialism? Or do you believe he saved the Establishment and preserved the status quo? Why?

5. Judging from the radical groups that gained large followings in the 1930s, are American institutions more endangered from the Left or from the Right? From those in power, from the poor, or from the middle class? Do the radical groups that have developed since the 1930s provide support for your opinion?

6. Would we be better off today if we had joined with other powers in actively opposing the aggressive moves of Japan, Italy, and Germany in the 1930s? If we had remained neutral not only in the 1930s but throughout World War II?

and secure the blessings of LiberTy for ourselves & Our posteriTy

CHAPTER 7

PROSPERITY IN ISOLATION
1919–29

THE SWING TOWARD CONSERVATISM

Postwar Reaction. Nineteen-nineteen was a year of disillusionment. During the war progressives, once satisfied with social legislation and national regulation of trusts, had raised their hopes for such fundamental changes as federal control of railroads, shipping, prices, and employment. John Dewey, America's most famous philosopher, had predicted in 1918 that "no matter how many among the special agencies for public control decay with the disappearance of war stress, the movement will never go backward." But during 1919 the movement toward a public-regulated economy not only receded but was lost altogether in a wave of reaction.

Like all sweeping changes in opinion, the swing to conservatism between early 1919 and 1920 had many causes. The unsatisfactory peace in Europe, publicized in the worst light by opponents of the League of Nations, cooled the popular enthusiasm that President Wilson had temporarily aroused. The result appears to have been an apathy about America's role in world affairs that carried over into domestic issues as well.

Along with this indifference to further reform there was undoubtedly a real fear on the part of middle-class Americans that revolution on the Russian model might spread. Socialism had ceased to be a utopian goal, safe to discuss at women's club meetings, and had become a gray, alien world of commissars and secret police. As a result, the unprecedented series of strikes used by labor in 1919 to keep wages abreast of soaring prices was widely regarded as a dangerous indication of revolutionary sentiment, inspired by the subversive activities of a foreign power. In some cases management publicly condemned the strikers as Reds.

Political demagogues were, of course, ready to ride to power by playing upon such fears. On January 1, 1920, agents of Attorney General A. Mitchell Palmer arrested nearly three thousand allegedly alien radicals and held them without hearings under the Sedition Act of 1918. Friends who subsequently inquired about those arrested were also jailed. The ailing President protested mildly against Palmer's activities, but the antiradical campaign gained momentum. Of the thousands of aliens rounded up by the Attorney General, 556 were deported, after trial, for radical activity.

Seventeen states passed "criminal syndicalist" laws providing for the arrest of agitators. The New York state legislature carried out a lengthy investigation of revolutionary radicalism and refused to seat Socialist representatives from New York

City. Meanwhile, Congress refused to admit Victor Berger from Wisconsin until that very moderate Socialist had again been elected by his Milwaukee constituents.

At the height of this "Red scare," the arrest and conviction of two alien anarchists, Nicola Sacco and Bartolomeo Vanzetti, for the murder of a factory paymaster and guard during a robbery in South Braintree, Massachusetts, turned out to be the *cause célèbre* of the 1920s. Because of the alleged bias of the judge and the prejudicial tactics of the prosecuting attorney at the trial, many liberals protested that the men had been convicted for their radicalism rather than for the stated crime. In the six years following their conviction in 1921, protest meetings took place all over the world, and men of international prominence like Albert Einstein and Anatole France gave their support to petitions urging clemency or a retrial. In Massachusetts, however, public opinion remained hostile; a special commission headed by the president of Harvard found that the trial had been fair and that the defendants were guilty; and on August 23, 1927, Sacco and Vanzetti were electrocuted in an atmosphere of martyrdom.

The most alarming aspect of the wave of anti-Red hysteria in the 1920s was not the injustices visited upon a few hundred leftists and aliens but the general suppression of free thought that accompanied the unrelenting efforts of the Attorney General and certain "patriotic" societies. Teachers became afraid to impart normal, necessary criticisms of American leaders and American society. Business employees were afraid to be associated with men or organizations branded by the superpatriots as subversive. Liberal journals were called revolutionary, and people were afraid to be seen reading them. Compared to the Red scare of the 1950s, that of the early twenties was less serious in its impact on government but probably more repressive in its effect on the ordinary citizen.

In the back country, especially in the South and a few parts of the Middle West, the hysteria gave a sinister impetus to the Ku Klux Klan, which was revived in 1915 "to unite white male persons, native-born Gentile citizens, who owe no allegiance of any nature to any foreign government, nation, institution, sect, ruler, person or people." The members were united against blacks, Catholics (who were held to owe allegiance to a foreign ruler), Jews, and foreigners. The Klan had shown little tendency to grow until the postwar anti-Red campaign got under way, but in 1920, under Edward Y. Clarke, a professional organizer and fund raiser, it quickly became a powerful force both socially and politically. By 1924 it had several million members. Since the initiation fee was $10, large resources were at the disposal of Klan leaders, who used them to influence—in some cases to control—state politics.

At the level of the local den, however, the Klan was largely an organization for leisure time enjoyment, community economic pressure, and irresponsible use of force. A congressional investigation revealed that blacks and foreigners were intimidated into selling property to Klan members at low prices and into avoiding business competition with them. Citizens defending blacks, foreigners, or Catholics might also incur the vengeance of the Klan. The hooded parades, secret meetings, fiery crosses, beatings, and lynchings were signs of the frustration of men in declining rural areas.

Against the ominous rise of lower middle-class reaction, the stuff of which fascism was to be made in Germany, must be placed the continuation of liberal and even radical farmer movements in the Northwest. Led by the old Non-Partisan League, a Farmer-Labor party ran second to the victorious Republicans in the election of 1920 in Minnesota, South Dakota, and Washington. Thus, the decentralized character of American politics sustained minority movements while making it difficult for them to win national power.

Triumph of the Conservatives. In the middle of the confusing year 1920 the two national conventions met to nominate candidates for the presidency. The leading Republican contenders—Governor Frank O. Lowden of Illinois and General Leonard Wood—fought each other to a deadlock. The compromise candidate supported by a group of business representatives and conservative congressional leaders was Senator Warren G. Harding of Ohio, a man virtually unknown to the American public but one who had the gracious, commanding look of a President. For Vice-President the convention nominated Calvin Coolidge, the Massachusetts governor famous for his stand against organized labor in the Boston police strike of 1919.

The Democrats had even greater difficulty in choosing a candidate. During thirty-seven indecisive ballots, Attorney General Palmer, the anti-Red champion, fought William G. McAdoo, the liberal ex-Secretary of the Treasury and son-in-law of Woodrow Wilson. Then the convention compromised on a progressive who had been twice reelected governor of Ohio, James M. Cox. While Cox was as little known to the general public as Harding, the Democratic ticket was strengthened by the vice-presidential nomination of Assistant Secretary of the Navy Franklin D. Roosevelt.

Partly in deference to President Wilson, Cox and Roosevelt made entry into the League of Nations a major issue of the campaign. The Republicans avoided commitment on the League question and instead advocated higher tariffs and tax reduction. Reading the popular temper correctly, they were extremely confident. During the campaign Harding stayed on his front porch in Marion, Ohio; his speeches, according to McAdoo, were "an army of pompous phrases moving across the landscape in search of an idea." In spite of—or perhaps because of—the assurance of victory, the Republicans were aided by a campaign fund of $8 million.

The Republican landslide was the greatest since the second election of James Monroe. Harding carried every state outside the "solid South," and there he carried Tennessee. He received 61 percent of the popular vote, as much as Franklin D. Roosevelt was to poll in his greatest victory. In Congress the Republicans could not score quite so great a sweep as the Democrats in 1936, because of the Democratic representatives from the South, but the Republican majority was 167 in the House and 22 in the Senate.

Harding Administration Scandals. Although Harding was probably not far below the average intelligence of the less prominent Presidents of the United States, he was lacking in ideas, vigor, and moral conviction. Easygoing and affable, he delegated too much responsibility. Harding appointed old friends to many important posts, though he offset these weak appointments by naming Charles E. Hughes Secretary of State; Andrew Mellon, Secretary of the Treasury; Henry A. Wallace, Secretary of Agriculture; and Herbert Hoover, Secretary of Commerce.

Harding's friends, with whom he often played poker late into the night, soon began taking bribes and misusing funds on a scale that could not be concealed. Late in 1922 Harding learned that Charles R. Forbes had stolen millions from the Veterans' Bureau. By the summer of 1923 there was a rumor that the House, now controlled by Democrats and Progressives, might try to impeach the President. But on August 2, in the midst of the increasing revelations of corruption, Harding died of an apoplectic stroke.

Ultimately investigations and trials revealed that Attorney General Harry M. Daugherty had profited from the enforcement of prohibition and the handling of alien property; Secretary of the Interior Albert B. Fall had received many thousands of dollars from oil men Harry F. Sinclair and E. L. Doheny for leasing them valuable government oil reserves in Teapot Dome, Wyoming, and in Elk Hills, California; Forbes had cost the taxpayers some $250 million more than necessary for hospitals and other veterans' benefits; and many lesser men had profited from the President's lack of judgment and rigor.

With Vice-President Calvin Coolidge now succeeding to the presidency, the Republican party had a man superbly qualified to make amends for the laxity of the Harding administration. Coolidge, a slight, dry-looking, diffident Vermonter who after graduation from Amherst had won success in Massachusetts law and politics, seemed to personify the traditional virtues of thrift and frugality. He would not be betrayed by his intimate friends, because he had none. At a time when business and most of the middle class seemed satisfied with the status quo, Coolidge could be relied upon not to rock the boat.

Republican National Policy. Led for eight years either by Harding, who had been installed by the right wing of the party, or by Coolidge, whom Hoover called a "real conservative," the Republican administration tried to lessen or remove controls over business activity. In this policy the President was often at odds with Democratic-Progressive coalitions in the House and the Senate, but the presidential powers of appointment and veto proved effective weapons in cutting down federal activities.

Ocean shipping presented special problems. At the end of the war the government owned some two million deadweight tons of hastily constructed freighters which were slow and inefficient in comparison with new turbine or diesel electric vessels coming from British and Continental yards. In addition, United States wages and manning requirements made it impossible for American ship owners to compete on an equal basis with foreign operators. To keep some of the ships at sea the Shipping Board for a decade pursued a policy of selling the freighters for $5 to $10 a ton and granting mail subsidies for operation on strategically important routes.

One of the first conflicts between the conservative President and the less conservative Congress was over the soldiers' bonus bill. This proposed legislation provided a twenty-year endowment policy totaling $1 for each day a veteran had served in the United States and $1.25 for each day overseas. President Harding in 1921 and President Coolidge in 1924 vetoed the bill; the Harding veto was sustained, but a more generous Congress overrode that of Coolidge.

Immigration Quotas. A major change in American political policy in the 1920s was the regulation of immigration on a quota basis. While the Chinese and Japanese had been excluded by diplomatic agreements and other Asian and African people had not attempted to immigrate in any large numbers, the United States had held the door open for most Europeans. Organized labor and "old stock" Americans had long tried to restrict the vast flood of newcomers, which in peaceful and prosperous years comprised more than a million annually. Finally, a combination of factors—resumption of heavy immigration from eastern Europe, unemployment at home, and the Red scare—led Congress to establish quotas based on the number of foreign-born residents in 1910. Opposed vigorously in Congress only by Catholics, the bill met a veto by Wilson. Passed again in the special session of 1921, it was signed by Harding. During the first year of operation the restrictions reduced immigration from around the million level to 300,000.

To organized labor and nativists, however, the number of "undesirable" or "unassimilable" immigrants from eastern Europe still seemed too large. The National Origins Act of 1924 set up a temporary quota of 2 percent of the foreign-born of 1890 and established a commission to work out quotas by a formula based on numbers of foreign-born over the whole range of United States census data. The bill excluded Orientals; Japan, which had been voluntarily restricting emigration to the United States, regarded this as an affront to national dignity, but the Japanese protest was brushed aside by Congress. Enacted into law in 1929, the final report of the Commission on National Origins reduced southern and eastern European quotas to negligible size and held the total of restricted immigrants to about 150,000 annually. Citizens of countries in the Western Hemisphere were exempted from restriction.

Tariffs, Taxes, and Federal Regulation. High tariff continued to be a major Republican policy. Ironically, the protectionist group in Congress in the early 1920s was led by Midwestern farmers who feared Canadian, Irish, and Argentine competition. Their first bill for increased agricultural duties was vetoed by Wilson on the grounds that American farmers also needed foreign markets. The Harding administration favored higher duties, but the increases in the Fordney-McCumber Tariff of 1922 were generally moderate. Although agricultural products gained protection, the principle of a tariff that would equalize prices of domestic and foreign products was generally maintained. The farm bloc managed to get manufactures like shoes and wagons on the free list, but some industries received very high protection. The Tariff Commission still had the right to recommend changes, and the President had the power to alter the rates by 50 percent. Neither Harding nor Coolidge made important use of this power.

The Republican Presidents appointed conservative, business-minded members to federal regulatory commissions. This led to such a relaxation in vigilance that, in the words of a famous authority, the Federal Trade Commission "tried to commit *hara-kiri*"—to cease functioning as a regulatory agency. Moreover, the antitrust division of the Justice Department seldom prosecuted mergers; the Federal Power Commission, established in 1920 to regulate interstate electric power, did little to justify its existence; and the efforts of the Interstate Commerce Commission to bring about railroad consolidation and recapture excess earnings were without significant effect.

Freed from fear of federal regulation, businessmen also were gradually relieved of the higher taxes of the war period. Andrew Mellon, formerly head of the Aluminum Company of America and one of the richest men in the world, believed sincerely that high income taxes retarded economic growth. As Secretary of the Treasury he immediately sponsored a tax bill that repealed the excess profits tax and sharply reduced the surtaxes on personal income. After amendments by the Republican farm bloc and by Democrats in the Senate, the Revenue Act of 1921 repealed the excess profits tax but cut the maximum surtax on personal income only from 65 to 50 percent. Nevertheless, since revenues steadily exceeded expenses, there was increasing pressure for tax reduction. By 1929 four subsequent revenue acts had reduced the maximum surtax to 20 percent and the effective initial rate to $3/_8$ of 1 percent. The tax on corporate income was slightly reduced, to 11 percent.

These tax reductions, which retarded repayment of the national debt and left it at $16 billion at the beginning of the Great Depression, have been vigorously criticized. Yet the administration faced a real economic dilemma. To have repaid the debt more rapidly would have released to the money markets as much cash as came from the untaxed savings of high incomes, if not more. Only if the government could have found a way to use the money so as to increase lower incomes or to pay it to some of the two million unemployed could the surplus have been kept from feeding the inflation in stocks and mortgage bonds. Such a fiscal policy would have been directly contrary to the firmly held beliefs of the conservative majority and, as an explicit policy, probably beyond the imagination of most of the more liberal minority.

One proposed use for federal funds which would not have involved the government in new types of business or competed with private industry was the support of farm incomes. Farmers had been led by the demands of World War I to expand wheat acreage, which in view of long-run trends was already excessive in 1914. After the collapse of the reconstruction boom in 1920, farm prices fell more than those of things the farmer had to buy, and both foreign and domestic markets for such staples as wheat and cotton declined. Farmers were not participating in the general prosperity.

A plan put forward by two farm machinery manufacturers in 1922 did not involve federal subsidy but merely required a federal marketing agency that could maintain a domestic price in excess of the world price. Written into the McNary-Haugen Bill and endorsed by practically all farmer organizations, the proposal was resisted by conservative Republicans as a dangerous extention of federal power. The bill was passed in 1926 and again in 1927 but killed both times by a Coolidge veto.

Although by the late 1930s the Farm Bureau Federation, the chief agricultural pressure group, was to seem conservative, in the 1920s it formed a rallying point for liberals. In spite of the conservative presidential leadership, progressives of both parties maintained their strength in Congress. The greatest obstacle to liberal victories during the decade was probably not the relatively small group of conservatives with substantial incomes but the general political apathy bred by prosperity from 1923 to

1929. Presidential elections drew only a little more than half the voters to the polls: Coolidge was sustained in the 1924 presidential election by a mere 28 percent of the possible electorate.

EXPANSION OF GOVERNMENT ACTIVITIES

Federal, State, and Local Change. Even within the administration, men like Charles E. Hughes and Herbert Hoover did not share the Coolidge standpat type of conservatism. Hoover, as Secretary of Commerce, tried to bring more efficiency into business operations. To avoid destructive competition he urged small companies to have trade associations administer their mutual concerns, and he invited them to post their prices with the Commerce Department and to refrain from secret rebates. To lower production costs he put his influence behind the movement for standard sizes. The number of shapes of bottles and the various sizes of bricks, for example, were both cut 90 percent. After unsuccessfully preaching self-regulation to the young air transport and radio industries, his department established regulatory agencies in 1926 and 1927 respectively. In these directions Hoover was a planner, but, as he saw it, he was using the power of government primarily to suggest better voluntary planning to private industry.

State and local authorities, still the most important forms of government, were led to greatly expand their operations. Increasing high-school education, in particular, demanded new buildings and bigger school budgets. Skyscrapers concentrated so many workers in the centers of the largest cities that new public transportation was required. On the other hand, automobiles moved so many families to the open areas of the cities or suburbs that new streets and sewers were continually needed. New York and some other states increased the scope and size of their expenditures for welfare. New laws or municipal ordinances regulating business practices, sanitation, and housing required new bureaus and squads of inspectors. From all these needs of a growing industrial society the expenses of government soared. Between 1922 and 1927 the annual cost of state and local government rose nearly 40 percent, and the rise had undoubtedly passed 50 percent by 1929. The debts of these governments increased even faster, up nearly 50 percent from 1922 to 1927 and perhaps by two thirds, had figures been collected, by 1929. It is also worth remembering that in 1929 these governments cost about two and a half times as much to run as the federal government and had about twice as many civilian employees, exclusive of school teachers. Thus what appears on the federal level to have been a period of low government expenditure and reduction of debt was *in toto* one of rapid increase in expenditure and dangerous accumulation of local indebtedness.

Security in the Pacific. While there was a vigorous movement for the League of Nations and world peace, most of the minority of Americans who thought about foreign relations probably wanted to avoid being involved in either European or Far Eastern affairs. The war against Germany was ended by a resolution of Congress on

July 2, 1921, and separate treaties were negotiated with the new governments of Germany, Austria, and Hungary, but Far Eastern problems were not settled.

Meanwhile the Navy Department had plans for building the world's largest battle fleet. In spite of congressional refusal to pass the big-navy bills, England and Japan were deeply worried over the possibility of having to compete with the United States in naval construction. Therefore, they readily accepted Secretary of State Hughes' invitation to meet in Washington in 1921 to discuss naval disarmament. Since a naval agreement would have to be linked with treaties establishing and guaranteeing Far Eastern arrangements, France, Italy, Belgium, the Netherlands, and Portugal, nations with Asiatic territories, were invited to the conference together with China.

Early in 1922 Secretary Hughes led the way to a naval agreement whereby England, Japan, and the United States scrapped hundreds of thousands of tons of battleships, afloat or in construction, and agreed to a 5–5–3 ratio for capital ships, with Britain and the United States at equal strength and Japan held to 60 percent of that tonnage. To secure Japan's interests in the western Pacific each party agreed not to fortify new bases or enlarge old ones. World War II was to demonstrate that this arrangement, as planned, gave Japan an initial supremacy in its nearby waters. After some argument, France and Italy joined in the treaty, each limiting the tonnage of its capital ships to 35 percent of the Anglo-American maximum. A new Four-Power Pact (United States, British Empire, France, Japan) replaced the Anglo-Japanese Alliance and pledged the powers to respect each other's possessions and rights in the Pacific. A Nine-Power Pact, also concluded during the Washington Conference, affirmed the sovereignty, independence, and administrative and territorial integrity of China. The American policy of an "open door" for Chinese trade was reaffirmed.

War Debts and International Cooperation. The Washington treaties established a system of security for Asia such as the Treaty of Versailles was presumed to have provided for Europe, but the latter had a major weakness: an unrealistic structure of reparations and war debts. In 1921 Germany was forced to accept a reparations commission bill for $33 billion, but no such sum could be transferred in a few decades from one European country to the others without severely disrupting the economies involved. Similarly the United States tried to collect war debts of $4.6 billion from England, $4 billion from France, and $2 billion from Italy. The European states advised a general cancellation of all international payments that would endanger normal economic growth, but Presidents from Wilson to Roosevelt insisted on the principle of collection.

Since such sums could be paid only in goods and since United States tariffs limited imports, payments were regularly more than balanced by new American lending and investment abroad. Throughout the decade bankers sold annually about $1 billion worth of foreign government, municipal, and corporate bonds to American investors. This was a profitable system for the bankers, and by giving foreigners dollars to spend, it allowed United States manufacturers to maintain large exports, but it meant that world financial stability depended on continued prosperity and an easy money market in the United States.

From the start, Germany was unable to pay the reparations assessed by the commission. In 1924 the so-called Dawes Plan, devised by Owen D. Young and Charles G. Dawes of the United States, cut reparations to what seemed like a manageable level, and in 1929 the Young Plan further reduced payments. By now the $33 billion bill had shrunk to about $2 billion. During the 1920s the Allies paid the United States about $2.6 billion in war debts, and the Americans loaned Germany some $2.5 billion, 80 percent of which went to the Allies. Therefore, in fact, there was nearly a mutual balancing. The Allies paid the United States, which loaned to Germany, which paid reparations to Allies, and the cycle continued. But the American investors and banks that had advanced the money were left with foreign bonds that soon defaulted on their interest payments.

Meanwhile, the United States pursued a rather uncertain course of international cooperation. Secretary of State Hughes started the practice of sending "unofficial observers" to League of Nations sessions and to meetings of the principal League committees, but isolationists in the Senate prevented the United States from joining the World Court. This, however, did not prevent Americans, as individuals, from serving as justices. In 1928 Secretary of State Frank B. Kellogg took the lead in negotiating a general agreement to outlaw war as an instrument of national policy. The Pact of Paris, or Kellogg-Briand Pact, was signed ultimately by all the great powers, but Kellogg regarded the pledge as more valuable for appeasing peace sentiment at home than for influencing foreign nations. Providing no means of applying collective sanctions against an aggressor, the pact was an idealistic but empty gesture.

Paradoxically, the idealistic foreign policy of Woodrow Wilson had left the United States deeply involved in the affairs of Caribbean countries. United States troops were in Haiti, Nicaragua, and the Dominican Republic, and diplomatic relations with Mexico had been suspended. On the South American mainland, hostility toward United States occupations interfered with both trade and investment.

Republican Leadership Reaffirmed. In the depression year of 1922 discontented agrarian and labor elements met in a Conference for Progressive Political Action. Continuing its meetings into 1924, the conference agreed to support the presidential nomination of Senator Robert M. La Follette at the Republican convention and, if defeated there, to organize a third party with La Follette as its candidate.

Obviously the progressive minority had no chance of winning the Republican nomination, but it might have been captured by the Democrats if that party had supported an advanced liberal ticket. The Democratic party, however, was disastrously split over such issues as prohibition, the Ku Klux Klan, Catholicism, and immigration restriction. Hampered additionally by a rule requiring a two-thirds majority for nomination, its convention took 103 ballots to select a relatively unknown New York corporation lawyer, John W. Davis, who failed to inspire enthusiasm in any faction.

When the Republican convention met and nominated Coolidge on the first ballot, the Progressives held their own convention and put forward La Follette. Supported by the American Federation of Labor, many Western farm organizations, and the Socialist party, La Follette ran on a platform advocating the type of action that

Europeans called social-democratic. Nationalization was to apply only to railroads and hydroelectric power; injunctions in labor disputes were to be effectively forbidden; and Congress was to be given power to overrule the Supreme Court.

Coolidge swept the election with 15,718,000 popular votes to 8,385,000 for Davis and 4,831,000 for La Follette. The latter carried only Wisconsin, and Davis won only the solid South. The Progressive party had failed to develop the strength necessary for survival.

Few American Presidents have enjoyed four such prosperous, peaceful, and generally pleasant years as those from 1924 to 1928. Coolidge could easily have been renominated and reelected had he chosen to run for a second elected term in 1928. But after keeping the bosses in doubt long enough to preserve his influence in the convention, Coolidge gave his support to Herbert Hoover. Quickly nominated, Hoover ran on a platform of continuing the Harding-Coolidge policies. With these, he said, "we shall soon, with the help of God, be in sight of the day when poverty shall be banished from this nation."

The Democratic managers probably had little hope of defeating a strong Republican, but they thought that an unusual candidate might bring new voters to the polls. Such reasoning may explain the swing to Governor Alfred E. Smith of New York, a Catholic of Irish immigrant parentage, who emphasized his origins by wearing a brown derby. The Democratic platform scarcely differed from the Republican, and on economic questions Smith differed little from Hoover. Smith made John J. Raskob, a fellow Catholic and chairman of the Finance Committee of General Motors, manager of the Democratic campaign. Raskob gave the utmost assurance to business that there would be no upsetting changes.

Aside from the immense support given the Republicans by the boom prosperity, the issues came to be Catholicism and prohibition. Smith could do nothing about the former except give assurances of his independence from Rome and his religious tolerance, and these apparently had little effect in the strongly Protestant back country. In the belief that labor and many businessmen were now in favor of repeal of the Eighteenth Amendment, Smith departed from the plank in the party platform that had been inserted to win the support of the dry South and campaigned strongly against prohibition.

While probably no candidate could have defeated Hoover in the year 1928, Smith lost or miscalculated on all fronts save one. His "me-tooism" in support of business probably changed few votes. His Catholicism and antiprohibition sentiments lost seven Southern states and, at the most, gained only two Northern ones. But he did have an appeal for the urban masses. This urban swing, scarcely noticeable in the Hoover landslide, was a portent of the basic change in party strength that was to come from the increase in urban Democrats in the decades ahead.

High Hopes for a Prosperous Nation. In his inaugural address Hoover said, "I have no fears for the future of our country, it is bright with hope." His *Memoirs* also show the high hopes with which he started his administration: "Mr. Coolidge was reluctant to undertake much that was either new or cost money, and by 1929 many things were already fourteen years overdue." He had a number of plans for bringing more efficiency into government activity, but his first major act, in calling a special congressional session to redeem Republican promises to farmers, unfortunately misfired. The President sponsored the Smoot-Hawley Tariff bill to raise the rates on agricultural products, but when the bill finally passed the Senate in June 1930, it carried higher rates on numerous manufactured products and raised the general level of rates on dutiable articles about 25 percent. Although this was not what the President had intended, to give assurance to business he signed the bill. Meanwhile, other nations had been raising their tariffs, some in retaliation for the United States' action, and the outlook for world trade and repayment of international obligations steadily grew darker.

In place of the McNary-Haugen scheme, the administration planned to help the farmer by the Agricultural Marketing Act of 1929. This originally provided for loans to aid cooperative selling, but progressives added a provision for the use of federal money to stabilize the market price of grain. For these purposes a Federal Farm Board was given a revolving fund of $500 million, the largest single appropriation up to that time for nonmilitary purposes. The plan for buying grain to raise domestic prices and reselling when the market could absorb the surplus might have worked for a time had there been rapid worldwide recovery in 1930. But since the trend toward oversupply in wheat already seemed clear, this cure through manipulating the market was at best a makeshift expedient.

In the effort to bring back prosperity after the onset of the depression in 1929, most of President Hoover's plans for efficiency and mild reform were abandoned. "Instead of being able to devote my four years wholly to these purposes," he lamented, "I was overtaken by the economic hurricane. . . . Then the first need was economic recovery and employment." Fearing that reform would upset business and deepen the depression, the President became as conservative as his predecessors.

SOCIAL CHANGE

Motorization and Urbanization.   While the advent of radio and progress in electronics promised great future changes, immediate changes in American society centered around the automobile. Up until World War I automobiles had been chiefly used for the recreation of the upper middle class. In 1917 fewer than one farm family in six had an automobile, and in the nation as a whole there were fewer than 5 million cars. As forms of transport, trucks and buses were negligible economically and socially.

By 1930 two thirds of America's farms—probably all the prosperous commercial farms—had automobiles, and the nation had about 23 million passenger cars. Since there were only about 26 million households, and many prosperous families in big cities did not use private automobiles, the United States had approached the goal of a car in the garage of every family that wanted one. Even more spectacular than the fivefold increase in passenger cars was a ninefold rise in the number of trucks. Nearly 4 million commercial vehicles, of which forty thousand were buses, signaled the beginning of the change to a society built around motor transport.

In the new geography main highway intersections would replace villages as shopping centers, cities would be within easy reach of farms, factories would move from congested cities to the country, and consolidated grammar and high schools would collect children by bus from miles around. Few places would remain remote from the pressures and advantages of an urbanized culture.

The "Automotive Social Ladder." One of the cultural pressures directly connected with the automobile was its rise as a sign of social status. The American automobile, to be sure, depreciated rather rapidly, and for reliable service, replacement was desirable in about five to seven years. But social considerations worked for even briefer ownership. To have a new car was a symbol of success and prosperity, and the bigger and more expensive the car the higher the presumed status of the owner. For urban and suburban apartment dwellers the automobile took the place of an elaborate house as a mark of social standing. Only farmers and the very rich seem to have been relatively immune to such pressures.

Quickly observing this "automotive social ladder," automobile manufacturers began to differentiate each year's model and to carry on the most intensive advertising of any makers of durable goods. While there were real physical and psychological satisfactions to be gained from a swift, smooth ride in a heavy, powerful car, the lure of social approval was perhaps the strongest force behind the continuous demand for new and bigger machines. Since buyers seldom had saved the money to pay cash, the automobile became the most important item in a rapid growth of installment buying.

While the spread of slums had shown the inadequacy of American municipal planning for nearly a century, the automobile more than the slum lay back of the rapid rise of planning commissions and authorities. Although zoning was initiated in New York in 1916 without particular regard to motor transport, that transport, by opening all areas to all types of use, led to the rapid spread of zoning to other cities. The steady migration to major metropolitan areas during the twenties also forced planning on reluctant municipal authorities. By the end of the decade 37 percent of the city population of the United States lived in zoned communities.

Automobiles and trucks required new bridges, tunnels, and thoroughfares into central city business districts. The Port of New York Authority, established by a "treaty" between New York and New Jersey in 1921, initiated interstate agencies to plan transportation. Generally, however, urban efforts to alleviate both traffic problems and slum congestion in the prosperous twenties could be characterized as too little and too late.

More Rights for Women. The Nineteenth Amendment, ratified by the states in 1920, established women's right to vote but was symbolic of much broader changes in feminine activity. The nineteenth-century image of the ideal woman had been of one waited on by servants, protected from the world, and limited in ideas and ability. Suffragettes before World War I were attacked as vigorously by other women who clung to the nineteenth-century ideal as by politicians who shied away from the challenge of a new electorate.

Early in the twentieth century upper middle-class women had started to lead a more vigorous, less sheltered life. They had learned to drive automobiles, smoke cigarettes, and embrace men in the modern ballroom dance. On a more serious level they went to college in increasing numbers, became doctors, dentists, and lawyers, promoted organizations for the general welfare, and took an active part in social reform. While the supply of cheap domestic help was drastically reduced, first by the war (which made much better paying jobs available for working women) and then by immigration restriction, the trend to smaller houses and apartments and the appearance of the vacuum cleaner and other housekeeping aids kept the middle-class housewife from becoming a drudge.

Both the rise of managerial and office employment in relation to that in the plant and the increases in trade and service in relation to manufacturing opened new job opportunities for women. There was, therefore, a gradual but steady rise in the percentage of working women, together with a shift in their activity from domestic service to store and office work. But in spite of these improvements in the range of economic opportunities, men were still paid more for the same types of jobs, and in many factories and low-price stores women worked long hours for very low wages.

Socially, married women working at white-collar jobs were no longer regarded as having lost some of their middle-class respectability. On the contrary, there was a tendency to admire them for their independence—the watchword of the "new woman," who reached maturity in the early 1920s. She was determined to live her life without regard to the older traditions of manners or morals. Freudian psychology was misused as a weapon for attacking the old double standard of sex relations and for proclaiming woman's equal right to infidelity and divorce. The more advanced also insisted on their right to go anywhere unchaperoned, to drink, smoke, and swear in public, and generally to behave as men did.

The decorous manners of the Victorian era seemed to disintegrate before the careless onslaught of the emancipated younger generation, and other social forces speeded the process. The heightened tempo of manufacturing, transportation, and communication was reflected in social life. The amenities of older societies seemed cumbersome and slightly ridiculous. Migration to cities and from one neighborhood to another led to easy acquaintance and friendship based largely on proximity or convenience rather than the old bonds of a shared past and common culture.

An Urban Black Society.   Since the beginning of the century there had been a steady migration of rural blacks to the cities, but World War i so increased the movement that the largest Northern cities—New York, Chicago, Philadelphia—became America's major centers of black population. Although he was frequently able to earn more money than he ever had before, the occupant of these black urban communities soon realized that he had not achieved the Promised Land. Usually he had to move into an overcrowded, delapidated tenement, where he replaced the most recent, poorest immigrant. And though the black was usually of old American stock, he found himself looked down on by the foreign-born white just as he had always been looked down on by the native white man. For a time in the 1920s the singers, dancers, and musicians of black Harlem, and some of its writers and artists as well, were "taken up" by white sophisticates and bohemians; but this fad did not last, nor did it touch the average black man.

There had never been much feeling of labor solidarity in the United States, and black workers in industrial centers were often resented as intruders who threatened white employment and white wage standards. Similar resentment led to attacks on blacks as the ghettos overflowed into white neighborhoods. In 1919 racial violence broke out in a score of cities all over the nation, and blacks learned that they could not rely on either police protection or justice in the courts.

In the early 1920s black activist organizations moved in two directions. With the support of white middle-class liberals, the National Urban League and the National Association for the Advancement of Colored People sought to establish for blacks the civil and political rights guaranteed by the Constitution. On this front, temporary legal victories were won in the *Sweet* case (1925), which upheld the right of the black to defend himself against violence, and in the *First Texas Primary* case (1927), which declared exclusion of black voters at the primary election stage in the democratic process to be unconstitutional. But the organization that represented the hopes and dreams of great numbers of working-class blacks was the Universal Negro Improvement Association, founded by the charismatic Jamaican, Marcus Garvey. Garvey called on the black man to take pride in his race and its history, to turn his back on white America, and to return to his African homeland. The practical NAACP worked for integration, the romantic Garvey for separation. Each side loathed the other.

Prohibition. Superimposed on this society that was undergoing fundamental and confusing changes was America's greatest experiment in increased government control of personal habits. Few nations have had a history of more consistent attachment to the consumption of alcohol than the United States. In the decades prior to 1918, however, there had been a trend toward more drinking of beer and wine and less recorded consumption of hard liquor, as well as a trend to various types of state prohibition. It seems possible that banning the purchase of hard liquor or making it difficult to obtain might have produced a more temperate nation without much public resistance, but this experiment was never tried. Instead, the combination of war hysteria over a shortage of grain, anti-German sentiment against the brewers, and the financing of temperance organizations by businessmen and others opposed to beer led to an effort to ban all alcoholic drinks.

The Eighteenth Amendment left interpretation of what was an "intoxicating" beverage to Congress. The Volstead Act of 1919, vetoed by Wilson and repassed by the necessary two-thirds majority, set the limit of alcoholic content at .5 percent. While farmers could continue to make wine and other drinks at home, as they always had, city dwellers were now denied the possibility of legally buying even the weakest form of beer. As a result, the big urban areas that had opposed the prohibition movement now refused to abide by the law. And as is usual under such circumstances, there was no difficulty in finding entrepreneurs ready to supply the illicit demand.

It is an interesting paradox of the triumph of the prohibitionists in Congress that, having passed the amendment and the Volstead Act, they settled back and made no great effort to enforce the law. The number of federal agents began at about 1500 and rose to only a little over 2800 at the peak. With a top salary of around $3000 it was not surprising that these men were often corruptible, but even had they been entirely diligent, they were too few even to check the imports of liquor. Furthermore, the local authorities in "wet" areas gave them little or no help. In 1923 New York state repealed its law for local enforcement, and politicians in other big metropolitan areas connived, almost openly, with the men supplying the liquor.

As a result, an illegal traffic in alcohol, liquor, and beer, worth hundreds of millions of dollars annually, fell into the hands of underworld leaders. The terms "racket" and "racketeer" came into use, and the newly powerful gangsters quickly branched out into other criminal activities, including bribery, extortion, arson, and murder.

"Where were the police?" one would logically ask. The answer often was: in the pay of racketeers. Al Capone, head of the liquor racket in Chicago, was as powerful politically as anyone in the municipal government of that metropolis, and he was the undisputed ruler of the suburban city of Cicero. In the suburbs of New York and other great cities the liquor interests often controlled county or municipal politics. The sheriffs and police chiefs received a portion of the weekly collections from speakeasies and worked against the occasional federal agent who sought to get evidence of violation of the law.

The national picture was confusing. In dry areas prohibition appeared to work at least as well as it had before the amendment. In wet urban areas, relatively less well represented in Congress, prohibition seemed to be undermining the moral values of both the young elite and honest government. Some manufacturers thought there was less drinking among their employees, while others were sure there was more. The Republican administration continued vaguely to sponsor "the noble experiment"; the Wickersham Commission, appointed by Hoover, gave an unfavorable report in January 1931 but illogically concluded that prohibition should be continued. In the end it was not moral or temperance issues but the depression and need for government revenue in the desperate year of 1932 that apparently tipped the balance in favor of legalizing the liquor business. There was no serious effort to substitute a new law permitting beer and wine for the unworkable Volstead Act. In 1933 the Eighteenth Amendment itself was quickly repealed by the Twenty-first, and the temperance problem was returned to the states.

ECONOMIC CHANGE

The Decline of Craft Unionism. World War I and the postwar boom brought union membership to a peak of five million workers in 1920, about 12 percent of the total labor force. While this was a record for the United States, in comparison with western Europe the level of organization was low. A major reason was that American labor organizations were largely limited to the skilled crafts and older types of industrial activity. The new mass production industries of the twentieth century, such as automobiles, chemicals, and electrical equipment, had successfully resisted efforts at organization.

The union situation of 1920 was essentially unstable. Many union members in war industries and postwar construction soon had to seek other jobs. Employer organizations, held back since 1917 by government policy and competition for workers, were now ready to marshal business-minded people against organized labor. During the Red scare it was easy to convince the middle class that unions had radical intentions.

The American Plan, which was sponsored by the National Association of Manufacturers, representing small and medium-sized business, and which was vigorously pursued by various trade and employer organizations, called for the open shop. Some of the organizations associated with the movement insisted that their members should not enter into any union contracts. Advertisements were placed in newspapers, denouncing the closed shop (one restricted to union members) as un-American. Labor spies were hired in larger numbers than before to detect union organizers.

One important "welfare" device for preventing the organization of workers by national unions was the employee representation plan or company union. The government demand that contractors in World War I enter into collective bargaining with their employees led 125 of the largest companies to organize their own unions with some 400,000 members. Since these unions and their officers were controlled and supported financially by the companies, they were not generally regarded as true representatives of labor. Yet in the twenties they constituted the one growing area of labor organization. By 1928 it was estimated that company union membership had grown to 1.5 million, half that of the AFL.

In addition to the American Plan and competing company unions, independent unions may also have been weakened by reforms in employee relations. In some big companies, the personnel departments that had been established during the war sought to decrease turnover and increase productivity by improving working conditions and proposing various measures to bolster workers' morale. But it may still be argued that the independent unions declined because of the depression of 1920 to 1922 and because business was growing away from the old skilled crafts. The immediate drop in union membership during those two years of depression was 1.4 million. Two hundred thousand more members were lost during the prosperous years from 1923 to 1929. By 1930 less than 7 percent of the labor force was organized in independent unions.

Only in coal and textiles were white labor leaders engaged in vigorous campaigns during the mid-twenties. Both industries had the same basic problems: Southern areas were not unionized, and Communists were undermining the existing union leadership. Although John L. Lewis was able to preserve the United Mine Workers' bargaining position in the older areas, he had to agree to wage cuts during the years of high national prosperity. Neither the United Textile Workers nor its Communist-led rival, the National Textile Workers' Union, was able successfully to invade the South and unionize the new mills. With lower wages in that region the industry continued to drift away from New England and the Middle Atlantic states.

As militancy declined in the ranks of labor, two trends were evident—one toward cooperation with employers, the other toward surrender of union leadership to racketeers. Where employers were small and often poorly informed, as in the garment industry, unions could help to improve shop practices and overall efficiency. Even some of the large railroads found that union-management cooperation increased productivity in their shops. But looking at the labor scene as a whole, the areas of advancing cooperation were small. In unions where the complacency of the mid-twenties made the members careless about attending meetings, dishonest local officials, supported by so-called gorillas, built up machines that the rank and file dared not oppose. Often these labor racketeers dealt secretly with employers, taking payments from them to prevent the union members from demanding wage increases. The twenties were not a decade of pleasant prosperity for organized labor.

Industrial Distress, Agricultural Depression. That symbol of modern mass production, the automated assembly line, was increasingly criticized in the twenties. The speed of the line was set by management, and with no independent unions to represent them, workers who could not maintain the pace were summarily fired. In addition, such plants generally had many workers under a single supervisor or foreman, who consequently had little contact with the men as individuals. While such big-plant assembly-line jobs involved only a small fraction of the labor force, to many artists and intellectuals they dramatized the plight of man in an impersonal, mechanized society.

Blacks who had come to industrial centers during the war and the postwar boom faced problems of a special type. Many companies would not hire them for anything but menial service jobs, and AFL unions would not accept them in the skilled crafts. This discrimination made many blacks quite ready to act as strikebreakers against organized white labor. A. Philip Randolph, one of the few influential black labor leaders, organized a union of Pullman Company maids and porters in 1925, but in spite of the all-black personnel on the cars, the Brotherhood of Sleeping Car Porters was unable at that time to displace a company union and force collective bargaining. Other efforts by Randolph to create a national organization of black unions were even less successful.

The poorer and the less efficient farmers also failed to share in the prosperity of the 1920s. Those who had been encouraged by the government to borrow money in order to bring more land under cultivation to meet the wartime demand now found themselves with heavy debts and a declining market. The hardest hit were wheat farmers in the Western prairie and plains states and cotton growers in the South. Mortgage foreclosures forced owners to become tenants, and losses on farm loans led to the closing of thousands of small banks in country towns. In the South black sharecroppers, particularly, were forced off the land and had to seek jobs in the growing cities.

During the decade advances in soil biology and chemistry made diversification of crops much safer than formerly; hybrid seeds were developed which could increase the yield and resistance to unfavorable weather of both corn and wheat; and all-purpose tractors were reduced in cost. But since few farmers had extra capital and the overly competitive situation failed to interest other investors, the new knowledge and technology were little used until World War II again brought high prices, rural prosperity, and a shortage of labor.

A Slower Rate of Growth. In the long run, economic growth depends upon the making of more and more capital goods such as buildings, factories, roads, and machines. For the decade 1919 to 1928 net capital formation (that is, the creation of new capital goods) in relation to national income was 14 percent less than in the previous decade and nearly 18 percent less than two decades earlier. During the years 1924 to 1929 the annual investment in new capital goods was actually falling. On the other hand, the income of the wealthiest classes was increasing and their savings were rising; these savings or funds for investment were by 1924 beginning to run ahead of the needs of industry and business for capital for physical expansion. In other words, there were more savings each year than there were productive new securities to be bought. As a result, investors were competing for the available securities, and the price of securities went up. A large part of the nation's savings were being used for speculation, while rising interest rates attracted unneeded billions from Europe.

But why should the rate of creation of capital goods slow down when there was plenty of saved money to pay for them? Two explanations can be offered. One is that since there was little change in real wages or salaries from 1924 to 1929, consumer demand did not rise rapidly enough to encourage industrial expansion. The other explanation is more speculative. Changes in technology occur in incalculable ways. Some that promise substantial profits require large new investments, as in the case of railroads, while others do not, as in the case of the phonograph. A series of technological innovations requiring large investment absorb savings and labor and produce an expanding economy; but few major capital-absorbing innovations in technology occurred in the 1920s. While some older developments such as electrification, roads for automobiles, and improvements in steel production were still going forward, after 1927 there was a slowing down of the combined rate of growth.

Technological Advance. Although the new technological developments of the 1920s did not actually increase the rate of capital investment, new devices were sought more vigorously than ever before. By 1929 about a thousand large firms were supporting some type of research. Better control of industrial products through careful cost accounting, spot testing, and laboratory analysis (collectively referred to as "quality control") also led to higher efficiency and productivity.

Radio broadcasting and air travel first reached the general public in this decade, and automobiles and electricity came into general use. Until 1919 the federal government forbade private use of radio. Broadcasts by Westinghouse's station KDKA of the presidential election of 1920 demonstrated the great public possibilities of the new medium of communication, and within the next few years the industry assumed the general pattern that was to remain for decades: competing national networks would subsist on substantial revenue from large advertisers, and high-priced performers would offer variety programs. By 1930 twelve million American families, about 40 percent of the total, could tune in stars like Rudy Vallee, Eddie Cantor, and sports announcer Graham McNamee on their radio sets.

The airplane, invented before World War I, had never attracted much interest in America. During the war the government made an effort to catch up with European development but produced few planes before the Armistice led to cancellation of contracts. The Post Office started an experimental airmail route between New York and Washington in 1918 and after six years extended service to Chicago and San Francisco. Meanwhile, commercial plane production was negligible, and flying was limited to selling rides at airfields and local fairs. In 1925 the government first made an effort to build commercial transport by allowing the Post Office to grant airmail contracts to private firms. The following year Congress gave general regulatory authority to the Commerce Department.

The regular use of air service in Europe and a series of spectacular overseas flights culminating in Charles A. Lindbergh's solo crossing of the Atlantic in 1927 gave some Americans confidence enough to travel by plane. Between 1928 and 1930 passengers increased from 1400 to 32,000, and revenue miles flown multiplied about thirty times to a total of 4.3 million. Although the young industry continued to grow during the depression, the 100 million passenger miles flown in 1940 were almost negligible compared to the 24 billion passenger miles by rail and the incalculable travel by private car.

In the automotive industry, even in the prosperous years of the 1920s, the smaller assemblers of cars had been dropping out. The early years of the depression reduced the number of competitors to fewer than a dozen, producing similar cars within four or five price ranges. Ford finally had to give up his famous Model T in 1927 and bring out the Model A, a car similar to those of his chief competitors. This episode temporarily convinced American manufacturers that in new cars the public wanted size and luxury rather than cheapness.

Both homes with electricity and total consumption of electrical energy doubled from 1920 to 1930. In urban and suburban areas five sixths of all residences came to have electricity, but farm electrification was only beginning. In 1920 1.4 percent of farms had electricity and by 1930 only 10 percent.

THE NEW ERA IN BUSINESS

Managerial Enterprise.   As usual in times of business prosperity, the number of firms grew faster than the population as a whole. In 1920 there were probably fewer than 2.5 million firms, in 1929 over 3 million. About two thirds of all firms were in trade and service, and very few of these had more than two or three employees. The overall growth figures, however, conceal a great deal of routine change. Every year of the twenties thirty to fifty thousand new firms started, and every year a slightly smaller number left the business scene. While adequately capitalized small companies that were started by men who knew the business they were entering had good chances of success, a large percentage of entrepreneurs lacked both qualifications. At the top, a few medium-sized or large firms disappeared each year through mergers, but these equaled only 1 or 2 percent of the new firms starting up.

The American business structure appeared to have reached a plateau of stability. Big companies continued to dominate highly capitalized manufacturing industries, railroads, and utilities. But the rise of true monopoly had been checked by antitrust laws. While in industries dominated by a few companies competition in price was avoided, competition in quality and marketing was generally vigorous.

By the 1920s the stock of most very large companies was widely held; neither the officers nor the directors of the company owned any considerable percentage of the shares. The chief officers were chosen from among men who had made successful careers in management and were professional executives rather than either relatives of an owner or large personal investors. The connection of such men with profit was indirect. Profit for the company was a mark of success, a guarantee of security, and a fund from which larger salaries could be drawn, but it did not directly enrich the professional manager. These men were interested in building strong organizations capable of weathering bad times, rather than in reaping quick profits in the market. They favored spending earnings for research, expert advice, and improvement of company morale, rather than using them to pay extra dividends to the stockholders. As a result, the common stock dividends of the biggest companies tended to move toward moderate, stable rates rather than to fluctuate with profits.

While scarcely a thousand companies were big enough to have professional, bureaucratic management remote from control by owners, the thousands of top executives of these big companies were leaders of business opinion. Executives commanded specialized knowledge and expert staff work; they hired the best lawyers, lobbyists, accountants, and engineers; and their assistants wrote for them speeches and articles analyzing business problems. Hence America seemed much more a land of big business than was the case statistically.

Shaping Public Opinion. George Creel's Committee on Public Information and similar European agencies during World War I provided a new emphasis on creating favorable opinion. About 1920 Edward Bernays and Ivy Lee began to call themselves public relations counselors. Soon the major advertising agencies also had public relations departments. The usual techniques were to publicize events that showed the client in a good light and to plant favorable stories in magazines. Much of the content of newspapers in the peaceful years of the twenties originated in public relations offices.

The value of the stockholder as a public relations resource was also exploited. By lowering the price of shares through splitting them two or more ways, and by aggressive selling to small investors, often through agents of the company, it was possible for a big corporation to acquire tens of thousands of new stockholders. American Telephone and Telegraph, which took a leading part in this movement, increased the number of its owners from 50,000 in 1920 to 210,000 in 1930. Stockholders were sent attractive annual reports and letters from the president designed to make them feel that they were an important part of the organization. In return many stockholders undoubtedly used their votes and influence for government policies favorable to the company.

Whether as a result of the new public relations, or prosperity, or for other less obvious causes, the American public seemed to have given up much of its traditional hostility to big corporations. Articles in praise of business signed by corporate leaders made popular reading in mass-circulation magazines, and business periodicals boasted of the dominance of the businessman and his values. In this friendly atmosphere business was bold in the use of direct influence in legislatures, in community pressures through business clubs, and in the use of advertising contracts to influence editors. A basic danger, as illustrated in the thirties, was that business developed no new progressive policy to go with its added responsibility.

Stock Market Boom and Bust. Besides lacking a suitable social philosophy, businessmen and their economic advisers lacked understanding of relationships in the economy. Consequently, the stock market boom from 1927 to 1929, though not reflected in any corresponding upswing in real capital formation, was not regarded as dangerous. Confidence that the severe business cycle was a thing of the past pervaded American finance.

With low taxes and with 5 percent of the wealthiest classes receiving about a third of disposable personal income, savings were large. Low corporate taxes allowed big companies to accumulate unprecedented cash surpluses. Both personal savings and corporate surpluses were used for speculation. Moreover, brokers, by means of loans, made it easy for investors of even modest income to purchase securities beyond their means. Investors could buy "on margin"—that is, deposit only a small percentage of the total price of a block of securities, with the broker advancing the rest of the money. The hope was, of course, that the price of the securities would rise and enable the investor to make a large profit on his small equity. Often brokerage houses and banks would lend three quarters of the cost of new securities, the customer depositing only a 25 percent margin. In practice, margins often were allowed to go down to 10 percent or less. Not only were both domestic and European banks happy to lend on this type of demand or call loan, but big business companies also employed unused reserves for stock market loans.

Since the public would readily buy the shares of railroad and public utility holding companies, ambitious entrepreneurs like the Van Sweringen brothers in Cleveland, Samuel Insull in Chicago, and S. Z. Mitchell in New York set up pyramids of one holding company on top of another. By selling stock in these companies to the public, the empire builders got the money to buy dozens of operating companies while keeping personal control of the organization through the top holding company. In theory, economies were being achieved through removal of wasteful competition, but in fact the savings were often consumed by greater managerial costs.

High-pressure selling by the agents of bankers and brokers led investors into buying many other questionable securities. Mortgages on the new urban hotels, apartments, and office buildings that were rising all over the nation were divided into small bonds for sale to investors. Ultimately these buildings would be needed, but in 1929 they were already outrunning the demand for such space. United States investment firms literally coaxed foreign governments into issuing bonds that could be marketed to the American public. And in spite of all this manufacture of new securities, the demand exceeded the supply and boosted the price of existing stocks higher and higher.

By the summer of 1929 many insiders, convinced that stock prices were too high in relation to earnings, started to sell. But thousands of speculators could only cling to the limb they were on and hope for some miraculous support. Late in October the limb broke in a series of panic days on the New York Stock Exchange. Stocks sank so fast that holders on margin were generally wiped out. Efforts by J. P. Morgan and Company to stabilize the market failed, and European banks began withdrawing $2 billion they had loaned on call. On October 29, the day of most extreme panic, 16 million shares were traded, and at times stocks could not be sold for want of buyers at any reasonable price. By November stocks had lost 40 percent of their September value.

Stunned by this disaster in what appeared to be stabilized prosperity, business and political leaders insisted that the economy was sound and that the market break would not affect industry. Only about half a million people had margin accounts, and only a million and a half had brokerage accounts of any kind. But since this small group included most of the chief accumulators and users of capital, their importance was not to be measured in numbers. Furthermore, the whole economy had become more closely geared to the stock market than ever before. In the collapse of values, corporations lost their surpluses; brokerage houses were unable to sell fast enough to cover their loans; banks in turn were left with demand loans that could be liquidated only at a fraction of their value; and foreign governments were no longer able to borrow on Wall Street.

CHAPTER 8

THE GREAT DEPRESSION AND THE NEW DEAL 1930–41

THE DOWNSWING

Increasing Force of the Depression.   In contrast to the severity of the stock market panic, the Great Depression began gradually. At the end of 1929 and the beginning of 1930 employment declined only slightly more than was seasonally normal. A Wall Street economist thought the collapse of inflated security values "a favorable development from the point of view of general business." Secretary of the Treasury Andrew Mellon saw nothing "in the present situation that is either menacing or warrants pessimism."

Influenced by the prevailing expressions of optimism, President Herbert Hoover sought to end the mild recession by encouraging appropriate business action and by implementing favorable government policies. In conferences with business leaders he urged them to maintain wages, prices, and plans for expansion. In return he promised to continue a normal program of public works; to raise tariffs; and to lower the Federal Reserve System's rediscount rate (the rate of interest at which banks could exchange customers' notes for currency at Federal Reserve Banks) in order to stimulate business activity by making credit more readily available. In addition, the Federal Farm Board, which had been created in 1929, was expected to support agricultural prices by lending funds to marketing cooperatives or to corporations set up by the cooperatives to stabilize the market; the loan funds would be used to purchase basic farm crops and livestock at marketing time so that markets would not be glutted.

The President, however, refused to face realistically the condition of the unemployed and, probably unaware of the weakness of the banks, continued to manipulate figures to encourage a false optimism; in the spring of 1930, just before business unemployment climbed sharply, he assured the nation: "The worst effects of the crash upon unemployment will have passed during the next sixty days."

The chief barrier to effective action in dealing with the advancing depression was that President Hoover, most economists, and practically all businessmen adhered to the traditional laissez-faire view that government should not interfere with business; thus they considered private investment the only road to national economic recovery.

They did not regard public works projects or other government programs as means of re-creating prosperity through increasing demand for goods and services. Furthermore, allied to the conservatives' failure to appreciate the possibilities of artificially increased demand was the traditional attitude that helping individuals by federal food or relief payments would undermine the initiative of the American people.

A slight upturn in early 1931 supported President Hoover's "wait-and-see" policy. But the business indexes soon started down again, and the international financial structure began to disintegrate. In June 1931, banks on the European continent failed; reparations and debt payments soon stopped, and by September England went off the gold standard (that is, refused to pay its foreign obligations in gold). In July President Hoover, with the agreement of England, France, and Germany, declared a one-year moratorium on European debt and reparation payments. He hoped that such a temporary lifting of the burden of intergovernmental debts would promote world trade and stimulate economic recovery. However, the European crisis resulted in continued gold withdrawals from banks in the United States, European sale of American securities, and the freezing of most foreign short-term loans owing to banks in this country. These events led to a contraction of bank loans in the United States and an end to the possibility of a quick return to prosperity. While the collapse of 1929 was initiated in the United States, descent into the deep trough from 1931 to 1933 was, as President Hoover claimed, precipitated by European events.

Initiation of the Welfare State.   Men of "the business world," wrote President Hoover, "threw up their hands and asked for government action." As voluntary action proved inadequate to counteract the deepening depression, Hoover moved step by step toward federal legislation. In December 1931 and January 1932 the President cooperated with leaders of the politically divided Senate and the Democratic House in creating the Reconstruction Finance Corporation (RFC). This conservatively managed agency, with resources of $2 billion, was to make loans to companies such as banks and railroads to prevent bankruptcy and forced liquidation. Aid was given to some five thousand medium-sized to large businesses to help them meet their pressing obligations, such as bond and mortgage interest or short-term debts. The philosophy of aid was to preserve those institutions whose operation was essential to the public and to other businesses; consequently, banks and railroads received the most aid while small business, in general, was not initially helped.

Until this time the "general welfare" clause of the Constitution had never been interpreted to mean maintenance of the economic system by congressional action. While later Democratic acts continuing the RFC and extending aid to agriculture and individuals were to push the doctrine much further, the nonpartisan RFC Act can be considered the beginning of the federal "welfare state" or "social capitalism." It demonstrated in the sphere of big business that an advanced industrial economy was so complexly interrelated that government could not stand by and see any essential parts break down.

Other recovery measures enacted in the spring of 1932 included the Glass-Steagall Act, which made government bonds and additional types of commercial paper acceptable as collateral for Federal Reserve notes—thus liberalizing the lending powers

INDEX OF COMMON STOCK PRICES, 1920–70

Years 1941–43 Equal 10

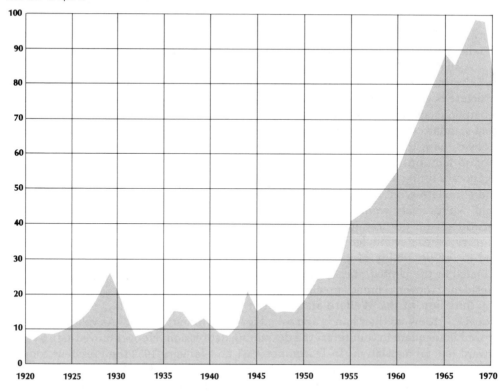

of banks—and made available to business about $750 million of the government gold supply. In July the Federal Home Loan Bank Act created twelve regional Federal Home Loan Banks to extend federal financial assistance to building and loan associations, savings banks, and insurance companies that were in trouble because of falling prices. But Democratic congressional efforts at direct aid to individuals were defeated by presidential vetoes. Hoover continued to view relief as a function of state and local governments, and consequently relief limped along on the basis of small RFC loans to the states.

Effects of the Depression. By the spring of 1932, conditions in the United States reached what seemed to be an intolerable impasse. Then, after remaining relatively unchanged for some nine months, the situation grew even worse. Yet in all this year of material, social, and moral prostration, there was never any threat of revolution, or even any important rise of radicalism in American politics. The American cultural traditions of self-help and individual responsibility seemed, for the most part, to make the sufferers feel guilty, and perhaps sullen and resentful, but not ready to fight for a new order.

The overall statement that unemployment rose to between a quarter and a third of the labor force gives too optimistic a picture of the effects of the depression on human beings. To begin with, total man hours worked in mid-1932 were only about 40 percent of those in 1929, and many experienced workers were being paid only five to ten cents an hour. Furthermore, destitute farmers were not considered unemployed, and people who had given up seeking work and students who stayed in school or college solely because they had no hope of finding jobs were not part of the "labor force." In general, the most easily replaceable workers, such as the unskilled, lost their jobs first, and what work remained was apportioned between management and skilled labor. Both managers and women office employees kept their jobs more often than workers in plants.

One-industry towns could be paralyzed by the failure of two or three local companies. By early 1932 the entire county of Williamson in southern Illinois had almost no employment. Some Appalachian mining cities had two or three hundred employed out of many thousands. If a community depended on industries making producers' goods, it usually suffered mass unemployment.

Without income or housing to hold them together, many families disintegrated. A father without a job, who washed dishes, made beds, sat around, and failed to provide food, lost status in his family. Sometimes his position became intolerable, and he was driven to suicide. Many more unemployed fathers and older children started drifting around the country, presumably looking for work but perhaps really seeking escape through activity. The drift of a million or more of these "migrants of despair" was aimless but generally toward warm areas, where each city tried to keep the wayfarers moving to somewhere else. Although in many cities they could get a meal, they could not stay.

In the larger cities the major burden of relief fell first on private donors and then on voluntary organizations, like the Red Cross, Salvation Army, Community Chest, and, as these exhausted their resources, on small local and state appropriations. Before the end of 1930, people who actually administered relief recognized that these resources were inadequate. "Local organizations," said C. A. Dykstra of Cleveland in 1932, "have tried to make $400 million play substitute for $20 or more billion, formerly paid in wages." In small cities conditions were often worse than in the major centers. A survey of fifty-nine cities of upstate New York in the winter of 1930–31 revealed that most of them had no relief programs. "By the fall of 1931," says Professor Irving Bernstein, "municipal relief—private and public—was bankrupt in virtually every city in the United States," and it is estimated that unemployment rose 50 percent in the next eighteen months.

The farming country presented the most outrageous paradox of all. With no effective means of controlling prices or production, farmers literally ruined each other. To keep his income up when prices were falling, each farmer tried to produce more and more, thus driving prices down still further until the value of some crops and animals was too low to justify taking them to market. And because gifts of food would potentially compete with sales, no permissible way was found to distribute and use agricultural surpluses. As a result, while a sheep raiser cut the throats of young lambs and threw them into a canyon because he could not afford to feed them, the families on bread lines ate soup. Southern sharecroppers fared worst of all. Owners unable to finance new crops left former tenants without food, and these rural areas generally lacked charitable or other relief organizations.

The Election of 1932. By the summer of 1932 the patience of various groups throughout the nation was becoming exhausted. Organized farmers in Iowa were violently enforcing a "farm holiday" on produce deliveries; an "expeditionary force" of several thousand veterans was encamped in Washington demanding cash payment of the World War I bonus; numbers of unemployed were killed by police in riots around Detroit; and some conservative editors were calling for a dictatorship to preserve the state.

Yet a majority of the leaders of both major parties conservatively opposed any substantial change in policy. Of the Democratic leaders only Governor Franklin D. Roosevelt of New York seemed to lean toward a more progressive approach, favoring the use of governmental power to whatever extent necessary and in whatever ways necessary to reverse the trend of economic events.

Franklin Delano Roosevelt, a fifth cousin of Theodore, had been brought up on a country estate above Poughkeepsie, New York, and educated at Harvard and at Columbia Law School. In 1910 he entered politics and was elected to the New York state assembly, where he stood for progressivism and reform and was an ardent supporter of Woodrow Wilson. President Wilson, aware of the personal charm of the big, strong-jawed, smiling young man, appointed Roosevelt Assistant Secretary of the Navy; the 1920 Democratic convention, needing the magic of the Roosevelt name, nominated him for the vice-presidency.

Shortly after his defeat as Cox's running mate Roosevelt contracted infantile paralysis, but by 1924 he had recovered sufficiently to appear, supported by crutches, at the Democratic convention and make the nominating speech for Alfred E. Smith. In 1928, at Smith's insistence, Roosevelt ran for governor of New York. Carrying the state by 25,000 votes while Smith lost it for the presidency marked Roosevelt as one of the coming men in the Democratic party. In 1930, after one term as a rather easygoing, liberal governor, he was reelected by a record-breaking 725,000 votes.

These repeated victories made him the party's logical candidate for the presidency in 1932, but Roosevelt, fearful of a strong undercurrent of conservative opposition, left nothing to chance. His able secretary, Louis M. Howe, planned and advised, and New York state Democratic chairman James A. Farley toured the country and talked to politicians. At the Democratic convention Farley skillfully negotiated with William Randolph Hearst and William G. McAdoo for California's support on the fourth ballot in return for the nomination of conservative House Speaker John Nance Garner for Vice-President. This shift swung Garner's state of Texas and other Southern states to the Roosevelt bandwagon, but Al Smith held on to his delegates and left Chicago without congratulating the nominee.

The Republicans had no recourse but to renominate Hoover, and, in truth, the prosperous people who financed and ran the national machinery in both parties probably thought that Hoover had done all that could be expected. Yet everyone knew he would not be a strong candidate with the public.

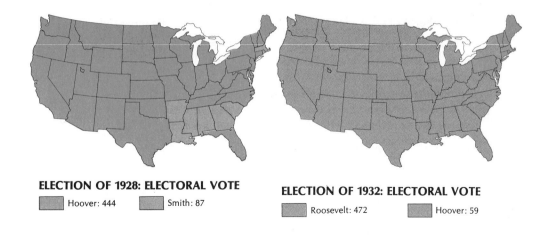

ELECTION OF 1928: ELECTORAL VOTE

■ Hoover: 444   ■ Smith: 87

ELECTION OF 1932: ELECTORAL VOTE

■ Roosevelt: 472   ■ Hoover: 59

The campaign mirrored the complete confusion in both parties regarding acceptable economic policy. The two platforms were nearly the same, and both candidates talked of public works and relieving misery while reducing spending and balancing the budget. But Garner was no doubt right when he told Roosevelt that to win "all you have to do is to stay alive until election day." Hoover probably gained no votes by his weary and often bitter campaign; on election day he polled 15,759,000 votes to Roosevelt's 22,800,000. While many middle-class voters supported Socialist party candidate Norman Thomas as the only candidate with a constructive program, Thomas failed utterly to attract the masses. His 881,951 Socialist votes were fewer than in 1920 and relatively less than half the Socialist vote in 1912. Some artists and intellectuals desiring a stronger protest supported William Z. Foster, the Communist, but his meager 102,785 votes indicated that few workers had supported him.

Bottom of the Depression. The depression reached its lowest ebb in the four months between the election and Roosevelt's inauguration. During this critical period there was little constructive leadership. Hoover thought that everything justifiable had been done in the domestic field and was interested in stimulating foreign trade. Roosevelt could not accept Hoover's analysis of the domestic situation and was not prepared to work for return to an international gold standard, the keynote of Hoover's plans. As the nation drifted without leadership, silver shirts, white shirts, khaki shirts, and other fascist organizations strove unsuccessfully for mass support. "Technocracy," a vaguely defined plan for placing control of the nation's means of production in the hands of technicians in order to realize the full efficiency of industrial equipment, created a midwinter furor, but it died quickly from lack of immediate, practical proposals. In general, the people waited patiently, putting their hopes in the new administration.

The final breakdown of commercial banking was responsible for bringing the economy to its lowest ebb. Of the 16,000 state banks of 1929 that were not members of the Federal Reserve System, nearly half had closed their doors by 1933. These banks had no system to save them, and many of their officers knew little about banking. Of the 7500 members of the Federal Reserve, about 1400 disappeared during the depression, demonstrating that even these banks were too small and poorly connected to stand the strain. Banks that failed drew away deposits kept in the banks of the larger cities. The first metropolitan area to buckle under the pressure was New Orleans. Early in February 1933 the governor of Louisiana declared a temporary "bank holiday," freezing loans and deposits.

Meanwhile, a senate committee investigating banking practices had uncovered dishonesty and evasion of responsibility in the highest circles. Major banks had lent money to their officers on no proper security, and bad securities had been sold to banks to save investment subsidiaries or affiliates from disaster. These and other questionable practices had been overlooked by federal examiners. Faced with such uncertainties, depositors began to withdraw their surplus cash from the banks and stuff it into safe deposit boxes.

Closing of the banks in Michigan in mid-February started a chain reaction that ended on March 4, 1933—the day of Roosevelt's inauguration—when Governor Lehman of New York and other governors joined in declaring a "bank holiday" to stop destructive runs as depositors rushed to withdraw savings. The banking crisis had, in turn, hurt business, and unemployment stood at somewhere between 14 and 17 million, perhaps as much as a third of the labor force. The economy was producing at about half the rate of 1929, and the trend was downward.

FDR: THE FIRST TERM

The Honeymoon.   Roosevelt's inaugural address on March 4, 1933, struck a note of hope. The nation was strong, he said, and would recover from this crippling depression: "The only thing we have to fear is fear itself—nameless, unreasoning, unjustified terror which paralyzes needed efforts to convert retreat into advance." He closed by affirming, "The people of the United States . . . have asked for discipline and direction under leadership. They have made me the present instrument of their wishes. In the spirit of the gift I take it."

The nation and Congress, which Roosevelt immediately called into emergency session, responded to his appeal, and quickly the pattern of the "New Deal" began to reveal itself. "Our greatest primary task," Roosevelt declared in his inaugural address, "is to put people to work." Preferably the employment should be by private firms, but if necessary the federal government should use its resources to provide employment on the most useful work projects that could be quickly devised. Second, the abuses that aggravated the depression must be corrected. Anyone guilty of criminal acts of financial or corporate manipulation must be punished. Banking laws should be made stricter in some respects, controls over the stock exchanges and the commodity markets should be tightened, and abuse of the holding-company device should be corrected by closer control of its use, especially in public utilities. After these emergency corrective measures had been taken, Roosevelt proposed a series of permanent steps to bring about a fuller development of the country and to make the lives of most Americans more secure and prosperous. Roosevelt referred to these three objectives of the New Deal as "Relief, Recovery, and Reform."

On March 6, before Congress met in special session, the President proclaimed a four-day national bank holiday and a four-day embargo on the export of gold, silver, and currency. Congress, convening on March 9, provided for the reopening of banks to relieve the financial emergency. The Emergency Banking Relief Act—enacted that day—confirmed the President's earlier actions and provided for the reopening of sound banks. At the same time Congress prohibited the use of gold except under license for export.

The special session of Congress subsequently was fed a stream of recovery measures drawn up by groups in the administration, often with differing philosophies; but with the force of the President behind them the bills were enacted by sweeping bipartisan majorities. By the time this famous "Hundred Days" or political "honeymoon" ended in June 1933, the basic emergency legislation was complete. The Federal Emergency Relief Administration (FERA) was created with $500 million in funds to be granted to states for direct relief. A Civilian Conservation Corps (CCC) was set up to put unemployed young men into camps to carry out reforestation and erosion-control projects. Beer and light wine with an alcoholic content of 3.2 percent or less by volume were legalized and repeal of the Eighteenth Amendment initiated (passage of the Twenty-first Amendment late in 1933 officially repealed prohibition).

Farm Relief. From the standpoint of loss in money income, farmers were the hardest hit of any occupational group. From 1925 on they were in a vicious circle of increasing overproduction of staple crops and declining prices; earnings were so low that grain and cotton farmers could not afford the investment needed to shift to other produce for which there was a better market. Depression turned hardship into disaster: total cash income for farmers fell from an average of nearly $11 billion per year in the late twenties to $4.7 billion in 1932. And even these figures fail to suggest the desperate straits of marginal cotton, corn, and wheat growers.

The Agricultural Adjustment Act of June 1933 contained the basic principle of subsequent farm legislation: the government should pay staple crop farmers to plant fewer acres, thus reducing output and raising the prices of farm products. Money to subsidize the farmers was to come from a tax on millers and other processors of staple products; in this way the law was self-supporting. To get the program going quickly, the Secretary of Agriculture arranged for the plowing up of millions of acres of cotton and the slaughter of six million pigs of less than usual market weights, the pigs to be put to uses other than providing human food. Although millions of Americans considered the destruction of food and cotton positively sinful as long as other millions were hungry and ill-clothed, agricultural prices and income did improve in 1934 and 1935.

Mortgage Refinancing. The government had to try not only to revive farm income but also to take care of hundreds of thousands of defaulted mortgages, both farm and nonfarm. In two initial acts creating the Federal Farm Mortgage Corporation and the Home Owners Loan Corporation, the government offered to refinance mortgages on long terms at low interest.

In addition, the Federal Housing Administration Act of 1934 introduced the guaranteed packaged mortgage—one that could be paid, principal and interest, by uniform monthly payments. This government guarantee of a high percentage of the total cost of homes in the low-price range constituted the most important change in the history of American home ownership. Now the man with a steady job could afford to build or buy, where he had had to rent before, and repayment of his obligations would occur automatically every month. This also marked an important step in the development of mass production of homes and long-term installment buying.

Regional Development.   One of the most revolutionary of the acts passed by the Hundred Days Congress initiated the redevelopment of an entire geographic region—the economically ailing seven-state Tennessee valley area.

The Muscle Shoals–Tennessee Valley Development Act of May 1933 created an independent public corporation, the Tennessee Valley Authority, which was given control of the government property at Muscle Shoals, Alabama, and the power to build and operate other dams and power plants on the Tennessee River and its branches wherever the authority thought advisable. In addition to generation and distribution of electric power, TVA was charged with controlling the flood waters of the Tennessee River and improving its navigation facilities, promoting the conservation of soil in the valley and aiding reforestation, and producing nitrates and other fertilizers for the improvement of the valley's agriculture. Government-financed improvements in the valley continued over the next generation, leading ultimately to industrial development as well as greatly increased animal husbandry.

Although the power dams, plants, and distribution systems of TVA were criticized by private power companies as unfair competition (the public facilities were not

TENNESSEE VALLEY AUTHORITY

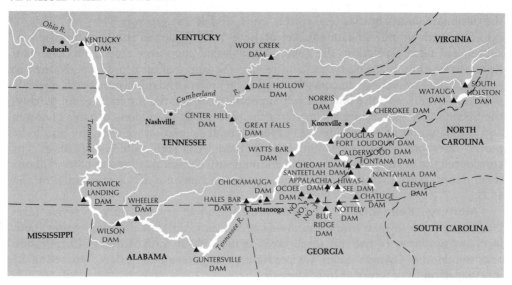

required to pay the same taxes as private companies, and they received other government subsidies), the constitutionality of the TVA was upheld by the Supreme Court in 1936. The following year President Roosevelt asked Congress to set up six additional regional river valley authorities, but Congress declined. The areas in which they were to be located were not quite such distinct units as the Tennessee valley, nor were the people of these other areas in such a distressed condition as those of the Tennessee valley had been in 1933. The general business outlook was brighter in early 1937, and the business community supported the widespread contention that private capital could develop these valleys as effectively as the federal government.

Partially thwarted in his larger conservation and development plans, the President succeeded in having the Civilian Conservation Corps plant a tree belt across the Great Plains, while the Department of Agriculture checked soil erosion by urging farmers to plow furrows at right angles to the slope of the land, a practice called contour plowing. Thus the New Deal period may be looked upon as the beginning of a heightened federal consciousness of ecological problems.

Industrial Recovery.   While banking, currency, mortgages, and agriculture had occupied the President's attention during the first weeks of his administration, he learned in April 1933 that unless he acted quickly Congress would pass a uniform thirty-hour-a-week law governing all industry. Because he regarded such a law as impractical, the President had his advisers prepare a substitute. The resulting National Industrial Recovery Act (NIRA), though hastily improvised, actually was the outgrowth of much thought by business, labor, and government about how to reconcile "free" private enterprise with effective control of wages and competition.

In many industries excess industrial capacity, unemployed labor, and nearly bankrupt firms had reduced the market to chaos. With women receiving as little as $5 for a full week's work, companies that tried to maintain fair labor standards found themselves undersold. The solution proposed in the act was to have each industry, probably through its trade association, agree to a code of "fair competition" defining wages, hours, and minimum prices. Labor would be represented in the making of such industry agreements by representatives of its own choosing without any pressure from the employer. The public would also be represented so that the interests of consumers would not be lost sight of. When all three parties were represented in the determination of policies for an industry, the government could overlook the fact that a price agreement would appear to be a clear "conspiracy to restrain trade" under the terms of the Sherman Antitrust Act. The National Recovery Administration (NRA) was set up to administer this section of the law.

The second section of NIRA set up the Public Works Administration (PWA) and authorized the expenditure of $3.3 billion for public works projects designed both to provide work for relief and to stimulate recovery.

The bill became law in June 1933, and the President appointed retired General Hugh S. Johnson as administrator of the first section. The negotiation of codes proved difficult and time consuming; in July 1933 President Roosevelt, in an attempt to speed matters, announced a blanket President's Reemployment Agreement governing wages and hours for those industries that could not agree upon a code. A blue eagle was adopted as the symbol of the cooperating firms; those that signed codes or the PRA were allowed to display it on their stores, plants, or merchandise, and the public was strongly urged not to patronize nonsigners. Within months millions of Americans were working under the soaring blue eagle. The original idea of cooperation between the employer, organized labor, and consumer representatives, however, was all but lost in the difficulties of reaching agreements. Furthermore, consumers were unorganized and unable to protect their interests as management and government drew up a flood of codes. As time passed, thousands of cases of noncompliance with codes were reported. Labor was extremely restive because industry often opposed union organization as authorized by NIRA, and the country was plagued by strikes. Employers began to fear that they had made a mistake in agreeing to negotiate with labor in drawing up the codes. The public also began to feel that it was being fleeced by prices that were rising faster than income.

Although the NRA contributed to the raising of wages from the low levels of 1932, did away with child labor, and in some industries helped small business to stay alive, the NIRA experiment illustrated the difficulty of suddenly regulating a complex economy. Furthermore, it failed to bring back prosperity. The United States Chamber of Commerce and labor leaders as diverse as William Green, John L. Lewis, and Sidney Hillman continued to support the NRA until the Supreme Court ruled the act unconstitutional, but business in general and the rising group in the Roosevelt administration had lost interest in it or become hostile toward it.

Devaluing the Dollar.　Controllable inflation, the President hoped, would raise farm prices and in general lighten the burden of debts in relation to income. The administration felt that such inflation could be stimulated either by heavy government spending or by altering the value of the dollar. Of the two possibilities, devaluing the dollar had the immediate advantages of not adding to government costs and of stimulating exports.

While the President was supporting the inflationist group in Congress, European nations were meeting in June-July 1933 to attack the worldwide depression by attempting to agree on stabilizing national currencies and restoring the international gold standard. However, contrary to this spirit, an amendment to the Agricultural Adjustment Act of May 1933 gave the President the right to inflate U.S. currency by issuing $3 billion in paper currency, freely coining silver, and devaluing the gold content of the dollar up to 50 percent. For the time being he did none of these things, waiting to see whether the AAA and the NRA would do the inflationary job, but neither would he enter into any international agreement fixing the value of the dollar. As a result, the London Economic Conference was a failure.

Although there was a sharp increase in manufacturing production, employment, and prices between March and July 1933—in part, the result of an effort to produce before the restrictive NRA codes went into effect—by autumn manufacturing and employment were declining, and wholesale prices had again leveled off. At this point the President decided to use his power to devalue the dollar in the expectation that the resulting inflation would lead to higher prices. He reduced the value of the gold content of the dollar to 59.06 cents, a degree of devaluation calculated to restore the price level of 1926. Prices rose slightly, but not nearly so much as the administration had expected; the President's monetary program had no significant effect.

Rise of Conservative Opposition. Early criticism of the New Deal had come primarily from advanced liberals and labor leaders. Some members of Congress, for instance, would have nationalized banking and railroads; these men and even more moderate liberals regarded the restoration of the banking system in relatively unchanged form as the loss of a great opportunity for progress toward a more stable economy. Organized labor was particularly dissatisfied with its treatment by the NRA, which in labor circles came to be called the "national run-around."

On the other hand, monetary manipulation during the last half of 1933 lost the President the support of many conservative Democratic leaders, who opposed any tinkering with the monetary system. Efforts at permanent reform of financial operations, as distinct from mere recovery, widened the rift between liberals and conservatives.

The reform program really began with the Federal Securities Act of 1933, by which the Federal Trade Commission was given the power to see that underwriters fully disclosed to investors all essential details pertaining to new securities issues. A further reform was effected by the Banking Act of June 1933, which divorced investment banking from commercial banking on the premise that the promoting and selling of new security issues by commercial banks gave them an improper amount of power over other businesses and was inconsistent with the policy of caution and prudence which banks should follow. The Banking Act also created the Federal Deposit Insurance Corporation (FDIC) to insure bank deposits up to established limits and prevent losses to depositors. Leading bankers vigorously opposed deposit insurance, and stricter regulation of the securities markets aroused more general business opposition.

The battle between liberals and conservatives was intensified when the Securities Exchange bill was before Congress in the spring of 1934. This bill called for the establishment of a three-member Securities and Exchange Commission to regulate the practices of stock exchanges, including the size of margins; to require full disclosure of details about all securities; and to enforce other parts of the Federal Securities Act of 1933. Stockbrokers and investment bankers complained strongly about the restrictions this legislation would place on them. But despite bitter debate in Congress the bill was passed in June 1934, and the die-hard opponents of all governmental regulation of the financial community were decisively defeated.

Another development in the spring of 1934 that alarmed some businessmen was adoption of the Reciprocal Trade Agreements Act, which gave the President power to make separate agreements with foreign nations to alter U.S. tariff rates by 50 percent in either direction. Even moderate Republicans denounced it as a surrender of power to the President. But the Democrats, with strong Southern support, held firm and enacted this change in American tariff policy.

In the course of debates over the Securities Act and the tariff, business arguments against the New Deal took their permanent shape. The government was condemned for creating a vast and irresponsible bureaucracy, for depriving individuals of their freedom and initiative, and for increasing the national debt. Direct relief, in particular, was condemned because it ran contrary to the deeply ingrained tradition that self-help was the basis of American greatness.

In August 1934 a group of wealthy Republicans and conservative Democrats formed the Liberty League to defend the rights and liberty of the individual against the New Deal. Backed by DuPont and General Motors executives, the League won the support of previous Democratic presidential candidates John W. Davis and Alfred E. Smith and many other conservative political leaders in both parties. The big city daily newspapers were moving in the same direction. Within a year, at least two thirds of the metropolitan dailies were strongly in opposition to the New Deal, and their influential columnists were attacking the "third-rate college professors" and other "impractical intellectuals" of the "Brain Trust" that was held to be guiding the policies of the administration.

Reliance upon the Masses. The business attack on the New Deal, though backed by adequate finances and the support of major newspapers, had the fatal weakness of lacking a positive philosophy. Business leaders could only ask the public again to put its faith in the self-regulating economy. That, in fact, the public would not trust self-regulation was shown in the election of 1934. Normally the administration party loses strength in Congress in the nonpresidential elections; the Democrats, however, gained nine seats in the House and nine in the Senate, with nearly 57 percent of the popular vote—an off-year administration victory unmatched since before the Civil War.

What had built the Democratic majority? The answer of a number of presidential advisers was that it was the voters' desire for security—for assurance that when unemployed or old they would be cared for. At this point, therefore, the New Deal became more equalitarian and humanitarian than any of the previous progressive movements.

In the spring of 1935 a new system of relief through useful work was instituted. Jobs ranging from mixing concrete to painting murals were to be created from an appropriation of nearly $5 billion. Pay would be at rates above relief but lower than approved for private employment. The Works Progress Administration lasted until World War II and spent some $11 billion. Although it could employ only from two to three million workers, it kept those with the more valuable skills from deteriorating through idleness. Other minor forms of aid were instituted to help students stay in school and to provide potential farmers with subsistence homesteads.

In the thirties women still were discriminated against by many employers, but their equality was recognized as never before. Indeed, most working women were far less interested in proving their independence than in earning a living wage and, frequently, in supporting or at least helping to support their families. One indication of the new status of women was Roosevelt's choice of a woman, Frances Perkins, as his Secretary of Labor.

In the President's mind, the most important legislation of this administration was the Social Security Act of 1935. This act created a Social Security Board to administer unemployment compensation, old-age security, and various social services. Payroll taxes were levied on both employers and employees to finance old-age pensions of from $10 to $85 per month for retired workers. Pensions under the new system would not begin until 1942, but meanwhile the federal government would assist the states in paying small pensions. In the beginning many groups, including farm and educational workers, were not eligible for pensions, but in succeeding years coverage was broadened and rates raised to compensate for inflation. The Social Security Act also extended federal-state unemployment insurance to 28 million workers and authorized money grants to states to assist them in relief of the blind, cripples, delinquent children, and other dependents. Now the power of Congess to legislate for the general welfare had a new meaning.

The Supreme Court: Challenge and Response. Early in 1935, with the Social Security bill on its way through Congress, the President regarded his program as virtually complete. Had the Supreme Court upheld the legislation of 1933 and 1934, the Roosevelt administration, like that of Woodrow Wilson, might have turned its attention to matters other than domestic reform. But the Supreme Court had four justices unalterably opposed to the New Deal, and two others, Owen J. Roberts and Chief Justice Charles E. Hughes, were very doubtful about the constitutionality of delegating congressional power to administrative agencies and using the commerce power to regulate conditions of production and trade within the states.

The crucial tests came in the spring of 1935, when the Court declared the NIRA and a number of other basic acts of the New Deal unconstitutional. There was little hope that those still to be tested, such as the Agricultural Adjustment Act, would fare any better. (The Supreme Court invalidated the first AAA in January 1936.)

The Court's failure to interpret the Constitution flexibly and to support the type of laws initially planned in cooperation with business leaders pushed the President toward further regulation. The influence of the administration was already behind Senator Wagner's National Labor Relations Act to replace the labor provisions of the outlawed NIRA. The Wagner Act created a new National Labor Relations Board (NLRB) for administrative purposes and upheld the right of employees to join labor organizations and to bargain collectively through representatives of their own choosing.

This support of labor was accompanied by other New Deal measures that antagonized conservatives. A new tax bill introduced in June 1935 had the announced purpose of shifting the tax burden from the poor to the rich. The "Soak the Rich Act" of 1935 actually made few changes in taxes on income under $50,000 a year, and the graduated corporation income tax stopped at 15 percent; but high surtaxes on very big incomes and on inheritance of estates further alarmed the wealthy over the "communistic" trend of the New Deal.

Attack by the rich probably strengthened support of the President. More politically dangerous was the attack on his policies by radical reformers. In his weekly radio broadcasts Father Charles E. Coughlin, a demagogic Catholic priest, first criticized the President for failure to take care of the rural poor and then progressed to a fascist type of attack on Jews and international bankers. In a more constructive vein, Dr. Francis Townshend of California advocated pensions of $200 a month for the elderly. But the most comprehensive political and economic appeal of the day came from Senator Huey P. Long of Louisiana. A mixture of machine politician and shrewd administrator who believed the depression could be cured by government spending, Long advocated a guaranteed minimum income and a capital levy on the rich to provide every family with a home, a car, and a radio. His simple country-boy manner and his slogan, "Every man a king," made him a real threat to Roosevelt's control of the Democratic party until Long was assassinated by a personal enemy in September 1935. Coughlin and other unorthodox reformers continued to keep the administration under fire, but without Long they lacked a strong political leader.

The Election of 1936. Many Republicans felt that with Alfred M. Landon, ex-governor of Kansas, they would defeat Roosevelt in 1936. The *Literary Digest's* poll of telephone subscribers, which indicated a Landon presidential victory, helped sustain this view. (Overlooked was the fact that Roosevelt supporters were not adequately represented among telephone subscribers.) Landon promised to do everything that the New Deal was doing for the common man but to do it in ways more satisfactory to business. The President responded with a more advanced liberalism than in earlier campaigns. In his acceptance speech he denounced the "economic royalists" and said that Americans, in their achievement of economic and social democracy, had a "rendezvous with destiny."

The result was the greatest landslide since 1920. Landon, with 16.7 million votes to the President's 27.8 million, carried only Maine and Vermont. The Coughlin group, supporting a radical farm leader, polled less than a million votes, and the Socialists' and Communists' votes were negligible. No President since Monroe had received such strong second-term support from the people.

THE LAST PHASE OF THE NEW DEAL

Battle over the Court. In a surprise move after the election of 1936 Roosevelt boldly attempted to use his great political strength and national popularity to alter the composition of the ultraconservative Supreme Court—and thus to liberalize the Court's attitude toward New Deal legislation.

In February 1937 the President presented Congress with a bill to reorganize the federal judiciary by adding up to fifty judges to the federal court system as a whole. The bill further proposed to increase the membership of the Supreme Court from nine to a maximum of fifteen by permitting the President to appoint one new justice for each justice over seventy who refused to retire. Roosevelt's ostensible argument for the bill was that federal judges were overworked and decisions too long delayed because the judiciary was "handicapped by insufficient personnel." Furthermore, the President contended that the aging judges were antiquated in outlook—"little by little, new facts become blurred through old glasses fitted, as it were, for the needs of another generation." For the lower courts Roosevelt's argument was valid, but the highest tribunal was not far behind in its case work, and the justices over seventy included some of the most vigorous and liberal members of the Court.

The magnitude of the change from nine to fifteen justices when no previous Congress had ever altered the size of the Court so drastically, and the doubtful sincerity of Roosevelt's argument for the major provision of the bill, reacted with unexpected strength against the administration. Liberal Democrats and progressive Republicans joined conservatives in opposing the measure. The press was violent in its denunciation, and public opinion polls showed popular distaste for so arbitrary an action by the President.

While Congress debated the President's "Court-packing" bill, the Court itself removed much of Roosevelt's reason for the bill by voluntarily liberalizing its stand on New Deal legislation. Justice Roberts and Chief Justice Hughes abandoned the conservative camp and joined Justices Brandeis, Cardozo, and Stone in reversing the legal doctrines of 1935 and 1936. In March 1937 the Court, by a five-to-four decision, upheld a Washington state minimum wage law for women although the previous year it had declared unconstitutional a similar law of the state of New York. In April the Court declared the National Labor Relations Act constitutional, and the next month it upheld the Social Security Act. Furthermore, Justice Van Devanter's resignation from the Court in May 1937 gave Roosevelt a chance to appoint a justice who would convert the liberal minority of the Court to a majority in future decisions. To succeed Van Devanter, Roosevelt appointed Senator Hugo L. Black of Alabama, an enthusiastic supporter of the New Deal.

In June 1937 the Senate Judiciary Committee reported the court reform bill unfavorably, and the Senate, after bitter debate, subsequently rejected the proposal by voting 70 to 20 to return it to the Judiciary Committee. Congress did, however, pass a Supreme Court Retirement Act permitting Supreme Court justices to retire, with full pay, at age seventy; it also passed a Judicial Procedure Reform Act which established reforms in the lower courts.

New Dealers found consolation for the defeat of the administration bill in the fact that the few years after defeat of the "Court-packing" plan saw a radical change in the complexion of the Supreme Court. A succession of deaths and resignations enabled Roosevelt to make eight new appointments to the Court and gave him the liberal tribunal which Congress had denied him.

A Government-Protected Labor Movement. Early in 1933 total independent union membership in the United States had fallen to less than 2.7 million, including about 2 million in the AFL. Unemployment had reduced company union membership to less than a million. The morale of union leaders was at a low ebb; in general their proposals for recovery were no more imaginative than Hoover's.

Section 7(a) of NIRA (granting to organized labor the right of collective bargaining through representatives of their own choosing) and the subsequent upswing in employment gave unions a chance to expand. Organizing drives and some help from the National Labor Board of the NRA raised total union membership to 3.6 million in 1935. Meanwhile, faced with the threat of being forced by code authorities to bargain collectively, the larger employers were setting up new company unions. By 1935 this type of membership had passed 2.5 million.

In the same year a group within the AFL, led by John L. Lewis of the United Mine

Workers, was urging the organization of all workers in a given industry—skilled or unskilled—into a single union. The AFL as a whole, however, was dominated by craft unions and officially opposed all moves toward industrial unionization.

The Wagner Act of 1935 gave industrial organizers new and potentially effective weapons. The powerful National Labor Relations Board created by the Act could, at the request of a union but not of an employer, hold a plant election; if the union received the vote of a majority of workers, it became the bargaining agent for all. Furthermore, the Board could determine the units—plants, companies, or industries—for election purposes, and it could prevent employers from interfering in any way with organizers or trying to influence the election. If the winning union was able to negotiate a closed-shop agreement, the employer was required to deduct union dues from the pay of all workers. But in view of the decisions of the Supreme Court in 1935 and 1936, even labor leaders regarded the law as probably unconstitutional.

Encouraged somewhat by the opportunities the new law might offer and much more by the sweeping reelection of a friendly President, the leaders of eight AFL unions defied the parent body and formed a Committee for Industrial Organization. Led by John L. Lewis, the CIO refused to compromise with the crafts, and the unions

Annual average of
EMPLOYMENT AND UNION MEMBERSHIP, 1920–70

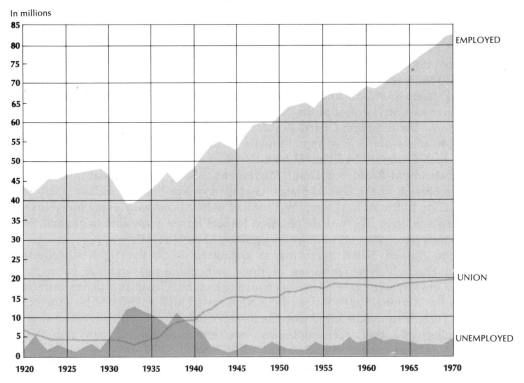

In millions

involved were expelled by the AFL in 1937. The following year the committee became the Congress of Industrial Organizations with Lewis as president and a membership roughly equal to that of the AFL.

While Lewis in 1936 wanted to use the government-supported power of labor to organize steel, the local unions in the automotive industries initiated action on their own front. Late in the year, when General Motors refused to recognize and bargain with the United Automobile Workers, union members in Flint, Michigan, occupied their plants. The sit-down strike left the workers in possession of valuable machinery, while food was brought in by their families. Efforts by local authorities failed to dislodge the workers, and the newly elected Democratic governor, Frank Murphy, refused to enforce court orders to remove them by using the state militia. Meanwhile, orders for cars were mounting as the motor industry enjoyed a return to prosperity, and President Roosevelt kept a steady pressure on General Motors to bargain with Lewis. As a result of both factors a settlement was reached that established a pattern of collective bargaining with the UAW. During the prosperous spring of 1937 similar agreements were worked out with the other motor companies except Ford.

In April the Supreme Court, under pressure from the "reform" bill in Congress, reversed its previous attitude and declared the Wagner Act constitutional. Even before this, the two major steel companies, also anxious to avoid a costly and perhaps useless strike, had signed agreements with the CIO. While Ford and the smaller steel companies violently resisted organization for some years more, by World War II they had all been forced into line by government action.

In spite of the sharp downswing of business and employment from mid-1937 to 1939, union strength continued to increase. Enthusiastic young organizers, government protection of the processes of organization and election, and compulsory bargaining were building a labor movement of unprecedented strength. In self-defense the AFL was forced to adopt the principle of industrial unionism and compete vigorously with the CIO. In 1940 there were nearly 9 million organized workers: over 4 million in the AFL, 3.5 million in the CIO, and a million in independent unions. Although substantially less than the 28 percent organized in Great Britain, the 30 percent in France, and the 50 percent in Australia and Denmark, the total of nonagricultural unionized employees was at a peak for the United States.

The Continuing Indian Problem. By the mid-twenties government policies concerning the 325,000 Indians scattered across the nation had obviously failed. The Dawes Act of 1887, providing for individual allotments of tribal land, had, through subsequent sale, fraud, and division by inheritance, reduced many Indian family holdings to acreages too small to sustain life, particularly in the semi-arid Southwest, where most Indians lived. The total acreage still owned by Indians had declined 60 percent since 1880, and a majority had a per capita income of under $200 a year.

But reform was a baffling problem. There were scores of tribes and languages. Sometimes two different dialects would be spoken in a single tribe. Almost a fifth of the Indians spoke no English. Some tribes were scattered and their members partially assimilated; others like the Navajos and Pueblos were intact and had many "full-bloods." Boarding-school education, which had been promoted by the Bureau of

Indian Affairs, alienated many children from their hereditary culture while failing to equip them for full participation in white society.

To reformers such as Charles J. Rhoads, John Collier, and the American Indian Defense Association, the best hope for the future appeared to be in strengthening tribal organization and restoring communal land holding. Rhoads, as Indian Commissioner in the Hoover Administration, failed to secure action, but in 1934 his successor, Collier, was influential in getting the Wheeler-Howard bill through Congress. For those tribes which voted to accept it, the Act ended further individual allotments and restored all remaining lands to tribal ownership. More land was to be purchased by the government to resettle landless Indians. Tribes were to be set up as corporations, able to draw on a $10 million revolving fund for new economic enterprises. Each cooperating tribe was also to draw up and ratify a constitution that would restore government by a tribal council.

The resulting policies, pursued by the Bureau over the next generation, were, on the whole, unsuccessful. The Act was, by congressional mandate, not applied in Oklahoma, where the "Five Civilized Tribes" lived and enjoyed some unevenly distributed wealth from oil. The Navajo tribe, numbering about a quarter of all Indians, refused to join. Application of the Act to most of the remaining tribes, with the addition of over 7 million acres of poor land, led to no considerable gain in prosperity for the Indians but to a great deal of trouble between the Indians, the paternalistic local agents, and the remote Bureau. In all, this well-intentioned policy came too late in the history of Indian-government relations to alter the results of decades of neglect and abuse in both policies and administration. By the mid-twentieth century, Indian grazing culture and white industrial society were so far apart that any assimilation could only be slow and difficult. Reconstitution of tribal society, on the other hand, was both artificial and—given the great differences among the Indian peoples—extremely difficult.

Black America. The depression decade was nearly spanned by a particularly flagrant denial of justice to nine young blacks accused early in 1931 of the rape of two white girls on a freight train in Alabama. Tried before an all-white jury in Scottsboro and defended only by inadequate counsel, eight of the nine were sentenced to death. In 1932 and 1934 the United States Supreme Court ordered retrials. Finally four of the prisoners were released, and in 1938 the Supreme Court refused to order a further trial for three sentenced to life and one to death. (Of these remaining four, two were paroled in 1944 and one in 1951; the fourth escaped in 1948.) During the thirties, the case achieved worldwide notoriety—thanks in part to the action of the legal bureau of the Communist party—and outside the South, at least, there was little doubt that the accused had suffered shocking injustice because of their race.

President Roosevelt appointed white race-relations counselors in many government departments, and as the urban black vote shifted dramatically from Republican to Democratic, Mary M. Bethune became Director of Negro Affairs in the National Youth Administration and Robert C. Weaver adviser to the Department of the Interior—the highest federal posts held by blacks since World War I. In *United States v. Classic* the Supreme Court made the state governments responsible for the conduct of party primaries and hence for the enforcement of constitutional rights in these contests, which were in fact the real elections in the solidly Democratic South. On the whole, however, the President was not prepared to battle Southern congressmen over enforcement of the rights of blacks, and New Deal housing policies actually increased segregation. But the plight of the poor black—and of the impoverished and neglected Indian—was publicized as never before, in part through the activities of the President's remarkable wife, Eleanor.

Toward the end of the period some progress was made toward equality of economic opportunity. The NAACP, directing its energy toward winning equal pay for black schoolteachers, had little immediate success, but in 1941 the federal district court for Virginia, at least, ordered equality by 1943. The CIO in principle admitted blacks to all its unions, though in the South they were often put into separate locals and denied true job equality. The growth of the new labor movement brought black workers into the mass production industries and in a few cases to minor administrative positions in big white companies.

Return to Depression. Aided by increased federal spending for WPA and payment of the remainder of the World War I soldier's bonus certificates (over the President's veto), 1936 and early 1937 were a period of returning prosperity. At this point the lack of any clear economic policy by either the administration or most of its critics was disastrously illustrated. To suit the conservatives in Congress, whose votes were needed to pass the Court bill, the President promised a balanced budget for 1937–38. His own fear of too strong a boom, even though six million were still unemployed, was shown when the Federal Reserve System took strong steps to tighten the money market.

As a result of this drastic reversal in federal policies, the sharpest business decline in American history began in July 1937 and reached bottom about mid-1938. Not until the beginning of 1940, when the European war and American rearmament had become important economic factors, was there a return to the business volume of 1937. The severity of the depression was about equal to that of late 1931. Unemployment rose above ten million, or a fifth of the labor force, and even with the return toward prosperity in 1940 over eight million people were still looking for jobs.

The renewed depression forced the government to institute new policies to promote recovery. Agricultural production had been sharply cut by a severe drought in 1934 and a more moderate one in 1936. In the latter year Congress passed a soil conservation act to check planting of soil-depleting crops and encourage planting of soil-restoring crops. As a result of these developments agricultural income, including government payments, stood up better than did the income of other sectors. In addition, the well-organized farmers won substantial new support in the Agricultural Adjustment Act of 1938. Soil conservation was to be encouraged by payments to staple crop producers agreeing to acreage allotments. Marketing quotas could also be imposed by the vote of two thirds of the growers of a staple crop. If Congress appropriated the money, farmers conforming to these regulations would be given "parity payments" whenever actual prices fell below "parity prices"—government-determined prices intended to keep the farmer's purchasing power at the 1909–14 level.

Crop loans were also available to all farmers of crops with marketing quotas, but those who did not accept the quota could borrow only 60 percent as much as could the cooperators. In spite of many loopholes and much subsequent criticism, this law remained the basic plan of agricultural support.

Wage and hour guarantees attempted in the NIRA were now incorporated in a Fair Labor Standards Act. The labor of children under sixteen was prohibited, the minimum wage was set at twenty-five cents an hour, and overtime was to be paid beyond forty-four hours a week. The Housing Act of 1937, now in operation, began the great task of slum clearance. Other parts of the federal budget, including public works and defense, were allowed to grow so that federal expenditures in 1939, more than 25 percent above 1938, were the highest of any peacetime year in previous American history.

Failure of the New Deal.   While the New Deal had greatly improved stability and security in the national economy, it had not brought satisfactory recovery. For the first time the gross national product per capita had failed to achieve a level higher than in the previous decade. What had been wrong? Several different answers were possible, depending upon different economic emphases.

It was possible, first of all, to emphasize the fact that from beginning to end President Roosevelt, either from conviction or for political expediency, held down spending and tried to balance the budget. Prior to the renewed depression of 1938, only 1934 and 1936 showed substantial increases in government spending in relation to receipts, and in both cases the level of spending dropped the following year. Put another way, the administration failed to make a clean break with the idea of the self-regulating economy and failed to develop a philosophy of where and how to spend. Yet while failing to spend at the level necessary to promote expansion, the government did not announce policies that encouraged expansion through investment by business.

Another line of reasoning pointed to the failure of NIRA and other legislation substantially to redistribute income so as to create sharply increased consumer demand. Still another was that by chance too few technological innovations occurred that offered profits in return for large capital investment.

Whatever approach one took, the disturbing question remained: How could a healthy economy be assured in time of peace?

THE APPROACH OF WORLD WAR II

Breakdown of the Security System.   Despite prevailing isolationist sentiment, the United States in the 1920s was part of a system of international security which rested on the Washington Treaties of 1922 governing Far Eastern relations (see p. 187); on the structure of international debt and reparations payments as worked out in the Dawes and Young Plans (see p. 188); and on the ability of the League of Nations—or its leading members, England and France—to police the settlement of Versailles. Between 1931 and 1935 this entire security structure was demolished, leaving the world perennially on the verge of war.

Partly because Russia had not been invited to take part in the Washington Conference, the treaties of 1922 did not bring peace to China. During the next decade Russia and China first combined to reunify China by defeating local warlords and then fought each other in an undeclared war. When peace was restored with Russia, the Chinese Nationalist leader Chiang Kai-shek tried to assert his power in southern Manchuria, long a Japanese sphere of influence. This gave the strongly imperialist Japanese army the excuse to overthrow the liberal ministry in Tokyo and to wage a war for complete control of Manchuria. The League of Nations, as well as individual countries like Britain and the United States, condemned the Japanese aggression, but Japan ignored the protests, completed its conquest of Manchuria, and in 1933 withdrew from the League. This demonstration that a great power could embark on aggression without meeting effective opposition from the strong members marked the beginning of the collapse of the League.

International debt and reparation payments depended upon continuing loans from the United States. With the collapse of the Wall Street security market it was only a question of time before payments ended. President Hoover's moratorium in 1931 temporarily eased the debt burden on European nations, but neither the Hoover nor the Roosevelt administration was ready to profit from the inevitable by canceling the war debts. After 1934 only Finland continued to pay, and another part of the World War I settlement had come to an end.

Meanwhile, Italy followed Japan's lead in aggressive expansion. In October 1935, the Italian fascist dictator Mussolini launched a wholesale invasion of the African kingdom of Ethiopia. President Roosevelt declared an arms embargo, and the League of Nations, under British pressure, condemned Italy as an aggressor and imposed economic sanctions. But because Britain and France were afraid of driving Germany and Italy into an alliance, the embargo did not include coal and oil. Furthermore, the League had little machinery for enforcing economic sanctions, and nonmembers like Germany and the United States largely ignored the prohibitions. As a result, the conquest of Ethiopia was quickly completed, and the authority of the League completely undermined.

The conflict over Ethiopia gave the new dictator of Germany, Adolf Hitler, his first big opportunity to use the military force he had been building up in defiance of the Versailles Treaty. In March 1936 Nazi troops marched into the Rhineland, which had been demilitarized by the Versailles Treaty. France mobilized 150,000 troops, but Britain refused to support the use of force to compel German withdrawal. Another World War I agreement had been smashed.

Why had the major military and naval powers of the world failed to enforce the peace? In the first place, Russia, the nation most feared in the long run by Great Britain, was not a party to the Western agreements. (The Soviet Union was not recognized by the United States until 1933.) The fact that Hitler was a professed enemy of Russia made it difficult for British governments, particularly the Conservative ones, to decide where the ultimate national interest lay. Yet even if the British decided to let Hitler gain strength, they did not want him too strong, and this weakened them in dealing with Italy. Another factor faced by both Britain and the United States was the strength of pacifist and neutralist movements in their own countries. A government embarking on vigorous policies that risked war might find itself lacking in the necessary legislative support. In France many conservatives in the army and the government feared communism much more than they feared Hitler's fascism.

Isolation and Neutrality. The breakdown of the world order led the United States both to strict isolationist legislation and to an effort to weld the Western Hemisphere into a self-sufficient defense system. The latter presented many difficulties. Aside from Canada, the nations of the Western Hemisphere were further removed from the United States by tradition and national culture than were the nations of northern Europe, and the capitals of the three largest South American powers, Argentina, Brazil, and Chile, were also farther removed geographically. Economically as well, the United States had more ties with Europe, and so did each of the major South American nations.

President Roosevelt's inaugural address in 1933 dedicated the United States to "the policy of the good neighbor"—nonaggression, nonintervention, and friendly cooperation to solve mutual problems in the Western Hemisphere. At the seventh Pan-American Conference meeting at Montevideo later the same year, the United States subscribed to a nonintervention pact adopted unanimously by the conference. But the attitude of the United States toward social democratic governments in the Caribbean area remained ambiguous. In the same year the new pact was adopted, Washington withheld recognition of a liberal government in Cuba which was opposed by the island's landed and business interests, and American warships surrounded the island. These actions, engineered by conservative State Department officials rather than President Roosevelt, led eventually to the overthrow of liberal government by military dictator Fulgencio Batista.

The President's long-range policy was reaffirmed the next year by abrogation of the Platt Amendment authorizing intervention in Cuba and by withdrawal of marines from Haiti. In 1936 the United States ratified a treaty restoring sovereign powers to Panama. Reciprocal trade agreements negotiated with six Latin American nations strengthened economic ties. While the bonds between "good neighbors" five thousand miles apart remained somewhat tenuous, the Roosevelt administration policy marked a great improvement over inter-American relations of the previous thirty years.

Though Americans in the mid-thirties were fully cognizant of the onrush of fascism in Europe, most of them were confident that the United States could remain a neutral bystander in the impending conflict. As Europe's crises deepened, determination mounted in the United States to "sit this one out." The hastily improvised Neutrality Act of 1935, reluctantly signed by Roosevelt, prohibited the export of arms or ammunition to belligerents and required the President to forbid American citizens to travel on the ships of belligerents except at their own risk. A "permanent" Neutrality Act in 1937 retained the earlier restrictions on loans and munitions in time of war and declared travel on belligerent vessels unlawful for American citizens. In addition it provided that for a period of two years belligerent nations could purchase goods, other than munitions, in the United States only on a "cash-and-carry" basis. During the Spanish Civil War of 1936–39, in which Germany, Italy, and the Soviet Union all took a hand, the United States remained resolutely neutral.

Rise of the Axis. In 1936 the presumed safeguards of the World War I diplomatic structure were finally swept away. In October and November Germany, Italy, and Japan entered into an anticommunist pact. These powers, having built new mechanized armies, were now too powerful for England and France to attack. Helped by German military engineers and scientists, Hitler had worked a diplomatic revolution that made defeated and penalized Germany the strongest nation in Europe.

Why had this happened? Causes may be traced far back, but three were abundantly clear in 1936: (1) Mutual distrust between England and France on one side and Russia on the other prevented the old World War I alliance against the central powers; (2) the United States could not be relied upon for active support; and (3) England and France had not kept up with military development. To make their plight worse, England and France guaranteed the independence of Czechoslovakia and, in 1939, of Poland, which they could not possibly defend against Germany. Faced with the choice of arming for possible war or muddling along in the hope that some change would occur in the German situation, the conservative leaders of the Western powers chose the latter course.

Large-scale Japanese inroads in northern China led President Roosevelt in a speech of October 1937 to test American sentiment by advocating a "quarantine" of aggressor nations. He quickly found that Congress was two to one against cooperation with the League of Nations in bringing effective sanctions against Japan. Underlying much of this isolationist attitude was an implicit confidence that England and France were still capable of controlling the situation. From 1938 on, however, as Germany continued to build up its mechanized army, the European situation was quite out of the preventive control of England and France. Hitler was ready to embark on a daring program of expansion, and his territorial demands were to prove limitless.

Hitler's first victim was his neighbor Austria, which Germany invaded and annexed in March 1938. After the Austrian coup, Hitler moved on to his next objective—the annexation of the Sudetenland, a German-speaking portion of Czechoslovakia. Hitler bluntly informed English Prime Minister Neville Chamberlain that he was determined to secure self-determination for the Sudeten Germans. Chamberlain in turn persuaded Édouard Daladier, the French premier, that a sacrifice on the part of Czechoslovakia would save the peace. In September 1938 Hitler, Mussolini, Daladier, and Chamberlain met in Munich and worked out the details of the surrender of the Sudetenland in return for Hitler's promise that he had no further territorial ambitions.

While the Munich Pact gave Britain precious time to build up its air force, British and French hopes that the agreement would appease Hitler's expansionistic cravings were shattered when in March 1939 the German army invaded and seized the remainder of the Czech nation. Mussolini seized Albania the following month, and the two dictators celebrated by signing a military alliance, the "Pact of Steel."

The shock of Hitler's callous violation of the solemn pledge made at Munich ended the appeasement policy of France and Great Britain. Britain launched a tremendous arms program, and in Paris Daladier obtained special emergency powers to push forward national defense.

It was Germany's aggression against Poland, however, that finally precipitated the Second World War. During the summer of 1939 Hitler made increasingly insistent territorial demands upon Poland while Chamberlain, with the French government concurring, warned the Nazi government that "in the event of any action which clearly threatened Polish independence" the British would "at once lend the Polish government all support in their power."

As German threats against Poland increased, Britain and France sought an alliance with the Soviet Union but refused to assent to its reannexation of the Baltic states. Meanwhile, the Nazi and Soviet foreign secretaries were secretly working out an agreement of their own; and on August 23, 1939, Russia and Germany signed a nonaggression pact. Russia reasoned that such a conflict would give the Soviet Union time to build up its armaments. The Soviet Union also secured German recognition of Soviet claims in eastern Poland and the Baltic states.

Now Hitler could attack Poland without fear of intervention by his great rival to the east. Without a declaration of war, Nazi troops crossed the Polish frontier on the morning of September 1, 1939, and the *Luftwaffe* began to bomb Polish cities. Hitler hoped that the appeasing governments of France and Great Britain would wring their hands and do nothing, but he miscalculated: the two Western democracies, knowing that their own time would come sooner or later, declared war on Germany on September 3. The Second World War had begun.

The Inactive War. War in Europe split American political opinion along new lines. Many liberals opposed defense spending because it would cut down on welfare appropriations. Conservatives who had vigorously opposed domestic spending were, in many cases, willing to support larger military appropriations. Public sentiment, disgusted by Europe's inability to keep the peace, was strongly against anything that would involve the United States in war.

From the start the President favored rearmament and aid to France and England. His political problem was to swing public and congressional opinion behind him. Plans for defense mobilization were drawn up but not acted upon. After the Munich Pact a White House Planning Conference led to a bill in 1939 appropriating a half billion dollars for defense. When polls early in 1940 showed public opinion 60 percent in favor of aid to England and France, the President secured a revised Neutrality Act that lifted the arms embargo for nations paying cash, but it still prohibited American ships from trading with belligerents and American citizens from traveling on belligerent vessels.

After the rapid conquest of Poland, Germany remained virtually inactive during the winter of 1939–40. This "Phony War" ended abruptly on April 9, 1940, when Germany simultaneously invaded Denmark and Norway. A month later Nazi armies invaded Belgium, France, and Holland, and in six weeks all had surrendered. After the fall of France the British rescued over 300,000 of their troops from the beach at Dunkirk, but they had to abandon practically all their equipment. The army returned to an island without land defense against armored columns. On June 10, when the defeat of France was certain, Italy came into the war on the side of Germany.

A Year of Decision. What should American policy be now that Hitler with his ally, Italy, controlled western Europe, and military men regarded the conquest of England as likely? The joint planners of the War and Navy Departments thought that the United States should husband its resources at home to prepare for attack. Isolationists, including many leading citizens and scholars, opposed any action that went beyond defense preparations. The President was for as much aid to Britain as he could arrange without being overridden by the antiwar majority in Congress.

The President's decision to take a chance on British survival through all-out U.S. aid was probably the most fateful one of the entire period. He could have pursued a more isolationist policy without alienating his political support. The policy he elected to pursue led almost inevitably to war. The overriding fact in the decisions of both Roosevelt and Wilson appears to have been an unwillingness to permit a Europe in which a militaristic Germany was the dominant power.

In a contest over policy involving military action the President has a great advantage over Congress. He can act and seek support later, whereas Congress, as a nonadministrative body, is always behind a rapid march of events. This is in effect what happened from June 1940 on. The President went ahead administratively to give England as much aid as possible. In so doing, he educated the public toward his point of view, and Congress was usually presented with actions already taken that would be hard to reverse.

In June, for example, Congress thought to restrict the President by passing a law forbidding him to give away military equipment unless the Army Chief of Staff and the Chief of Naval Operations certified it as not essential to the national defense. But on September 2 an executive agreement was signed with England transferring fifty overage American destroyers in return for British bases in Newfoundland, Bermuda, and the Caribbean. Since the bases increased American security, this action was obviously not a violation of the law, yet it tied the United States to the defense of the British Empire and marked the end of any pretext of neutrality. Germany did not declare war at this time because it did not want the United States in the war. But later in the same month Germany, Italy, and Japan formed a military alliance obviously aimed at the United States.

These critical strokes of foreign policy took place during the presidential campaign of 1940. Four days before the Republican convention met in June, the President appointed Republican leaders Henry L. Stimson and Frank Knox to his cabinet as Secretaries of War and of the Navy. Two days before the convention France surrendered. The general confusion favored the internationalists. As none of the leading Republican contenders developed decisive strength, Wendell L. Willkie, a businessman who sympathized with Roosevelt's foreign policy, was skillfully maneuvered to victory. As in 1936, the Republicans had gone far away from the principles of their center and right wing to attract marginal Democratic votes.

The national emergency led the President to seek a third term. Through the manipulations of Harry Hopkins, representing the President, the Democratic bosses were reluctantly forced to accept Henry A. Wallace, the controversial Secretary of Agriculture, for the vice-presidency.

During the campaign both those favoring all-out aid to Britain and those opposed to risks that might lead to war were nationally organized. The journalist William Allen White of Kansas headed a Committee to Defend America by Aiding the Allies, and business leader Robert E. Wood of Illinois was chairman of the isolationist America First Committee. The effect of the controversy on the campaign was not immediately clear, since both candidates were internationalists. But by October, as Great Britain withstood Germany's bombing attacks and was not invaded, the argument that aid to Britain was more important than keeping out of war lost its immediate urgency. When public opinion pollsters found that the number of those favoring foreign aid had declined to less than half the voters, Willkie shifted his ground. Having failed to gain support on the issues of the third term and mismanaged defense, Willkie now attacked Roosevelt as a warmonger. Alarmed by the apparent success of the Willkie strategy, the President was pushed further and further away from his true beliefs. Just before election he told his listeners: "I have said this before, but I shall say it again and again and again: Your boys are not going to be sent into any foreign wars." In his mind, conflict resulting from an attack on the United States would not be a "foreign" war.

The Democratic vote was slightly below that of 1936 and the Republican 5.5 million larger, but Willkie won only 82 electoral votes to Roosevelt's 449. The total minor party vote fell below 200,000. It was hard to call the result a referendum on any policy, since there had been no substantial disagreement; but it could be read as a vote of confidence in Roosevelt personally, or, as Republicans saw it, as proof of the strength of habitual patterns of voting and the Democratic political machine. To the President, it was support for more vigorous foreign aid and military preparation.

Characteristically, the President had put political and foreign problems ahead of domestic ones. By August Congress had appropriated some $16 billion for defense—enough, if it could be used, to move toward a war footing. The following month Congress agreed on a bipartisan basis to a selective service (draft) act. But meanwhile the essential economic organization for defense faltered. Production, the President felt, could be called into existence later when needed.

This was, of course, far from true. Coordination of production was in the hands of a nearly powerless National Defense Advisory Commission. In the words of Donald Nelson, its coordinator for procurement, the commission "began to stagger in the late summer and early autumn of 1940. In November it was punch drunk. It did not fall flat on its face until five days before Christmas." Its successor, the Office of Production Management, had little more success.

The basic difficulty was that private industry did not want to be regimented in time of peace, and, for fear of strengthening the isolationists, the President was reluctant to ask Congress for the necessary power. Fortunately, however, the United States had great capacity for manufacturing the automotive and other steel equipment needed for this war. Incentives such as quick tax write-offs and long-term contracts stimulated big business to undertake much of the new construction that had to precede mass production of military equipment.

By December 1940 the opinion polls indicated around 60 percent of the American people were in favor of helping Great Britain even at the risk of war. Thus, when Churchill told Roosevelt that British credit for the purchase of war supplies was nearing exhaustion, Roosevelt believed he had popular support for extending more liberal, outright aid. A bill was quickly drawn up and introduced in Congress calling for "munitions of war and supplies of many kinds to be turned over to those nations which are now in actual war with aggressor nations," to be paid back in goods and services at the end of the war. Opposed by Republican leaders, the bill had the compulsion of the situation behind it. On March 11 "Lend-Lease" became law, and the next day the President asked Congress for an initial $7 billion to implement the policy. (Total Lend-Lease aid to all the Allies through the course of the war amounted to over $50 billion.)

The United States had already broken the laws of neutrality beyond repair by aiding only one side and keeping the vessels of the other out of the western Atlantic. Lend-Lease marked the point of no return on the road to war. The bill committed American industrial power, nearly equal to that of all the rest of the world, to the defeat of Germany.

CHAPTER 9

THE AGE OF ANALYSIS

THE INNER REVOLUTION

New World of Uncertainty. In the late nineteenth century, middle- and upper-class Americans subcribed to well-defined values of Christian morality and the doctrine of self-improvement through the use of reason and will. They viewed the physical universe as a coherent, understandable system regulated by simple laws which were rapidly being learned. As a result of the firm beliefs of American society, parents and teachers tended to be authoritative, and political and economic leaders tended to be dogmatic.

During the first two decades of the twentieth century, this system of beliefs was attacked from every side. New scholarship cast doubt upon the literal truth of the Bible. Psychology first questioned the older theories of learning and mental discipline and then, through Freud and John B. Watson, attacked reason itself. Furthermore, understanding of the nature of the physical world was lost to all but scientists by the discovery that only mathematics provided a reliable guide to the behavior of matter. None of these new ideas were satisfactory substitutes for the old "truths"; the new world of science was based on uncertainty and on a continual search for answers that could, at best, be only partial.

In the first two decades of the twentieth century only scientists, clergymen, professors, and other intellectuals were much troubled by the changing bases for belief. Only in the 1920s was the impact of the new ideas felt in middle-class child rearing, education, and popular thought. But when this stage was reached, the total effect on the educated American amounted to a revolution in ideas and attitudes.

Changes in Education. The mid-nineteenth-century American view was that education should be directed toward primarily moral or religious rather than intellectual ends. The philosophy of Horace Mann, the most famous American educator of the period, was a "blend of natural law, faith in progress, capitalistic morality, and liberal Protestantism." The teacher's role was to see that the pupils memorized passages that inculcated abstract truths.

But in the late nineteenth century American scholars returned from German universities with new conceptions of psychology and elementary education. By 1900 some progressive parents were applying the new psychology to child rearing: children were to be trained by reason and interest rather than by display of parental authority. Confined to a few advanced families before World War I, these principles of letting the child experiment and learn for himself were widely held among the urban middle class of the 1920s.

A radically progressive approach to education based on the new psychology was advanced by John Dewey (see pp. 156–57). Before World War I the impact of Dewey's teachings was limited to some private schools and the public systems in a few cities, but in the 1920s his principles became dominant in the major teachers colleges and spread throughout the public school system as theory, if not as practice. Dewey's *Democracy and Education,* written in 1916, was the most influential guide; the Progressive Education Association, formed in 1919, was the major pressure group; and Teachers College of Columbia University was the chief training center for progressive educators.

Often allied with progressivism were new movements for efficiency and utility in education. School superintendents applied business methods of "job-analysis" to their schools. The intellectual worth of teachers was often neglected, while they were rated by their efficiency in performing the "housekeeping" necessities of the school. The idea of preparing the student for daily life, rather than requiring him to master a body of knowledge, led a writer in 1922 to divide school activities into four major categories: health, fundamental processes, civic and social relations, and recreation. Of these, only the second embraced conventional learning.

From the emphasis on utility came a great growth of vocational education on the secondary level. The Smith-Hughes Act of 1917, granting federal aid to vocational education, started a rapid spread of special high schools and manual or trade departments in older schools. More and more a distinction was made between the minority in high school who expected to go to college and the majority who should substitute the development of practical skills for "book learning."

In the 1930s the extreme child-centered philosophy was superseded by a community-centered approach. No doubt the depression put emphasis on social and community duties, but, in addition, child centeredness had been pushed to such chaotic extremes that even Dewey had become critical of the results. The newer view stressed good group relations among students and teachers, and schools responsive to the needs and problems of the community. Although it partially restored discipline, this approach did not necessarily place more emphasis on academic learning.

Statistics can only partly suggest the low but improving quality of teaching in the interwar period. In 1920 the average teacher's salary was $871 a year, and the usual school was a small rural building with one or two teachers. The average teacher did not have a college education and was not paid enough to support a family. As a result, most teachers were young single women teaching school until they married or found a more promising job. By 1930 the situation had improved somewhat. The average salary had risen to $1400—still inadequate for a middle-class family—and buses were introducing the consolidated school. By 1940 consolidated schools, with their greater degree of specialization among teachers, were becoming the rule in the more populous areas; a majority of the children were in urban schools; and teachers' salaries had risen about 25 percent in purchasing power.

College education followed many of these same trends. There was a decided shift away from the traditional classical program: schools of education in which physical education could be a major subject multiplied; women were offered courses in home economics; and most major universities started schools of commerce or business. For students who wanted a mixture of liberal arts and "useful" subjects, junior colleges offered two-year certificates. In 1920 there were only fifty-two such colleges; by 1930 there were ten times that number.

Although many regarded these developments as a lowering of the standards of college education, colleges and universities showed substantial development as centers of learning and research. The 1920s was the first full decade in which general research was supported by massive endowments such as those of the Carnegie and Rockefeller Foundations. Increasing private donations and state grants enabled American universities to rival those of Europe as centers of research. And at the same time more and more Americans were going to college. In 1920, 8 percent of young people aged 18 to 21 were in college; in 1930, over 12 percent; and in 1940, nearly 16 percent. College degrees were becoming increasingly important in securing jobs and gaining social prestige.

The Attack on Rationality. While the pragmatic philosophy that underlay progressive education emphasized the use of reason to alter tradition, psychological theories that emerged in the 1920s questioned man's ability to reason objectively. The founder of behaviorism, John B. Watson, who denied the existence of consciously directed reason, had a powerful influence on academic psychology; and the ideas of Sigmund Freud, a Viennese physician and neurologist, had a profound social impact. In his brilliant writings Freud popularized the idea that people were impelled to think and act in certain ways by unconscious pressures rather than by logical reasoning. Freud further held that these irrational, unconscious urges were of a "sexual" nature, although he used the term "sex" broadly to include many cravings for pleasure not normally thought of as sexual. Thus, to Freud, what appeared to be rational behavior was often merely the disguise for a mixture of erotic urges and childhood attitudes which, though they were unrecognized by the individual, influenced his behavior in many ways.

One of the great appeals of Freudianism was that it offered help to people who were emotionally disturbed. By a patient's free association of ideas in the presence of a psychoanalyst, together with the scientific interpretation of his dreams, it might be possible to bring the disturbing elements to conscious recognition and thus to lessen or end his feeling of conflict or anxiety.

Early Freudian doctrines lent themselves to a completely sexual view of man's conduct; their emphasis on the *libido,* man's instinctive sexual drive, plus Freud's denial of the validity of religious feelings had a profound effect upon the thinking of well-educated people all over the Western world. It turned older theological doctrine upside down: Freudianism placed no emphasis on abstinence and little on reason and offered salvation through indulgent secular "confession." People who sought Freudian therapy did not necessarily discard their religious faith, and a few clergymen managed to reach a compromise with the new doctrine, but again the scientific approach had weakened or contradicted the values of the nineteenth century.

Freudianism provided an excellent weapon for attacking Victorian formalities, rural Protestant virtues, older educational ideas, and limitations on women's activities. Leading intellectuals like Walter Lippmann, Harold Lasswell, and Jerome Frank applied it to politics, public opinion, and the law with the general effect of further weakening rationality and traditional standards. Magazines and books were full of the new language of psychiatry, and many well-educated people enjoyed being amateur Freudian analysts. Well-informed parents now worried about the danger of suppressing their children's urges, and the child-centered home joined the child-centered school in relaxing discipline.

Physical and Social Theory. A further attack on the nineteenth-century belief that man was on the verge of understanding the nature of things came from physical science. Over the half century before 1920 a brilliant group of European physicists and mathematicians demonstrated that man could not perceive the nature of physical reality or picture its workings by the ordinary three-dimensional images of the mind; only mathematics had a logic that could handle the four or more dimensions of physical problems. Furthermore, they discovered that matter was not solid substance but a system of electrical energy, and that the only guides to this reality were mathematical equations and readings of complicated electrical recording devices. Discoveries in the infinitesimal world of the atom and the infinite world of outer space made reflective men uncertain whether reality is precise and orderly or, at least, whether man's imagination is capable of grasping its order, if there is one. In 1930 the English physicist Sir James Jeans suggested that reality as men were accustomed to thinking of it might be only an illusion.

Some writers predicted that the scientific uncertainty that was brought to the reading public in the late 1920s would lead to a new age of faith. But the immediate effect seemed to be a move in the opposite direction. Like the earlier evolutionary theory, the new science undermined theology without offering anything positive to replace it. Furthermore, the highly abstract characterizations of God that seemed to suit the physical theories were without much appeal to Americans.

The effect of mathematical logic and the changes in scientific knowledge was also upsetting to the social sciences and philosophy. Society no longer seemed so simple as it had at the beginning of the century. If general social laws were to be discovered, it would only be by highly complex and sophisticated methods. As a result, American social scientists turned to improving their methods and trying them out on limited, carefully defined problems, rather than elaborating general systems. Philosophers, also discouraged by the mysterious character of reality, turned to studies of method. "How can any kind of truth be established?" became their major question. The testing of various systems of logic and representation consumed their time, and the main body of philosophers lost interest in general systems of thought.

While the social sciences as a whole continued their pursuit of more sophisticated methods, the depression brought the pressure of immediate, practical problems to bear on economic thinking. A few academic social scientists embraced Marxism and gave up hope for the capitalist system, but the number was surprisingly small. The majority turned to solutions of the type that were given a rounded theoretical formulation by the British economist John Maynard Keynes.

Keynes' ideas brought the first major revision of economic theory in the twentieth century. Furthermore, they offered a more realistic view of the operation of the entire economy than had existed before. His major work, *The General Theory of Employment, Interest and Money,* published in 1936, shifted the main theoretical emphasis from supply and demand to income and investment, or from the mechanics of the market to the distribution of income. Keynes' most important conclusions were: (1) that increasing the income of the poor stimulated demand, while increasing the income of the rich promoted saving; (2) that increased demand, not increased saving, led to new business investment (his major revision of older theory); (3) that total income could only increase from such investment; (4) that if the functioning of the undisturbed free market did not provide adequate business investment to maintain a sufficient flow of income, government was the only agency with sufficient spending power to see that this result was achieved.

Obviously these doctrines implying higher wages and government investment were resisted by conservatives. But the theory was already being applied in fact by the New Deal, although President Roosevelt did not subscribe to Keynesianism or any other economic theory. By the end of World War ii the prosperity induced by government spending and massive redistribution of income downward was so obvious that politicians of both major parties implicitly acted on the Keynesian assumptions, and academic economists gradually made Keynes' ideas the starting point for their new theoretical models. These things would have happened without Keynes, but he supplied the rationale for the capitalist revolution that emerged from the disaster of the Great Depression.

The Increasingly Social Gospel.   While the pressures of clergymen for sweeping social reform lessened in the prosperous 1920s, religious groups became increasingly concerned with secular matters. Urban churches, in particular, acquired game rooms, gymnasiums, and lecture halls and seemed to be shifting their emphasis from worship to social service and recreation. By the end of the decade the Federal Council of Churches of Christ, the liberal ecumenical organization, had commissions for such diverse matters as international justice, social service, race relations, and Christian education. The National Catholic Welfare Conference, formed to help carry out social obligations of the Catholic Church, became a powerful force with a large staff of experts on legislative matters. Missionary activities also were increasingly secularized. By 1920 effectively organized Protestant and Catholic missions in non-Christian areas were emphasizing "civilizing" education, medical care, and various other services.

The increasingly social orientation of the leading Protestant churches was resisted by fundamentalists—Protestants who believed in the literal interpretation of the Bible as a historical record and prophecy, as well as a guide to faith and morality. The conflict between fundamentalism and current scientific views, either religious or secular, was dramatized by the Scopes trial in 1925. John Scopes, a science teacher in a Tennessee high school, was charged with violating a state law forbidding the teaching in public schools of any theories denying the Biblical account of the creation of man—Darwin's theory of evolution in particular. With his prosecution led by William Jennings Bryan, who championed the literal interpretation of the Bible, and his defense conducted by the famous liberal lawyer Clarence Darrow, Scopes was convicted of violating the Tennessee law and fined $100, but the penalty later was set aside. The Scopes trial attracted more national and worldwide attention to American fundamentalism than did any other event of the period between the wars.

Equally fundamentalist but with a quite different mission and influence were the ethnic churches in the urban centers. Each immigrant group quickly established its own congregations, which were centers of neighborhood social life and for the preservation of national customs and ceremonies. Wise Catholic bishops usually appointed priests of the same nationality as the parishioners. Second- and third-generation immigrants often supported their churches and church schools more to preserve their national cultures than because of particular denominational faith.

As the old-stock white middle class deserted the cities, more and more urban Protestant churches became black. The original Southern Baptist denomination spawned numerous cults and sects, whose small churches provided centers where the members, often from the same areas of the South, could rejoice in the promise of a better life to come. This emphasis on the hereafter rather than the now made the black churches, as a whole, a conservative influence, tending to reconcile parishioners to their earthly lot.

Except in the South the Protestant church in America had been mainly supported by the urban middle class. Neither farmers in remote areas nor working-class city dwellers generally made the effort necessary to participate in the activities of a Protestant church, but for status-seeking members of the middle class, particularly in suburban areas, the church had a definite social value. It was a place to meet leading citizens and develop friendships through cooperation in religious endeavors. Consequently, the great growth of the urban and suburban middle class and the spread of the automobile to outlying areas led to a steady increase in church membership up to 1929. By 1926, 46 percent of the population were church members.

These reasons for growth go far to explain why the Great Depression reversed the trend in membership. People with only shabby clothes and no money for the collection plate did not want to appear before their more prosperous neighbors. The depression may actually have increased religious feeling, but between 1930 and 1934 the income of Protestant churches declined 50 percent. For the decade as a whole church membership fell about 6 percent. That the decline was caused by financial hardships is further indicated by the rapid growth in membership in the prosperous years that followed World War II.

The Great Depression brought liberal Catholic, Jewish, and Protestant organizations closer together. In 1931 the National Catholic Welfare Conference, the General Conference of Rabbis, and the Federal Council of Churches of Christ joined in a conference on Permanent Preventatives of Unemployment. Such efforts were continued by an interfaith Committee on Religious Welfare Activity. Despite vocal opposition from conservatives who wanted their churches to refrain from raising political and social questions, liberal religious journals became increasingly secular in content and more concerned with economic problems. But in spite of social criticism by a small group of religious leaders, parish churches and their ministers tended to remain quite conservative.

MASS COMMUNICATION

Newspapers. The newspaper continued to be the principal reading matter of adult Americans. Where personal interests were involved, such as in attitudes toward the New Deal, readers were obviously prepared to disagree with their newspapers. But by subtle selection and handling of news and comment the papers and press associations undoubtedly influenced readers to accept the ideas of publishers and editors.

The major trends in the period between the wars were toward papers that were less directly competitive and more elaborate. While newspaper chains stopped growing in the 1930s, another ultimately more important limitation on competition came from the merger of competing papers within the same city. In 1930 nine tenths of the cities with a population of more than 100,000 had two or more directly competing papers, but of the smaller cities only a fifth had such morning or evening competition.

In the larger cities competition of a sort was often maintained by an all-day tabloid competing against single full-sized morning and evening papers. The first American tabloid newspaper was the *New York Daily News,* started by Joseph M. Patterson in 1919. Easy to read on subways and buses, by 1924 the *News* had the largest circulation in the city. Other publishers quickly copied Patterson's innovation, and by 1940 there were nearly fifty tabloids.

Another form of potential competition whose effects on the full-sized daily were hard to measure was radio news. To protect themselves, many papers—250 by 1940—bought control of radio stations. In spite of the obvious fact that radio could deliver news more quickly, intimately, and dramatically, the effect of news broadcasts on newspaper circulation was not severe. As the public received increasing amounts of news, it appeared to gain more interest in local, national, and international events and to spend more time learning about them.

Improvements in technology and press services produced better quality newspaper illustrations, more detailed last-minute news, and an increase in special departments and columns. The humorous columnist like "Mr. Dooley," or Will Rogers, his counterpart in the 1920s, was an old feature, but the column of serious general comment was an innovation in the twenties. People bought papers just to read some favorite columnist like Heywood Broun or Walter Lippmann. The more popular writers were distributed by press syndicates to newspapers all over the United States.

Magazines. The increasing public appetite for current events was fed by the rise of weekly news magazines. In 1920 only the *Literary Digest,* which took its material on current events largely from the newspapers, was important in this weekly field. In 1923 *Time,* smartly written under the direction of editors Briton Hadden and Henry Luce, made an immediate hit and inspired two other news weeklies. Following English patterns, the weekly picture magazine *Life* was started by the Luce organization in 1936. It also attracted imitators.

Throughout the 1920s the aged *Saturday Evening Post* was supreme among general weekly magazines. Closely mirroring the interests of the satisfied middle class, it mixed good popular fiction with inspirational articles about business leaders and the virtues of the American way of doing things. During the 1930s the *Post,* by turning more liberal, managed to hold much of its circulation, but competitors in its own field as well as other types of magazines were weakening its position.

Surrounded by hundreds of magazines and other sources of news and comment, the educated man of the 1920s frequently felt unable to keep up with what was being written. To help him, Mr. and Mrs. De Witt Wallace started *The Reader's Digest,* a reprint of what they considered the most important magazine articles of the preceding month. As the popularity of their digest grew, they also commissioned articles and condensed books for quick reading. Ultimately *The Reader's Digest* became the most widely read magazine in the world.

Radio. In August 1920, Station WWJ of the Detroit *News* began commercial broadcasting. The mass development of radio was retarded by many problems, including the control of necessary patents by American Telephone and Telegraph, General Electric, and Westinghouse, and the unwillingness of Associated Press, the largest news service, to have its releases broadcast. But in 1926 A. T. & T. agreed to permit network broadcasting by renting its wires, and the same year AP, pressed by Hearst's International News Service and other competitors, amended its rules to allow broadcast of important news. Between 1926 and 1929 three national radio networks were created. Advertising agencies now brought their big clients to the networks, and radio quickly achieved the form that was to characterize it during the next generation.

By 1940 four fifths of American households had radios. These families heard Hoover, Roosevelt, and other political leaders put forth their views; Franklin Roosevelt, in particular, capitalized on his charming radio personality and the pseudo-intimacy of home reception in his "fireside chats."

Since advertisers dictated what was to be performed, there was little sponsorship for serious drama or literature during the popular hours. The leading stars of screen and stage appeared on radio, but usually as special attractions in the middle of variety shows. The only obvious effect of radio on its listeners was to make American culture more uniform in language, humor, and material goals.

THE ARTS

During the prosperous twenties, patronage of the arts was more widespread than ever before, but the Great Depression brought five grim years when most painters, sculptors, and serious composers could sell practically nothing. Rescue came in 1935 from the Federal Arts Project, a branch of WPA. Forty thousand destitute actors, musicians, writers, and painters were employed at from $60 to $100 a month, and they quickly produced an unprecedented amount of music, drama, and other art for audiences that ran into the millions. This financial support, meager as it was, won many artists back from rebellion to a more balanced judgment of American society.

Painting. While a number of major American artists continued to work in one or another of the modes of abstract painting launched earlier in Europe (see pp. 161–62), during the reaction of the 1920s against prewar enthusiasms nonrepresentational painting failed to attract young artists, and it diminished in popularity during the depression. A group including Charles Sheeler and Georgia O'Keefe, whose work was better received by the public, emphasized the abstract aesthetic form in machinery, architecture, and nature. Their craftsmanship was exacting, their themes recognizable, and their forms sharply bounded and precise.

The main body of important American painting during the interwar period, however, illustrated a more conventional type of painting which had close enough contact with reality to permit social observations. Thomas Hart Benton, Grant Wood, and John Steuart Curry dealt with the rural sights and characters of the Midwest, both pleasant and unpleasant. In contrast to the Midwesterners there existed a group of painters who similarly concentrated on the American scene but explored the problems of urban life. Ben Shahn, William Gropper, and Philip Evergood were among those stimulated by a strong sense of social justice, engendered primarily by the depression, and they sought to use art as a "social weapon"; in their paintings they protested against political corruption, slums, and strikebreaking. Whereas the ashcan school of the early twentieth century (see p. 161) had seen poverty as picturesque or inescapable, these angry painters of the 1930s saw it as an inexcusable result of capitalism.

Never before in American history had so many young men sought careers in art. The prosperity of the middle twenties produced one great wave, which ended for the majority in poverty and nonproductivity during the first half of the 1930s. The second major upswing came in 1935 with the Federal Arts Project. Partly because the subsidized painters had to do so many community murals and other public pictures, and partly because there was a general return to an appreciation for things American, this art tended to embrace the national past. It cannot be said with assurance that during these twenty years any great masterpieces were executed by American painters, but the total product of the abler artists was larger and more impressive than in previous generations.

Music. The development of the phonograph and the radio gave composers and performers of serious music a vastly expanded audience. By the 1920s phonographs and records had achieved an accuracy of reproduction that made them acceptable to fine musicians. Undoubtedly many more people than ever before became acquainted with operas, symphonies, and other classical works.

Although composers, like other artists, had reacted before the war to the new scientific attitude of experimentalism, trying dissonant, multitonal, nonrhythmic compositions, this avant-garde had few representatives in the United States. Instead, an upsurge in American composition drawing on native materials produced works ranging from simple blues and popular songs through more sophisticated show tunes and the jazz-based dance music of Duke Ellington to concertos and symphonies. Jazz—which has been called both the major black contribution to American culture and the only purely American contribution to the arts—was already mature in 1920. During the following decade the musical comedies of American composers Irving Berlin, George Gershwin, Jerome Kern, and Cole Porter captivated the Western world. Carrying the same motifs to a higher plane of serious composition, George Gershwin wrote *Rhapsody in Blue* (1924), *An American in Paris* (1928), and *Porgy and Bess* (1935), all of which won worldwide acclaim. Aaron Copland, Roy Harris, the black composer William Grant Still, and other Americans also wrote ballet scores and symphonies giving classic form to American rhythms and melodies.

The stage—and particularly the musical stage and the bandstand—offered the American black his best opportunity to escape from poverty and social invisibility. At a time when practically all sports were still segregated, white jazz musicians looked to the great black jazz men for both instruction and inspiration, and in the thirties blacks and whites played jazz together publicly as well as privately. Paul Robeson achieved stardom both as actor and as singer; Robeson and the contralto Marian Anderson won wide acclaim in the concert hall.

Literature and Drama. Writers of the 1920s experienced a growing dissatisfaction with and alienation from American society and twentieth-century values. In particular, they were disillusioned by the ease with which Woodrow Wilson and other world leaders had converted moral idealism into a zeal for war; they were alienated by the triumph of materialism and business values in the postwar period; and they were exasperated by the smug self-satisfaction of the American upper classes. "The younger generation," wrote Harold Stearns, "*is* in revolt; it *does* dislike almost to the point of hatred and certainly to the point of contempt the type of people dominant in our present civilization."

In *This Side of Paradise* F. Scott Fitzgerald complained that the young writers "had grown up to find all Gods dead, all wars fought, all faiths in men shaken." They deplored American materialism, prosperity, Puritanism, and conformity—in short, much of the national heritage. But unlike the confident prewar novelists, they did not preach reform, for they saw no immediate way of correcting the situation. This prevailing nonsocial attitude was sweepingly expressed by the leading drama critic, George Jean Nathan: "What concerns me alone is myself and a few close friends. For all I care the rest of the world can go to hell at today's sunset."

To escape from America writers moved to the relative isolation of Greenwich Village in New York City or to the more complete separation of Paris. That critic H. L. Mencken's pungent but superficial and nihilistic attacks on American values were widely read in both his *American Mercury* magazine and in book form revealed the desire of many intellectuals to divorce themselves from most traditional American attitudes.

Yet from this alienated generation of writers came as much good drama, poetry, and fiction as the United States had ever seen. Novelists denounced the world in vigorous new prose, used new literary techniques, and wrote with frankness and sincerity. Ernest Hemingway, who gave currency to the phrase "the lost generation," brilliantly pictured its disillusioned, cynical, expatriate society in *The Sun Also Rises* (1925) and traced the causes of that disillusionment and cynicism in his novel of World War I, *A Farewell to Arms* (1929). But by 1940 in *For Whom the Bell Tolls* Hemingway had moved gradually to a more positive position of affirming the need for the social solidarity of free men against totalitarianism.

Other writers exposed the contradictions and hypocrisies of American culture. *An American Tragedy* (1925), which portrayed a young American hopelessly confused by the false social and religious values of his environment, marked the summit of

Theodore Dreiser's career. Sinclair Lewis wrote all of his important attacks on American society during the 1920s. *Main Street* (1920) satirized the small town of the Middle West, where "dullness made God." *Babbitt* (1922) parodied the self-satisfied, conformist, materialistic American businessman so successfully that "Babbitt" and "Babbittry" were added to the dictionary. *Arrowsmith* (1925) depicted an America which placed frustrating impediments in the path of a doctor devoted to medical research. *Dodsworth* (1929) satirized the American woman, picturing Fran Dodsworth as a pampered, selfish, superficial, pretentious snob. Sherwood Anderson in *Winesburg, Ohio* (1919) and in subsequent books showed from a Freudian viewpoint how middle-class morals and customs produced a neurotic society. Perhaps the most brilliant attacks on the lack of proper values among the American upper class were in F. Scott Fitzgerald's *This Side of Paradise* (1920) and *The Great Gatsby* (1925).

The continuing black protest against the injustice of American life and the growing sense of black racial unity were reenforced for a brief period in the twenties by white writers in search of new themes and forms of expression. Urban communities of educated blacks had, from the beginning of the century, produced an increasing volume of prose and poetry. The discovery, about 1925, of this literature by white novelists and critics such as Sherwood Anderson and Carl Van Vechten called the attention of their readers to what came to be called the Harlem Renaissance. While recognition and attendant pride undoubtedly stimulated black creativity, the sudden flood of publicity produced the false impression that the black literary movement was a new, brief phenomenon. In fact, James Weldon Johnson's novel, *The Autobiography of an Ex-Colored Man* was first published in 1912; Langston Hughes' remarkable output of prose and poetry, fiction and nonfiction, extended into the 1960s; and other writers of the Harlem Renaissance, like Countee Cullen, Alain Locke, Claude McKay, and Jean Toomer, were by no means limited to the last half of the 1920s. As a group, perhaps their greatest achievement was to portray the world of the American black man and woman as they knew it.

In contrast to the preoccupation of writers in the twenties with individual emotional adjustment as seen in the light of new psychologies, the Great Depression inevitably brought a return to social problems. Poverty amidst plenty was the writers' lot as well as that of the masses. John Dos Passos, an alienated member of the upper middle class who had begun an attack on American capitalism in *Three Soldiers* (1921), achieved his best work in a trilogy, *U.S.A.*, published between 1930 and 1935. His picture of American capitalism was far from objective, but the writing was sincere and powerful.

John Steinbeck's *The Grapes of Wrath* (1939), a chronicle of the misery of a family of Oklahoma tenant farmers who migrate to California in search of work, is a graphic description of the contrast between prosperous, propertied Americans, protected by the machinery of government, and the migratory unemployed. Accounts of suffering based on experience rather than observation include Henry Roth's *Call It Sleep* (1934), an autobiographical account of childhood in the slums of New York, and Richard Wright's *Native Son* (1940), a picture of white oppression drawn by an angry black man. The strength of both springs from the deep emotional understanding of the authors.

Three men who placed less emphasis on immediate political problems produced notable work between 1929 and 1941. James T. Farrell's three-volume *Studs Lonigan* (1932–1935) showed the failure of the traditional character-building institutions—the home, the school, and the church—to prevent the moral ruin of a young Irish-American in Chicago. William Faulkner published a dozen volumes dealing both realistically and symbolically with the failure of Southern society to adjust to the twentieth century. His vivid portrayals of the inner life of very diverse characters in an imaginary Mississippi county were relatively timeless and uninfluenced by the depression. Thomas Wolfe, regarded by many critics as a major figure, wrote four autobiographical novels between 1929 and his death in 1938. Combining both an obsession with his own emotional responses and a devotion to America, his long, loose-jointed books were unique in a decade largely given over to novels of social analysis.

The twenties in particular were a time of continuing achievement in American poetry. T. S. Eliot, expatriate but still an American citizen, published *The Waste Land* (1922), a poem of despair that exerted tremendous influence. Hart Crane's major work, *The Bridge,* appeared in 1930. In addition to some of the older poets, Wallace Stevens, William Carlos Williams, Robinson Jeffers, E. E. Cummings, and Marianne Moore were all writing poetry of the first rank.

In drama the postwar rebellion against the world in general and America in particular also produced important work. The eleven plays of Eugene O'Neill, from *Beyond the Horizon* (1920) to *Mourning Becomes Electra* (1931), all strongly influenced by Freudian psychology, marked the first major American contribution to serious theater. A number of other dramatists, including Sidney Howard, Maxwell Anderson, Elmer Rice, and Robert Sherwood, joined in this remarkable upsurge. During the depression a new playwright, Clifford Odets, wrote a strong drama, *Waiting for Lefty* (1935), in praise of collective action and the labor movement; and late in the decade there was a shift from anticapitalist plays to antifascist and antiwar themes. The most talented woman playwright of the times was Lillian Hellman, a severe critic of much in American life. But, all in all, neither American drama nor poetry and fiction in the depression period equalled in originality or vigor the work of the twenties.

Motion Pictures.   D. W. Griffith's silent movie, *Broken Blossoms,* starring Lillian Gish, was widely acclaimed in 1919 by critics as marking the emergence of a new art form, said by the *Literary Digest* to be as important as music or poetry. Unfortunately, technological success and the work of this one middle-aged pioneer were not followed by a great burst of high-quality motion picture composition, directing, and acting.

The motion picture as an art medium was subordinated to business interests in marketing the film. The major production studios owned chains of theaters and controlled the circulation of pictures. With an investment of $2 billion to protect by 1930, the managers of the industry were unwilling to risk films that might not appeal to a major part of the American public; consequently, motion pictures of the twenties were massive spectacles of courts and armies directed by Cecil B. DeMille, sentimental melodramas starring Mary Pickford, breathtaking exploits by Douglas Fairbanks, Sr., or romantic seductions by Rudolph Valentino. Charlie Chaplin, producing and directing his own pictures, continued in his comedies of the underdog to protest against the current trends of both American society and Hollywood film production.

In the last three years of the 1920s sound and then color made the motion picture potentially the equal of the stage. As a result, local and traveling stock companies and vaudeville practically disappeared, and the professional stage became restricted to a few of the largest cities. From the 1920s to the 1950s the motion picture was the standard form of dramatic entertainment in the United States.

Although the artistic quality of the best pictures of the 1930s was unquestionably superior to that of the previous decade, the industry still feared realism and dealt only occasionally and cautiously with social problems. Accepted doctrine was that the audience wanted to escape into a dream world of wealth and high adventure. Consequently, with a few exceptions, the motion picture was a conservative force substituting imaginary satisfactions for worries about the daily problems of life. Produced by businessmen, pictures inevitably glorified material values and preserved the legendary American success story during the grim years of unemployment.

Architecture. To many Europeans the most important American artistic achievement of the 1920s was the skyscraper. Many European cities regulated the height of buildings, and none had the urge for lofty display that seized American business. As land values rose in U.S. cities, it became economical to increase the height of buildings in the most valuable locations, but the heights achieved in the 1920s far exceeded the economic need. The advertising value that accrued to the company that built a towering building and the extra amount that tenants were willing to pay for the prestige and convenience of such lofty offices led to a race for height that culminated in the 1200-foot Empire State Building, begun in 1929.

The architectural design that was dominant in skyscraper architecture by the late 1920s resulted partly from the New York Zoning Act of 1916, which forced setbacks in buildings rising above certain heights. The plans of the Finnish architect Eliel Saarinen, who designed a series of blocks diminishing in size as the building rose, with windows set in vertical panels between continuous strips of stone or concrete, became a general model for skyscraper design.

During both prosperity and depression, older styles of architecture dominated the design of most public buildings and homes. The Capitol in Washington, D.C., was rebuilt by the Hoover and Roosevelt administrations in the classical Greco-Roman style, the style also chosen for most post offices and state buildings. During the 1920s hundreds of thousands of new homes were built by the well-to-do, but they or their architects and builders generally preferred to adopt some past style rather than to experiment with the unfamiliar problems of "modern." Needless to say, the builders of small homes, many without architects, eschewed experimentation.

THE PERIOD AS A WHOLE

By 1940 the scientific and technological basis for a new era in the world's history had been achieved, but emotional and institutional adjustment had not taken place. "The old has lingered on as the new has appeared," wrote Walton Hamilton in 1938, "the industrial landscape is all broken up with fault lines. . . . A lingering culture—fiction, drama, music, poetry—tries vainly to bring itself alongside current industrial fact."

Economic failure was accompanied by intellectual and spiritual troubles affecting the entire Western world. Among the elite of all leading nations the scientific, pragmatic attitude had displaced the traditional "natural" or religious values of the nineteenth century. What had seemed simple and reasonable to their grandfathers seemed infinitely complex and uncertain to men of the second quarter of the twentieth century. School and church, once the guardians of basic beliefs, were now confused and tended to become followers of the new trends rather than sources of authority.

The spiritual uncertainty of the times deeply affected artists and scholars; yet both these groups reacted so vigorously against the obvious shortcomings of their environment that American productivity in both art and scholarship reached new levels. The 1930s, in particular, was a decade of realistic and sharpened probing into American problems.

BIBLIOGRAPHY

William E. Leuchtenberg, *The Perils of Prosperity: 1914–1932** (Chicago: University of Chicago Press, 1959) and Harold E. Faulkner, *From Versailles to the New Deal* (New York: U.S. Publishers Association, 1951) are good general accounts of the swing toward conservatism in the 1920s. On political and social thought see Eric F. Goldman, *Rendezvous with Destiny: A History of Modern Reform,** abr., rev. ed. (New York: Vintage Books, 1956), and Richard Hofstadter, *The Age of Reform: From Bryan to F. D. R.** (New York: Vintage Books, 1966). Arthur M. Schlesinger, Jr., *The Crisis of the Old Order** (Boston: Sentry Editions, 1957) is a provocative discussion from a Democratic viewpoint, as is Karl Schriftgiesser's more journalistic account, *This Was Normalcy* (Boston: Little, Brown, 1948). William Allen White, *A Puritan in Babylon** (Capricorn Books, 1965), is a good picture of Coolidge and his times. On the antiforeign reaction see: Kenneth T. Jackson, *The Ku Klux Klan in the City** (New York: Oxford University Press, 1969). For continuing progressivism see Kenneth MacKay, *The Progressive Movement of 1924* (New York: Octagon Books, 1966); B. C. and Fola La Follette, *Robert M. La Follette 1855–1925,* vol. 2 (New York: Macmillan, 1953); and Oscar Handlin, *Al Smith and His America** (Boston: Little, Brown, 1958). The best general economic account of the period just prior to the Great Depression is

George Soule, *Prosperity Decade: From War to Depression, 1917–1929** (New York: Harper & Row, 1968). An entertaining, journalistic, but essentially accurate picture of the period 1919 to 1939 is in two books by Frederick Lewis Allen: *Only Yesterday: An Informal History of the Nineteen Twenties** (New York: Harper & Row, 1931, and later editions); and *Since Yesterday, 1929–1939,** (New York: Bantam Matrix, 1965). John K. Galbraith, *The Great Crash 1929,** 2nd. ed. (Sentry Editions, 1969) is both lively and authoritative. For labor history see Irving Bernstein, *The Lean Years: A History of the American Worker, 1920–1933** (Baltimore: Pelican Books, 1960).

Black experience from the earliest days is covered in John Hope Franklin, *From Slavery to Freedom: A History of American Negroes,** 3rd. ed. (New York: Vintage Books, 1967) and August Meier and Elliott M. Rudwick, *From Plantation to Ghetto: An Interpretive History of American Negroes,** enlarged ed. (New York: Hill & Wang, 1970). *The Black Worker: The Negro and the Labor Movement** (New York: Atheneum, 1968) is an account by Sterling D. Spero and Abram L. Harris written in 1931. (Harris became one of the earliest black professors at a major white university.) Also by a black professor is Vishnu V. Oak, *The Negro's Adventure in General Business* (Westport, Conn.: Negro Universities Press, 1949); see also: Ivan H. Light, *Ethnic Enterprise in*

America: Business and Welfare among Chinese, Japanese and Blacks (Berkeley & Los Angeles: University of California Press, 1972). Elliott M. Rudwick, W. E. B. Du Bois: Propagandist of Negro Protest, 2nd ed. (Philadelphia: University of Pennsylvania Press, 1969) is a good biography. Writing from many periods is collected in Black Nationalism in America* (Indianapolis and New York: Bobbs-Merrill, 1970), edited by John H. Bracey, Jr., August Meier, and Elliott Rudwick. On civil and criminal rights see Bernard H. Nelson, The Fourteenth Amendment and the Negro Since 1920 (New York: 1946, reprint by Russell and Russell, 1967); and Dan T. Carter, Scottsboro: A Tragedy of the American South* (New York: Oxford University Press, 1971). The Harlem Renaissance is seen in proper perspective by a black professor, Kenny J. Williams, They Also Spoke: An Essay on Negro Literature in America, 1787–1930 (Nashville, Tenn.: Townsend Press, 1970). A famous summary of the black position in society at the end of the interwar period is Gunnar Myrdal, An American Dilemma: The Negro Problem in Modern America,* 2 vols. (New York: Torchbooks, 1969); this has been abridged by Arnold M. Rose as The Negro in America* (New York: Torchbooks, 1964).

Harris G. Warren, Herbert Hoover and the Great Depression* (New York: W. W. Norton, 1964) and Albert U. Romasco, The Poverty of Abundance: Hoover, the Nation, the Depression* (New York: Oxford University Press, 1968) are judicious accounts. A brief and recent survey of the period 1929–45 is Thomas C. Cochran, The Great Depression and World War II* (Glenview, Ill.: Scott, Foresman, 1968). More detailed are Basil Rauch, The History of the New Deal 1933–1938* (New York: Capricorn Books, 1963) and William E. Leuchtenberg, Franklin D. Roosevelt and the New Deal, 1932–1940* (New York: Torchbooks, 1963). Two more volumes by Arthur M. Schlesinger, Jr., The Coming of the New Deal* and The Politics of Upheaval* (Boston: Sentry Editions, 1965) take the Age of Roosevelt to 1936. Three volumes by Frank Freidel bring his biography, Franklin D. Roosevelt (Boston: Little, Brown, 1952–56) to 1932. A good, objective biography is James M. Burns, Roosevelt: The Lion and the Fox* (New York: Harvest Books, 1956). Legislative opposition is ably discussed in James T. Patterson, Congressional Conservatism and the New Deal* (Lexington: University of Ken-

tucky Press, 1967). All types of conservative criticism are included in Edgar E. Robinson, The Roosevelt Leadership, 1933–1945 (New York: Plenum Publishing, 1955). Roosevelt's strongest opponent on the left is covered well and in detail in T. Harry Williams, Huey Long* (New York: Bantam Books, 1970). Many of Roosevelt's associates wrote memoirs: of these Frances Perkins, The Roosevelt I Knew* (New York: Harper & Row, 1964) is favorable and Raymond Moley, After Seven Years* (Lincoln, Neb.: Bison Books, 1971) is critical. Robert E. Sherwood, Roosevelt and Hopkins: An Intimate History, rev. ed. (New York: Harper & Row, 1950) is strong on foreign affairs, while John M. Blum, From the Diaries of Henry Morgenthau, Jr., 3 vols. (Boston: Houghton Mifflin, 1959–67) is chiefly domestic. A good study of the judiciary is C. Herman Pritchett, The Roosevelt Court: A Study in Judicial Politics and Values, 1937–1942* (Chicago: Quadrangle Books, 1969). For an analysis of important changes in the patterns of voting see Samuel Lubell, The Future of American Politics* (New York: Harper & Row, 1966).

There is a considerable literature on Indian history since the 1920s. Good general accounts are Harold E. Fey and D'Arcy McNickle, Indians and Other Americans* (Harper & Row, 1971) and Hazel W. Herzberg, The Search for Indian Identity (Syracuse: Syracuse University Press, 1971). On the immediate effects of New Deal policies see: T. H. Haas, Ten Years of Tribal Government and the Indian Reorganization Act (Washington: Government Printing Office, 1947).

For a history of foreign policy friendly to Roosevelt see Allan Nevins, The New Deal and World Affairs (New York: U.S. Publishers Association, 1950); for a critical one see Charles A. Beard, President Roosevelt: A Study in Appearances and Realities (Hamden, Conn.: Shoe String Press, 1968). More detailed discussion of the American entrance into World War II, favorable to the President, is in William L. Langer and S. Everett Gleason, The Challenge to Isolation: 1937–1940: The World Crisis and American Foreign Policy (New York: Harper & Row, 1952) and The Undeclared War: September 1940–December 1941 (Gloucester, Mass.: Peter Smith, 1953).

Broadus Mitchell, Depression Decade, 1929–1931* (New York: Torchbooks, 1969) is an economic account built around New Deal legislation. John D. Black, *Parity, Parity, Parity* (Cambridge: Harvard Committee on Research in the Social Sciences, 1942) discusses agricultural policies. The effects of NIRA on small business is seen in Louis Galambos, *Competition and Cooperation: The Emergence of a National Trade Association* (Baltimore: The Johns Hopkins Press, 1966), and on big business in Sidney Fine, *The Automobile Under the Blue Eagle: Labor Management and the Automobile Manufacturing Code* (Ann Arbor: University of Michigan Press, 1963). Labor history is treated in Walter Galenson, *The CIO Challenge to the AFL* (Cambridge: Harvard University Press, 1960); Irving Bernstein, *Turbulent Years: A History of the American Worker, 1933–1941** (Sentry Editions, 1969); and Sidney Fine, *Sit-Down: The General Motors Strike of 1936–1937* (Ann Arbor: University of Michigan Press, 1969). A comprehensive but uninterpretive social and economic picture of the 1930s is Dixon Wecter, *Age of the Great Depression, 1929–1941** (Chicago: Quadrangle Books, 1971).

For a general discussion of cultural and intellectual trends between the wars see Merle E. Curti, *The Growth of American Thought* (New York: Harper & Row, Publishers, 3rd. ed., 1964), Henry Steele Commager, *The American Mind** (New York: Bantam Books Inc., 1950), and Eric F. Goldman, *Rendezvous with Destiny: A History of Modern American Reform,** abr., rev. ed. (New York: Vintage Books, 1956). Morton White, ed., *The Age of Analysis** (New York: New American Library, 1955) is lively on trends in philosophy. On religion see Robert M. Miller, *American Protestantism and Social Issues, 1919–1939* (Chapel Hill: University of North Carolina Press, 1958). Robert Lekachman, *The Age of Keynes: The Times, Thought and Triumph of the Greatest Economist of Our Age** (Vintage Books, 1966) is good and readable on the economic shortcom-

ings of the New Deal. Lawrence A. Cremin, *The Transformation of the School: Progressivism in American Education 1876–1957** (Vintage Books, 1966) is an excellent account with major emphasis on the 1920s and 1930s; Isaac L. Kandel, *American Education in the Twentieth Century* (Cambridge: Harvard University Press, 1957) is a brief general history. Volumes I and II of Erik Barnouw, *A History of Broadcasting in the United States,* 3 vols. (New York: Oxford University Press, 1966–70) are journalistic in approach but the best source.

For a general discussion of twentieth-century developments in painting see John H. Bauer, *Revolution and Tradition in Modern American Art** (New York: Praeger, 1951). Oliver W. Larkin, *Art and Life in America,* rev. ed. (New York: Holt, Rinehart and Winston, 1960) devotes Book Six to a provocative survey of the period 1930–45. There is no detailed work on the architecture of the period, but some discussion is included in James M. Fitch, *American Building: The Historical Forces That Shaped It* (Boston: Houghton Mifflin, 1948). Gilbert Seldes in *The Public Arts** (New York: Simon and Schuster, 1956) gives a highly personal interpretation of moving pictures, radio, and theater. Lewis Jacobs, *Rise of the American Film,** Studies in Culture and Communication Series (New York: Teachers College, Bureau of Publications, Columbia University, 1968) is an excellent scholarly account covering social as well as artistic aspects. For some modern criticism of cinema in the thirties see James Agee, *Agee on Film,** 2 vols. (New York: Grosset & Dunlap, 1969). There are many books on the literature of the period. For an introduction see Alfred Kazin, *On Native Grounds** (New York: Anchor Books, 1958).

*Denotes a paperback.

4

AN ERA of waR, abundanCe, & disSenSion

Historians FREQUENTLY TALK OF THE NEED TO HAVE PERSPECTIVE ON A period in order to understand it. The passage of time allows the historically unimportant to fade and partisanship to weaken. And it does more than that. It may alter the meaning of a historical era.

Take the years since the Second World War. In the early postwar years most Americans felt that they were on the verge of a golden age. Not only had the enemies, Germany and Japan, been utterly defeated, but the depression which the ending of war production had been expected to bring had failed to occur. Instead, the United States entered upon a new era of prosperity. The abundance that poured each year from farms and factories seemed to justify all the faith that Americans had traditionally placed in hard work, efficiency, and simply getting the job done. And it was true that the almost uninterrupted prosperity after 1941 dramatically improved the standard of living of the average citizen. The American worker now lived better than any other worker in the world in all history. In 1958 an hour of labor bought a meal for the average American worker, while earning a meal took a West German worker 131 minutes, a Belgian 200 minutes. Even traditionally disadvantaged American blacks were starting to participate in the new prosperity.

Today in the 1970s, however, we are beginning to see the period after 1945 with new eyes—eyes conditioned by developments of the intervening years. Many Americans are asking whether the production of more and more goods is not exacting too high a cost. As the smog created by automobiles and industries makes the air unbreathable, and the cities become clogged with traffic, and the woods and wilds are denuded for lumber or stripped bare for coal, and the rivers are turned into sewers, Americans question the hitherto unquestioned value of economic growth. (It is ironic, too, that without increasing wealth the problems of the environment and of the society cannot be attacked with any hope of success, for all the remedial measures cost money.)

The age-old justification for industrialization—indeed, its historic promise—was that more goods meant a more enjoyable life for the masses of people. But it was becoming evident that materialism breeds materialism without fostering the values, like cooperation and kindness, that leisure and wealth are supposed to encourage. There was even some evidence that abundance divides a society rather than unites it. Now the person who does not like blacks, or Jews, or Italians can move away from them—to a different neighborhood, to the suburbs, or to another part of the country. In earlier times people generally could not afford to do that; they had to learn to live with differences. In short, in a society of abundance people can indulge their prejudices, creating golden ghettos in which all the neighbors have the same backgrounds, the same attitudes, and the same credit cards.

Other developments which the 1940s had called successes a longer perspective turned into problems. During the administration of Franklin Roosevelt the growth of the power of the presidential office had been hailed as a means for achieving needed reforms, uniting the country, and providing moral leadership. Harry

Truman, John F. Kennedy, Lyndon Johnson, and Richard Nixon all followed Roosevelt's example in their own expansion of presidential power. Indeed, one of the principal criticisms of Dwight Eisenhower as President was that he did not make full use of the authority of his office. But by the 1970s senators of both parties were expressing alarm at the unceasing inflation of the powers of the President, particularly in foreign affairs. After all, during the years since Franklin Roosevelt, two Presidents had committed the country to major wars in Asia without a congressional declaration of war.

In the minds of many Americans the Second World War marked the end of isolationism: the United States, with its great industrial power, was at long last taking its rightful place as the leader of the Western world. And the nation moved swiftly into the center of world politics, committing itself not only to the defense of western Europe but to the active defense of endangered countries of Asia as well. This revolution in foreign policy was praised as evidence that the proper conclusion had been drawn from the failure of the Western democracies to stand up to Hitler in the years before World War II. This was the lesson that persuaded the Truman adminstration that the United States must fight in Korea and the Johnson administration that it must fight in Vietnam. Only gradually did it become clear that the Communist world was not analogous to the Nazi state, that it was as deeply riven by national rivalries as the capitalist world. And by the time this new lesson was being absorbed, the old policies of the Cold War had committed America to costly involvement in Southeast Asia.

As recently as 1961 President John F. Kennedy was still giving eloquent voice to that sense of power and purpose that victory in World War II had created and prosperity at home had sustained. The United States, he said at his inauguration, would "pay any price, bear any burden, meet any hardship, support any friend, oppose any foe to assure the survival and the success of liberty." Ten years later another President was recognizing the inappropriateness of such an optimistic commitment. In his first State of the World address, Richard Nixon pointed out that "America cannot—and will not—conceive *all* the plans, design *all* the programs, execute *all* the decisions and undertake *all* the defenses of the free nations of the world." Over a year earlier he had begun to withdraw troops from South Vietnam, troops whose advance guard had been sent there in 1962 by Kennedy. Although Nixon's policy was certainly not a return to the isolationism of the 1930s, the United States in the 1970s was clearly revising, if not reversing, the expansionist policy of the preceding quarter century. That fact alone could not help but influence the way Americans would evaluate those twenty-five years.

As David Potter has written in an earlier part of this book, each era attacks its immediate problems, leaving to the future the working out of the inevitable irony that the solutions of one era produce the problems of the next. And there was irony in those years. In 1945 the United States stood at the height of its economic and military power, confident and proud after the total victory over the Axis. That very confidence and pride caused it to assume more economic commitments, take on more treaty obligations, and fight more wars. Few of these decisions were wrong in themselves; each could be justified by events at the time. But by 1971 it was clear that the country could not simultaneously wage war in Asia and carry out major reforms at home. In the minds of Americans the Vietnam War was not another World War II, that "good" war for which all could justify sacrifice. It was not even a Korean War, the "police action" which few had liked but which had been at least terminable. Rather, it was a war that no one wanted but that could not be ended.

Nor was the war the only frustration. It was not at all evident that even peace with abundance could end social problems like racial discrimination and urban crime, as many had once thought. It was even open to question, paradoxically enough, whether abundance could end poverty—at least through the methods and devices that have been used thus far. For despite an annual gross national product of over a trillion dollars and a succession of antipoverty, welfare, and housing programs, the slums multiplied, and millions remained poor.

In a sense, too, the irony of the era of war and abundance lay behind the so-called generation gap. It made a big difference whether you were an adult in 1945 or whether you became one at the end of the 1960s. For these were two quite different Americas, and each saw the other through different eyes. Only by knowing the history of both could the differences between them be understood.

FOR THOUGHT AND DISCUSSION

1. What does the experience of the past years of war reveal about the relationship between domestic and foreign policies? Which has more influence on the other?

2. Does the fact that the Supreme Court changes from conservative to liberal and back again call into question its authority? Is it proper for Presidents to seek to change the outlook of the Court through appointments?

3. Could a "Marshall Plan" for Asia be as successful as the one carried out in Europe? Ought one to be tried?

4. Why do many historians today, contrary to general opinion during his administration, rank Harry Truman as a great President? Why do some revisionist historians view Dwight Eisenhower's presidency as better for the country than Lyndon Johnson's?

5. How do you account for the growing popular and governmental concern for the position of blacks in American society since 1940?

6. Is American society more diverse and open in the 1970s than it was in previous periods? What standards of comparison would you use?

do ❋ oRdain

& esTablish this ConsTituTion

for the United States of America.

CHAPTER 10

THE PRICE OF POWER
1941–48

THE CHALLENGE

Roosevelt's Dilemma. The Lend-Lease Act of March 1941 was only the first step that President Roosevelt was prepared to take in order to help Britain resist German aggression. Although he probably overestimated the strength of the vocal isolationist minority, he estimated correctly the great reluctance of most Americans to become directly involved in a war. As a result, in his pursuit of what he thought was the defense of American interests, he was not always open and candid. Sometimes he acted secretly, as he did in late April 1941, when he ordered a naval patrol of the North Atlantic to help the British detect German submarines. Other times he acted as boldly as he thought the majority of the people would permit, as in July, when American troops were ordered to Iceland to relieve the British in protecting it from German invasion.

When Hitler, in a surprise move, invaded the Soviet Union on June 22, 1941, Roosevelt followed Churchill in welcoming a new fighting force in the war against Germany, even though few military advisers believed the Russians could hold out more than three months against the German blitz. Acutely aware of the weakness of British and Russian defenses, Roosevelt, in early July, asked Congress for an extension of the draft law and repeal of the prohibition on overseas service for draftees. Isolationists branded the request as yet another of the President's covert efforts to get the United States into war, but after acrimonious debate the draft extension passed by a single vote in the House of Representatives.

On August 9–12 Roosevelt and Prime Minister Churchill met secretly on the U.S.S. *Augusta* in Argentia Bay, Newfoundland. The result was the Atlantic Charter, setting forth the aims of the war: no territorial changes would be made in favor of the victors, and all nations would be protected in their right to choose their own governments, without fear of aggressive threats. When announced on August 15, this meeting between a technical neutral and an active belligerent brought loud protests from isolationists in the United States. Nevertheless, upon his return home Roosevelt asked for increased appropriations for Britain and the Soviet Union.

Undeclared War. When in September a German U-boat attacked the American destroyer *Greer,* which, unbeknown to the American public, was sending the British navy information about German submarines, Roosevelt seized the opportunity to issue a "shoot-on-sight" order to the navy and asked Congress for authority to arm American merchant ships. With American naval vessels shooting without even waiting to be attacked, it was only a matter of time before a serious incident occurred. On October 17 the American destroyer *Kearny* was torpedoed and damaged off Iceland; eleven Americans were killed. Less than three weeks later the *Reuben James* was sunk by a German U-boat with the loss of 115 lives. Yet most Americans seemed to support the President's policy, and in early November Congress authorized Roosevelt to arm merchant vessels and permit their entry into the war zone. Although the fight in Congress had been bitter, the House victory was 212 to 94, far greater than the single-vote margin of the previous summer.

By the end of November 1941 Hitler's armies were deep inside the Soviet Union, seemingly on their way to an early victory, and Japan was obviously readying itself for an offensive against the British and Dutch colonies in Southeast Asia. The President's dilemma was acute. He could not dispel the nagging fear that Russia and Britain, despite American aid, might yet be overwhelmed by the Germans—an event which would leave the United States alone to face Germany. At the same time he knew that Americans were so divided over the struggle in Europe that he dare not try to lead them immediately into full-scale war against Hitler.

Japanese-American Relations, 1940–41. Since the early 1930s, Japanese expansionism on the Asian mainland had met gradual but increasing American opposition. Finally in 1939 the United States began to restrict the flow to Japan of some strategic war materials, like oil and scrap iron. But Roosevelt would not embargo all war materials, as some of his advisers urged, because he feared that too strong a stand would push the Japanese into an adventure against the oil-rich and defenseless Dutch East Indies. Yet he believed some measures were necessary to warn Japan of American opposition to aggression. The Japanese response was to move into northern Indochina in the summer of 1940 and to join the Tripartite Pact with Germany and Italy in September 1940.

By early 1941 the Japanese and American positions in Asia were irreconcilable; Japan's minimum demand was that the United States cease its aid to Chiang Kai-shek, while the United States insisted that Japan end its war against China. During 1941 diplomatic efforts aimed at softening the two positions proved to be in vain. Japanese militarists believed that war was the only answer to America's interference with Japanese ambitions in Asia, and the military's hand was strengthened in April 1941, when the Soviet Union promised to remain neutral in the event of a Japanese-American war. Japan's fear of a two-front war was thus reduced, while Hitler's earlier promise to support Japan in a war against the United States made it clear that the United States would be the one forced to fight on two fronts.

Japanese ambitions became clearer and more alarming in July, when Japanese military units invaded southern Indochina in obvious preparation for an attack upon the Dutch East Indies. In retaliation the United States, Britain, and the Netherlands cut off all vital military supplies to Japan.

On September 6, 1941, Japan's Supreme War Council voted for war if American aid to China did not cease within six weeks. Before the six weeks elapsed, General Hideki Tojo became premier. Though convinced that war was inevitable, Tojo sent a personal representative, Saburo Kurusu, to Washington in early November for further fruitless talks with the Americans. By the end of the month Americans knew, from their breaking of the Japanese codes, that war was coming, but they did not know where in the Pacific it would start. On November 24 American naval authorities sent out warnings of war with Japan to the commanders at Pearl Harbor and Manila. On November 27 these bases were warned again, this time that "An aggressive move by Japan is expected within the next few days." On December 1 the emperor gave his consent to war; already a Japanese task force was steaming across the northern Pacific for a surprise attack on Pearl Harbor. In Washington, the two Japanese envoys, Kurusu and Ambassador Nomura, continued their inconclusive talks with Secretary of State Cordell Hull.

Pearl Harbor. The time was 7:50 on Sunday morning, December 7, 1941. In the sky over Oahu island, Captain Nakaya of the Japanese navy wrote in his log:

> Pearl Harbor is still asleep in the morning mist. The orderly groups of barracks, the wriggling white line of the automobile road climbing up to the mountaintop; fine objectives in all directions. . . . Inside the harbor were important ships of the Pacific fleet, strung out and anchored two ships side by side in an orderly manner.

Ten minutes later the first wave of Japanese planes struck the great American base. The surprise was complete; some American sailors thought the first bombs were accidentally dropped from American planes. Although the Americans fought back fiercely, the losses sustained were enormous: all eight battleships, the main object of the attack, were put out of action. Two never saw action again. Except for three aircraft carriers, which happened to be at sea, the whole Pacific fleet was damaged or destroyed. Almost all the aircraft, most of which did not even get off the ground, were knocked out. More than 2400 Americans were killed and 1200 wounded; the Japanese lost twenty-nine airplanes, five midget submarines, and one fleet submarine. Considering the extensive damage, the attack on Pearl Harbor was one of the cheapest victories in the history of warfare.

Despite the devastating success of the raid, the decision to attack Pearl Harbor was a colossal blunder. For some time the administration had feared that by attacking British and Dutch possessions in Asia without involving the United States, the Japanese would make it impossible to unify America behind a war to halt their aggression. After December 7, however, Americans were united in their opposition.

The strike against Pearl Harbor was only one part of an audacious grand plan to destroy British, Dutch, and American power in the western Pacific. Soon after the bombing of Pearl Harbor, Japanese planes attacked the Philippines. Though this time there had been some warning from Hawaii, the Americans were again caught unready. On December 8 the Japanese attacked Hong Kong, Borneo, the Malay Peninsula, and the American island outpost of Guam. The boldness and power of the Japanese advance were brought home on December 10, when Japanese land-based bombers sank the British battleship *Prince of Wales* and the battle cruiser *Repulse* off the coast of Malaya. Never before had air power destroyed a free-moving battleship; the age of the airplane in naval warfare had arrived. Successful amphibious landings in the Philippines and elsewhere also attested to the Japanese' command of the most advanced methods of offensive warfare.

The day after the attack on Pearl Harbor, Congress, at the President's request, voted for war with Japan with only one dissenting vote. On December 11, Hitler fulfilled his promise to the Japanese by declaring war on the United States; Italy followed soon thereafter. The dilemma was resolved. The United States was now in a position to use to the fullest its great power against aggressor nations in both Asia and Europe.

After the initial shock had passed, many Americans grew suspicious that the astonishing success of the Japanese assault must have resulted from traitorous acts, but exhaustive investigations on the part of both the navy and Congress produced no evidence to support such allegations. The fact is that most military experts seriously underestimated Japan's ability to mount the kind of elaborate, multipronged assault of which Pearl Harbor was but a part. The commanders at Pearl Harbor were lax in taking precautions after the war warnings of November, but these defects add up to nothing more sinister than inefficiency and carelessness.

WAR IN TWO HEMISPHERES

Creation of the Grand Alliance. Within two weeks after Pearl Harbor Winston Churchill and his chief military advisers arrived in Washington for extended discussions with the President and American military leaders about the long-range strategy of the two-front war in which both countries were now engaged. The basic decision of the conference, as General Marshall later reported, was that "Germany is still the prime enemy and her defeat is the key to victory. Once Germany is defeated the collapse of Italy and the defeat of Japan must follow." Roosevelt, despite pressure to do otherwise, never deviated from this decision, even though Japan appeared to be the greater immediate menace to the United States. The two allies also agreed to pool their resources and military equipment for the duration of the struggle. Finally, the conference created a Combined Chiefs of Staff in Washington to plan and coordinate global strategy. As a public manifestation of the new association, Churchill, Roosevelt, Maxim Litvinov (representing Stalin), and the representatives of twenty-three other nations at war with one or more Axis powers signed the Declaration of the United Nations on New Year's Day, 1942.

As the arsenal of the alliance, the United States in subsequent months worked out new Lend-Lease agreements with the principal allies. According to these agreements, the costs of the war were to be borne in proportion to ability to pay. By the end of the war in 1945, the United States contributed over $50 billion in Lend-Lease, the bulk of which went to Great Britain. In return, the Allies provided $8 billion in goods or services to the United States.

Holding the Line. The first months of 1942 were filled with one Japanese success after another. (As a gesture of defiance the United States dispatched General James Doolittle to lead a small, carrier-borne air strike against Tokyo in April, but its military value was nil.) In a matter of months the Japanese overran all of Southeast Asia. In February they took the great British naval base of Singapore; in March, Java, the main island of the Dutch East Indies. Another Japanese army, meanwhile, had overrun Siam and Burma and now stood poised on the borders of India. By the end of March the Japanese controlled the western half of the Pacific from the Kuriles to the Solomons, as well as the islands and mainland of Southeast Asia from Indochina to India. In the Philippines all American resistance ceased on May 6.

Strenuous American efforts in the middle of 1942 managed to stop, but not roll back, the Japanese advance. In May the naval-air Battle of the Coral Sea halted the southward naval advance, and the following month an American victory over a large Japanese naval task force off Midway Island ended the eastward thrust. Japanese losses at the Battle of Midway were so extensive that thereafter the imperial navy was on the defensive. The third effort to contain the Japanese advance comprised a series of combined land and sea operations on and around the little-known, jungle-covered island of Guadalcanal in the Solomons. The first precarious American landing on Guadalcanal took place on August 7, 1942, but it was not until the fifth major sea and air encounter on November 13–14, 1942, that the southern Solomons rested securely in American hands.

As in the Pacific, the first year of war in Europe brought almost uninterrupted setbacks for the Allies on both land and sea. That spring and summer German submarines sank Allied tankers and merchantmen before the eyes of civilians on the shores of New Jersey and Florida. By the middle of 1942 shipping losses reached a new peak of 4.5 million tons, or more than in all of 1941; yet in the same six months only twenty-one U-boats were sunk. At the conclusion of eleven months of war and after a furious program of shipbuilding, Allied tonnage was less than it had been on the day Pearl Harbor was bombed. Although losses were gradually reduced, the submarine menace hung over Allied preparations for counteraction until the middle of 1943.

The Turning Point. In the month of November 1942, Allied forces around the globe assumed the offensive, which they never lost thereafter. November had witnessed the victory on Guadalcanal. At about the same time the Russians, after a heroic defense of Stalingrad on the Volga, seized the offensive against the Germans. On November 8, American forces commanded by General Dwight D. Eisenhower invaded the French colonies of Morocco and Algeria with surprise landings from a giant armada of 500 warships and 350 transports and cargo ships. The Vichy French offered only scattered resistance. Total Allied casualties amounted to fewer than two thousand.

The immediate purpose of the North African landings was to catch the German armies, under General Erwin Rommel, in a giant squeeze; only a week before, General Bernard L. Montgomery's British Eighth Army had begun an offensive at El Alamein in Egypt. As Rommel's forces retreated westward before Montgomery along the North African coast in December and January, they backed up against the now well-established American forces in Algeria and Tunisia. By the early spring of 1943 Rommel's once invincible Afrika Korps was no more. German losses in Africa reached 350,000.

With all of North Africa in Allied hands, the next target was Sicily, and by the time the Sicilian campaign was concluded at the end of August 1943, Italy was out of the war. A new Italian government joined the Allies in the war against Germany, but the Nazi forces quickly disarmed the Italians, thereby rendering the diplomatic coup a military nullity. Despite three amphibious invasions of the Italian peninsula, stubborn German resistance and the Italian mountains kept the Allies fighting in Italy until May 2, 1945.

Setting the Goals of War. In January 1943, soon after the consolidation of the Allied landings in North Africa, Roosevelt and Churchill met in the Moroccan city of Casablanca to discuss war aims. It was at this meeting that Roosevelt, after consulting with Churchill, announced that only unconditional surrender of Germany and Italy would be acceptable to the Allies. Later critics would argue that such uncompromising terms stiffened German resistance and prolonged the war. Certainly the Nazi propaganda machine played upon the argument that victory for the Allies spelled annihilation for the Germans. But at the time Roosevelt was careful to say that unconditional surrender "does not mean the destruction of the population of Germany, Italy, and Japan, but it does mean the destruction of the philosophies of those countries which are based on conquest and the subjugation of other people." Actually, it appears doubtful that the statement influenced German resistance very much; certainly it produced exactly the opposite effect upon the Italians, who surrendered with alacrity nine months later.

Late 1943 saw several meetings of the Big Three powers. At the end of October the foreign ministers of the United States, Great Britain, and the Soviet Union met for the first time in Moscow. There it was agreed that the three nations would consult on "all matters relating to the surrender and disarmament" of their common enemies. They also recognized a need for setting "the earliest possible date" for the planning of an international organization of the "peace-loving states." Victory, in short, was already being anticipated.

En route to a meeting with Stalin in Teheran, Iran, Churchill and Roosevelt stopped at Cairo on November 22–26, 1943, to confer with the Nationalist Chinese leader Chiang Kai-shek. The three allies agreed to prosecute the Pacific war until Japan was forced into unconditional surrender. They also agreed that Manchuria, Formosa, and the Pescadore Islands, earlier seized by Japan, should be returned to China after the war.

The Teheran Conference of November 28–December 1, 1943—the first personal encounter between Stalin, Churchill, and Roosevelt—resulted in no new decisions, although Roosevelt did secure from Stalin, as Hull had from Molotov a month earlier, a promise of Russian help against Japan soon after the end of the war against Germany. Convinced of the need to have Stalin's friendship in the postwar world, Roosevelt did his best to charm the dictator and to dissipate Stalin's obvious suspicion of the two English-speaking allies.

The Battle for Production. In a very real sense the turning of the tide of war from constant defeat to persistent victory was attributable to the astounding production which flooded from American factories and farms. At Teheran even Stalin acknowledged that without American production the Allies would not be winning the war.

Conversion of the economy to full wartime production did not really begin until after Pearl Harbor. During 1940 and 1941 Roosevelt created several agencies, headed by businessmen and labor leaders, to speed up and coordinate production; but when the Japanese struck, the level was still far from satisfactory. In January 1942 Roosevelt set up the War Production Board with Donald M. Nelson as chief and, though this more centralized control was the best arrangement yet, the organization of production did not achieve optimum efficiency until the creation of the Office of War Mobilization in May 1943 under James F. Byrnes, former Democratic senator from South Carolina.

While building up an armed force of some fifteen million men and women, the United States undertook to expand its productive capacity to feed, clothe, supply, house, and transport this army as well as make sizable support contributions to the British and Russian armies spread around the globe. To meet this gargantuan assignment required not only the expenditure of billions of dollars but also the execution of a host of plans and arrangements. Priorities for materials had to be established, raw materials gathered, labor recruited to replace the men inducted into the armed services, and civilian industries converted to war work. The automobile industry, for example, was given over entirely to the manufacture of tanks, trucks, and other military vehicles. The aviation industry expanded its working force from 49,000 in 1939 to a peak of 2.1 million in November 1943, when it employed over 12 percent of the total number of workers in manufacturing. To keep supplies moving, the total tonnage of American shipping increased over five times between 1939 and May 1945. Whole new industries sometimes had to be created: the production of synthetic rubber was inaugurated when the Japanese cut off the major source of natural rubber from Southeast Asia. The volume of industrial production increased so rapidly that by October 1943 some cutbacks were made to prevent surpluses.

Between 1939 and 1946 agricultural production increased some 30 percent, even though the labor force on farms *fell* more than 5 percent. As a result, not only was the United States able to keep the armed forces well supplied with food, but the nation as a whole ate better than ever before, and the Allies were able to draw upon the American larder during the war and after.

The Home Front. Because the needs of the armed forces came first, many kinds of civilian goods ranging from automobiles to toasters were unobtainable, and necessities in short supply like coffee, sugar, meat, and butter were rationed in order to ensure equitable distribution. Housing, especially in areas where new war plants went up, was hard to obtain, and housing conditions were crowded and substandard. Bus and train travel was dirty, uncomfortable, and overcrowded, if available for a civilian at all. Many commodities still obtainable on the home front declined in quality but not in price as manufacturers tried to get around price controls. However, the average citizen did not suffer unduly. As Director of War Mobilization Byrnes said in January 1945, "It is not as if the civilian economy has been starved. Some items are short. But on the whole the volume of consumption has risen. . . . Our level of living is higher than in 1929 or 1940."

Industrial labor was certainly better off. Unemployment dropped from 9 million in July 1940 to 780,000 in September 1943. And though prices rose by about 30 percent between 1939 and 1945, wages rose faster, increasing about 70 percent, thanks to raises and overtime pay. The need for additional labor was so great that at one point the government undertook a house-to-house survey to find workers for war industries; by the middle of 1944 war workers accounted for some 45 percent of the nation's labor force, which included millions of women and teenagers (aged 14–17).

Although more workers went out on strike during the war years than during the depression years, the number was less than 2.5 million in any one year and only a small proportion of the total labor force. Only occasionally did the President have to seize plants in order to keep production going. The most notable labor dispute was with John L. Lewis, who twice in 1943 led his United Mine Workers in strikes against government restraints on wage increases. In retaliation, Congress in June 1943 enacted a general antilabor law, the Smith-Connally Act, which authorized the President to seize any plant where a strike threatened to interfere with the war effort and which imposed criminal penalties on those who called such strikes. Roosevelt vetoed the bill as extreme, but Congress quickly overrode his veto.

The job of fitting a free labor force to the needs of war production was formidable. A War Manpower Commission, created in 1942, undertook this task by freezing workers to their jobs unless more important war work required them elsewhere. To handle disputes between labor and management, now that strikes were voluntarily banned, the President set up the War Labor Board. The board also attempted to hold the line on wages in order to keep prices level, although it did permit a 15 percent increase to make up for the rise in the cost of living. In the main, the War Labor Board, which settled thousands of labor disputes amicably during the war years, refused to permit the emergency to be used as an excuse for eroding the gains made by organized labor in the previous decade. As a result, union membership increased from nine million in 1940 to almost fifteen million in 1945.

Controlling Inflation. Simply because there was so much money and so few consumer goods, the control of prices was a major problem. Essentially, prices were kept under control by two methods—increased taxes and a price freeze. The Office of Price Administration, which was in charge of controlling inflation, failed to put a tight lid on prices until late in 1942 so that some prices, notably those of foods, rose alarmingly through most of that year. Thereafter, however, controls were more effective. Prices in general did not rise more than 30 percent between 1940 and the end of the war.

Because Congress would not follow through on legislation, taxation was not so steep as the administration had hoped. Only the Revenue Act of 1942, which increased corporate, private income, and excise taxes, took much of a bite out of civilian purchasing power. In that act, for the first time, the income tax reached into the pockets of the average citizen. About fifty million income-tax payers were recorded in

1943 as compared with thirteen million in 1941. Congress refused to heed Roosevelt's demand for a further increase in taxes in 1943. Yet in spite of government spending at a rate as high as $100 million a year, about 40 percent of the cost of the war was paid for out of taxes, a proportion which had never been achieved in any previous American war.

Civil Liberties.   Fearful of sabotage, the government early in 1942 ordered the rounding up of some 110,000 Japanese living on the West Coast, even though some two thirds of them were American citizens. Although no specific acts of sabotage could be charged against them, these people were held in "relocation centers" in the interior for most of the war. This action of the government, though generally supported at the time and subsequently upheld by the Supreme Court, was later condemned as an indefensible act of racism, since mere Japanese ancestry was the basis for the internment. Ironically, the Japanese in Hawaii, who made up a much larger proportion of the population, were not affected by the order. No comparable interference with civil liberty was taken against Americans of German and Italian ancestry, nor did the population at large indulge in irrational attacks on Germans like those that had marred the domestic record during the First World War. But *native* minorities did suffer. Large numbers of whites attacked blacks in Detroit in 1943, and whites in other cities resorted to violence against blacks. During the last two years of the war, white servicemen and civilians also harassed young Mexican-Americans in the Los Angeles area in what came to be called the "zoot-suit riots," after the extravagant styles worn by many Mexican-American youths. Later, these incidents were seen to mark the beginning of overt Mexican-American self-consciousness, which by the late 1960s became the Chicano movement. (See p. 324.)

By and large, the position of blacks improved during the war. Thousands moved into Northern cities seeking the new job opportunities. By April 1944 a million more blacks were employed in civilian jobs than in 1940; during the same period the number of blacks in skilled jobs and foreman positions doubled. Under pressure from black leaders the federal government also undertook to make jobs available. The President in June 1941 created a Fair Employment Practices Committee to investigate charges of discrimination against minorities on defense jobs. In 1943 the committee was granted enforcement authority.

The Election of 1944.   In the midst of the Second World War, as in the Civil War, the nation conducted a presidential election. The Republicans, who after Pearl Harbor strongly supported the war effort, now entertained high hopes for victory, since in the congressional elections of 1942 they had gained forty-seven seats in the House and nine in the Senate, dropping the Democratic majority in the House to its lowest level since Roosevelt first took office. Prominently considered for the Republican nomination was Thomas E. Dewey, who had gained national renown as the first Republican since 1920 to be elected governor of New York state. Dewey spoke for the same internationalist wing of the party that had supported Wendell L. Willkie in 1940, but he did not suffer from Willkie's close identification with the administration. Moreover, Dewey, unlike Willkie, enjoyed the support of the professionals in the party. As a result, the convention nominated Dewey on the first ballot—with only a single dissenting vote. John A. Bricker of Ohio, who as a Midwesterner and an isolationist brought balance to the ticket, received the vice-presidential nomination. The party platform was internationalist in content, but the convention's enthusiasm for Bricker betrayed the persistence of isolationism in Republican ranks.

Roosevelt waited until just a week before the Democratic convention met in July before he indicated his willingness to seek the nomination. The real battle in the convention then raged around the choice of his running mate. Roosevelt's own choice, though not a strong one, was incumbent Vice-President Henry Wallace, but Wallace was unacceptable to conservatives within the party. The President's second choice was James F. Byrnes, the efficient and capable Director of the Office of War Mobilization; however, labor leaders and liberals in general opposed Byrnes as antiblack and perhaps antilabor. As a consequence, before the convention actually voted, party leaders and the President had decided upon Harry S. Truman as a compromise candidate. Truman, a senator from Missouri, was chairman of a Senate investigating committee that had gained national acclaim for its honest and efficient policing of government war contracts.

His head filled with plans for the postwar settlement, Roosevelt's heart was not in the hustings. Nevertheless, early in the campaign he made one of the most effective political speeches of his career and by the vigor of his few campaign speeches effectively countered Republican charges that he was physically incapable of enduring another term of office. As usual Roosevelt won, though by a smaller margin in the popular vote than ever before, receiving 25.6 million votes to Dewey's 22 million. The Democrats retained control of both houses, gaining twenty-four new seats in the House of Representatives.

Island Hopping in the Pacific.　When the last Japanese resistance ended on Guadalcanal in February 1943, the United States began the long push northward toward Japan. The task was essentially one for the navy and the marines, since the Japanese were dug in on a multitude of small islands scattered throughout the western Pacific. One by one through 1943, Japanese island fortresses fell to air and amphibious attack, often only after terrible loss of life: the central Solomons in the summer, eastern New Guinea in the fall, and the Gilbert Islands in the late fall. As the great naval task forces of the United States moved northward, other Japanese outposts were bypassed, their garrisons still intact; cut off from supplies, they would eventually have to surrender without bloodshed. By the end of June 1944 the capture of Saipan in the Marianas placed the air force's giant new B-29 bomber within easy striking distance of Tokyo itself. Systematic bombing of Japan's home islands from Saipan began in November 1944.

The Invasion of Europe.　Meanwhile, preparations were well under way for the long-awaited frontal assault upon Hitler's Fortress Europe. Ever since the middle of 1942 Stalin had been urging the western allies to open a second front, but aside from the invasion of Italy, which was obviously peripheral, their response had been confined to bombings of the Third Reich. Nevertheless, by the middle of 1943 these air attacks were formidable. In one week in July 1943, for example, the combined British and American air forces dropped eight thousand tons of bombs on Hamburg,

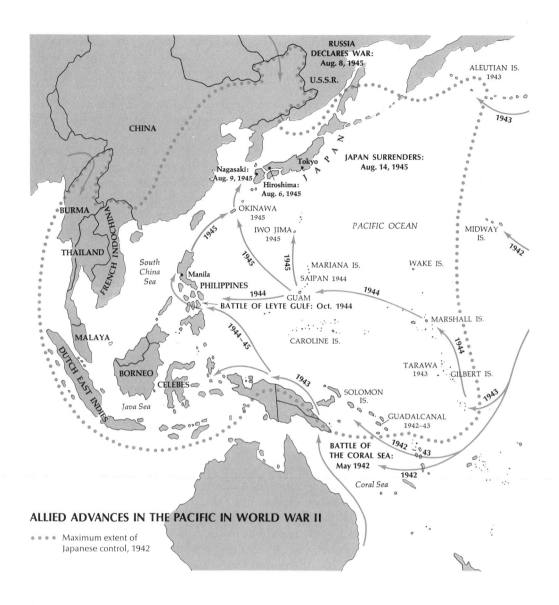

RUSSIA
DECLARES WAR:
Aug. 8, 1945

U.S.S.R.

ALEUTIAN IS.
1943

1943

CHINA

J A P A N

Tokyo
JAPAN SURRENDERS:
Aug. 14, 1945

Nagasaki:
Aug. 9, 1945
Hiroshima:
Aug. 6, 1945

BURMA

FRENCH INDOCHINA

OKINAWA
1945

IWO JIMA
1945

PACIFIC OCEAN

MIDWAY
IS.

1942

THAILAND

1945

1945

1945

MARIANA IS.
SAIPAN 1944

WAKE IS.

South
China
Sea

Manila
PHILIPPINES

1944

GUAM

1944

BATTLE OF LEYTE GULF: Oct. 1944

MARSHALL IS.

MALAYA

CAROLINE IS.

1944

DUTCH EAST INDIES

1944–45

BORNEO

CELEBES

Java Sea

1943

SOLOMON
IS.

TARAWA
1943

GILBERT IS.

1943

GUADALCANAL
1942–43

1942   43

BATTLE OF
THE CORAL SEA:
May 1942

1942

Coral Sea

ALLIED ADVANCES IN THE PACIFIC IN WORLD WAR II

• • • •   Maximum extent of
Japanese control, 1942

devastating three quarters of the city. Later, fifty other large German cities each
received a similar pounding. More than 300,000 Germans died in these uninterrupted
raids, which by 1944 were deliberately aimed at workers' homes as well as factories in
an effort to destroy German morale as well as German industrial capacity. The raids
cost the Anglo-American air forces some 21,000 bombers and their crews.

On December 6, 1943, in appointing Dwight D. Eisenhower Supreme Allied
Commander of the West, the Combined Chiefs of Staff told him: "You will enter the
continent of Europe and, in conjunction with other Allied Nations, undertake

ALLIED ADVANCES IN EUROPE IN WORLD WAR II

••••• Maximum extent of Axis control, 1942

UNITED KINGDOM

D-DAY: June 6, 1944

Brest

Paris

FRANCE

Neutral

Hamburg
GERMANY
Berlin

GERMANY SURRENDERS: May 7, 1945

Vienna

Warsaw

1944
1944
1945

U.S.S.R.

Leningrad

Moscow

Stalingrad

1942

1943

Budapest

1945

ITALY

Rome

Naples

GREECE

1944

1944

ALLIED INVASION OF NORTH AFRICA: Nov. 8, 1942

Casablanca   Oran   Algiers

1942

1942

MOROCCO

1943

Bizerte

SICILY

INVASION OF SICILY: July 10, 1943

INVASION OF ITALY: Sept. 3, 1943

TUNISIA   Tripoli

ALGERIA

1943

1943

1942

El Alamein

BRITISH DRIVE: Oct. 1942

LIBYA   EGYPT

operations aimed at the heart of Germany and the destruction of her armed forces."
For months before the actual invasion began and while supplies, shipping, and men
were being accumulated in England, Allied planes bombed and strafed German
positions along the Channel coast. The Nazis could not help but know in general what
was impending, but thanks to superb Allied counterintelligence, they misjudged the
exact point of the attack on D-day, June 6, 1944. The main concentration of Allied
troops was north of the Cotentin peninsula in Normandy, where the massive invasion
force quickly established five connected beachheads. Within two weeks a million

troops landed and moved inland; by the end of July both the British and American armies had broken out of their coastal positions and were striking north and west. On August 15 a new American army invaded southern France, and on August 25 Paris fell to French and American troops.

Concomitantly with the Allied invasion of June 6, the Russians launched a broad offensive on the eastern front, bringing their armies to the Baltic and into Poland and Romania by the end of the summer. By late autumn of 1944 the armies of the Grand Alliance were poised to strike into Germany from both east and west.

Despite the overwhelming land and air power being brought against it, Germany made two desperate attempts to forestall the inevitable. The first was a new secret weapon, a fast-flying rocket bomb, the V-2. (The V-1 or "buzz bomb," used somewhat earlier, was a jet-driven aerial bomb and not a rocket.) The first V-2s landed in England in August. Traveling faster than the speed of sound, the V-2 was impossible to intercept, and it hit without warning. Before the launching bases could be destroyed by Allied bombers, the murderous V-2 attacks killed some eight thousand Britons.

The other desperate German effort was a great counteroffensive mounted on December 16, 1944, against the American forces in the Ardennes forest of Belgium. The Battle of the Bulge, as it came to be called, caught the Americans by surprise and forced them to retreat. As a result the whole Allied timetable in the west was set back over six weeks. The first Allied troops did not cross the Rhine until March 7, 1945, when the bridge at Remagen, one of the few remaining Rhine bridges, was unexpectedly taken by soldiers of the American Ninth Armored Division. By that time the Russians stood on the banks of the Oder River, less than forty-five miles from Berlin.

The Big Three at Yalta.   As the coils of Allied power tightened around Germany, Roosevelt, Stalin, and Churchill met on February 4–11, 1945, at Yalta, a resort town in the Crimea. Desirous of securing Russian aid against the Japanese and of bringing the Soviet Union into a new world organization, Roosevelt did his best to assure Stalin that the United States recognized Russia's special interests in Europe. It was agreed that the new government of Poland would be the one established at Lublin by the Russians and not the one in exile in London. But it was also agreed that final recognition of the Lublin government would await "free and unfettered elections." Also, pending the signing of a German peace, Poland would receive German territory to compensate for portions of eastern Poland taken by Russia in 1939.

Russian insistence upon a large figure for German reparations was also favorably received by the Americans, though no final commitment was made. Stalin asked for and received cession of the Kurile Islands from Japan and concessions and bases in China. In return, Stalin agreed to participate in the new world organization and to enter the war against Japan within three months after the defeat of Germany.

Despite later criticisms, the so-called concessions by Roosevelt do not seem excessive in the context of February 1945. Poland, after all, was in Russian hands, and Russian military assistance against Japan then seemed eminently desirable and worth the granting of Japanese territory to the Soviet Union. Furthermore, Chiang Kai-shek later consented to the concessions Roosevelt agreed to support in Stalin's behalf.

The End of the Third Reich.   Soon after the Yalta Conference, on April 12, 1945, Franklin D. Roosevelt died at Warm Springs, Georgia. A surprised and shaken Harry S. Truman assumed the presidency the same day. Roosevelt's death plunged the nation and the peoples of the Allied world into sorrow, but the military machine FDR had helped to forge drove on to total victory over Germany and Italy.

With the Russians already fighting in flaming, bombed-out Berlin, Adolf Hitler on April 30 committed suicide in his underground bunker beneath the Reichs chancellery; faithful guards burned his body. Nazi Germany outlasted its founder by no more than a week. On May 2, Admiral Karl Doenitz, whom Hitler had named as his successor, tried to surrender to the British while continuing the war against the Russians, but Field Marshal Bernard L. Montgomery contemptuously rejected this last attempt to divide the Western and Eastern allies. Germany surrendered unconditionally to all the Allied powers on the morning of May 7, 1945.

The United Nations Organization and Potsdam.   FDR's death left President Truman to complete the task Roosevelt had considered preeminent: the convocation of the representatives of the Allied nations at San Francisco to draw up a charter for a new world security organization. The completed Charter of the United Nations was signed by all fifty Allied countries on June 26, 1945. Despite America's long history of isolationism and its rejection of the League of Nations after World War I, the Senate agreed to American membership in the UN after only six days of debate and with only two dissenting votes.

President Truman was also called upon to represent the United States at the last conference of the Big Three powers at Potsdam, Germany. Since no final decisions on Germany had been made at Yalta and since the United States still wanted Russia's support against Japan, Truman, Stalin, and Churchill (later replaced by Clement Attlee, representing the newly elected Labour government in Britain) met outside ruined Berlin on July 17, 1945. Differences between East and West were more evident than before; wranglings frequently occurred over details and the meaning of previous agreements. The two Western allies were deeply suspicious of Russian policy in Poland, which Stalin seemed intent upon making a Russian satellite despite agreement on its independence at Yalta. Stalin also insisted that the new border between Germany and Poland was final, though at Yalta the border had been considered only temporary. Furthermore, the tentative agreements on reparations Stalin now insisted were final. All three powers agreed that Germany should remain united, although, for purposes of temporary military administration, each of the three powers (later France was added) would occupy a separate zone. Berlin itself was to be occupied jointly by the victors. Even though Russia had not yet entered the war in the Pacific, the conference issued a demand for Japan's unconditional surrender.

The End of the War with Japan.   As the European war reached its climax in the summer and fall of 1944, the American air force and navy moved ever closer to the Japanese home islands. In October, American troops sloshed ashore on the island of Leyte in the Philippines in a move that caught the superior Japanese forces completely by surprise. In the naval encounters in the Battle of Leyte Gulf the American forces utterly defeated the last important remnants of the Japanese fleet. At the end of

February 1945, after successful invasions of Luzon and Mindanao, General Douglas MacArthur, the resourceful American commander in the Pacific, announced the capture of Manila. Just three years had elapsed since he had been ordered by President Roosevelt to leave the Philippines in the face of the Japanese invasion.

That same month of February 1945 the marines landed on Iwo Jima, only five hundred miles from Japan itself. After defeating its stubborn defenders in bloody fighting, the Americans used the airfield for fighters flying protection for the planes bombing Japan. On March 9, B-29s from Saipan dropped a record load of firebombs on Tokyo, igniting the wooden and paper houses of the city; the resulting holocaust was rivaled only by that at Hiroshima five months later.

Even as fierce fighting continued on the Philippines, the Americans invaded Okinawa, close to the home islands. Once again, as at Tarawa in the Gilberts and Iwo Jima in the Bonins, the Japanese dug in and fought virtually to the last man, while Kamikaze (Japanese suicide pilots) hurled their planes at the Americans, sinking thirty-four ships of the invading fleet. By the end of the campaign in June 1945, some 110,000 Japanese had died on Okinawa; fewer than 8000 had been taken prisoner. The 49,000 American casualties were the heaviest of any engagement in the Pacific theater and a grisly prefiguring of the costs to be expected from the contemplated assault on the Japanese home islands.

That dreaded encounter, however, never came; at 8:15 A.M. on August 6, 1945, a single B-29 dropped a single atomic bomb on the industrial city of Hiroshima. The tremendous blast waves, fire waves, and radiation leveled 60 percent of the city and killed over seventy thousand people outright; ten thousand more were never found. Because the bewildered Japanese did not surrender immediately, on August 9 a second nuclear bomb was dropped on Nagasaki with equally devastating consequences. A day before, on August 8, the Soviet Union fulfilled its promise by declaring war on Japan and invading Manchuria. Japan's leaders, recognizing that their country faced certain destruction and heeding the emperor's pleas that no more lives be sacrificed, surrendered unconditionally on August 14. The official surrender took place on September 2 aboard the battleship *Missouri* anchored in Tokyo Bay.

The story of the development of the nuclear bomb began in August 1939, when President Roosevelt received a letter from Albert Einstein informing him that the splitting (fission) of the nucleus of an atom of uranium seemed possible. The consequent release of energy, Einstein wrote, would be enormous. Fearful that Nazi scientists might develop such a bomb, the administration in 1940 began the Manhattan Project to try to beat them to it. Working secretly in a squash court under the stands of the football stadium at the University of Chicago, a team of scientists in December 1942 successfully constructed the first nuclear pile. Once it had been shown that a nuclear reaction could be controlled, the engineers took over, constructing plants at Oak Ridge, Tennessee, and Hanford, Washington, for the manufacture of materials needed for assembling a bomb. After more than $2 billion had been invested in the great gamble, the first test of the bomb took place successfully on July 16, 1945, in the desert outside Alamogordo, New Mexico. The secret of the project had been kept so well that Harry Truman did not learn of it until he became President.

The job of building the bomb was so complicated and time-consuming that the two bombs used against Japan were the total world supply. Later it was learned that the Germans had lagged far behind the United States and Great Britain in the development of nuclear fission and probably would not have been able to construct a bomb for months or perhaps years. But no matter who made the first bomb, once its devastating power had been released, the world could not be the same again. Thus, simultaneously with the coming of peace, the world entered the age of nuclear power—an age which would be at once an era of promise and of fear.

FROM PEACE TO COLD WAR

Reconversion. Soon after the surrender of Japan, the dismantling of the great military establishment began. By January 1946, in response to public clamor at home and unrest among the troops still stationed around the globe, the government was discharging members of the armed forces at the rate of 35,000 a day; by the end of 1946 the armed forces were less than 80 percent of wartime strength. Simultaneously with the discharging of soldiers, the government began the cancellation of war contracts; $35 billion worth were dropped within a month after the surrender of Japan. The end of war work and the glutting of the labor market with discharged veterans seemed to many to presage a severe depression, but billions of dollars of personal savings and the rapid transition to peacetime production made it turn out otherwise. Instead, inflation became the principal economic problem in ensuing years.

The ending of overtime work at war plants and the upward movement of prices in 1945 and 1946 provoked organized labor into a wave of strikes. In October 1945, for example, the number of man-days lost through strikes doubled over September. It continued to rise until February 1946. All told, about 4.5 million workers went out on strike in 1946. Since the strikes were usually for increased wages, the federal government ran into difficulties trying to hold the line on prices. Demands by Congress and the public for tax reductions also meant increased pressure on prices. In November 1945 Congress cut income taxes by some $9 billion and repealed the wartime excess-profits tax as an inducement to increased production.

The big issues of 1946 were prices and labor unrest. The Truman administration tried to hold the line on prices by continuing wartime price controls, but businessmen, most Republicans, and other large sectors of the population were anxious to remove all wartime restrictions. The results were inadequate price-control legislation and a steadily rising price curve. With the election of a Republican Congress in November 1946, the Truman administration gave up and abolished virtually all controls over prices. Nevertheless, shortages of all kinds of goods persisted, with the result that prices in 1947 continued to rise to new heights almost every month. Despite the high prices, or perhaps because of them, employment remained high and business activity good. Undoubtedly many workers, especially unorganized labor and white-collar workers, suffered from the steady increase in the cost of living, but the country as a whole enjoyed a boom.

In February 1946, before it was clear that a boom would be the shape of the postwar era, Congress passed the Employment Act, which placed responsibility upon the federal government for the prevention of mass unemployment and economic depression. Although no specific measures were spelled out in the Act (because of the need to win conservative support), it did create a Council of Economic Advisors to the President. In a sense the Act was a reflex from the days of the depression, showing the continuing effect of the New Deal revolution.

Truman versus a Republican Congress.   Opposition to price controls, support of labor control bills, and demand for tax reductions marked a rising conservative tide across the country and in the Congress. This conservatism was clearly reflected in the congressional elections of 1946. Brandishing the slogan "Had Enough?" the Republicans elected majorities in both houses for the first time since 1928. First on the agenda of the new Eightieth Congress was legislation to control labor unions, which since the end of the war had been disrupting the economy through nationwide strikes. Earlier in 1946 Truman had vetoed a severe antilabor law, even though he himself, beset by a national railroad strike in May 1946, had threatened to draft rail workers into the army. In June 1947 the new Republican Congress, under the leadership of conservative Senator Robert A. Taft, passed the Labor-Management Relations, or Taft-Hartley, Act. Truman returned the bill with a stinging veto message, but Congress quickly overrode the veto.

The Taft-Hartley Act attempted to meet two public complaints against labor. In an effort to deal with nationwide strikes that disrupted the economy, the act empowered the President to force a union to accept a sixty-day "cooling-off period" before striking. If at the end of the cooling-off period the dispute was not settled, the employer's last offer would have to be presented to the workers for a secret vote. The act was also intended to reverse the alleged favoritism of New Deal legislation toward labor by listing a number of unfair union practices: it banned the closed shop, permitted employers to sue unions for broken contracts or strike damages, required unions to make their financial statements public, forbade union contributions to political campaigns, limited the "check off" system whereby employers collected union dues, and required union leaders to take oaths that they were not Communists. Despite the opposition of labor organizations and of many liberal Democrats, the Taft-Hartley Act has remained unchanged, a measure of the American people's conviction in the postwar era that national labor unions, like business, need some kind of public control.

Although Truman and the Republican Eightieth Congress rarely agreed on domestic policies, on defense and foreign policy they often did (see below, pp. 271–73). The army, navy, and air force were merged into the Department of Defense under the National Security Act of July 1947. James V. Forrestal, former Secretary of the Navy, became the first Secretary of Defense.

Russian Expansionism.   Even before the Potsdam Conference in July 1945, there had been signs that the Allied unity displayed at Yalta was superficial. Before his death, for example, Roosevelt had warned Stalin that the Yalta agreements concerning Poland must not be ignored. Stalin's initial refusal to send Foreign Minister Molotov to the UN conference in April 1945 also aroused Western suspicions of Russian intentions about the postwar world, while the abrupt stopping of Lend-Lease in early May raised doubts in Russian minds about Western friendship. At Potsdam Stalin insisted on having his way in Poland and with German reparations, which the Russians considered imperative for the rebuilding of their devastated country. During the last half of 1945 and most of 1946, at the United Nations and at meetings of the Council of Foreign Ministers to draw up peace treaties with the lesser enemy states, the West and Russia clashed repeatedly; each saw the other as increasingly threatening or uncooperative. Obviously the two sides had different views of the future of Europe, and especially of Germany.

Particularly ominous for the peace of the postwar world was the Soviet Union's refusal to withdraw its troops from Iran, which the Russians and the British had jointly occupied during the war. Only vigorous protests by the United States and the United Nations impelled a Russian withdrawal in late May 1946. To the Russians the important point was that they had withdrawn under pressure; to the West, and particularly the Americans, it was the necessity to threaten the Russians that was significant. Two months later, in early August, the Soviets demanded slices of Turkish territory and a share in the control of the Dardanelles. To many Western observers Russian behavior announced a resurgence of historic czarist ambitions.

Actually, Soviet conquests already far exceeded any dreams of the czars: Russian armies stood as far west as Berlin and central Germany, and all of eastern Europe lay under their control. Indeed, throughout the forties and early fifties it was the presence of large Russian armies in central Europe at a time when the West had long since demobilized its wartime forces that sustained the suspicions and fears of Western leaders. Today the likelihood of a Russian military advance against western Europe seems slight, but to a generation that had seen Russian power move from east to west against Hitler, that likelihood was ever present. Moreover, although Yugoslavia was not occupied by Russian troops, it was then firmly Communist under the leadership of Marshal Tito. Indeed, in 1946 Tito was more truculent in his dealings with the West than was Stalin himself. The same month that the Soviets served their demands upon Turkey, Tito's planes on two different occasions shot down unarmed American transport planes which had accidentally crossed the Yugoslav frontier. It was Yugoslavia, not Russia, that was supplying Communist-led guerrillas fighting against the British-dominated Greek government.

Churchill, now out of office because of a Labour party victory, gave voice to the concern of the Western nations. At Fulton, Missouri, on March 5, 1946, with President Truman sitting conspicuously on the platform, Churchill called attention to the "iron curtain" which "has descended across the continent" from "Stettin in the Baltic to Trieste in the Adriatic." Moreover, he went on, "Nobody knows what Soviet Russia and its Communist international organization intends to do in the immediate future, or what are the limits, if any, to their expansive and proselytising tendencies." Meanwhile, the Soviets in the UN turned down the American plan for international control of nuclear energy. Since under the plan the United States would have voluntarily surrendered its monopoly of nuclear power, Americans took the Soviet rejection as another sign that the Soviets were not interested in peace and order in the world. The Russians, apparently, saw the American plan as a way of denying them their own nuclear bomb. On both sides, suspicions grew.

The Problem of Germany.   The major European dispute between East and West concerned the future of Germany. In the view of the Western powers, particularly the United States, the revival of a united Germany had been agreed upon at Yalta and reaffirmed at Potsdam. But Russian insistence upon large German reparations could only mean that Stalin intended to keep Germany weak and without hope of recovery for the foreseeable future. As a result the Russians obtained very little in the way of reparations from the Western occupation zones, though in their own zone they carted eastward everything they could.

By the fall of 1946 Secretary of State James F. Byrnes was convinced that the Russians did not really want a reunited and independent Germany and were using the continued division of Germany as a means of impeding German recovery. He therefore persuaded the British to merge their zone with that of the Americans. (The French, as skeptical of German unification as the Russians, did not join the other Western allies until 1949.) However, in merging the Western zones, Byrnes was helping to divide Germany ever more permanently between East and West. Thus, in Germany as in the United Nations, the Cold War had obviously come into being by the end of 1946. Increasingly in the years ahead, West Germany (which became independent as the German Federal Republic in 1954) would be viewed by the West as the chief bulwark against Russian expansion into western Europe, while the Soviet Union would see it as the chief threat to Russian hegemony in eastern Europe.

The Containment Policy.   For a time after World War II it seemed that the Russians might well be in a position to extend their influence into western as well as eastern Europe. Economically and militarily prostrate from their struggles, the nations of western Europe were in poor position to defend themselves against Soviet military force and subversion. In France and Italy strong Communist parties seemed on the verge of taking power either through the ballot box or by force. In Greece Communist-led guerrillas fought pro-Western government forces for control of the country. Even Great Britain, presumably one of the principal victors of the war, was on the verge of bankruptcy. Economically bled, Britain could no longer sustain its traditional role as guardian of Greek independence; in February 1947 the British announced the imminent withdrawal of aid. In Turkey, too, an unstable government was being pressured by the Soviets for territorial grants and administrative concessions in the Dardanelles.

In Asia and Africa the steady drive for independence had already begun. With their lack of experience in democratic procedures and their difficulties of maintaining stability in the midst of poverty and strife, the new nations were ripe for Communist revolution or subversion, either of which, American leaders anticipated, would make them allies of the Russians.

The American response to this global Communist threat was the establishment and gradual implementation of the policy of "containment." As publicly announced in July 1947 in an article by State Department aide George F. Kennan, "The main element of any U.S. policy toward the Soviet Union must be that of a long-term, patient but firm and vigilant containment of Russian expansive tendencies." While accepting—though not entirely—the accomplished fact of Soviet control over eastern Europe, the policy of containment sought to hold the line against the further extension of Soviet power, military or political.

The Truman Doctrine.   Even before the containment policy was officially enunciated, the Truman administration had taken steps to stem the Communist advance. After much soul-searching and consultation with congressional leaders of both parties, President Truman urged the United States to take up the burden of aid to Greece and Turkey. In a historic address to Congress and the nation on March 12, 1947, he called for $400 million in economic and military aid for the two beleaguered countries to save them from "aggressive movements that seek to impose upon them totalitarian regimes." His proposal was opposed by conservatives, who protested the cost, and by liberals and left-wingers, who denounced it as warmongering. However, all recognized that this "Truman Doctrine," pledging aid to nations resisting aggression or subversion, signaled a sharp departure from the whole previous practice of American foreign policy. For the first time in peace, the United States was being asked to commit its military might (though that part of the proposal was underplayed by the President) and economic power to the defense of countries outside the Western Hemisphere. By a vote of 67 to 23 in the Senate in April and 287 to 107 in the House in May the Republican Congress sanctioned the new turn in foreign policy by voting the funds.

The Marshall Plan.   An immediate Soviet military invasion was not the greatest threat to western Europe in the first postwar years. It was the legacy of war—persistent poverty, widespread misery, and mass unemployment—in which communism found its greatest ally, especially in countries like Italy and France, where economic and political instability was an open invitation to subversion. Therefore, to stimulate European recovery, the Truman administration began plans for extending massive economic assistance. The idea—first suggested in a speech by Under Secretary of State Dean Acheson—was brought to the attention of the world, and Europe in particular, in a Harvard commencement address delivered by Secretary of State George C. Marshall on June 5, 1947.

Marshall's speech offered American economic aid to any European nation seriously interested in restoring the shattered economy of Europe, including those nations closely associated with Soviet Russia. The nations of western Europe accepted the suggestion with enthusiasm, but Russia, after some preliminary exploration, compelled its allies to stay out of the scheme, on the excuse that the Marshall Plan was a cover-up for American imperialistic designs. The proposal also evoked widespread opposition in the United States, from both the right and the left, but leading Republicans, notably Senator Arthur H. Vandenberg, championed it from the outset. Calling the idea a "calculated risk" to "help stop World War III before it starts," Vandenberg countered assertions that it was a gigantic "international WPA" or a "Socialist blueprint." As presented to Congress in December, the measure envisioned the expenditure of $17 billion over a four-year period, with $6.8 billion to be spent in the fifteen months following April 1, 1948.

During the fall and winter of 1947 the continued decline of the European economy and the many stories of starvation and misery in western Europe gave substance to the argument for United States assistance. But equally influential were the continued signs of Soviet pressure. For example, in February 1948 a Communist workers' coup thrust democratic Czechoslovakia behind the Iron Curtain, and in March reports of a Russian advance to the West circulated among government officials. Furthermore, a Communist victory appeared to be a real possibility in the Italian elections coming up in April. Responding to these pressures and to others from an anxious administration, Congress on April 2, 1948, passed the European Recovery Act or Marshall Plan, granting to the President about 90 percent of the funds he had requested for the first year. Though Congress refused to commit the United States to anything thereafter, subsequent grants were made on an annual basis.

The full four-year plan was never carried out because the Korean War intervened, but the $12.5 billion extended to sixteen western European countries achieved the purpose of reviving the European economy. Between 1948 and 1951 production of all the countries rose about 37 percent. With a more prosperous economy and resultant political stability, the internal threat of communism receded noticeably. Moreover, the international cooperation fostered by the plan afforded the European nations a new insight into the advantages of closer economic union. That insight bore fruit in the 1950s with the formation of the European Coal and Steel Community and, later, the Common Market or European Economic Community.

Point Four. In his inaugural message of January 1949 President Truman added another dimension to America's commitment to the improvement of the world's economy. As "Point Four" of his foreign policy statement, he announced that the United States was undertaking "a bold new program for making the benefits of our scientific and industrial progress available for the improvement and growth of under-developed areas." In subsequent years American technicians traveled around the globe helping primitive farmers become less so, installing better means of disease prevention and cure, and in general helping to bring the labor-saving and life-saving technology of the West to Asia, Africa, and Latin America.

NATO. Soon after the European Recovery Program went into effect, the East-West conflict over Germany reached its most dangerous stage. In July 1948 the Soviets, vexed by the frictions arising from joint administration of Germany and hoping to force Western evacuation of Berlin, ordered a blockade of all ground communication with the city, which lay deep in the Soviet zone. Faced with the prospect of war if they forced their way to Berlin, the Western Allies instead instituted a gigantic airlift to fly in supplies and food. Although the Russians did not molest the airlift, they did not agree to ending the blockade until May 1949. Meanwhile the airlift had proved its ability to sustain the West Berliners and the Western right of access to Berlin.

The Berlin blockade reinforced the American belief in the need for closer military cooperation among the western European nations. The Brussels Pact of March 1948 had already created a defensive alliance among Great Britain, France, Belgium, Luxembourg, and the Netherlands. Toward the end of 1948 the United States encouraged widening the Brussels Pact alliance to include other nations rimming the North Atlantic. In the spring of 1949, twelve countries, including Canada and the United States in the New World, joined the North Atlantic Treaty Organization, which in 1952 expanded to include Turkey and Greece and in 1955 West Germany.

With the signing of the treaty in April 1949, the United States, for the first time in peace, obligated itself to come to the assistance of European nations. This was the strongest commitment yet assumed in the course of the diplomatic revolution that had begun only four years earlier with the ratification of the United Nations Charter. The NATO treaty encountered only slight opposition in the Senate, which ratified it on July 21, 1949. In early 1951 General Dwight D. Eisenhower was appointed Supreme Commander of the new integrated defense force to be fashioned out of the national armies of the twelve signatories.

THE ASIAN REVOLUTION

The Overthrow of Colonialism. If the results of the war in Europe dropped unexpected problems into the laps of Americans, the consequences of the war in western Asia constituted a revolution. The great colonial powers, though victors in the war, lost virtually all their Asian possessions within five years after the defeat of the Japanese. When the British returned to Malaya and Burma, the Dutch to the East Indies, and the French to Indochina, they were greeted with demands for independence and sometimes by open military rebellion.

One by one the European nations made the only possible response; they got out of Asia. The United States, acting on a prewar promise, led the movement by granting final independence to the Philippines on July 4, 1946. Britain followed next, finally reducing its once vast empire in Asia to a few pin points on the map, like Hong Kong and Singapore. But not all the European powers recognized the shape of the future as clearly as Britain. The Dutch did not transfer power to the new nationalist government of the United States of Indonesia until 1949, and the French sacrificed the flower of their officer corps and thousands of young men in a futile struggle to suppress the nationalist movement in Indochina until 1954. The liquidation of colonialism was the first part of the Asian revolution.

The Transformation of Japan. The second part of the revolution in Asia was the American occupation of Japan. Although ostensibly representing all the Allied powers, General Douglas MacArthur, the American occupation commander, in reality was the supreme authority in that country, and his policy was dictated by the United States. Aside from stripping Japan of all its colonies, including Formosa and Korea, the United States deliberately undertook to destroy the old Japan. Thoroughgoing land reform, which spread land ownership more widely than ever before, improved the lot of the peasantry. A new democratic constitution, in which the emperor was reduced from a god to a mere symbol of national unity, also removed the army from politics. Women were enfranchised for the first time and given greater freedom in society and within the family. As Edwin O. Reischauer, an authority on Japanese history and ambassador to Japan under the Kennedy administration, once wrote: "During the early post-war years in Japan, MacArthur played the role not only of the most radical American revolutionary of modern times but also of the most successful."

When the Korean War broke out in 1950 (see pp. 276–78), the United States and its non-Communist allies in the war against Japan hastened to conclude peace with the Japanese, despite the objections of the Soviet Union. The peace treaty was signed in September 1951, and in a separate agreement the United States was permitted to retain military bases in Japan. As with Germany, the United States also encouraged its former enemy in Asia to rebuild its dismantled military machine as a defense against communism.

The Rise of Chinese Communism. The third prong of the Asian revolution was the Communist conquest of China. When World War II ended, China was accorded the status of a great power, receiving, for example, a permanent seat on the Security Council of the United Nations. With the Japanese defeat, most people assumed that Generalissimo Chiang Kai-shek's Nationalists would reinforce their rule over all China. Even Stalin at the close of the war recognized Chiang's Nationalist government, not Communist leader Mao Tse-tung's, as the rightful regime. But the Chinese Communists had a sizable army and a government in northwestern China and were stronger than many observers thought.

At first the United States helped Chiang in his effort to spread his military authority over all of China. When that failed, the United States attempted through most of 1946 and 1947 to find a basis for agreement between Chiang and Mao Tse-tung; in December 1945 President Truman had dispatched General George C. Marshall to China, where he worked for over a year on such a mission, but without success. By late 1947 the two sides were fighting it out in open civil war, during which Chiang's lack of support from the masses of the Chinese people became increasingly evident.

By the close of 1949 the Nationalists had been forced to flee to the island of Formosa (Taiwan), some one hundred miles off the coast. In October 1949 the Soviet Union extended diplomatic recognition to the new People's Republic of China, and in February 1950 the two Communist powers signed a mutual assistance agreement and pact of alliance. Thus, just as the end of the Berlin blockade and the creation of NATO marked the ebbing of the Communist danger in western Europe, the Cold War came to Asia.

THE DEMOCRATS STAY IN

The Miracle of 1948. By 1948 Harry Truman had warmed up well to the role of President, which had been thrust upon him so suddenly three years before, and he was eager to try himself before the electorate. Although opposed by many Democrats who thought he lacked popular appeal (according to opinion polls, his presidency was approved by only 36 percent of the people in April 1948), the President controlled the July Democratic convention, which dutifully renominated him on the first ballot, naming Senator Alben W. Barkley of Kentucky as his running mate. When the Republican Congress was called into special session by Truman that summer and refused to enact his liberal program, Truman went into the campaign talking about the "do-nothing" Eightieth Congress.

In the election Truman faced a serious loss of votes from both the right and left wings of his party. Because the Democratic convention adopted a strong civil rights plank, several Southern states bolted Truman and put forth their own States' Rights party candidate, Governor J. Strom Thurmond of South Carolina. Thurmond, it was expected, would cut deeply into Truman's support in the Deep South. The candidacy of Henry A. Wallace on the newly formed Progressive party ticket promised to draw away left-wing and liberal votes, for Wallace campaigned vigorously against the administration's containment policy, contending that it was anti-Russian and would lead to war instead of peace.

The Republicans, more confident of victory than at any time since the Great Depression, nominated for President their 1944 standard bearer, Governor Thomas E. Dewey of New York, with Governor Earl Warren of California as the vice-presidential nominee. Dewey's campaign was a model of caution; sure of victory, he preached unity and the need for efficiency. Accepting all of the New Deal reforms, even though they were also Truman's stock in trade, Dewey simply said he would administer them better. Even commentators opposed to Dewey conceded, along with the public opinion polls, that a Republican victory was foreordained. Harry Truman, though, was not convinced. He barnstormed around the country, attacking the Republican Congress for being against the people's interests. Republicans, he said, were "old moss backs . . . , gluttons of privilege . . . , all set to do a hatchet job on the New Deal." He traveled some 32,000 miles and made 356 speeches, far exceeding the campaign effort of Dewey, his overly confident and much younger opponent.

Election night brought the big surprise: Truman never lost the slight lead he gained in the early returns. By next morning the miracle had occurred; Harry Truman was elected by two million votes. Truman's vigorous appeals to popular memories of the Great Depression and his uncompromising defense of the New Deal had apparently struck fire in millions of voters (though 700,000 who cast votes for state candidates did not even bother to vote for President). Moreover, by emphasizing the decline in farm prices under Republican farm legislation, Truman actually recaptured the farm vote, which Roosevelt had lost in 1940 and 1944. Dewey ran better than Republican congressional candidates, probably because of Truman's vigorous attacks on the Eightieth Congress. Not surprisingly, the Democrats gained seventy-five new seats in the House and nine in the Senate. Although Truman lost four Southern states (thirty-nine electoral votes) to Thurmond, he had shown that a united South was not necessary for a Democratic victory, especially since his Southern losses were more than made up for in the North by urban black votes. Henry Wallace's candidacy, which at one time had been viewed as a threat to Democratic strength in Northern cities, affected Truman's total hardly at all.

The Fair Deal. In his inaugural speech in January 1949, Truman spoke of his program as the "Fair Deal"; in effect, it was a continuation and extension of the New

Deal. It called for civil rights legislation, a national health program, aid for public education, and support for low-income housing. Truman also asked for repeal of the Taft-Hartley Act and enactment of a new farm subsidy program (the Brannan Plan), but the Congress, despite its Democratic complexion, would agree to neither. A coalition of Republicans and conservative Southern Democrats killed off not only civil rights legislation but most of the other measures of the Fair Deal. On the other hand, in 1949 Truman did succeed in obtaining a housing act and a minimum-wage increase to 75 cents an hour. In 1950 Congress also agreed to broadening Social Security coverage, placing some ten million more persons under the benefits of the system.

After 1949 Truman was increasingly plagued by revelations of corruption in his administration. Although none of the disclosures compared with the Teapot Dome scandals of the twenties, many officials, especially in the Internal Revenue Service, were proved in court to be corrupt. Moreover, some White House officials turned out to have rather casual standards of proper behavior for government officers. In short, the Republican charge that the Democrats had been too long in control of the executive branch of government seemed to have some validity. But an issue of foreign policy was to supersede corruption as a Republican weapon against the administration.

The Outbreak of the Korean War. When in 1945 the United States and the Soviet Union occupied the former Japanese colony of Korea, they arbitrarily divided the country between them along the 38th line of latitude. Originally intended to be temporary, the line, in the suspicious atmosphere of the Cold War, hardened into a border between two Korean regimes—the North under Russian tutelage and the South under American. Because each of the Korean regimes wanted to unite the peninsula under its own rule, border clashes were frequent. When the Americans withdrew their troops from South Korea in 1949, they carefully refrained from leaving behind any offensive weapons like tanks or heavy artillery for fear that the strongly nationalist president of South Korea, Syngman Rhee, would attempt to conquer North Korea by force of arms.

The Russians, withdrawing at about the same time, left a well-trained and heavily equipped North Korean army behind and may even have encouraged the North Koreans to attempt unification by force. In any event, on June 25, 1950, the North Korean army stormed across the 38th parallel, quickly overwhelming the thin South Korean defenses. The next day, before the rapidly advancing invaders, Rhee's government fled the capital of Seoul. Thereupon, the Truman administration, faced with a naked act of military aggression, decided to commit the United States to South Korea's defense, even though the American army then comprised no more than ten and one half infantry divisions and one armored division. On June 30, when it became evident that American air and naval support alone could not save the South Koreans, the first U.S. ground troops landed in Korea. Prodded by the United States, the United Nations on June 27 branded the North Koreans as aggressors and called upon all member states to "furnish such assistance to the Republic of Korea as may be necessary to repel the armed attack and to restore international peace and security to the area." On July 7 General Douglas MacArthur was designated United Nations commander in chief. Although all during the fighting in Korea, American and South

Korean troops made up the great preponderance of UN forces, by the end of 1950 some twenty nations had sent some kind of support. Because the Russians had been boycotting the Security Council in protest against the West's refusal to admit Communist China to the UN, their representative was not present to veto the resolution which propelled the United Nations into the war.

For over two months the American and South Korean forces suffered uninterrupted defeats as the powerful North Korean armies pushed them down the peninsula into a small pocket around the port city of Pusan. Then on September 15, 1950, in a surprise maneuver, General MacArthur led a successful amphibious landing at Inchon on the west coast, far behind the North Korean lines. A simultaneous drive from the Pusan area caught the Communists in a giant pincer movement. By October 1 the United Nations forces were on the verge of crossing the 38th parallel into North Korea. When they did, a new phase of the war in Asia opened.

On November 26, as units of the United Nations forces approached the Yalu River—the border between Korea and Communist China—large contingents of Chinese "volunteers" ambushed them, compelling the UN troops to retreat. Thereafter, increasing numbers of Chinese poured across the Yalu, and the UN troops were once again pushed far south of the 38th parallel. Thus deprived of total victory, General MacArthur asked for permission to bomb the Chinese in what he called their "sanctuary" across the Yalu. The Truman administration turned down his request on the ground that such action might well invoke the Sino-Soviet mutual assistance pact and thus bring on a war with the two chief Communist powers.

But if the nation was spared a world war, a limited war far from American shores produced frustrations that made the Korean struggle immensely unpopular. Public opinion polls indicated that after January 1951 Truman never again received the support of a majority of the American people. Many spoke bitterly of "Truman's War." A draft board in Montana went so far as to refuse to draft any more men until General MacArthur was authorized to bomb as he saw fit in China.

As the leading advocate of striking directly against China, MacArthur inevitably came into fatal clash with the administration. When a letter written to the House Republican minority leader was released to the press—a letter in which MacArthur charged administration "diplomats" with fighting the Asian war "with words" rather than "with arms" and declared that "there is no substitute for victory"—President Truman on April 11, 1951, summarily removed the general from his commands in Korea and Japan. The nation was surprised and shocked. The President was widely attacked and MacArthur accorded a hero's welcome when he returned to the United States. After an address by the dismissed general before Congress, a Senate investigation exhaustively inquired into the removal. At the end of several weeks of hearings, during which the pitch of emotionalism gradually declined, the Senate committee agreed with General Omar Bradley when he said that MacArthur's policy would have extended the fighting to the mainland of Asia, which would "involve us in the wrong war, at the wrong place, at the wrong time, and with the wrong enemy."

The Effects of the Korean War. By demonstrating that aggression could be halted if the nations of the world were determined to do so, the Korean War stimulated

THE KOREAN WAR

- - - - Armistice Line: June 26, 1953

▼▼▼▼▼ Pusan perimeter: Farthest advance of North Korean forces, Sept. 1950

•••••• Farthest advance of United Nations forces: Nov. 1950

the expansion of America's armed forces and put life into the recently created NATO. Domestically the Korean "police action," as Truman once called the war, forced the administration to institute economic controls, but not to the extent of World War II. Although both income and excise taxes went up in 1950 and a new excess profits tax became law in 1951, there was enough military production by the end of 1952 to permit the easing of many of the economic controls. Indeed, the war had pushed the nation into a new boom, quickly ending the recession of 1948–49. Thus, conditions of life in the United States were such that many Americans, who had no relatives in Korea hardly knew there was a war at all. That such was the case only made the war more unpopular among those who did have sons fighting overseas.

The End of the Korean Fighting.   Once the Chinese intervention demonstrated that the whole peninsula could not be united under Syngman Rhee, the Truman administration sought to end the fighting as soon as possible. By the end of 1952, strengthened UN forces had pushed the Chinese northward to the region of the 38th parallel. Although the United States was prepared to strike a truce at that point, the Communists held off. An armistice was not signed in Korea until the middle of 1953 under the Eisenhower administration.

The Great Fear.   Between 1949 and 1954 the nation was gripped by a pervasive fear that communism was about to subvert the Republic. Any program or any idea traceable to Communist ideology became suspect; merely being accused of having been a Communist was sometimes enough to condemn a man to loss of job or friends. A veritable witch hunt for traitors and disloyal citizens was carried out by government and by private groups. Actually, throughout the whole period the number of disloyal persons discovered in positions of trust was insignificant.

The Great Fear grew out of the deteriorating international situation of 1946 and 1947, when some Communists in the United States, Canada, and Britain showed that regardless of their formal citizenship, they owed first loyalty to the Soviet Union. In 1947 the federal government instituted a program to check on the loyalty of government employees, and many public educational institutions, like the University of California, demanded oaths of loyalty from their faculties. Congressional investigations in 1947 and 1948 revealed evidence of spying in government by Communists during the 1930s. The most notable instance was the case of Alger Hiss, a former high-ranking member of the State Department, who was accused of heading an espionage ring in the 1930s that passed on classified documents to the Soviets; his two trials in 1949–50 for perjury (the statute of limitations prevented indictment for espionage) aroused wide public concern over Communist influence in government.

Hiss' trial and conviction, like other revelations about Communists in government, concerned espionage prior to 1945, but in 1950 the FBI revealed that American spies had transmitted secret A-bomb data to the Russians in 1945 and 1946. Several Americans, including Julius and Ethel Rosenberg, were tried and convicted for espionage. The Rosenbergs, whose cause the Communists tried vainly to make into a new Sacco-Vanzetti case, were executed in 1953.

To these and other sensational revelations of Communist activity in the United States, the Congress responded with the Internal Security (or McCarran) Act of 1951, passing it over Truman's veto. The new law required Communist and Communist-front organizations to register with the government and to identify as Communist all their mail and literature; it also forbade employment of Communists in defense work and barred anyone who had belonged to a Communist or fascist organization from entering the country. The most drastic of all provisions and the one which measured the extremity of congressional concern was the authorization for the government to place Communists, citizens and aliens alike, in concentration camps whenever a national emergency occurred.

The Rise and Fall of McCarthy. The person who more than any other exacerbated the Great Fear during these years was Joseph McCarthy, a Republican senator from Wisconsin. McCarthy first came into national prominence in February 1950 when he charged in a speech at Wheeling, West Virginia, that fifty-seven or more Communists were then working in the State Department. "In my opinion," he said, "the State Department, which is one of the most important government departments, is thoroughly infested with Communists," and it was all the fault of Secretary of State Dean Acheson, that "pompous diplomat in striped pants, with a phony British accent." A Senate investigating committee later exonerated the department, but McCarthy continued to make similar unsubstantiated charges of Communists in government, occasionally naming a name but citing numbers by the score. In the context of the Great Fear, his spectacular, headline-making accusations often gained credence. Occasionally he was courageously repudiated and criticized, but most government officials, including his fellow senators, feared to gainsay him; to do so laid his accusers open to charges of being "soft" on communism.

McCarthy's attacks on the State Department and other agencies of the executive branch continued even under Eisenhower's Republican administration. Indeed, during the 1952 campaign Eisenhower hesitated to criticize the senator publicly even though it was widely known that Eisenhower deeply resented the scurrilous attacks that McCarthy had made upon General George C. Marshall, a man Eisenhower greatly admired. As late as January 1954 a Gallup public opinion poll showed that 50 percent of the American people favored McCarthy's activities and only 29 percent opposed him, although by then the senator had driven from the State Department almost all its experts on China on the grounds that they had "lost" China to the Communists.

McCarthy's power to frighten came to an abrupt end in 1954 when he obliquely attacked President Eisenhower and directly assailed Secretary of the Army Robert Stevens as an "awful dupe" of the Communists. McCarthy's now-apparent demagoguery caused his popularity to plummet. Coming under senatorial investigation himself for his unmannerly conduct, McCarthy was "condemned" for his behavior by sixty-seven senators in December 1954, although a mere twelve months before only one senator had been willing to stand out against an appropriation for McCarthy's Committee on Government Operations. The senator's influence abruptly collapsed. Soon thereafter he went into a physical decline, dying in May 1957.

McCarthy's fall marked the end of the Great Fear. A product of that fear and not a cause of it, McCarthyism could last only so long as Americans believed that the internal menace of communism was greater than the external threat. By 1954 they no longer thought so.

CHAPTER 11

COLD WAR AND HOT WAR
1947–72

THE REPUBLICAN INTERLUDE

The Election of 1952. As early as 1950, leading Republicans, especially those of an internationalist persuasion, had been talking of Dwight D. Eisenhower as the ideal candidate for the party in 1952. Still incredibly popular because of his war record, Eisenhower also possessed political appeal because his rise from poor boy in Kansas to international renown seemed to epitomize the American dream. When his name was first suggested for the nomination, Eisenhower announced he was not interested, but in July 1952, after much public and private pressure, he resigned his command of the NATO forces and agreed to try for the nomination.

His most formidable opponent was Senator Robert A. Taft of Ohio, conservative in domestic affairs and neo-isolationist. Twice Taft had been turned down in favor of Dewey; now the senator's supporters, who were legion, felt Taft's chance had come. But the convention nominated Eisenhower on the first ballot, with Senator Richard M. Nixon of California as his running mate. As a congressman a few years earlier, Nixon had gained national renown as a member of the House Un-American Activities Committee that unmasked Alger Hiss.

After Harry Truman took himself out of the race, the Democrats centered their attention upon new prospects, notably Adlai E. Stevenson, governor of Illinois. Although Stevenson was not sure he wanted to run, the July convention "drafted" him on the third ballot. In an effort to heal the wounds from the party split over civil rights in 1948, the convention nominated a Southerner, Senator John J. Sparkman of Alabama, for Vice-President.

From the outset Eisenhower was the favorite. While Stevenson was compelled to defend the Truman administration, the Republicans fiercely attacked it for alleged corruption, for coddling Communists in government, and, above all, for the Korean War. Late in the campaign Stevenson's manager, referring to the Republican barrage of criticism, remarked: "We are suffering from a new kind of KKK—Korea, Communism, and corruption." Stevenson, however, proved to be an admirable candidate. His speeches were undoubtedly the most sophisticated addresses heard from a presidential candidate since the days of Woodrow Wilson. His ratings on the public opinion polls steadily rose during the campaign, but never to the level of Eisenhower's.

Toward the end of October Eisenhower capitalized on the pervasive discontent over Korea by promising that, if elected, he would personally make a trip to the battlefront in an effort to bring the fighting to an end. Even the prosperous times, which ordinarily would have worked to the advantage of the incumbent party, could not overcome the force of the Korean issue.

Eisenhower scored a sweeping personal victory with 442 electoral votes to Stevenson's 89 and almost 34 million popular votes to Stevenson's 27 million. Eisenhower's popular vote ran 15 percent ahead of his party's vote for Congress, for the Republicans captured both houses by only slim majorities (and, in fact, lost that control to the Democrats in the mid-term elections two years later). Another measure of Eisenhower's victory was that he broke into the Democratic South, capturing not only border states like Maryland and Missouri, and Tennessee and Virginia, but Texas and Florida as well. Even in the traditionally isolationist Middle West Eisenhower won easily despite his record as an internationalist. Blacks, rural Southerners, and the big city voters in the North remained loyal to the Democrats, but close postelection analyses showed that Eisenhower won support from all classes and income levels. A striking measure of his popularity was that perhaps as much as a quarter of his popular vote came from people who had voted for Truman in 1948.

The First Eisenhower Administration. Many Americans, knowing Eisenhower's long record as a military man, anticipated a stern and exacting leader of Congress and the nation. In fact, Eisenhower turned out quite the opposite. Basically he conceived the President's functions to be quite distinct from those of Congress; he generally refused even to comment upon legislation while it was passing through the legislative mill.

The first administration was intended to be a businessman's government in the best sense of the phrase: it would not be subservient to business, but it would do its best to encourage business. Thus all economic controls left over from the Korean War were abolished early in February 1953. Similarly, government enterprises which

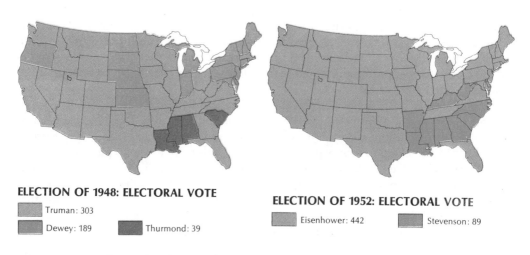

ELECTION OF 1948: ELECTORAL VOTE

Truman: 303

Dewey: 189   Thurmond: 39

ELECTION OF 1952: ELECTORAL VOTE

Eisenhower: 442   Stevenson: 89

competed with private business were dropped. A balanced budget became the guiding aim of the administration under the leadership of Secretary of the Treasury George C. Humphrey. When he took office, Eisenhower cut over a billion dollars from Truman's foreign aid budget, but in the main he would not let the drive for economy endanger the national security. If there were any choice, the administration generally gave preference to business over government. Thus it awarded an electric power contract to a private utility instead of to the Tennessee Valley Authority; and in 1956 the Atomic Energy Commission authorized the private development of electric power through nuclear energy.

In at least two respects the Republicans carried on New Deal–Fair Deal policies without question. One was in showing a willingness to use federal authority to counteract the recession of 1954, and the other was in expanding the coverage of the Social Security system in 1953. Eisenhower also tried to overcome the isolationism that still persisted among many Republicans; indeed, it was to advance the cause of internationalism that he had run in the first place. But it required all of Eisenhower's prestige to prevent the passage in 1954 of the so-called Bricker Amendment, which would have limited the treaty-making power of the government and enlarged congressional control over foreign relations. Although advanced as a means of preventing the treaty-making power from being abused, this proposed amendment to the Constitution would have seriously handicapped the President's handling of foreign affairs.

The Election of 1956.   Normally, in view of Eisenhower's immense popularity, his renomination in 1956 would have been unquestioned. But in September 1955 the President suffered a severe heart attack which incapacitated him for two months. Although his steady recovery emboldened the party leaders to call once again for his nomination, the President himself withheld his consent until February 1956. That summer he was renominated along with Richard M. Nixon. The Democrats also renominated Adlai Stevenson, who this time had eagerly sought the nomination.

Eisenhower won again. The Republican campaign capitalized on "peace and prosperity," but the victory is better explained by the character of a man who could inspire millions of voters to display campaign buttons reading "I like Ike." Eisenhower's personal popularity won him 457 electoral votes to Stevenson's 73. That it was a personal victory was attested by the fact that Eisenhower failed to bring a Republican Congress into office with him. The Democrats continued to control the Senate and the House. Ike ran 6.5 million votes ahead of Republican congressional candidates. Not since 1848 had a President failed to carry with him at least one house. For a popular President such a failure was unprecedented.

Working with Democrats.   Throughout his second term Eisenhower was confronted with Democratic majorities in both houses. (In the elections of 1958 these majorities reached numbers not seen since the mid-1930s.) Believing his presidential role as one of resisting a "wasteful" Democratic Congress, Eisenhower regularly vetoed government salary increases and demands for tax cuts during the 1958 recession. Despite the Democratic majorities, all save one of Eisenhower's vetoes of antirecession measures held.

One of the three principal pieces of legislation of Eisenhower's second term was the Labor-Management Reporting and Disclosure Act (1959), growing out of Senate committee hearings on racketeering, corruption, and extortion in labor unions. The others were the Civil Rights Act of 1957 and the National Defense Education Act of 1958 (see pp. 286 and 290). The labor act followed the thinking of the Taft-Hartley Act, assuming a divergence of interest between union members and leaders. Senator John L. McClellan, whose committee held the hearings, and Representative Philip M. Landrum, who sponsored the bill in the House, were Southern Democrats, so the bill also symbolized the Republican–Southern Democratic alliance that usually supported the President on labor and financial measures. The Landrum-Griffin Act, as it was also called, among other things set up a "bill of rights" to protect union members against assessments and coercion by labor leaders; required unions to make public, largely for the benefit of their members, all expenditures and all payments made to officers; and provided that unions must hold regular elections of officers.

THE SECOND RECONSTRUCTION

The 1954 Decision. On May 17, 1954, in handing down a decision in *Brown* v. *Board of Education of Topeka,* the Supreme Court of the United States unanimously concluded "that in the field of public education the doctrine of 'separate but equal' has no place." In the middle of the twentieth century, "separate education facilities are inherently unequal," the Court concluded. In thus overturning the decision in *Plessy* v. *Ferguson* (1896), on which all Southern states rested the validity of their segregated public facilities, the Court opened a new chapter in the history of black people in America.

For over a decade the Supreme Court had been invalidating state laws which discriminated on grounds of race, but the school decision shocked the South. Although a few border-state communities like Baltimore and Washington, D.C., began desegregation of schools in 1954, in most of the South the decision met stiff and determined resistance. By the middle of 1956 only some 350 school districts out of 6300 were desegregated in the South, and none of these desegregated districts was located in the middle or Deep South.

Southern Resistance. In 1957 Southern opposition to school desegregation reached the point of clashes with federal military power. Under a plan of gradual desegregation worked out by the local school board and the federal district court, nine Negro students were scheduled to enter Central High School in Little Rock, Arkansas, in the fall of 1957. But Arkansas' Governor Orville Faubus used state troops to bar their entrance. Faced with state defiance of federal authority, President Eisenhower sent in United States paratroopers to enforce the orders of the federal court. For several weeks soldiers with fixed bayonets escorted the black students to classes, and federalized Arkansas troops later remained to patrol the school grounds for the entire school year.

If the breakdown of orderly processes of law in Arkansas shocked the nation and the world, in the South the use of federal troops temporarily stiffened resistance.

"Massive resistance" statutes, as they were called, were hastily enacted in a number of states, resulting in the closing of schools in Little Rock and in three communities in Virginia. By 1959, though, the more moderate people in Arkansas and Virginia accepted at least token desegregation in preference to no public schools at all. And in 1960 and 1961 token desegregation came to the Deep Southern states of Louisiana and Georgia, particularly in the big cities of New Orleans and Atlanta.

The determined opposition of segregationist leaders and White Citizens Councils in the Deep South was not to be broken so easily, however. In September and October 1962, a transfixed nation watched as the state of Mississippi, through its elected officials, defied a federal court order requiring the University of Mississippi to permit a black man, James Meredith, to enroll as a student. The federal authorities tried their best to avoid the use of armed force by working behind the scenes to secure compliance with the court. But Governor Ross Barnett's public statements of defiance encouraged thousands of segregationists, including many students, to attack physically the federal marshals assigned to protect Meredith upon his arrival at the university. As a result of the vehemence of the attack, President John F. Kennedy dispatched thousands of federalized Mississippi national guardsmen and regular army troops to the university town of Oxford to restore peace and to insure the execution of the court's orders. Meredith entered the university as its first known black student.

Prior to the riots, desegregation at the state college and university level had been proceeding almost without incident in the Southern states, excepting Alabama and South Carolina. Thereafter, every state moved to integrate all levels of education, though primary and secondary schools had little more than token integration until 1968. Between then and 1971 the proportion of black children doubled in Southern schools heretofore wholly white, reaching 39 percent. This was a greater increase and a larger proportion than that for the nation as a whole. By 1971 only 14 percent of black children in the South were still in schools that were entirely black. In short, the movement toward integration in the South had proceeded further than it had elsewhere in the country.

Even so, resistance continued. The principal evidence was the growing number of private, all-white schools in the South. In 1971 it was estimated that about 4 percent of school-age children attended such schools.

A New Civil Rights Movement. The decline of segregation in the South during the 1950s and 1960s was hastened by a rising militancy among Southern blacks in opposition to segregation. One of the most influential, as well as most successful, was the boycott of local buses in Montgomery, Alabama, by the fifty thousand black residents. The boycott against segregation on the buses began in December 1955. Although it brought hardship to the blacks who ordinarily depended upon public transportation to get to work, it was sustained for almost a year. One of the leaders of the movement was the Reverend Martin Luther King, Jr., a young Southern black, who became nationally known for his remarkably effective oratory and his moral leadership, based upon the principle of nonviolence. His successes at Montgomery and in other causes in behalf of equality and justice, in the North as well as in the South, brought him worldwide recognition and, in 1964, the Nobel Peace Prize.

Segregation of bus passengers was declared unconstitutional by the Supreme Court in November 1956.

The slow pace of desegregation also provoked the federal government to take action against discrimination. In August 1957, Congress, after much debate, passed the first civil rights act since the days of Reconstruction. Its purpose was to protect the voting rights of blacks; though the provisions were weaker than those originally advocated by the Eisenhower administration, they empowered federal judges to jail for contempt anyone—including state officials—who prevented a qualified person from voting. The law also created a temporary Civil Rights Commission to investigate violations of civil rights and to make recommendations for new legislation. (The Commission was continued into the 1970s.)

A second civil rights act, against which Southerners filibustered unsuccessfully, was passed in 1960 to further protect the voting rights of blacks. It was not until the Johnson administration, however, that a voting rights bill was passed that substantially increased voting by blacks in the South. (See pp. 300–01.) From 1960 on, blacks themselves undertook new ways of attacking segregation in the South: there were "sit-ins" at segregated lunch counters and bus depots, "wade-ins" at segregated beaches, and even "pray-ins" at segregated churches, all aimed at nonviolent achievement of integration.

Simultaneously with the antisegregation movement in the South, Northern blacks in cities like New York and Chicago campaigned against segregated public schools. Northern segregation resulted from residential patterns rather than from laws, but the effects were often the same. Blacks demanded, with some success, that their children be accepted in white schools outside their local districts, where the schools were often crowded and run-down or under-financed. When in the early 1970s the federal courts used compulsory busing to bring about racial mixture in Northern schools, as it had done in the South, strong white opposition exploded. When the issue reached the Supreme Court, the new Nixon-appointed Chief Justice, Warren Burger, wrote a decision supporting busing as a legitimate tool for breaking down segregated education. But a Gallup poll reported in November 1971 that 76 percent of Americans opposed busing as a means of bringing about integration, and during the 1972 campaign busing was an issue even when candidates avoided it. In some cities, including San Francisco and Pontiac, Michigan, parents who opposed busing for racial reasons boycotted the schools in the fall of 1971. And in 1972 white parents boycotted a school in Brooklyn, N.Y., to which black children were being bused. It was like Little Rock all over again.

THE NEW ACTIVIST SUPREME COURT

If in the 1930s the Supreme Court was the center of controversy because of its conservatism, in the 1950s and 1960s it was the object of both criticism and praise because of its willingness to innovate. That willingness, as we shall see, was also the prime source of the strong desire on the part of the first Nixon administration to change its outlook by new, conservative appointments. In at least two different fields the Court exceeded even its customary importance as the final arbiter of American law.

Renewed Interest in Individual Rights. One of these fields was civil rights and individual liberties. The most striking instance was the 1954 decision in which the Court struck down segregated education. But there were other examples, too.

During the 1950s the Court spoke out clearly in defense of individual rights even when the accused were Communists. In the case of *Yates* v. *U.S.* (1957) the Court seriously modified the *Dennis* v. *U.S.* decision of 1951, upholding the conviction of eleven Communist leaders for conspiring to overthrow the government by force in violation of the Smith Act. Chief Justice Vinson had stated in his 1951 decision that government could act if only "a highly organized conspiracy" to overthrow in the future were established; the *Yates* decision distinguished between "advocacy of forcible overthrow as mere abstract doctrine" (which is within the free speech protection of the First Amendment) and "advocacy which incites to illegal action" (proscribed by the Smith Act). Thus mere advocacy of a theoretical desirability of violence was now not sufficient for conviction. Moreover, "mere membership or the holding of office in the Communist party" was held not to be sufficient proof of specific intent to "incite" persons to overthrow the government.

In the same year, in *Watkins* v. *U.S.*, which concerned a defendant who had admitted past Communist activities but had refused to disclose names of Communist associates, the Court, in effect, warned congressional investigating committees that not every kind of question asked of a witness was constitutionally permissible. A citizen has the right to be fully informed of the purpose of an inquiry before being obliged to supply information; Congress is not a "law enforcement or trial agency" authorized "to expose the private affairs of individuals without justification." Congress, the Court held, must respect the constitutional rights of witnesses, which include freedom of speech, of political belief, and of association, and protection from self-incrimination. Here the Court was boldly protecting the rights of the individual citizen against one of the oldest and most treasured powers of Congress: the necessary authority of a legislature to secure facts for the writing of legislation.

In two other areas the Court also intervened in behalf of individual rights. The first was in regard to religion in the public schools. In *Engel* v. *Vitale* (1962) the Court held that a school-sponsored prayer in the classroom was a violation of the doctrine of separation of church and state. It constituted, the Court held, an establishment of religion, which is prohibited by the First Amendment. A year later in the case of *Abington Township* v. *Schempp,* the Court went a step further and ruled that the required reading of the Bible in public-school classrooms also violated the First Amendment. Although both of these decisions aroused much popular and congressional opposition, efforts to have the decisions overruled by an amendment to the Constitution failed.

The second area concerned the rights of citizens charged with crimes. In a series of cases beginning with *Gideon* v. *Wainwright* (1962) and culminating in *Miranda* v. *Arizona* (1966), the Court held that the police must not infringe in any way on an individual's right to be presumed innocent until proved guilty. The *Gideon* decision, overturning a twenty-year rule, concluded that paupers had the right to a lawyer even if the court had to pay his fee. In the *Miranda* decision the Court ruled that an accused person could not be questioned by the police unless his lawyer was present. Although many police officials angrily contended that these decisions hindered the conviction of known criminals, defenders of civil liberties hailed the decisions as landmarks in the protection of the individual against arbitrary power. A continuation of this line of reasoning in a case in 1972 was of particular significance because by then four members of the court were appointees of the Nixon administration, which had been among the prominent critics of the Court's liberal view of individual rights in criminal cases. In a 7–2 decision, the Court held that in all cases, including minor crimes (misdemeanors), in which jail sentences resulted, a defendant must be provided with counsel if he is too poor to pay for a lawyer. Only forty years before, a person convicted of a capital crime could be executed even though he had been unable to afford a lawyer. Now a defendant could not be sent to jail for drunken driving if he did not have a lawyer to defend him at his trial.

The Rights of Urban Dwellers. The Court's decisions in *Baker* v. *Carr,* handed down in March 1962, and in *Reynolds* v. *Sims* two years later, were freighted with almost as much significance for the future as the *Brown* decision on segregation in 1954. The *Baker* case concerned the refusal of Tennessee to reapportion its legislative seats in accordance with changes in the distribution of population. The Court decreed that districts of markedly unequal populations constituted an inequity for which the courts could rightly be expected to provide a remedy. For a number of years, as population flowed from the rural areas to the cities, urban dwellers had smarted under the failure of their growing numbers to be reflected in increased representation in the state legislatures. It was well known that rural-dominated legislatures simply refused, as in the case of Tennessee, to reapportion seats, for to do so might mean loss of rural control. Until the *Baker* decision the courts had always held that such inequity was a "political" question beyond their jurisdiction. The *Reynolds* decision extended the reasoning of the *Baker* decision to include the upper as well as the lower houses of the state legislatures. These decisions opened up the possibility that with equitable apportionment of representation the cities would be able to get a better hearing in the state legislatures for their many and worsening problems (see pp. 317–19).

The effects of the *Baker* decision were soon apparent. In a number of states where rural dominance in politics had long depended upon underweighting urban populations, the impact of the decisions was almost immediately evident in the new political strength of cities. Atlanta, for example, suddenly gained new strength in the Georgia legislature. In 1967 a reapportioned Tennessee legislature succeeded in repealing the antievolution statute passed in 1925, during the heyday of rural domination of the legislature. By 1971 more than half the states had reapportioned their legislatures, though some of the new plans had been thrown out by the courts as inadequate.

SPUTNIK AND ITS REPERCUSSIONS

Americans had always prided themselves on their technological progress; they were justly pleased to be the first nation to split the atom and to fuse hydrogen. They liked to think of themselves in science and technology, as in standard of living, as second to none. Then came October 4, 1957.

On that day the Soviet Union placed the first Sputnik, a man-made satellite, into orbit around the earth. It took four more months for the United States to put a far smaller vehicle into space. By then the Russians had put into orbit a second satellite, large enough to carry a live dog. This initial superiority of Russian rocketry shook both the administration and the American people.

With the scientific and, to a lesser degree, the political prestige of both countries hinging upon successfully orbiting hardware, satellites were hurled into the skies in profusion during 1958 and in subsequent years. By 1961 the most obvious consequence of the first Sputnik was that the United States had mounted six separate series of rocket probes, each more ambitious and scientifically sophisticated than the preceding one. In 1961 President John F. Kennedy announced the beginning of the most dramatic of all the rocket series—Project Apollo, which was designed to land a man on the moon by 1970. Despite some cutbacks in funds during the middle 1960s and the death of three astronauts, American successes in orbiting man-carrying satellites around the earth and in landing vehicles on the moon itself put the United States on a par with, if not ahead of, the U.S.S.R. In December 1968, well ahead of the deadline President Kennedy had set, two American astronauts landed on the moon; other American visits to the lunar surface followed during the next few years.

The Military Impact of Sputnik. A factor in most Americans' dismay over the initial Russian successes in space rocketry was the fear that the United States was vulnerable to a new kind of military attack. Prior to the orbiting of Sputnik i, the Eisenhower administration had depreciated Russian boasts of being able to shoot off nuclear-tipped missiles that could reach the United States from bases in the Soviet Union. At that time American military missile capability was unable to reach more than five hundred miles. The Russians proved their claim with the orbiting of Sputnik i; the immediate American response was congressional and public clamor for a crash program to catch up with the Russians. In early 1958 Congress and the administration responded with a $1.27 billion program for accelerating missile development; in the budget of 1958–59 President Eisenhower proposed the largest peacetime military expenditures in American history.

As a result of the new and feverish interest in military rocketry, the United States developed a whole new spectrum of weapons. It included short- and medium-range rockets which could be used against planes, troop formations, and ships, and giant intercontinental ballistic missiles (ICBM), which could span oceans at speeds in excess of fifteen thousand miles per hour and devastate cities with their nuclear warheads. Perhaps the closest to an invulnerable weapon was the 1500-mile-range Polaris missile, which was designed to be fired from a submerged nuclear-powered submarine. Such a submarine could remain submerged for months at a time without refueling and would present an almost impossible target for an enemy to locate and destroy. One measure of the character of the missile race between the two superpowers was that in the late sixties even the Polaris missile was being replaced by the more powerful and longer-range Poseidon missile; by the early seventies the Poseidon was being replaced by the more sophisticated Trident.

Behind the missile race was the recognition that an all-out attack by nuclear-tipped missiles could devastate the whole country in a matter of an hour or so. In a war of nuclear missiles the principal defense was threat of retaliation from secure bases, as invulnerable to surprise attack as engineers and scientists could make them; for once the first attack had been launched there would be no time for mobilization. In addition to the submarine missiles, the United States also sank ICBMs in great protective concrete emplacements in the ground in order to have them operational even after a direct enemy strike. Meanwhile, military authorities on both sides developed an antimissile missile (ABM)—a projectile that would be able to knock an enemy missile out of the sky before it could reach its target. By 1970 Moscow was ringed by ABMs and the United States had ABMs around some of its missile sites. On their missiles, both sides were also beginning to use multiple warheads that could be independently targeted in order to complicate the work of the ABMs.

As weapons of nuclear power became ever more complicated—and more expensive—Congress and a sizable portion of the public began to have doubts that so much power was actually necessary to maintain the balance of terror. It was in the context of astronomical, escalating costs for the new missile systems that the disarmament agreements between the United States and the Soviet Union in 1972 had such great importance (see p. 311).

The Impact on Education.   The space and missiles races were only the most obvious consequences of Sputnik I. Another was the spurring of a thorough reassessment of the state of American education. Understandably proud of their long history of success in mass education, Americans were shocked to find that the Soviet Union seemed to be doing better in training scientists and engineers. Actually, even before Sputnik began to circle the earth, some educators and others had been calling for more rigorous training and for more emphasis upon science and mathematics in the curricula of the nation's schools. These critics made much of recent reports on Russian education that showed the large amount of time spent on science, mathematics, and languages in the Soviet schools. Soon after Sputnik went up, schools around the country began to revise their curricula to put more emphasis upon these subjects.

The administration and Congress responded to the national concern in September 1958 by enacting the National Defense Education Act, which suggested in its title the newly discerned connection between the defense of the country and its schools. The law originally provided for financial encouragement to instruction and study in science, mathematics, and modern foreign languages, but that encouragement was soon extended to virtually all fields. In the first ten years of the law more than 1.5 million college students received $1.3 billion dollars in low-interest loans to continue their education, while some 27,000 fellowships were granted to graduate students for advanced work. The Act was the first major federal effort in behalf of higher education since the College Land Grant Act of 1862. As the Johnson administration would show (see p. 300), the interest in federal support of higher education was only beginning. The reaction to Sputnik sparked a reevaluation of education—its goals and methods—that was still underway in the early 1970s.

A NEW ERA IN FOREIGN AFFAIRS

The Death of Stalin. In January 1953 a Republican administration took office in Washington; on March 5 Joseph Stalin died in Moscow; and in July the Korean War came to a halt. These events, coming so close together, marked a new era in the Cold War. Although no single Soviet leader emerged immediately to inherit Stalin's enormous personal power, the new Russian leaders demonstrated more flexibility and resourcefulness in foreign policy than Stalin had. Notable in this regard was Nikita Khrushchev, who became head of the Communist party in 1953 and premier in 1958. Unlike Stalin, the new Soviet leaders traveled widely outside Russia, selling Communism energetically; in 1959 Khrushchev visited the United States.

The Eisenhower administration also sought to alter foreign policy by taking a new approach. Despite his overall commitment to the major policies of the Truman administration, John Foster Dulles, the new Secretary of State, hoped to do more than merely contain communism. Toward the end of 1953, for example, he tried unsuccessfully to badger the European nations into a new defense community which would include a rearmed Germany. A looser grouping, agreed upon in 1954, did provide for a revived German army to be included in NATO.

On the other side of the world in Asia, soon after Communist-led Vietnamese guerrillas drove the French from Indochina in 1954, Secretary Dulles moved to counter further Communist expansion by the formation of the Southeast Asia Treaty Organization (SEATO). It was modeled after NATO but was conspicuously weaker on at least two counts: the signatories were required only to consult, not to take action, in the event of attack, and the organization failed to include the chief powers of the region. Composed of Thailand, Australia, New Zealand, the Philippines, Pakistan, Britain, France, and the United States, SEATO did not include India, Indonesia, Ceylon, and Burma, all of which refused invitations to join.

Dulles also hoped to use the threat of American nuclear capability as a means of countering the superior manpower of the Communist bloc. But his threat of "massive retaliation" in the event of aggression was weakened by the fact that the Soviet Union also possessed the new weapons of war. In 1949 the Soviet Union exploded successfully a nuclear bomb of its own and in 1953 added a thermonuclear (hydrogen) bomb to its arsenal. (The United States detonated its first thermonuclear device in 1952.) Hence any use of nuclear weapons against the Soviet Union or its allies would presumably set off a war of catastrophic proportions.

The acquisition of nuclear weapons by the Soviet Union spurred arrangements for a meeting of the heads of government of the United States, Great Britain, France, and the Soviet Union. A meeting at the summit, as Winston Churchill called it, took place in the summer of 1955 at Geneva, Switzerland. Little was achieved concretely, but Eisenhower's suggestion that the United States and the U.S.S.R. exchange plans of their military establishments and permit aerial photography of each other's bases seemed, for a while, like a promising idea. Even though the Russians saw little merit in Eisenhower's "open skies" proposal, the suggestion made evident the American President's sincere and anxious search for a way out of the terrible nuclear impasse between the two giant powers.

Crisis in the Middle East; The Hungarian Revolt. The foreign policies of both the United States and Russia were tested more severely in November 1956. Early that month Israeli, French, and British military forces invaded Egypt. All three countries had deep grievances against Colonel Gamal Nasser's nationalistic regime. Nasser had long been a champion of Arab opposition to Israel, refusing to recognize that new country and constantly threatening invasion, and earlier in 1956 he had seized the Suez Canal, contrary to Egypt's treaty obligations. Without informing their ally the United States, Britain and France, ten days after Israel invaded Egypt, dropped paratroopers on the Suez area, quickly overwhelming the inefficient Egyptian army. At almost the same time, the Soviet Union ruthlessly suppressed a widespread and heroic revolt of the Hungarians against Communist rule.

Both the Suez and Hungarian invasions took the United States by surprise. The administration opposed both, but its power over the Soviets was nil. The opposition of the United States to the Suez adventure was more successful, both because the United States was an ally of Britain and France and because world opinion and the United Nations vehemently condemned it. Piously, the Soviet Union added its voice to that of the United States. Britain, France, and Israel, heeding the United Nations resolution for a cease-fire, withdrew their troops.

The immediate consequence of the Suez crisis was that Egypt drew closer to the Soviet Union, and Communist penetration of the Middle East seemed imminent. Reacting to this development and in response to a request from the President, Congress in March 1957 passed a resolution affirming America's intention to aid any country in the Middle East which seemed to be threatened by a Communist coup, internal or external. The first test of what came to be called the Eisenhower Doctrine occurred in July 1958, when American marines landed in Lebanon to forestall a possible invasion from neighboring Syria, then a satellite of Nasser's and judged to be overly friendly toward the Soviet Union. The pro-Western regime in Lebanon was not overthrown, and by the end of October 1958 all American troops had withdrawn.

The Middle East crisis of 1956–58 brought the Eisenhower administration full circle. Once hopeful of avoiding "brush-fire wars," it found itself dispatching troops to trouble spots much as Truman had done in Korea. It was also evident after 1956 that Moscow was not the only source of instability in the world. Rising nationalism in Asia, Africa, and even the Americas presented new problems and dangers. Khrushchev was adept at winning friends in the new regions, and he consciously identified his country with the fierce opposition of the former colonial peoples to their old rulers. In part to offset Khrushchev's successful international salesmanship, the President in December 1959 and through the first half of 1960 embarked upon extensive good-will tours of the Middle East and Southeast Asia, Latin America, and eastern Asia. Although the first two tours were eminently successful, the last, to Asia, proved much less so; anti-American riots in Japan prevented the President from visiting that country at all.

The U-2 Incident. Even before the Tokyo riots of June 1960, other events seriously tarnished the American image abroad and further impaired Soviet-American relations. Early in 1960 the President, still hopeful of being able to arrange some kind of disarmament agreement with Khrushchev, had agreed to another summit meeting in Paris. But just before the conference opened, the Russians announced the shooting down of a high-flying American espionage plane deep inside the Soviet Union. At first the American officials denied the accusation, but after the Russians triumphantly produced the plane and its pilot, who was still alive, the United States shamefacedly admitted undertaking this and other flights over the Soviet Union. Outraged, Khrushchev called off the summit meeting, deliberately insulting Eisenhower in the process. In their propaganda around the world the Russians made the most of the American admission. The incident of the U-2, as the special plane was called, dealt a heavy blow to American prestige and honor. The flight was not only contrary to standard usages under international law, but the United States had been caught in an official lie which undermined its credibility before the world.

Troubles with Castro. American relations with Cuba also deteriorated seriously in 1960. On January 1, 1959, a young revolutionary, Fidel Castro, succeeded in overthrowing the corrupt dictatorship of General Fulgencio Batista. At first the new government enjoyed the support of the American people, who welcomed Castro when he visited the United States soon after assuming power. But when it became evident that the social revolution Castro proclaimed also included the confiscation of American property and the wholesale execution of the "enemies of the revolution," the attitude of the American people and their government cooled noticeably. By early 1960 over a billion dollars worth of American property had been confiscated without compensation, and a steady stream of refugees from Cuba entered Miami. Furthermore, Castro made no secret of his friendship with the Soviet Union, with which he concluded trade agreements. In retaliation, late in May 1960 the United States ended all economic aid to Cuba, and in July, at the recommendation of an angry Congress, the President cut imports of Cuban sugar by 95 percent. Since the United States was Cuba's principal customer and sugar the island's chief export, this action hurt. The Castro regime became increasingly anti-American.

The Election of 1960. Because the recently ratified Twenty-second Amendment limited Presidents to two terms, the Republicans in 1960 did not have to wait to learn if Eisenhower would run for a third term. Vice-President Richard M. Nixon was the choice of most party leaders, including the President. Nixon was nominated on the first ballot, and Henry Cabot Lodge, the United States ambassador to the United Nations, was chosen as his running mate.

The front-runner at the Democratic Convention was Massachusetts Senator John

F. Kennedy, who had shown strength in a number of state primaries. Thanks to a well-prepared campaign and a highly organized staff, Kennedy was nominated on the first ballot. Astutely, he urged the nomination of his erstwhile opponent, Senator Lyndon Johnson of Texas, for second place on the ticket. The Democrats wrote a deliberately liberal platform, including support of the Supreme Court decision on desegregation.

Since both candidates were in their youthful forties, the campaigning was strenuous, despite extensive use of television and jet travel. Nixon personally visited all fifty states and Kennedy appeared in forty-four. The candidates also inaugurated a series of four joint appearances on television, which helped Kennedy, since he had enjoyed less national recognition than Nixon.

Kennedy also ran under the handicap of being a Roman Catholic. Although the Republicans officially did not allude to his religion or use it against him, a number of private persons and organizations did question the fitness of a Catholic in the presidency. Kennedy met the prejudice head-on, candidly and without rancor. "I am not the Catholic candidate for President," he said at one point in the campaign. "I do not speak for the Catholic Church on issues of public policy, and none in that Church speaks for me. . . . Are we to say that a Jew can be elected Mayor of Dublin, a Protestant be named foreign minister of France . . . but a Catholic cannot be President of the United States?" Subsequent analyses showed that Kennedy's religion was the central issue for most voters.

The election turned out to be one of the closest in American history, with Kennedy winning by fewer than 113,000 votes out of a record 68.6 million votes cast. At least 4.5 million Protestants who had voted for Stevenson voted for Nixon, it has been estimated, but Kennedy's Catholicism brought out new Catholic voters, and he won support from some Eisenhower Protestants; few Republican Catholics shifted. Lyndon Johnson was essential in helping to stem the Southern Protestant opposition to a Catholic President. Kennedy's election finally disproved the political platitude that a Catholic could not be elected President, the Constitution notwithstanding.

ELECTION OF 1960: ELECTORAL VOTE

Kennedy: 303   Nixon: 219   Byrd: 15

Vote divided (Kennedy and Byrd)

Vote divided (Nixon and Byrd)

Although a shift of merely twelve thousand votes in five states would have given Nixon an electoral college majority, the congressional elections were one-sidedly Democratic. At that level, at least, it was clear that the country was still strongly Democratic.

THE KENNEDY ADMINISTRATION

Limited Success with Congress. In keeping with the youthful, vigorous image he had projected during the campaign, John Fitzgerald Kennedy called his program "The New Frontier." More eloquent than any President since Woodrow Wilson, more concerned with elevating and educating the people than any President since Theodore Roosevelt, Kennedy entered office surrounded by driving intellectuals and men of high purpose. But he soon found that the conservative Congress was decidedly cool, if not hostile, to his program. Twice during 1961 and 1962 Congress rejected his bills for medical care for the aged and federal aid to education. Congress also voted down his recommendation for a new cabinet post of urban affairs. In the first two years of his administration, Congress gave the President only a part of his requests for tax reforms; in 1963 it refused to act on his request for an income tax cut of $11 billion, which Kennedy had strongly urged as a necessary stimulus to the economy.

Like Roosevelt and Truman before him, Kennedy discovered that a heavily Democratic Congress was no guarantee that a Democratic President would be able to enact his program. Most of the slowness or hostility of Congress centered in the House of Representatives, which was dominated by conservative Southern Democrats and Republicans, often working in coalition. In the congressional elections of 1962 the President vigorously campaigned for a Democratic Congress, and, contrary to the usual results of mid-term elections, the Democrats lost very few seats in the House and actually gained some in the Senate. Yet the result for the President's program was largely negative. At the time of Kennedy's death by assassination on November 22, 1963, Congress had failed to pass a single major piece of the legislative program he had enunciated the previous January.

The administration's principal legislative success had come in the previous year. The Trade Expansion Act of 1962 was important because it marked an even more significant departure from protectionism than the Reciprocal Trade Act of 1934. It gave the President new and unprecedentedly wide powers to cut tariff rates, although for decades Congress had jealously guarded its prerogatives in this field. The act also provided for federal aid to business firms and workers adversely affected by the resulting increased competition from abroad. Kennedy correctly hailed the act because it provided means for increasing the rate of American economic growth through the expansion of American exports. By permitting the importation of certain foreign goods, especially those from the booming European Common Market (composed of France, Italy, West Germany, and the Benelux countries) and from Japan, the administration hoped to secure important and wider markets for American goods abroad, while increasing, through competition, the efficiency of industry at home.

Several times Kennedy publicly denied that his administration harbored any of that hostility toward business usually associated with the Democratic regimes of Roosevelt and Truman. But the business community clearly felt uneasy about Kennedy's leadership—particularly after he used threats of government intervention and harassment to force United States Steel to rescind its price increases in the spring of 1962.

Losses and Gains in Foreign Affairs. The Kennedy administration's foreign policy record was mixed. At his death the long-term problems of the Cold War were still unresolved and some new ones had been added. Germany and Berlin were still divided, and the several thousand advisers and support troops that Kennedy had sent to South Vietnam to help its anti-Communist government fight Communist rebels constituted only the beginning of a much larger involvement to come (see p. 304).

During the early days of his administration, Kennedy launched the Alliance for Progress in Latin America, a long-range economic aid program designed to combat the conditions of poverty that contributed to the spread of communism and denied a decent living to millions. Through technical advice, loans, and grants, the Alliance endeavored to help Latin Americans help themselves in effecting land reform, improving farming techniques, and accelerating industrial development.

The Alliance's laudable aim of not permitting United States funds to be used to bolster undemocratic or unpopular regimes was not easily put into practice. Military juntas in Argentina, Brazil, and Peru in 1962 and in the Dominican Republic in 1963 interfered with or actually overthrew constitutional governments, thereby bringing into serious question the political stability and commitment to constitutional and democratic procedures of those nations. It could be said, though, that the Alliance at least ended the long neglect of Latin America, whose leaders and intellectuals both resented United States indifference and feared its power and its intentions. In 1965 President Johnson admitted that the program would have to continue for twenty years instead of the original ten before it could be properly evaluated. By 1970 the rate of economic growth among members of the Alliance was higher than it had been in the early years of the program, but the average still fell below the planned-for 2.5 percent per year. A continuing problem was the unwillingness of governments in Latin America to encourage birth control, despite the impact of one of the highest birth rates in the world.

During the Kennedy administration the storm center of Latin American affairs proved to be Cuba. In April 1961, Kennedy ill-advisedly lent token naval support to an invasion of Cuba by a small group of anti-Castro Cuban refugees at a place called Bay of Pigs. But the effort to overthrow Castro's avowedly Communist regime ended in fiasco when the 1500-man invasion force was easily defeated and its members killed or captured. The United States suffered grievously in prestige because it had once again, as in the U-2 incident, contravened the normal procedures of international law and had broken its own agreements under the inter-American security system. The immediate result was the strengthening of the Castro regime and the tightening of Cuba's connection with the Soviet Union.

How close that Russo-Cuban tie actually was became painfully clear in the summer and fall of 1962, when the Soviet Union began supplying the island nation with large amounts of economic and military aid. Then, in early October, American reconnaissance planes photographed Soviet medium-range missile sites under construction on Cuban soil. Alarmed at what he termed the upsetting of the "nuclear status quo" in the world, Kennedy on October 22, 1962, declared a naval quarantine of Cuba, broadcasting to the world and particularly to the Soviet Union the American intention to risk war rather than to permit a buildup of Soviet missile power in Cuba, only ninety miles from the United States.

The carefully considered confrontation brought the world to the very brink of nuclear war; but within three days the Russians agreed to withdraw their missiles in exchange for an American agreement not to support any future invasion of Cuba. Although Soviet technicians and support troops remained temporarily on the island, the extension of Soviet missiles to the Western Hemisphere had been stopped.

Then and later Kennedy was criticized for risking a world holocaust in order to show the Russians how determined he was; but most observers in the United States and western Europe praised his coolness and his success in dealing with the crisis. In any event, he did not gloat over the Soviet retreat. Instead he continued to seek ways of breaking the circle of mutual suspicion that perpetuated the Cold War; and his success in making some accommodations with the Russians suggests that the ordeal of the missile crisis of 1962 marked a significant shift in Soviet-American relations. His most concrete accommodation was the working out of a limited test-ban treaty with the Russians during the summer of 1963. The treaty, which was ratified overwhelmingly by the Senate in October 1963, prohibited any testing of nuclear weapons in the atmosphere, in outer space, or under water. Although the stockpiles of nuclear weapons on both sides continued to grow, the test-ban treaty promised to reduce the contamination of the atmosphere and showed that careful and limited negotiations with the Russians could bear fruit. The United States and the Soviet Union also agreed to establish a so-called hot line, or direct teletype circuit, between the Kremlin and the White House, to be used for instant communication between the two superpowers in the event of an international emergency in which it was important to know each other's intentions. The "hot line" proved valuable at the outbreak of the Arab-Israeli war of June 1967, when the leaders of the U.S.S.R. and President Johnson used it to assure each other of their common desire to refrain from direct intervention in the war.

The Assassination of President Kennedy. On November 22, 1963, in Dallas, Texas, to the horror of a stunned nation and a shocked world on both sides of the Iron Curtain, an assassin's bullet turned to ashes the shining but unfulfilled promise of John Fitzgerald Kennedy. In the short time that he had been before the world, his youthful vigor, self-deprecating wit, and incisive intellect had won favor among Americans of all political persuasions. Young adults especially were deeply affected by this novel political figure who spoke inimitably to and for their generation. Foreign nations, from leaders to ordinary citizens, responded to his image of the United States as a nation compassionate toward the weak, imaginative in confronting old problems, and firm in leadership. His low-keyed eloquence and bright intelligence moved people in all walks of life, from affluent suburbanites to the inner-city poor. His death seemed horrifying even to an age hardened to violence and inured to irrationality.

JOHNSON AND DOMESTIC AFFAIRS

The Transfer of Power. Within ninety-eight minutes of Kennedy's death, Lyndon Baines Johnson was sworn in as President. Johnson was a quite different man from the wealthy, Eastern-bred, sophisticated Kennedy. Born in Texas in modest circumstances in 1908, Lyndon Johnson had spent almost all his adult years in the swirling politics of Texas and Washington, first as a member of the House of Representatives in the Roosevelt era and then as senator and majority leader during the Eisenhower years.

"The Great Society." In his State of the Union message in January 1964, President Johnson called for "a war against poverty" as the central goal of his administration. The Economic Opportunity Act, passed in August 1964, was only the first of the legislative steps to be taken in that war. The act recognized that most of the poverty in the nation resulted from lack of education and training among the unemployed rather than from a dearth of jobs. The law appropriated almost a billion dollars for agencies and programs designed to retrain the workless in order to fit them for the more highly skilled jobs available in an advanced society. The name the President gave to his program was the Great Society, which he defined as "a place where men are more concerned with the quality of their goals than the quantity of their goods."

Johnson's long and distinguished career in the legislative branch gave him an understanding of Congress that enabled him to push through legislation that had been stalled for half a year under Kennedy. Within Johnson's first year in office, Congress passed the first reduction in income taxes in thirty years, the Economic Opportunity Act already mentioned, the long-pending foreign-aid bill, the Higher Education Facilities Act, and the strongest and most far-reaching civil rights act ever put into law (see p. 301). Not all the measures that were asked for the Great Society were enacted that first year; but the record made clear that in his dealings with Congress, Johnson was highly successful, despite the handicap of following a martyred President.

President in His Own Right. Inasmuch as Johnson was advocating the same kind of a liberal program advanced by Democratic Presidents since Franklin Roosevelt, conservatives in the Republican party were convinced that, to win the presidency in 1964, the G.O.P. had to put forward a candidate with a different political philosophy from that of Eisenhower and Dewey, who had represented the Eastern, liberal wing of the party. For too long, conservative Republicans contended, the party had been merely an echo of the Democrats; victory would come, they added, only if the voters were presented with a real choice.

The man the conservatives selected as their standard-bearer was Barry Goldwater, a senator from Arizona, who, ever since his election to the Senate in 1958, had been publicly opposing the liberal point of view and the liberal programs which had long dominated both parties. In 1963, for example, he said that social security should be voluntary and that the TVA should be sold. As a result of careful organization and arduous preconvention campaigning, the Goldwater forces won the Republican nomination for their candidate. The platform of the party reflected his philosophy: it called for an end to deficit spending, further tax reduction, and a more militant foreign policy, which it characterized as a "dynamic strategy aimed at victory," a reference to the increasingly frustrating war in Vietnam (see pp. 304 and 306).

There was no doubt, of course, that Lyndon Johnson would be the Democratic candidate, though his selection of Hubert Humphrey as running mate came as something of a surprise, since Humphrey had long been associated with the more liberal wing of the party, toward which Johnson was not thought to be favorably disposed. The platform was as liberal as Humphrey ever was, stressing civil rights for blacks, medical insurance for the aged, full employment, and aid to education; also, it denounced not only the Communist party but such supernationalistic organizations as the John Birch Society and the Ku Klux Klan. The contest between the Republican and Democratic parties, in short, was unusually ideological for an American presidential campaign, since it was devoid of the usual balancing of philosophies in candidates and platforms.

Johnson proved to be not only the more relaxed and experienced campaigner but also the more popular. His margin of votes was the largest in U.S. history, topping even Franklin Roosevelt's in 1936. He carried 44 states and won 295 seats in the House of Representatives and 68 seats out of 100 in the Senate. Goldwater's record as a believer in military solutions to problems of foreign policy, such as that in Vietnam, and his repudiation of the social gains of the New Deal lost him many votes among moderate Republicans, the poor, the aged, and ethnic minorities. Not surprisingly, Johnson's proportion of the black vote in the big cities of the North and in several Southern states reached as high as 90 and 95 percent. Farmers, too, voted Democratic, because they feared that Goldwater's laissez-faire views would jeopardize the government support program for agriculture. Four of the six states Goldwater carried were in the Deep South, where it was believed that his position on the rights of black Americans (he had voted against the Civil Rights Act of 1964) was less dangerous to white supremacy than that of Johnson. He also endeared himself to the white South by his emphasis upon states' rights and his steady denunciations of centralization of power in Washington.

The debacle that the Republicans suffered in 1964 was somewhat repaired in the November elections of 1966, when the party was able to win forty-seven new seats in the House of Representatives and eight new governorships. That almost all the Republican winners had either opposed Goldwater's nomination in 1964 or simply ignored his conservative ideology in 1966 indicated once again how damaging the party's shift to the right two years before had been.

Constructing the Great Society. Thanks to his overwhelming victory at the polls in 1964, Johnson found that the legislation he wanted was passed quickly by the new Congress. To continue the war against poverty, the legislators appropriated $1.1 billion to alleviate rural poverty in Appalachia and $3.3 billion for the economic development of depressed urban areas. At the President's urging, Congress in 1965 also authorized rent subsidies to the poor living in privately owned housing. The program was designed to help low-income people living outside public housing. Johnson called the Act "the single most important breakthrough" in housing legislation. That same year Johnson secured the passage of the Medicare bill, which provided for medical aid for persons over sixty-five through the social security system—a measure that Kennedy had advocated earlier but that had twice failed to get through Congress. Johnson also redeemed Kennedy's 1960 pledge to revise the immigration laws in order to remove the discrimination against immigrants from eastern and southern Europe that had been a part of national policy since the 1920s. The Immigration Act of 1965 provided for the elimination by 1968 of quotas based on national origin but retained a ceiling on the total number of immigrants to be admitted each year.

The Education President.   Johnson's most dramatic and path-breaking contribution was in education. For years the role of the federal government in supporting education had been vehemently debated, without either side being able to prevail. Under Johnson the question was settled positively; from now on it would be a question only of how much support the federal government ought to provide. The National Defense Education Act of 1964, for example, offered federal support for the teaching of the humanities as well as the sciences in college. Federal support of education no longer needed to be confined to subjects useful in repelling foreign threats, as it had at the passage of the first NDEA under Eisenhower in 1958.

The Elementary and Secondary Education Act of 1965 was also a landmark measure. It provided for the expenditure of over one billion dollars for improving education in schools below the college level and, also for the first time, permitted federal money to be granted to private church-supported schools. For thirty years the major stumbling block in the path of federal aid to education had been the demand of such schools—principally Roman Catholic—for funds and the refusal of many people to countenance such aid on the ground that it would violate the traditional separation of church and state. These obstacles were transcended in the Act by confining the federal funds to nonreligious expenditures, while justifying such grants as aid to pupils rather than as aid to religious institutions. In the Higher Education Act of 1965, the federal government for the first time provided scholarships for college students in an effort to realize President Johnson's goal of making it financially possible for any young American to attend college. The Act also constituted a continuation of the long-term trend toward popularization of higher education that had begun in the 1920s and had been continued by measures such as the G.I. Bill, which had offered financial aid to World War II veterans wishing to attend college.

A Southern President and Black America.   John F. Kennedy's moving television appeal to Americans in 1963 to accept the moral challenge of full equality for blacks justly earned him the distinction of being the first President in the twentieth century to attack the question of discrimination against black Americans in clearly moral terms. But to Lyndon Johnson must go the credit for the most sweeping attack on unequal treatment of the black mounted by any President at any time. The Civil Rights Act of

1964 really originated under the Kennedy administration, but it remained for Johnson to push it through a three-month filibuster in the Senate. The Act prohibited racial discrimination in public places, in employment, and in labor unions. As a sanction of compliance, it provided for the withholding of federal funds from any state that practiced racial discrimination. Since much federal money went to support schools, hospitals, and other state services, this provision gave bite to the law. The Act also sought to get around the literacy requirements for voting, which were often used in the South as a means of disfranchising blacks. It provided that any adult with a sixth-grade education was presumed to be literate. The immediate effect was to open public accommodations in many cities of the South for the first time in the twentieth century—though not much was changed in the rural and small-town South—and to increase voting by blacks in many communities.

It is also worth noting that the Civil Rights Act of 1964 was the broadest statement of American belief in equality ever enacted. It not only prohibited racial discrimination, but it outlawed discrimination in employment for reasons of sex, nationality, and religion as well. The federal government was now committed to enforcing equality of treatment for two of the most visible groups in the United States—blacks and women.

The Johnson administration also pushed through a new voting bill in 1965. Despite protections for black voters in the acts of 1957, 1960, and 1964, blacks were still being kept from the polls in the South by subterfuge, intimidation, or outright refusal by state officials. The Voting Act of 1965 provided for federal officers to register black voters in any county in which the Justice Department found less than 50 percent of the eligible voters actually participating in presidential elections. A striking measure of how far the country had come on the question of federal power as well as on the rights of blacks was that in 1890 a similar bill by Representative Henry Cabot Lodge had been denounced and killed in the Senate for being a "Force Bill." In 1965 such a bill seemed a mild and necessary measure to most of the country. As a result of the protection and support provided by the law, registration drives over the subsequent years brought millions of black voters into the political process. By 1970 about two thirds of the eligible black adults in the South were registered, a proportion that had not been achieved since the days of Reconstruction. As a result, in that same year Alabama counted 105 black elected officials—the second highest number in the nation. One consequence of the new interest in black voting was the large number of black elected officials throughout the country. By 1970 there were almost two hundred black state legislators, though as recently as 1962 there were only fifty-two. Eighty-one cities were headed by black mayors in 1971.

Voting rights were not the only concern of the white Southerner in the White House. In 1967 President Johnson asked Congress to enact a civil rights bill that would end discrimination in the sale and rental of housing, one of the bases for all-black schools in the North as well as a major handicap to blacks in achieving equality of opportunity. Congress was slow to move on the measure until the assassination of Martin Luther King, Jr., on April 4, 1968, impelled it to action. King was undoubtedly the leading black in the nation, uncompromising in his commitment to the achievement of equality through nonviolence. He was shot by a white racist while participating in a protest movement in behalf of striking black garbage collectors in Memphis. The civil rights bill that King's death hastened to the President's desk outlawed discrimination on racial grounds in the sale and rental of about 80 percent of the housing in the country. A similar bill had failed of passage in 1966 because of Northern objection to such legislation. This was the last piece of civil rights legislation in the Johnson or in the first Nixon administration.

Johnson also took pride in appointing the first black to the cabinet (Robert C. Weaver as Secretary of Housing and Urban Development) and the first to the Supreme Court (Thurgood Marshall).

Two Steps Forward, One Backward. Despite the administration's commitment to civil rights and the passage of four civil rights acts since 1954, resistance to acceptance of blacks as equals persisted in the South and caused large-scale riots in Northern cities. White violence against black demonstrators in Alabama in the spring of 1965 caused President Johnson to send federal troops into his native South to provide the protection that George C. Wallace, Alabama's segregationist governor, would not. In the elections of 1966 strong segregationists won the governorships in Alabama and Georgia.

In the summers of 1964, 1965, and 1966 riots broke out in the black ghettos of several Northern cities, during which rioters attacked the police, burned large areas, and looted stores. In Los Angeles in 1965 the violence resulted in $40 million in property damage, almost four thousand arrests, over a thousand wounded, and thirty-four deaths. Black demonstrators in Chicago in 1966, protesting against segregated housing, encountered a high degree of hatred and physical violence from whites.

In the spring and summer of 1967, riots in varying degrees of severity occurred in more than thirty cities. In Detroit and Newark alone, 68 persons lost their lives, about 1400 others were injured, and almost 7000 were arrested. Property damages from looting and burning were estimated in hundreds of millions of dollars. In April 1968 the assassination of Martin Luther King, Jr., sparked another outburst of black rage in some 125 cities across the country. This time, Washington, D.C., Baltimore, Chicago, and Kansas City, Missouri, were conspicuous for the level of damage and violence. All told, 46 persons were killed, more than 2600 injured, and some 22,000 arrested. Property losses were put at $45 million.

During the late 1960s and early 1970s there were signs in various Northern cities that as the movement for racial equality sought to break down housing barriers or to desegregate schools with enrollments based on segregated housing patterns, white resistance would become stronger rather than weaker. The failure of Congress to pass an open housing bill in 1966—the first civil rights bill to fail in almost ten years of the Black Revolution—was one sign. Another was the approval that greeted the Nixon administration's slowdown on implementation of school integration in 1969 and after.

Progress in the direction of equality for blacks had been made, to be sure. More blacks were voting in the South than in a century. The whole legal basis of segregation in the South was gone, and by 1972 school integration throughout the region had moved far beyond mere tokenism. Although blacks still experienced a higher rate of unemployment than whites, in 1970 that disparity, for the first time, was less than 100 percent. Between 1960 and 1970 the proportion of blacks who had purchasing power equivalent to $10,000 in 1969 dollars rose from 9 percent to 24 percent. That increase was considerably greater than the doubling that took place over the same period for whites. Yet it was still true that blacks, constituting only 11 percent of the population, made up 30 percent of those who were below the official government poverty line.

Equality would become a reality for all Americans when the war against poverty was won. That job, however, entailed more than the removal of legal barriers to opportunity. It would require an assault upon a century of accumulated discrimination against blacks in housing, education, and jobs. By the end of the Johnson administration that battle had merely been begun, and it was clear that neither most white Americans, nor the Nixon administration, wanted to press the struggle very hard.

"Let Us Continue." With these words Lyndon Johnson announced his support of John F. Kennedy's policies after the assassination in Dallas. The same words might be used to sum up the deeper springs of Johnson's policies, for the new President was also following in the path of Franklin Roosevelt's New Deal, during which he had first entered national politics. Indeed, Johnson's programs in education and civil rights went beyond anything done under the New Deal; the Housing and Urban Development Act of 1968, which provided $5.3 billion over a three-year period for new housing, especially for low-income families, made New Deal housing expenditures seem paltry. Yet Lyndon Johnson's Great Society never went beyond the New Deal in concept—it simply moved forward in the direction the New Deal had pointed.

It was not, however, the limited imagination of the architects of the Great Society that diminished it in the eyes of the American people and brought it to an unexpected close. It was the inability of the President to end the Vietnam War. Dissatisfaction was already evident in the elections of 1966, when the Republicans picked up forty-seven seats in the House and three in the Senate. By the end of November 1967, according to a Gallup poll, only 38 percent of the American people were satisfied with the President's handling of his office, though three years before he had been elected in a historic landslide. To understand what one historian has called "the tragedy of Lyndon Johnson," we have to look at foreign affairs—an area of presidential activity where Johnson was neither expert nor happy.

JOHNSON, NIXON, AND THE WAR

The Dilemma of Vietnam. If Johnson was responsible for the enactment of much of the liberal legislation that Kennedy could not get through, he benefited, in turn, from his predecessor's superior handling of foreign affairs. Indeed, looking back on their administrations, it appears that Kennedy's successes lay principally in foreign affairs while Johnson's enduring monuments are probably found in his domestic programs. One advantage that Johnson inherited from Kennedy was a more relaxed and understanding relationship with the Soviet Union. The Cold War still remained, but it had obviously been moderated as a result of Kennedy's resistance to Russian pressures, as in Cuba, at the same time he was working out accommodations to lessen tensions, like the test ban treaty, an agreement to sell wheat to Russia, and his conversations with the Russians to limit the spread of nuclear weapons.

It was in Southeast Asia that Kennedy's policies ill served his successor. When the French withdrew from their former colony of Indochina in 1954, after defeat by Vietnamese nationalists and Communists under the leadership of Ho Chi Minh, the country was divided into two parts. The northern half was frankly Communist, the southern strongly anti-Communist. The Geneva agreement of 1954, which established the division, also called for unification of Vietnam within two years on the basis of free elections. But since it appeared that the elections would result in the triumph of Ho Chi Minh in both sections of the country, the Eisenhower administration encouraged the establishment of an independent republic in south Vietnam, as part of its global strategy to prevent the spread of communism.

In retrospect the American commitment to resist the spread of Communist power everywhere was based upon an overly simple analysis. Events would show that not all Communist governments were under the control or discipline of Moscow, as many United States officials in the 1950s and even into the 1960s insisted they were. Nor was it evident that a world order of peace depended, as Secretary of State Dean Rusk asserted during the Johnson years, upon resistance at any cost to any form of aggression by Communists. Nor was it accurate to see the war in Vietnam as simply a replay of the Korean conflict. The war in Vietnam began as a civil war—largely directed against the tyrannical rule of Ngo Dinh Diem, the first of the South Vietnamese presidents whose governments were supported by the United States.

During the Eisenhower administration the United States, which had heavily subsidized the unsuccessful French war against Ho, sent economic and military aid to the South. As the situation there continued to deteriorate, President Kennedy in 1962–63 rapidly increased the number of military advisers, helicopters, and other forms of military assistance, though the actual fighting was still left in the hands of the South Vietnamese. Johnson, in the campaign of 1964, promised to keep the United States free from a land war in Asia while continuing to support South Vietnam's resistance to the local guerrillas of the National Liberation Front or Viet Cong and the Communist troops sent from the north.

By early 1965, however, the likelihood of military and therefore political defeat in the south became so great that President Johnson sharply increased the American commitment to contain communism in Asia. In February 1965 he ordered the first bombing of bases and supply dumps in the north. Later that year he not only increased the number of American military personnel in the south but also authorized for the first time the direct engagement of the enemy by American ground troops.

This new turn in American involvement in the war had several consequences. For one thing, by 1966 the military presence of some 400,000 United States troops removed the possibility that the Communist-led guerrillas could take over the south as long as the Americans remained. It also meant that the war was now being fought largely by Americans, though some 500,000 South Vietnamese troops were also mobilized.

Second, the ever-increasing bombing of North Vietnam alarmed many European allies of the United States, who feared that Communist China or the Soviet Union, which supported the northern regime, would feel compelled to enter the war. Such an act would, of course, involve a direct confrontation between the great powers and perhaps lead to a nuclear war.

Third, within the United States, the Johnson policy of gradually but relentlessly escalating the war divided the American people. Few Americans wanted a full-scale war against China or the Soviet Union, yet it seemed that the policy might lead in that direction. Also many Americans had voted for Johnson in preference to Goldwater in 1964 on the ground that the war would not be expanded if Johnson were elected, and they now felt that he had misled them. Others found Johnson's policy faulty on moral grounds, contending that the regime in South Vietnam was representative of neither its people nor their national aspirations; and still others opposed his policy on the more pragmatic level that the United States was overextended in commitments and power in Vietnam.

Advocates of American abandonment of the long involvement in Vietnam grew in number as the war dragged on. Most Americans, to be sure, supported the general policy of containing communism in Asia, just as they had supported it in Europe. But as the cost of that containment mounted and the connection between the interests and safety of the United States and the interminable war became less and less clear, many Americans began to think that the price was too high. Even those who accepted the administration's claim that the war was primarily a defense against aggression from the north could not help but recognize that, even in 1968, with over a half million American troops in Vietnam, victory was still not in sight. Although President Johnson insisted that American withdrawal could mean national ignominy and national danger, the direct interest of the United States in the war was never spelled out. The administration relied more and more upon the argument that the war involved the prestige of the United States and the "credibility" of its word among its allies.

The effect of the war on American foreign relations elsewhere was evident when Johnson dispatched several thousand marines in 1965 to prevent an alleged Communist coup from overturning the government of the Dominican Republic in the Caribbean. Although the troops were withdrawn within a year, the United States had once again violated its pledge not to intervene in the affairs of Latin American nations. The consensus was that Johnson had intervened out of fear of another Cuba near American shores. Though the evidence of Communist power in Santo Domingo was slight, the President was not willing to take the chance that the non-Communists could remain in control without help from the United States. In the context of the frustrating war in Vietnam and the continued existence of a Communist regime in Cuba, even the slightest threat of yet another Communist regime in the Western Hemisphere seemed too risky to contemplate.

On the other hand, when war between Egypt and Israel became imminent in May and June of 1967, the United States hesitated to get involved, despite moral and perhaps legal obligations to support Israel against a military threat to its survival. Undoubtedly the heavy involvement in Vietnam played an important part in the decision to go slowly in trying to prevent the outbreak of hostilities in the touchy Middle East. Consequently, the United States was unable to prevent the brief war, which began in early June 1967.

At home it was also evident that the rising cost of the war—at least $20 billion a year—was stiffening resistance in Congress and across the country to further expenditures in behalf of the Great Society. In November 1967, Senator Eugene McCarthy, a liberal Democratic senator from Minnesota, announced that he would run in the upcoming primaries against the President in order to provide an alternative on the question of the war. By this time the high cost of the war in both money and men, as well as its persistence, had aroused much public hostility, even within the President's own party. Yet few thought McCarthy's challenge would seriously affect the President or the continuance of the war.

On January 29, 1968, at the beginning of Tet, the Vietnamese lunar New Year, the Viet Cong and the North Vietnamese launched a major offensive against thirty provincial capitals held by South Vietnamese forces. The power of the attack took the Americans and their Vietnamese allies by surprise. At one point fighting was going on within the American Embassy in Saigon itself. Although a shaken administration bravely announced the Tet offensive a complete failure, few believed it; after all, the military and the government had been announcing for months that the war was being won.

That March, Senator McCarthy received almost as many votes in the New Hampshire Democratic primary as the President of the United States. For months the President had been unable to appear in public without insulting harassment and even danger to his person from the opponents of the war, and this new measure of public repudiation put unendurable pressure upon him. He could either abandon the war—a policy he had resolutely refused to consider—or abandon the presidency. In a surprise television announcement at the end of March, Johnson removed himself from consideration for renomination, at the same time announcing a partial cessation of the bombing of North Vietnam. Although the war had already killed hundreds of thousands of Vietnamese and thousands of Americans, the presidency and the political career of Lyndon Johnson were perhaps its most spectacular casualties.

Yet Johnson's withdrawal from political life was only the first of the shocks that preceded the election of 1968. Five days later, Martin Luther King, Jr. was assassinated in Memphis, Tennessee—an event, as we have already noted, which caused violence to erupt in over a hundred cities. Then two months after that, in the midst of the furious primary campaign for the Democratic nomination which Johnson's retirement had begun, Senator Robert Kennedy of New York, brother of the assassinated President, was himself shot and killed by a fanatical anti-Zionist. Kennedy, who had become almost as widely idolized as his brother, was well on his way to being the Democratic presidential nominee. He already was a recognized champion of those who wanted to end the war in order to move toward new domestic reforms.

The Election of 1968. The death of Robert Kennedy assured the nomination of Vice-President Hubert Humphrey as Democratic presidential candidate, but not until after the passions stirred up by Vietnam had disrupted the party convention in Chicago. Thousands of disenchanted young people—both moderates who had worked in Senator McCarthy's primary campaign and radicals out to "confront" the Establishment—demonstrated in the streets until they were brutally dispersed by the police in full view of television news cameras. The sight of the bloody clashes shocked the American people. Neither the Democratic platform, which offered no significant alternative to the Johnson war policies, nor the candidate, who was identified with those policies, provided a rallying point for opponents of the war.

Meanwhile, the Republican convention had nominated Richard Nixon, who had survived not only his defeat by John Kennedy in 1960 but the subsequent loss of a race for the governorship of California. Since then he had worked hard at building support within the party and keeping in the public eye through meetings with world leaders. Recognizing that he must win a substantial number of Southern votes, Nixon chose Spiro Agnew, governor of the border state of Maryland, as his running mate.

The campaign was complicated by the candidacy of George Wallace of Alabama, who ran on the American Independent party ticket. No one expected him to win; but he clearly threatened Humphrey in the traditionally Democratic South, and the enthusiasm he stirred in some Northern states reflected the opposition of many blue-collar workers to the Democratic stand on civil rights. There was a possibility that he could prevent either major candidate from winning a majority of the electoral vote and thereby throw the election into the House of Representatives.

The campaign revolved around the war overseas and the social problems at home. Nixon stressed the alarming increase of violence in the cities, which he attributed to the leniency of the Democratic administration toward demonstrators and rioters and of the Supreme Court toward criminals. Playing upon the public's fears, he promised to end the "permissiveness" that, he insisted, fostered lawlessness. Although he had supported the aims of the war against communism in Southeast Asia since his own vice-presidency, he promised to bring the conflict in Vietnam to an end, though he declined to say how. In the television appearances on which he chiefly relied, he shunned the issue of integration, which was unpopular among many whites, and concentrated on "law and order," about which there could be little controversy. Generally, he portrayed himself as a leader dedicated to national unity and international peace.

Burdened with the Johnson record on Vietnam, Humphrey finally announced that, if elected, he would stop the bombing of the north. As election day approached, his popular support rose steadily, bolstered by the efforts of his powerful allies in organized labor to win working-class voters back from George Wallace. Just before the election President Johnson announced the cessation of American bombing in North Vietnam.

Given the shambles at the Democratic convention, the election was remarkably close. Nixon won by only a half million votes out of 73 million cast. He carried thirty-two states, however, to Humphrey's fourteen. Nixon won seven Southern states, Wallace five, and Humphrey one—Texas. But while the outcome indicated that the Democrats could no longer count on even a majority of Southern states in a presidential election, the vote for Congress showed that most Americans still voted Democratic. Both House and Senate remained comfortably in Democratic hands.

Nixon and the War. The political destruction of Lyndon Johnson and the mood of the country during the campaign made it clear to the new President that the public would no longer stand for the emotional and financial drain of an endless Asian war. Within six months after taking office, Nixon announced that he would withdraw 25,000 troops from Vietnam over the next ninety days. Thus began the policy of gradual withdrawal that was to continue for the next four years. Meanwhile, the South Vietnamese army was further trained and equipped to carry on the war by itself; this policy President Nixon called Vietnamization.

Nixon's willingness to use American power to insure the success of his policy marked a new high in brinkmanship. In the spring of 1970 he ordered American forces to support a South Vietnamese invasion of neighboring Cambodia (and eventually of neighboring Laos) in order to destroy enemy supplies and troop buildups. This action, taken at a time when the war was supposedly "winding down," outraged those Americans who saw it as expanding the conflict. When, in the same week as the invasion, four students were killed by national guardsmen during an antiwar demonstration at Kent State University in Ohio, students at almost three hundred colleges and universities went on strike. American troops were subsequently withdrawn, but both Cambodia and Laos remained in the theater of war.

As he continued to remove American ground troops from Vietnam, Nixon also continued the negotiations in Paris that President Johnson had agreed to in 1968. But neither side would accept the other's demands; and in the early spring of 1972 North Vietnamese troops launched a powerful assault across the demilitarized zone in the north and the Cambodian border in the west. To support the reeling South Vietnamese forces, President Nixon widened the war once again. He ordered stepped-up bombing raids against North Vietnam, including the capital, Hanoi, and the major port, Haiphong, neither of which had been bombed since 1968, and the rail lines from China. He also ordered the navy, for the first time, to mine Haiphong harbor. His intention was to cut off the military supplies from the Soviet Union and China that made such offensives possible. China and Russia denounced the American "aggression" but took no other action.

The President was gambling for high stakes. In November he would be up for reelection. If the war was still going on then, his Democratic opponent would have an enormous advantage with an electorate that was clearly sick of the war. Yet if he withdrew all American power from Southeast Asia and the Saigon regime collapsed under Communist pressure, he would be held responsible. Thus he needed to continue to withdraw the troops, but he also needed some assurance that Saigon could survive.

To critics of his policy, it seemed that Nixon was following the tactics of the Johnson administration and trying to bomb the North Vietnamese into an acceptable settlement. By 1970 more tons of bombs had been dropped on the small country of Vietnam than had been dropped on Germany and Japan in all of World War II, and the raids of 1972 were setting new records in sheer destructiveness. Yet after all the punishment, the Viet Cong and the North Vietnamese continued to fight and continued to score successes in the south.

Diplomatic Breakthroughs. In the summer of 1971 the President made the dramatic announcement that he had accepted an invitation to visit the People's Republic of China, which had been secretly arranged by Henry Kissinger, the President's trusted advisor on foreign policy. The implications of the trip, which took place in February 1972, were far-reaching. It ended twenty years of frigid enmity between the two powers. It also ended American opposition to the seating of Communist China in the United Nations: Communist China took the place of Chiang Kai-shek's China on the Security Council and on the Assembly in the fall of 1971. And the visit concluded China's long isolation; by 1972, for example, Japan was opening commercial and diplomatic negotiations with the Chinese.

Nixon's visit did not convert China and the United States into instant allies. Diplomatic recognition did not immediately follow, and the United States pledged itself to maintain its treaty obligations to Chiang Kai-shek's regime on Taiwan, even though Communist China claimed the island. Yet a new era in the relations between the United States and the Communist powers seemed to have begun. This was confirmed when the White House announced that, within two months after his visit to Peking, President Nixon would visit Moscow as well.

Behind this about-face by the long-time anti-Communist, Richard Nixon, and the leaders of the two largest Communist states was the hostility between the Russians and the Chinese. China, as the weaker of the two Communist giants, wanted a counterweight in the form of better relations with the United States. Russia, on the other hand, feared that the United States and China might combine against it. As a result, President Nixon was welcomed in both capitals, even as his bombers unloaded unprecedented tons of explosives on his hosts' ally, North Vietnam.

The new relationships gave Nixon an opportunity to appeal privately to China and the Soviet Union to put pressure on North Vietnam to conclude the war on terms the United States could accept. Since American troops were steadily being removed (the last ground combat forces were withdrawn in August 1972), his desire for an end to hostilities was clear. At the same time, the continued bombing of North Vietnam made it equally clear that he intended to keep up the pressure until his minimum conditions were met.

Four years after taking office, Richard Nixon had indeed reduced American involvement in Vietnam; few American casualties were being suffered. But the cost of the war continued to run in the billions of dollars annually, and the destruction in Vietnam and in the rest of Indochina went on. This was true even though in January 1973, the United States and the Vietnamese all signed a cease-fire agreement in Paris after intensive and lengthy negotiations as well as a resumption of the heavy bombing of North Vietnam in late December. As a result of the Paris agreement, the American bombings stopped in all of Vietnam and all Americans who were held as prisoners were released by March 1973. American planes, however, continued to bomb in Cambodia in an effort to prevent the collapse of the government there and to bring about a cease-fire between government and anti-government forces. In short, even with all American troops and prisoners of war out of Vietnam, the longest war in United States history still dragged on, though its purpose was now more obscure than ever.

Domestic Flexibility.   As in foreign affairs, so in domestic affairs, Nixon surprised friend and foe alike with his ability to abandon or drastically modify attitudes and principles he had held during a lifetime in public affairs. When he took office he proclaimed an end to federal deficits, and for two years he insisted that he would never impose economic controls. But in 1970, for the first time in nine years, inflation wiped out the gain in median income for a family of four, and since the economy was sluggish as well as inflationary, government tax receipts fell below expectations. (Unemployment was up from 3 million in 1968 to over 5 million in 1971.) In August 1971 the President ordered a freeze on prices, wages, and rents, and three months later he set up agencies to police observance of federal economic guidelines. Thus, having for years pronounced himself an opponent of the "New Economics," he ended up embracing Keynesian theory and the familiar Democratic belief that government has a responsibility to regulate the economy. And with the spiraling cost of the Vietnam War, by 1972 his administration ran up not only the largest budgetary deficit since the Second World War but two of the largest in American history.

Nixon also showed his flexibility by recommending that the federal government provide a minimum income of $1600 for every family of four on welfare. Since the idea had been advocated by liberals years earlier, many Democrats could support it in principle, but liberal senators rejected the $1600 figure as inadequate. No agreement was reached and so no new welfare program was enacted before Congress adjourned. Another Democratic idea that Nixon sought to make a part of what he called his "New American Revolution" was that of sharing federal revenues with the states and cities. A revenue-sharing bill was finally passed in September 1972.

In June 1972 the President signed a landmark bill providing for the first time that nearly every college and university would receive some federal money. It also provided that, as a matter of policy, any student needing money to attend college could obtain a loan of up to $1400 a year. Public colleges and graduate schools were prohibited from discriminating against women students on pain of loss of federal funds.

The Act also marked the first interference by Congress in the school desegregation issue: it prohibited any new court-ordered school busing for purposes of racial balance until June 1974. The President angrily denounced the provision for not prohibiting present as well as future court-ordered busing on any grounds and promised to carry the busing issue—merely a new form of the old segregated school issue—into the presidential campaign.

In 1969 Congress went along with the President's recommendations for a tax cut in an effort to stimulate the economy. It also accepted presidential proposals in making the Postal Service an independent agency and in establishing the National Rail Passenger Corporation (Amtrak) to reorganize and run the nation's passenger rail service. Congress, however, went far beyond his lukewarm recommendations on the improvement of the environment. It passed, at the end of the 1972 session, a $24.6 billion sewage treatment bill that was vetoed by the President on the ground that such an expenditure was inflationary. Nixon had recommended only $6 billion. Congress, in a rare exhibit of independence, quickly overrode the veto.

Despite the liberal character of some of Nixon's policies, both foreign and domestic, his administration frankly repudiated the liberalism of the Kennedy and Johnson years in other areas, particularly in civil rights. The conservatism was manifested most ideologically in the speeches of Vice-President Spiro Agnew, who went out of his way to castigate liberals—especially reporters and commentators critical of the administration—as dangerous to America and to condemn youthful protestors and demonstrators for their lack of discipline and lack of respect. The President himself spoke out against laws making abortion easier to obtain, and he vetoed a bill that would have provided federally supported child-care centers for working mothers, arguing that such measures weakened traditional family ties.

Nixon's first Attorney General, John Mitchell (who had been his campaign manager in 1968), considered the Supreme Court decisions protecting the rights of accused persons to be too lenient and sought to slow down school integration in the South. His efforts in this direction were rejected by the federal courts, as was his use of wiretapping without court orders in the name of national security.

Nixon appointed a new Chief Justice in 1969, but his next two nominees for the Supreme Court—Southern "strict constructionists," to use the President's description—were rejected by the Senate as inadequately qualified. Before his first term was completed, however, he appointed three more justices, all with records that revealed conservative legal philosophies. They soon began to make their views felt. In June 1972, for example, the Court for the first time in eighteen years was unable to render a unanimous decision on school desegregation because two of the new justices voted against the majority.

For facing up to the changed international realities of the 1970s, the first Nixon administration was likely to go down in history as among the important influences in moderating the Cold War. After the Moscow meetings in the spring of 1972, the Soviet Union and the United States agreed to new limitations on missiles and submarines, as well as on joint explorations of space. By 1972 few Americans continued to look on China as the Great Red Menace a whole generation of Americans had been taught to fear. To have been instrumental in bringing about such an alteration in the world scene was no mean achievement, even if, on the domestic front, the Nixon record was thin in significant accomplishment and short on recognition of the legitimate claims of minorities and of the importance of civil liberties to all Americans.

The Avalanche of 1972. For a long time, Richard Nixon had made clear that he intended to run again for President. Before the Republican Convention met in August he had also made evident that he wanted his vice-president, Spiro Agnew, again as his running mate. The Democrats, however, could not settle as easily upon Nixon's opponent. Hubert Humphrey, who had only narrowly been defeated by Nixon in 1968, was eager to try again. But before the Democratic Convention met in July, George McGovern, senator from South Dakota, and long an outspoken opponent of the war in Vietnam, showed that he was a favorite in the various state primaries. Those victories won him the nomination on the first ballot. The Democratic Convention itself was unusual that year since its members had been selected by a new process which guaranteed representation to ethnic minorities, women, and young people. This new kind of party convention—more serious and dedicated to the question of political issues than any convention since the Progressives' in 1912—enthusiastically supported McGovern's liberal posture. The platform promised a quick end to the war, a deep reduction in military expenditures, tax revision, and increased expenditures on social services.

The vice-presidential candidate that the convention named, Thomas Eagleton, senator from Missouri, however, was soon compelled to resign because he admitted to having undergone psychological treatment in recent years. Sargent Shriver, a brother-in-law of John F. Kennedy, was named in Eagleton's place. This unexpected change gave a setback to the hitherto highly successful McGovern organization from which it never recovered. As the weeks of the campaign passed, it became clear that McGovern was really the nominee of only a minority of his party and that his very liberal position on tax reform, welfare, and particularly on reductions in military spending, were frightening many traditional Democrats into the Nixon camp. Roman Catholics, working men, Southerners, and ethnic groups were clearly unhappy about McGovern. Rather than putting Nixon on the defensive for failing to end the war after four years in office, McGovern found himself on the defensive for being less than candid in his handling of the resignation of Eagleton and in being less than informed in proposing welfare and tax reform programs that he later had to withdraw. Although McGovern publicized certain dubious actions by lesser officials in the Nixon administration or campaign, the country did not seem to think that McGovern's charges were worth taking seriously. Moreover, when George Wallace was definitively removed from the

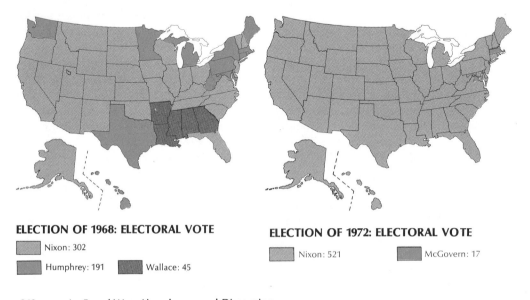

ELECTION OF 1968: ELECTORAL VOTE

Nixon: 302

Humphrey: 191   Wallace: 45

ELECTION OF 1972: ELECTORAL VOTE

Nixon: 521   McGovern: 17

campaign in May because of permanent paralysis after an attempt upon his life, the Wallace supporters moved to Nixon, not McGovern. The President's stand against busing in school integration, and a "hard line" on urban crime and on welfare won the support of many white Southerners and traditional Democrats in the cities of the North.

The enormous lead that the polls showed for Nixon over McGovern early in the campaign continued to election day. As a result the President left to Vice-President Agnew and other subordinates the actual campaigning. Nixon probably made fewer campaign speeches than Franklin Roosevelt did in 1944 in the midst of the Second World War. Although President Nixon and his foreign policy advisor Henry Kissinger worked hard to arrange an agreement with North Vietman to end the war before the election, the foot-dragging of South Vietnam prevented that feather from being added to the President's cap.

The results of the election made clear that he did not need an end to the war in order to win one of the biggest victories in American history: 49 states and 61 percent of the popular vote. McGovern, by winning only Massachusetts and the District of Columbia, was as badly defeated as Alf Landon in 1936. Those who had contended that McGovern would be the "Democratic Goldwater"—too far out of the mainstream of either party to be able to win—proved to be right. Nixon completed the breakup of the Democratic Solid South, which Harding had begun in 1920. He captured, with large majorities, every one of the former states of the Confederacy, a feat never before achieved by a Republican president. Significant for the future politics of the South was the election of three Republican Congressmen from Mississippi and Louisiana for the first time since Reconstruction.

Yet it would be a mistake to see Nixon's victory as a Republican resurgence. Indeed, Nixon's campaign had concentrated on "reelecting the President," rather than on winning a Republican majority. In his few campaign speeches the President rarely mentioned his party and in some Southern states Nixon campaigners refused to help Republican candidates who were running against conservative Democrats. The result was that the Democrats continued to control both houses of Congress by substantial majorities, as they had done since 1957. Most Americans, it would seem, were still Democrats, but they apparently did not see George McGovern as their kind of Democratic president.

From Landslide to Watergate. Nixon's overwhelming victory at the polls promised a powerful, even a dominating presidency in his second term, despite continued Democratic control of Congress. But an event of the 1972 campaign, which had been brushed aside at the time, turned the great Nixon victory into ashes within months after his inauguration.

On June 17, 1972, as the Democratic National Convention was approaching, five men were arrested while breaking into the Democratic headquarters in Washington. They were caught attempting to install electronic spying devices to listen in on Democratic plans. The headquarters were located in a large complex of buildings at the edge of the Potomac River called the Watergate. The Democrats naturally sought to make the break-in a political issue, but no connection between the Republicans or other supporters of the President and the burglars could then be established. Soon after the burglars were convicted in early 1973, however, the involvement of White House officials in the Watergate break-in became known. The Senate moved to set up a special investigating committee and at public hearings before that committee in May and June important members of the Nixon administration were implicated. John Mitchell, once Attorney-General under Nixon and the man who had masterminded the President's first election, was linked to Watergate in sworn testimony. He and Nixon's former Secretary of Commerce were also indicted for other election irregularities. Moreover, on April 30, just before the Senate investigation got under way, Nixon's two chief White House aides resigned, along with lesser officials, two of whom confessed to participating in the plot to break into the Watergate and to conceal the White House's complicity after the burglars were arrested.

The revelations were at once shocking and unprecedented in American political history; for weeks in the spring of 1973, as resignations followed revelations, the government seemed to be almost paralyzed. *The New York Times* spoke darkly of the White House's "subverting America." And there was sufficient truth in the charge to make it more than journalistic sensationalism. Persons high in the government had even used supposedly nonpolitical agencies like the FBI and CIA in seeking to bring about the reelection of the President. Despite much rhetoric emanating from the Nixon administration in support of "law and order," some officials in that administration had been countenancing breaking the law for purely political ends. Some officials had been willing to commit perjury to secure the President's reelection—and did, by their own admission.

The Aftermath. The effects of Watergate were immediately discernible in the changed relationship between President and Congress. For years the power and prestige of the presidency had been growing at the expense of Congress. The process had begun during the Depression under Franklin Roosevelt and had continued, even accelerated, during the Cold War and the war in Vietnam. The great Nixon electoral victory in 1972 promised that the process would continue. Watergate and popular dissatisfaction with the unending involvement in Southeast Asia, however, brought a sharp reversal. Congress, it is true, failed to override a presidential veto in early 1973, but both Houses of Congress refused funds to continue the bombing in Indochina, where the cease-fire did not apply. This was the first time that the House had ever voted against the war in Indochina.

The long-range consequences of Watergate would have to wait upon the full revelations of the extent of the Administration's involvement, which might even reach the President himself. But whatever new information might come to light from the various investigations under way, by the early summer of 1973 there was already enough known to differentiate Watergate from the Harding Administration's Teapot Dome or the Star Route Frauds of the Grant Administration. In those scandals men had traded government privileges for personal profit. In the Watergate no personal profit was involved, but something much more sinister: the willingness to break the law, to commit perjury, and to lie by those charged with upholding the law—all in the name of reelecting a president.

Reassuring in the whole thing, however, was the way in which the crimes and the later "cover-up" were revealed. The newspapers, the judiciary, and members of the two major political parties—all parts of the established system—contributed to the exposure. Diligent reporters, particularly from the Washington *Post,* dug up part of the story, while a persistent and conscientious federal judge, John Sirica, presiding at the trial of the five burglars, forced out other clues. The natural interest of the Democrats in exploiting these revelations, for partisan if for no other reasons, made certain that the leads provided by the press and the court would be fully and thoroughly investigated. Watergate revealed undoubted defects in American political practices, but at least it also showed that institutions charged with correcting such abuses were functioning as expected.

CHAPTER 12

TOWARD 2000: CHANGING SOCIETY AND CHANGING VALUES

THE PROBLEMS OF PROSPERITY

The Affluent Society.   The massive unemployment of the Great Depression—which the New Deal as late as 1939 was unable to reduce below 17 percent of the total labor force—evaporated in the war boom. Although some unemployment occurred during the several postwar recessions, the percentage of jobless workers never again reached as high as 8 percent. After 1940 high productivity and prosperity were the dominant social facts. Goods spilled out of American factories and farms in ever increasing volume and variety. Between 1940 and 1960 the gross national product, after price changes are discounted, rose 114 percent, though the population grew less than 36 percent. In 1971 the gross national product passed $1 trillion; as recently as 1960 it had been "only" $500 billion.

Other periods in American history—the 1920s, for example—had been notable for their prosperity, but the novelty of the decades between 1945 and 1965 was that the lower-income groups, as well as the upper-income levels, shared in it. Millions of American families moved up the income ladder. Income distribution, it is true, remained unequal—in 1962, for example, 5 percent of families received almost 20 percent of personal income. Yet there was a tendency in the direction of equality; during the 1930s, the top 5 percent of income receivers had taken almost 27 percent of personal income.

The improving economic position of the average American was clear from the statistics. Weekly wages of workers in manufacturing, for example, increased 16 percent between 1947 and 1957 and another 17 percent between 1960 and 1969 even after price changes are taken into account. Another general measure of improved living standards was the increase in home ownership. In 1940 less than 44 percent of American families, including farmers, owned their own homes; by 1960 the figure was almost 62 percent. (Between 1960 and 1970, however, the figure rose only slightly.)

Persistence of Poverty.   Despite the evidence of an improving standard of living and the decline in the proportion of the poor, there were still dark spots in the society of affluence. By the 1960s and 1970s these dark spots were major social issues. One warning of the paradox of poverty in the midst of plenty was voiced as early as 1958 by economist John Kenneth Galbraith in *The Affluent Society.* Galbraith pointed out that the public sector of the economy—schools, hospitals, roads, sanitation, mental health, and other public services—was not participating in the new prosperity. Although expenditures for education, health, and highways were much higher than in 1940, schools were still crowded, the number of beds in mental hospitals was grossly insufficient, and the roads were jammed with cars. Because affluent Americans found all kinds of luxury commodities attracting their increased dollars—from electrically driven toothbrushes to elaborate mechanical toys—not much more money than before was left in the citizen's pocket to finance the public services. Despite their prosperity, in short, Americans were still finding taxes too high and social welfare too expensive.

Galbraith went on to point out that poverty in the United States was no longer an economic problem but a social one; the poor remained so because they could not participate in the booming economy. Generally, they were unable to earn an adequate living because of lack of education, illness, or old age or because they were geographically isolated in economic backwaters like Appalachia or rural New England.

Galbraith's warning was emphasized and clothed in dramatic language in Michael Harrington's *The Other America,* published in 1962. Harrington argued that the poor were all over the country but that the prosperous simply did not see them. The poor consisted of the millions of blacks in the ghettos of the great Northern cities; the hundreds of thousands of Southern sharecroppers, existing in rural poverty; the thousands of migratory workers of the West, brown, white, and black; and the millions of people over sixty-five who lived on low incomes, often less than $1000 a year. It was recognition of the sharp contrast between the lot of poor people and the affluence of American society in general that goaded the nation into undertaking antipoverty measures in the 1960s. But the difficulty of eradicating poverty and the unwillingness of better-off Americans to change their old habits caused issues like welfare programs and minimum income proposals to remain subjects of debate in the 1970s. The redistribution of wealth, it was becoming clear, was not an easy thing to bring about.

The Decline of the City.   Since 1920 a majority of Americans have lived in towns or cities of 2500 population or greater. By 1970 almost three fourths of all Americans lived in urban areas, and the trend appeared irreversible, with each census reporting a decline in the rural population. During the fifties and sixties the kinds of urban areas in which Americans chose to live began to change. Central metropolitan districts did not keep up with general urban growth: between 1950 and 1960, for example, the aggregate total population of cities over 100,000 increased merely 9.3 percent, and four out of five of the giant cities of over one million actually *decreased* in population. The continuing increase in urbanization, in short, was the result of people moving from the country or small towns to suburbs, rather than simply to big cities.

Many people, of course, were also deserting the central cities for the suburbs. This movement began in earnest in the 1920s, but by the fifties it was a mass exodus. In 1953 the editors of *Fortune* compared the suburban migration to the great immigration from Europe in the early years of the twentieth century. About as many people—1.2

million—moved to the suburbs that year as entered the United States in 1907. And the census of 1970 made it clear that the trend was continuing. Between 1960 and 1970, 61 of the 153 cities of 100,000 or more lost population. For many it was the first loss of population since the beginning of the urbanizing movement in the nineteenth century. In 1970 less than a third of Americans lived in central cities, while more than two fifths lived in surrounding suburbs.

This development challenged Americans with new problems. Because the central city was still the place in which the suburbanite earned his living, millions of Americans traveled daily as much as fifty miles from home to work and back again, creating an urgent need for safe and efficient means of commuter transportation. But because large numbers of commuters preferred automobile travel over train or bus service, expensive highways built to speed travel were often choked with slow-moving cars, many of them carrying only the driver. The consequent demand for parking facilities alone—not to mention the multiplying demands for new expressways and freeways—ate significantly into the prime real estate of the great cities, thus cutting into the tax base that was needed for increased urban expenditures. Moreover, commuter trains, forced to compete with the automobile, found it more and more difficult to make a profit or even to survive, and many were forced to reduce or discontinue their service. Yet much of the metropolitan labor force still depended on the commuter lines for daily transportation, and as a consequence a number of state and local governments faced pressures to subsidize the commuter lines in one way or another. The Urban Mass Transportation Assistance Act of 1970 brought some federal money for mass transportation to the beleaguered cities, but the need far outran the remedy. The automobile was still a difficult competitor to overcome, as became evident soon after the opening of San Francisco's new, computerized Bay Area Rapid Transportation system (BART) in 1972. It was not clear that BART could attract sufficient regular riders to become self-supporting.

The flight to the suburbs was both a symptom and a cause of the decline of the city as a place of human habitation. Insofar as the city became the home of the poor—it was middle-class families that fled the overcrowded schools, substandard housing, and polluted air—metropolitan residential areas deteriorated still more. High land prices, caused in part by land speculation and by rapid, unplanned growth, created a big obstacle to the construction of adequate low- and middle-income housing. Nonexistent or poorly enforced building and housing codes, haphazard zoning laws, and the profits to be made from slum real estate further contributed to the continual rotting of the core cities in America's metropolitan areas. When the Housing Act of 1968 authorized 1.7 million units—mainly low- and moderate-income—over the next three years, it was estimated that at least six million were needed. Added to the problems of housing were those of overcrowded, understaffed urban schools and the fact that large areas of modern cities were generating increasing rates of crime, including juvenile delinquency.

These perplexing urban problems stimulated attempts to restore the nation's cities to economic and social health. Under the generic term "urban renewal," many cities attempted to rehabilitate run-down neighborhoods by land clearance and new construction or by renovating existing structures and bringing such areas into conformity with zoning, housing, health, and safety standards. Cities used their power of condemnation and subsidies from the federal government to clear substantial areas, in many of which low-cost public housing for people meeting certain standards of need was built; in 1962, 1200 local authorities operated half a million dwelling units.

But despite the success of urban renewal projects in several of America's metropolitan areas, progress was slow. Land clearance ran into vexing legal delays; the relocation of former tenants was a continuing source of irritation; and renewal critics attacked everything from spiraling costs to the aesthetic and social drawbacks of the new construction. They charged that several billions already spent to rejuvenate America's cities had helped only to destroy their individuality; they called the new middle-income housing "a marvel of dullness and regimentation"; and in 1962 some critics correctly predicted that new low-income projects would themselves be slums by the 1970s.

One device that the Johnson administration pushed in 1966 to encourage better housing for the poor was rent subsidies that would permit poor people to live in nongovernment housing even if the rents were higher than they could afford. Another was to provide federal funds for the renovation of older houses and tenements in established neighborhoods in order to escape the asceptic, often starkly unattractive housing projects.

Since coordination of the many efforts to deal with the problems of the decaying city was paramount, Congress in 1965 created a new cabinet post for urban development and, in 1966, another for transportation. The latter was designed to encourage and coordinate efforts in behalf of better intra- and interurban transportation, since the automobile had itself become a problem of urban living.

The Dominance of White Collars. During most of America's history the majority of workers have been farmers, miners, fishermen, and factory workers—that is, blue-collar workers. But ever since the opening of the twentieth century, an increasing proportion of the labor force has comprised white-collar workers—that is, managers, clerks, professionals, government employees, and self-employed proprietors. In 1970, for example, white-collar workers constituted 50.8 percent of the nonagricultural labor force, blue-collars 34.5 percent, and service workers (policemen, bank tellers, domestics, and others) 10.5 percent. The growth of a white-collar class meant that an increasing number of people were being supplied with goods by an ever smaller proportion of agricultural and manufacturing employees. It also measured the maturity of the economy, since only a highly mechanized and skilled society could achieve such a division of labor. By 1970 less than 5 percent of the working force was in agriculture, but 18 percent of the labor force was employed by government—in a society that prided itself on being the antithesis of socialistic! (In officially Communist Yugoslavia in 1972, 20 percent of the work force was employed by the government.)

White-collar predominance also testified to the consumer nature of the economy. Whereas in previous history most paid labor was employed in making new goods, by the end of the 1950s most working people were consuming goods, helping others consume goods, or performing a service.

In a society of consumers and white-collar workers the emphasis was on personal relations; people, not things, were the objects of work. As David Riesman pointed out in his influential book *The Lonely Crowd* (1950), sometimes this emphasis on people ended in outright psychological manipulation, as occurred in certain types of selling and advertising. But even when persuaders were not at work, there was still a tendency for Americans to be concerned with other people and what they thought about each other.

Traditionally, white-collar workers have resisted joining unions, even though white-collar pay is often inferior to industrial wages. In 1958, for example, only 12 percent of all unionized workers were employed in nonmanual occupations. The growth in the white-collar class thus seemed to explain, at least partly, the stagnation in labor organizing in the 1950s. Despite its organizing drives and its power, organized labor in the 1960s barely kept pace with the growing size of the labor force. In 1964, for example, about 30 percent of nonagricultural workers were in unions; four years later the proportion was down to 28 percent.

A large part of the white-collar class was composed of women, who after 1940 entered the labor force in ever-increasing numbers. Indeed, between 1950 and 1970 some 13.2 million women joined the labor force as compared with only 9.5 million men. And among these working women were growing numbers of wives and mothers; by 1970 over two fifths of all married women were employed in paying jobs. Almost a third of women with children under six were working, and that figure included only married women whose husbands were present. In short, women now constituted the largest source of new workers in the economy.

Women entering the labor force, however, were frequently compelled to accept jobs that paid less or were otherwise less rewarding than their education or training warranted. This was especially true of college-educated women, who, proportionately, returned to work in larger numbers than their noncollege sisters. Furthermore, the needs of the economy apparently did not encourage women to develop their powers. In the 1950s women made up a smaller proportion of all college students than they had in the 1920s; and fewer women, proportionately, were entering graduate schools. By the 1970s, however, there was some reason to believe this pattern was changing (see p. 323).

Automation and Technological Unemployment. Automation, which was introduced into an increasing number of industrial processes during the postwar years, promised to displace human labor faster and more widely than any mechanical process ever known before. Automation differed from ordinary mass production in that men were no longer necessary for the continual operation of the machines. Instead, electronic devices made the machines self-regulating, much as a thermostat turns the heat on and off in a room as the temperature changes. The most advanced form of automated machine was the computer, which performed thousands of tasks, such as mathematical calculations, within a matter of seconds. Although the machine appeared to have the capacity to "think"—that is, to make decisions—actually it had already been "instructed" in the possible answers to any question it might be asked as well as with the reasons why, in a given circumstance, one answer should have been selected over another. Its "thinking," therefore, was really an incredibly rapid electronic canvassing of all the alternatives, from which the best answer was selected.

Labor unions estimated that in the six years prior to 1961, 1.5 million blue-collar workers were dropped from manufacturing, chiefly because of automation. The widespread introduction of a rather simple mechanical device like the self-service elevator displaced forty thousand operators in New York City alone. Many jobs, especially those involving personal service, would never be automated, but in the 1960s industries like chemicals were already highly automated.

In the early 1960s labor unions were attempting to work out arrangements to prevent the introduction of automation from causing wholesale dismissals. Usually these arrangements took the form of creating funds, to which employers contributed, for retraining workers for new jobs. By 1970, however, the fears about automation that had bedeviled the 1960s had subsided in the face of reality. There were severe limits to the replacement of human workers by machines.

The Corporate Economy.   Behind the drive to mechanization and automation lay the willingness of business and government to invest ever-increasing amounts of money in scientific and technological research for the improvement of methods and techniques. During the 1950s outlays for research and development rose faster than the gross national product, reaching $12 billion in 1959. (By 1971 the investment had reached $28 billion.) About half the total was contributed by the federal government. A new and fruitful relationship developed between business and government on the one hand and the universities on the other. Recognizing that research was one of the sources of new products and techniques and therefore of increased productivity, both business and government, through research grants and consulting contracts, drew heavily upon the knowledge and skills of the intellectual community. One of the unexpected consequences of the Vietnam War was that universities, under pressure from students, moved to reduce these connections.

The rapidly growing economy of the 1950s and 1960s was highly institutionalized. The individual entrepreneur or operator, so celebrated in national mythology, was still in evidence, but he was no longer a significant figure in the operation of the economy. In 1958 there were some five million individually owned businesses outside of farming, mining, and fishing, but this figure left 85 percent of all economically engaged persons working for someone else. The largest businesses, of course, were corporations, but the economy was actually dominated by only a tiny fraction of them. In 1968, for instance, 18 percent of America's corporations received 91 percent of the total income of corporate enterprises. Indeed, it was the large corporation that made the heavy investments in research and development that were playing such a large part in maintaining prosperity.

These large corporations, in turn, were encouraged to grow larger by the expanding economy. With the federal government now acknowledging its responsibility to prevent or at least mitigate a depression, corporate businesses could afford to be less cautious in their operations and therefore to keep investment in the economy high. Moreover, the enormous military spending, which exceeded $88 billion annually by 1970, acted as a further incentive to corporate activities and profit accumulation.

Government, despite its acknowledged role as a regulator of the economy, is also a partner in the economy. The more than $200 billion annual budgets of the federal government constitute a significant part of the gross national product, and the close links forged between business and government in military and space activities constitute a novel concentration of power. President Eisenhower, in his farewell address to the American people in 1961, called attention to the dangers:

> . . . This conjunction of an immense military establishment and a large arms industry is new in the American experience. . . . We recognize the imperative need for this development. Yet we must not fail to comprehend its grave implications. . . . In the councils of government, we must guard against the acquisition of unwarranted influence, whether sought or unsought, by the military-industrial complex. The potential for the disastrous rise of misplaced power exists and will persist.

The New Agriculture. Farming, like industry, also witnessed a revolution in productivity, upon which rested the prosperity and high standard of living of the postwar decades. In 1960, for example, an hour of industrial employment bought 2.2 pounds of round steak; in 1929 the same amount of labor bought only 1.2 pounds.

If, as these figures indicate, American farming was highly productive, it was also backward, inefficient, and a cause of poverty for millions of people who still clung to traditional ways of working the land. Even though the number of farmers has been steadily declining ever since the 1920s, in 1961 1.6 million farm families, or 44 percent of the total number, earned so little from agriculture that they had to engage in other kinds of employment to make ends meet. These people—black sharecroppers in the South, migrant farm laborers, and farmers on marginal lands in Appalachia and elsewhere—actually lived more meanly than welfare recipients in the great cities. It was the efficient farmers, constituting less than two fifths of the total, who produced 87 percent of all agricultural commodities. The other 2.2 million farms could lie fallow and not be missed.

The highly efficient farms were actually a product of the high government price supports, which encouraged large capital investment. It was this high capitalization that explained the enormous increase in productivity. In 1960 some five million tractors were in use on American farms, and thousands of mechanical cotton pickers displaced many thousands of Southern black workers who left agriculture to seek wider opportunities in Northern cities. New seeds, new machines, and new chemicals of all kinds also gave impetus to the farm revolution of the postwar years. Chemicals are used not only to kill harmful insects but to hasten crop maturity, to kill weeds, to defoliate plants in order to facilitate harvesting, or to inhibit growth in crops like tobacco where only certain kinds of leaves are desired. The chemical industry also developed new feeds for chickens, which speed up growth and make it possible to raise broilers from egg to maturity in eight to nine weeks. The disastrous effects of some of these chemicals upon wildlife have posed a serious dilemma for a society wanting cheap and abundant food and wildlife at the same time.

The most important consequence of the changes in agriculture after 1945 is that the family farm as it has been known in the United States since the beginning has almost disappeared. Between 1949 and 1959 some 1.2 million farm families simply left agriculture; by 1960 less than 8 percent of the American population lived on farms. By 1970 the proportion was less than 5 percent, yet the value of total farm production rose about 20 percent in the same ten-year period. During the 1950s and 1960s governmental policies in support of agriculture had helped transform the nature of farming. In most cases either a farmer was a large-scale operator with a large capital investment, or he ceased to be a farmer altogether.

The New Equality.   One consequence of the affluence that was characteristic of the years from 1945 to 1970 was a growing demand from the disadvantaged for a greater share in the prosperity. This certainly lay behind the upswell in civil rights movements in the 1950s and 1960s; it was undoubtedly a part of the new demand for wider opportunities from other "minority" groups like women, Mexican-Americans (Chicanos), and Indians.

Women, it is true, outnumbered men, but in their limited opportunities for jobs and prestige, they were like ethnic or racial minorities. They were like minorities, too, in that they often did not assert themselves. These were among the arguments in Betty Friedan's *Feminine Mystique* (1963), which sparked the new feminist movement of the late 1960s and early 1970s. Beginning as only a weak voice in a society largely complacent about women's rights, the movement by 1972 was compelling a new recognition of women's quest for equality. It produced a whole range of organizations from militant to moderate, with Betty Friedan's National Organization for Women (NOW), founded in 1966, the most widespread. In 1972 the movement helped push through Congress a women's equal-rights amendment to the Constitution.

Thanks to the Civil Rights Act of 1964 and executive orders prohibiting discrimination on grounds of sex as well as race or religion, the federal government forced open new jobs for women in private employment, while insisting that public institutions increase their proportion of women employees, especially in high-level jobs. The new drive to expand women's opportunities saw traditionally male occupations like those of army general, telephone lineman, jockey, air-tower controller, and FBI agent being filled by women either for the first time or in unprecedented numbers. The new women's organizations also mounted a successful campaign to change state laws to make abortions and birth control information easier to obtain; and they aroused a new popular demand for—and, in some instances, succeeded in gaining government support for—child-care centers, so that mothers could have a true choice as to whether or not to seek employment. Although not many more women were actually elected to national political office than in previous years, women participated in politics on a greater scale than ever before. At the Democratic Convention in 1972, for example, about 35 percent of the delegates were women—a proportion previously unheard of—and a black woman, Representative Shirley Chisholm of New York, was placed in nomination for President. Even at the Republican Convention, which had no minimum quota for women delegates, women made up almost 30 percent of the membership. Although women workers were still concentrated in low-paying and low-prestige jobs, the new push for equality suggested that in the course of the 1970s that situation would be changing.

The Black Revolution by its example also spurred into visibility a large minority heretofore almost unknown to most Americans: the Mexican-Americans, who numbered as many as ten million. Though they were principally concentrated in the Southwest, hundreds of thousands lived in the Detroit–Chicago area, so that their disadvantaged social and economic position was not simply a regional problem. The new Chicano organizations, however, were most active in the Southwest. In Texas, for example, the Raza Unida party was sometimes successful in local politics. Some of the militant Chicano groups in California went beyond demanding representation in governmental agencies and in private industries and took part in the antiwar movement.

Cesar Chavez was perhaps the best known of the Chicano leaders, principally because of his successful organizing of the California grape pickers, most of whom were Mexican-Americans. His grape boycott in the years 1965 to 1969 compelled the grape growers to recognize the union and to bargain with it. More Mexican-Americans were now entering the universities and politics, particularly in the Southwest, suggesting that soon they would play a role in the life of the region commensurate with their numbers.

The newest minority group to assert itself in the late 1960s was also the oldest—the Indians. Books by militant friends of the Indian, like Alvin Josephy's *Red Power* (1971), or by Indians themselves, like *Custer Died for Your Sins* (1969), by Vina Deloria, Jr. brought the Indian's outlook and sometimes his resentments to a wider public, and the federal government took some steps to recognize the just claims of Indians for fairer treatment. (The occupation of Alcatraz Island in San Francisco Bay by a group of Indians in 1971 showed that some thought the government was moving too slowly.) Under President Johnson the Bureau of Indian Affairs was headed by an Indian for the first time.

In June 1970 President Nixon proclaimed "that the historic relationship between the Federal Government and the Indian communities cannot be abridged without the consent of the Indians." His announcement ended the policy, begun under the Eisenhower administration, of turning the Indians off the reservations into society. That same year, as a recognition of past injustices to the Indian, the Nixon administration returned 48,000 acres of land around Blue Lake, New Mexico, which had long been sacred to the Taos Pueblo Indians. Indians were still often caught between two cultures, without much preparation or opportunity to move into the mainstream of American economic life—if that was what they wished to do—but at least more recognition was being given to their situation as a separate culture than at any time since the Indian Reorganization Act under the New Deal.

The new emphasis upon equality during the 1960s also caused new black nationalist or separatist groups to come to the fore. The Black Muslims, a religious society founded by Elijah Muhammad during the 1930s, attracted national attention in the mid-1950s when the remarkably articulate Malcolm X became head of the Muslims in Harlem. The Muslims preach a form of Islam in religion and black separatism in social policy. After he had turned away from the narrow nationalism of Elijah Muhammad, Malcolm X died a martyr in the cause of human rights at the hands of an assassin in 1965.

Perhaps the most militant of the nationalist groups was the Black Panther party, which began in the Oakland, California, ghetto in 1966. A former convict of enormous literary talent, Eldridge Cleaver, was the best known spokesman of the party; his book *Soul on Ice* is one of the classics of the Black Revolution of the 1960s, along with Malcolm X's *Autobiography.* Cleaver fled to Algeria in 1968 after a series of confrontations between police and Panthers. By 1972 the Panthers were less involved in confrontations with police and more concerned with educational and breakfast programs for black children in the urban ghettoes.

A third figure of prominence in the new black nationalism in the 1960s was Stokely Carmichael, who in 1966, at twenty-four, became head of the Student Nonviolent Coordinating Committee (SNCC). His slogan "Black Power" aroused a new sense of self-awareness and pride in many young blacks and a sense of identification and cohesion among blacks of all ages. As a leader, Carmichael did not last into the 1970s, but his idea of Black Power, along with the activities of other nationalist groups, brought a new positive emphasis upon blackness and African origins among dark-skinned Americans.

To realize their commitment to equality Americans still had a long way to go, as the slow if steady progress in the achievement of the rights of black Americans made evident. But by the 1970s the ideal of equality for all groups was being pressed as never before in American history. It promised hope as well as conflict in the years ahead.

ARTS AND EDUCATION

The Theater and the Novel.   Over the last quarter century the Broadway theater continued to be dominated by crowd-pleasing musicals and light comedies. The musicals (*My Fair Lady, Fiddler on the Roof*) were written and produced for the affluent middle class, whose members could afford the ever-higher prices. A refreshing exception was *Hair,* which spoke for youth and enjoyed years of success at home and abroad after opening on Broadway in 1967. In recent years most of the successful comedies seem to have been written by Neil Simon. New dramatists of stature included Arthur Miller (*All My Sons,* 1947; *Death of a Salesman,* 1949; *A View from the Bridge,* 1955), Tennessee Williams (*The Glass Menagerie,* 1944; *A Streetcar Named Desire,* 1947; *Cat on a Hot Tin Roof,* 1955; *Sweet Bird of Youth,* 1959), and Edward Albee (*The American Dream,* 1961; *Who's Afraid of Virginia Woolf,* 1962).

Live theater showed its vitality off Broadway—around Manhattan (as in Joseph Papp's exciting productions in Central Park) and in cities and university towns around the country, where young playwrights and young performers experimented and learned their crafts. In New York black writers, actors, and directors combined their talents to create black theater.

World War II produced its share of novels, among them John Hersey's *A Bell for Adano* (1944), Irwin Shaw's *The Young Lions* (1948), Norman Mailer's *The Naked and the Dead* (1949), James Jones' *From Here to Eternity* (1951), and—ten years later, for another generation—Joseph Heller's *Catch-22.* Mailer went on to write more novels and then to move over into a highly personal form of journalism that produced, among other works, *Armies of the Night* (1968), his remarkable account of his own participation in an antiwar demonstration at the Pentagon.

The quarter century saw the last works of a number of novelists of the first and second rank—Faulkner, Hemingway, Dos Passos, Steinbeck, John O'Hara. Some of the best of the new writers carried on in the realistic tradition: Saul Bellow (*The Adventures of Augie March,* 1953; *Herzog,* 1964), for example, and Bernard Malamud (*The Assistant,* 1957; *A New Life,* 1961). Others began in the tradition and then moved away from it: Mailer, and Philip Roth, who followed a brilliant short story collection (*Goodby, Columbus,* 1959) with two traditional novels and then swerved to the wild sexual excess of *Portnoy's Complaint* (1969), the vitriolic political satire of *Our Gang* (1971), and the fantastic metamorphosis of *The Breast* (1972). John Updike, a virtuoso performer, moved in and out of the realistic tradition with *Rabbit Run* (1960), *The Centaur* (1963), and *Rabbit Redux* (1971).

The two best-known black novelists of the period were Ralph Ellison (*Invisible Man,* 1952) and James Baldwin (*Go Tell It on the Mountain,* 1953; *Another Country,* 1962), who also spoke bitingly to white America in his essays (*Nobody Knows My Name,* 1961; *The Fire Next Time,* 1963).

The Movies. The years after 1945 saw the decline of the movie industry, as television transfixed the American public. Many movie theaters closed down, and the Hollywood lots either went unused or turned out films for TV. (The number of movie houses went from 18,600 in 1948 to a low of 9,200 in 1963; by 1967 they were up to 12,000.) In the sixties, however, producers—especially young, independent producers—became aware that there was one sizable segment of the population that did not want to stay home nights and stare at the set. Reared on television, the young were ready to leave it to their parents. Many members of the new audience were college students or recent graduates. To reach them, the movies had to grow up.

The best of them did. As in the theater and the novel, censorship was virtually dead—a development conservatives blamed on the "permissiveness" of the Supreme Court—and this permitted a new realism and a new frankness of both theme and treatment. More significant, perhaps, was the new sophistication the audience demanded. Westerns could still succeed, but to do so they must either laugh at their own clichés (*Cat Ballou*) or create characters instead of cardboard cutouts (*Butch Cassidy and the Sun Dance Kid*). War, long the subject of romantic or chauvinist epics, came in for ironic attack in movies like *Dr. Strangelove, Catch-22,* and *M*A*S*H.*

Some of the best of the new movies were addressed directly to the young. *The Graduate* came to be looked on as a classic statement of what young people held against their parents and what they thought of themselves. *Easy Rider* offered a sympathetic view of the drug culture in idyllic settings. Young movie-goers were enraptured by the visually striking space adventure, *2001.* If some older fans were troubled by the moral ambiguities in the new films and wondered whether there was, in fact, anything particularly grown-up or sophisticated about clinical studies of loveless sex and celebrations of violence, by the 1970s the movies were an important emotional and intellectual experience for a great many young Americans.

Along with the new realism in the movies there came a few attempts to portray race relations honestly, but for black audiences the big screen, like the small screen, remained oppressively white. By the seventies, however, a number of movies made expressly for black audiences (*Shaft, Super Fly,* and *Sounder*) had scored impressive successes. Some blacks as well as whites deplored the separatism and the racial chauvinism sometimes involved, but others cheered the fact that there were finally some movie heroes and heroines for the black fan to identify with.

Architecture, Painting, and Sculpture. During the 1940s the "international" architectural style of the 1930s became more rectangular, more severe, and colder than ever. The most influential figure was Ludwig Mies van der Rohe, who had arrived from Germany in 1936. The classic example of his work is the austerely rectangular, rational, and eminently functional campus of the Illinois Institute of Technology in Chicago. His influence is best seen in New York's Lever House and the Secretariat building of the United Nations. The contrast between Mies and Frank Lloyd Wright is evident in Wright's great round, spirally Guggenheim Museum and Mies' box-like Seagram building, both built in New York in 1958.

By the mid-fifties Mies' harsh, geometric forms were being modified. Edward Stone introduced concrete screening, courts, ponds, and ornamented façades, as in his American Embassy building in New Delhi and in his John F. Kennedy Center for the Performing Arts in Washington, D.C. (1971). Another leader of the new decorative architecture, Eero Saarinen, son of Eliel Saarinen (see p. 242), displayed in his TWA terminal at Idlewild Airport and his earlier hockey rink at Yale University a genius for radically new roof design. The work of the Nisei, Minoru Yamasaki, continued Saarinen's reconciliation of the old and the new, as in his light and airy Science Building at the Seattle World's Fair of 1962.

The architecture of the 1960s and 1970s took full advantage of new technologies in steel and concrete. One of the most striking examples of the new emphasis upon outside trusses for large structures was the athletic facility at the Phillips Exeter Academy in New Hampshire, completed in 1971. Giant trusses supported the roofs of the gymnasium, swimming pool, and skating rinks to provide an enormous amount of uninterrupted interior space. The architects, Kallman, McKinwall, and Knowles, had employed similar giant outside trusses in their new Boston City Hall, which opened in 1969. The city hall was conspicuous, too, for its massive open courtyards among closely built old buildings in downtown Boston.

Business enterprises also employed the new spacious architecture in their headquarters and plants, usually in the countryside around metropolitan centers. American Can Company, for example, built a modern structure on landscaped grounds in Greenwich, Connecticut, and Olivetti Typewriter and Computer put up an innovative plant designed by Louis Kahn near Harrisburg, Pennsylvania.

In the late 1960s the new affluence gave impetus to the tall building. Both San Francisco (TransAmerica Building, 1971) and Chicago (John Hancock Building, 1968) boasted of the first tapered skyscrapers in the country—the radical design provided greater stability. Until the opening of the World Trade Center in New York City in 1971, the John Hancock Building superseded the Empire State Building as the tallest building in the world; but, when it is completed in 1973, Chicago's Sears Building will take honors as the world's tallest.

In painting the flight from objective representation, barely noticeable in the 1930s, became almost headlong in the forties. In the fifties abstract expressionism was in (and was to enjoy a modest revival again in the seventies); in the sixties came op art and pop art. Painting as a business boomed, with dealers and investors trying to guess which of the painters in each new school would produce work that might increase in value. One whose work did increase in value, and whose reputation kept pace, was the "action" painter, Jackson Pollock. Another was Willem de Kooning, who presented in canvas after canvas his deeply personal vision of *Woman*. Artists like Mark Rothko and Barnett Newman juxtaposed blobs and blocks of color in works that overwhelmed the viewer by their sheer size.

If the abstract expressionists and the op artists turned away from the world of things, the pop artists embraced it. Their works took off from, or duplicated, the familiar: beer cans, soup cans, cartons, hamburgers, comic-strip characters, photographs of movie queens. Often they made three-dimensional forms and then painted them, so that it was difficult to distinguish between painters and sculptors. Claes Oldenburg's distinctively "tired" or "melted" artifacts, such as toilets and sinks, reminded the viewer of the earlier surrealist paintings of Salvador Dali.

Sculptors of the sixties also made life-size manikins of plaster, plastic, and other materials and sometimes created dramatic scenes incorporating groups of these sculpted figures, clothed and painted, and real furniture—tables, chairs, and so on. And sculptors worked with "found" objects, sometimes combining or otherwise altering them, sometimes merely mounting them. Finally, there was art that fit none of the old categories: combinations of color, sound, and movement; self-destroying works; "happenings" in which living people took part; and such phenomena as piles of dirt, curtained canyons, and long trenches dug in deserts.

Meanwhile, older traditional artists survived, and new ones emerged. The painter Ben Shahn, for example, retained his concern with social problems and his representational technique until his death in 1972. Larry Rivers stayed close enough to the objective reality of the human figure to communicate, wryly, with the viewer. And the most popular artist of distinction in recent times, Andrew Wyeth, worked in the tradition of the meticulous realists of the nineteenth century.

The Educational Revolution. If, as we have seen, Sputnik sparked a new interest in education on all levels, by the 1960s that interest had taken on a life of its own. In 1970, 47 percent of students who entered the fifth grade in 1962 went on to college as compared with 21 percent of those who entered the fifth grade in 1942. That same year, 1970, 2.6 million students graduated from high school, and 2 million enrolled in some institution of higher learning. Never before had a college education seemed so necessary to the average American. In itself this drive to college was at once a sign of the affluence of American society and a measure of the need for highly trained personnel in an advanced economy.

Although some observers feared that the rising demand for college education must result in lowered academic standards, most colleges apparently did not think so, for existing facilities were expanded and new institutions were founded across the nation during the 1960s. New York State, for example, by 1967 had surpassed California with the largest state system of higher education, enrolling 200,000 students in its several branches of a state university system that had only started in 1947. It was reported, moreover, that each week in 1967 saw a new institution of higher learning being founded in the United States. Indeed, the expansion of state systems—with junior colleges, liberal arts colleges, and graduate and professional schools—posed a new and serious threat to even the best of the long established private institutions as they all competed fiercely for high quality students and faculty. But if higher education by the middle 1960s was one of the great "growth" industries of the economy, by the early 1970s that growth had slackened considerably thanks to some of the unforeseen consequences of that unprecedented expansion.

The state systems, for example, became so large that students began to protest that they were being lost in the rush to "greatness." First of several spectacular manifestations of student concern was a series of student protests and riots on the Berkeley campus of the University of California in 1964, which brought that huge educational complex to a halt for several days. Though the upheavals at Berkeley and other institutions caused administrators and faculty to think afresh about their enterprise, this did not prevent even more massive disruptions at Columbia University in 1968 and at Harvard in 1969, to mention only two of the more prominent. Indeed, between January and June 1968, the National Student Association counted 221 major demonstrations at 101 colleges and universities, involving some 40,000 students. By this time the protests were against the continuation of the war as well as the impersonality of the large educational institution and the alleged irrelevance of higher education. Suddenly, the American student long known for his docility and lack of interest in social protest was aroused. That the phenomenon was not simply related to the war was evident from the riots and disturbances on many campuses in foreign countries in 1968 and 1969. For several days, for example, the whole university system of Paris was brought to a halt by student rebellion.

The student demonstrations in the United States reached a peak in August 1971, with the bombing of a computer center at the University of Wisconsin in which a graduate student was killed. Thereafter, the demonstrations as well as the violence subsided sharply. During the academic year 1972 most college campuses were undisturbed by the interruptions of classes and academic routine that had been almost standard at dozens of campuses for half a decade. The reasons for the decline of the demonstrations are not clear, though administrative and curricular changes along the lines demanded by student protesters undoubtedly helped. Certainly the violence on campus and the repeated interruptions of classes made many students increasingly intolerant of them. University administrations and faculty also became more adept at defusing or countering demonstrations than had been the case in the beginning.

One consequence of the student demonstrations was a more fundamental rethinking of the goals and nature of university education than even Sputnik had spurred. Some educational authorities as well as lay citizens began to question seriously the value of a liberal arts education for all of the more than 50 percent of high-school students who go on to college each year. Students and trustees, though often at loggerheads in the past, came together in questioning the educational value of academic tenure. The continuing high cost of education assured that these and other questions would be issues for years to come.

A CHANGING SOCIETY

The Culture of Youth. The questioning of the universities and education in general was only a part of the alterations taking place among young people during the sixties and after. If any date can be selected for the beginning of an increasing self-consciousness among young people who found American society hypocritical and misdirected, it was the summer of 1964. That was the time when hundreds of white students, predominantly from Northern and Western colleges and universities, descended on Mississippi and other parts of the South to work for the black civil rights movement. Although some were disillusioned by that foray against injustice, many went on to other causes, particularly the movement to end the war in Vietnam. It was this cause that most affected their generation, through the draft, the casualty lists, the emigrations to Canada, the desertions to Sweden; and it was this cause that mobilized their forces. In October 1967 a confrontation at the Pentagon involved some 35,000 people, most of them young. Later, several antiwar demonstrations attracted over 100,000 participants.

It would be a mistake, however, to see the rise of a self-conscious youth movement as simply a consequence of political events or as a political event in itself. At bottom it was a criticism of American society; not infrequently it went beyond criticism to outright rejection of the values of that society. (For a tiny revolutionary minority, rejection meant destruction by bombing.) The dress that many young people assumed—pseudo-proletarian blue jeans, denim shirts, and work boots; fringed jackets and Indian headbands; flamboyant colors and designs—set them apart from the "straight" world, even as it revealed their own conformity. An even bolder rejection of contemporary mores by young men was the wearing of long hair, a practice that developed in the mid-sixties. (Fashion designers and the straight society—including in many cases the parental generation—first fought the revolution in dress and hair styling, then adapted it to their own uses. Whether this was victory or a defeat for the young, it undeniably showed their influence and their ability to provide alternatives in life style.)

Behind the casual dress, however, lay a greater significance: an emphasis upon equality, which denied deference, rank, and hierarchy. People, the young insisted, should be recognized for their individual human dignity and not for what society said they were. The new equality was evident in the impatience of most college-age students with the traditional distinctions of race and sex. Even in many Southern universities young people were much less racially prejudiced than their elders. The decline in deference was often stigmatized by Establishment spokesmen like President Nixon and Vice-President Agnew as a result of "permissiveness." Yet it was clearly part and parcel of the broader world movement, of which anticolonialism was an example, which was demanding that hitherto disadvantaged people be given a chance to participate in the making of decisions that affect them, whether in education, in government, or in society in general. It was seen in the United States, too, not only in movements in behalf of blacks and women but also in demands by students for a role in college curricular development and governance, in demands by homosexuals for freedom from harassment, and in new protest organizations among welfare recipients.

Equality has long been an accepted American value, even if its attainment has not been fully realized. But young people did not simply ask that the adult world live up to its own standards; they began to question seriously some of the values of the going society. Perhaps the most significant difference between young people and their elders was the emphasis the young placed upon feeling and emotion. To most of the young, adults seemed to be afraid of their feelings, of their bodies, of their urges, while the young gloried in sensation, paradox, and imagination. Hence the interest in mysticism, Zen Buddhism, and the writings of off-beat psychologist R. D. Laing. With their emphasis upon the value of emotion and feeling, the young exhibited a new romanticism. That had been the interest and message, too, of the young Romantic poets and writers of early nineteenth-century Europe in their revolt against the reason and reasonableness of the eighteenth century. Certainly the emphasis upon feeling helps to explain the interest in hallucinatory drugs and particularly a drug like marijuana, which enhances feelings and the imagination while dulling reason and rational thought. (Nineteenth-century Romantics like Samuel Coleridge and Thomas de Quincey got "high" on drugs for imaginative experience, too.) The consumption of alcohol—the most "successful" drug of all time—continued to far outrun the use of marijuana, but the general rise in the use of drugs throughout society was undoubtedly another measure of youth's influence. A further sign of the deep interest in feeling among the young was the enormous popularity of loud, rhythmic "rock" music and the vigorous, body-contorting, often erotic dancing that accompanied it. These dances made the foxtrot and the ballroom dancing of the previous generation seem to be—as in a sense they were—out of a different culture.

The greater freedom between the sexes that young people now experienced was also a part of the new emphasis upon feeling, sensation, and personal relations. Now that pregnancy was controllable by the contraceptive pill, many college students saw no reason to deny their feelings and postpone sexual relations until marriage. Although the 1960s saw greater freedom and even emphasis upon sexuality and nudity in public than any previous period, the saturation of the society with sex in magazines, advertising, TV, and movies should not be seen as stemming from the young. Most of the young spurned the "blue" movies and the porno shops, which they saw as selling sex rather than enjoying it. To the young it was the enjoyment of sex that was important, not its public expression and availability.

A Testing Time. A keynote in arguments between the generations was "deferred pleasure," the phrase young people used to describe (as well as deride) the adults' argument that some things had to be postponed before they could be enjoyed. It was the rebuttal of the young that life was now, not tomorrow. They saw no need to wait until they had a good job and a bank account before they saw the world, lived with their beloved, followed their impulses. For them, making and saving money, working hard for a home in the suburbs, did not represent the good life. Worthwhile living meant doing what interested you rather than what paid well, having satisfying relationships with people rather than competing with them.

To many adults, particularly those who had memories of the Great Depression, this was a shockingly impractical philosophy. Some were quick to charge that it would survive only so long as its exponents were being subsidized by their parents or at least knew that they could always turn to their parents in time of financial need. Yet young people were often showing a surprising ability to live their philosophy year after year without help from home.

Whether a fundamental change was under way in American society, the seventies might show. Would the end of the war and the draft remove the rallying point for young political activists? The society at large gave recognition to the seriousness and responsibility of the young when the voting age was lowered to eighteen in 1971 by the passage, in record time, of the Twenty-sixth Amendment. Even more significant was the fact that by 1972 over half the states, including California and New York, went on to lower the age of majority from twenty-one to eighteen in all or almost all legal matters. But while young people played a vigorous role in the primary campaign of George McGovern, political activity by the young in 1972 was less evident than it had been in 1968.

Would a serious economic depression convert the young idealists into practical careerists? For some, the tightening of the job market at the beginning of the seventies made opportunities to earn money less easy to take for granted and a bank account more important; but the new willingness to do menial work stood many in good stead.

There was also the question of whether the more visible, more articulate members of the youth culture—like the beats of the fifties and the hippies of the sixties—were, in fact, an unrepresentative minority. Most young people had never participated in the criticism of American society, its values and its standards. Most had not demonstrated against the war in Vietnam or campaigned for Eugene McCarthy or Robert Kennedy or George McGovern. The majority of those who went to college did so in order to get ahead and do better than their parents. Many young people worked for the reelection of Nixon and Agnew. And many of the noncollege-student majority of young people heartily disliked the youth culture.

Yet a change had already taken place. After the 1960s the young had an identity and a self-consciousness that people of their age in America had never felt before. They may not have been more intelligent or more gifted on the average then previous generations; but they were certainly better educated, and teachers and employers testified to their intellectual and organizational abilities. Although there had always been generation gaps, never before had the young side been so penetratingly critical. Events would soon reveal what its ultimate contribution to the democratic experience would be.

BIBLIOGRAPHY

The classic account of the coming of the war is the very full William L. Langer and S. Everett Gleason, *The Undeclared War, 1940–41* (New York: Harper & Row, 1953); more readable and as reliable for the Pacific side is Samuel E. Morison, *The Rising Sun in the Pacific* (Boston: Little, Brown, 1948). Full on diplomacy as well as authoritative is Herbert Feis, *The Road to Pearl Harbor* (Princeton: Princeton University Press, 1950). A popular but painstaking and fascinating reconstruction of the attack on Pearl Harbor is Walter Lord, *Day of Infamy* (New York: Holt, Rinehart and Winston, 1957). An intriguing and penetrating study of the causes for the surprise on December 7 is Roberta Wohlstetter, *Pearl Harbor: Warning and Decision* (Stanford: Stanford University Press, 1962). James MacGregor Burns, *Roosevelt: The Soldier of Freedom* (New York: Harcourt Brace Jovanovich, Inc., 1970) completes his readable biography of Roosevelt on a more critical note than most in dealing with foreign policy.

Herbert Feis has devoted himself in several volumes to detailing authoritatively the diplomatic history of the war and immediate postwar years. A central volume in his series is *Churchill-Roosevelt-Stalin* (Princeton: Princeton University Press, 1957). Robert Sherwood, *Roosevelt and Hopkins*, rev. ed. (New York: Harper & Row, 1950) is less objective but more interesting and filled with fascinating selections from the sources. One of the major revisionist works on FDR's handling of foreign affairs is Gabriel Kolko, *The Politics of War* (New York: Vintage Books, 1970). Chester Wilmot, *The Struggle for Europe* (New York: Harper & Row, 1952) is highly interpretive, but soundly based on the sources and very critical of American policy. The story of the creation of the nuclear bomb is told in Lansing Lamont, *Day of Trinity* (New York: Atheneum, 1965).

Eric Goldman, *The Crucial Decade and After* (New York: Vintage Books, 1960) sums up in lively and lucid prose the major events between 1945 and 1960. Although pedestrian in presentation, the *Memoirs* of Harry Truman, 2 vols. (Garden City, N.Y.: Doubleday, 1958), are a must for the years immediately after the war. The only good biographies of Truman are by friendly journalists, of which the best is Cabell Phillips, *The Truman Presidency* (New York: Macmillan, 1966). An excellent collection of important documents, some not previously published, along with commentary, is Barton J. Bernstein and Allen J. Matusow, eds., *The Truman Administration: A Documentary History* (New York: Harper & Row, 1966). For recent criticisms of the Truman years see also Barton J. Bernstein, ed., *Politics and Policies of the Truman Administration* (Chicago: Quadrangle Books, 1970). One of the most important as well as highly readable studies of postwar politics is Samuel Lubell, *The Future of American Politics,* 2nd ed. (Garden City, N.Y.: Anchor Books, 1956). A scholarly study, critical of both sides in the controversy over Korea, is John W. Spanier, *The Truman-MacArthur Controversy and the Korean War* (Cambridge, Mass.: Harvard University Press, 1959). Richard Rovere, *Senator Joe McCarthy* (New York: Harcourt Brace Jovanovich, Inc., 1959) is the best, albeit hostile, study of the Wisconsin senator. Michael Paul Rogin, *The Intellectuals and McCarthy: The Radical Specter* (Cambridge, Mass.: The M.I.T. Press, 1967) puts McCarthy into a broader context of political and intellectual history. For the national obsession with Communists, see Earl Latham, *The Communist Controversy in Washington: From New Deal to McCarthy* (Cambridge, Mass.: Harvard University Press, 1966).

Of a number of general studies of international relations in the postwar years, the following are readable and reliable: Louis J. Halle, *The Cold War as History* (New York and Evanston: Harper & Row, 1967); Stephen E. Ambrose, *The Rise to Globalism: American Foreign Policy Since 1938* (Baltimore: Penguin Books, Inc., 1971); John Lewis Gaddis, *The United States and the Origins of the Cold War, 1941–1947* (New York: Columbia University Press, 1972). Two books that try to look at Russian as well as U.S. policy are Walter LaFeber, *America, Russia, and the Cold War, 1945–1966* (New York: John Wiley, 1967), and Adam Ulam, *Expansion and Coexistence* (New York: Praeger, 1968). A valuable introduction to the problems facing underdeveloped nations is Robert L. Heilbroner, *The Great Ascent* (New York: Harper & Row, 1963).

Indispensable sources for the revolution in foreign policy in the postwar years and interesting in themselves are *The Forrestal Diaries,* edited by Walter Millis (New York: Viking Press, 1951) and *The Private Papers of Senator Vandenberg,* edited by Arthur H. Vandenberg, Jr. (Boston: Houghton Mifflin, 1952). In somewhat shrill tones, Norman A. Graebner, *The New Isolationism* (New York: Ronald, 1956) tells the story of the fight for internationalism in the 1950s.

The only critical biography so far of Eisenhower is Marquis Childs, *Eisenhower: Captive Hero* (New York: Harcourt Brace Jovanovich, Inc., 1958) but it is thin and somewhat partisan. More friendly is Arthur Larson, *Eisenhower: The President Nobody Knew** (New York: Scribner's Sons, 1968). Full of accurate and important private information on the administration is Robert J. Donovan's friendly report, *Eisenhower: The Inside Story* (New York:Harper & Row, 1956). Emmet Hughes, *The Ordeal of Power* (New York: Atheneum, 1963) is from inside the administration, too, but from a disenchanted member. The best entry into the various elections of this period or any other is the recent Arthur M. Schlesinger, Jr. *et al.,* eds., *History of American Presidential Elections, 1789–1968,* 4 vols. (New York: Chelsea, 1971). The campaigns of 1960 and 1964 have been reported in readable if purplish prose in Theodore White, *The Making of the President, 1960** (New York: Atheneum, 1961) and *The Making of the President, 1964** (New York: Atheneum, 1965). For a similar treatment of the election of 1968 but from the view of English journalists, see Lewis Chester *et al., An American Melodrama* (New York: Viking Press, 1969).

The best biography of Kennedy prior to the presidency is James MacGregor Burns, *John Kennedy: A Political Profile* (New York: Harcourt Brace Jovanovich, Inc., 1960). His presidency has been detailed by admiring former associates in Theodore C. Sorenson, *Kennedy** (New York: Bantam, 1965) and Arthur Schlesinger, Jr., *A Thousand Days* (Boston: Houghton Mifflin, 1965). More critical is Richard J. Walton, *Cold War and Counter-Revolution: The Foreign Policy of John F. Kennedy* (New York: Viking Press, 1972). The best study so far of Johnson is R. D. Novak and R. Evans, *Lyndon B. Johnson: The Exercise of Power* (New York: New American Library, 1966), which is critical but fair. More from the inside is Eric F. Goldman, *The Tragedy of Lyndon Johnson** (New York: Dell, 1969). The best book on any recent President is Garry Wills, *Nixon Agonistes: The Crisis of the Self-Made Man** (Boston: Houghton Mifflin, 1970), which puts Nixon in a broad ideological framework. Richard M. Nixon, *Six Crises** (Garden City, N.Y.: Doubleday, 1962) gives much background on the President.

Books on the Vietnam War are numerous. The best introductory volume is George M. Kahin and John W. Lewis, *The United States in Vietnam** (New York: Dell, 1967). For the view of an insider who turned against the war, see Townsend Hoopes, *The Limits of Intervention** (New York: McKay, 1969), and for the background of the war, John T. McAlister, Jr. *Viet Nam: The Origins of Revolution** (New York: Alfred A. Knopf, 1969) and Bernard Fall, *The Two Viet-Nams,* 2nd ed. (New York: Praeger, 1966).

The literature on the cultural ıd social issues of these years is growing ɒy leaps and bounds. Well written, idiosyncratic, and full of flavor is William L. O'Neill, *Coming Apart: An Informal History of America in the 1960's* (Chicago: Quadrangle, 1971); it has much on the culture, particularly of youth. Jane Jacobs, *The Death and Life of Great American Cities** (New York: Random House, 1961) is one of the most provocative books on the problem of the city. Broader in scope and packed with information is Mitchell Gordon, *Sick Cities** (Baltimore: Penguin, 1964). Herman P. Miller, *Rich Man, Poor Man** (New York: Crowell, 1971) intelligently analyzes the distribution of wealth and poverty. An excellent analysis of the economy during the Eisenhower years is Harold G. Vatter, *The U.S. Economy in the 1950's* (New York: Norton, 1963). The changing character of agriculture if vigorously and closely examined in Edward Higbee, *Farms and Farmers in an Urban Age* (New York: Twentieth Century Fund, 1963).

Books on black America proliferate. A good introduction to the issues is Charles E. Silberman, *Crisis in Black and White** (New York: Random House, 1964). More scholarly and narrower in scope is Benjamin Muse, *The American Negro Revolution: From Non-Violence to Black Power, 1963–1967** (Bloomington, Ind.: Indiana University Press, 1968). Indispensable as well as readable are several books by black leaders: Martin Luther King, Jr., *Stride Toward Freedom: The Montgomery Story** (New York: Harper & Row, 1958); Malcolm X, *Autobiography of Malcolm X** (New York: Grove Press, 1965); Eldridge Cleaver, *Soul on Ice** (New York: Dell, 1968). On the women's movement a good introduction to the literature is the collection, Betty Roszak and Theodore Roszak, eds., *Masculine/Feminine** (New York: Harper & Row, 1969). Juanita Kreps, *Sex in the Marketplace** (Baltimore: The Johns Hopkins Press, 1971) is a good, brief introduction to the economic position of women. A recent, convenient introduction to Chicanos is Joan Moore, *The Mexican American** (Englewood Cliffs, N.J.: Prentice-Hall, 1970); the standard history is still Carey McWilliams, *North from Mexico** (Boston: Houghton Mifflin, 1948).

*Denotes a paperback.

APPENDICES

THE DECLARATION OF INDEPENDENCE
In Congress, July 4, 1776.

*The unanimous Declaration
of the thirteen united States of America,*

When in the Course of human events, it becomes necessary for one people to dissolve the political bands which have connected them with another, and to assume among the Powers of the earth, the separate and equal station to which the Laws of Nature and of Nature's God entitle them, a decent respect to the opinions of mankind requires that they should declare the causes which impel them to the separation.

We hold these truths to be self-evident, that all men are created equal, that they are endowed by their Creator with certain unalienable Rights, that among these are Life, Liberty and the pursuit of Happiness. That to secure these rights, Governments are instituted among Men, deriving their just powers from the consent of the governed, That whenever any Form of Government becomes destructive of these ends, it is the Right of the People to alter or to abolish it, and to institute new Government, laying its foundation on such principles and organizing its powers in such form, as to them shall seem most likely to effect their Safety and Happiness. Prudence, indeed, will dictate that Governments long established should not be changed for light and transient causes; and accordingly all experience hath shown, that mankind are more disposed to suffer, while evils are sufferable, than to right themselves by abolishing the forms to which they are accustomed. But when a long train of abuses and usurpations, pursuing invariably the same Object evinces a design to reduce them under absolute Despotism, it is their right, it is their duty, to throw off such Government, and to provide new Guards for their future security.— Such has been the patient sufferance of these Colonies; and such is now the necessity which constrains them to alter their former Systems of Government. The history of the present King of Great Britain is a history of repeated injuries and usurpations, all having in direct object the establishment of an absolute Tyranny over these States. To prove this, let Facts be submitted to a candid world.

He has refused his Assent to Laws, the most wholesome and necessary for the public good.

He has forbidden his Governors to pass Laws of immediate and pressing importance, unless suspended in their operation till his Assent should be obtained; and when so suspended, he has utterly neglected to attend to them.

He has refused to pass other Laws for the accommodation of large districts of people, unless those people would relinquish the right of Representation in the Legislature, a right inestimable to them and formidable to tyrants only.

He has called together legislative bodies at places unusual, uncomfortable, and distant from the depository of their Public Records, for the sole purpose of fatiguing them into compliance with his measures.

He has dissolved Representative Houses repeatedly, for opposing with manly firmness his invasions on the rights of the people.

He has refused for a long time, after such dissolutions, to cause others to be elected; whereby the Legislative Powers, incapable of Annihilation, have returned to the People at large for their exercise; the State remaining in the mean time exposed to all the dangers of invasion from without, and convulsions within.

He has endeavoured to prevent the population of these States; for that purpose obstructing the Laws for Naturalization of Foreigners; refusing to pass others to encourage their migrations hither, and raising the conditions of new Appropriations of Lands.

He has obstructed the Administration of Justice, by refusing his Assent to Laws for establishing Judiciary Powers.

He has made Judges dependent on his Will alone, for the tenure of their offices, and the amount and payment of their salaries.

He has erected a multitude of New Offices, and sent hither swarms of Officers to harass our people, and eat out their substance.

He has kept among us, in times of peace, Standing Armies without the Consent of our legislatures.

He has affected to render the Military independent of and superior to the Civil Power.

He has combined with others to subject us to a jurisdiction foreign to our constitution, and unacknowledged by our laws; giving his Assent to their acts of pretended Legislation:

For quartering large bodies of armed troops among us:

For protecting them, by a mock Trial, from Punishment for any Murders which they should commit on the Inhabitants of these States:

For cutting off our Trade with all parts of the world:

For imposing taxes on us without our Consent:

For depriving us in many cases, of the benefits of Trial by Jury:

For transporting us beyond Seas to be tried for pretended offences:

For abolishing the free System of English Laws in a neighbouring Province, establishing therein an Arbitrary government, and enlarging its Boundaries so as to render it at once an example and fit instrument for introducing the same absolute rule into these Colonies:

For taking away our Charters, abolishing our most valuable Laws, and altering fundamentally the Forms of our Governments:

For suspending our own Legislatures, and declaring themselves invested with Power to legislate for us in all cases whatsoever.

He has abdicated Government here, by declaring us out of his Protection and waging War against us.

He has plundered our seas, ravaged our Coasts, burnt our towns, and destroyed the lives of our people.

He is at this time transporting large armies of foreign mercenaries to compleat the works of death, desolation and tyranny, already begun with circumstances of Cruelty & perfidy scarcely paralleled in the most barbarous ages, and totally unworthy the Head of a civilized nation.

He has constrained our fellow Citizens taken Captive on the high Seas to bear Arms against their Country, to become the executioners of their friends and Brethren, or to fall themselves by their Hands.

He has excited domestic insurrections amongst us, and has endeavoured to bring on the inhabitants of our frontiers, the merciless Indian Savages, whose known rule of warfare, is an undistinguished destruction of all ages, sexes and conditions.

In every stage of these Oppressions We have Petitioned for Redress in the most humble terms: Our repeated Petitions have been answered only by repeated injury. A Prince, whose character is thus marked by every act which may define a Tyrant, is unfit to be the ruler of a free people.

Nor have We been wanting in attentions to our British brethren. We have warned them from time to time of attempts by their legislature to extend an unwarrantable jurisdiction over us. We have reminded them of the circumstances of our emigration and settlement here. We have appealed to their native justice and magnanimity, and we have conjured them by the ties of our common kindred to disavow these usurpations which, would inevitably interrupt our connections and correspondence. They too have been deaf to the voice of justice and of consanguinity. We must, therefore, acquiesce in the necessity, which denounces our Separation, and hold them, as we hold the rest of mankind, Enemies in War, in Peace Friends.

We, therefore, the Representatives of the united States of America, in General Congress, Assembled, appealing to the Supreme Judge of the world for the rectitude of our intentions, do, in the Name, and by authority of the good People of these Colonies, solemnly publish and declare,

That these United Colonies are, and of Right ought to be Free and Independent States; that they are Absolved from all Allegiance to the British Crown, and that all political connection between them and the State of Great Britain, is and ought to be totally dissolved; and that as Free and Independent States, they have full power to levy War, conclude Peace, contract Alliances, establish Commerce, and to do all other Acts and Things which Independent States may of right do. And for the support of this Declaration, with a firm reliance on the Protection of Divine Providence, we mutually pledge to each other our Lives, our Fortunes and our sacred Honor.

JOHN HANCOCK	GEO. TAYLOR
BUTTON GWINNETT	JAMES WILSON
LYMAN HALL	GEO. ROSS
GEO. WALTON	CAESAR RODNEY
WM. HOOPER	GEO. READ
JOSEPH HEWES	THO. M'KEAN
JOHN PENN	WM. FLOYD
EDWARD RUTLEDGE	PHIL. LIVINGSTON
THOS. HEYWARD, Junr.	FRANS. LEWIS
THOMAS LYNCH, Junr.	LEWIS MORRIS
ARTHUR MIDDLETON	RICHD. STOCKTON
SAMUEL CHASE	JNO. WITHERSPOON
WM. PACA	FRAS. HOPKINSON
THOS. STONE	JOHN HART
CHARLES CARROLL	ABRA. CLARK
OF CARROLLTON	JOSIAH BARTLETT
GEORGE WYTHE	WM. WHIPPLE
RICHARD HENRY LEE	SAML. ADAMS
TH. JEFFERSON	JOHN ADAMS
BENJ. HARRISON	ROBT. TREAT PAINE
THOS. NELSON, JR.	ELBRIDGE GERRY
FRANCIS LIGHTFOOT LEE	STEP. HOPKINS
CARTER BRAXTON	WILLIAM ELLERY
ROBT. MORRIS	ROGER SHERMAN
BENJAMIN RUSH	SAM'EL. HUNTINGTON
BENJA. FRANKLIN	WM. WILLIAMS
JOHN MORTON	OLIVER WOLCOTT
GEO. CLYMER	MATTHEW THORNTON
JAS. SMITH	

THE CONSTITUTION OF
THE UNITED STATES OF AMERICA

We the People of the United States, in Order to form a more perfect Union, establish Justice, insure domestic Tranquility, provide for the common defence, promote the general Welfare, and secure the Blessings of Liberty to ourselves and our Posterity, do ordain and establish this Constitution for the United States of America.

ARTICLE I.
Section 1.

All legislative Powers herein granted shall be vested in a Congress of the United States, which shall consist of a Senate and House of Representatives.

Section 2.

The House of Representatives shall be composed of Members chosen every second Year by the People of the several States, and the Electors in each State shall have the Qualifications requisite for Electors of the most numerous Branch of the State Legislature.

No Person shall be a Representative who shall not have attained to the Age of twenty five Years, and been seven Years a Citizen of the United States, and who shall not, when elected, be an Inhabitant of that State in which he shall be chosen.

Representatives and direct Taxes shall be apportioned among the several States which may be included within this Union, according to their respective Numbers, which shall be determined by adding to the whole Number of free Persons, including those bound to Service for a Term of Years, and excluding Indians not taxed, three fifths of all other Persons.[1] The actual Enumeration shall be made within three Years after the first Meeting of the Congress of the United States, and within every subsequent Term of ten Years, in such Manner as they shall by Law direct. The Number of Representatives shall not exceed one for every thirty Thousand, but each State shall have at Least one Representative; and until such enumeration shall be made, the State of New Hampshire shall be entitled to chuse three, Massachusetts eight, Rhode-Island and Providence Plantations one, Connecticut five, New-York six, New Jersey four, Pennsylvania eight, Delaware one, Maryland six, Virginia ten, North Carolina five, South Carolina five, and Georgia three.

When vacancies happen in the Representation from any State, the Executive Authority thereof shall issue Writs of Election to fill such Vacancies.

The House of Representatives shall chuse their Speaker and other Officers; and shall have the sole Power of Impeachment.

Section 3.

The Senate of the United States shall be composed of two Senators from each State, chosen by the Legislature thereof, for six Years; and each Senator shall have one Vote.

Immediately after they shall be assembled in Consequence of the first Election, they shall be divided as equally as may be into three Classes. The Seats of the Senators of the first Class shall be vacated at the Expiration of the second Year, of the second Class at the Expiration of the fourth Year, and of the third Class at the Expiration of the sixth Year, so that one third may be chosen every second Year; and if Vacancies happen by Resignation, or otherwise, during the Recess of the Legislature of any State, the Executive thereof may make temporary Appointments until the next Meeting of the Legislature, which shall then fill such Vacancies.[2]

No Person shall be a Senator who shall not have attained to the Age of thirty Years, and been nine Years a Citizen of the United States, and who shall not, when elected, be an Inhabitant of that State for which he shall be chosen.

The Vice President of the United States shall be President of the Senate, but shall have no Vote, unless they be equally divided.

The Senate shall chuse their other Officers, and also a President pro tempore, in the Absence of the Vice President, or when he shall exercise the Office of President of the United States.

The Senate shall have the sole Power to try all Impeachments. When sitting for that Purpose, they shall be on Oath or Affirmation. When the President of the United States is tried the Chief Justice shall preside: And no Person shall be convicted without the Concurrence of two thirds of the Members present.

Judgment in Cases of Impeachment shall not extend further than to removal from Office, and disqualification to hold and enjoy any Office of honor, Trust or Profit under the United States: but the Party convicted shall nevertheless be liable and subject to Indictment, Trial, Judgment and Punishment, according to Law.

Section 4.

The Times, Places and Manner of holding Elections for Senators and Representatives, shall be prescribed in each State by the Legislature thereof; but the Congress may at

---

[1]"Other Persons" being black slaves. Modified by Amendment XIV, Section 2.

[2]Provisions changed by Amendment XVII.

any time by Law make or alter such Regulations, except as to the Places of chusing Senators.

The Congress shall assemble at least once in every Year, and such Meeting shall be on the first Monday in December, unless they shall by Law appoint a different Day.[3]

Section 5.

Each House shall be the Judge of the Elections, Returns and Qualifications of its own Members, and a Majority of each shall constitute a Quorum to do Business; but a smaller Number may adjourn from day to day, and may be authorized to compel the Attendance of absent Members, in such Manner, and under such Penalties as each House may provide.

Each House may determine the Rules of its Proceedings, punish its Members for disorderly Behaviour, and, with the Concurrence of two thirds, expel a Member.

Each House shall keep a Journal of its Proceedings, and from time to time publish the same, excepting such Parts as may in their Judgment require Secrecy; and the Yeas and Nays of the Members of either House on any question shall, at the Desire of one fifth of those Present, be entered on the Journal.

Neither House, during the Session of Congress, shall, without the Consent of the other, adjourn for more than three days, nor to any other Place than that in which the two Houses shall be sitting.

Section 6.

The Senators and Representatives shall receive a Compensation for their Services, to be ascertained by Law, and paid out of the Treasury of the United States. They shall in all Cases, except Treason, Felony and Breach of the Peace, be privileged from Arrest during their Attendance at the Session of their respective Houses, and in going to and returning from the same; and for any Speech or Debate in either House, they shall not be questioned in any other Place.

No Senator or Representative shall, during the Time for which he was elected, be appointed to any civil Office under the Authority of the United States, which shall have been created, or the Emoluments whereof shall have been encreased during such time; and no Person holding any Office under the United States, shall be a Member of either House during his Continuance in Office.

Section 7.

All Bills for raising Revenue shall originate in the House of Representatives; but the Senate may propose or concur with Amendments as on other Bills.

Every Bill which shall have passed the House of Representatives and the Senate, shall, before it become a Law,

be presented to the President of the United States; If he approve he shall sign it, but if not he shall return it, with his Objections to that House in which it shall have originated, who shall enter the Objections at large on their Journal, and proceed to reconsider it. If after such Reconsideration two thirds of that House shall agree to pass the Bill, it shall be sent, together with the Objections, to the other House, by which it shall likewise be reconsidered, and if approved by two thirds of that House, it shall become a Law. But in all such Cases the Votes of both Houses shall be determined by yeas and Nays, and the Names of the Persons voting for and against the Bill shall be entered on the Journal of each House respectively. If any Bill shall not be returned by the President within ten Days (Sundays excepted) after it shall have been presented to him, the Same shall be a Law, in like Manner as if he had signed it, unless the Congress by their Adjournment prevent its Return, in which Case it shall not be a Law.

Every Order, Resolution, or Vote to which the Concurrence of the Senate and House of Representatives may be necessary (except on a question of Adjournment) shall be presented to the President of the United States; and before the Same shall take Effect, shall be approved by him, or being disapproved by him, shall be repassed by two thirds of the Senate and House of Representatives, according to the Rules and Limitations prescribed in the Case of a Bill.

Section 8.

The Congress shall have Power To lay and collect Taxes, Duties, Imposts and Excises, to pay the Debts and provide for the common Defence and general Welfare of the United States; but all Duties, Imposts and Excises shall be uniform throughout the United States;

To borrow Money on the credit of the United States;

To regulate Commerce with foreign Nations, and among the several States, and with the Indian Tribes;

To establish an uniform Rule of Naturalization, and uniform Laws on the subject of Bankruptcies throughout the United States;

To coin Money, regulate the Value thereof, and of foreign Coin, and fix the Standard of Weights and Measures;

To provide for the Punishment of counterfeiting the Securities and current Coin of the United States;

To establish Post Offices and post Roads;

To promote the Progress of Science and useful Arts, by securing for limited Times to Authors and Inventors the exclusive Right to their respective Writings and Discoveries;

To constitute Tribunals inferior to the supreme Court;

To define and punish Piracies and Felonies committed on the high Seas, and Offences against the Law of Nations;

To declare War, grant Letters of Marque and Reprisal, and make Rules concerning Captures on Land and Water;

To raise and support Armies, but no Appropriation of

---

[3]Provision changed by Amendment XX, Section 2.

Money to that Use shall be for a longer Term than two Years;

To provide and maintain a Navy;

To make Rules for the Government and Regulation of the land and naval Forces;

To provide for calling forth the Militia to execute the Laws of the Union, suppress Insurrections and repel Invasions;

To provide for organizing, arming, and disciplining, the Militia, and for governing such Part of them as may be employed in the Service of the United States, reserving to the States respectively, the Appointment of the Officers, and the Authority of training the Militia according to the discipline prescribed by Congress;

To exercise exclusive Legislation in all Cases whatsoever, over such District (not exceeding ten Miles square) as may, by Cession of particular States, and the Acceptance of Congress, become the Seat of the Government of the United States, and to exercise like Authority over all Places purchased by the Consent of the Legislature of the State in which the Same shall be, for the Erection of Forts, Magazines, Arsenals, dock-Yards, and other needful Buildings;—And

To make all Laws which shall be necessary and proper for carrying into Execution the foregoing Powers, and all other Powers vested by this Constitution in the Government of the United States, or in any Department or Officer thereof.

Section 9.

The Migration or Importation of such Persons as any of the States now existing shall think proper to admit, shall not be prohibited by the Congress prior to the Year one thousand eight hundred and eight, but a Tax or duty may be imposed on such Importation, not exceeding ten dollars for each Person.

The Privilege of the Writ of Habeas Corpus shall not be suspended, unless when in Cases of Rebellion or Invasion the public Safety may require it.

No Bill of Attainder or ex post facto Law shall be passed.

No Capitation, or other direct, Tax shall be laid, unless in Proportion to the Census or Enumeration herein before directed to be taken.

No Tax or Duty shall be laid on Articles exported from any State.

No Preference shall be given by any Regulation of Commerce or Revenue to the Ports of one State over those of another: nor shall Vessels bound to, or from, one State, be obliged to enter, clear, or pay Duties in another.

No Money shall be drawn from the Treasury, but in Consequence of Appropriations made by Law; and a regular Statement and Account of the Receipts and Expenditures of all public Money shall be published from time to time.

No Title of Nobility shall be granted by the United States: And no Person holding any Office of Profit or Trust under them, shall, without the Consent of the Congress, accept of any present, Emolument, Office, or Title, of any kind whatever, from any King, Prince, or foreign State.

Section 10.

No State shall enter into any Treaty, Alliance, or Confederation; grant Letters of Marque and Reprisal; coin Money; emit Bills of Credit; make any Thing but gold and silver Coin a Tender in Payment of Debts; pass any Bill of Attainder, ex post facto Law, or Law impairing the Obligation of Contracts, or grant any Title of Nobility.

No State shall, without the Consent of the Congress, lay any Imposts or Duties on Imports or Exports, except what may be absolutely necessary for executing its inspection Laws: and the net Produce of all Duties and Imposts, laid by any State on Imports or Exports, shall be for the Use of the Treasury of the United States; and all such Laws shall be subject to the Revision and Controul of the Congress.

No State shall, without the Consent of Congress, lay any Duty of Tonnage, keep Troops, or Ships of War in time of Peace, enter into any Agreement or Compact with another State, or with a foreign Power, or engage in War, unless actually invaded, or in such imminent Danger as will not admit of delay.

ARTICLE II.

Section 1.

The executive Power shall be vested in a President of the United States of America. He shall hold his Office during the Term of four Years, and, together with the Vice President, chosen for the same Term, be elected, as follows:

Each State shall appoint, in such Manner as the Legislature thereof may direct, a Number of Electors, equal to the whole Number of Senators and Representatives to which the State may be entitled in the Congress: but no Senator or Representative, or Person holding an Office of Trust or Profit under the United States, shall be appointed an Elector.

The Electors shall meet in their respective States, and vote by Ballot for two Persons, of whom one at least shall not be an Inhabitant of the same State with themselves. And they shall make a List of all the Persons voted for, and of the Number of Votes for each; which List they shall sign and certify, and transmit sealed to the Seat of the Government of the United States, directed to the President of the Senate. The President of the Senate shall, in the Presence of the Senate and House of Representatives, open all the Certificates, and the Votes shall then be counted. The Person having the greatest Number of Votes shall be the President, if such Number be a Majority of the whole Number of Electors appointed; and if there be more than one who have such Majority, and have an equal Number of Votes, then the House of

Representatives shall immediately chuse by Ballot one of them for President; and if no Person have a Majority, then from the five highest on the List the said House shall in like Manner chuse the President. But in chusing the President, the Votes shall be taken by States, the Representation from each State having one Vote; A quorum for this Purpose shall consist of a Member or Members from two thirds of the States, and a Majority of all the States shall be necessary to a Choice. In every Case, after the Choice of the President, the Person having the greatest Number of Votes of the Electors shall be the Vice President. But if there should remain two or more who have equal Votes, the Senate shall chuse from them by Ballot the Vice President.[4]

The Congress may determine the Time of chusing the Electors, and the Day on which they shall give their Votes; which Day shall be the same throughout the United States.

No Person except a natural born Citizen, or a Citizen of the United States, at the time of the Adoption of this Constitution, shall be eligible to the Office of President; neither shall any Person be eligible to that Office who shall not have attained to the Age of thirty five Years, and been fourteen Years a Resident within the United States.

In Case of the Removal of the President from Office, or of his Death, Resignation, or Inability to discharge the Powers and Duties of the said Office, the Same shall devolve on the Vice President, and the Congress may by Law provide for the Case of Removal, Death, Resignation or Inability, both of the President and Vice President, declaring what Officer shall then act as President, and such Officer shall act accordingly, until the Disability be removed, or a President shall be elected.

The President shall, at stated Times, receive for his Services, a Compensation, which shall neither be encreased nor diminished during the Period for which he shall have been elected, and he shall not receive within that Period any other Emolument from the United States, or any of them.

Before he enter on the Execution of his Office, he shall take the following Oath or Affirmation:—"I do solemnly swear (or affirm) that I will faithfully execute the Office of President of the United States, and will to the best of my Ability, preserve, protect and defend the Constitution of the United States."

Section 2.

The President shall be Commander in Chief of the Army and Navy of the United States, and of the Militia of the several States, when called into the actual Service of the United States; he may require the Opinion, in writing, of the principal Officer in each of the executive Departments, upon any Subject relating to the Duties of their respective Offices, and he shall have Power to grant

---

Reprieves and Pardons for Offences against the United States, except in Cases of Impeachment.

He shall have Power, by and with the Advice and Consent of the Senate, to make Treaties, provided two thirds of the Senators present concur; and he shall nominate, and by and with the Advice and Consent of the Senate, shall appoint Ambassadors, other public Ministers and Consuls, Judges of the supreme Court, and all other Officers of the United States, whose Appointments are not herein otherwise provided for, and which shall be established by Law: but the Congress may by Law vest the Appointment of such inferior Officers, as they think proper in the President alone, in the Courts of Law, or in the Heads of Departments.

The President shall have Power to fill up all Vacancies that may happen during the Recess of the Senate, by granting Commissions which shall expire at the End of their next Session.

Section 3.

He shall from time to time give to the Congress Information of the State of the Union, and recommend to their Consideration such Measures as he shall judge necessary and expedient; he may, on extraordinary Occasions, convene both Houses, or either of them, and in Case of Disagreement between them, with Respect to the Time of Adjournment, he may adjourn them to such Time as he shall think proper; he shall receive Ambassadors and other public Ministers; he shall take Care that the Laws be faithfully executed, and shall Commission all the Officers of the United States.

Section 4.

The President, Vice President and all civil Officers of the United States, shall be removed from Office on Impeachment for, and Conviction of, Treason, Bribery, or other high Crimes and Misdemeanors.

ARTICLE III.

Section 1.

The judicial Power of the United States, shall be vested in one supreme Court, and in such inferior Courts as the Congress may from time to time ordain and establish. The Judges, both of the supreme and inferior Courts, shall hold their Offices during good Behaviour, and shall, at stated Times, receive for their Services, a Compensation, which shall not be diminished during their Continuance in Office.

Section 2.

The judicial Power shall extend to all Cases, in Law and Equity, arising under this Constitution, the Laws of the United States, and Treaties made, or which shall be made, under their Authority;—to all Cases affecting

---

[4]Provisions superseded by Amendment XII.

Ambassadors, other public Ministers and Consuls;—to all Cases of admiralty and maritime Jurisdiction;—to Controversies to which the United States shall be a Party;—to Controversies between two or more States;—between a State and Citizens of another State;—between Citizens of different States,—between Citizens of the same State claiming Lands under Grants of different States, and between a State, or the Citizens thereof, and foreign States, Citizens or Subjects.[5]

In all Cases affecting Ambassadors, other public Ministers and Consuls, and those in which a State shall be Party, the supreme Court shall have original Jurisdiction. In all the other Cases before mentioned, the supreme Court shall have appellate Jurisdiction, both as to Law and Fact, with such Exceptions, and under such Regulations as the Congress shall make.

The Trial of all Crimes, except in Cases of Impeachment, shall be by Jury; and such Trial shall be held in the State where the said Crimes shall have been committed, but when not committed within any State, the Trial shall be at such Place or Places as the Congress may by Law have directed.

Section 3.

Treason against the United States, shall consist only in levying War against them, or in adhering to their Enemies, giving them Aid and Comfort. No person shall be convicted of Treason unless on the Testimony of two Witnesses to the same overt Act, or on Confession in open Court.

The Congress shall have Power to declare the Punishment of Treason, but no Attainder of Treason shall work Corruption of Blood, or Forfeiture except during the Life of the Person attainted.

ARTICLE IV.

Section 1.

Full Faith and Credit shall be given in each State to the public Acts, Records, and judicial Proceedings of every other State. And the Congress may by general Laws prescribe the Manner in which such Acts, Records and Proceedings shall be proved, and the Effect thereof.

Section 2.

The Citizens of each State shall be entitled to all Privileges and Immunities of Citizens in the several States.

A Person charged in any State with Treason, Felony, or other Crime, who shall flee from Justice, and be found in another State, shall on Demand of the executive Authority of the State from which he fled, be delivered up, to be removed to the State having Jurisdiction of the Crime.

---

[5]Clause changed by Amendment XI.

No Person held to Service or Labour in one State, under the Laws thereof, escaping into another, shall, in Consequence of any Law or Regulation therein, be discharged from such Service or Labour, but shall be delivered up on Claim of the Party to whom such Service or Labour may be due.

Section 3.

New States may be admitted by the Congress into this Union; but no new State shall be formed or erected within the Jurisdiction of any other State; nor any State be formed by the Junction of two or more States, or Parts of States, without the Consent of the Legislatures of the States concerned as well as of the Congress.

The Congress shall have Power to dispose of and make all needful Rules and Regulations respecting the Territory or other Property belonging to the United States; and nothing in this Constitution shall be so construed as to Prejudice any Claims of the United States, or of any particular State.

Section 4.

The United States shall guarantee to every State in this Union a Republican Form of Government, and shall protect each of them against Invasion; and on Application of the Legislature, or of the Executive (when the Legislature cannot be convened) against domestic Violence.

ARTICLE V.

The Congress, whenever two thirds of both Houses shall deem it necessary, shall propose Amendments to this Constitution, or, on the Application of the Legislatures of two thirds of the several States, shall call a Convention for proposing Amendments, which, in either Case, shall be valid to all Intents and Purposes, as Part of this Constitution, when ratified by the Legislatures of three fourths of the several States, or by Conventions in three fourths thereof, as the one or the other Mode of Ratification may be proposed by the Congress; Provided that no Amendment which may be made prior to the Year One thousand eight hundred and eight shall in any Manner affect the first and fourth Clauses in the Ninth Section of the first Article; and that no State, without its Consent, shall be deprived of its equal Suffrage in the Senate.

ARTICLE VI.

All Debts contracted and Engagements entered into, before the Adoption of this Constitution, shall be as valid against the United States under this Constitution, as under the Confederation.

This Constitution, and the Laws of the United States which shall be made in Pursuance thereof; and all Treaties made, or which shall be made, under the Authority of the United States, shall be the supreme Law of the Land; and the Judges in every State shall be bound thereby, any Thing in the Constitution or Laws of any State to the Contrary notwithstanding.

The Senators and Representatives before mentioned, and the Members of the several State Legislatures, and all executive and judicial Officers, both of the United States and of the several States, shall be bound by Oath or Affirmation, to support this Constitution; but no religious Test shall ever be required as a Qualification to any Office or public Trust under the United States.

ARTICLE VII.

The Ratification of the Conventions of nine States, shall be sufficient for the Establishment of this Constitution between the States so ratifying the Same.

done in Convention by the Unanimous Consent of the States present the Seventeenth Day of September in the Year of our Lord one thousand seven hundred and Eighty seven and of the Independence of the United States of America the Twelfth[6] IN WITNESS whereof We have hereunto subscribed our Names,

GEORGE WASHINGTON,
President and Deputy
from Virginia

---

[6]The Constitution was submitted on September 17, 1787, by the Constitutional Convention, was ratified by the conventions of several states at various dates up to May 29, 1790, and became effective on March 4, 1789.

New Hampshire
JOHN LANGDON
NICHOLAS GILMAN
Massachusetts
NATHANIEL GORHAM
RUFUS KING
Connecticut
WILLIAM S. JOHNSON
ROGER SHERMAN
New York
ALEXANDER HAMILTON
New Jersey
WILLIAM LIVINGSTON
DAVID BREARLEY
WILLIAM PATERSON
JONATHAN DAYTON
Pennsylvania
BENJAMIN FRANKLIN
THOMAS MIFFLIN
ROBERT MORRIS
GEORGE CLYMER
THOMAS FITZSIMONS
JARED INGERSOLL
JAMES WILSON
GOUVERNEUR MORRIS

Delaware
GEORGE READ
GUNNING BEDFORD, JR.
JOHN DICKINSON
RICHARD BASSETT
JACOB BROOM
Maryland
JAMES MCHENRY
DANIEL OF ST. THOMAS
 JENIFER
DANIEL CARROLL
Virginia
JOHN BLAIR
JAMES MADISON, JR.
North Carolina
WILLIAM BLOUNT
RICHARD DOBBS
 SPRAIGHT
HU WILLIAMSON
South Carolina
J. RUTLEDGE
CHARLES C. PINCKNEY
PIERCE BUTLER
Georgia
WILLIAM FEW
ABRAHAM BALDWIN

AMENDMENTS TO THE CONSTITUTION

[AMENDMENT I]

Congress shall make no law respecting an establishment of religion, or prohibiting the free exercise thereof; or abridging the freedom of speech, or of the press; or the right of the people peaceably to assemble, and to petition the Government for a redress of grievances.

[AMENDMENT II]

A well regulated Militia being necessary to the security of a free State, the right of the people to keep and bear Arms, shall not be infringed.

[AMENDMENT III]

No Soldier shall, in time of peace be quartered in any house, without the consent of the Owner, nor in time of war, but in a manner to be prescribed by law.

[AMENDMENT IV]

The right of the people to be secure in their persons, houses, papers, and effects, against unreasonable searches and seizures, shall not be violated, and no Warrants shall issue, but upon probable cause, supported by Oath or affirmation, and particularly describing the place to be searched, and the persons or things to be seized.

[AMENDMENT V]

No person shall be held to answer for a capital, or otherwise infamous crime, unless on a presentment or indictment of a Grand Jury, except in cases arising in the land or naval forces, or in the Militia, when in actual service in time of War or public danger; nor shall any person be subject for the same offense to be twice put in jeopardy of life or limb; nor shall be compelled in any criminal case to be a witness against himself, nor be deprived of life, liberty, or property, without due process of law; nor shall private property be taken for public use, without just compensation.

[AMENDMENT VI]

In all criminal prosecutions, the accused shall enjoy the right to a speedy and public trial, by an impartial jury of the State and district wherein the crime shall have been committed, which district shall have been previously ascertained by law, and to be informed of the nature and cause of the accusation; to be confronted with the witnesses against him; to have compulsory process for obtaining witnesses in his favor, and to have the Assistance of Counsel for his defence.

[AMENDMENT VII]

In Suits at common law, where the value in controversy shall exceed twenty dollars, the right of trial by jury shall be preserved, and no fact tried by a jury, shall be otherwise re-examined in any Court of the United States, than according to the rules of the common law.

[AMENDMENT VIII]

Excessive bail shall not be required, nor excessive fines imposed, nor cruel and unusual punishments inflicted.

[AMENDMENT IX]

The enumeration in the Constitution, of certain rights, shall not be construed to deny or disparage others retained by the people.

[AMENDMENT X]

The powers not delegated to the United States by the Constitution, nor prohibited by it to the States, are reserved to the States respectively, or to the people.[7]

[AMENDMENT XI]

The Judicial power of the United States shall not be construed to extend to any suit in law or equity, commenced or prosecuted against one of the United States by Citizens of another State, or by Citizens or Subjects of any Foreign State.[8]

[AMENDMENT XII]

The Electors shall meet in their respective states, and vote by ballot for President and Vice-President, one of

---

[7]The first ten amendments were all proposed by Congress on September 25, 1789, and were ratified and adoption certified on December 15, 1791.

[8]Proposed by Congress on March 4, 1794, and declared ratified on January 8, 1798.

whom, at least, shall not be an inhabitant of the same state with themselves; they shall name in their ballots the person voted for as President, and in distinct ballots the person voted for as Vice-President, and they shall make distinct lists of all persons voted for as President, and of all persons voted for as Vice-President, and of the number of votes for each, which lists they shall sign and certify, and transmit sealed to the seat of the government of the United States, directed to the President of the Senate;—The President of the Senate shall, in the presence of the Senate and House of Representatives, open all the certificates and the votes shall then be counted;—The person having the greatest number of votes for President, shall be the President, if such number be a majority of the whole number of Electors appointed; and if no person have such majority, then from the persons having the highest numbers not exceeding three on the list of those voted for as President, the House of Representatives shall choose immediately, by ballot, the President. But in choosing the President, the votes shall be taken by states, the representation from each state having one vote; a quorum for this purpose shall consist of a member or members from two-thirds of the states, and a majority of all the states shall be necessary to a choice. And if the House of Representatives shall not choose a President whenever the right of choice shall devolve upon them, before the fourth day of March next following, then the Vice-President shall act as President, as in the case of the death or other constitutional disability of the President.—The person having the greatest number of votes as Vice-President, shall be the Vice-President, if such number be a majority of the whole number of Electors appointed, and if no person have a majority, then from the two highest numbers on the list, the Senate shall choose the Vice-President; a quorum for the purpose shall consist of two-thirds of the whole number of Senators, and a majority of the whole number shall be necessary to a choice. But no person constitutionally ineligible to the office of President shall be eligible to that of Vice-President of the United States.[9]

[AMENDMENT XIII]

Section 1.

Neither slavery nor involuntary servitude, except as a punishment for crime whereof the party shall have been duly convicted, shall exist within the United States, or any place subject to their jurisdiction.

Section 2.

Congress shall have power to enforce this article by appropriate legislation.[10]

---

[9]Proposed by Congress on December 9, 1803; declared ratified on September 25, 1804; supplemented by Amendments XX and XXIII.

[10]Proposed by Congress on January 31, 1865; declared ratified on December 18, 1865.

[AMENDMENT XIV]

Section 1.

All persons born or naturalized in the United States, and subject to the jurisdiction thereof, are citizens of the United States and of the State wherein they reside. No State shall make or enforce any law which shall abridge the privileges or immunities of citizens of the United States; nor shall any State deprive any person of life, liberty, or property, without due process of law; nor deny to any person within its jurisdiction the equal protection of the laws.

Section 2.

Representatives shall be apportioned among the several States according to their respective numbers, counting the whole number of persons in each State, excluding Indians not taxed. But when the right to vote at any election for the choice of electors for President and Vice-President of the United States, Representatives in Congress, the Executive and Judicial officers of a State, or the members of the Legislature thereof, is denied to any of the male inhabitants of such State, being twenty-one years of age, and citizens of the United States, or in any way abridged, except for participation in rebellion, or other crime, the basis of representation therein shall be reduced in the proportion which the number of such male citizens shall bear to the whole number of male citizens twenty-one years of age in such State.

Section 3.

No person shall be a Senator or Representative in Congress, or elector of President and Vice President, or hold any office, civil or military, under the United States, or under any State, who, having previously taken an oath, as a member of Congress, or as an officer of the United States, or as a member of any State legislature, or as an executive or judicial officer of any State, to support the Constitution of the United States, shall have engaged in insurrection or rebellion against the same, or given aid or comfort to the enemies thereof. But Congress may by a vote of two-thirds of each House, remove such disability.

Section 4.

The validity of the public debt of the United States, authorized by law, including debts incurred for payment of pensions and bounties for services in suppressing insurrection or rebellion, shall not be questioned. But neither the United States nor any State shall assume or pay any debt or obligation incurred in aid of insurrection or rebellion against the United States, or any claim for the loss or emancipation of any slave; but all such debts, obligations and claims shall be held illegal and void.

The Congress shall have power to enforce, by appropriate legislation, the provisions of this article.[11]

[AMENDMENT XV]

Section 1.

The right of citizens of the United States to vote shall not be denied or abridged by the United States or by any State on account of race, color, or previous condition of servitude.

Section.

The Congress shall have power to enforce this article by appropriate legislation.[12]

[AMENDMENT XVI]

The Congress shall have power to lay and collect taxes on incomes, from whatever source derived, without apportionment among the several States, and without regard to any census or enumeration.[13]

[AMENDMENT XVII]

The Senate of the United States shall be composed of two Senators from each State, elected by the people thereof, for six years; and each Senator shall have one vote. The electors in each State shall have the qualifications requisite for electors of the most numerous branch of the State legislatures.

When vacancies happen in the representation of any State in the Senate, the executive authority of such State shall issue writs of election to fill such vacancies: *Provided,* That the legislature of any State may empower the executive thereof to make temporary appointments until the people fill the vacancies by election as the legislature may direct.

This amendment shall not be so construed as to affect the election or term of any Senator chosen before it becomes valid as part of the Constitution.[14]

---

[11]Proposed by Congress on June 13, 1866; declared ratified on July 28, 1868.

[12]Proposed by Congress on February 26, 1869; declared ratified on March 30, 1870.

[13]Proposed by Congress on July 12, 1909; declared ratified on February 25, 1913.

[14]Proposed by Congress on May 13, 1912; declared ratified on May 31, 1913.

[AMENDMENT XVIII]

Section 1.

After one year from the ratification of this article the manufacture, sale, or transportation of intoxicating liquors within, the importation thereof into, or the exportation thereof from the United States and all territory subject to the jurisdiction thereof for beverage purposes is hereby prohibited.

Section 2.

The Congress and the several States shall have concurrent power to enforce this article by appropriate legislation.

Section 3.

This article shall be inoperative unless it shall have been ratified as an amendment to the Constitution by the legislatures of the several States, as provided in the Constitution, within seven years from the date of the submission hereof to the States by the Congress.[15]

[AMENDMENT XIX]

The right of citizens of the United States to vote shall not be denied or abridged by the United States or by any State on account of sex.

Congress shall have power to enforce this article by appropriate legislation.[16]

[AMENDMENT XX]

Section 1.

The terms of the President and Vice President shall end at noon on the 20th day of January, and the terms of Senators and Representatives at noon on the 3d day of January, of the years in which such terms would have ended if this article had not been ratified; and the terms of their successors shall then begin.

Section 2.

The Congress shall assemble at least once in every year, and such meeting shall begin at noon on the 3d day of January, unless they shall by law appoint a different day.

---

[15]Proposed by Congress on December 18, 1917; declared ratified on January 29, 1919; repealed by Amendment XXI.

[16]Proposed by Congress on June 4, 1919; declared ratified on August 26, 1920.

Section 3.

If, at the time fixed for the beginning of the term of the President, the President elect shall have died, the Vice President elect shall become President. If a President shall not have been chosen before the time fixed for the beginning of his term, or if the President elect shall have failed to qualify, then the Vice President elect shall act as President until a President shall have qualified; and the Congress may by law provide for the case wherein neither a President elect nor a Vice President elect shall have qualified, declaring who shall then act as President, or the manner in which one who is to act shall be selected, and such person shall act accordingly until a President or Vice President shall have qualified.

Section 4.

The Congress may by law provide for the case of the death of any of the persons from whom the House of Representatives may choose a President whenever the right of choice shall have devolved upon them, and for the case of the death of any of the persons from whom the Senate may choose a Vice President whenever the right of choice shall have devolved upon them.

Section 5.

Sections 1 and 2 shall take effect on the 15th day of October following the ratification of this article.

Section 6.

This article shall be inoperative unless it shall have been ratified as an amendment to the Constitution by the legislatures of three-fourths of the several States within seven years from the date of its submission.[17]

[AMENDMENT XXI]

Section 1.

The eighteenth article of amendment to the Constitution of the United States is hereby repealed.

Section 2.

The transportation or importation into any States, Territory, or possession of the United States for delivery or use therein of intoxicating liquors, in violation of the laws thereof, is hereby prohibited.

Section 3.

This article shall be inoperative unless it shall have been ratified as an amendment to the Constitution by conventions in the several States, as provided in the Constitution, within seven years from the date of the submission hereof to the States by the Congress.[18]

[AMENDMENT XXII]

Section 1.

No person shall be elected to the office of the President more than twice, and no person who has held the office of President, or acted as President, for more than two years of a term to which some other person was elected President shall be elected to the office of the President more than once. But this Article shall not apply to any person holding the office of President when this Article was proposed by the Congress, and shall not prevent any person who may be holding the office of President, or acting as President, during the term within which this Article becomes operative from holding the office of President or acting as President during the remainder of such term.

Section 2.

This article shall be inoperative unless it shall have been ratified as an amendment to the Constitution by the legislatures of three-fourths of the several States within seven years from the date of its submission to the States by the Congress.[19]

[AMENDMENT XXIII]

Section 1.

The District constituting the seat of Government of the United States shall appoint in such manner as the Congress shall direct:

A number of electors of President and Vice President equal to the whole number of Senators and Representatives in Congress to which the District would be entitled if it were a State, but in no event more than the least populous State; they shall be in addition to those appointed by the States, but they shall be considered, for the purposes of the election of President and Vice President, to be electors appointed by a State; and they shall meet in the District and perform such duties as provided by the twelfth article of amendment.

Section 2.

The Congress shall have power to enforce this article by appropriate legislation.[20]

---

[17]Proposed by Congress on March 2, 1932; declared ratified on February 6, 1933.

[18]Proposed by Congress on February 20, 1933; declared ratified on December 5, 1933.

[19]Proposed by Congress on March 24, 1947; declared ratified on March 1, 1951.

[20]Proposed by Congress on June 16, 1960; declared ratified on April 3, 1961.

[AMENDMENT XXIV]

Section 1.

The right of citizens of the United States to vote in any primary or other election for President or Vice President, for electors for President or Vice President, or for Senator or Representative in Congress, shall not be denied or abridged by the United States or any state by reason of failure to pay any poll tax or other tax.

Section 2.

The Congress shall have the power to enforce this article by appropriate legislation.[21]

[AMENDMENT XXV]

Section 1.

In case of the removal of the President from office or his death or resignation, the Vice President shall become President.

Section 2.

Whenever there is a vacancy in the office of the Vice President, the President shall nominate a Vice President who shall take the office upon confirmation by a majority vote of both houses of Congress.

Section 3.

Whenever the President transmits to the President pro tempore of the Senate and the Speaker of the House of Representatives his written declaration that he is unable to discharge the powers and duties of his office, and until he transmits to them a written declaration to the contrary, such powers and duties shall be discharged by the Vice President as Acting President.

Section 4.

Whenever the Vice President and a majority of either the principal officers of the executive departments or of such other body as Congress may by law provide, trans-

mit to the President pro tempore of the Senate and the Speaker of the House of Representatives their written declaration that the President is unable to discharge the powers and duties of his office, the Vice President shall immediately assume the powers and duties of the office as Acting President.

Thereafter, when the President transmits to the President pro tempore of the Senate and the Speaker of the House of Representatives his written declaration that no inability exists, he shall resume the powers and duties of his office unless the Vice President and a majority of either the principal officers of the executive department or of such other body as Congress may by law provide, transmit within four days to the President pro tempore of the Senate and the Speaker of the House of Representatives their written declaration that the President is unable to discharge the powers and duties of his office. Thereupon Congress shall decide the issue, assembling within 48 hours for that purpose if not in session. If the Congress, within 21 days after receipt of the latter written declaration, or, if Congress is not in session, within 21 days after Congress is required to assemble, determines by two-thirds vote of both houses that the President is unable to discharge the powers and duties of his office, the Vice President shall continue to discharge the same as Acting President; otherwise, the President shall resume the powers and duties of his office.[22]

[AMENDMENT XXVI]

Section 1.

The right of citizens of the United States, who are 18 years of age or older, to vote shall not be denied or abridged by the United States or any state on account of age.

Section 2.

The Congress shall have the power to enforce this article by appropriate legislation.[23]

---

[21]Proposed by Congress on August 27, 1962; declared ratified on January 23, 1963.

[22]Proposed by Congress on July 6, 1965; declared ratified on February 10, 1967.

[23]Proposed by Congress on March 23, 1971; declared ratified on June 30, 1971.

PRESIDENTS, VICE-PRESIDENTS, AND CABINET MEMBERS

President and Vice-President	Secretary of State	Secretary of the Treasury	Secretary of War
George Washington (F) .... 1789 J. Adams .... '89	T. Jefferson .... '89 E. Randolph .... '94 T. Pickering.......... '95	A. Hamilton .... '89 O. Wolcott........... '89	H. Knox .... '89 T. Pickering.......... '95 J. McHenry .... '96
John Adams (F)................ 1797 T. Jefferson (R^J)........... '97	T. Pickering.......... '97 J. Marshall .... '00	O. Wolcott........... '97 S. Dexter .... '01	J. McHenry .... '97 J. Marshall .... '00 S. Dexter .... '00 R. Griswold........... '01
Thomas Jefferson (R^J) .... 1801 A. Burr (R^J) .... '01 G. Clinton (R^J)............. '05	J. Madison........... '01	S. Dexter .... '01 A. Gallatin........... '01	H. Dearborn .... '01
James Madison (R^J) .... 1809 G. Clinton (R^J)............. '09 E. Gerry (R^J)............. '13	R. Smith............ '09 J. Monroe............ '11	A. Gallatin........... '09 G. Campbell .... '14 A. Dallas .... '14 W. Crawford......... '16	W. Eustis .... '09 J. Armstrong......... '13 J. Monroe .... '14 W. Crawford......... '15
James Monroe (R^J) .... 1817 D. Tompkins (R^J) .... '17	J. Q. Adams.......... '17	W. Crawford......... '17	I. Shelby............ '17 G. Graham........... '17 J. Calhoun .... '17
John Quincy Adams (NR)........... 1825 J. Calhoun (R^J) .... '25	H. Clay............. '25	R. Rush............. '25	J. Barbour........... '25 P. Porter .... '28
Andrew Jackson (D) .... 1829 J. Calhoun (D) .... '29 M. Van Buren (D)................ '33	M. Van Buren........ '29 E. Livingston .... '31 L. McLane .... '33 J. Forsyth .... '34	S. Ingham .... '29 L. McLane .... '31 W. Duane........... '33 R. Taney............ '33 L. Woodbury........ '34	J. Eaton............ '29 L. Cass .... '31 B. Butler............ '37
Martin Van Buren (D) .... 1837 R. Johnson (D)...................... '37	J. Forsyth .... '37	L. Woodbury........ '37	J. Poinsett .... '37
William H. Harrison (W)............ 1841 J. Tyler (W)................. '41	D. Webster .... '41	T. Ewing .... '41	J. Bell.............. '41
John Tyler (W and D)............. 1841	D. Webster .... '41 H. Legare........... '43 A. Upshur .... '43 J. Calhoun .... '44	T. Ewing .... '41 W. Forward.......... '41 J. Spencer........... '43 G. Bibb............. '44	J. Bell.............. '41 J. McLean........... '41 J. Spencer........... '41 J. Porter .... '43 W. Wilkins ,........ '44
James K. Polk (D) .... 1845 G. Dallas (D)...................... '45	J. Buchanan.......... '45	R. Walker........... '45	W. Marcy........... '45
Zachary Taylor (W)................ 1849 M. Fillmore (W)................. '49	J. Clayton........... '49	W. Meredith .... '49	G. Crawford .... '49
Millard Fillmore (W)................ 1850	D. Webster .... '50 E. Everett........... '52	T. Corwin .... '50	C. Conrad .... '50
Franklin Pierce (D) .... 1853 W. King (D) .... '53	W. Marcy........... '53	J. Guthrie........... '53	J. Davis............. '53
James Buchanan (D)................ 1857 J. Breckinridge (D) .... '57	L. Cass .... '57 J. Black .... '60	H. Cobb .... '57 P. Thomas .... '60 J. Dix............... '61	J. Floyd............ '57 J. Holt.............. '61
Abraham Lincoln (R).............. 1861 H. Hamlin (R) .... '61 A. Johnson (U).................. '65	W. Seward.......... '61	S. Chase............ '61 W. Fessenden .... '64 H. McCulloch .... '65	S. Cameron .... '61 E. Stanton .... '62
Andrew Johnson (U) 1865	W. Seward.......... '65	H. McCulloch .... '65	E. Stanton .... '65 U. Grant............ '67 L. Thomas .... '68 J. Schofield .... '68

Party affiliations: D, Democratic; F, Federalist; NR, National Republican; R, Republican; R^J, Republican (Jeffersonian); U, Unionist; W, Whig.

350

Secretary of the Navy	Attorney General	Postmaster General	Secretary of the Interior
	E. Randolph.............. '89		
Established	W. Bradford............. '94		
April 30, 1798	C. Lee .... '95		
B. Stoddert.............. '98	C. Lee .... '97		
	T. Parsons.............. '01		
B. Stoddert.............. '01	L. Lincoln............... '01		
R. Smith................ '01	R. Smith .... '05		
J. Crowninshield .... '05	J. Breckinridge........... '05		
	C. Rodney .... '07		
P. Hamilton............. '09	C. Rodney .... '09		
W. Jones................ '13	W. Pinkney .... '11		
B. Crowninshield........ '14	R. Rush .... '14		
B. Crowninshield........ '17	R. Rush .... '17		
S. Thompson............. '18	W. Wirt................. '17		
S. Southard .... '23			
S. Southard .... '25	W. Wirt................. '25	*Cabinet status since* *March 9, 1829*	
J. Branch................ '29	J. Berrien................ '29	W. Barry................. '29	
L. Woodbury............. '31	R. Taney................ '31	A. Kendall .... '35	
M. Dickerson............ '34	B. Butler .... '33		
M. Dickerson............ '37	B. Butler .... '37	A. Kendall .... '37	
J. Paulding.............. '38	F. Grundy............... '38	J. Niles .... '40	
	H. Gilpin .... '40		
G. Badger............... '41	J. Crittenden .... '41	F. Granger .... '41	
G. Badger............... '41	J. Crittenden .... '41	F. Granger .... '41	
A. Upshur .... '41	H. Legare .... '41	C. Wickliffe .... '41	
D. Henshaw............. '43	J. Nelson................ '43		
T. Gilmer .... '44			
J. Mason .... '44			
G. Bancroft.............. '45	J. Mason .... '45	C. Johnson.............. '45	*Established* *March 3, 1849*
J. Mason .... '46	N. Clifford .... '46		
	I. Toucey................ '48		
W. Preston.............. '49	R. Johnson .... '49	J. Collamer.............. '49	Thomas Ewing .... '49
W. Graham .... '50	J. Crittenden .... '50	N. Hall .... '50	A. Stuart................ '50
J. Kennedy............... '52		S. Hubbard .... '52	
J. Dobbin .... '53	C. Cushing............... '53	J. Campbell .... '53	R. McClelland .... '53
I. Toucey................ '57	J. Black .... '57	A. Brown .... '57	J. Thompson .... '57
	E. Stanton............... '60	J. Holt .... '59	
G. Welles .... '61	E. Bates .... '61	H. King.................. '61	C. Smith................. '61
	T. Coffey................ '63	M. Blair.................. '61	J. Usher.................. '63
	J. Speed................. '64	W. Dennison............. '64	
G. Welles .... '65	J. Speed................. '65	W. Dennison............. '65	J. Usher................. '65
	H. Stanbery .... '66	A. Randall .... '66	J. Harlan .... '65
	W. Evarts .... '68		O. Browning .... '66

PRESIDENTS, VICE-PRESIDENTS, AND CABINET MEMBERS

President and Vice-President	Secretary of State	Secretary of the Treasury	Secretary of War	Secretary of the Navy
Ulysses S. Grant (R) . . . . . 1869 S. Colfax (R) . . . . '69 H. Wilson (R) . . . . '73	E. Washburne. . '69 H. Fish . . . . '69	G. Boutwell . . . . '69 W. Richardson . '73 B. Bristow . . . . . '74 L. Morrill . . . . . . '76	J. Rawlins. . . . . . '69 W. Sherman . . '69 W. Belknap . . . '69 A. Taft . . . . . . '76 J. Cameron. . . . '76	A. Borie . . . . . . '69 G. Robeson . . . '69
Rutherford B. Hayes (R) . . 1877 W. Wheeler (R) . . . . '77	W. Evarts . . . . . . '77	J. Sherman. . . . . '77	G. McCrary . . . '77 A. Ramsey . . . . '79	R. Thompson. . '77 N. Goff . . . . '81
James A. Garfield (R) . . . . . 1881 C. Arthur (R) . . . . '81	J. Blaine. . . . . . . '81	W. Windom . . . '81	R. Lincoln . . . . . '81	W. Hunt . . . . . . '81
Chester A. Arthur (R) 1881	F. Freling- huysen. . . . . . '81	C. Folger . . . . . . '81 W. Gresham . . . '84 H. McCulloch. . '84	R. Lincoln . . . . . '81	W. Chandler. . . '81
Grover Cleveland (D) . . . . . 1885 T. Hendricks (D) . . . . '85	T. Bayard. . . . . . '85	D. Manning . . . '85 C. Fairchild. . . . '87	W. Endicott. . . . '85	W. Whitney . . . '85
Benjamin Harrison (R) . . . . . 1889 L. Morton (R) . . . . '89	J. Blaine. . . . . . . '89 J. Foster. . . . . . . '92	W. Windom . . . '89 C. Foster . . . . . . '91	R. Proctor . . . . . '89 S. Elkins . . . . . . '91	B. Tracy . . . . . . '89
Grover Cleveland (D) . . . . . 1893 A. Stevenson (D). . . . . '93	W. Gresham . . . '93 R. Olney . . . . . . '95	J. Carlisle. . . . . . '93	D. Lamont. . . . . '93	H. Herbert . . . . '93
William McKinley (R) . . . . . 1897 G. Hobart (R). . . . . '97 T. Roosevelt (R). . . . . '01	J. Sherman . . . . '97 W. Day . . . . . . '97 J. Hay. . . . . '98	L. Gage . . . . '97	R. Alger . . . . '97 E. Root. . . . . . . '99	J. Long. . . . . '97
Theodore Roosevelt (R) . . . . 1901 C. Fairbanks (R) . . . . '05	J. Hay. . . . . '01 E. Root. . . . . . . '05 R. Bacon . . . . . . '09	L. Gage . . . . '01 L. Shaw . . . . . . '02 G. Cortelyou. . . '07	E. Root. . . . . . . '01 W. Taft. . . . . . . '04 L. Wright. . . . . . '08	J. Long. . . . . '01 W. Moody. . . . . '02 P. Morton . . . . . '04 C. Bonaparte. . . '05 V. Metcalf . . . . . '07 T. Newberry. . . '08
William Howard Taft (R) . . 1909 J. Sherman (R). . . . . '09	P. Knox . . . . '09	F. MacVeagh . . '09	J. Dickinson . . . '09 H. Stimson . . . . '11	G. Meyer . . . . . . '09
Woodrow Wilson (D) . . . . . 1913 T. Marshall (D) . . . . '13	W. Bryan . . . . . . '13 R. Lansing . . . . '15 B. Colby . . . . . . '20	W. McAdoo . . . '13 C. Glass. . . . . . . '18 D. Houston. . . . '20	L. Garrison . . . . '13 N. Baker . . . . . . '16	J. Daniels. . . . . . '13
Warren G. Harding (R) . . . . 1921 C. Coolidge (R) . . . . '21	C. Hughes. . . . . '21	A. Mellon . . . . . '21	J. Weeks. . . . . . . '21	E. Denby . . . . . . '21
Calvin Coolidge (R) . . . . 1923 C. Dawes (R) . . . . '25	C. Hughes. . . . . '23 F. Kellogg . . . . . '25	A. Mellon . . . . . '23	J. Weeks. . . . . . . '23 D. Davis . . . . . . '25	E. Denby . . . . . . '23 C. Wilbur . . . . . '24
Herbert Hoover (R) . . . . 1929 C. Curtis (R). . . . . '29	H. Stimson . . . . '29	A. Mellon . . . . '29 O. Mills. . . . . . . '32	J. Good. . . . . '29 P. Hurley. . . . . . '29	C. Adams . . . . . '29
Franklin D. Roosevelt (D). . 1933 J. Garner (D). . . . . '33 H. Wallace (D) . . . . '41 H. Truman (D). . . . . '45	C. Hull. . . . . '33 E. Stettinius . . . '44	W. Woodin. . . . '33 H. Morgen- thau . . . . . . '34	G. Dern . . . . '33 H. Woodring . . '36 H. Stimson . . . . '40	C. Swanson. . . . '33 C. Edison . . . . '40 F. Knox . . . . . . '40 J. Forrestal. . . . . '44
Harry S. Truman (D) . . . . . . 1945 A. Barkley (D) . . . . '49	J. Byrnes . . . . . . '45 G. Marshall. . . . '47 D. Acheson. . . . '49	F. Vinson . . . . . '45 J. Snyder . . . . . . '46	R. Patterson . . . '45 K. Royall . . . . . . '47	J. Forrestal. . . . . '45

Party affiliations: D, Democratic; R, Republican.

Attorney General	Postmaster General	Secretary of the Interior	Secretary of Agriculture	Secretary of Commerce and Labor	
E. Hoar .... '69 A. Ackerman ... '70 G. Williams .... '71 E. Pierrepont ... '75 A. Taft......... '76	J. Creswell .... '69 J. Marshall .... '74 M. Jewell ..... '74 J. Tyner....... '76	J. Cox......... '69 C. Delano ..... '70 Z. Chandler ... '75			
C. Devens...... '77	D. Key........ '77 H. Maynard. .. '80	C. Schurz ..... '77			
W. Mac- Veagh..... '81	T. James....... '81	S. Kirkwood... '81			
B. Brewster.... '81	T. Howe ...... '81 W. Gresham ... '83 F. Hatton...... '84	H. Teller ...... '81	*Cabinet status since Feb. 9, 1889*		
A. Garland .... '85	W. Vilas....... '85 D. Dickinson .. '88	L. Lamar...... '85 W. Vilas....... '88	N. Colman .... '89		
W. Miller...... '89	J. Wanamaker.. '89	J. Noble....... '89	J. Rusk........ '89		
R. Olney ...... '93 J. Harmon...... '95	W. Bissell ..... '93 W. Wilson..... '95	H. Smith ...... '93 D. Francis..... '96	J. Morton...... '93		
J. McKenna.... '97 J. Griggs ...... '97 P. Knox .... '01	J. Gary .... '97 C. Smith ...... '98	C. Bliss .... '97 E. Hitchcock... '99	J. Wilson ..... '97	*Established Feb. 14, 1903*	
P. Knox .... '01 W. Moody..... '04 C. Bonaparte... '07	C. Smith ...... '01 H. Payne...... '02 R. Wynne ..... '04 G. Cortelyou... '05 G. Meyer...... '07	E. Hitchcock... '01 J. Garfield ..... '07	J. Wilson ...... '01	G. Cortelyou... '03 V. Metcalf ..... '04 O. Straus...... '07	
G. Wicker- sham........ '09	F. Hitchcock... '09	R. Ballinger.... '09 W. Fisher ..... '11	J. Wilson ...... '09	C. Nagel ...... '09	
J. McReynolds . '13 T. Gregory..... '14 A. Palmer ..... '19	A. Burleson.... '13	F. Lane......... '13 J. Payne....... '20	D. Houston.... '13 E. Meredith.... '20	**Secretary of Commerce** *Established March 4, 1913* W. Redfield.... '13 J. Alexander ... '19	**Secretary of Labor** *Established March 4, 1913* Wm. Wilson ... '13
H. Daugherty.. '21	W. Hays ...... '21 H. Work ...... '22 H. New .... '23	A. Fall .... '21 H. Work ...... '23	H. C. Wallace.. '21	H. Hoover..... '21	J. Davis .... '21
H. Daugherty.. '23 H. Stone ...... '24 J. Sargent...... '25	H. New .... '23	H. Work ...... '23 R. West .... '28	H. C. Wallace.. '23 H. Gore .... '24 W. Jardine..... '25	H. Hoover..... '23 W. Whiting.... '28	J. Davis .... '23
W. Mitchell.... '29	W. Brown ..... '29	R. Wilbur ..... '29	A. Hyde....... '29	R. Lamont..... '29 R. Chapin ..... '32	J. Davis .... '29 W. Doak ...... '30
H. Cummings . '33 F. Murphy..... '39 R. Jackson ..... '40 F. Biddle ...... '41	J. Farley....... '33 F. Walker...... '40	H. Ickes .... '33	H. A. Wallace.. '33 C. Wickard .... '40	D. Roper ...... '33 H. Hopkins.... '39 J. Jones........ '40 H. A. Wallace.. '45	F. Perkins ..... '33
T. Clark .... '45 J. McGrath..... '49 J. McGranery .. '52	R. Hannegan .. '45 J. Donaldson... '47	H. Ickes........ '45 J. Krug........ '46 O. Chapman... '49	C. Anderson... '45 C. Brannan .... '48	H. A. Wallace.. '45 W. A. Harri- man .... '46 C. Sawyer ..... '48	L. Schwellen- bach .... '45 M. Tobin...... '48

PRESIDENTS, VICE-PRESIDENTS, AND CABINET MEMBERS

President and Vice-President	Secretary of State	Secretary of the Treasury	Secretary of Defense[1]	Attorney General	Postmaster General
			Established July 26, 1947 J. Forrestal[2] .... '47 L. Johnson[2] .... '49 G. Marshall[2] ... '50 R. Lovett[2] ..... '51		
Dwight D. Eisenhower (R)................. 1953 R. Nixon (R)............ '53	J. Dulles....... '53 C. Herter...... '59	G. Humphrey.. '53 R. Anderson... '57	C. Wilson ..... '53 N. McElroy .... '57	H. Brownell ... '53 W. Rogers ..... '57	A. Summer- field .... '53
John F. Kennedy (D) ...... 1961 L. Johnson (D).......... '61	D. Rusk....... '61	D. Dillon...... '61	R. McNamara.. '61	R. Kennedy.... '61	J. Day......... '61 J. Gronouski... '63
Lyndon B. Johnson (D) .... 1963 H. Humphrey (D)....... '65	D. Rusk....... '63	D. Dillon...... '63 H. Fowler ..... '65 J. Barr......... '68	R. McNamara.. '63 C. Clifford..... '68	R. Kennedy.... '63 N. Katzenbach . '65 R. Clark .... '67	J. Gronouski... '63 L. O'Brien ..... '65 W. Watson .... '68
Richard M. Nixon (R) ..... 1969 S. Agnew (R) .... '69	W. Rogers..... '69	D. Kennedy ... '69 J. Connally .... '70 G. Schultz..... '72	M. Laird ...... '69	J. Mitchell ..... '69 R. Kleindienst . '72	W. Blount ..... '69 *Abolished Aug. 8, 1970*

Party affiliations: D, Democratic; R, Republican.

[1]The Department of Defense, established during the Truman Administration, was a combination of the Departments of War and the Navy.

[2]Appointed during the Truman Administration.

Secretary of the Interior	Secretary of Agriculture	Secretary of Commerce	Secretary of Labor	Secretary of Health, Education, and Welfare	Secretary of Housing and Urban Development	Secretary of Transportation
				Established April 1, 1953		
D. McKay .... '53 F. Seaton ..... '56	E. Benson .... '53	S. Weeks ..... '53 L. Strauss .... '58 F. Mueller .... '59	M. Durkin.... '53 J. Mitchell .... '53	O. Hobby .... '53 M. Folsom.... '55 A. Flemming . '58		
S. Udall ...... '61	O. Freeman... '61	L. Hodges.... '61	A. Goldberg .. '61 W. Wirtz ..... '62	A. Ribicoff ... '61 A. Celebrezze. '62		
S. Udall ...... '63	O. Freeman... '63	L. Hodges.... '63 J. Connor..... '65 A. Trow- bridge ...... '67 C. Smith ..... '68	W. Wirtz ..... '63	A. Celebrezze. '63 J. Gardner.... '65 W. Cohen .... '68	*Established Sept. 9, 1965*	
					R. Weaver.... '66 R. Wood ..... '68	*Established Oct. 15, 1966*
						A. Boyd...... '66
W. Hickel .... '69 R. Morton .... '71	C. Hardin .... '69 E. Butz........ '71	M. Stans ..... '69 P. Peterson ... '71	J. Hodgson ... '69	R. Finch...... '69 E. Richardson. '71	G. Romney ... '69	J. Volpe ...... '69

PARTY DISTRIBUTION IN CONGRESS

CONGRESS	YEAR	PRESIDENT	SENATE			HOUSE		
			Majority Party	Minority Party	Others	Majority Party	Minority Party	Others
1	1789–91	F (Washington)	Ad 17	Op 9	0	Ad 38	Op 26	0
2	1791–93	F (Washington)	F 16	R^J 13	0	F 37	R^J 33	0
3	1793–95	F (Washington)	F 17	R^J 13	0	R^J 57	F 48	0
4	1795–97	F (Washington)	F 19	R^J 13	0	F 54	R^J 52	0
5	1797–99	F (J. Adams)	F 20	R^J 12	0	F 58	R^J 48	0
6	1799–01	F (J. Adams)	F 19	R^J 13	0	F 64	R^J 42	0
7	1801–03	R^J (Jefferson)	R^J 18	F 14	0	R^J 69	F 36	0
8	1803–05	R^J (Jefferson)	R^J 25	F 9	0	R^J 102	F 39	0
9	1805–07	R^J (Jefferson)	R^J 27	F 7	0	R^J 116	F 25	0
10	1807–09	R^J (Jefferson)	R^J 28	F 6	0	R^J 118	F 24	0
11	1809–11	R^J (Madison)	R^J 28	F 6	0	R^J 94	F 48	0
12	1811–13	R^J (Madison)	R^J 30	F 6	0	R^J 108	F 36	0
13	1813–15	R^J (Madison)	R^J 27	F 9	0	R^J 112	F 68	0
14	1815–17	R^J (Madison)	R^J 25	F 11	0	R^J 117	F 65	0
15	1817–19	R^J (Monroe)	R^J 34	F 10	0	R^J 141	F 42	0
16	1819–21	R^J (Monroe)	R^J 35	F 7	0	R^J 156	F 27	0
17	1821–23	R^J (Monroe)	R^J 44	F 4	0	R^J 158	F 25	0
18	1823–25	R^J (Monroe)	R^J 44	F 4	0	R^J 187	F 26	0
19	1825–27	C (J. Q. Adams)	Ad 26	J 20	0	Ad 105	J 97	0
20	1827–29	C (J. Q. Adams)	J 28	Ad 20	0	J 119	Ad 94	0
21	1829–31	D (Jackson)	D 26	NR 22	0	D 139	NR 74	0
22	1831–33	D (Jackson)	D 25	NR 21	2	D 141	NR 58	14
23	1833–35	D (Jackson)	D 20	NR 20	8	D 147	AM 53	60
24	1835–37	D (Jackson)	D 27	W 25	0	D 145	W 98	0
25	1837–39	D (Van Buren)	D 30	W 18	4	D 108	W 107	24
26	1839–41	D (Van Buren)	D 28	W 22	0	D 124	W 118	0
27	1841–43	W (W. Harrison)						
		W (Tyler)	W 28	D 22	2	W 133	D 102	6
28	1843–45	W (Tyler)	W 28	D 25	1	D 142	W 79	1
29	1845–47	D (Polk)	D 31	W 25	0	D 143	W 77	6
30	1847–49	D (Polk)	D 36	W 21	1	W 115	D 108	4
31	1849–51	W (Taylor)						
		W (Fillmore)	D 35	W 25	2	D 112	W 109	9
32	1851–53	W (Fillmore)	D 35	W 24	3	D 140	W 88	5
33	1853–55	D (Pierce)	D 38	W 22	2	D 159	W 71	4
34	1855–57	D (Pierce)	D 40	R 15	5	R 108	D 83	43
35	1857–59	D (Buchanan)	D 36	R 20	8	D 118	R 92	26
36	1859–61	D (Buchanan)	D 36	R 26	4	R 114	D 92	31
37	1861–63	R (Lincoln)	R 31	D 10	8	R 105	D 43	30
38	1863–65	R (Lincoln)	R 36	D 9	5	R 102	D 75	9
39	1865–67	R (Lincoln)						
		R (Johnson)	U 42	D 10	0	U 149	D 42	0
40	1867–69	R (Johnson)	R 42	D 11	0	R 143	D 49	0
41	1869–71	R (Grant)	R 56	D 11	0	R 149	D 63	0
42	1871–73	R (Grant)	R 52	D 17	5	D 134	R 104	5
43	1873–75	R (Grant)	R 49	D 19	5	R 194	D 92	14
44	1875–77	R (Grant)	R 45	D 29	2	D 169	R 109	14
45	1877–79	R (Hayes)	R 39	D 36	1	D 153	R 140	0
46	1879–81	R (Hayes)	D 42	R 33	1	D 149	R 130	14
47	1881–83	R (Garfield)						
		R (Arthur)	R 37	D 37	1	R 147	D 135	11
48	1883–85	R (Arthur)	R 38	D 36	2	D 197	R 118	10
49	1885–87	D (Cleveland)	R 43	D 34	0	D 183	R 140	2
50	1887–89	D (Cleveland)	R 39	D 37	0	D 169	R 152	4
51	1889–91	R (B. Harrison)	R 39	D 37	0	R 166	D 159	0
52	1891–93	R (B. Harrison)	R 47	D 39	2	D 235	R 88	9

CONGRESS	YEAR	PRESIDENT	SENATE			HOUSE		
			Majority Party	Minority Party	Others	Majority Party	Minority Party	Others
53	1893–95	D (Cleveland)	D 44	R 38	3	D 218	R 127	11
54	1895–97	D (Cleveland)	R 43	D 39	6	R 244	D 105	7
55	1897–99	R (McKinley)	R 47	D 34	7	R 204	D 113	40
56	1899–01	R (McKinley)	R 53	D 26	8	R 185	D 163	9
57	1901–03	R (McKinley)						
		R (T. Roosevelt)	R 55	D 31	4	R 197	D 151	9
58	1903–05	R (T. Roosevelt)	R 57	D 33	0	R 208	D 178	0
59	1905–07	R (T. Roosevelt)	R 57	D 33	0	R 250	D 136	0
60	1907–09	R (T. Roosevelt)	R 61	D 31	0	R 222	D 164	0
61	1909–11	R (Taft)	R 61	D 32	0	R 219	D 172	0
62	1911–13	R (Taft)	R 51	D 41	0	D 228	R 161	1
63	1913–15	D (Wilson)	D 51	R 44	1	D 291	R 127	17
64	1915–17	D (Wilson)	D 56	R 40	0	D 230	R 196	9
65	1917–19	D (Wilson)	D 53	R 42	0	D 216	R 210	6
66	1919–21	D (Wilson)	R 49	D 47	0	R 240	D 190	3
67	1921–23	R (Harding)	R 59	D 37	0	R 303	D 131	1
68	1923–25	R (Coolidge)	R 51	D 43	2	R 225	D 205	5
69	1925–27	R (Coolidge)	R 56	D 39	1	R 247	D 183	4
70	1927–29	R (Coolidge)	R 49	D 46	1	R 237	D 195	3
71	1929–31	R (Hoover)	R 56	D 39	1	R 267	D 167	1
72	1931–33	R (Hoover)	R 48	D 47	1	D 220	R 214	1
73	1933–35	D (F. Roosevelt)	D 60	R 35	1	D 310	R 117	5
74	1935–37	D (F. Roosevelt)	D 69	R 25	2	D 319	R 103	10
75	1937–39	D (F. Roosevelt)	D 76	D 16	4	D 331	R 89	13
76	1939–41	D (F. Roosevelt)	D 69	R 23	4	D 261	R 164	4
77	1941–43	D (F. Roosevelt)	D 66	R 28	2	D 268	R 162	5
78	1943–45	D (F. Roosevelt)	D 58	R 37	1	D 218	R 208	4
79	1945–47	D (F. Roosevelt)						
		D (Truman)	D 56	R 38	1	D 242	R 190	2
80	1947–49	D (Truman)	R 51	D 45	0	R 246	D 188	1
81	1949–51	D (Truman)	D 54	R 42	0	D 263	R 171	1
82	1951–53	D (Truman)	D 49	R 47	0	D 235	R 199	1
83	1953–55	R (Eisenhower)	R 48	D 47	1	R 221	D 212	1
84	1955–57	R (Eisenhower)	D 48	R 47	1	D 232	R 203	0
85	1957–59	R (Eisenhower)	D 49	R 47	0	D 232	R 199	0
86	1959–61	R (Eisenhower)	D 62	R 34	0	D 280	R 152	0
87	1961–63	D (Kennedy)	D 65	R 35	0	D 261	R 176	0
88	1963–65	D (Kennedy)						
		D (Johnson)	D 68	R 32	0	D 258	R 177	0
89	1965–67	D (Johnson)	D 68	R 32	0	D 295	R 140	0
90	1967–69	D (Johnson)	D 64	R 36	0	D 248	R 187	0
91	1969–71	R (Nixon)	D 57	R 43	0	D 243	R 192	0
92	1971–72	R (Nixon)	D 54	R 44	2	D 254	R 180	0

Ad: Administration; AM: Anti-Masonic; C: Coalition; D: Democratic; F: Federalist; J: Jacksonian; NR: National Republican; Op: Opposition; R: Republican; R^J: Republican (Jeffersonian); U: Unionist; W: Whig.

PRESIDENTIAL ELECTIONS*: ELECTORAL AND POPULAR VOTE

Presidential Candidate[1]	Electoral Vote	Popular Vote	Presidential Candidate[1]	Electoral Vote	Popular Vote
1789[2]: 11 States			S. Johnston	2	
GEORGE WASHINGTON	69		*Independent-Federalist*		
John Adams	34		C. C. Pinckney	1	
John Jay	9		*Independent-Federalist*		
R. H. Harrison	6				
John Rutledge	6		**1800[2]: 16 States**		
John Hancock	4		THOMAS JEFFERSON	73	
George Clinton	3		*Republican*		
Samuel Huntington	2		Aaron Burr	73	
John Milton	2		*Republican*		
James Armstrong	1		John Adams	65	
Benjamin Lincoln	1		*Federalist*		
Edward Telfair	1		C. C. Pinckney	64	
(Not voted)	12		*Federalist*		
			John Jay	1	
1792[2]: 15 States			*Federalist*		
GEORGE WASHINGTON	132				
Federalist			**1804: 17 States**		
John Adams	77		THOMAS JEFFERSON	162	
Federalist			*Republican*		
George Clinton	50		C. C. Pinckney	14	
Republican			*Federalist*		
Thomas Jefferson	4				
Aaron Burr	1				
			1808: 17 States		
1796[2]: 16 States			JAMES MADISON	122	
JOHN ADAMS	71		*Republican*		
Federalist			C. C. Pinckney	47	
Thomas Jefferson	68		*Federalist*		
Republican			George Clinton	6	
Thomas Pinckney	59		*Independent-Republican*		
Federalist			(Not voted)	1	
Aaron Burr	30				
Anti-Federalist			**1812: 18 States**		
Samuel Adams	15		JAMES MADISON	128	
Republican			*Republican*		
Oliver Ellsworth	11		DeWitt Clinton	89	
Federalist			*Fusion*		
George Clinton	7		(Not voted)	1	
Republican					
John Jay	5		**1816: 19 States**		
Independent-Federalist			JAMES MONROE	183	
James Iredell	3		*Republican*		
Federalist			Rufus King	34	
George Washington	2		*Federalist*		
Federalist			(Not voted)	4	
John Henry	2				
Independent					

*Source: U.S. Bureau of the Census, *Historical Statistics of the United States, Colonial Times to 1957* (Washington, D.C., 1960).

[1]Excludes unpledged tickets and minor candidates polling under 10,000 votes; various party labels may have been used by a candidate in different states; the more important of these are listed.

[2]Prior to the election of 1804, each elector voted for two candidates for President; the one receiving the highest number of votes, if a majority, was declared elected President, the next highest, Vice-President. This provision was modified by adoption of the Twelfth Amendment which was proposed by the Eighth Congress, December 12, 1803, and declared ratified by the legislatures of three fourths of the states in a proclamation of the Secretary of State, September 25, 1804.

[3]No candidate having a majority in the electoral college, the election was decided in the House of Representatives.

Presidential Candidate[1]	Electoral Vote	Popular Vote	Presidential Candidate[1]	Electoral Vote	Popular Vote
1820: 24 States			**1848: 30 States**		
JAMES MONROE	231		ZACHARY TAYLOR	163	1,360,967
Republican			*Whig*		
John Quincy Adams	1		Lewis Cass	127	1,222,342
Independent-Republican			*Democratic*		
(Not voted)	3		Martin Van Buren		291,263
			Free Soil		
1824: 24 States			**1852: 31 States**		
JOHN QUINCY ADAMS	84[3]	108,740	FRANKLIN PIERCE	254	1,601,117
Andrew Jackson	99[3]	153,544	*Democratic*		
Henry Clay	37	47,136	Winfield Scott	42	1,385,453
W. H. Crawford	41	46,618	*Whig*		
			John P. Hale		155,825
1828: 24 States			*Free Soil*		
ANDREW JACKSON	178	647,286			
Democratic			**1856: 31 States**		
John Quincy Adams	83	508,064	JAMES BUCHANAN	174	1,832,955
National Republican			*Democratic*		
			John C. Frémont	114	1,339,932
1832: 24 States			*Republican*		
ANDREW JACKSON	219	687,502	Millard Fillmore	8	871,731
Democratic			*American*		
Henry Clay	49	530,189			
National Republican			**1860: 33 States**		
William Wirt	7		ABRAHAM LINCOLN	180	1,865,593
Anti-Masonic			*Republican*		
John Floyd	11		John C. Breckinridge	72	848,356
Nullifiers			*Democratic (South)*		
(Not voted)	2		Stephen A. Douglas	12	1,382,713
			Democratic		
1836: 26 States			John Bell	39	592,906
MARTIN VAN BUREN	170	765,483	*Constitutional Union*		
Democratic					
William Henry Harrison	73		**1864: 36 States**		
Whig			ABRAHAM LINCOLN	212	2,206,938
Hugh L. White	26	739,795[4]	*Republican*		
Whig			George B. McClellan	21	1,803,787
Daniel Webster	14		*Democratic*		
Whig			(Not voted)	81	
W. P. Mangum	11				
Anti-Jackson			**1868: 37 States**		
			ULYSSES S. GRANT	214	3,013,421
			Republican		
1840: 26 States			Horatio Seymour	80	2,706,829
WILLIAM HENRY HARRISON	234	1,274,624	*Democratic*		
Whig			(Not voted)	23	
Martin Van Buren	60	1,127,781			
Democratic			**1872: 37 States**		
			ULYSSES S. GRANT	286	3,596,745
1844: 26 States			*Republican*		
JAMES K. POLK	170	1,338,464	Horace Greeley	[5]	2,843,446
Democratic			*Democratic*		
Henry Clay	105	1,300,097	Charles O'Conor		29,489
Whig			*Straight Democratic*		
James G. Birney		62,300	Thomas A. Hendricks	42	
Liberty			*Independent-Democratic*		

[4]Whig tickets were pledged to various candidates in various states.

[5]Greeley died shortly after the election and presidential electors supporting him cast their votes as indicated, including three for Greeley, which were not counted.

PRESIDENTIAL ELECTIONS: ELECTORAL AND POPULAR VOTE

Presidential Candidate[1]	Electoral Vote	Popular Vote
B. Gratz Brown	18	
Democratic		
Charles J. Jenkins	2	
Democratic		
David Davis	1	
Democratic		
(Not voted)	17	
1876: 38 States		
RUTHERFORD B. HAYES	185	4,036,572
Republican		
Samuel J. Tilden	184	4,284,020
Democratic		
Peter Cooper		81,737
Greenback		
1880: 38 States		
JAMES A. GARFIELD	214	4,453,295
Republican		
Winfield S. Hancock	155	4,414,082
Democratic		
James B. Weaver		308,578
Greenback-Labor		
Neal Dow		10,305
Prohibition		
1884: 38 States		
GROVER CLEVELAND	219	4,879,507
Democratic		
James G. Blaine	182	4,850,293
Republican		
Benjamin F. Butler		175,370
Greenback-Labor		
John P. St. John		150,369
Prohibition		
1888: 38 States		
BENJAMIN HARRISON	233	5,447,129
Republican		
Grover Cleveland	168	5,537,857
Democratic		
Clinton B. Fisk		249,506
Prohibition		
Anson J. Streeter		146,935
Union Labor		
1892: 44 States		
GROVER CLEVELAND	277	5,555,426
Democratic		
Benjamin Harrison	145	5,182,690
Republican		
James B. Weaver	22	1,029,846
People's		
John Bidwell		264,133
Prohibition		
Simon Wing		21,164
Socialist Labor		

Presidential Candidate[1]	Electoral Vote	Popular Vote
1896: 45 States		
WILLIAM McKINLEY	271	7,102,246
Republican		
William Jennings Bryan	176	6,492,559
Democratic[6]		
John M. Palmer		133,148
National Democratic		
Joshua Levering		132,007
Prohibition		
Charles M. Matchett		36,274
Socialist Labor		
Charles E. Bentley		13,969
Nationalist		
1900: 45 States		
WILLIAM McKINLEY	292	7,218,491
Republican		
William Jennings Bryan	155	6,356,734
Democratic[6]		
John C. Wooley		208,914
Prohibition		
Eugene V. Debs		87,814
Socialist		
Wharton Barker		50,373
People's		
Joseph F. Malloney		39,739
Socialist Labor		
1904: 45 States		
THEODORE ROOSEVELT	336	7,628,461
Republican		
Alton B. Parker	140	5,084,223
Democratic		
Eugene V. Debs		402,283
Socialist		
Silas C. Swallow		258,536
Prohibition		
Thomas E. Watson		117,183
People's		
Charles H. Corregan		31,249
Socialist Labor		
1908: 46 States		
WILLIAM HOWARD TAFT	321	7,675,320
Republican		
William Jennings Bryan	162	6,412,294
Democratic		
Eugene V. Debs		420,793
Socialist		
Eugene W. Chafin		253,840
Prohibition		
Thomas L. Hisgen		82,872
Independence		
Thomas E. Watson		29,100
People's		
August Gillhaus		14,021
Socialist Labor		

[6]Includes a variety of joint tickets with People's party electors commited to Bryan.

Presidential Candidate[1]	Electoral Vote	Popular Vote	Presidential Candidate[1]	Electoral Vote	Popular Vote
1912: 48 States			Norman Thomas		267,835
WOODROW WILSON	435	6,296,547	*Socialist*		
Democratic			Verne L. Reynolds		21,603
Theodore Roosevelt	88	4,118,571	*Socialist Labor*		
Progressive			William Z. Foster		21,181
William Howard Taft	8	3,486,720	*Workers*		
Republican			William F. Varney		20,106
Eugene V. Debs		900,672	*Prohibition*		
Socialist					
Eugene W. Chafin		206,275	**1932: 48 States**		
Prohibition			FRANKLIN D. ROOSEVELT	472	22,809,638
Arthur E. Reimer		28,750	*Democratic*		
Socialist Labor			Herbert Hoover	59	15,758,901
			Republican		
1916: 48 States			Norman Thomas		881,951
WOODROW WILSON	277	9,127,695	*Socialist*		
Democratic			William Z. Foster		102,785
Charles Evans Hughes	254	8,533,507	*Communist*		
Republican			William D. Upshaw		81,869
A. L. Benson		585,113	*Prohibition*		
Socialist			William H. Harvey		53,425
J. Frank Hanly		220,506	*Liberty*		
Prohibition			Verne L. Reynolds		33,276
Arthur E. Reimer		13,403	*Socialist Labor*		
Socialist Labor					
			1936: 48 States		
1920: 48 States			FRANKLIN D. ROOSEVELT	523	27,752,869
WARREN G. HARDING	404	16,143,407	*Democratic*		
Republican			Alfred M. Landon	8	16,674,665
James M. Cox	127	9,130,328	*Republican*		
Democratic			William Lemke		882,479
Eugene V. Debs		919,799	*Union*		
Socialist			Norman Thomas		187,720
P. P. Christensen		265,411	*Socialist*		
Farmer-Labor			Earl Browder		80,159
Aaron S. Watkins		189,408	*Communist*		
Prohibition			D. Leigh Colvin		37,847
James E. Ferguson		48,000	*Prohibition*		
American			John W. Aiken		12,777
W. W. Cox		31,715	*Socialist Labor*		
Socialist Labor					
			1940: 48 States		
1924: 48 States			FRANKLIN D. ROOSEVELT	449	27,307,819
CALVIN COOLIDGE	382	15,718,211	*Democratic*		
Republican			Wendell L. Willkie	82	22,321,018
John W. Davis	136	8,385,283	*Republican*		
Democratic			Norman Thomas		99,557
Robert M. La Follette	13	4,831,289	*Socialist*		
Progressive			Roger Q. Babson		57,812
Herman P. Faris		57,520	*Prohibition*		
Prohibition			Earl Browder		46,251
Frank T. Johns		36,428	*Communist*		
Socialist Labor			John W. Aiken		14,892
William Z. Foster		36,386	*Socialist Labor*		
Workers					
Gilbert O. Nations		23,967	**1944: 48 States**		
American			FRANKLIN D. ROOSEVELT	432	25,606,585
			Democratic		
1928: 48 States			Thomas E. Dewey	99	22,014,745
HERBERT HOOVER	444	21,391,993	*Republican*		
Republican			Norman Thomas		80,518
Alfred E. Smith	87	15,016,196	*Socialist*		
Democratic					

PRESIDENTIAL ELECTIONS: ELECTORAL AND POPULAR VOTE

Presidential Candidate[1]	Electoral Vote	Popular Vote	Presidential Candidate	Electoral Vote	Popular Vote
Claude A. Watson *Prohibition*		74,758	Richard M. Nixon *Republican*	219	34,108,546
Edward A. Teichert *Socialist Labor*		45,336	Harry F. Byrd *Independent*	15[x]	116,248
			Orville Faubus *States' Rights*		214,549
1948: 48 States			Eric Haas *Socialist Labor*		46,560
HARRY S. TRUMAN *Democratic*	303	24,105,812	Rutherford B. Decker *Prohibition*		46,203
Thomas E. Dewey *Republican*	189	21,970,065	Farrell Dobbs *Socialist Workers*		39,541
J. Strom Thurmond *States' Rights*	39	1,169,063	Charles L. Sullivan *Constitution*		19,570
Henry Wallace *Progressive*		1,157,172	J. Bracken Lee *Conservative*		12,912
Norman Thomas *Socialist*		139,414			
Claude A. Watson *Prohibition*		103,224			
Edward A. Teichert *Socialist Labor*		29,244	**1964: 50 States and D.C.**		
Farrell Dobbs *Socialist Workers*		13,613	LYNDON B. JOHNSON *Democratic*	486	43,126,506
			Barry Goldwater *Republican*	52	27,176,799
1952: 48 States			Eric Haas *Socialist Labor*		45,186
DWIGHT D. EISENHOWER *Republican*	442	33,936,234	Clifton DeBerry *Socialist Workers*		32,705
Adlai E. Stevenson *Democratic*	89	27,314,992	Earle H. Munn *Prohibition*		23,267
Vincent Hallinan *Progressive*		140,023	John Kasper *States' Rights*		6,953
Stuart Hamblen *Prohibition*		72,949	Joseph B. Lightburn *Constitution*		5,060
Eric Haas *Socialist Labor*		30,267			
Darlington Hoopes *Socialist*		20,203	**1968: 50 States and D.C.**		
Douglas A. MacArthur *Constitution*		17,205	RICHARD NIXON *Republican*	301	31,770,237
Farrell Dobbs *Socialist Workers*		10,312	Hubert Humphrey *Democratic*	191	31,270,533
			George Wallace *American Independent*	46	9,906,141
1956: 48 States			Hennings Blomen *Socialist Labor*		52,588
DWIGHT D. EISENHOWER *Republican*	457	35,590,472	Dick Gregory *Freedom and Peace*		47,097
Adlai E. Stevenson *Democratic*	73[7]	26,022,752	Fred Halstead *Socialist Worker*		41,300
T. Coleman Andrews *States' Rights*		107,929	Eldridge Cleaver *Peace and Freedom*		36,385
Eric Haas *Socialist Labor*		44,300	Eugene McCarthy *New Party*		25,858
Enoch A. Holtwick *Prohibition*		41,937	Earle H. Munn *Prohibition*		14,519
			Charlene Mitchell *Communist*		1,075
1960: 50 States					
JOHN F. KENNEDY *Democratic; Liberal*	303	34,227,096			

[7] One Democratic elector voted for Walter Jones.

[x] Byrd's electoral count includes the votes of fourteen unpledged electors from Mississippi and Alabama, in addition to one vote pledged to Nixon but cast for Byrd by an Oklahoma elector.

JUSTICES OF THE UNITED STATES SUPREME COURT

NAME	Terms of Service[1]	Appointed By	NAME	Terms of Service[1]	Appointed By
Chief Justices in Capital Letters			*Chief Justices in Capital Letters*		
John Jay, N.Y.	1789–1795	Washington	Henry B. Brown, Mich.	1891–1906	B. Harrison
James Wilson, Pa.	1789–1798	Washington	George Shiras, Jr., Pa.	1892–1903	B. Harrison
John Rutledge, S.C.	1790–1791	Washington	Howell E. Jackson, Tenn.	1893–1895	B. Harrison
William Cushing, Mass.	1790–1810	Washington	Edward D. White, La.	1894–1910	Cleveland
John Blair, Va.	1790–1796	Washington	Rufus W. Peckham, N.Y.	1896–1909	Cleveland
James Iredell, N.C.	1790–1799	Washington	Joseph McKenna, Cal.	1898–1925	McKinley
Thomas Johnson, Md.	1792–1793	Washington	Oliver W. Holmes, Mass.	1902–1932	T. Roosevelt
William Paterson, N.J.	1793–1806	Washington	William R. Day, Ohio	1903–1922	T. Roosevelt
John Rutledge, S.C.[2]	1795	Washington	William H. Moody, Mass.	1906–1910	T. Roosevelt
Samuel Chase, Md.	1796–1811	Washington	Horace H. Lurton, Tenn.	1910–1914	Taft
Oliver Ellsworth, Conn.	1796–1800	Washington	Charles E. Hughes, N.Y.	1910–1916	Taft
Bushrod Washington, Va.	1799–1829	J. Adams	Willis Van Devanter, Wy.	1911–1937	Taft
Alfred Moore, N.C.	1800–1804	J. Adams	Joseph R. Lamar, Ga.	1911–1916	Taft
John Marshall, Va.	1801–1835	J. Adams	Edward D. White, La.	1910–1921	Taft
William Johnson, S.C.	1804–1834	Jefferson	Mahlon Pitney, N.J.	1912–1922	Taft
Brockholst Livingston, N.Y.	1807–1823	Jefferson	James C. McReynolds, Tenn.	1914–1941	Wilson
Thomas Todd, Ky.	1807–1826	Jefferson	Louis D. Brandeis, Mass.	1916–1939	Wilson
Gabriel Duvall, Md.	1811–1835	Madison	John H. Clarke, Ohio	1916–1922	Wilson
Joseph Story, Mass.	1812–1845	Madison	William H. Taft, Conn.	1921–1930	Harding
Smith Thompson, N.Y.	1823–1843	Monroe	George Sutherland, Utah	1922–1938	Harding
Robert Trimble, Ky.	1826–1828	J. Q. Adams	Pierce Butler, Minn.	1923–1939	Harding
John McLean, Ohio	1830–1861	Jackson	Edward T. Sanford, Tenn.	1923–1930	Harding
Henry Baldwin, Pa.	1830–1844	Jackson	Harlan F. Stone, N.Y.	1925–1941	Coolidge
James M. Wayne, Ga.	1835–1867	Jackson	Charles E. Hughes, N.Y.	1930–1941	Hoover
Roger B. Taney, Md.	1836–1864	Jackson	Owen J. Roberts, Penn.	1930–1945	Hoover
Philip P. Barbour, Va.	1836–1841	Jackson	Benjamin N. Cardozo, N.Y.	1932–1938	Hoover
John Catron, Tenn.	1837–1865	Van Buren	Hugo L. Black, Ala.	1937–1971	F. Roosevelt
John McKinley, Ala.	1838–1852	Van Buren	Stanley F. Reed, Ky.	1938–1957	F. Roosevelt
Peter V. Daniel, Va.	1842–1860	Van Buren	Felix Frankfurter, Mass.	1939–1962	F. Roosevelt
Samuel Nelson, N.Y.	1845–1872	Tyler	William O. Douglas, Conn.	1939–	F. Roosevelt
Levi Woodbury, N.H.	1845–1851	Polk	Frank Murphy, Mich.	1940–1949	F. Roosevelt
Robert C. Grier, Pa.	1846–1870	Polk	Harlan F. Stone, N.Y.	1941–1946	F. Roosevelt
Benjamin R. Curtis, Mass.	1851–1857	Fillmore	James F. Byrnes, S.C.	1941–1942	F. Roosevelt
John A. Campbell, Ala.	1853–1861	Pierce	Robert H. Jackson, N.Y.	1941–1954	F. Roosevelt
Nathan Clifford, Me.	1858–1881	Buchanan	Wiley B. Rutledge, Iowa	1943–1949	F. Roosevelt
Noah H. Swayne, Ohio	1862–1881	Lincoln	Harold H. Burton, Ohio	1945–1958	Truman
Samuel F. Miller, Iowa	1862–1890	Lincoln	Frederick M. Vinson, Ky.	1946–1953	Truman
David Davis, Ill.	1862–1877	Lincoln	Tom C. Clark, Texas	1949–1967	Truman
Stephen J. Field, Cal.	1863–1897	Lincoln	Sherman Minton, Ind.	1949–1956	Truman
Salmon P. Chase, Ohio	1864–1873	Lincoln	Earl Warren, Cal.	1953–1969	Eisenhower
William Strong, Pa.	1870–1880	Grant	John Marshall Harlan, N.Y.	1955–1971	Eisenhower
Joseph P. Bradley, N.J.	1870–1892	Grant	William J. Brennan, Jr., N.J.	1956–	Eisenhower
Ward Hunt, N.Y.	1873–1882	Grant	Charles E. Whittaker, Mo.	1957–1962	Eisenhower
Morrison R. Waite, Ohio	1874–1888	Grant	Potter Stewart, Ohio	1958–	Eisenhower
John M. Harlan, Ky.	1877–1911	Hayes	Byron R. White, Colo.	1962–	Kennedy
William B. Woods, Ga.	1881–1887	Hayes	Arthur J. Goldberg, Ill.	1962–1965	Kennedy
Stanley Matthews, Ohio	1881–1889	Garfield	Abe Fortas, Tenn.	1965–1970	Johnson
Horace Gray, Mass.	1882–1902	Arthur	Thurgood Marshall, Md.	1967–	Johnson
Samuel Blatchford, N.Y.	1882–1893	Arthur	Warren E. Burger, Va.	1969–	Nixon
Lucius Q. C. Lamar, Miss.	1888–1893	Cleveland	Harry A. Blackmun, Minn.	1970–	Nixon
Melville W. Fuller, Ill.	1888–1910	Cleveland	Lewis F. Powell, Jr., Va.	1971–	Nixon
David J. Brewer, Kan.	1890–1910	B. Harrison	William H. Rehnquist, Ariz.	1971–	Nixon

[1]The date on which the justice took his judicial oath is here used as the date of the beginning of his service, for until that oath is taken he is not vested with the prerogatives of his office. Justices, however, receive their commissions ("letters patent") before taking their oath—in some instances, in the preceding year.

[2]Acting Chief Justice; Senate refused to confirm appointment.

POPULATION OF THE UNITED STATES: 1800–1880

Division and State	1800	1810	1820	1830	1840	1850	1860	1870	1880
UNITED STATES	5,308,483	7,239,881	9,638,453	12,866,020	17,069,453	23,191,876	31,443,321	39,818,449	50,189,209
New England	1,233,011	1,471,973	1,660,071	1,954,717	2,234,822	2,728,116	3,135,283	3,487,924	4,010,529
Maine	151,719	228,705	298,335	399,455	501,793	583,169	628,279	626,915	648,936
New Hampshire	183,858	214,160	244,161	269,328	284,574	317,976	326,073	318,300	346,991
Vermont	154,465	217,895	235,981	280,652	291,948	314,120	315,098	330,551	332,286
Massachusetts	422,845	472,040	523,287	610,408	737,699	994,514	1,231,066	1,457,351	1,783,085
Rhode Island	69,122	76,931	83,059	97,199	108,830	147,545	174,620	217,353	276,531
Connecticut	251,002	261,942	275,248	297,675	309,978	370,792	460,147	537,454	622,700
Middle Atlantic	1,402,565	2,014,702	2,669,845	3,587,664	4,526,260	5,898,735	7,458,985	8,810,806	10,496,878
New York	589,051	959,049	1,372,812	1,918,608	2,428,921	3,097,394	3,880,735	4,382,759	5,082,871
New Jersey	211,149	245,562	277,575	320,823	373,306	489,555	672,035	906,096	1,131,116
Pennsylvania	602,365	810,091	1,049,458	1,348,233	1,724,033	2,311,786	2,906,215	3,521,951	4,282,891
South Atlantic	2,286,494	2,674,891	3,061,063	3,645,752	3,925,299	4,679,090	5,364,703	5,835,610	7,597,197
Delaware	64,273	72,674	72,749	76,748	78,085	91,532	112,216	125,015	146,608
Maryland	341,548	380,546	407,350	447,040	470,019	583,034	687,049	780,894	934,943
Dist. of Columbia	8,144	15,471	23,336	30,261	33,745	51,687	75,080	131,700	177,624
Virginia	886,149	983,152	1,075,069	1,220,978	1,249,764	1,421,661	1,596,318	1,225,163	1,512,565
West Virginia	....	....	....	....	....	....	....	442,014	618,457
North Carolina	478,103	555,500	638,829	737,987	753,419	869,039	992,622	1,071,361	1,399,750
South Carolina	345,591	415,115	502,741	581,185	594,398	668,507	703,708	705,606	995,577
Georgia	162,686	252,433	340,989	516,823	691,392	906,185	1,057,286	1,184,109	1,542,180
Florida	....	....	....	34,730	54,477	87,445	140,424	187,748	269,493
East South Central	335,407	708,590	1,190,489	1,815,969	2,575,445	3,363,271	4,020,991	4,404,445	5,585,151
Kentucky	220,955	406,511	564,317	687,917	779,828	982,405	1,155,684	1,321,011	1,648,690
Tennessee	105,602	261,727	422,823	681,904	829,210	1,002,717	1,109,801	1,258,520	1,542,359
Alabama	1,250	9,046	127,901	309,527	590,756	771,623	964,201	996,992	1,262,505
Mississippi	7,600	31,306	75,448	136,621	375,651	606,526	791,305	827,922	1,131,597
West South Central	....	77,618	167,680	246,127	449,985	940,251	1,747,667	2,029,965	3,334,220
Arkansas	....	1,062	14,273	30,388	97,574	209,897	435,450	484,471	802,525
Louisiana	....	76,556	153,407	215,739	352,411	517,762	708,002	726,915	939,946
Oklahoma	....	....	....	....	....	....	....	....	....
Texas	....	....	....	....	....	212,592	604,215	818,579	1,591,749
East North Central	51,006	272,324	792,719	1,470,018	2,924,728	4,523,260	6,926,884	9,124,517	11,206,668
Ohio	41,365	230,760	581,434	937,903	1,519,467	1,980,329	2,339,511	2,665,260	3,198,062
Indiana	5,641	24,520	147,178	343,031	685,866	988,416	1,350,428	1,680,637	1,978,301
Illinois	....	12,282	55,211	157,445	476,183	851,470	1,711,951	2,539,891	3,077,871
Michigan	....	4,762	8,896	31,639	212,267	397,654	749,113	1,184,059	1,636,937
Wisconsin	....	....	....	....	30,945	305,391	775,881	1,054,670	1,315,497
West North Central	....	19,783	66,586	140,455	426,814	880,335	2,169,832	3,856,594	6,157,443
Minnesota	....	....	....	....	....	6,077	172,023	439,706	780,773
Iowa	....	....	....	....	43,112	192,214	674,913	1,194,020	1,624,615
Missouri	....	19,783	66,586	140,455	383,702	682,044	1,182,012	1,721,295	2,168,380
North Dakota	....	....	....	....	....	....	4,837	2,405	36,909
South Dakota	....	....	....	....	....	....	....	11,776	98,268
Nebraska	....	....	....	....	....	....	28,841	122,993	452,402
Kansas	....	....	....	....	....	....	107,206	364,399	996,096
Mountain	....	....	....	....	....	72,927	174,923	315,385	653,119
Montana	....	....	....	....	....	....	....	20,595	39,159
Idaho	....	....	....	....	....	....	....	14,999	32,610
Wyoming	....	....	....	....	....	....	....	9,118	20,789
Colorado	....	....	....	....	....	....	34,277	39,864	194,327
New Mexico	....	....	....	....	....	61,547	93,516	91,874	119,565
Arizona	....	....	....	....	....	....	....	9,658	40,440
Utah	....	....	....	....	....	11,380	40,273	76,786	143,963
Nevada	....	....	....	....	....	....	6,857	42,491	62,266
Pacific	....	....	....	....	....	105,871	444,053	675,125	1,148,004
Washington	....	....	....	....	....	1,201	11,594	23,955	75,116
Oregon	....	....	....	....	....	12,093	52,465	90,923	174,768
California	....	....	....	....	....	92,597	379,994	560,247	864,694
Alaska	....	....	....	....	....	....	....	....	33,426
Hawaii	....	....	....	....	....	....	....	....	....

POPULATION OF THE UNITED STATES: 1890-1970

Division and State	1890	1900	1910	1920	1930	1940	1950	1960	1970
UNITED STATES	62,979,766	76,212,168	92,228,622	106,021,568	123,202,660	132,165,129	151,325,798	179,323,175	203,184,772
New England	4,700,749	5,592,017	6,552,681	7,400,909	8,166,341	8,437,290	9,314,453	10,509,367	11,847,186
Maine	661,086	694,466	742,371	768,014	797,423	847,226	913,774	969,265	993,663
New Hampshire	376,530	411,588	430,572	443,083	465,293	491,524	533,242	606,921	737,681
Vermont	332,422	343,641	355,956	352,428	359,611	359,231	377,747	389,881	444,732
Massachusetts	2,238,947	2,805,346	3,366,416	3,852,356	4,249,614	4,316,721	4,690,514	5,148,578	5,689,170
Rhode Island	345,506	428,556	542,610	604,397	687,497	713,346	791,896	859,488	949,723
Connecticut	746,258	908,420	1,114,756	1,380,631	1,606,903	1,709,242	2,007,280	2,535,234	3,032,217
Middle Atlantic	12,706,220	15,454,678	19,315,892	22,261,144	26,260,750	27,539,487	30,163,533	34,168,452	37,152,813
New York	6,003,174	7,268,894	9,113,614	10,385,227	12,588,066	13,479,142	14,830,192	16,782,304	18,190,740
New Jersey	1,444,933	1,883,669	2,537,167	3,155,900	4,041,334	4,160,165	4,835,329	6,066,782	7,168,164
Pennsylvania	5,258,113	6,302,115	7,665,111	8,720,017	9,631,350	9,900,180	10,498,012	11,319,366	11,793,909
South Atlantic	8,857,922	10,443,480	12,194,895	13,990,272	15,793,589	17,823,151	21,182,335	25,971,732	30,671,337
Delaware	168,493	184,735	202,322	223,003	238,380	266,505	318,085	446,292	548,104
Maryland	1,042,390	1,188,044	1,295,346	1,449,661	1,631,526	1,821,244	2,343,001	3,100,689	3,922,399
Dist. of Columbia	230,392	278,718	331,069	437,571	486,869	663,091	802,178	763,956	756,510
Virginia	1,655,980	1,854,184	2,061,612	2,309,187	2,421,851	2,677,773	3,318,680	3,966,949	4,648,494
West Virginia	762,794	958,800	1,221,119	1,463,701	1,729,205	1,901,974	2,005,552	1,860,421	1,744,237
North Carolina	1,617,949	1,893,810	2,206,287	2,559,123	3,170,276	3,571,623	4,061,929	4,556,155	5,082,059
South Carolina	1,151,149	1,340,316	1,515,400	1,683,724	1,738,765	1,899,804	2,117,027	2,382,594	2,590,516
Georgia	1,837,353	2,216,331	2,609,121	2,895,832	2,908,506	3,123,723	3,444,578	3,943,116	4,589,575
Florida	391,422	528,542	752,619	968,470	1,468,211	1,897,414	2,771,305	4,951,560	6,789,443
East South Central	6,429,154	7,547,757	8,409,901	8,893,307	9,887,214	10,778,225	11,477,181	12,050,126	12,804,552
Kentucky	1,858,635	2,147,174	2,289,905	2,416,630	2,614,589	2,845,627	2,944,806	3,038,156	3,219,311
Tennessee	1,767,518	2,020,616	2,184,789	2,337,885	2,616,556	2,915,841	3,291,718	3,567,089	3,924,164
Alabama	1,513,401	1,828,697	2,138,093	2,348,174	2,646,248	2,832,961	3,061,743	3,266,740	3,444,165
Mississippi	1,289,600	1,551,270	1,797,114	1,790,618	2,009,821	2,183,796	2,178,914	2,178,141	2,216,912
West South Central	4,740,983	6,532,290	8,784,534	10,242,224	12,176,830	13,064,525	14,537,572	16,951,255	19,322,458
Arkansas	1,128,211	1,311,564	1,574,449	1,752,204	1,854,482	1,949,387	1,909,511	1,786,272	1,923,295
Louisiana	1,118,588	1,381,625	1,656,388	1,798,509	2,101,593	2,363,880	2,683,516	3,257,022	3,643,180
Oklahoma	258,657	790,391	1,657,155	2,028,283	2,396,040	2,336,434	2,233,351	2,328,284	2,559,253
Texas	2,235,527	3,048,710	3,896,542	4,663,228	5,824,715	6,414,824	7,711,194	9,579,677	11,196,730
East North Central	13,478,305	15,985,581	18,250,621	21,475,543	25,297,185	26,626,342	30,309,368	36,225,024	40,252,678
Ohio	3,672,329	4,157,545	4,767,121	5,759,394	6,646,697	6,907,612	7,946,627	9,706,397	10,652,017
Indiana	2,192,404	2,516,462	2,700,876	2,930,390	3,238,503	3,427,796	3,934,224	4,662,498	5,193,669
Illinois	3,826,352	4,821,550	5,638,591	6,485,280	7,630,654	7,897,241	8,712,176	10,081,158	11,113,976
Michigan	2,093,890	2,420,982	2,810,173	3,668,412	4,842,325	5,256,106	6,371,766	7,823,194	8,875,083
Wisconsin	1,693,330	2,069,042	2,333,860	2,632,067	2,939,006	3,137,587	3,434,575	3,951,777	4,417,933
West North Central	8,932,112	10,347,423	11,637,921	12,544,249	13,296,915	13,516,990	14,061,394	15,394,115	16,324,389
Minnesota	1,310,283	1,751,394	2,075,708	2,387,125	2,563,953	2,792,300	2,982,483	3,413,864	3,805,069
Iowa	1,912,297	2,231,853	2,224,771	2,404,021	2,470,939	2,538,268	2,621,073	2,757,537	2,825,041
Missouri	2,679,185	3,106,665	3,293,335	3,404,055	3,629,367	3,784,664	3,954,653	4,319,813	4,677,399
North Dakota	190,983	319,146	577,056	646,872	680,845	641,935	619,636	632,446	617,761
South Dakota	348,600	401,570	583,888	636,547	692,849	642,961	652,740	680,514	666,257
Nebraska	1,062,656	1,066,300	1,192,214	1,296,372	1,377,963	1,315,834	1,325,510	1,411,330	1,483,791
Kansas	1,428,108	1,470,495	1,690,949	1,769,257	1,880,999	1,801,028	1,905,299	2,178,611	2,249,071
Mountain	1,213,935	1,674,657	2,633,517	3,336,101	3,701,789	4,150,003	5,074,998	6,855,060	8,283,585
Montana	142,924	243,329	376,053	548,889	537,606	559,456	591,024	674,767	694,409
Idaho	88,548	161,772	325,594	431,866	445,032	524,873	588,637	667,191	713,008
Wyoming	62,555	92,531	145,965	194,402	225,565	250,742	290,529	330,066	332,416
Colorado	413,249	539,700	799,024	939,629	1,035,791	1,123,296	1,325,089	1,753,947	2,207,259
New Mexico	160,282	195,310	327,301	360,350	423,317	531,818	681,187	951,023	1,016,000
Arizona	88,243	122,931	204,354	334,162	435,573	499,261	749,587	1,302,161	1,772,482
Utah	210,779	276,749	373,351	449,396	507,847	550,310	688,862	890,627	1,059,273
Nevada	47,355	42,335	81,875	77,407	91,058	110,247	160,083	285,278	488,738
Pacific	1,920,386	2,634,285	4,448,660	5,877,819	8,622,047	10,229,116	15,114,964	21,198,044	26,525,774
Washington	357,232	518,103	1,141,990	1,356,621	1,563,396	1,736,191	2,378,963	2,853,214	3,409,169
Oregon	317,704	413,536	672,765	783,389	953,786	1,089,684	1,521,341	1,768,687	2,091,385
California	1,213,398	1,485,053	2,377,549	3,426,861	5,677,251	6,907,387	10,586,223	15,717,204	19,953,134
Alaska	32,052	63,592	64,356	55,036	59,278	72,524	128,643	226,167	302,173
Hawaii	. . . .	154,001	192,000	255,912	368,336	423,330	499,794	632,772	769,913

imperialism, 130, 136, 140–141; as Secretary of State, 143, 144; and Taft, 121

Bryant, William Cullen, 66

Bulge, Battle of the, 264

Bull Moose party. *See* Progressive party

Bull Run: first battle of, 6; second battle of, 9

Bureau of Corporations, 119

Burger, Warren, 286

Burke Act, 60

Burlingame Treaty, 68

Burma, 256, 273, 291

Burns, James McGregor, 176

Burnside, Ambrose E., 9

Business: and the Eisenhower administration, 282–283; in Gilded Age, 39–40, 62–63; during Great Depression, 202–203, 208, 211, 214, 221; under Kennedy, 296; in Progressive Era, 109, 110, 118

Busing, 286, 310

Buzz bomb (V-1), 264

Byrnes, James F., 258, 261, 270

Cable, George Washington, 94

California, University of, 89, 279, 329

Cambodia, 308–309

Cameron, Simon, 45

Canada: American desire to annex, 128, 129; and Communism, 279; NATO, 273; and Taft, 121

Cantor, Eddie, 197

Capitalism: finance, 51–52; industrial, 38–39, 52; venture, 16

Capone, Al, 194

Cardozo, Benjamin, 217

Caribbean, 139–140

Carmichael, Stokely, 325

Carnegie, Andrew, 45, 46, 48, 49, 110

Carnegie Foundation, 158, 232

Carnegie Steel Company, 49, 52

Carpetbaggers, 25, 26

Carranza, Venustiano, 141–142

Casablanca Conference, 257

Castro, Fidel, 293, 296

Cather, Willa, 162

Catholic Church. *See* Roman Catholic Church

Central Pacific Railroad, 16, 43, 44

Ceylon, 291

Cezanne, Paul, 162

Chamberlain, Neville, 225, 226

Chancellorsville, Battle of, 6, 9

Chandler, Zachariah, 64

Chaplin, Charlie, 241

Charter of the United Nations, 265, 273

Chateau-Thierry, 148

Chautauqua movement, 96–97

Chavez, Cesar, 324

Chiang Kai-shek, 223, 253, 257, 264, 274, 309

Chicago, Illinois, 53, 54, 286

Chicago, University of, 266

Chicanos, 260, 323, 324

Child Labor Act, 167

Child labor laws, 114, 126

Children's Bureau, 122

China: Communist, 274, 277, 305, 308, 309; and Rutherford Hayes, 68; and Japan, 253, 254; Open Door, 137; and Russia, 223, 264; Washington Conference, 187; World War II, 257

Chisholm, Shirley, 323

Chisholm Trail, 58

Churchill, Sir Winston, 228, 252, 255, 257, 264, 265, 269, 292

Churchill, Winston (novelist), 162

City, 317–319

Civilian Conservation Corps (CCC), 209, 211

Civil Rights Acts: (1875), 81; (1957), 284, 286; (1960), 286; (1964), 298, 300–303, 323

Civil Rights Commission, 286

Civil Service Act, 69–70

Civil Service Reform Act, 64

Civil War: and black Americans, 20–21; causes, 2, 3; problems of the Confederacy, 12, 13; emancipation and reconstruction, 18, 19; industry, 39; sea power, 13–15; Virginia front, 6–9; in the West, 9–11; and women, 17–18

Clarke, Edward Y., 181

Clayton Antitrust Act, 54, 125–126

Cleaver, Eldridge, 325

Clemenceau, Georges, 150

Cleveland, Grover, 70–72, 75, 77, 130, 132

Closed shop, 195

Cochran, Thomas C., 34

Cold Harbor, Battle of, 11

Cold War, 248, 267–273, 274, 276, 303, 311

Collier, John, 220

Collier's, 113

Colombia, 139

Colonialism, overthrow of, 273–274

Columbia School of Mines, 94

Columbia University, 89, 329

Columbian Exposition, 161

Combined Chiefs of Staff, 255, 262

Commager, Henry, 176

Committee of Industrial Organization (CIO). *See* Congress of Industrial Organizations (CIO)

Committee on Public Information, 149

Committee on Religious Welfare Activity, 235

Common Market. *See* European Common Market

Commons, John R., 85, 111

Communism: in China, 274; Cold War, 268–273; in Czechoslovakia, 272; and the Great Fear, 279–280; in

Hungary, 292; and Japan, 274; in labor, 268; Marshall Plan, 271; in Middle East, 292; after death of Stalin, 291; and Supreme Court, 287; in Vietnam, 304, 305, 309. *See also* Red scares

Community Chest, 205

Concord Summer School of Philosophy and Literature, 89

Conference for Progressive Political Action, 188

Congress: 1877–1900, 62, 72; 1919–1929, 183; influenced by business, 110; and military action policy, 227; and the Supreme Court, 287

Congress of Industrial Organizations (CIO), 218, 219, 221

Conkling, Roscoe, 34, 64, 67, 68

Containment policy, 270–271

Cooley, Charles Horton, 85

Coolidge, Calvin, 182, 183, 188–189

Copland, Aaron, 238

Coral Sea, Battle of, 256

Cornell, Alonzo B., 67

Cornell, Ezra, 47

Cornell University, 89

Corporations: 1960s, 321

Cotton, 13

Coughlin, Charles E., 215, 216

Council of Economic Advisors, 268

"Court-packing" bill, 216–217

Cox, James M., 182

Coxey, Jacob S., 77

Cram, Ralph Adams, 161

Crane, Hart, 241

Crane, Stephen, 94, 95

Crédit Mobilier, 29, 43

Creel, George, 149

"Criminal syndicalist" laws, 180

Crocker, Charles, 43

Crocker Company, 43

Croly, Herbert, 167–168

Cuba: 1930s, 224; American desire to annex, 128, 129; Castro, 293; independence, 136; and Kennedy, 296–298; Spanish-American War, 131, 133; Treaty of Paris (1898), 134

Cullen, Countee, 240

Cullom Committee, 50

Cummings, E. E., 241

Curry, John Steuart, 238

Curtis, George William, 66

Curtis, William, 70

Czechoslovakia, 225, 272

Daladier, Edouard, 225

Danish West Indies (Virgin Islands), 128

Dardanelles, 269

Darrow, Clarence, 163, 234

Darwin, Charles, 45

Darwinism. *See* Evolution, theory of; Reform Darwinism; Social Darwinism

Garraty, John, 55
Garvey, Marcus, 193
Gas Ring, 65
General Conference of Rabbis, 235
General Electric, 237
General Motors Corporation, 219
General Theory of Employment, Interest and Money, The, 234
Generation gap, 249, 332
Geneva Agreement of 1954, 304
George, Henry, 49–50, 66, 86, 93
Georgia: desegregation, 285
German Federal Republic, 270
Germany: Berlin blockade, 272; Cold War, 269, 270; during Great Depression, 203; NATO, 291; U.S. and Samoa, 130; World War I, 142, 143, 144, 146–148, 151, 186–188; after World War I, 186–188; World War II, 225–227, 252, 253, 257, 264, 265
Gershwin, George, 238
Gettysburg, Battle of, 6, 9
Gibbons, James Cardinal, 53, 92
G.I. Bill, 300
Gideon v. *Wainwright*, 288
Gilbert Islands, 130, 261, 266
Gilded Age, 33–35, 83, 93, 97
Gilman, Daniel Coit, 33–34
Gladden, Washington, 92, 159
Glass-Steagall Act, 203
Godkin, E. L., 34, 66, 83
Gold mining, 56
Gold Standard, 209, 212
Gold Standard Act, 80
Goldwater, Barry, 298–299
Gompers, Samuel, 55, 115, 126
Good Neighbor Policy, 224
Gorgas, Josiah, 15
Gorman, Arthur P., 64, 67
Gould, Jay, 41, 53
Grand Alliance, 255, 264
Grand Army of the Republic, 63, 71
Grandfather Clause, 125
Grange, 73–74
Grant, Ulysses S., 9–12, 28–30, 68
Great Britain: 1930s, 219, 223; Brussels Pact, 272; U.S. Civil War, 13–14; Communism, 279; during Great Depression, 203; international arbitration, 29; Japan, 253; League of Nations, 151; Lend-Lease, 255; naval alliance between U.S. and, 131; nuclear weapons, 291; SEATO, 291; Suez Canal crisis, 292; U.S. and Samoa, 130; Washington Conference, 187; World War I, 142–143, 147, 187; World War II, 225, 226, 228, 252, 263
Great Depression, 162, 185, 202–203, 234, 235, 237–238
"Great Fear," 279–280
"Great Society," 298–300
Great Southwestern Strike, 53
Greece, 269, 270, 271, 273
Greeley, Horace, 29–30

Green, William, 212
Greenback Labor party, 69
Greenbacks, 17, 19, 68, 70
Griffith, D. W., 241
Gropius, Walter, 161
Guadalcanal, 256, 261
Guam, 134, 254
Guggenheim Museum, 327
Guiteau, Charles J., 69

Hadden, Briton, 236
Hague Tribunal, 140
Haiti, 141, 188
Hamburg, 261
Hammer v. *Dagenhart*, 126
Hampton, Wade, 81
Hancock, Winfield Scott, 69
Hanna, Marcus Alonzo, 77, 79, 110, 115
Harding, Warren G., 182–183
Harlem Renaissance, 240
Harper's Ferry, 9
Harriman, Edward H., 41, 106
Harrington, Michael, 317
Harris, Joel Chandler, 94
Harris, Roy, 238
Harrison, Benjamin, 71–72, 75–76
Harte, Bret, 94
Harvard University, 84, 94, 329
Hatteras, 14
Havemeyer, Henry O., 45, 49
Hawaii, 130, 136, 254
Hay, John, 137, 139
Hayes, Rutherford B., 30, 66–68
Haymarket Riot, 54
Hay-Pauncefote Treaty, 139
Hearst, William Randolph, 131–132, 141, 151, 206
Hegel, Georg Wilhelm Friedrich, 89
Heller, Joseph, 325
Hellman, Lillian, 241
Hemingway, Ernest, 239
Hepburn Act, 116
Herron, George, 159
Hersey, John, 325
Higher Education Act, 300
Higher Education Facilities Act, 298
Hill, James J., 41, 106, 110
Hillman, Sidney, 212
Hiroshima, 266
Hiss, Alger, 279, 281
History, view of, in Progressive Era, 164–166
Hitler, Adolf, 223, 225, 226, 252–253, 255, 261, 265
Hobart, Garret A., 77
Ho Chi Minh, 304
Holmes, Oliver Wendell, Jr., 90, 166
Home Owners Loan Corporation, 209
Homer, Winslow, 96
Homestead Act, 57
Hong Kong, 254, 273
Hood, John B., 12
Hooker, Joseph, 9

Hoover, Herbert, 148, 176, 182, 186; and Great Depression, 202–203; as President, 189–190, 206–207, 223
Hopkins, Harry, 227
Hopkins, Mark, 43
Hot line, 297
House Un-American Activities Committee, 281
Housing Acts: (1937), 222; (1968), 318
Housing and Urban Development Act, 303
Howe, Louis M., 206
Howells, William Dean, 94, 95
Huerta, Victoriano, 141
Hughes, Charles Evans, 145, 182, 215, 217
Hughes, Langston, 240
Hull, Cordell, 254, 257
Hull House, 111
Humphrey, George C., 283
Humphrey, Hubert H., 299, 306–307, 311
Hundred Days, 209
Hungary, 187, 292
Huntington, Collis P., 43

Iceland, 129, 252, 253
Idealism, 89, 111–112
Immigration: Chinese, 68; in Progressive Era, 111, 153–154; quotas, 184
Immigration Act (1965), 300
Impeachment, 28
Imperialism, 130, 134
India, 256, 291
Indian Affairs, Bureau of, 219–220, 324
Indian Reorganization Act, 60, 324
Indians: civil rights movements, 323; Gilded Age, 58–60; (1900–1917), 125; and the New Deal, 219–220, 221; in the 1960s, 324
Individualism: Hegelian idealism, 89; and religion, 91; and Social Darwinism, 84; Sumner, 84
Indochina, 253, 256, 273, 291, 304
Industrialism: in Gilded Age, 15–16, 33, 39–40, 83–84; 1920s and 1930s, 175; railroads, 41–42; and religion, 91–92
Industrial Revolution, 38–41
Industrial Workers of the World, 120, 149
Inflation, 212, 259, 267
Inness, George, 95
Insull, Samuel, 200
Intercontinental ballistic missiles (ICBM), 289
Interior, Department of the, 60
Internal Security Act, 279
International News Service, 237
Interstate Commerce Act, 50, 71
Interstate Commerce Commission (I.C.C.), 116, 122
Ireland, Archbishop John, 92
Iron Curtain, 269, 272